HISTORIA RELIGIONUM

VOLUME II

RELIGIONS OF THE PRESENT

HISTORIA RELIGIONUM

HANDBOOK FOR THE HISTORY OF RELIGIONS

EDITED BY

C. JOUCO BLEEKER
Professor of the History
and the Phenomenology of Religions
in the University of Amsterdam

AND

GEO WIDENGREN
Professor of the History and Psychology of Religions
in the University of Uppsala

VOLUME II

RELIGIONS OF THE PRESENT

LEIDEN
E. J. BRILL
1971

PRINTED IN THE NETHERLANDS

TABLE OF CONTENTS

JUDAISM

BY

R. J. ZWI WERBLOWSKY

Jerusalem

I. The Essence of Judaism

Methodological reflections

In order to comprehend a religious phenomenon adequately and from the "inside" as it were, it is necessary to understand first how the tradition of the community and the consciousness of its members relate to their own past. How does the religious community view the historical continuity of which it assumes itself to be part, and how does it define its place in that continuum? Writing the history of a religion "past and present," inevitably means more than merely adding a chapter on the present to those dealing with the past. In fact, the past appears differently from the shifting vantage points of successive presents, even as the present is evaluated differently according to the different normative interpretations which members of a religious community give to their past. Hence also the observation that the history of a religion, like that of a people, has to be written by every generation anew—which is tantamount to saying that it is liable to be antiquated as soon as it is written.

The present work provides an instructive illustration of this methodological difficulty. The "Religion of Israel," as a religion of the past, is allotted in it about twice as much space as "Judaism," which is classified among the religions of the present. To the historian who looks not *at* Judaism but *into* Judaism (not to say *from* Judaism), the division is about as meaningful as that between Vedic Religion or Apostolic Christianity (religions of the past) on the one hand, and, on the other hand, Hinduism or the Christian Church (religions of the present) respectively. In fact, from the point of view of the Jew, Judaism and the Religion of Israel are the same, and what is called the religion of (Biblical) Israel is but one chapter of a long and variegated historical continuum. No doubt it is legitimate to enquire whether the activity of Ezra (see above, Volume I, p. 223) does not mark a cesura rahter than a smooth transition, and similarly one may ask whether the secularisation of modern post-emancipation Jewry (see below, p. 26) does not represent a serious break in historical continuity. But whereas terms such as "continuity" and "discontinuity" are notoriously difficult to define (apart from being, on occasion, also emotionally loaded), it should be comparatively easy to describe the relationship of a religious group both to its actual history and to its notion (or "image") of history. The divergent ways in which the same events and facts can be regarded by different traditions are well illustrated by the manner in which Christians and Jews respectively view the life and ministry of Jesus. For the former there is a straight line running from the Old Testament through the events recorded in the Gospels right up to the life of the Church today. Post-biblical Jewish religion, which is called "Judaism" to distinguish it from the religion of Biblical Israel, is considered as a sideline which branches off the main road at its most important juncture. For the Jewish consciousness, on the other hand, there is no break at all in the line leading from the Bible to the Scribes, Pharisees, Rabbis and later teachers of Judaism.

If the historian's own locus in time is a matter of crucial relevance for his manner of perceiving history, it is even more decisive for his perception of the "essence" of a religion. For the historian is not content with an arbitrary, horizontal cross-section at some point in time (even his own time) which would yield him a synchronic essence. As a historian of religion he is committed to a diachronic view, made up of successive phases all equally and "essentially" meaningful. As a matter of fact the history of every religion is so rich and varied that we simply cannot take in all its manifestations and stages of development at one synoptic glance. Yet we often like to think that somehow all these are expressions of one underlying idea or type, variations as it were on one basic theme. There is, consequently, a tendency to consider each religion as characterised by a specific structure, and one proceeds to regard all its varied manifestations as stamped with this specific character and exhibiting its unique essence. As it happens, the essence ascribed to any particular religion is often the projection of the typology required by a philosopher's system (as e.g. in the case of Hegel), or else it is alleged to be the result of the historian's phenomenological insight. But in the latter case we are, as often as not, caught in a circular argument. For either the phenomenological essence is a *vaticinium post eventum*, in which case a subsequent development may modify it, or else it is an *a priori* insight, in which case it is a dogmatic affirmation which almost of necessity leads to selective qualification of at least some phenomena as marginal, as aberrations and as not of the essence. Surely the essence of Christianity would be described very differently if Arianism or Monophysitism had become its dominant doctrinal form. Whether or not a certein tendency or movement survives, whether a certain "alien" influence is absorbed and integrated or, conversely, resisted and rejected may be a matter of historical accident no less than of immanent necessity dictated by the essence of the religion concerned—unless we consider whatever has happened as being *ipso facto* of the essence. The historian of Christianity writing in 1969 has no certain way of telling whether the fashionable theology "after the death of God" is a curious aberration and a passing fad, incompatible with the essence of Christianity, or whether it will turn out to be a significant chapter in the history of Christian experience and theology (i.e. the Christian verbalization of experience).

These somewhat general and deliberately inconclusive reflections have been premised to our account of Judaism because they highlight the inherent limitations of the undertaking. Depending on whether Judaism is held to be a body of religious and moral teaching (e.g. "ethical monotheism") or the history of a particular and chosen people, the assimilationist ideology of the Reform Movement of the 19th century (see below p. 43) and the nationalist revival known as Zionism respectively will be judged very differently. In fact, if the election and destiny of Israel as a people are taken seriously and as being of the "essence" of Judaism, then even the so-called secular Israelites form an essential part—theologically speaking—of the religious (and not merely of the social) history of the Jews. Bearing in mind the aforementioned reservations, we may, perhaps, venture to delineate the essence of Judaism with reference to the community which is its bearer (Israel, the Jews, Jewry), the Divine Being whose will transforms this community into a religious body, and the nexus between the two.

Peoplehood and Religion

As a group which emerged towards the end of the second millenium B.C. in the Near East and developed its historical and cultural character in the period 1000-600 B.C., the Jews were always fiercely conscious of being set apart from all other nations. This distinctness was understood as due to a specific religious vocation and destiny. This calling, however, was that of a people, viz. of the descendants of Abraham who had grown into "a great and mighty nation" because

God knew their ancestor "that he will command his children and his household after him, and they shall keep the way of the Lord to do justice and judgment" (Gen. 18:18-19). As a people called to be "a kingdom of priests and a holy nation" (Exodus 19:6) it knew that it was destined "to dwell alone and shall not be reckoned among the nations" (Numbers 23:6) even as "the Lord alone did lead him" (Deut. 32:12). No doubt the formation and development of this basic religious consciousness passed through many stages, but the curious fact is that our extant records do not reflect this process—at least not clearly and deliberately. The biblical books do not describe how the characteristic Israelite identity developed, and which inner factors and outer pressures shaped it. They present the specific religio-national consciousness of Israel and its underlying theology in a more or less crystallised form, and it is in this form that they determined the history of later Judaism. In the Jewish self-understanding Israel is a natural community ("the seed of Abraham") whose natural existence has a religious significance and purpose. This religious—one is tempted to say "supernatural"—quality of the natural existence of the Jewish people expresses itself, among other things, in the observance of a discipline of life, the purpose of which is not so much to procure salvation as to sanctify. Whilst the historian is undoubtedly correct in maintaining that the Jewish people gave birth to Judaism, it is no less true that this people is a people born of religion. A 10th century theologian and Aristotelian philosopher, Rabbi Sa'adyah Gaon, expressed this traditional awareness in the trenchant formula: "this nation is a nation solely by virtue of its *Torah*."

This combination of natural viz. ethnic community and religious calling places Judaism in a unique position between the great universalist religions and the ancient tribal or civic religions. The latter were based on natural groups or political units, whilst the former have no immediate place for the natural community in their religious sociology. The *samgha* is no people, the Church is the "people of God" in a metaphorical sense only, and even the Muslim *ummah* is a very different concept from that of the Hebrew *'am*, *'om* or *goy*. In the case of Israel the identity of peoplehood and religion is not adventitious. It is not the result of the absorption by a people of an extant religion, but the people and its religion seem to have grown together. It was God who had called the ancestor out of Ur of the Chaldees and bade him leave his country and his kindred and his father's house for the land that he would show him. Later he called the ancestor's descendants, by now a small people, out of their bondage in Egypt and confirmed his covenant with them at Mount Sinai. This, at any rate, is how Israel subsequently came to see its beginnings. The interesting thing about ethnic particularism as expressed theologically in the concepts of covenant and election, is its universalistic exclusiveness. Even though all people walk every one in the name of his God (who is, anyway, sheer vanity and nothingness), Israel confesses that its Lord alone is the God of heaven and earth and all the fullness thereof. "For all the gods of the nations are idols, but the Lord made the heavens ... Give unto the Lord, O ye families of the peoples, give unto the Lord glory and strength ... Say among the nations that the Lord reigneth; he shall judge the nations righteously" (Psalm 96: 5-10). And the verse which speaks of Israel's election to be a kingdom of priests and a holy nation is preceded by the words "for all the earth is mine."

Whilst "absolute monotheism" may not be the most adequate term to render the ancient Jewish, pre-philosophical, idea of God, it is certainly better and less misleading than any other. Old Testament scholars have been at pains to show that monotheism was a relatively late development, decisively influenced by the prophets and definitely crystallising during and after the Babylonian exile. Historians who do not share the simplistic evolutionist schemas will find the problem more complex. Evidently the God of the ancient Israelites has no history, though he creates history and intervenes in it, and hence has no theogony or mythology. Nothing can be told of him, except of his dealings with his creation in general and with man in particular. In the divine sphere he stands absolutely alone and no other divine being is associated with or subordinated to him—whatever the traces and echoes of earlier Semitic mythologies that may still be preserved in biblical language. No doubt the belief in one God articulated itself more clearly and distinctly as time went on, but this articulation would not have taken place if a certain conception had not been present, at least implicitly, from the very beginning. Whether this beginning is dated with the Patriarchs or with Moses is immaterial for our present purpose. In any event the prophets seem to have appealed to what they held to be the traditional values of Israel when they inveighed against departures from the purity of the faith and fidelity to the covenant. The settlement in Canaan confronted the previously semi-nomadic tribes with novel aspects of life: the power of the earth, the mystery of fertility, dependence on the rains, and all the other realities and cultural (including religious) patterns that go with a sedentary, agricultural civilisation. The struggle that ensued is recorded in the books of *Joshua*, *Judges*, *Samuel* and *Kings*, as well as in the collections of prophetic speeches. In the end the Israelites realised that Yahweh, the God of their fathers, whom they knew as having guided them in the desert, was in fact the same as the dispenser of fertility and rain (Hosea 1:10). He was also the same that demanded justice and lovingkindness of a people and of rulers that began to be increasingly influenced by the habits and morals of the petty monarchies of the ancient Near East. As time went on they had to learn that this God resented worship that was not backed by obedience and righteousness. Finally they were warned that if they would not learn their lesson in time they would have to learn it he hard way, in exile and tribulation. It was true that they were a chosen people, but this chosenness was a double-edged sword (cf. Amos 3:2). In the southern kingdom the divine election and covenant came to include also the royal dynasty of David and God's chosen city Jerusalem. All these were covenanted to God in a special relationship the validity of which was everlasting, much like that of the similar covenant with nature (cf. Jeremiah 31: 34-35; 33: 20-21, 25-26), and there was no escape or respite from the required loyalty. Even unfaithfulness could not dissolve the covenant; it would only bring chastisement. Israel was God's chosen spouse (as a favourite metaphor of the prophets put it); as such they could be neither widowed nor divorced, but only bidden to return God's love and to return *to* God's love. These notions became deeply rooted attitudes after the destruction of the First Temple, last but not least because the prophetic prediction of defeat, exile and subsequent restoration had confirmed their message, strengthened the belief in the special destiny of the Jewish people, and rendered the certainty of ultimate salvation beyond destruction and catastrophy less incredible than it might otherwise have been. Yet it would be a mistake to assume that only the deportation to Babylonia "proved" as it were the validity of the prophets' monotheism and convinced the people of the falseness of idolatry. In point of fact the destruction of Jerusalem could have been accounted for equally well on polytheistic premisses (cf. Jeremiah 44). It was the traditional monotheism of Israel which weighted the scales in favour of the prophetic interpretation of events and their claim that injustice, oppression and "whoring after strange gods" were disastrous aberrations from the path which Israel should walk.

Monotheism

This one God to whom Israel owed allegiance was an intensely personal God. Hence Jewish monotheism was exclusive, i.e. a positive relationship to a distinct and jealous God with a distinct name ("Yahweh, he is God"), and very unlike the monotheism by inclusion which occasionally develops as a syncretistic or philosophical synthesis of higher paganism. There the divine has many names and many manifestations. For classical Judaism, however, monotheism was by exclusion: Yahweh *or* Ba'al. And in the hoped for day in the future "Yahweh will be one and his name one" (Zach. 14: 9). This tradition of radical monotheism evidently renders it difficult for Judaism to seek a syncretistic answer to the questions posed by the existence of other religions. But God is not only arithmetically one; he is "one" in the sense of unique—and hence incomparable, wholly other, spiritual and transcendent. It is not without reason that Deut. 6: 4 "Hear O Israel, Yahweh is our God, Yahweh is One" has become the central confession of Judaism; these words were on the lips of hundreds of thousands of martyrs, and are still repeated every morning and evening, as well as on his deathbed, by every practising Jew.

However, it was not theoretical monotheism as belief in the existence of a supreme being that gave Judaism its distinctive quality, but practical monotheism as a relationship to an active, self-revealing and demanding God. Relationship with such a God meant loving and fearing him, doing his will, obeying and serving him. This in turn meant abiding by all the laws and commandments (prescriptions and prohibitions) which God had laid down and which formed an integral part of his Covenant with the people as solemnly ratified at the great theophany on Mount Sinai. In later times this theophany came to be known as the "Giving of the Law", and the term *Torah* became one of the most central concepts of Judaism. Of course "Law" is only one of the many meanings in the semantic spectrum of *Torah* as understood in later Judaism. *Torah* is doctrine, guidance, instruction, teaching. It can mean the Pentateuch, the Bible, revelation, or traditional religion as a whole. It is against the wider background of the Jewish theology of the "Word" or Scripture as God's revealed will that the translation "Law"—introduced by hellenistic Jewry—acquires some measure of legitimacy. In rabbinic Hebrew the term *halakhah* was used for that aspect of *Torah* which is law, whilst *aggadah* designates all non-legal lore—exegetical, edifying, homiletic, moralizing and theological. The various codifications of the ancient laws, commandments and ordinances, interpreted and administered by the priests, were probably accompanied from the very beginning by oral traditions without which they could never have been applied to the ever changing concrete situations. Consequently, after the final amalgamation of the various codes and other narrative traditions into one holy book, the notion of an "Oral Law," complementing and interpreting the written *Torah*, became one of the major doctrines of later Judaism.

Religious authority

Just as the notion of a chosen people walking in God's way and obeying his voice implies a canonical tradition laying down the law and the commandments, so also the existence of such a literature implies rules and procedures for authoritative interpretation. In fact, the locus of religious authority in later Judaism is in the sphere of the interpretation of the Law. Originally this was part of the function of the priests, but after the return to Jerusalem of the several groups of Babylonian exiles and the establishment of the Second Temple, there emerged a new type of bearer of religious authority: the non-sacerdotal "master" viz. teacher and expositor of the Law. The "scribes" and their successors, the rabbis, ultimately supplanted the priesthood, especially after the latter lost the social and institutional base of their authority with the destruction of the Temple by the Romans in 70 A.D. The sages and teachers suceeded not only the priests; they were also held to be the heirs of the prophets. With the cessation of charismatic apostolic prophecy, bringing in vision or word the divinely inspired message, the task of formulating, expounding and preaching the fundamental religious values and their practical application devolved on the scribes and sages. Prophecy degenerated into visionary apocalyptic, and in its own time the Talmud could rightly claim that "the sage was superior to the prophet." It is a curious fact that this development took place at a time when the power as well as the social and political significance of the priesthood had reached unprecedented heights. In the time of the Second Temple the priesthood was considered a hereditary hierarchy officiating by divine right, though later it became increasingly unpopular as it compromised itself religiously as well as politically. In due course rabbinic authority developed a theory and practice of legitimation. Unlike the priesthood of the "House of Aaron" which officiated in virtue of biological succession, rabbinic authority was conferred by ordination which was held to have been transmitted in an unbroken successsion going back to Moses himself. By the time that formal ordination ceased to be practised, rabbinic authority was established strongly enough to persist and operate on a theoretically more informal basis and without a regular hierarchy. The prestige conferred by learning and expert knowledge of the Law determined a rabbi's influence and his place in the informal hierarchy. Charismatic personalities whose authority was based on saintliness or other personal qualities and spiritual gifts were not unknown, but they could rarely compete for the authority and leadership enjoyed by the rabbi as scholar and teacher of the Law.

Scriptures and religious literature

The sacred tradition, the expounding and interpreting of which was the chief task of religious authority, consisted of the Scriptures and the Oral Law. The most authoritative part of Scripture was the *Torah* i.e., the Pentateuch which was held to have been verbally revealed to Moses on Sinai and which was canonized after the return from the Babylonian exile. The collections of historical accounts and prophetic speeches known as "The Prophets," and certain other writings known as "Hagiographa" were canonized much later, and the final establishment of the canon took place only after the destruction of the Second Temple. The canon of Hebrew Scripture does not include the writings known as Apocrypha and Pseudepigrapha, many of which figure in the "Old Testament" of the Catholic Church. Jewish tradition distinguishes several levels of authority and inspiration in Scripture, and only the five books of Moses are considered to be the very word of God and hence the source and guarantee of the permanent and immutable validity of the revealed Law. For this reason Jewish orthodoxy to this very day has great difficulty in coming to terms with biblical criticism, particularly as applied to the Pentateuch.

The "Oral Law" as developed by the Pharisaic teachers and their successors, the Tannaim and Amoraim, took the form of scriptural exegesis and of more or less systematic arrangement of the body of law as discussed in the rabbinic schools. All these were originally memorized, but subsequently the "oral" teaching too, both *mishnah* and *gemara*, was committed to writing. The *mishnah* is a summary codification of rabbinic law as it had evolved by the second century of the Christian era. The *gemara* is composed in the form of a "Hansard" reporting the at times wide-ranging discussions of the Mishnaic text that went on in the rabbinic academies. The results of centuries of analysis and elaboration of detail are embodied in the *Talmud*, the great compilations of rabbinic (particularly legal) lore made in the academies of Palestine and Babylonia. Whereas the *halakhah* dominates the Talmud, *aggadah* figures more prominently in the collections of moralising and edifying homilies known as *midrash*. Both together form the inexhaustible storehouse of tradition, wisdom, guidance and instruction to which Judaism turned for elucidation of God's revelation. Theologically speaking the Talmud as the "Oral Law" is second only to the Bible, yet it may almost be said to be primary since Rabbinic Judaism views the Bible only through the Talmud whose categories of thought, theological perspective and legal interpretations are normative and determine the understanding of Scripture. The Talmud in its turn became a canonical text and gave rise to commentaries and supercommentaries. The accumulating halakhic material inspired attempts at systematic codifications as well as a vast literature of *responsa*. In fact, the *responsa* are in many ways the most illuminating part of Jewish literature, since they show the practice of rabbinic Judaism "in action" as it were and at grips with the varying historical and social conditions of the Jewish communities all over the world. The validity of a halakhic ruling was always tested against the standards and principles of the Talmud, and *halakhah* as such, whilst flexible to a point, is characterised by a relatively firmer authority, greater rigidity and fuller articulation than the non-legal part of religious teaching. The latter exists in a more unofficial or fluid state, accepted by a kind of tacit assent and hallowed by tradition, but usually unsupported by formal discipline and ecclesiastical authority.

Philosophical and theological literature may be considered an outgrowth of *aggadah*. The latter, though neither codified nor considered absolutely binding in the same sense in which a halakhic ruling is, was sufficiently authoritative to require religious thinkers to take account of it when elaborating their philosophical systems. Hence the systematic philosophical theology that developed in the Middle Ages strove to bring its doctrines into alignment with the aggadic and halakhic traditions. Conversely it may be said that the Jewish thinkers strove to bring traditional aggadic and halakhic teaching into alignment with contemporary philosophical systems. In any case religious thought remained bound—at least formally—to a traditional literature and had to justify itself by means of (often allegorical) interpretation of authoritative texts. Nevertheless a distinct type of philosophical, non-midrashic and non-homiletical literature developed to which was added, in due course, the mystical literature of the kabbalists (see below, p. 23). Kabbalistic writings exhibit both the homiletic form of the *midrash* and the systematic character of philosophical literature. Whilst the *halakhah* provided the body of Jewish religious life, *aggadah*, philosophy and mysticism provided its soul viz. the articulation of its self-understanding and interpretation until the modern period. Mention should also be made of another type of literature which is in many ways the chief source and expression of Jewish religiosity. This is the liturgy whose beginnings go back to the period of the Second Temple and to whose basic core the generations added successive layers of devotional and liturgical compositions.

The preceding survey has attempted to present the framework within which the essence of traditional Judaism should be seen. This attempt inevitably focussed on one particular form of Judaism and is, therefore, open to the charge of arbitrariness. In fact, as the sequel will show, there is hardly a statement about details of doctrine regarding the Deity, man, eschatology etc. taken from one authoritative source which could not be controverted by quotations from another source. There is hardly an idea or doctrine that cannot be found in the vast library of Jewish thought, and hence no writer can escape the awkward necessity of concentrating on what he considers to be the "main trend", and treating other forms of religious life and thought as marginal or secondary. A few examples must suffice by way of illustration. The conception of a transcendent God has been held to be absolutely fundamental to Judaism. Yet the idea of God as taught by some of the great Hasidic masters comes very close to what is generally called pantheism. The great mystical theologian and founder of the *Habad* school of Hasidism, R. Shneour Zalman of Lyady (1747-1813) is a case in point. The verse Deut. 4: 39 ("Know therefore ... and consider it in thine heart, that the Lord he is God ... there is none else") which is usually and correctly translated so as to express the rejection of paganism by biblical monotheism, is interpreted by R. Shneour Zalman as meaning "there is *nothing* else" i.e., God is everything and there is nothing that is not God. The point here is neither that R. Shneour Zalman's opponents accused him of pantheistic heresy, nor that his teaching is a long way indeed from both the biblical and the classical rabbinic conception of God, but the more important—and perhaps disconcerting—fact that no historian of Judaism can dismiss *Habad* Hasidism as "un-Jewish." When moving from theological doctrines to the basic self-understanding of the Jewish Community we encounter similar variety. 19th century liberal Judaism denied the national character of the Jewish community and insisted on its purely denominational nature (cf. below, p. 43), thus placing itself in opposition to both traditional theology and the modern nationalist (i.e. Zionist) interpretation of Jewish existence.

Messianism

Among religous beliefs linking theological dogma with the experience of history none is, perhaps, as instructive as the doctrine of the Messiah. The assertion that messianism was of the essence of Judaism has frequently been made by both Jewish and Christian authors. For the latter this was the most facile method of focussing the essence of Judaism on that one point where it could most easily be confronted with Christianity, i.e. the religion which claimed that the promised Messiah had in fact come. For many Jewish thinkers messianism was not only the promise and hope that kept Judaism alive in an abyss of humiliation, persecution and massacre, but also the ultimately universalistic sanction of an apparently particularistic religion. Yet the role and significance of the messianic idea in Judaism vary according to circumstances. Evidently the tribes that settled in Canaan had no need of messianism. Theirs was not the experience of hope but that of the fulfilment of the promises made to the Patriarchs. The author of the violently antimonarchical diatribe I Samuel 8 surely did not look forward to a messianic king as the consummation of all hopes. In fact, the messianic ideology developed only after kingship had been firmly established in Israel. This "kingship ideology" seems to have been indebted to Canaanite notions regarding the role of the king in maintaining the harmony between human society on the one hand and the forces of nature and the supernaturals on the other. As the Lord's anointed or "son" of God, the king fulfilled a cosmic function whose centre of gravity shifted, as time went on, from the cosmogonic foundation of the ideal state of affairs to an eschatological one. As the careers of the successive kings became more and more disappointing and historical reality corresponded less and less to the ideal of perfect blessing and prosperity, the notion of salvation was projected on the future, when the Lord's anointed, the messianic king of the house of David, would preside over a perfected world such as foretold by the prophets. In fact, the covenant with David had become so deeply rooted in the consciousness of the people that a messianic world was unthinkable without a scion of the house of

David ruling over it. The ancient liturgical benediction, recited after the reading of the Lesson from the Prophets, recalls God's faithful promises, prays for Israel's return to Zion, "the home of our life", and then continues: "Gladden us, O Lord our God, with Elijah the prophet, thy servant, and with the kingdom of the house of David, thine anointed. Soon may he come and rejoice our hearts. No stranger shall sit upon his throne, nor shall others any longer inherit his glory, for by thy holy name thou didst swear unto him that his light should not be quenched for ever."

Whilst messianic belief and hope were entertained by all Jews, the details varied greatly at different periods and with different thinkers. Moreover, it was not only the details which varied but also the function and significance of the "messianic complex" as a whole within the totality of the Jewish faith. Time and again messianic fervour, nourished by ancient or more recent apocalyptic texts, would explode into messianic movements which, as a rule, petered out after the failure, death or disappearance of the messianic pretender, precursor of prophet. Others would cultivate messianic hope but at the same time neutralize its dangerous potential by keeping it in eschatological "deep freeze". Others again would move the messianic complex to a subordinate position, considering the quest of spiritual perfection (e.g. the philosophical piety of Maimonides or the ascetic piety of Bahya; see below, pp. 21-3) or the devout and conscientious observance of the divine commandments (as in the halakhic piety of rabbinic Judaism) as being the essence of religious faith and practice. The words with which the greatest Jewish philosopher of the Middle Ages concludes his brief exposition of traditional eschatology are instructive in this respect: "All these things [*scil.* the details concerning the messianic era] nobody knows what they will be like ... and in any event their exact manner of happening and other details are no basic principle of religion. Therefore one should not spend one's time on such aggadic statements and ... [apocalyptic] texts, or consider them as fundamental, for they are conducive neither to the fear nor to the love of God."

Maimonides's reserved attitude towards apocalyptic messianism certainly cannot be taken as representative of the historical fullness of Judaism, yet he does seem to express one of its major trends. It is a trend in which the emphasis is on a religious life focussed on the love and the fear of God as actualised in the service of God i.e., in obedience to his revealed will and law. "Blessed is our God who hath created us for his glory and hath separated us from them that go astray, and hath given us the true Law and planted everlasting life in our midst. May he open our heart unto his Law, and place his love and fear within our hearts, that we may do his will and serve him with a perfect heart" (from the daily liturgy). It is this attitude which seems in many ways characteristic of what is historically the most widespread and most representative form of Judaism: rabbinic Judaism. For this reason our presentation of Judaism takes as its point of reference rabbinic Judaism as it has existed for about two thousand years and as it has crystallised in a rigid pattern of orthodoxy in the 16th-18th centuries. It is unnecessary to emphasise that this orthodoxy, which exhibits the dominant features of rabbinic Judaism, is not the whole of Judaism. Yet even even other, including modern, forms of Judaism cannot ignore this point of reference and very often they articulate and define their own positions by way of a polemical or critical demarcation over against rabbinic Judaism.

II. The History of Judaism

Return from the Babylonian exile

Some of the stages in the development of Judaism have already been adumbrated in the preceding section. The destruction of the Temple in Jerusalem by Nebuchadnezzar in 587 B.C. (see Vol. I, p. 296) though it marked the end of an era in the history of the Jews and their religion, was not the end of their history. On the contrary, the disaster confirmed the prophecies of Micah, Jeremiah and others. During the "Babylonian exile" the Jews learned to live as a minority, enjoying greater or lesser autonomy within the larger, ungodly, pagan political state. The loss of political independence caused Jewish society to organise itself as a religious community, bound together by their faith in the unbroken validity of God's covenant with them and in the unfailing promise of a divinely operated restoration. The experience of the Babylonian exile gave rise to patterns of faith and forms of organization that enabled Judaism to survive the much longer and more gruelling exile that followed on the destruction of the so-called Second (actually the third, Herodian) Temple by the Romans in 70 A.D. When Cyrus issued an edict in 538 B.C. permitting the rebuilding of the Temple in Jerusalem and the return of the exiled Jews to their homeland, the prophetic prediction of a future restoration received triumphant vindication. The idea took root that a special divine providence watched over the fortunes of the Jewish people, and that whatever calamities would befall them, the promise of ultimate deliverance would never fail them. As a matter of fact only a small number of exiles returned to Jerusalem, but Judaea and the far flung diaspora—from Persia and Babylonia in the east to Egypt in the west—now formed part of one *oikoumene* (at first Persian and then, after the conquests of Alexander the Great, Greek-Hellenistic) and hence no profound differences or separations arose. The returning exiles brought with them the "*Torah* of Moses" which henceforth functioned as the "book of the law of God" to be interpreted by the competent authorities. Observance of the Sabbath, the prohibition of inter-marriage and other rules were strictly enforced. A liturgy of prayer began to develop alongside the sacrificial cult of the priests in the Temple. This liturgy was in use in small groups outside the capital, but subsequently established itself even within the Temple precincts. After the destruction of the Second Temple it was the Synagogue which survived as the major and most potent religious institution. Together with the liturgy of the synagogue there also developed the beginnings of a type of religious teaching that was neither priestly nor of the traditional type of lay "Wisdom". The teaching that evolved was based on an increasingly intensive "interpretation" of the Law of Moses, and it took place in a liturgical setting (reading of the Law, accompanied by oral translation and interpretation, in the synagogue) as well as in schools. In both cases the scribe, and his successor the rabbi, supplanted the priest. Yet there could be little doubt that the "return to Zion", heralded with such sanguine enthusiasm by the second Isaiah, turned out to be less than perfect. The restoration of the Davidic dynasty proved abortive, the majority of the people continued to live in the diaspora, and politically as well as morally and individually it was painfully evident that if there was such a thing as a golden age it was in the future. The problem of individual eschatology became no less pressing than that of the collective, national expectation, and doctrines which subsequently came to be formulated in greater detail (the immortality of the soul, resurrection of the dead, last judgment etc.) may well have begun to evolve at that period.

Hellenism

The conquests of Alexander the Great substituted a Greek for the Persian *oikoumene*. The contact with Hellenism, like that with other cultures, helped to sharpen the consciousness of ethnic and religious distinctness of the Jews and their sense of a unique religious calling, but it was not without its dangers. The process of hellenization, though opposed by the pious faithful, also found eager supporters in certain priestly and aristocratic circles. There is good reason to believe that the revolt of the Maccabees (167 B.C.) did not begin as an insurrection against the policies of Antiochus IV Epiphanes, but rather as a civil war of the orthodox against the Jewish hellenizers. The steadfastness of the many martyrs who refused to apostatise during Antiochus's attempt to enforce pagan Hellenism and the subsequent victory of the Maccabees left Palestinian Jewry strong enough to absorb Greek influences without danger of being engulfed by them. The extent and depth of hellenistic influence on Judaism are difficult to gauge. Whilst material life (including synagogue architecture and tomb inscriptions) became predominantly Greek and the Hebrew language absorbed many Greek words (even as designations of major Jewish institutions such as the *sanhedrin*), its effects in the sphere of religious thought and institutions are less easy to determine. It is not impossible that the legal as well as ethical teachings of the early Palestinian rabbis owe something to hellenistic thought. Hellenistic influences are evident also in some of the apocrypha and pseudepigrapha which were not admitted to the canon of Scripture and many of which have survived only in Greek versions. Outside Palestine Greek had become the language of the Jews, and as early as the 3rd century B.C. the Jews of Egypt used a Greek translation of the Bible (the Septuagint). It is not surprising, therefore, that diaspora Jewry became more easily and more strongly hellenised, sharing in the civilisation of the environment, assimilating to it, and yet remaining obstinately different. This, incidentally, led to the first historically recorded manifestations of both literary anti-semitism and anti-Jewish rioting. In the eyes of the pagan gentiles, the Jewish worship of an invisible and imageless God was tantamount to atheism, and Jewish cohesion and aloofness was considered a symptom of anti-social misanthropy. Alexandria was the capital of that Jewish hellenism of which Philo is the noblest representative. Here Jewish philosophers came profoundly under the influence of all that was best and spiritual in hellenistic thought and piety. Under the impact of Greek (platonic and stoic) philosophy they began to translate traditional Jewish symbols into Greek idiom, and at times it is difficult to determine whether they used Greek thought to elucidate Judaism or whether they reformulated Judaism as a hellenistic philosophy. However that may be, Philo's harmonisation of revelation and philosophy, i.e. of the Bible and hellenistic thought (and especially the monotheistic tendencies of the latter) proved of far reaching consequence for the history of Christian thought, and hence for western civilisation, although his influence on Judaism was negligible. Philo, not unlike many of the apocryphal books of the Old Testament, disappeared from the Jewish horizon and had to be "re-discovered" at a later period. A great deal of Jewish hellenistic writing, whether philosophical (Philo) or historical (Josephus) was apologetic and propagandistic in character, endeavouring to prove to the gentiles the superiority and excellence of the Jewish laws and teachings. Although this apologetic literature made no impression on the pagan world, the hellenistic period provides a classic illustration of the capacity of Judaism to enrich, without losing, itself by contact with a universal civilisation.

Sects

Apart from Hellenism, there existed many other influences, trends, groups and sects, and towards the end of the Second Temple—by which time the Jewish *oikoumene* had become that of the Roman Empire—Judaism presented a variegated picture. The Samaritans, according to the official Jewish view (ii Kings 17; Nehemiah 6), were descendants of the heathen colonists whom Sargon II had settled in Samaria after the fall of the Northern Kingdom; they subsequently adopted some features of Israelite religion, thus producing a syncretistic religion of their own. According to their own tradition (which may contain some truth), the Samaritans are descendants of that part of the population of the Northern Kingdom which remained in the country after the deportation of the majority of the ten tribes. By the 5th century B.C. the schism was complete and subsequently developed into permanent hostility. (Relations only changed when part of the small Samaritan community of Nablus settled in the state of Israel after 1948). Whilst the Samaritans thus stood outside the politico-religious structure of the Jewish people, the Essenes—who are probably identical with the Qumran Covenanters, i.e. the sect whose writings have been found in caves in the Judaean desert near the Dead Sea—were a voluntary association distinguished by a semi-monastic discipline, a *halakhah* which differed in some respects from that of the Pharisaic teachers, and characteristic theological doctrines which included predestinarian beliefs, a dualism dividing the children of light from the children of darkness, frequent baptismal ablutions and an emphatic repudiation of the priestly and political authorities that held power in Jerusalem. The Sadducees were a priestly and "upper class" party, opposed to the usurpation of religious authority by the Pharisaic "lay" scholars who interpreted Scripture, by means of what they alleged to be the "Oral Law", in a progressive and adaptive manner. Although the Pharisees were themselves an *élite* as regards meticulous observance of the Law, and hence were "separated" (*parush* = "separate," Pharisee) from the majority of ordinary laymen, the mass of the people nevertheless sympathised with them and tended to accept their leadership. The destruction of the Temple by Titus (70 A.D.) spelled the cessation of sectarianism and the uncontested ascendancy of Pharisaism. The Pharisees and their successors, the rabbis and "doctors of the Law," were the only spiritual force capable of guiding the people. Henceforth, and until the beginning of the modern period, Judaism is identical with rabbinic Judaism. The only exception proves the rule, since Karaism (see below, p. 21) was a sectarian protest against rabbinism.

Rabbinic Judaism

Rabbinic Judaism and rabbinic literature have been briefly characterised above, pp. 7. Although supreme authority was for some time vested in the hereditary "patriarchs" of Palestinian Jewry (much as later communal authority among the semi-autonomous Jewry of the Sassanian Empire was vested in the hereditary exilarchs—both being considered to be descended from the House of David), rabbinic leadership was socially democratic even if élitist in its intellectual and moral demands. Of the "three crowns" of royalty, priesthood and *Torah*, the latter was considered the noblest and it was there for the taking by anyone who showed willingness and aptitude to endure the long and strenuous course of study, memorise the increasing mass of the "Oral Law" (which was not committed to writing until a later date), and learn to compare and sift the many opinions emitted in the schools and academies of Palestine and Babylonia. Many of the early sages were artisans, though at a later period scholars were granted certain privileges (e.g. tax exemption) and in the Middle Ages a salaried rabbinate with fixed emoluments came into being. In the hands of the rabbinic teachers the whole of life became a system of behaviour commanded by God. To live by the Law was to do God's will, to walk in his way, to further his purpose and thereby to achieve individual salvation and blessedness as well as prepare the way for the

Messiah. It is understandable that rabbinism, whose highest ideal and consuming desire was precisely this life of joyous obedience, developed a real passion for the business of ascertaining God's will in all possible circumstances. From Scripture and traditional premisses, and by the accepted rules of interpretation and deduction, the "disciple of the sages" was always engaged in discovering the specific application of the divine law to each and every situation that occurred or might conceivably occur. As a result rabbinic Judaism was primarily concerned with the formulation of rules and norms that would relate human behaviour to the revealed will of the Creator. No doubt the rabbis also taught faith and doctrine, exhorted the people to persevere in their fidelity to the Law in the love of God and in constant readiness for martyrdom, kept alive the messianic hope in the heart of a persecuted nation living precariously in the midst of a hostile (at first pagan and later Christian) environment, and strengthened their consciousness of being a chosen people, distinct from all others and the object of God's love and promise. Yet although the rabbis were also preachers and spiritual guides, they were first and foremost lawyers. The old institution known as the Sanhedrin was a legislative and judicial body, halfway between a parliament and a supreme court. The adage that rabbinic Judaism was not interested in orthodoxy (right faith) but in orthopraxis (right action) is, like most antithetical epigrams, at best a misleading half-truth, but it contains enough truth to emphasise a tendency which could, on occasion, go to extreme lengths. The strenuous intellectual labour of *Talmud Torah* (the study of the Law) became the ideal business of life and a supreme religious value in itself. Study tended to become a sort of sacramental activity in which the Jew communed with God through his revealed logos, the *Torah*. The negative side of this development was a hypertrophy of rabbinic casuistry about legal and ritual minutiae which continued to proliferate as time went on and which often bordered on the absurd.

But however absurd in its extremes, any limits set to this development would have been arbitrary and even more absurd. If you are supposed to abstain from work on the Sabbath, then you must also define what constitutes work. Where is the thin line of division between harvesting, reaping and plucking ears of corn? There were thousands of problems of this kind, because the whole of life had to be sanctified by being made subject to the Law. The house had to be a house of God, the table an altar, the market place an expression of justice. There is hardly an act which a practising Jew can perform (including dressing or cooking a meal) to which some religious duty or prohibition is not attached. The Jew does not merely want to do the right and lawful thing, and to avoid sin. He positively wants to do God's will and therefore desires that every act should be a divine commandment. The Hebrew term *miṣwah* which is used for "good deed" or "religious act" means literally "commandment." The rabbis counted 613 positive and negative commandments (not counting their subdivisions and ramifications) which they related to the 613 parts of the body recognised by their anatomy. To make sure that all life was hallowed, the rabbis ordained blessings to be recited on all possible occasions: when eating, drinking, putting on new clothes, seeing beautiful objects, smelling a flower, hearing sad news and so on. When the occasion was the performance of a positive commandment, the benediction contains the words "...who has sanctified us by his commandments and commanded us to...".

The redaction of the Palestinian Talmud took place ca. 400 A.D., that of the Babylonian Talmud during the 5th-6th centuries. In due course the rabbis succeeded in imposing the Talmud on practically the whole of Jewry from Persia to the east to Spain in the west. Whatever variations there existed, were matters of custom, liturgical usage and minor differences of interpretation, as e.g. the differences between the Sephardi (Spanish) and Ashkenazi (German) traditions in Europe or the various local traditions (e.g. the Yemenite) in the Orient. This unifying pattern of belief and practice provided the widely scattered Jewish diaspora not only with a spiritual home but also with an armour that both isolated and protected it until the dawn of the modern period.

Philosophical Theology

Within the firmly established framework of rabbinic Judaism, significant changes occurred as regards its intellectual and spiritual articulation during the Middle Ages. One of the most important developments was the rise of a philosophical theology. In the wake of the Muslim thinkers who examined their own faith in terms of the Greek philosophy which they had re-discovered and further developed, the Jewish theologians too began to discuss fundamental beliefs in the light of of Neo-platonism and Aristotelianism, and with the rigorous discipline of philosophical logic. There was also the apologetic stimulus and the necessity of upholding one's faith against competing religions claiming equally divine revelations and authoritative scriptures as their foundations. The only common ground on which argument could move was that of rational thinking and, if possible, rational proof. There were, moreover, internal Jewish conflicts that stimulated reflection. Whereas occasional messianic and gnostic movements, often led by *illuminati* and abetted by political confusion and turmoil, quickly disappeared, the Karaite ("Scripturalist") sect which recognised the authority of the Bible only and denied that of rabbinic tradition, presented a more serious challenge. In actual fact the Karaites too had to evolve canons of interpretation and a legal tradition of their own, but their criticism could only be met by a systematic and convincing statement of the orthodox faith. As Karaite criticism was essentially rational, holding up to scorn the crudely anthropomorphic style of much aggadic literature, the anti-Karaite struggle stimulated not only biblical exegesis but also rational theological thinking. Among the problems discussed by the philosophers were the nature of revelation; knowledge and faith, and their relation to each other; the nature of the human personality and its relation to God; the existence and attributes of God; the createdness or eternity of the world; providence and theodicy. The assumption underlying this philosophical effort was that reason was not only competent to deal with these problems but was, in fact, required to do so as a religious duty. Reason was man's noblest part; through it alone he was the image of God and capable of communing with his Creator. The exercise of the rational faculty, i.e. the pursuit of philosophy, thus became transfigured with the halo of religious contemplation. Whereas for the talmudist rabbi the highest form of religious meditation had been the study of the Law, for the philosopher it was the comtempleation of the eternal forms. Many of the principles of the Jewish faith were formulated with dogmatic precision during that period, though it should be remembered that these discussions were carried on between philosophical thinkers and not between official theologians authorised to lay down the truth and to pronounce anathemas.

The greatest and most influential medieval philosopher, Moses Maimonides (1135-1204), also happened to be one of the most illustrious talmudists, and his systematic code of rabbinic law was more honoured in orthodox circles than his controversial philosophical *magnum opus* "The Guide for the Perplexed." Maimonides was particularly emphatic in his struggle against anthropomorphism, and his doctrine of attributes rules out everything that even faintly suggests corporeality or multiplicity in God, that is, in fact, all positive attributes. Since biblical and rabbinic literature are teeming with anthropomorphic expressions, allegorical interpretation is resorted to (as in the case of Philo) in order to make the hallowed texts agree with philosophical truth. The latter should be "known" and not merely believed, and it is the intellect alone which, if properly developed, is man's immortal part. The belief in a Messiah who rebuilds the Temple and rules over an Israel restored to its ancient homeland is expressly affirmed but does not, so one feels, form an organic and essential part of this philosophical system. Maimonides believed that the law revealed in the *Torah* provided the kind of physical and moral discipline most apt to assist the development of man's higher (i.e. rational) faculties and to lead him to true contemplative knowledge and communion with God. This stage of being lovingly united to God, the consummation of the *amor intellectualis dei*, is, according to Maimonides, identical with prophecy. A messianic world is one where peace, prosperity and orderly government prevent all distractions and render the undisturbed philosophical life possible. The doctrine of the resurrection of the dead, a major Jewish dogma since the time of the Pharisees and affirmed in the daily liturgy, is formally accepted by Maimonides though it does not fit in very well with his attitude and system as a whole. Violent controversies ensued as an orthodox, anti-philosophical reaction set in, inspired by the not unreasonable fear that a system which allegorised away all "awkward" traditional beliefs and which explained many of the laws of the *Torah* as mere symbolic reminders of certain philosophical truths would ultimately undermine Jewish practice and religion. The criticism of philosophical intellectualism was stated even before it reached its apogee with Maimonides. Yehudah ha-Levi, a profound religious thinker and the greatest of all medieval Hebrew poets (d. 1148) defended the specificity of religious experience and religious life. Centuries before Pascal he formulated the distinction between the God of Aristotle, who is at best a "first cause" or "prime mover," and the God of Abraham who is the Living God experienced in personal relationship and in revelation. Religion is based not on speculative knowledge of causes but on miracles, though ha-Levi is careful to point out that religion, whilst not rational, is not anti-rational. Judaism is not based on universal reason but on the particular historical experience of a particular historical people. Ha-Levi's theology is a theology of the *ekklesia Israel*. The destiny of this mystical and at the same time natural (and indeed racial) community is linked to a unique, chosen and promised land, and the yearning for Zion suffuses both ha-Levi's thought and his poetry. Less historically minded than ha-Levi, but also less intellectualistic than Maimonides, is the 11th century ascetic and spiritual writer Bahya ibn Pakuda. His *Book of the Duties of the Heart* moves in the familiar medieval Neoplatonic tradition and testifies to the profound influence exerted by Sufi spirituality on Jewish pietist circles, though Bahya's Jewish heritage makes him recoil from the extreme asceticism and the ideal of the "annihilation in unity" of the human soul preached by the Sufis. Perhaps Bahya's spirituality should be described as ascetic piety rather than mysticism, since his ladder of perfection culminates not in extatic union with God but in a consuming love of God, "the longing of the soul and its yearning for the creator, so that it may cleave to his supreme light." As in the case of Maimonides, and unlike Yehuda ha-Levi, Bahya's spirituality lacks the historical awareness that looms so large in traditional Judaism. No doubt Bahya sincerely believed in the election of Israel, the coming of the Messiah and the ingathering of the exiles to the Holy Land, but in the dynamics of his system these hardly play any role. The predominance of one particular concern pushes others into the background without actually denying them. A spirituality concerned with the perfection of the individual—whether in terms of intellectualist mysticism, as in the case of Maimonides, or in terms of pietist mysticism, as in that of Bahya—tends to become indifferent to history both as a reality and as a religious category. It was one of the achievements of the Kabbalah that it combined mysticism with the historical, and indeed messianic, orientation of Judaism.

Mysticism and Kabbalah

The Kabbalah (literally "tradition," for its adepts believed that their esoteric doctrines went back to Moses and the Patriarchs) is but one phase, albeit the most important and far-reaching in its effects, in the history of Jewish mysticism. The Old Testament apocrypha and pseudepigrapha already suggest the existence of circles cultivating visionary experiences. The Essenes too seem to have had doctrines of a more esoteric nature. In the talmudic period an extatic mysticism was practised in certain circles in which cosmological doctrines and gnostic notions combined with elements from the vision of the Divine Throne (the *Merkabah* or "chariot") described by Ezekiel. As the climax of his extatic ascent, the *Himmelsreise der Seele*, the visionary beheld the awesome splendour and numoinous majesty of the Divine Throne. It appears that this type of mysticism was practised also in rabbinic circles, though it was treated with the greatest discretion and only very few and obscure allusions to it are found in the Talmud. Some of these traditions, however, survived and combined with other influences (including Neoplatonic speculations) to produce the Kabbalah *sensu stricto*. The gnostic character of this curious theosophical system which developed in the 12th and 13th centuries in Southern France and in Spain, is due mainly to its conception of the divine *pleroma* as consisting of a number of dynamic factors (similar to the "aeons" of the ancient gnostics) whose interactions constitute the fullness of the Life Divine. This mystical pleroma, its inner dynamisms and its relation to the human world can only be described in symbolic language and intended in symbolic acts. Here the kabbalistic exegesis of Scripture and the kabbalistic interpretation of the symbolic significance of the ritual acts prescribed by the Law, combine with the philosophico-gnostic theosophy of the Kabbalah. The divine and the human spheres are interdependent. The fallen state of the world and Israel's suffering in particular reflect a fatal disruption within the inner life of the Godhead. Conversely, human sinfulness can provoke and perpetuate this disruption, even as devout observance of the commandments and religious meditation can heal it. Every act and thought thus has cosmic significance, and it is Israel's task to promote redemption by contemplative efforts and a holy life. Thus for the kabbalist the religious life was not merely a matter of doing God's will or acquiring merits; it was a series of significant performances transformed into mystically redemptive acts by virtue of contemplative concentration. No doubt this mythological and theurgic mysticism often bordered on magic, but it placed the religious life of the individual and of the community on a cosmic stage on which the struggle for the wholeness of God and his creation was played out as Israel, sinful but struggling and suffering, was pitted against the nations of the world who were the very substance of demonic evil. After the expulsion of the Jews from the Iberian peninsula at the end of the 15th century, the sharpened experience of crisis and an intensified expectation of the messianic advent increased the influence and significance of the Kabbalah and led to the great kabbalistic revival whose centre was in Galilee. According to the thoroughly gnostic mythology of Isaac Luria (d. 1572), a pre-cosmic catastrophe had occurred even before Adam's fall, in the very heart of God's creative manifestation.

This "breaking of the vessels"—precosmic as far as God is concerned, cosmic as regards the actual state of creation, historic as regards the fate of Israel, individual as regards the soul of sinful man—can only be healed by Israel bending all its energies to lifting the fallen sparks of the divine light-essence out of the demonic abyss into which they had fallen and restoring them to their source. This task can only be accomplished by a life of ascetic sanctity, mystical meditation and the strict fulfilment of the divine Law, the latter corresponding in mystical analogy to the structure of the cosmos. The messianic fervour of the period combined with the magical tendencies of kabbalistic theurgy exploded in the messianic movement that centered round Sabbatai Sevi of Smyrna (d. 1676). The movement and its aftermath gave rise to mystical heresies advocating the conquest of evil not by observance of the Law but, on the contrary, by a deliberate descent into the realm of evil, impurity and sin. These antinomian doctrines and the sects that practised them in the wake of the abortive messianic movement, plunged Judaism into a prolonged crisis which, in the long run, limited the influence of the Kabbalah but also served as a catalyst in engendering the Hasidic revival (see below).

The mighty messianic awakening, its miserable failure, and its aftermath of apostasy, mystical antinomianism and nihilism, created the need for a new spiritual and emotional focus that would satisfy the religious longing of the masses. The answer was given by Israel Ba'al Shem Tov (d. 1760) and his disciples. The "Hasidic" movement which quickly spread in Eastern Europe taught a religious inwardness whose supreme value was communion with God. This experience of communion could be of an enthusiastic or a contemplative nature, but it was far removed both from the arid intellectualism and legalism of the talmudists and from apocalyptic messianism. Hasidism left the body of traditional law, customs and beliefs intact (apart from minor changes in liturgy and ritual), but as a movement of the unlettered masses, led by charismatic individuals and grouping itself in conventicles distinct from the established congregations with their traditional rabbinic leadership, it was at first fiercely opposed by the official establishment. In the end Hasidism did not become a dissident sect; it remained a movement within traditional Judaism. But the original mystical impetus soon spent itself. The idea of charismatic leadership degenerated into a theological version of the "cult of personality" (the hasidic leader acting as a mediator between the faithful and God and posing as a worker of miracles) and led to the establishment of hereditary dynasties and hasidic "courts." With the general deterioration of the situation of the Jews of eastern Europe, Hasidism became—in the eyes of the pioneers of enlightenment—the very incarnation of obscurantism, superstition and imperviousness to change.

Enlightenment and Reform

Whilst Hasidism spread in Eastern Europe, Western and Central Europe witnessed a growing tendency to grant the Jews civil rights and emancipation. The emerging Jewish bourgeoisie in Prussia and elsewhere easily responded to those ideas of the enlightenment that seemed to offer them tolerance and to promise their harmonious absorption into the life of the larger society (which at that time still was a Christian society). Lessing's friend Moses Mendelssohn (1729-1786) prepared the way for this development, which gathered impetus in the 19th century, by translating the Bible into literary German: a symbolic exodus of the Jew from the ghetto of his Jewish-German jargon to the promised land of civilisation. Mendelssohn held that Judaism was a "revealed legislation" and not a dogmatic system of beliefs. According to him the Jewish "faith" was that of enlightened liberal rationalism, and hence there was no reason why the Jews should not be admitted, as citizens, to civil rights whilst maintaining, as a religion, their distinctive ritual laws and customs. Mendelssohn's own children and grandchildren failed to see the necessity of a distinctive and "segregationsist" ritual law when the essential beliefs were those of enlightened liberalism; they and many others accordingly embraced, in a perfunctory way and as an act of social assimilation, the dominant religion. The progress of emancipation throughout Europe in the wake of the French revolution and after the Napoleonic conquests, integrated the Jews more and more within their surrounding host society (in spite of the original tendency to grant them "everything as citizens but nothing as Jews," and in spite of several reactionary setbacks in the 19th century). The traditional conception of Jewry as a distinct, separate and indeed segregated society was increasingly felt to be socially unreal, and morally and intellectually indefensible. Emancipation, assimilation, liberalism, enlightenment, rationalism and (later) historical criticism combined to create a climate in which "reform," i.e. liberal modernism seemed to many Jews to offer a way of preserving a Jewish religious identity whilst otherwise becoming part of the surrounding civic society. By relinquishing many of the traditional beliefs and practices, Reform Judaism lost the power to oppose effective resistance to the radical assimilationist trend, and hence its success in Europe remained limited whereas in the more pluralistic society of the U.S. it succeeded to a remarkable degree. In Eastern Europe orthodoxy remained impervious to any change or modern influence. Reacting against the danger of encroaching secular enlightenment, an ethico-pietistic (*musar*) revival swept many of the talmudic schools. The influence of this movement is still strongly noticeable in rabbinic circles and talmudic academies. In Germany the "neo-orthodoxy" founded by S. R. Hirsch (d. 1888) sought to combine strict ritual and dogmatic orthodoxy with participation in the civic, cultural and even national life of the host country. Unlike the orthodoxy of eastern Europe which rejected all secular studies and knowledge, western neo-orthodoxy welcomed them albeit with many mental reservations; thus e.g. biblical criticism or evolutionist biology are still avoided. Thinkers outside the orthodox fold have used, and are using, current philosophical systems (in the 19th century Kantian and Hegelian, in the 20th century neo-Kantian, pragmatist and existentialist) as a basis for their philosophies of Judaism.

Zionism

A major change occurred towards the end of the 19th century, as the experience of antisemitism, and the gradual realisation of the impossibility or failure of social emancipation (at first more evident in eastern Europe, but revealed to Theodore Herzl, the founder of Zionism, in the west during the Dreyfus affair) prepared the way for a national-territorialist solution of the "Jewish problem." Supernatural messianism had ceased to be an inspiring force, but the traditional messianic hope and longing for a redemptive restoration combined with a secular conception of Jewish "auto-emancipation" to produce the Zionist movement. The dedication of Zionist pioneers in reclaiming the malaria-ridden marshy swamps and the barren deserts of the ancient homeland, the situation created by the greatest catastrophe in the history of a people used to catastrophes and martyrdom — the extermination of six million Jews in Europe during World War II, and the heroic resistance of the Jews of Palestine to the invading armies of seven Arab states resulted in a new fact in the history of Judaism: the State of Israel. The European holocaust and the elimination, under Soviet Communism, of the great reservoir of Russian Jewry as a potent force in Jewish life, have resulted in a polarisation of Jewry in two main centres: Israel and the U.S. Their situation will be reviewed below, pp. 42 ff.

III. The Doctrine of God

From what has been said in the preceding paragraphs it should be obvious that the traditional conception of God is essentially an "operational" one: God is the one who is served in loving obedience. He is the redeemer who chose Israel to be his people, and who revealed to them his Law. He is the creator and ruler of the world. He is not an anonymous cosmic principle but "the God of our fathers" and "Yahweh is his name." The Bible describes him as transcendent, spiritual, utterly non-mythological, yet also intensely personal and, indeed, "jealous." He is not merely existing, creating and acting, but is also turned towards man, calling for his co-operative response, demanding of him to "listen" i.e., to obey. This human vocation devolved in a unique sense upon Israel as God's elect people. "Our Father and our King" has become a standard liturgical formula, expressing a sense of both loving intimacy and unquestioning subjection. The "I-Thou" relationship with God which Martin Buber has analysed and which the liturgical formula using the second person ("Blessed art thou...") inculcates, means that transcendence is experienced as charging Israel with the duty to respond, i.e. with *responsibility*. Failure to respond, that is infedility to the Covenant and disobedience to the Law, is visited by divine wrath and punishment. Biblical language is unashamedly anthropomorphic and remains so even in its anti-anthropomorphic disclaimers (cf. the so-called prayer of Solomon at the dedication of the Temple: "Behold, the heaven of heavens cannot contain thee, how much less this house that I have builded" I Kings 8:27). Philo of Alexandria was surely not the first to have felt that Scripture modelled its speech concerning God too much on human, all-too-human forms of expression. By means of allegorical exegesis he endeavoured to lift anthropological speech to a higher spiritual level, stressing God's utter transcendence which cannot be grasped by discursive thinking though it can be incompletely approached in the extasy of contemplation. The Palestinian rabbis, on the other hand, continued the Biblical tradition of boldly speaking of God in human terms. For only by adhering to anthropomorphic (or anthropopathic) imagery is it possible at all to bring out the relevance and meaningfulness of the reality of God to human lives. On the one hand the rabbis used all sorts of circumlocutions for God (such as Heaven, the Power, the Holy One Blessed Be He, etc.) to increase the awe of his Holy Name, but on the other hand they were at pains to bring God near to even the humblest heart and understanding. If necessary, Scripture could be made to show that God suffers together with his children in exile, weeps over the destruction of the Temple, rejoices over piety and good works, wears phylacteries like every good Jew, takes part in learned rabbinic discussions about niceties of ritual law, and eagerly looks forward to receiving prayers. More particularly he demonstrates moral values in order to teach his children the proper way of the imitation of God: "even as he is merciful, so be ye merciful; even as he visiteth the sick, so go ye and visit the sick." The aggadic expositions of the rabbis lacked systematic elaboration and theological method; generally they moved on the level of popular homiletics, imaginative moralising, and the kind of half-mythical symbolic thinking whose inner coherence becomes evident (to us moderns) only after careful analysis. In this manner the rabbis succeeded in expressing in simple but concrete language the apparent paradoxes of faith: the unfathomable mystery of the Godhead and its clear, ethical character; God's remoteness and his nearness; his forgiving love and the terror of his judgment, and many more "dialectical" polarities of this kind. Their theological thinking was thus unsystematic, but it possessed an organic unity of its own.

The anthropomorphism of rabbinic language, together with the esoteric literature of circles of extatic mystics in which mention seemed to be made of a vision of the "measure" and dimensions of the Godhead (see also above, p. 23-4 on the Merkabah mystics) could not fail to bring about a reaction. Karaite rationalism and sarcasm (see above, p. 21) forced the rabbinic thinkers to "purge" the idea of God of homiletic and folkloristic anthropomorphisms, and to re-formulate it in philosophical terms. Here Maimonides (see above, p. 21) was the most influential thinker. All positive attributes of God had to go overboard, and even such innocent statements as God is "great," "good," "powerful" and the like were held to be pregnant with heresy unless re-interpreted in terms of a "negative theology." How it is possible to pray to such a Deity and to trust in him is another problem, and in this truly impressive part of Maimonides's philosophy the almost unbridgeable gulf between the philosopher's God and that of the devout, simple believer becomes glaringly apparent.

The influence of the "negative theology"—both that of the Neoplatonic tradition and that of Maimonides—is evident in the Kabbalah (see above, p. 24), for the kabbalistic doctrine of God combines philosophical and gnostic elements. The classical Kabbalah was aware of the difference between the living, dynamic God of religion and the conceptually purified God of the *theologia negativa*. We have seen how on a certain level of abstraction monotheism can become "monolithic" and static, devoid of vitality. The divine has become a "state" and has ceased to be a "process." The kabbalists therefore distinguished between two aspects of the divine: the hidden and unknowable *deus absconditus*, and the manifest, self-revealing, accessible God of religious experience. Of the former not even existence can be predicated; he (or rather "it") is the paradoxical fullness of the great divine Nothing. The kabbalists called it *En Sof*, the "Infinite." It is so hidden in the mystery of its nothingness that it is not even mentioned in the Bible, let alone addressed in prayer or accessible in contemplation. The Bible, God's Word, is by definition nothing but the revelation or self-manifestation of God. In fact, an existing God means a manifest, revealed and related God. The process of manifestation, i.e. revelation or emerging relatedness, is thus identical with the process by which the divine "Nothing" comes as it were into "Being." The text of the Bible, read superficially, seems to describe the creation of the world and God's first dealings with it; the kabbalist's eye pierces through this layer of meaning to the esoteric level which for him is the ultimately significant one. What Scripture tells us is the process of divine becoming and of the inner-divine life. For in the depths of the divine hidenness, all turned in upon itself, there occurs a primordial initial wrench by which it begins to turn outwards, to unfold, to exist. Here existence is literally an *ex-stare*, a process of extraversion in the intraverted *En Sof*. This initial movement is described in the *Zohar* (the most important kabbalistic text) in a highly mystical passage as the concentration or crystallisation of energy in one luminous point which bursts the closed confines of *En Sof*.

Here we come to the second main feature of kabbalistic theology: its continual use of the term "emanation" instead of "creation." But although the term is borrowed from Neoplatonic tradition, its purpose is not to mediate between the spiritual One and the material many by introducing a number of intermediaries, but rather to describe the procession of the fullness of the divine Being from the *Ungrund* of its Nothingness. The World of Emanation is thus very Godhead, and its totality is described as a complex organism of ten potencies or foci (*sefiroth*). These potencies are not ten gods, but ten aspects, stages or manifestations of the Deity revealing itself. The dynamic interrelations of the *sefiroth* make up the intensely dramatic inner life of the Godhead which, in spite of its complexity, is essentially one. The mystery of the unity within the Godhead is described in frankly erotic imagery as the union between male and female *sefiroth*. One cannot but sympathisise with the orthodox critics who complained that the *sefiroth* were even worse than attributes, for both the dualism of the hidden and the manifest God, and the doctrine of *sefiroth* looked dangerously like departures from strict Jewish monotheism. The kabbalists, who had some of the greatest luminaries of orthodox talmudic learning in their camp, replied that they were speaking of a profound mystery, and that the mystical understanding of the divine unity in all its manifestations was precisely their main concern.

The details of the kabbalistic system with its strange mythological symbolism and audacious erotic imagery need not be described here in detail. Suffice it to say that what began as a highly esoteric doctrine finally became a generally accepted framework within which the fate and destiny of Israel and the practice of the Law acquired a new historical, and indeed cosmic, meaning. Hasidism, for all its "internalisation" of kabbalistic theosophy, did not produce any revolutionary doctrine of God, except in its more pantheistic trends (see above, p. 11). Modern orthodoxy has stuck to the traditional formulations, whilst non-orthodox thinkers have sought to formulate Jewish theology in the language of their contemporary philosophies. Whilst modern secularism and Zionist nationalism enable many Jews to identify with Judaism as an historical (as distinct from a denominational) entity which does not necessarily involve theological beliefs, Reform Judaism, for all its modern liberalism, insists on a religious definition of Jewish existence and retains the term "God" in its liturgy. "Progressive revelation" is asserted in contradistinction to the belief in a supernatural and unique revelation as affirmed by orthodoxy. The obvious weaknesses and contradictions of such a theology (or lack of theology) have not yet been sufficiently explored by Reform thinkers with the sole exception of M. Kaplan and his Reconstructionist Movement which frankly adopt an antisupernaturalist and thoroughly pragmatist and humanistic attitude.

IV. Ritual, Liturgy and Ethics

"The catechism of the Jew is his calendar." This dictum of S. R. Hirsch (see above, p. 27) fairly sums up the Jewish conception of life as an incessant service of God, closely related to the daily round and the annual cycle. Already the biblical stratum of Judaism enables us to distinguish between various types of cultic activity. Thus there are symbolic acts which express the fundamental awareness of the group in the ways peculiar to ritual and myth. The Sabbath is an outstanding example, since in this particular sign of the Covenant (Exodus 31: 16) the Jew testifies, by his abstention from creative work, to his creatureliness and to God's sovereignty as the Lord of creation (Exodus 10: 11) and as the Lord of History (Deut. 5: 15). There are rites regulating the relation of the group and of its individual members to God, such as e.g. the annual ritual of Atonement. The bringing of the first fruits and similar customs belong in the same category. Their purpose is to testify to the divine ownership of the national territory: the people hold their land from their liege lord, God (cf. Leviticus 25: 23). There are feasts and fasts keeping alive the understanding of God's mighty deeds in history, and revitalising the conscioussness of historic solidarity with the past and the future. A remarkable example is the annual Passover celebration commemorating the Exodus from Egypt. Originally perhaps of diverse origins—an agricultural festival and a nomadic rite—the Passover became charged with essentially historic significance, and developed into the most intimate, moving and impressive Jewish domestic celebration. According to a rabbinic formulation "every man in every generation should consider himself as if he had gone out of Egypt." On Passover the Jew re-lives the beginnings of his people as the revelation of the meaning of history as the liberation of slaves to the dignity of children of God and to the freedom which is the gift of God and the service of God. For there is only one road from Egypt to the Promised Land: the road past Sinai, and indeed, the Pentecost, another ancient festival connected with the agricultural cycle, in due course became "the feast of the Giving of our Law." Another instance of the tendency to "hisoricise" original nature festivals is given by the Bible itself. The autumn festival of Tabernacles, whose connection with the harvest and with the rains of the coming season is attested by the bunch of four plants carried by the worshippers (cf. Leviticus 23: 40), is accounted for as follows by the biblical writer: "Ye shall dwell in booths seven days... that your generations may know that I made the children of Israel to dwell in booths when I brought them out of the land of Egypt" (Leviticus 23: 42-43). There are commandments fostering certain attitudes and values, and prohibitions designed to prevent a lowering of the moral and spiritual level. Among these are regulations prohibiting intercourse with the pagan population of Canaan, and similarly in the post-biblical period many prohibitions were enacted expressly for the purpose of limiting contacts between Jews and gentiles. The many dietary laws serve the double purpose of submitting the whole of life, even on its purely vegetative level, to the discipline of sanctification (cf. Leviticus 11: 43-47; 20: 23-26) and of preventing commensality with non-Jews. The dietary laws as still practised by observant Jews prohibit the eating of certain ("unclean") animals and prescribe the manner of preparation of certain otherwise permitted foods (e.g. the way of slaughtering the "clean" animals, the salting of meat to draw out the blood (cf. Genesis 9: 4; Leviticus 17: 14), and the strict separation of milk and meat products (based on a rabbinic extension of the prohibition Exodus 34: 26 and elsewhere). On several fastdays in the year—days of penitence or national mourning—neither food nor drink may be taken, whilst on the Sabbath and festival days the enjoyment of food is considered a religious duty. Thus even when eating, mating or dressing the Jew must realise that every part of his life is under a divine charge: it can be debased or hallowed. Other prohibitions and prescriptions are more immediately concerned with social and moral values such as social justice, charity, love of one's fellow man and personal holiness. Marriage, though essentially a legal ceremony, is also a religious rite, but divorce, which has to take place in a rabbinic court to make sure it complies with all the requirements of talmudic law, is a purely legal act. To marry and beget children is considered a supreme religious duty. Every child of a Jewish mother is born into the Covenant of Israel, but male children are circumcised on the eighth day. Circumcision is, therefore, not so much an initiation as the conferring of the "sign of the Covenant." The significance of the rite as a mark of belonging to the Jewish people is such that it is practised even by Jews who otherwise neglect all traditional observances. Non-Jews who wish to convert are received in the fold and "under the wings of the divine presence" after baptismal immersion and (in the case of males) circumcision. Children are trained to perform all religious rites and customs, but only after the age of thirteen (boys) or twelve (girls) are they legally obliged to their observance. Rabbinic law exempts women from many positive commandments and also restricts their study of the *Torah* to the minimum necessary for the fulfilment of their religious and domestic duties. This, together with the fact that women do not actively participate in public worship (though they may attend services, seated in a separate section or gallery, apart from the men) gives traditional Jewish worship a markedly masculine character. Modern non-orthodox congregations permit mixed seating and in some cases also encourage active participation by women in the prayer service.

Prayer is taken for granted throughout the history of Judaism, although opinions regarding its nature, meaning, value and efficacy have varied with the times and with the philosophical outlook and religious temperament of the thinkers concerned. The efficacy of petitionary prayer is traditionally affirmed in spite of the grave theological problems raised by this doctrine. Rabbinic teaching considers prayer as a divine commandment: God desires man to express his love of him, dependence on him, and longing to commune with him in this form. For the kabbalist mystics prayer was the highest and most intense form of mystical communion. The ancient Rabbis deduced the duty of daily prayer from the more general Biblical injunction "to serve him with all thine heart." "Which is the service of the heart?" they asked, and replied "this is prayer." The order and character of prayer was regulated by the Rabbis so as to include praise, thanksgiving and petition. The proportion of these elements and their detailed contents originally varied with the individual worshipper, but in time a relatively fixed liturgy developed. Jewish tradition insists on the value of public worship, and full liturgical proceedings are only possible in the presence of the "Congregation of Israel" which must be represented by a quorum of at least ten adult males. Only when no such quorum is available should the three statutory daily prayers be said privately. The basis of the liturgy is the *Shema* (Deuteronomy 6: 4-9; see above, p. 7) set in a framework of appropriate prayers, and the *'amidah* consisting of nineteen (on the Sabbath and feast days of seven) benedictions and petitions. These, together with certain psalms and a considerable body of ancient and later liturgical compositions (hymns, devotions, penitential prayers) constitute the traditional liturgy. This liturgy also contains the "implicit theology" of traditional Judaism, and expresses the basic beliefs of Israel and the yearnings of the individual and the people: redemption and resurrection, prosperity and blessing, the aspiration for nearness to God, forgiveness of sins and the restoration to national independence in the promised land, the messianic age and the coming of the Kingdom. On the Sabbath and certain other days the public service includes readings from the Pentateuch and the Prophets. (In earlier times the prophetic lesson provided the text for the sermon). No less significant than the synagogue is the home as the locus of religious performance and domestic ritual. In modern, non-orthodox Judaism this aspect of tradition has been lost and the centre of gravity of religious performance has shifted from the home to the synagogue and from the individual as an actively practising member to professional ministers.

It should be obvious from the above that in a system in which all commandments and prohibitions are thought to emanate directly from God and to be laid down in authoritative codes, the distinction between ritual and ethics cannot be strictly maintained. Nevertheless an awareness of the difference between these two spheres seems to have been alive at all times. Even without committing oneself to the patently exaggerated view which describes the Old Testament prophets as the pioneers of an ethical religiosity in opposition to the ritualism of the priests, it is evident that prophetic preaching emphasised the primacy of moral and social values above cultic performance. The ancient Rabbis too recognised a "heavenly law" that went beyond the positive law administered by man (though the latter was divinely revealed) and which the truly righteous would conscientiously heed. In fact, the righteous man will seek not to move on "the line of the law" but to realise the ideal norm of which the strict law is often merely the extreme outer limit. The tendency to stress ritual piety to the neglect of spiritual or ethical values has been the theme of many writers and preachers, including Bahya's *Duties of the Heart* (see above, p. 23) and the founders of the *musar* movement in the nineteenth century (see above, p. 27). The Talmud explicitly distinguishes between the duties of man towards God alone, and his duties towards his fellowman (which, of course, are by definition also duties towards God). The Day of Atonement, whose sacramental quality expiates transgressions of which one sincerely repents, is effective only as regards sins committed towards God alone. Sins against one's fellow-man require reconciliation with the latter before the religious dimension of such sin can be expiated by the Day of Atonement.

The acute awareness of the Jews of being a distinct group, separate from all the nations—the latter often being identified with the principle of evil—has produced a double standard of morality: one for the in-group and the other for the out-group. In fact, it was his analysis of Judaism which provided Max Weber with a paradigm for his distinction between *Innenmoral* and *Aussenmoral*. Both types are "ethical" in the sense of being determined by specific, religiously sanctioned criteria. But they are nonetheless different, and this fact in itself is sufficient to make them appear unethical on any definition that equates morality with universality. Here, it would seem, the conflicting claims of Jewish particularism and Jewish universalism have not yet come to terms.

The basic "myth" of Judaism is that God made a Covenant with a particular people, chose them to be "a kingdom of priests and a holy nation," and revealed to them his Law. All the rest is an attempt to explain, rationalise, elaborate, justify. All myths are likely to suffer from too much explanation, and the Jewish myth is no exception. Modern thought has aggravated the crisis. The mystery—and scandal! —of election has made even some Jewish thinkers fight shy of what seems to them a chauvinistic particularism. No doubt chosenness makes sense only if there is a God who does the choosing, even as revelation is possible only where there is a God who does the revealing. The modern mind, however, trained by history, anthropology and biblical criticism may have some difficulty in finding a satisfactory paraphrase for revelation, let alone for the revelation of a Law. It is no less difficult to explain a concept of election that includes a particular destiny and a universal calling, the agony of the "suffering servant" and a messianic promise. It may be even more difficult to speak of a transcendent God who is also a personal God, addressing man, claiming him, and imposing upon him a destiny and a vocation. Perhaps it is wiser to acknowledge the mystery and leave it at that. But the historian of religion does not deal with the mystery but with the ways in which people—believers and thinkers, participants and victims—have lived, interpreted and verbalised their experience of it. Hence a few more words must be said about the doctrines of Judaism.

V. Creation, the Nature of Man, and the Last Things

Whatever the account of creation given in the first chapters of Genesis may originally have intended to convey, it certainly established the notion of a unique, omnipotent and sovereign spiritual God. Later generations interpreted the text as teaching a *creatio ex nihilo*, a doctrine subscribed to even by theologians who otherwise followed Aristotle. Man, according to this account, is constituted of the same stuff as the rest of creation ("dust from the earth") but is, at the same time, distinguished from it by certain special qualities. Neither the biblical nor the rabbinic sources enlarge on the precise meaning of the statement that man was created in the image of God, though the Rabbis emphasise that this is man's title to excellence. Man's god-likeness enables him to exercise dominion over creation and to create himself, albeit not *ex nihilo*. The nature of man was defined differently at different periods and in terms of the psychological concepts provided by current philosophies. Thus the doctrine of man of the medieval thinkers is indebted to Neoplatonic and Aristotelian psychology, and hence they distinguish not only between body and soul but between different faculties and different kinds of soul (e.g. vegetative, animal, rational). In philosophical anthropology the notion of intellect (*nous*) played a major role. To what extent this supernal soul was not only of heavenly origin but actually a divine or near-divine emanation was a matter of dispute between philosophical and mystical theologians, though the extreme view which considers the human soul as being of divine substance was rarely held. The ancient Rabbis adopted the Platonic doctrine of the pre-existence of souls, but the belief in *metensomatosis* (also known as metempsychosis or transmigration of souls) penetrated rabbinic Judaism only under the influence of the kabbalistic movement. The essential feature of rabbinic anthropology was not the opposition body-soul (let alone flesh-spirit of matter-spirit), but the doctrine of the "two inclinations": the good *yeṣer* and the *evil yeṣer*. Man is thought to be capable, under the guidance of the Law and with God's assured help, to choose the good and to overcome the temptations and the pull of the evil inclination. Freedom of choice and moral responsibility have been characteristic of most Jewish thinking on the subject, giving it a distinctly "Pelagian" flavour. The story of Eden and of Adam's fall have never played the role in Judaism which they have e.g. in Christian theology. The idea of original sin, though not unknown in rabbinic sources, is rather marginal and never calls into question man's capacity to determine his fate in this world and in the world to come. The notion of original sin is more prominent in kabbalistic literature, where it forms part of the gnostic mythology describing the mystery of the inner divine life and its relation to the world of man. The kabbalists went to considerable lengths in elaborating the analogy between the divine macrocosm and the human microcosm. It is precisely because the human frame is the microcosmic image of God, that man's actions, by the laws of the universal interrelation of all things, can have such tremendous repercussions in the divine sphere. Original sin is the primeval disruption of the inner-divine unity wrought by man, even as man's task is the restoration of this mystical unity. It should be added that when rabbinic and kabbalistic texts speak of "man," they generally refer to the Jew. Non-Jewish humanity is, more often than not, either completely outside their ken or else explicitly identified with the substance of evil and the sphere of the reprobate. There are, of course, many exceptions to this rule, but by and large the loneliness and suffering of Israel, the "sheep among seventy wolves," could not fail to be reflected in the anthropology of the ancient and medieval thinkers.

Man's contact with the transcendent God is, according to the biblical and rabbinic view, in love, fear and obedience. The medieval philosophers identified the prophetic charisma with that of the enlightened philosophical intellect, and considered it as the highest stage of spiritual perfection and of communion with God. Whilst illuminations and supernatural intimations were held to be possible and, indeed, to be vouchsafed to extraordinary individuals, they were never considered as a source of legitimate authority. In rabbinic Judaism religious authority was a function of scholarship, and decisions regarding religious law and conduct had to be arrived at by the accepted methods of argument and deduction. According to a charming Talmudic legend God himself submitted with good grace when a rabbinic decision, arrived at by a majority vote after proper discussion ran counter to his own view as made known by miracles and a "heavenly voice." Ethical and mystical manuals nevertheless prescribed disciplines of meditation and of ascetic piety designed to lead the soul to the highest stages of humility, love of God, mystical communion and illumination by the Holy Spirit.

Man's contact with the world is based on the assumption that nature runs an as a whole predictable course according to laws which the creator has implanted in it. God, of course, is sovereign ruler and can change the normal course of events or interfere with it (miracles), but as a rule the stability and regularity of the created order can be relied upon. In the Middle Ages this traditional view was philosophically re-formulated in terms of a natural causality willed and ordained by God, the supreme First Cause. Only few thinkers felt impelled (under obvious Sufi influence) to deny causality and natural laws because, in their view, such an independent causal nexus would impair the sovereign, free and absolutely unconditional and unlimited providence of God. An obvious corollary of this view was ascetic quietism since all action implied the choice of ends, the adoption of means, and the belief in the causal nexus between means and ends. Whilst there are various types of quietism and almost all of them can be instanced in Jewish history, yet is is fair to say that rabbinic Judaism leans towards activism. Both in his practical and in his more specifically religious life (i.e. fulfilling one's moral obligations in providing for one's needs and those of one's dependents, and working out one's salvation by right behaviour and the fulfilment of God's commandments) the Jew is bidden to act, and to act morally and repsonsibly. As we have seen, the kabbalists transposed this practical activism to the sacramental and semi-magical level of mystical action. Whilst ascetic tendencies and movements were not unknown and at times were even prominent, (as penitential exercises, as a discipline of simplicity and humility, as a means of subjugating the body in order to achieve moral and spiritual perfection, or as a mystical technique for achieving illumination), rabbinic Judaism does not disapprove of the enjoyment of the good things of life. Gratification should not be suppressed but hallowed by the discipline and the restraint imposed by the Law. The enjoyment of food and drink may be a positive religious duty (e.g. on the Sabbath and feast days) although gluttony is forbidden. Erotic contacts and thoughts outside marriage are strictly prohibited, but celibacy is severely discouraged on both moral and theological grounds, and marriage is considered a major religious duty. Sexual intercourse within marriage (limited by periods of purification after menstruation) is justified not merely by the purpose of procreation but also as an expression of mutual love between husband and wife. The kabbalists went even further than that and transposed the traditional rabbinic doctrine on a mystical level. On the basis of their theosophical doctrine of a male and female aspect within the Godhead and their conception of the holiness of wedlock, they taught a kind of mystical metaphysics of the sexual act.

Since biblical times it was generally held that man's welfare both on this earth and in the hereafter depended on his religious and moral behaviour. The obvious logical and empirical difficulties of this belief have been discussed at great length—from the book of Job onwards—in theological and religious literature. Whilst many refinements, special considerations and supplementary doctrines were advanced (e.g. that the righteous suffer for all their sins here on earth so as to qualify for perfect bliss after death; that suffering might be due to sins commited during a previous incarnation; that Israel's suffering is a mystery connected with the larger drama of cosmic restoration and reflecting the suffering of God himself), the basic principle was, as a rule, never seriously questioned.

It is evident that Judaism too had to develop and formalise a doctrine of the "last things" with a view to answering questions of both personal and collective destiny. In the period of the Second Temple, earlier beliefs originating in the ancient kingship ideology and in prophetic visions of a glorious restoration and a golden age combined with new influences and ideas. Beliefs and hopes were current regarding a national restoration under a victorious military leader or through miraculous intervention from above. The ideal redeemer would be a Davidic king, or a heavenly being referred to as the "Son of Man." Redemption could thus mean a better and more peaceful world, or the utter end and annihilation of "this age" and the ushering in, amid catastrophe and judgment, of a new era and "a new heaven and a new earth." The chaotic welter of of these ideas is visible in the apocryphal books of the Old Testaments and in the New Testament writings, as well as in later Jewish apocalyptic literature. The original biblical tradition of thinking about the future in social, collective and historical terms was now further complicated by new patterns of thought. The increasing preoccupation with the destiny of the individual, together with the demand for a satisfactory account of the ways of divine justice in meting out reward and punishment, led to the adoption of the originally Persian idea of the resurrection of the dead. In spite of its objectionable irrationality to modern, "enlightened" minds, this idea had the advantage of implicitly safeguarding the biblical integral conception of the human personality as an animated body or flesh vivified by the spirit. Resurrection, if it means anything at all, can only mean that to define anybody you have to define him as a particular "body." The other point about the traditional belief in resurrection is that it keeps to the pattern of a final consummation of the process of history: at the end of days God will inaugurate the New Era of his Kingdom.

The doctrine of immortality is opposed to the idea of resurrection in both respects. In the first place it tends to regard the soul, a kind of independent spiritual substance, as the essential part of man. The body is merely its material clothing, and a vile and inferior one at that. The doctrine of immortality also lifts individual eschatology out of the historical, messianic context, since the course of history as such becomes irrelevant to the fate and destiny of the individual soul. The tension between these incompatible anthropological doctrines is illustrated by the compromise solution which says that at the resurrection the human soul will be returned to a so-called spiritual or glorified body. At least three different strands thus went into making up the thread of what became traditionally accepted eschatology: (1) the messianic era of national restoration, including the rebuilding of the Temple, (2) the new *aeon* of God's Kingdom, including the resurrection of the dead, (3) a celestial hereafter in which the soul eternally enjoys the blessed vision. Medieval writers tried to harmonise and systematise the various and partly contradictory eschatological traditions. Thus the messianic expectation became a kind of Millenarianism. The messianic era would be followed by the Great Judgment, the Resurrection and the New Era. Meanwhile individual Jewish souls are provisionally judged after death and go to Heaven (also "Paradise"), or to purgatory where they atone for a maximum of one year for the sins committed on earth. From this disincarnate state they will be called to final judgment and resurrection. For the kabbalists heaven and purgatory were too static as means of reward and punishment; they merely settled accounts, as it were, but did not allow for more active change. They therefore accepted the belief in *gilgul* or transmigration of souls (see above, p. 37) which they regarded as a further manifestation of God's love for his creatures. Even after death, God is prepared to give sinful man a fresh start and the possibility not only to expiate and repair past sins but also to acquire further merits and to contribute to his perfection and that of the cosmos. According to most kabbalists three times is the maximum number of *gilgul*. As in most religions, the rather lurid descriptions of hell to be found in medieval texts were understood either more or less literally according to the degree of sophistication or religious temperament of the believer. Nineteenth century liberal theologians tried to explain hell and purgatory away but continued, with remarkable inconsistency, to cling to the belief in an eternal blessedness in one form or another.

As regards the messianic age, ancient and medieval apocalyptic literature supplied plentiful details, but these were as a rule not given official dogmatic sanction (see above, pp. 12-3). In general it may be said that messianic belief always included the actual physical liberation of Israel from persecution and bondage, its return to its ancient homeland, the restoration of the Davidic dynasty, the re-building of the Temple in Jerusalem and the recognition by all nations of Israel's election and calling. Whatever the spiritual significances attached to these hopes, they were never allowed to dissolve the concrete historical core into pure spirituality. Even the mystical interiorisations of Judaism never lost their touch with reality—a reality of which anti-semitism, physical persecution, social discrimination and moral humiliation always formed part—and hence redemption from sin and evil was always regarded as connected with the conquest of evil in the historical, i.e. the political and social, sphere. For some thinkers historical messianism was a major concern; they obviously thought in terms of an historical salvation and the Kingdom of God. For others, including Maimonides, the messianic kingdom was merely the background for the ideal contemplative life. In Lurianic kabbalism (see above, p. 24) the messiah is no redeemer at all in the normal sense of the word; his appearance merely signifies that Israel has achieved its great cosmic task of repairing the primordial catastrophe or fall. For some of the 18th and 19th century Hasidim who sought mystical communion with God almost to the point of a submergence of consciousness in the Divine, historical categories were evidently less relevant. Certain modern trends (assimilationist, socialist and nationalist viz. Zionist) provided secular variants or substitutes for the historical ideals of religious messianism.

VI. Contemporary Judaism

The beginnings of modern Judaism have been briefly described above, pp. 26-7. Emancipation (though only partially successful) and the disintegration of the traditional medieval patterns, rationalism, the experience of modern antisemitism culminating in the Communist persecution of Judaism and the Nazi extermination of European Jewry, the new secular nationalism merging with age-old messianic longings, the secularisation of the modern world and the progress of religious reform—all these produced a situation radically different from that which Judaism had known in the past.

Reform Judaism (see above, p. 26) rejected rabbinic ritualism and orthodox particularism, and sought to define its religious content as an enlightened, progressive, universalistic, ethical and "prophetic" monotheism. The prayer service was adapted to modern taste (e.g.

increasing substitution of the vernacular for the traditional Hebrew, the use of organ music), ritual laws which hindered free social intercourse with gentiles were declared to be no longer obligatory, and items of an "archaic," "particularistic" or "nationalistic" character (such as e.g. the hope of a return to Zion and the restoration of the Temple and its cult) were deleted from prayerbook and creed. The original radicalism of the Reform Movement subsequently gave way to a more positive evaluation of the halakhic tradition, and contemporary Reform shows attempts to revive traditional symbols and rituals whilst many Reform leaders are actively committed to Zionism and the State of Israel. The following excerpts from two official statements may serve to illustrate the change that took place in American Reform Judaism in half a century. The "Pittsburgh Platform" of 1885 declared:

> We recognise in the Mosaic legislation a system of training the Jewish people for its mission during its national life in Palestine, and today we accept as binding only its moral laws, and maintain only such ceremonies as elevate and sanctify our lives, but reject all such as are not adapted to the views and habits of modern civilization... We hold that all such Mosaic and rabbinical laws as regulate diet, priestly purity, and dress originated in ages and under the influence of ideas entirely foreign to our present mental and spiritual state ... Their observance in our days is apt rather to obstruct than to further modern spiritual elevation... We recognize, in the modern era of universal culture of heart and intellect, the approaching of the realization of Israel's great messianic hope for the establishment of the kingdom of truth, justice and peace among all men. We consider ourselves no longer a nation, but a religious community, and therefore expect neither a return to Palestine, nor a sacrificial worship under the sons of Aaron, nor the restoration of any of the laws concerning the Jewish state... We reassert the doctrine of Judaism that the soul is immortal, grounding this belief on the divine nature of the human spirit... We reject as ideas not rooted in Judaism the beliefs both in bodily resurrection and in Gehenna and Eden... as abodes for everlasting punishment and reward."

The "Columbus Platform" of 1937 breathes a very different air. "The Torah, both written and oral, enshrines Israel's ever-growing consciousness of God and of the moral law. It preserves the historical precedents, sanctions and norms of Jewish life, and seeks to mould it in patterns of goodness and holiness." Judaism being "the soul of which Israel is the body" the Reform rabbis assembled at Columbus recognise "in the group-loyalty of Jews who have become estranged from our religious tradition a bond which still unites them with us," and affirm "the obligation of all Jewry to aid in [Palestine's] upbuilding as a Jewish homeland by endeavouring to make it not only a haven of refuge for the oppressed but also a center of Jewish culture and spiritual life." The pluralistic denominationalism which is characteristic of North America has given Reform Judaism there a scope and possibilities which it found neither in Europe nor in Israel.

Orthodoxy in eastern Europe remained static and impervious to change. In the west it reasserted itself after the first shock, and while developing a keener understanding of the problems and challenges of the modern age, defended the validity and unbroken authority of traditional Law and observance. Both types of orthodoxy are represented in Israel and the U.S. where they show signs of growing strength and increasing militancy. In Israel in particular, where the orthodox rabbinate enjoys a legally recognised status and authority, much of the public and private life of even the non-orthodox majority is subject to religious jurisdiction and pressures (e.g. no civil marriage is possible in Israel; almost complete cessation of public transport on the Sabbath). In matters of faith and doctrine orthodoxy remains faithful to the traditional rabbinic and medieval positions. Its efforts at "modernisation" take the form of using technological devices to solve practical problems posed by ritual law. E.g. milking cows is not permitted on the Sabbath, but an electric milking installation regulated not by human hands but by an automatic clock set before the beginning of the Sabbath may solve the halakhic problem at an orthodox dairy farm.

Conservative Judaism occupies a half-way position between orthodoxy and reform, attempting as it does to affirm the values and traditions of historical Judaism without accepting them in their totality as obligatory and unchanging. The theoretical foundations of this ideology were laid in the second half of the 19th century by the scholars of the Breslau Rabbinical Seminary in Germany, who argued that Judaism, having never been static, would have to develop and change also in the present and the future, albeit in an organic and responsible manner and with a sense of loyalty and commitment to the past. This school of "Historical Positive Judaism" eventually led to the "Conservative Judaism" of the U.S. which neither repudiates nor accepts the absolute authority of traditional *halakhah* and dogma, steering its course by *ad hoc* decisions rather than by dogmatic statements of principles. In the U.S. these three trends have assumed the character of three denominations. Although each has international affiliations,

Reform and Conservative Judaism are less important in European countries where the official religious establishment is orthodox even though the majority of the Jews are indifferent or, at any rate, neither practising nor orthodox.

In addition to these major religious trends, mention should also be made of manifestations and expressions of a personal religious outlook which understands itself as essentially Jewish whilst remaining completely free of denominational affiliations. Martin Buber (d. 1965) is the best known example of such an individual thinker who is, at the same time, an exponent of Jewish thought. But perhaps the most surprising development of the modern period is the emergence of secular Judaism, i.e. an apparently paradoxical yet none the less historically valid form of Jewish (cultural, ethnic, national) identification which is religiously indifferent or even—as in the case of e.g. Zionist Marxists—antireligious. Judaism, it is argued, exists as a historical entity with a national, social and ethical essence. For obvious historical reasons this essence articulated itself in the past in religious forms. With the fading out of religion from modern civilization, a secular re-interpretation of Judaism and its historical essence is necessary and legitimate. Much of the contemporary national culture of Israel is based on this premiss. It is hardly necessary to point out that the religious Jew will reject the ideology and very definition of a secular Judaism even though he may, paradoxically enough, consider this secular Judaism as an inalienable part of that mystical body which is historical Israel. To the extent that modern theology tends to evaluate the phenomenon of secularism as such in a positive perspective, Jewish religious thinking too need not necessarily repudiate secular Judaism as heresy or apostasy. In fact, the great mystical theologian of the last generation and Chief Rabbi of Palestine, A. I. Kook (d. 1935) interpreted secular Jewish nationalism and socialism precisely in such a theological perspective as a necessary aspect of the essentially dialectical process by which the Jewish vocation and destiny were being fulfilled.

No doubt this state of affairs raises many questions. How will Israel emerge from its present revolutionary situation as a traditional religion and a secular society; as a Jewish state which must include Muslims, Christians and others as "Israelis," and as the religion of a minority of British, French or American citizens; as a particular people and the bearer of a universal destiny; as a nation that has experienced the ultimate depths of agony as well as the fulfilment of age-old hopes;

as a witness of the vindication of its history as well as of the realisation that ultimate salvation may be beyond history? Only the historians of the future will perhaps be able to attempt answers to these questions.

VII. The Scientific Study of Judaism

The scientific study of Judaism is fairly recent. It is true that scholarship was always highly regarded among the Jews, but their learning was mainly scholastic in character. Accounts of Judaism, whether by Jewish or gentile scholars, were systematic or descriptive rather than historical. Historical interest was exceptional among Jews, and even where it existed, traditional religious belief severely limited its critical scope or the possibility if its free expression. The struggle for civil emancipation and the movement for religious reform in the 19th century produced the *Wissenschaft des Judentums* as a programme for the scientific study of the religion, literature, and history of the Jews in accordance with the recognised scholarly methods of historical and philological research. Originally its inspiration was apologetic: Judaism had a proud past (hence antisemitic arguments about Jewish inferiority were unfounded), it had evolved in various forms throughout its history (hence reform and change were legitimate), and it had often existed in close cultural contact with the surrounding civilisations (hence there was no reason for denying the Jews civil rights). The movement spread from Germany to Italy, France, England and the U.S., and a parallel school, writing in Hebrew, emerged in eastern Europe. The main emphasis was on the history of literature (biblical, post-biblical, rabbinic, philosophical and liturgical) but the apologetic, ideological and intellectual bias of the period inevitably influenced the direction and the results of these scholarly efforts. "Jewish Studies" in the modern sense, whilst continuing the scholarly tradition founded in the 19th century, have added a stronger emphasis on social and economic history to the originally more literary pre-occupations, have refined their methods of philological analysis and historical interpretation, have added vastly to the known sources of Judaism (discovery and examination of libraries and manuscripts) and have embraced within their scope phenomena which for apologetic or other reasons had received insufficient attention. E.g. the history of Jewish mysticism and the Kabbalah, treated as negligible or contemptible by the rationalism of the 19th century, has established itself in the 20th century as a major field in the study of Judaism.

Non-Jewish scholars too have contributed to the study of Judaism, albeit mainly in narrowly specified areas and often with a markedly polemical slant. Old Testament studies were always cultivated by Christian scholars, but the underlying assumption was that the Hebrew Scriptures were but a preparation for the New Testament, and that post-biblical and pharisaic Judaism was a sterile, decadent and inferior type of religion. The same tendency is noticeable in the work of many specialists in the Second Temple and New Testament periods. Here the emphasis was on Jewish Hellenism and apocalyptic as a background for the New Testament. Rabbinic Judaism was studied less for its own sake than as a backdrop (and a foil) against which to view early Christianity. The emancipation of the history of religions, as a scientific discipline, from its parent science, theology, has considerably benefited the study of Judaism.

BIBLIOGRAPHY

A bibliography, for non-hebraists, of the history of Judaism is difficult to compile, since Hebrew is not only the language of most of the religious texts and documents but also that of a considerable part of the most authoritative and up-to-date scholarly research. The renaissance of modern Hebrew in the last decades and the development of centres of learning in Israel have resulted in an increasing use of Hebrew in publications (periodicals, monographs, doctoral dissertations, annotations and commentaries to critical editions of texts and documents) dealing with Judaism in all its aspects. The following list of recommended books does not, therefore, aspire to be sufficient; it merely wants to help the reader to orient himself further.

Texts

The Bible (Soncino Books of the Bible, Hebrew text and English translation and commentary, 14 vols., 1943-52. Editor: Rev. Dr. A. Cohen. This ed. is useful because the commentary summarizes the views of the classical Jewish commentators and hence illustrates how the Jews read and understood the Scriptures).

The Babylonian Talmud, transl. into English with notes, glossary and indexes under the editorship of Isidore Epstein; 34 vols. and index volume, 1935-52.

The Midrash, transl. into English with notes, glossary and indexes under the editorship of H. Freedman and M. Simon, 10 vols., 1939.

The Zohar, transl. by H. Sperling and M. Simon, 5 vols., 1949.

The Authorised Daily Prayer Book of the United Hebrew Congregations of the British Empire, transl. by S. Singer and with historical and explanatory notes by Israel Abrahams, London, 1922.

Anthologies

BARON S. and BLAU, J., *Judaism: Rabbinical and Talmudic Period*, 1954.

GLATZER, N. N., *Hillel the Elder: the emergence of classical Judaism*, 1966.
——, *Faith and Knowledge: the Jew in the Medieval World*, 1963.
——, *The Dynamics of Emancipation: the Jew in the modern age*, 1965.
——, *In Time and Eternity: a Jewish Reader*, 1961.
HERTZBERG, A., *Judaism*, 1961.

General works of Reference

The Jewish Encyclopaedia 12 vols., New York, 1901-6. (Antiquated in many respects but still excellent).
WERBLOWSKY, R. J. Z. and WIGODER, G., (edd.) *The Encyclopedia of the Jewish Religion*, 1966.
FINKELSTEIN, L., *The Jews: Their History, Culture and Religion*, 2 vols., 3rd ed., 1960.

History

BARON, S., *A Social and Religious History of the Jews*, 2nd ed., 1952ff., 12 vols. and 2 index vols. (The modern standard work).
ROTH, C., *A Short History of the Jewish People.*

History of Religion, Theology and Philosophy

FINKELSTEIN, L., *The Pharisees* 2 vols., 3rd ed., 1962.
MOORE, G. FOOT, *Judaism in the First Centuries of the Christian Era*, 3 vols, 1927-30.
SCHUBERT, K., *Die Religion des nachbiblischen Judentums*, 1955.
SCHECHTER, S., *Some Aspects of Rabbinic Theology*, 1909.
——, *Studies in Judaism* 1st-3rd Series, 1896-1924.
GUTTMANN, J., *Philosophies of Judaism*, 1964.
VAJDA, G., *Introduction à la Pensée Juive du Moyen Age*, 1947.
——, *L'Amour de Dieu dans la Théologie Juive*, 1957.
SCHOLEM, G., *Major Trends in Jewish Mysticism*, 3rd ed., 1956.
WIENER, M., *Jüdische Religion im Zeitalter der Emanzipation*, 1933,
HERTZBERG, A., *The Zionist Idea*, 1959.
EPSTEIN, I., *The Faith of Judaism: an interpretation for our times*, 1954.
——, *The Jewish Way of Life*, 1946. (Both works present the strictly orthodox point of view).
KOHLER KAUFMANN, *Jewish Theology, Systematically and Historically Considered*, 1918 (Reform point of view).
BAECK, L., *The Essence of Judaism*, 1948.
HESCHEL, A., *God in Search of Man: A Philosophy of Judaism*, 1955.
HERBERG, W., *Judaism and Modern Man: An Interpretation of Jewish Religion*, 1951.
ROTH, L., *Judaism: a Portrait*, 1960.
JACOBS, L., *Principles of the Jewish Faith: An Analytical Study*, 1964.

CHRISTIANITY

BY

C. W. MÖNNICH

Amsterdam, Holland

I. The Essence of the Christian Religion

God is *persona* and can only be contacted as *persona*: all attempts to fathom the most essential characteristics of the Christian religious sphere lead to this conclusion. Now a *persona* is not the same thing as a personality. The latter word signifies especially an inner structure: behind the external phenomena of word, gesture, stature, behaviour can be discerned the inside, the hidden motivation, the invisible heart. But *persona* refers to the external; in origin it is the mask and consequently the actor and the dignitary. Juridical terminology retains this significance in such a word as legal person. Now the classical use of the word *persona* in Christianity implies this external and juridical meaning rather than that of personality. God is intrinsically invisible, unknowable and impenetrable. Even in Christian mysticism, as can be discerned in one of its fathers, the author of the Pseudodionysian writings (about 500), God remains the absolutely transcendental and inaccessible; union with Him is nothing other than an indication of a situation on the frontier of religious existence, and that frontier cannot be crossed by any creature. Union is always hampered by the proviso "only as far as it is attainable." Within Christian religiousness, revelation is not the opening of a path which leads to the inner nature of God; it is the appearance of God's *persona* and hence the path of intercourse between God and mankind. From what God does and says, man can infer what God's will is, but he cannot go back beyond that revelation. Admittedly this revelation discloses God's disposition, just as man's reaction to this revelation discloses his disposition. But the attention of the Christian faith is focussed on the function of God and man in their mutual relationship: Lord and servant, Saviour and one in danger. The issue is the relationship of partners; hence revelation is simply the establishment of that relationship by God.

This relationship is brought about by the initiative taken by the sovereign God. He is first to act, and if his servants fail to fulfil his commandment, again it is God who, in rejecting and renewing the relationship, once more raises the point of his sovereign power. God is revealed as the Lord in creation, sustenance and renewal; these conceptions express the character of the Christian experience of God better than the terms of election and covenant. The well-known formula that God is the completely Other cannot be considered adequate. In the Christian context God is never merely the completely Other: He is the Other primarily in that He stands opposite man, being as well our partner as the Inaccessible. A God-in-himself has little or no significance for the Christian faith.

God is sovereign. Therein lies also his exclusivity. Christianity has never abandoned this Jewish heritage (the dogma of the trinity and of the incarnation have, as we shall see below, a different purport and do not diminish the exclusivity of the Christian God). It is insufficient to say that the Christian religion is monotheistic; in tenor the religious philosophy of the Graeco-Roman world is also monotheistic. The multiplicity of gods was looked upon as personifications of characteristics or functions of the one divine being, and for various thinkers of that age this was not merely a philosophical abstraction, but a religious experience. But the Christian invocation "one God" is primarily an echo of the first commandment of the Decalogue and the "Hear, O Israel" of Deut. 6.4. God has no equals, only servants and friends; the inhabitants of heaven, the angels, and of the earth, mankind. They are his creatures and hence can at once be characterised as non-divine within the Christian religiousness.

If God is *persona*, so is man. That God is Lord is not a secondary qualification which can be added to His first one: "He is," but the expression is a tautology. Likewise the qualification "The creature is servant" is also a tautology, and does not express a special quality. To be non-divine immediately implies being subject to God the Lord. This explains why the Christian faith can conceive of a "divine" retinue of the Lord and even borrow such terms as "divine" and "deification" from a non-Christian religious sphere to indicate creatures. But "divine" does not imply that man shares in a divine substance, it implies that through obedience as servant of God man is included in the work and companionship of God. The denotation of God as substance—discussed further in the section on the Christian doctrine—is a rather late auxiliary line of Christian theology, and here "substance" has a different meaning from that usual in philosophy.

The exclusivity of God in the Christian religiousness has had its repercussions on the Christian cosmology: namely, it has desacralised the world in principle. In their defense against the non-Christian religiousness with which the Christian faith was confronted in the ancient world and later in the missionary field, the Christians always emphasised that the forces of nature were not divine, but creatural. They have no right to sacrifice and prayer, cult and worship; they need not be feared, they are subservient to man. If they appear overwhelming, there may be some demons involved, but these demons, no matter how dangerous they may be, are also apostatical creatures, overcome by Christ. Another explanation is God's wrath at the disobedience of man. Gods are either devils or dead people who are worshipped instead of God by apostatical people influenced by satanical temptation. It is remarkable how eagerly the ancient Christian polemists accepted the theories of Euhemerism—a phenomenon that prevailed until the late Middle Ages. Only when paganism sought revenge for its defeat and the feelings of lust and unrest, born of the distress and difficulties of precarious life in the second half of the Middle Ages, began to fasten on to the now almost unrecognisable, older divine powers, was there any question of a new sacralisation, to wit the belief in devils, witches and wizards. And then the consequences of the witch hunt became manifest. Strangely enough, in such a religiously conservative country as Spain, the Inquisition hunted down heretics and Jews, but not witches, and that at a time when the witch hunt in Germany, England and France assumed alarming proportions.

The desacralisation of the forces of nature resulting from the belief in God's exclusivity and the conception that the creation was for the sake of man enabled the Christian religion, with its possibilities of adaptation, to survive the great revolution that had been taking place in Western spiritual life since the 17th century. But the exclusivity of the Christian God also rendered impossible the religious tolerance prevailing in the Roman world, which found its scientific support in the philosophy of that time. Tolerance towards other religions is not an impossibility within Christendom; no one, according to one of the opinions held during the period of persecution, can be forced to believe. On the other hand it was held that the non-believer is the rejected one. Moreover the theocratic idea that God is the Lord in all aspects of human existence profoundly influenced the development of the Cristian religion. In the long run that undeniably fostered intolerance: the sufferance of one rejected by God is an affront to the sovereign God. For that matter, tolerance did not spring from Christianity itself, but was imposed on it by non-Christian powers. This again was an instance of the adaptability of Christianity.

In Judaism the notion that God can only be known through his relationship to his created servants is usually expressed in the conception of a covenant between Him and his servants. This notion is not unknown to Christianity, but more essential is the idea of God's kingdom, which was already clearly evolved in the Jewish apocalyptical teaching. God is the faithful, just Lord, who makes his faith and righteousness the basis of the existence of God's people and to this attaches his promise of preservation. The redemption of that promise is the primary fact of the Christian faith: the King of God's realm has appeared; he is Jesus, called therefore the Anointed, the Christ. This King sent by God to deliver his people heralds the new age or eon of salvation: the age of peace, righteousness, health, joy, in short the eternal life intended by God. In him are discernible the features expressed by prophets and apocalyptics: the King of Israel, the obedient servant who fulfils God's righteousness, the Son of Man, the new man, etc. In a word: he is the fulfilment of God's promises and the fulfiller of the Law.

A new age opens up, the old age is past. This defines history. In Christianity, history's entry into the religious field of vision is the result of the appearance of the King of the new eon. That is the new world epoch in which God's peace shall prevail. But the conception of history as the course of God's dealings with the generations of mankind, within the Christian field of vision, is of Judaistic origin. God's revelation is not primarily thought of as occurring in a timeless and spaceless environment, nor in an inconceivable time, for instance a mythical primeval age, nor in an undeterminable heavenly or paradisical space, but in a concrete human world. God reveals himself as the God of the fathers, mentioned by name, and He wishes to maintain a relationship with their children. Places and vicissitudes of men are mentioned. Religious celebrations are linked up preferably with historical events, real or assumed. It began with the story of God's activities involving his people, the children of Abraham, Isaac and Jacob. History is the history of man in which God effects a change. In other words: time is punctuated by the coming of the moment chosen by God to mark the beginning of a new era. In the apocalyptic teaching this conception is stylised as a division into world periods;

the last period will be the age of deliverance. This expectation is fulfilled by the coming of Christ, and hence the apocalyptic conception is often reduced to two periods: the old and the new. Christ's arrival heralds the beginning of a new eon. But the issue here is not a moment, but a period of time. The new time has come, but is not yet visible to everyone. This distinction lends a further dimension to the end of times. The question as to how long it will be before Christ has fully revealed his glory has occupied the minds long enough (and still is being discussed in small groups), but it ranks second to the expansion itself.

There are various aspects to the concept of the Kingdom of God in the Christian belief. Firstly it is a purely religious concept: It is connected with the story about the coming of Christ, his death and resurrection; admittance to the kingdom is granted through baptism after man has forsworn evil and has been freed from the devil by exorcism; man is preserved in it by the presence of God's Spirit, which passes on and confirms Christ's message and which brings about the works of the Kingdom of God; by means of the sacramental supper man is brought into the presence of the King. History and ritual form a whole here. Baptism means being buried with Christ (according to Paul's interpretation), and being resurrected with him (non-Paulinistic, but generally accepted in the Church); Holy Communion anticipates the gathering of Christ and his followers in the fulfilment. The story of Christ is not so much portrayed as actualised in the ritual by Christ himself. Secondly, however, the idea of the kingdom of God expresses more than a sacral community. The terminology of the Christian faith is political and juridical rather than religious. The kingdom of God is reminiscent of the ancient kingdoms of Israel and Juda. Jesus is the King from the house of David. There is a Law which must be fulfilled and it is its moral aspect that is emphasised. There is mention of reconciliation, redemption, justice and justification. And although Christ's kingdom is not of this world, that only means that it is not of the old world, that it belongs to the new eon heralded by his coming. Now even though one believes that these and similar expressions are largely metaphorical, it still is true that in the Christian faith—in this respect, too, indebted to the prophetic vision of Judaism—the essential element is the moral obligation to care for your fellowman. Indeed, the fulfilment of that obligation alone will bestow God's joy on the world. In the last parable of Jesus' eschatological sermon (Matthew 25, 31-46) the "nations" (gentiles) can find the criterion for their preservation in their behaviour towards suffering man.

The pivot of the Gospel is righteousness: the mutual faithfulness of God and man in their relationship. The believer must realise the demands of God for the salvation of his fellow-man. But there is yet another aspect to this moral side of the question. The Christian faith assumes that its adepts are also personally involved in God's righteousness and at all levels of God's kingdom: the ritual and narrative, the political and moral. Man's admittance to the Kingdom through baptism is a question of grace, but it does not take place regardless of the volition of the person to be baptised. This has led to difficulties in the baptismal practice of Christianity; in the case of infant baptism the substitute faith of the parents or godparents or of the entire church is usually assumed. With regard to the political aspect the church has, on the one hand, allowed itself to be moulded into a sacral department of the state (e.g. the Roman imperial church or the Lutheran national churches in the 17th century), and on the other it has itself gone so far as to imagine the realm of the emperor to be the realm of God and his Anointed (e.g. Byzantium and certain medieval emperors of Germany) The earth has been sanctified by the coming of Christ, and in that light the political order prevailing on earth is easily consecrated as being part of the kingdom of God. In the Middle Ages the image employed was that of a body with two sides, State and Church.

At the same time, however, government and society can themselves be criticised by the Christian conscience. This phenomenon has occurred during the most divergent circumstances and periods: thus in the Byzantine empire the criticism came from the contemplative monks and in the Reformation from the farmers led by Thomas Münzer. Often that protest is directed against certain moral aspects of life upheld by the state. Then it can closely resemble criticism of what is sometimes called a world-minded church: that is a church whose institutionalisation has become closely bound up with the political power, with the concommittant social, economic and financial means, and this can be felt to be an injustice by those not in power.

Such criticism—and also purely moral criticism of the behaviour of the people—is often uttered by individual prophets, though the institutional church administration can also voice it. There have always been prophets, sometimes denounced as heretics, but sometimes accepted officially by the Christian community during their lifetime or afterwards. Their appearance is one of the essential elements of the Christian religion, characterised as it is, after all, by prophetism.

In addition, however, it has its equally essential institutional form, though this can differ in type. In other words: up till now some kind of ecclesiastical institution has *quocumque modo* proved to be essential to the Christian faith. This is based on the idea of Christ's kingship and the notion that the Christian lives in a new eon that is only accepted as reality by faith and is not yet visible to everyone. This period is anyhow the period of Christ's kingship. But man, even the believer, isis still menaced by the powers of darkness of the old period. In it the invisible Christ is present in the person of the official leader of the Christian congregation. Various duties are assigned to this leader—the bishop in the Catholic world, otherwise a board appointed to govern one or more congregations. This leader protects the congregation against the assaults of the Ruler of this world, hence he is its shepherd in Christ's stead. He directs the life of his herd. He is the authorised expounder of Christ's message because he is the successor of the apostles. It means that through the Holy Ghost, the work they took over from Christ is still being carried out. In short the congregation is usually thought to be grouped institutionally around an official, a charismatic deputy of the Lord, or else it considers itself as a whole to be official and priestly.

Because of this charismatic character, it is always possible that individuals who are charismatically talented may emerge; the prophets, the mystics, the ascetics, who operate legitimately within the Christian church as members of a monastery, and also independently in or outside the church, as for example the hermit or, in a non-Catholic context, the lay preacher. From this sector groups usually of a sectarian character can be formed by followers of the inspired individual.

There is another phenomenon connected with the conception of God as *persona*. The issue in the religious knowledge of God is not, at least not primarily, a philosophical or scientific knowledge, but man's involvement with his God. In other words: the most urgent question is that of communication: how can I meet God? The answer is first and foremost: there where He is to be found. If the godhead is thought to be an eternal being, as the nameless One elevated above all that is divided, as in the neo-Platonic mysticism, then He will be found in the realm of the mind and not in that of matter. The mind is part of an undivided reality, it unites the multiplicity of the material phenomena into entities, ideas, conceptions, and in this way man can proceed towards the sought-for and desired godhead. In other words, in such a context God can be found in the eternal being of the Spirit by the human mind which, surmounting discursive reasoning, can essay the synthesis of ideas. But if God is *persona*, then the point of encounter is given on the level of the reality of this *persona*. God is there where he speaks with man as *persona*. We have already seen that the issue in this concept of person is not a being which manifests itself in such a manner that we would have the right and the possibility to inquire what could be hiding behind the mask, behind the functionary. From the religious viewpoint, the *persona* comprises the entirety, the entire God, the entire man. But man is a being of flesh and blood, he has a material life and that is essential to his existence. He is a body. But he is also a soul, and his association with his God has a spiritual character. Here, again, he can not be qualified as a substance with a synthetic predicate: a being, which is mind. He is the servant of God, as a totality, with body and mind. It follows then that he meets his God in his own physical-mental world. But, as we have seen, God determines the location of this meeting. He indicates the spot on earth where He is to be found. There He speaks fully, because He is *persona* there, just as He is to be found by the angels in heavenly guise though equally as *persona*.

An essential feature of the Christian religion is, therefore, that materiality is highly valued: in the communication between God and man, materiality is implicit. The Kingdom of God is being established on earth; the King of that realm is a man, He is present through His word and the sacraments, and His kingdom comprises more than a ritual ceremony. It claims justice in human society and man's rules of conduct necessary for the obedience to God's word. Something similar can be seen in the eschatology. The issue is the resurrection of the fiesh, not, or not merely, the immortality of the soul.

But all that is material was created and hence qualified as subservient to God. God's creatures, however, are differentiated; three persons are concerned in the relationship of God and creation. There is a relationship between God and the one spoken to by Him, hence an appointed and chosen person, who can be an individual or a collective body. At the same time this elected person is, by his selection, brought into a relationship with a third party: in that way his relationship with God is further defined. Examples are: God—Moses, the prophets, the priests, the kings—the people; but also, and this has become very important for Christianity: God—God's people—the nations. In the last of days, according to late-prophetic conviction, the nations will come to Zion and serve the God of Israel. This expresses the conviction that the heathens would become part of God's people. In principle, the belief in the Messiah makes the gentile a member of God's people in the new eon. As such, however, the gentile is no longer obliged to observe the rites of the old Israel, for his coming to the Messiah is the very sign of the new eon, whereas the old ritual is the sign of God's people in the old eon. Consequently Christianity, a Palestinian Jewish sect in origin, separated from Judaism and they became two different religions, though with a common Holy Scripture of which the Christian exegesis has been canonised in the New Testament, and a number of common religious conceptions, but with diverging beliefs regarding the fundamental questions of deliverance and future.

Secondly, in this trilateral relationship between God and mankind lay the starting point for the propagation of Christianity. Now that the coming of Christ has in principle made it possible for the heathen to become one of God's people, it is the duty of the Christians to bring this about by proclaiming the message of his coming to distant peoples. Distant peoples: this implies that with the advent of the new eon the space within which God's work is manifested is thrown wide open—the ends of the earth have seen the salvation of this God. Christ is Lord of the entire world, his messengers go abroad to bring the nations to the God of Israel. A remarkable thing in this connexion is that at the end of the second century the word "diaspora" was still used by the Christians as an alternative to the word "catholic." In the diaspora the Word has been heard, and in consequence what originally lay beyond the little circle about the God of Israel has become orientated towards that same God. The dispersed peoples have become the universal and one people of God.

The expansion of Christianity into a world religion proves it was capable of carrying out this apostolic programme. Started as the religion of a Jewish minority, it was nevertheless able to take root in a differently constituted Graeco-Roman culture, even to adopt a number of the latter's fundamental ideas, including religious ones, and simultaneously adapt them to its own basic conceptions. The most important from the point of view of religion is perhaps the conception of justice, since it provided a point of contact with the moral aspects of Christianity. In the Christian literature a universal, non-Christian tenet is used to define it: to give every man his due. In this way non-Jewish Christian thought and experience assimilates the judgment of God, primeval element in the eschatology: God rewards each man according to his works. But at the same time Christianity includes in the notion of justice defined as *justitia distributiva* the idea of God's faith, which is fundamental to the Jewish conception of justice: God is faithful and does not abandon the work of his hands. This aspect is evaluated as love, and this love is effectuated in the coming of Christ, his (Jewish) commandment to love God and one's neighbour, and in his care for the church and the world.

This capacity for adapting and converting what the Christians meet within a non-Christian world is one of the prime features of the Christian religion. This was what enabled it to cope with the situation in which it was placed when, still a minority that was all but unrepresented in some regions, it received the patronage of the Roman authorities and expanded into the official religion of the empire. In the East the tradition could be continued, in the West Christianity found its place in the constitution of the Germanic kingdoms. It survived feudalism, and since the twelfth century it succeeded in making itself indispensable in the world of urban trade and industry which conflicted with the agrarian feudalism. It witnessed the loss of large areas, especially in the eastern part and along the southern shore of the Mediterranean, where Islam spread. But in north-western, northern and north-eastern Europe it expanded far beyond the outermost limits of either the Roman or the Carolingian empire. It experienced great schisms in the Middle Ages between the Greek and Latin forms of Christianity, a schism rooted mainly in the alliance of Church and State, and in the sixteenth century within western Christendom between Reformation and Catholicism, a schism which went much deeper, also from a religious viewpoint, than that between the eastern and western church after 1054. Nevertheless it managed to hold its position in spite of apparent weakening when the modern age dawned with its entirely different world image of both cosmology and geography. When the western hemisphere was discovered Christianity succeeded in asserting itself there in the newly conquered lands as an essential part of the "establishment". The subjected peoples had also to accept it. The same holds good for Australia, where the last great phase in the expansion of Christianity was completed in the nineteenth century. Only in Asia and Africa has it gained little hold.

Now the comment on all this could be: Christianity was the religion of the conquerors. They exported it along with their power, and where that power proved inadequate, as in seventeenth century Asia, or was extended at a time when this religion had lost a considerable portion of its hold over the conquerors themselves as in nineteenth century Africa, Christianity failed to take root. Even then, however, its capacity for adaptation and transformation proved to be great. Christianity found fertile soil among the subjected peoples of the conquered areas and did not remain the religion of the rulers only.

This phenomenon is based on a characteristic already discernible in the Jewish religion: religion and the culture of the "Establishment" are not identical. They can appear in opposition to each other, as evidenced in the prophetic and apocalyptic traditions. God is Lord of the entire world: where ever people are, He is their God. Moreover in this religion the believer is considered to be personally involved in his belief, as we have seen. This means, in turn, that in the tensions between the upholders of the established order in state and society and the opposition, inspiration can be found by both parties in their Christianity. In fact the ambivalence of Christianity is asserted here: a God who is spirit, but also body, a future that has commenced but must still come, an essentially institutionary character but also a free prophetism, the belief in an eternal and immutable truth which nevertheless is conceived of as a human being (Jesus Christ). It is this ambivalence, which at times becomes ambiguity and antithesis, that has enabled Christianity to expand and persist in the most divergent circumstances. On the whole there was little danger of a blurring of the boundaries in the direction of syncretism. The aforesaid exclusivity of God prevented this.

II. Historical Development

Shortly after the death of Jesus—which cannot be dated precisely—Christianity spread out beyond the frontiers of Palestine, first mainly through the synagogues in the diaspora and later also, and finally exclusively, outside that context. The Catholic church, which developed towards the end of the first and especially in the course of the second century, is not the only shoot from the old root. A development also took place within the Jewish milieu, mainly in Jerusalem at first and thereafter when this group fled to Transjordania during the siege of Jerusalem in that country. This branch remained isolated from what took place elsewhere in the Roman empire; in fact clear traces of it disappear in the third century. Seen from the viewpoint of the Catholic church, it resembled a sect and was of no importance for the development of catholicism. In addition there was Gnosticism, which accepted and adapted Christian conceptions and traditions and formed Christian-Gnostic groups, a process which reached its climax in the second century. In this period we see how certain heathen-Christian groups (i.e. Christian congregations whose members did not reach Christianity via the synagogues) acquire a more clearly defined profile, partly through their repulsion of the Gnostics on the one hand and attacks from the synagogue on the other. They were centred around the originally Jewish Holy Scriptures ("Law and Prophets" as they are usually termed, or briefly: "The Scripture"), which are authoritatively interpreted by the Christian—apostolic—tradition as being fulfilled in Christ. This interpretation was finalised in the acceptance of a number of writings attributed to the apostles or their disciples (the Gospels, the Acts, the Epistles, and finally one Revelation) which together form the list or canon of the apostolically authorised exegesis in liturgy. Secondly the preaching was laid down in a summary of what non-Christians were taught in preparation for their baptism, the so-called Rule of Faith from which the various forms of the profession of faith were to grow, but which was basically the same everywhere. Thirdly the episcopal office acquired increasing significance, both as the office that had to safeguard the congregation against the powers assailing it (reversion to the older religions, deeds considered a sin in Christianity, heresies, discouragement induced by the tensions arising from Christian isolation) and also as the unchanging office of doctrinal authority based on the apostolic tradition in face of the independent prophets who, as bearers of the Holy Ghost, threatened to follow their own course with respect to the institutional holders of office.

This catholicism had to hold its ground against both the synagogue and the non-Christians. The break with the synagogue is clearly approaching in the epistles of Paul and also in the Gospel of John, though neither Paul nor John was an opponent of the synagogue in the way the later Christians were. The conflict with the synagogue centred on the issue of the interpretation of the Scriptures, whether they can only be understood in the light of Christ's deeds and subsequently of the meaning of the Law. It was a different matter with paganism. Here it was a question of suspicion regarding the new sect that was not recognised as Jewish and that clearly was averse to the non-Jewish religiousness and also to a large extent to the non-Christian way of life. Christendom was a religious minority with a divergent pattern of life that had become isolated. The non-Christian opinion was unfavourable. Scholars believed that the history of Jesus the Messiah was a fable. Others feared and despised Christianity as the religion of atheism, since it contested non-Christian religiousness and refused to make offering to the emperor's image; as the religion of misanthropes, since Christians lived apart and held that all who did not believe in Christ lived in darkness and were doomed; as the religion of practitioners of incest. This was an accusation made repeatedly against other minority groups living in a certain degree of isolation and later was made by the Christians against the Jews. As for the Christians, this accusation could have been based on the fact that they called each other brother and sister and in religious community gave each other the kiss of peace. They were also feared and despised as cannibals; the accusation of infanticide is of the same nature as that of incest and likewise was made against others. Here the conception of the Last Supper as the eating and drinking of Jesus' body and blood could have formed the motive. The many catastrophic disasters during the later imperial age, such as famine, wars, epidemics, led the stricken to seek a scapegoat, which as usual was found in isolated minority groups. Opposition to this trend was offered by the Apologists, the most important of whom was Justin Martyr (died about 165). They tried to demonstrate firstly that the Christian belief did not form a threat to the state and could offer the authorities protection and reconciliation with God, and secondly that it was rational and pagan religiousness irrational. These two motives are important: the first gave an impetus to the preparations for assuming religious leadership within the polity, the second placed Christian religiousness and its conceptions over and against the prevailing philosophical way of thinking. The Christians learned how to use the Graeco-Roman culture's most important set of concepts to serve their faith.

The first phase of intellectual maturity was reached by Christianity in its catholic form at the beginning of the third century. In Egyptian Alexandria Origenes was at work, and he was the most important Greek theologian of antiquity and the great exegetic testator, whose treasures were exploited down to the end of the Middle Ages, albeit anonymously and via divers mediaries. In the west Rome was the most important congregation, but the intellectual nucleus lay for the time being in North Africa, in Carthage where Tertullian and, a generation after him about the middle of the third century, Cyprian worked. From this region was to emerge the greatest father of the Western Church, AUGUSTINE.

The course of development progressed quietly on the whole during the first half of the third century. It was only under Decius (249-251) that widespread persecution broke out. Previous persecutions, although often very violent, had been of a local and sporadic nature. In the fifty years after Decius new persecutions occurred repeatedly which were not systematically carried through, finally culminated in the persecution begun in 303 under Diocletian (284-305). In the war of succession to this emperor, the western rulers Constantine and Licinius granted tolerance to the Christian religion, perhaps for reasons of propaganda against the East, where the majority of the Christians lived but where violently anti-Christian potentates ruled. After Constantine the Great's definitive victory and apart from a brief pagan reaction under Julian the Apostate (361-363), Catholicism more and more acquired the character of the actual state religion, until finally Theodosius the Great (379-395) made it the only religion tolerated in his empire.

In the course of the fourth century, though of older origin, the monastic system developed: representatives of the Christian life's difference from the world. These hosts of ascetics provided the church with large numbers of picked troops for the maintenance of the Christian order among the believers and in the Christian commonwealth. On the other hand from among the ascetics there emerged ever and again those prophets who resisted the identification of the existing order with the church, or the degeneration of the church into nothing more than a sacral and ritual instrument. All the great reformations in the church, including that of the sixteenth century, have emanated from the monastery. The origins of the ascetic movement are not clear in all respects. With regard to the religious aspect a link may be found in Christian eschatology; as for the sociological aspect, like phenomena in Judaism (Essenes, the groups made known in the Dead Sea Scrolls) and paganism (Neo-Pythagorians, certain cynic philosphers) probably made their influence felt. The origin lay in Egypt on the border between the cultivated land and the desert, and very soon afterwards similar phenomena appeared in Palestine and Syria. The hermit was probably the earliest ascetic, but soon colonies of hermits appeared and joined together under a uniform pattern of life. Rules for the coenobite way of life were drawn up (Gr. *koinos bios*, communal life); and in the west more than the east this form prevailed, though the anchorite seclusion of the hermits or desert-dwellers never died out entirely (*anachorein*—to withdraw apart).

The basic rule of asceticism is that the kingdom of God is not of this world. Property is repudiated and also sexuality, which often is thought to be a satanical menace. To poverty and chastity was soon added a third ascetic requisite, obedience; obedience to the experienced ascetic, whose acolytes had to obey his commands, and then to the leader of the monastic community, the abbot. The classical rules for the sect were drawn up by the Egyptian Pachomius and the Cappadocian Basil of Caesarea. In the west this was done by Benedict of Nursia in central Italy, founder of the Benedictine order which, repeatedly reformed as regards the *opus dei*, the liturgy of the hours of prayer, was the only western order to last until the creation of the mendicant friars, who lived according to different principles.

Monasticism rendered the Christian church an inestimable service in christianising the rural areas. The ancient ecclesiastical Christianity was mainly an urban phenomenon, but asceticism gravitated first towards the uncultivated regions and later those regions also defined as uncultivated from the viewpoint of urban culture, namely the estates practising large-scale agriculture. Usually the monks occupied the position of landed proprietor and did not personally work on the land. For that matter their minutely organised and exacting daily schedule of prayer did not offer them much opportunity for such activity. In any case ascetism opened up the path towards the christianisation of the rural areas. It was from the monasteries, too, that missionaries went out to bring Christianity to northern and central Europe, and in the process the Greek and Latin worlds collided.

Meantime, ever since the recognition by Emperor Constantine, Christianity had to fight hard to preserve its doctrine, in order to preserve its identity. Already in the century preceding its recognition by the imperial government a battle had had to be fought against heresies, especially that of the Gnostics, and they had been successfully barred out. But that does not mean there was no need continually to present the content of the Christian message in such a way that the new, non-Jewish public of the Christian mission could understand it. The terminology of Greek philosophy was used for the preaching of that message, and moreover certain thoughts and conceptions from the world of the mystery religions found their way into the church. On closer inspection, however, we see that in a Christian context this borrowed material acquired a meaning different to that which it had

had in its original framework. This will be discussed in greater detail below. In the period during which the church was recognised by the governing authority and slowly but surely became monopolised by it, the struggle for the purity of doctrine took on sharper contours. The tendency of the later emperors further to centralise the empire had its repercussions in the church, especially since they found in it one of the most powerful cohesive forces in the state. Catholicism was able to settle accounts with its old enemies more easily than in former days. In principle it could count on the government's law-enforcing power, which forbade the public appearance and sometimes even the existence of pagan, heretical or gnostic communities and rites and made it difficult for the synagogues. But at the same time differences of opinion within the church on the related complex of ideas about salvation and the doctrine concerning God, Christ and the Holy Ghost sharpened into disputes and threatened the peace of the state. During the fourth and succeeding centuries the government repeatedly intervened in the discussions within the Catholic church, exiled bishops, favoured certain currents, granted and confiscated property and so caused more unrest in the church than there had ever been before.

It was during this period that the first great synods were held under imperial rule, meetings summoned by the emperor to decide on matters pertaining to the church as a whole. But the empire of Constantine or Theodosius was not destined to go on forever. The ancient structure of the western half of the empire disintegrated in the course of the fifth century, and the spoils were divided among the Germanic victors, who were Arian or non-Christian, in any case non-catholic. They were converted to the Catholicism of their subjects in the course of the fifth and sixth centuries, but the monarch's relationship to the church differed from that of the emperors. No longer was the church the priestly body whose duty it was to safeguard the Christian order in the state. Rather was it the property of the ruler. This difference became very important with respect to the dissimilar development of the church in the east and the west.

In the east the old imperial structure remained intact. The leading bishop, of Constantinople, was in fact an official of the sacral emperor and became even more so when the other old patriarchates—Alexandria in Egypt, Antioch in Syria, and Jerusalem—were lost to the Byzantine empire as a result of Islam's conquests. The church there did manage to remain in existence to some degree, since Islam was generally more tolerant to Christianity than vice versa, but it could no longer form a counterweight to Constantinople, which in fact dominated church life as organ of the state. The only spiritual counterweight was offered by the monks. In the west, however, an urge to reform the church developed steadily from the tenth century on, emanating mainly from the abbey of Cluny in Burgundy. The aim was to release the church from the state patronage, give Rome the spiritual leadership and simultaneously develop the church's own political power. This development took place mainly in the twelfth and thirteenth centuries. By accepting the supremacy of Rome, the regional churches gained a certain degree of individual independence with regard to their rulers. This course of events gave rise to many problems. It led to a series of conflicts between the rulers and the pope or curial prelates in the regional churches, the most important of which was that between the pope and the German emperor. This conflict was waged over the question of the ruler's right to appoint bishops, to invest them with crosier and ring. It was a question with immediate political consequences, since the bishops themselves were usually rulers over large territories. This so-called War of Investiture ended in a compromise. The rulers had to recognise the independence of the bishop, but the pope was not able to regulate his appointment entirely according to his own wishes.

With the increasing prestige of Rome after the eleventh century, the relations between the church in the east and in the west similarily became more difficult. Ever since antiquity the heads of Rome and Constantinople had repeatedly banned one another from the ecclesiastical communion. In 1054 a similar breach occurred once more. In the following centuries the opinion that this was the origin of the schism (known as the Eastern schism) gained ground, when the gap between the two parts of Christendom was made definitive by the crusades.

These expeditions, masked as military pilgrimages and undertaken by western nobles to occupy the holy places in Palestine and seize territories in the Middle East, caused a definitive alienation between eastern and western Christendom. The first crusade was the answer to the appeal of the Byzantine emperor, who was menaced on his eastern and southern frontiers by the advancing forces of Islam. Very soon, however, the westerners realised that the projected occupation could best be effected by conquering Constantinople. This was accomplished during the fourth crusade (1204), which ended in the Byzantine throne being occupied by a western prince (the eastern emperor had his seat in Nicea) and, especially, in the latinisation of the church of Constantinople. This deed of violence turned the alienation between the two halves of Christendom into an unbridgeable schism. The differences in the historical development of the east and the west in the political, social and cultural fields were considerable, and since Christianity comprised not only a religious group but a whole society, the religious difference also increased in significance with the passing of centuries. Now when it became ever more manifest during the course of the crusades that the issue also was a conflict between the two areas of the Mediterranean, in which the west soon came to look on the east as a conquered province, the Byzantine empire lost all feelings about Christian solidarity, undermined as it was by the interests of the crusaders and their backers, especially such Italian commercial centres as Venice and Genoa. Constantinople did make a few attempts to ease its desperate plight due to Islamic invaders by approaching Rome about an ecclesiastical union, notwithstanding contrary political interests and the hostile attitude of its own population, but all these attempts failed. The negotiations of the councils of Lyons (1274) and Florence (1435) achieved nothing. The sum total of the crusades as far as Greek Christendom was concerned can be expressed in the slogan that echoed in the streets of Constantinople during its last siege in 1453: better Turkish than popish.

There were Christian churches in the Islamic countries, some originating from schisms in ancient days, e.g. Nestorian and Monophysite. They were widely disseminated. The Nestorians, who dated from the fifth century, had their churches as far away as China and Malacca, while the Monophysites were largely the inspirers of the church of Ethiopia, where Christianity penetrated from Egypt. But the greatest expansion of eastern Christendom was in the direction of Russia. There, according to the notion of Russian Orthodoxy, was to be found the third Rome, after the ancient Rome and Constantinople.

The history of western Christendom is determined by the political and economical development of the Middle Ages in the west, where since the twelfth century the cities with their new economic power and the culture founded on it gradually ousted the feudal system. The significance of that development for Christendom becomes manifest on considering how an unmistakable, often heretical resistance arose to the established church with its orthodoxy and institutions. On the one hand there was a reversal to the apostolic poverty among the

Apostolic Brothers and Waldenses, and on the other there was the influence of the Albigenses and other older movements that reached the west from the east via the Balkans and were important especially in southern France. But the rise of the mendicant orders is also a sign of this new power in western and southern Europe. Dominicus, a travelling preacher from Spain who wished to convert the Albigenses, is the father of the Dominican Order, the Order of Preachers, and Francis, born in Assisi in Italy, of the Franciscan Order or Friars Minor. Their spirituality was largely opposed that of the feudal Benedictines, bound to their monastery, and the Cistercians and Norbertines, groups which came into being in the twelfth century as rivals of the Benedictines but inspired by Benedictine rules. The principle difference lies in the fact that the new orders of the thirteenth century no longer acknowledge the *stabilitas loci*, the restriction to one place, just as a city dweller is not tied to the soil.

When the first great universities began to develop in urban surroundings, the mendicant orders of Dominicans and Franciscans quickly discovered in them the natural milieu for their theology. In many respects the new bourgeois culture was very critical of the old agrarian-feudal pattern of Christian civilisation, and here the said orders found their challenge: Can Christianity maintain itself even under these circumstances? Theology removed from the monasteries to the university, and in theologics the mendicant orders tried to formulate the answer. Noteworthy Franciscans were first of all the Englishman ALEXANDER OF HALES, BONAVENTURA (died 1274) and thereafter JOHANNES DUNS SCOTUS (died 1308), while of the Dominicans, after ALBERT THE GREAT, THOMAS AQUINAS is by far the most important (died 1274). These scholastics—scholasticism simply means the theological study practised at the university—tried to find the answer to the new situation in west European culture. They endeavoured to fuse all knowledge of that time into one great system, in which wordly and theological knowledge would ultimately blend in harmony. The great scholastics of the thirteenth century had in mind a magnificent synthesis of belief and science, but by the end of the Middle Ages, in fact ever since the fourteenth century, this synthesis was contested. The great thinkers of the Franciscan school, for example JOHANNES DUNS SCOTUS and WILLIAM OF OCCAM, stressed God's unfathomable will and power rather than the rational equilibrium in the world emanating from God's thought. Old religious notions were broached which can also be traced outside the framework of the scientific assimilation of the religious data and the philosophy of the world. As for that scientific work, theological circles began to get accustomed to the idea that theology and philosophy, religious insight and human intellect can follow different and diverging paths, and this was of importance in the New Age. On the one hand, therefore, was created the feeling that the content of the Christian faith cannot be overtaken by ratio and also that the contrary should not be allowed to influence the scientific way of thought that was rapidly conquering the world of nature. On the other hand there arose a need to investigate the concept of God along new lines, but soon it appeared that a synthesis of theology and philosophy was a difficult undertaking, a sign that the Christian religion was no longer able to encompass life in its entirety.

The first signs of this are found grosso modo in the evolution of western European life, including that in Italy, since the beginning of the fourteenth century. Already in the previous century the new ascetic groups of the mendicant orders represented a different type of spirituality and mentality than the older groups, which had had their natural milieu in a mainly agrarian and feudal society. The mendicant orders, in their turn, were the result of an initial urban-cultural development in the twelfth century. BERNARD OF CLAIRVAUX (d. 1153) was, in a certain sense, a man of two ages—theologically conservative, organiser of a regime still bound to the monastery, but with a new spirituality—and he revealed new mystic nuances in his experience concerning Christ. But in the thirteenth century there was born in the circles of the new scientific theology a renewed interest in the mysticism of DIONYSIUS THE AREOPAGITE. On the one hand it satisfied the desire for a philosophical extension, since this mysticism operated to a large degree with the most mature techniques of the ancient philosophy, and on the other hand it was also able to satisfy the desire for a more intense personal experience of the encounter with God. This mysticism reached its climax in RICHARD OF ST. VICTOR (died 1173) and especially BONAVENTURA, general of the Franciscans and contemporary of THOMAS AQUINAS, who, for that matter, also wrote commentaries on DIONYSIUS. Alongside of it, however, there existed other forms of personal or group spirituality in which great interest was shown in Christ's love, in his suffering and humanity. It was a religiousness characterised by great fears and great tenderness, which was much more subjectively charged than was formerly the case in Christian life and which accordingly was less constrained and institutional. This of course aroused the anxiety of the ecclesiastical authorities and rulers: the Inquisition grew steadily in importance.

The greater tensions in spiritual life were even further increased by the world situation. In the middle of the fourteenth century the Black Death raged across Europe, a pest epidemic for which there was no remedy and which spread rapidly because of the greater mobility of life in those days. Powerless in face of this plague, man sought its cause in the wrath of God and in satanical powers. Belief in the devil became more virulent than ever, and people sought their salvation among the heavenly hosts, angels, and especially popular saints. Since time immemorial a saint was thought to have the power of healing, and the possession of his relic acquired the character of a means of defence against the evil snares of the devil and his companions. At the same time the mortal fear of physical and spiritual dangers led to ever more intense ascetism and to hatred of the institutional powers in the church. This process also had its beginning in the twelfth but was greatly accelerated after the thirteenth century. Groups that sought an isolated position soon found themselves on the brim of sectarism and were branded as heretics. This phenomenon even occurred in an extreme wing of the Franciscans, among the fraticelli for instance. The people lived in fear of the judgment of God. Already in 1260 the prophecy of the apocalyptic JOACHIM OF FIORE (d. 1202) that the world would soon come to an end had caused great consternation, and both about the middle and at the end of the fourteenth century unbridled ascetic-apocalyptic movements came into being.

The feeling of uneasiness about life was intermingled with a feeling of uneasiness about the church. At the beginning of the thirteenth century the pope, influenced by the French king, moved his residence to Avignon just beyond the border of what was French territory at that time but under French pressure. This "Babylonian exile" of the pope (1309-1377) was followed by the so-called western schism (1378-1417), when Europe was divided between dependence on a pope enthroned in Rome and on one who resided in Avignon. That caused profound spiritual confusion in daily life, because in the west even more than in the east the pope was recognised as the spiritual leader of all Christians. All that came of the reforming councils held in the first half of the fifteenth century was that the papacy came out the winner and that the necessary reforms were not put into operation. More than ever before the pope had become an Italian ruler, though for the religious life of most Rome remained the holy city of Peter, prince of the apostles.

All this prepared Christendom for the great changes that were to occur in the Modern Age. From the middle of the fifteenth century on they clearly took place. In the east Islam not only conquered all of Asia Minor, but also Greece and a large section of the Balkans after the fall of Constantinople in 1453. On the whole the old Christian church managed to hold out, but the centre of gravity of orthodoxy in the east was shifted to Russia. In the west, however, the last remnants of Moslim sovereignty in the Iberian peninsula were cleared away by a Christendom that was both militant and conservative. From the global point of view, this Christendom was the most important one as regards the expansion of the religion: the last large-scale conversion to Christianity followed on the Hispano-Portuguese conquests in Central and South America. Once more and for the last time on such a large scale Christianity demonstrated its capacity for adaptation. Imposed from above by the conquerors, it absorbed the old indigenous religions in the long run and destroyed all that could not be interpreted as or transformed into Christian forms of religion and devotion.

This Iberian Catholicism, particularly the Spanish, exercised the greatest pressure on the papacy, and the difficulties of the western leader of Christendom, victor after the failure of the said reforming councils, are largely attributable to the political complications of this period. Meanwhile it became increasingly more obvious that spiritually the Middle Ages were passing. In Italy, playground of a number of larger and smaller political and military powers which could not claim a legitimate tradition, there came into being a humanism that broke away from traditional patterns of thought, drew its inspiration from the human spirit and found nourishment in a new experience of classical antiquity, or what was presented to be so. It disposed radically of more and more of the older scholastic sciences: the world experienced a rebirth, a renaissance. But there still was no escape from Christianity, either politically or socially: society of that day cannot be conceived of without the church. But the discontent with the ecclesiastical Christianity that had existed since the fourteenth century certainly did not diminish, and the victory of the Renaissance popes over the councils and the new spiritual climate of humanism did not wipe out the restless, tormented religiousness. The conflict broke out violently in the second and third decades of the sixteenth century. The occasion—not the cause—was the action of the German Austin friar Martin Luther. He was inspired to a new theological approach, which taught that man can only find peace with God in justification through Christ and his work alone, not through anything he could accomplish in the way of religious merit himself. Justification through faith alone, in Christ alone, through mercy alone. In the long run he and many others realised that this implied that the traditional church had become impure. The Bible constituted the documentation of this new line of thought. It was stripped of the exegesis made by man and claimed to be infallible, and was no longer considered an element in a system of acts and thoughts, but was made the basis of all thoughts and all actions to the exclusion of all the rest. Humanism was of assistance especially because its interest in philology opened up the knowledge of the basic languages, Hebrew and Greek and, to a lesser degree, because of its criticism of the old scholasticism and of the excesses of the superstitious devotions among the people often sustained by ecclesiastical authorities. However, the specifically Lutheran way of thinking was never essentially influenced by the religiousness of humanism itself. This religiousness was interested in the Christian way of life as taught by the Man Christ, which derived in part from the medieval practical mystical piety, and manifested universalistic tendencies which sought knowledge of the true God even outside the historical Christendom, allowing, for example, Socrates a place in heaven.

Luther's action soon was emulated by others elsewhere, in Switzerland by Zwingli who was influenced more by humanism, elsewhere especially by spiritualists who offered resistance to the established Christianity. These people, who thought mainly along apocalyptic lines, normally took as their starting point the fact that the spirit of God revealed itself immediately in the heart of God's friends and that the period of the church's external means of mercy had passed or that these means had become senseless in the demonised church. They advocated anabaptism (baptism of adults) and rejected the established hierarchy. Extatic and apocalyptic religious phenomena occurred in their circles. Their rejection of the existing religious order, in which church and state were close allies, rendered them politically suspect. Consequently they suffered the most severe persecution, whereas the reformation of Luther and Zwingli was acknowledged by rulers or municipal authorities and by and large was politically acceptable. The spiritualists cannot be classified under one social or doctrinal denominator. They comprised vigorous revolutionary-apocalyptic movements in the Low Countries which resulted in the founding of the Kingdom of Zion in Munster (Westphalia) in 1534-1535 as well as retiring, pious persons, peasant rebels as well as secluded scholars. They are a sign of the fierceness of the religious eruption in the sixteenth century and equally of its disorientation. They came into conflict not only with the Catholic magistrature, but also with the new Protestant rulers and by all they were ruthlessly persecuted. It was not till about the middle of the sixteenth century that a section of the old anabaptists began to navigate less stormy waters, thanks to the organising work of Menno Simons (d. 1561), while spiritualism found its successor in the continued influence of humanism. The latter was to have a long tradition particularly in the Netherlands which even Calvinism could not destroy.

Lutheranism took root mainly in the countries with a predominantly agrarian economy, such as Germany and the Scandinavian countries, whereas the Calvinistic reformation determined the protestant Christianity of countries with a marked commercial character situated along the new trading routes to America and India, such as France, Flanders and the Netherlands. CALVIN, who was born in northern France and died in Geneva (1564), advocated a theology that differed as to shades of meaning rather than principles from the newer theology inaugurated by Luther. In actual fact he differed more from ZWINGLI. But he was more concerned with honouring God by placing a Christian hall-mark on the entire life of the community, and he had more opportunity for doing so. He had a clearer vision of the conception of theocracy: God is the king of state and church, and even though he could not fully realise his ideal in Geneva, the model he aimed at retained its great significance in the development of Calvinism. Incidentally it is remarkable that, from a world-wide viewpoint, it was actually in America that his thoughts produced the most important practical results. In France itself Catholicism soon regained the upper hand, as in Flanders. In the Netherlands an older tradition of practical piety such as that of the Brethren of the Common Life and of the humanist minded circles retained a certain amount of influence in the mainly tolerantly inclined ruling caste of the big merchants. There part of the Calvinist programme was put into affect, especially during the Eighty Years War, even though the Calvinists definitely formed a minority group. A true theocracy was, however, never created. But in New England in particular, a Calvinist Puritanism mainly of English extraction placed a much clearer stamp on life there.

In England a national church came into being which had a Catholic structure though traces of moderate Calvinism can be discerned in it. For political and personal reasons King Henry VIII broke away from Rome, but did not go as far as to tolerate protestantism at home. A Protestant reaction under Edward VI was followed by a Catholic, pro-Roman one under Mary Tudor. Then Elizabeth I consolidated the Anglican Church. This was not to the liking of everyone. Pro-Calvinists, especially from the commercial and industrial sectors though also the lower nobility, who were puritans by nature and sometimes allied to certain spiritualistic movements, formed opposition groups. Some of these fled the country and went directly or via the Netherlands to seek their liberty in America.

The religious wars which ravaged central and western Europe from roughly the middle of the sixteenth to the middle of the seventeenth century can only with ample reserve be qualified as such, because even in the period of the reformation the new religiousness was conceivable only within the context of a Christian society and Christian governments, whose activities and hence also wars appeared to be involved in the cause of their confessions. In the course of the sixteenth century a number of monarchs and rulers sided with the reformation, whilst elsewhere—specifically under the most powerful rulers—Catholicism held its ground. The Catholic church equibalanced the shock of the reformation in the second half of the sixteenth century with the Council of Trent and also with the rise of a number of new forces of the counterreformation, of which the Jesuits were the most important new organisation. In the fields of science, mission and pastoral care they defended the church and enhanced Rome's significance as headquarters of the church. Likewise in the second half of the sixteenth century Protestantism formulated its classical creeds, signs of its consciousness of its proper nature, but also an arming for self-preservation.

The results of the religious wars were divergent. In France the struggle resembled a civil war more than anything else. It ended with the victory of Henry of Navarre, Henry IV, who achieved a certain religious peace by promulgating the Edict of Nantes (1598) which maintained the status quo: the Protestant religion was allowed in those regions where it was already known, but Catholicism was to remain predominant. In the Netherlands the character of these wars was mainly that of rebellion against Spain. Since the southern Netherlands remained in the power of Spain, Protestantism gained no foothold there. In Germany the violence of war raged most furiously. There the confessions of the native and foreign rulers were diametrically opposed, and immeasurable damage, both material and spiritual, was suffered by this country, where the witch-hunt reached its climax precisely in the first half of the seventeenth century. Nevertheless the contours of the new Europe slowly but surely emerged—and hence also the position of Christianity. The Peace of Munster in 1648 was the important turning point.

"Whose the region, his the religion" (*cujus regio, ejus religio*): this was essentially the church policy of those days. This policy implied that the churches had to be considered established powers, which in turn meant that the division in western European Christendom acquired an institutional character. On the whole the leaders of those churches aimed at making their "establishment" as strong as possible, both by means of the church orders and by teaching and theology, which became scholastic in character. But other spiritual forces were at work which were influenced by certain tendencies already discernible in medieval scholasticism and the humanism of the fifteenth and sixteenth centuries. The industrial and commercial world of western Europe needed a different science than that offered by the rigidifying orthodoxy. The expansion of the earthly and cosmic horizons demanded a new manner of controlling nature, and science found new, experimental methods, evolved a new natural science and also acquired a new knowledge of the human body. Not that the great thinkers of the seventeenth century were anti-Christian as a rule. DESCARTES, for example, felt that his mathematical method could provide a new basis for faith, and the English philosophers, less naive on the one hand, accepted the official church of their country as part of the society or, more naive on the other, looked upon religion and science as two incompatible but nevertheless co-existent quantities. More important for the future of the religion, however, was the fact that English thinkers applied empirical psychological analysis to the study of the processes of thought and, in general, the life of the spirit, including its religious life. Pioneer work on these lines was carried out by JOHN LOCKE (d. 1704).

However, the Christian religion could not be completely restrained within the rigorous and rigid objectivistic framework of ecclesiastical officiality. There was a fear of externalisation and a desire to experience the encounter with God personally. This new trend was remarkable.

Its phenomena could be found in the Protestant confessions, in both Lutheran and Calvinist circles where the term pietism was used. But similar phenomena could also be discerned in Catholicism, for example the rise of certain devotions such as that of the Sacred Heart, or of mystical-quietistic movements such as that of MME DE GUYON. The most impressive of all, however, was the Port-Royal circle in France, the counterpart of pietism, where the great mathematician and scientist BLAISE PASCAL opposed the efforts of the Jesuits to stipulate possibilities of life by means of a compromise between the demands of the age and the demands of the church's ethics, but also against the idea that the God of the philosophers was the God of Abraham, Isaac and Jacob, the Father of Jesus Christ.

Ever since the seventeenth century and especially since the end of the wars of religion, western Christianity has been faced with the demand for tolerance towards divergent convictions. This demand has a complicated background. In the first place a certain indifference towards the religions was manifested already in early Italian humanism; BOCCACCIO recorded the story of the three rings which LESSING later used in his Nathan der Weise. But a tolerant mentality towards religious differences also evolved in the northern humanism of such people as Erasmus: the main issue was the practice of living a Christian life in neighbourly love, the realisation of the simple science of Christ as opposed to the complicated scholastic speculations on dogma. Shortly after ERASMUS, JEAN BODIN lumped all religions together and belittled their differences. Furthermore, there was the spiritualistic criticism on all forms of institutional religions implying that in a new era they would disappear. In the second half of the seventeenth century however, there was a growing opinion that the wars of religion signified the failure of the confessions, and the conception of tolerance became a serious point of discussion: the people had different confessions and would simply have to find a way of living together in peace. This new vision was made possible by the newer sciences and concomitant philosophy. In it a very successful conception was offered of the world and of life: it was possible to control the new horizons with the help of this new science. This totality admitted of a certain conception of God, but it scarcely applied to the God of the Christian faith and left very little room for the old dogmas. The reformatory and counter-reformatory problems of sin, law, justification, mercy and the relevant views of man as the rejected and saved were no longer analogous to what the man of the new age experienced of himself and his world, and in the so-called Deism he found a satisfactory alternative to the failing confessions. God caused the world, it is now evolving and man as creature has the faculty of maintaining himself and attaining happiness. Life has no need of supranatural assistance, and hence Christianity in its true form is not a matter of mystery but of human development.

The crisis experienced by Christianity in the eighteenth century was that, although the churches were on the whole accepted by the ruling authorities as indispensable elements of society ("If there were no God, He would have to be invented"), they were undermined externally by a certain tolerance based on deistic indifference among the intellectuals and by a considerable amount of apostasy among the lower strata of society. When the Wesleys began their propagation of the Gospel among the paupers of the nascent industrial revolution, they encountered many who had never been in a church and were entirely ignorant of the message of the Gospel. Moreover the churches came into contact with all shades of pietism which did not reject the official dogma, but placed personal religious experience above outward appearance. In this period the expansive Christian activities of evangelisation and missionary work were carried out mainly by para-ecclesiastical groups, such as Wesley's Methodists, Franck's workers among the orphans, Zinzendorf's Moravian Brethren, the pietistical circles of the Bible Societies. Here in particular the apostolic impulse emanated from the old prophetic notion of personal responsibility before God.

The spirit of the age also affected Catholicism. The influence of the Jesuits was removed by their dissolution in 1773. The hatred against them was based partly on a typical Catholic anti-clericalism which was embodied in a man like VOLTAIRE, but also was felt by politicians, for they feared the power of the cleric even while considering the church indispensable to the state.

For that matter a parallel phenomenon was to be found in Russian orthodoxy. There the official church became more and more controlled by the ruling authorities, and the true religious life together with the pastoral care found support, as of old, among the ascetics, the staretsi and the so-called Old Believers.

All these factors made the breech between contemporary spiritual life and Christianity even more manifest. Politically it was expressed in the separation between church and state effected during the French revolution. A reaction followed at the beginning of the nineteenth century, heralded already by Napoleon's Concordat, which did great damage to the church, but which was not carried through, except in such old Catholic countries as Austria, Italy, Spain and Portugal. In the second half of the nineteenth century the church was nearly everywhere in fact and in law separated from the state. There were some exceptions, even in the non-Catholic world, the most important being those churches which had been state churches since the sixteenth century in countries not ravaged by the revolution, namely England and the Scandinavian countries.

In various respects the position of Christianity in the nineteenth century caused a division of minds which, though hopeless at the time, appeared less definitive in the second half of the twentieth century. In the western Catholic camp the centralisation of the church in Rome continued. The 1848 revolution induced Pope Pius IX to adopt a conservative policy which became increasingly marked during his very long period of office (1846-1878). Moreover the Catholic theological views were made more and more subservient to the juridical aspects: a centuries-old process in which the framework of Christian life was determined by the *Corpus iuris canonici*, which increased in importance during the Curia's reactionary conflict with the spirit of the age. Consequently it is understandable that the almost monolithic isolation of Roman Catholicism could hold out for a long time and also that many, no longer socially bound to obedience, turned their backs on the church. The instruments in which old Catholic convictions (the immaculate conception of Mary, the infallibility of official, "ex cathedra" truths proclaimed by the doctrinal office of the pope), were "proclaimed" dogma's, have a juridical character. Pope Pius XII's proclamation in 1950 of Mary's physical ascent to heaven is a late echo of the nineteenth century.

Protestantism was much less monolithic. At the beginning of the nineteenth century stood Fr. Schleiermacher, whose theological views, whether accepted or contested, determined the character of the theology passed on from the previous century. His ideas did not proceed from the thought that God reveals Himself: he was inclined to label that ill-begotten and now inacceptable metaphysics. He chose his starting point in the religious man and in his possibilities of experiencing religiously the total reality, the universum as he liked to term it. That universum is no longer a reality in face of a transcendental God, as alleged by the older theologians, but a different and, in his view expressed especially in his earlier writings, a better word for God. It is the reality on which he knows he is entirely dependent, if he is able to develop fully his religious talent (present in every man), and hence he seeks to attain his place determined by that universum. According to this view, the main feature of the theology is sought in the pious heart of man, and in the nineteenth century this proved to be a very fruitful conception. In addition it should be remembered that, in a world in which the church as objective institution steadily receded from its position as one of the established powers that determined life, great difficulties were bound to arise for the older objectivism. Gradually it was looked upon as naive, the religious man was left to his own resources more than ever and found scarcely any support in the Establishment. This growing uncertainty was a pre-eminent reason for the search for new paths that was evidenced in the formation of numerous sects precisely in the nineteenth century (pietistic currents, chiliastic groups, secession within the church, apocalyptical movements such as that of the Mormons, etc.), but also in the Dane SÖREN KIERKEGAARD, who in diverse respects was the very opposite of SCHLEIERMACHER. In KIERKEGAARD the believing individual finally came into conflict with the established church. He knew that man cannot be absorbed in any system whatsoever and realised that he was judged according to his existence. Though little esteemed in his own time, he has become the classical precursor of the religiousness prevailing in the first half of our century.

But not every one tried in his own way to distantiate himself from bourgeois idealism. It still held its power to fascinate, especially as regards its scientific consequences. It had no room for the old metaphysics, in which for centuries faith had found its philosophical foundation. With the progress of natural science in the nineteenth century this idealism became more and more a matter of dispute, matter and man as a form of matter attracted increasing attention, and these facts had a strengthening rather than a weakening effect on the tendency in theological studies to place the Christian religion on a new basis. In accordance with the philosophical and scientific thought of the day, there was a desire to settle accounts with the old supranaturalism; what we are concerned with in science and life is this nature and this world. The Bible became a collection of documents manifesting a religiousness of the past: these biblical writings are human testimonials which should therefore be studied from an historical-critical viewpoint. One of the earliest and most sensational publications in this field was "Das Leben Jesu" by D. F. STRAUSS (orig. 1835). In it the story of the Gospel becomes a myth, that is to say the idea is presented in the form of an historical narrative. This viewpoint aroused a storm of protest, and further historical-critical research made Strauss's work outdated, a normal occurrence in scientific studies. But in principle the research continued along the same lines, and the Old Testament was similarly dealt with. The same approach was applied to the history of Christianity. In fact the normal methods of historical research were applied to the history of the church and of the religious phenomena which can be classified under the term "Christian."

Consequently room was made for a new opinion about the non-biblical religions. The origins of their scientific study certainly go back further than the nineteenth century; under Deism study was already being done in that field. The present work is not the place to investigate that development of the history of religions in greater detail. This young branch of theological interest is important as a sign of a new mentality: in principle Christian thought is given the opportunity to pass scientific judgment on non-Christian religions. The basic assumption here is the recognisability and kinship of religious phenomena, because they are human phenomena.

Behind all these many activities, scientific in aim but rooted in a certain conviction about belief, lay the revolution in which Christianity became involved in the nineteenth century. It had lost its former character of popular belief, and the churches, which gradually dropped out of the natural context of society, became more like associations of co-religionists, even among the followers of the old creeds. The retention of confession became more and more a matter of personal decision. The various branches of western, non-Roman Christianity were often engaged in mutual and fierce conflicts, but looking back on them today they greatly resemble one another, because all of them were confronted with the fact that being a Christian had become a matter of personal volition in the nineteenth century. Whether one's thoughts were conservative or progressive, orthodox or liberal and modern, the believing individual made his own decision. Even the most traditional Christianity was not the inevitability it had been as social and cultural phenomenon in the preceding centuries.

Entirely in keeping with the aforesaid tendencies of personal conscientious decision and the related subjective religiousness, the missionary activities were mainly undertaken by associations that were often interconfessional and more or less pietistic, or even by individuals. To a large extent the church developed into a sort of coordinating body, whereas the religious life proper took place in associations of congenial religious people. This trend was most clearly evidenced in the Netherlands, but occurred elsewhere too. Within Anglican Christianity there developed a high church section which sought a rapprochement with the Roman Catholic church. Other movements also came into being, as in Germany where the union of Lutherans and Reformed Churches was imposed from above, this definitely strained relationships in certain areas. Such phenomena occurred also in France and elsewhere.

The change in mental climate which made itself felt about the end of the century influenced religious life insofar as modernism lost its former optimistic outlook and began to place more emphasis on man's sin and God's mercy, but the actual religious life did not succeed in finding a new ecclesiastical basis. This was not accomplished until the period between the two world wars when the oecumenical movement got under way. At first in three branches: the life and work of Christians, the faith and the church order, missions. At the big conference held im Amsterdam in 1948 these groups were fused in the World Council of Churches.

For Catholicism, which recognised the bishop of Rome as its spiritual leader, the "aggiornamento," the bringing-up-to-date, was not really initiated until the pontificate of John XXIII. The turning point came with the Second Vatican Council (1962-1965), which caused a commotion about many matters in the Catholic Church. Since then its relations with other Christian churches has become much more positive.

In the nineteenth century Pan-Slavism became an important element in eastern Christendom, especially in Russia. An almost Messianic role was attributed to the Slavonic Christians. In a world which, Christian or not, had lost the consciousness of redemption through Christ, they confirmed and proved the truth of the Gospels. The movement was primarily a matter of philosophers and writers, who often in practice mistrusted the official leaders of the Russian church and were mistrusted by them in turn. In the footsteps of Russian policy, these leaders endeavoured to expand their influence in the other eastern churches. But this was not what the Pan-Slavs aimed at in their programme. They more inclined to be apocalyptical romantics who gave form to a Christian Messianism through their literary imagination. Their ideas exercised a certain amount of influence in the west, especially in the period between the two world wars.

The second important fact in the history of Russian Christianity was the Russian revolution, which severed the bonds between the church and state and restricted the influence of the church. Especially in the beginning the church suffered persecution, and a rather intensive atheistic propaganda was carried on. However, its attitude, especially during the Second World War, has demonstrated that it can be considered one of the country's moral forces. The Russian church also is in contact with the Oecumenical movement.

III. The Conception of God

All who think of God, think of something living, said Augustine, and whoever thinks of Him in the right way, thinks of him as Life itself. The expression "the Living God" repeatedly occurs in the Bible. Without doubt Christianity is not the only religion which conceives of God as the force of life itself. The term must therefore be defined more specifically. To begin with, this God is experienced as God of the entire world: He created it and gave it life. This act of creation is not made conceivable or intuitively understandable in ritual. No sacred marriage takes place between the heavenly deity and the mother-goddess earth, but the earth is itself product of God's Word. To be precise, God is the absolutely only one, the invisible Lord of heaven and earth, Spirit invisible and uncreatural.

Firstly, in this divine exclusivity Christianity found a link with the monotheistically-inclined philosophical culture of the world in which it first appeared, and its spiritual character made possible an identification with such philosophical concepts as being, reason and cause. Secondly this conception of God contains the grounds for the conflict about the desacralisation of nature and human life: apart from this God no other divine powers are at work. If we consider how often this theme recurs in the preaching and the synodal resolutions of Antiquity and the early Middle Ages, we realise that the spiritual leaders primarily endeavoured to educate their believers in this direction. It was only in the second half of the Middle Ages and under the pressure of circumstances that it appeared that the fear of the demonic forces in nature and life definitely had not disappeared and could react dangerously.

But Christianity, being in this respect the inheritor of a prophetic-apocalyptic Judaism, is not primarily a religion that is interested in preserving life as a phenomenon of nature. This God is not primarily Lord of the vital forces of the cosmos, but of man to whom He reveals himself as the just one. As a just one rather than as Spirit or Reason, which was the principal characteristic of divine substance in the philosophy of the Graeco-Roman world. God reveals himself in his Word as the God who fulfils his promise of the renewal of the world of man. The church's teaching was focused on this, not on giving an insight into the religious significance of the cosmos. The central fact was that God reveals himself as the saviour of man's endangered existence: in doing so He appears as the Lord who founds his kingdom of justice by sending the Messiah.

God, the Lord of the people of his servants, reveals his sovereignty to the greatest extent in their preservation, by fulfilling the promise made to the patriarchs. Hence He is a God of history. His eternity is not timelessness, and time is not an adumbration of eternity or of immutability, as PLATO conceives time in the *Timaeus*. God is eternal because He is present in every earthly situation. He is eternal because He is present in the earthly, new age of the Messiah. Paul's comment on the words of the prophet "In a time of favor have I answered you, in a day of salvation have I helped you" (Isaiah 49, 8) was "behold, now is the acceptable time; behold, now is the dat of salvation" (2 Cor. 6, 2). This same notion is expressed in the opening words of the Fourth Gospel: "and the Word became flesh, and dwelt among us" (John 1, 14).

In God's presence among mankind lies the true character of the Christian conception of God. It does not imply that God, as it were, reflects Himself in the existence of his believers, but that He himself is present only and exclusively in the human Messiah Jesus. This means that God's *persona* is identical to the man Jesus Christ, and hence this man can wholly and to the exclusion of all others be called God. The complete qualification of Jesus as God, the Word become flesh, occurs only twice in the New Testament, namely John 1 and John 20, 28. In the latter passage Jesus is addressed as "My Lord and my God." The man Jesus, exclusive embodiment of God's sovereignty, must be addressed as "God." He is God's act for his people and so identical to God. Hence the qualification "The man Jesus Christ is God" has been preserved. He is entirely God, one in being with the heavenly Father, and entirely man, one in being with us, as the now classical formula has it. Nevertheless he is one person.

In him dwells all the fulness of the Godhead bodily, as is said in the Epistle to the Colossians (2, 9).

Though Christ is conveived of as the God-man and though he is different from mankind in that respect (he conquered death and as the new Adam has received a name which is above every name, the name of Lord (Philipp. 2,6-11)), he is not held to be isolated from his people. He is the first fruits of the dead (I Cor. 15, 20-23). God's *persona* also continues to be present among that people, who can therefore be characterised as having become the body of Christ. However, since Christ's own body remains invisible with the Father since his ascension to heaven and his people on earth are still visible, the problem arises how this invisible humanity of God in Christ is present among his people. The question can be formulated thus: how can that body of Christ, which is his people, be a living body that continues his work? The answer has been found in a conception which, like the primitive Christian elements of the conception of God, is of Jewish extraction. God's spirit is the breath of life which God has breathed into his creatures (Ps. 104, 29 et seq.; cf. Gen. 2, 7). In keeping with prophetism, this Spirit of God becomes the breath of life of the new life, that of righteousness under the Messiah. Thus to the Father and the Son is added the Holy Ghost, which is similarily conceived of as a *persona* in the meaning of the word defined above. It is the presence of God and God's Anointed among his people and is consequently equally and absolutely God in being.

In this way and also because of certain formulas in the New Testament there came into being the conception of the Trinity, though there is no elaborated doctrine about the Trinity in the New Testament itself. No one has ever contested that God is one and unique; on the contrary, this conception has been anxiously safeguarded. But He is a living God, there is a movement of life in Him. Better still, He Himself is the life which makes human life living by creating, judging and renewing it to eternal life. The latter does not mean primarily immortality. The expression means, in the first place, that human life shall no longer be threatened by the forces which can lead to man's downfall, and of those forces death is "the last enemy" (I Cor. 15, 26). Admittedly the classical forms of the preaching of the trinity derive from Greek philosophy, at least as far as the terminology is concerned, but they should be interpreted within the context of biblical preaching, as appears repeatedly in theological and especially homiletic literature. Then they reveal a pattern clearly divergent from this philosophy, which can be explained from the biblical data of this conception of God.

IV. Worship

Given its conception of God, Christianity might be expected to seek in its worship the realisation of the Messianic kingdom in human existence. Now this realisation has not only ritual aspects, it has first and foremost ethical and dogmatic ones. In the prophetic-apocalyptic tradition of the oldest congregations reflected in the New Testament, it is understandable that the requirement of righteousness and mercy towards anyone in need is emphatically postulated, but equally that the study of the Scriptures (the Law and the Prophets, as the sacred books of Israel are called) occupies a foremost position. The Scriptures are studied to reveal their Messianic content, their testimonial about Christ. That is why the doctrine and the liturgy cannot be separated. Moreover it should be borne in mind that the first Christian congregation was nothing but a Jewish sect, which adhered firmly to the Jewish temple worship. Furthermore it had a synagogal character, what was even more cogent for the Christians outside Jerusalem, and principal ingredients of the synagogal services (reading of the Scriptures accompanied with their interpretation, psalms, prayers) were retained. Church architecture only acquired a temple-like character later and never completely. In the first place a church is a house of the Lord in which his people join Him and is not a sanctuary in the strict sense of the word. Later during the Christianisation of pagans, a non-Christian temple could seldom be utilised as a church.

Not only are the doctrine and the liturgy closely allied, the same applies to the ethics and the liturgy. Whoever gains admittance to the church through being baptised does not automatically received eternal life, but is transferred into a renewed existence of obedience to God and must bear the full responsibility of the freedom inherent in it. In other words, he must fulfil the confession of his baptism in doctrine and life.

A. *Cult*

In principle the Christian rites are concentrated around three nuclei: the ritual of baptism, of Mass and of the canonical hours.

Since time immemorial baptism has been felt to be the act which transfers man from death, the old life without Christ, to a new existence orientated towards eternal life. It is a sacrament, in other words a hidden act of God, invisible to man, which is accomplished in the visible act of the church. It is best to view the entire ritual, and not just the immersion in or sprinkling with water, as Baptism. Ancient baptism should be visualised as follows. Accompanied by the prayers and fasting of the congregation (fasting which counts as repentence and as preparation for the expected new life, but which also has an ascetic purport in this sense that one has to learn to break away from his former ways of life), the prospective recipient is prepared for baptism. This is done mainly by instruction in the message of Christianity: the person to be baptised is sometimes called briefly catechumen, i.e. one who is being taught. The ceremony itself comprises a series of actions: the exorcism of the devil, the profession of faith, the immersion or affusion, the laying-on of the hands, by which the newly baptised receives the Holy Ghost. Then the recipient, who has removed his clothing at the beginning of the rite, is given new, white clothing and is led to the meeting place of the congregation, where he now may partake of the sacred meal, communion.

The purport of the sacrament, therefore, is not merely the forgiving of sins, but primarily the introduction to the new life, the existence with Christ in the new eon. Complications arose, however, as soon as Christianity became an essential ingredient of society. People are born into society, and the same holds good for a Christian society. Through his very birth a man is absorbed, as it were, in the circle of those who already belong to the church in one way or another. This changed the significance of baptism to a certain extent. It can most clearly be discerned in the development of the baptism of children. At an early period, at least as early as the second half of the second century, children must have been baptised. Probably the children were looked upon as elements of the social family-milieu and, when that family was Christian, as future members of the church. Moreover baptism, the opening up of the new life, was also held to be a prerequisite for victory over death. In the ancient world the eve of Easter day was generally accounted the day of baptism, but when a life was in danger baptism could be held on other days. Considering the high rate of child mortality in the ancient world, it is only natural that parents had their children baptised. The possibility of doing so lay in the conviction that in this sacrament it was the invoked, three-in-one-God who realised the salvation granted in the performance of the baptism. Man does not make the baptism, neither does the performer nor the recipient by his volition, but God. However, the ritual itself has retained the character of a baptism for adults adapted to children.

On the whole, child-baptism has remained customary in most Christian churches. Nevertheless this institution has been opposed at times, especially during the Reformation. The baptism of adults was advocated, because the baptism of the old church was considered demonic, because that church did not possess the Holy Ghost and because man must himself choose God and have this choice sealed by his baptism. From these Anabaptists emerged both the Mennonites, who baptise adults only, and indirectly the Baptists. Even today there are groups which only recognise adult baptism and which rebaptise new members already baptised elsewhere.

The second nucleus of rites can be found in the Mass, a word that is not used here exclusively to indicate the Roman Catholic type of worship, but which in this connexion also encompasses the often divergent Sunday services of churches born of the Reformation.

The classical Catholic service can be divided into two parts: there is a preliminary service (the service of the Word) and a celebration of communion. The first is concentrated on the reading and interpretation of the Scriptures, answered by the prayers and psalms of the congregation. The forerunner of this form was primarily the service of the synagogue. The second part, however, goes back to the service at home, the celebration of communion, the commemoration and presentation of the Lord's Supper in which the Lord, Himself invisible, presents himself to his people by the sacramental acts performed at table.

This Holy Communion is the second great sacrament of Christianity. It belongs to the earliest ingredients of the Christian rites and is derived from the last supper partaken of by Jesus and his disciples on the eve of his death. In this respect it refers to Jesus' suffering and death, but is not purely a commemorative meal. Already in the earliest communication about the Lord's Supper handed down by Paul (I Cor. 10, 16 et seq.; 11, 23-27), the meal is the remembrance and proclamation of the death of the Lord and simultaneously the partaking of the body of Christ. Here the multiple meaning of the expression "body of the Lord" plays an important part. Firstly the congregation is accounted the body of the Lord; secondly it is of importance that communion at table renders the partakers one community through the host who distributes the gifts; thirdly it must be mentioned that by his death and resurrection, hence by giving his life, Christ granted his people salvation and a new life. This division into three, later more systematised, has been important from the very beginning. The term "commemorate, remembrance" implies that the believers are aware of being transposed into the presence of their Lord, who initiated this meal and who comforted them with the promise to return (by this Holy Communion the death of the Lord is shown till he comes, 1 Cor. 11, 26). Since, however, all life in the new eon emanates from Him and His death is the basis of salvation, He is both host and food at Holy Communion: "This is my body, this is my blood" are the words used in reference to the bread and wine of the Last Supper.

The distinctive aspects of the sacrament of communion as regards "body" were not the only factors which made different accentuations of the Lord's Supper possible. The remarkable character of the Christian conception of sacrament also made its influence felt. Above it has been described as the invisible act of God in the visible act of the church. In the Christian view, that invisibility not only signifies spiritual as opposed to perceptible, but also and primarily what is still latent as opposed to what presently will be revealed. Hence the sacrament has always been of a rather provisional character, it anticipates the achievement of eternal life, the life in paradise (often conceived of as a meal). Secondly the sacrament is thought to come into being through God's Word joining the elements. God's word spoken over the visible signs—water, bread, wine, oil, etc.—remains the principal fact of the sacrament, not the rite itself, which derives its proper meaning from the utterance of God's word. However, the fact that this Word has a physical structure means that not only is a representation given in Communion of the completion, but Christ is thought to be actually present, albeit in the hidden form of the church's visible act.

Consequently the sacrament can sometimes be conceived of more as a reference, a preaching of what Christ has done and still will do, though sometimes the emphasis is placed mainly on the presence of Christ in the sacrament. The interpretation of the sacrament can therefore range widely from an almost pure symbolism, in which the congregation of believers who have gathered in remembrance of Christ receive most attention, to an ultra-realistic conception which, though not accredited in theology, emerges in certain popular devotions, such as the miracles of bleeding wafers. Almost always the churches themselves have emphasised in one way or another the actual presence of Christ in the hidden form of bread and wine. The western Catholic church did so by means of the concept "transubstantiation" which though derived from medieval philosophy may not be regarded as philosophical. It means that the words, spoken by Christ over bread and wine at the Last Supper, said by the priest over the elements make Christ really present, even though the outward forms of bread and wine remain unchanged. In this way the mystery is retained in the sacrament. Materially the eastern church thinks in the same way, and moreover the churches of Reformation have, in diverse variants, retained the idea that Christ himself is present, in other words the real subject of the celebration.

The third nucleus of the Christian rites is contained in the so-called canonical hours, or fixed prayers at certain hours of the day. Certain forms of canonical hours were already known in the synagogue as morning and evening prayers, and Christian groups adopted this custom at an early stage. Those prayers were often also chants; it is hardly possible to draw a clear, liturgical distinction between prayer and hymn. The Psalter in particular is used in these hour-services, though the ancient hymns were also intended for the canonical hours insofar as they were not merely literary works, such as the verses of Gregory of Nazianzus or of Prudentius. In the Middle Ages song-like elements first found their way into the Mass.

The canonical hours flourished and expanded greatly especially among the ascetics. Their interest in them was based on a complicated network of motives. Firstly there is the "pray and work." Man, who belongs to God, must receive everything from his God. He must ask and praise his God for it. He must appeal to God for mercy and praise His name, and within that framework of prayer and eulogy he must perform his work. Whatever he does, he does because he has received the command and the power to do so from his Lord, and the purpose is the glorification of the name of God. In a world which looked upon work as nothing but trouble and misery and thought human freedom was based on leisure time, the prayers of the canonical hours resembled the protest of people who had learned to understand their lives to be primarily servitude to God. Servants must obey, and the spiritual leader of a group of ascetics (abbot, literally father) must see to it, as God's representative, that this obedience is maintained. Hence the canonical hours are also an exercise in obedience, because of their strict schedule and the considerable demands they make on the attention and the mnemotechnics of the participants at these canonical prayers. Here prayer becomes work. But there was another motive. The obedience to God is that of a soldier to his commander, and the soldier's task is to maintain God's order. Tertullian already described these canonical hours as *stationes*, watch-duty: by prayer one watches over the world against the assaults of the demons. Consequently-praying and keeping watch are closely interrelated. The devil can attack the sleeper, but is driven off and kept at a distance by the praying watchman. This theme recurs again and again in the hymns of the canonical hours.

For centuries the service of the canonical hours consituted the ascetic's "actual" work of God. No change in this occurred until the rise of the mendicant orders, whose ascetism was organised on different lines and who looked upon preaching and teaching as a means of warding off the evil powers. Nevertheless the service of the canonical hours never entirely fell into disuse. In the Breviary Catholicism provided an abridgment of the canonical hours for those who were prevented by their activities from adhering to the customary choral prayers (i.e. service of canonical hours held in the choir of the monastery church or in the chapter pews of a minster). In Protestantism this service can be found in the home prayers in the morning and evening and at table, and moreover in the morning and evening church services, the matins and vespers, which are usually of a rather intimate nature in smaller gatherings.

The church year or calendar grouped about the two great festivals of Christmas and Easter, has also ritual importance. These events are not original elements of the Christian celebrations. The earliest, still Jewish group of Christians celebrated the Jewish festivals and honoured the "day of Resurrection," i.e. the day after Sabbath, the first day of the week, as a special day with a morning prayer and a ritual meal. As the gap between synagogue and church widened, there arose the need to celebrate the great Jewish festival pesach separately since Christ's suffering and victory had taken place during the Passover period. His death and resurrection could be attributed the same meaning of salvation celebrated by the synagogue at pesach. The preparations for baptism on the eve of Easter in which the congregation took part by means of prayer and fasting gave rise to the period of Lent or Passion-time which forms the introduction to Easter, the feast of the resurrection. Of Jewish origin is the period succeeding the Passover, which lasts for seven weeks and is terminated by Pentecost in the synagogue and Whitsuntide in the church: the story of the pouring out of the Holy Ghost is linked up with Pentecost in Acts 2, 1. For several centuries this Easter cycle was the only liturgical festive period, and this Easter festival is still the most important one in folklore of oriental Christianity, including the Russian.

The festival of Christ's nativity originated in Egypt, and the old name Epiphany still reveals that the sixth of January is celebrated as the appearance of the Lord. It rivalled with the Egyptian feast of the Nile waters. In the occident the day of Christ's birth was fixed on 25 December which largely ousted 6 January as the Nativity festival; 25 December was originally the festival especially celebrated in Rome of the Invincible Sun. Later in the christianised Germanic territories it managed to replace the mid-winter feast. This festival is similarily preceded and succeeded by special weeks. Some weeks previously—the number differs in east and west—there is a period of Advent which originally was also a preparatory period of fasting. After the Nativity come the New Year's celebration and the festival of Epiphany or the three Kings, and this period continues till the beginning of Lent, which marks the opening of the Easter cycle. The period between the end of the Easter cycle (Whitsuntide or its octave eight days later when the Trinity is celebrated) and the beginning of the Advent is not of a specially festive character.

There is a second principle on which the church calendar is drawn up, the celebration of the saints on the days on which they "rested with the Lord"; the day on which they died is accounted the day on which they were born into eternal life. As early as the second century the days of the martyrs were recorded for the purpose of such commemoration; we know the day on which many died, but not the year. Specifically the martyr is through the medium of the Holy Ghost witness ("martus") of Christ's triumph. Stephen, the first Christian martyr, saw on his death the heavens open up and Christ as victor on the right hand of God (Acts 7, 55).

Since the church year is, in fact, the ritual of the new eon of the Lord in which the believers are made witnesses by the Holy Ghost of Christ's victory, it is understandable that the anniversaries of the martyrs and their successors, the saints, found a place in the church calendar. Nevertheless no official church ritual for them has been evolved, and neither is this the case with the great festivals of Christmas, Easter and Whitsuntide, whose structure is still that of the Mass. The commemoration of the saints is celebrated in the customary rites of canonical hours and Mass, and they are only mentioned in prayer, hymn and possibly hagiography. In Protestantism the calendar of the saints has largely fallen into disuse, and traces of it are only to be found in ecclesiastical-traditionalistic Lutheranism and Anglicanism.

The saints perform an important function in Christianity, for confidence is placed in their intercession. They occupy a prominent position in both eastern and western Catholicism. As remarked above, the martyrs were the first to receive the devote attention of the faithful. Their importance lay not so much in their courageous stand against their persecutors as in the fact that their constancy proved that they possessed the Holy Ghost and hence were witnesses of Christ's victory over death and the devil. Since the church encompassed, in principle, all who shared eternal life with Christ, hence also the saints assembled around Christ in heaven, the martyrs were looked upon as people who admittedly were no longer on earth, but who were nevertheless allied to the church on earth and could intercede powerfully with Christ. Besides the bearer of the Holy Ghost could forgive sins. Those who had been weak in the days of persecution and had submitted to an anti-Christian measure of the government appealed to the martyrs, who had remained faithful, for forgiveness and reacceptance in the church community. This had given rise to many conflicts with the official church leaders, but the conviction that because of their possession of the Holy Ghost the martyrs could give assistance did not weaken. Later when the function of the martyrs was taken over by the ascetics, also people who had overcome the world by the power of God's spirit, assistance was given by them. Another factor was that people saw the sign of the devil in all the distresses of illness and danger and appealed to the saints for assistance against them. This was often done besides their graves, and so there evolved the cult of their relics.

In a certain sense the saints took on the role of helpful divine powers from an older religious life, and consequently many legends of the saints contain parallels with ancient myths and sagas. The devotion paid to Mary is at least partly an instance of this. Since God was thought to be masculine (Father, Son and Holy Ghost), the mother figure satisfied a certain religious need. But it would be absolutely incorrect to equate Mary with the mother-goddesses known in the non-Christian world around the Mediterranean and later too in the Celtic, Germanic and Slavonic religious worlds. In the first place Mary has never been accounted a divine figure: she is a human being, the first to receive salvation from Christ, the pre-eminent saint, but nowhere in the liturgy or theology does she transcend the limits of her creatural being. She is honoured as the Mother of God, but this is in honour of Christ as God and not of Mary as goddess, at least in the preaching and teaching of the church. Her intercession is held to be powerful, and she has been the subject of a great deal of devotion. This devotion has increased steadily right up to recent times, as is evidenced by the church festivals and the fact that in the nineteenth and twentieth centuries Roman Catholicism judged it beneficial to dogmatise the Mariology to some extent, e.g. in 1854 the dogma of the Immaculate Conception of Mary: Mary was not born in original sin; in 1950 the dogma of Mary's physical ascension to heaven. Moreover the devotional attention paid to Mary was considerably strengthened by the appearances of Mary for example in Lourdes in 1858 to Bernadette Soubirous and in Fatima in 1917.

The climax of the worship of the saints that is in the piety of the people, occurred in the later Middle Ages, when the people whose existence was threatened on all sides sought helpers in their need. The Reformation looked upon the greatly increased tendency to turn to the saints as an attack on the sovereignty of God's power and mercy and a detraction from the honour of Christ. Consequently it took a firm stand against the worship of saints.

The extent to which the Reformation endeavoured to reduce the prevailing religious phenomena characterised by it as "human institutions," is not manifested merely in its attitude to the worship of the saints. It is also expressed in its doctrine concerning the sacraments. It has been pointed out above that the conception of sacrament has a rather wide scope. Originally various church acts were indeed distinguished, for example baptism, Holy Communion, preaching, charity and suchlike, but the word "mystery," *mysterium* is used by preference to indicate that God's act is accomplished in all these acts. Only in the Middle Ages, and mainly in western scholastic thought, the need arose to systematise this sacramental action of the church. In the course of the twelfth century seven sacraments were distinguished (baptism, confirmation, penance, communion, the consecration of priests, marriage and the sacrament of the sick or extreme unction) and in addition other acts of a less clearly sacramental character were described as sacramentalia. The definition which originally prevailed was that of Augustine: "the Word (of God) comes to the element and it becomes a sacrament which therefore is also, as it were, a visible word"—a definition retained during the Middle Ages and still held to be the correct definition of a sacrament by Luther. In it all emphasis is not placed on the elements, as though these automatically became sacraments in themselves through their ritual use, but on the Word of God, of which the other figuration is that of preaching and teaching. Nevertheless signs were present even in ancient times that the sacrament was definitely looked upon as a particularly religious, redeeming act, and then the church ritual transformed the elements into instruments of salvation. The priest performs the consecrating act, the Word of God referred to by Augustine becomes part of the rite and is no longer the really constitutive factor in the sacrament. As the Middle Ages passed, the sacraments developed into sacred acts *sui generis* in theology and to a much greater degree in popular devotion and church practise. This can be discerned in the Holy Communion and also in other sacraments. The doctrine of transubstantiation, the way in which the priest performed the communion (e.g. in the silent Masses) and the treatment of the consecrated host (reservation and adoration) gave rise to the idea that the sacrament was a mystery in which the people were a nominal, but certainly not a real, constitutive factor. The belief in miracles which was attached to the consecrated elements particularly in the late Middle Ages demonstrated that clearly the conception of sacrament could develop in the direction of a separate sacred and sanctifying act alongside the Word of God and could sometimes surpass the latter. The Reformation opposed this trend. The number of sacraments was reduced to the two inaugurated by Christ, baptism and communion, and the others, which Catholic theology wished to attribute to Christ's inauguration, were termed institutions of man and not Christ. In the late Middle Ages and influenced by western theology, the eastern church also acknowledged the seven sacraments.

B. *Ethics*

In the introduction to this fourth section, ethics and liturgy were said to be closely related. The man whom God calls and makes a new creature, whose belief is confirmed by baptism, is placed in a situation in which, on the one hand, he is aware of salvation and, on the other, knows that this salvation leads to freedom. He is able to live under God's Law. The second factor is that although the believer is placed in the new life and the new age that were initiated by Christ, the reality is still a hidden one visible only through faith. It will only become completely visible in the fulness of time and at a juncture in time determined by God. Hence the Christian life is determined not only by faith, but also by hope. The third factor in Christian ethics is that the fulness of time hoped for by the believer is not his own personal and therefore isolated salvation, but the revelation of God's kingdom of peace for the entire world. He is not a member of an isolated group of chosen people who are not related to the rest of mankind, for the selection must be looked upon as God's appointment of servants who will be instrumental in the realisation of His kingdom. That will encompass the entire world. All the ends of the earth shall see the salvation of this God. Election applies primarily to Christ, the concentration of the chosen people, and hence also the believers who are made members in Christ. This elected Christ has been sent to the world, and his people are also sent to that world where the message of salvation has not yet been heard nor formed, but which is God's own world. This is where charity assumes its place in Christian ethics.

The connexion between the liturgy and Christian ethics lies in the religious tension contained in the idea that the kingdom of God began with Christ, but that its completion still lies in the future. The inspirative power of Christian ethics is contained in the first fact, and the form of its experience is in the liturgy. But the state of incompletion, the latency of God's kingdom, implies the task of propounding the reality of God's love in the world of today.

This love, conceived of as God's will to preserve his creatures, is the sum total of the Law—a conception derived from the faith of Israel. When asked which commandment was most important, Jesus replied "Hear, O Israel: 'The Lord our God, the Lord is one; and you shall love the Lord your God with all your heart, and with all your soul, and with all your mind, and with all your strength.' The second is this, 'You shall love your neighbour as yourself. There is no other commandment greater than these.'" (Marc. 12, 29-31). In his version, Matthew adds (Matth. 22, 40): "On these two commandments depend all the law and the prophets." These passages are based on Deut, 6, 4 et seq. and Levit. 19, 18. For the sake of God's love, God who so loved the world that He gave it His only begotten son (John 3, 16), the faithful must love their neighbours. Now the word "neighbour" raises a problem. In the passage in Levit. 19, 18, the neighbour is a member of the same people. The New Testament word really is "neighbour." The prophetic preaching, however, has brought the world of nations within Christendom's field of vision, and so the duty of neighbourly love has acquired a wider meaning. For in Christ has appeared the Lord of the entire world, and hence the partition between Jew and heathen has been removed (cf. Ephes. 2, 11-20). In this eschatological perspective the word "neighbour" has the content of "fellow-man," the alien is also a fellow-man. It is remarkable that in the parable of the good Samaritan (Luke 10, 30-37) the neighbour of the Jewish victim of the thieves is the stranger, a notion also expressed in the parable in Matthew about the last judgment, in which the nations who never knew the Lord gained admittance to His kingdom because of their love for their fellow-man in need (Matth. 25, 31-46).

The above-mentioned elements of the ethical system admit of so much latitude in their practical realisation that the results are sometime contradictory. In the introduction to this article attention has already been drawn to the peculiarity that Christianity has become the religion of the greatest world-conquerors, whose activities were definitely not unmarked by violence. For that matter, this is not the only paradox of Christian ethos. Another is the often conservative trait, peculiar to a religion which has been part of state and society for centuries, a trait which can be justified ideologically by the fact that Christianity legitimises its endeavours by reference to the truth made known to the patriarchs by God, or received from Christ by the apostles who passed it on unchanged, whereas the church preaching is first and foremost directed towards the future. The same paradox manifests itself in a slightly different guise when the church, controlled by the leading groups in society, practises charity towards the poor and assists them, but maintains the class barrier and has no feeling of solidarity towards them, while at the same time there can be believers who are sympathetic towards the poor and who consequently turn against the church leaders. In both cases the parties concerned believe that the issue is the Christian ethos. Such contradictions have not made Christianity an impossibility. On the contrary, it has saved it from being identified with a fixed social or cultural pattern. The aforementioned capacity of Christianity for adapting itself to the most divergent circumstances, which is so remarkably at odds with the strict exclusivity of its conception of God, is related to this phenomenon. The real issue is the polarity between the conviction that God's kingdom has come in Christ—a conviction which the history of Christianity has shown to be definitely conservative in its effects—and the conviction that God's judgment lies in the future completion—a conviction which has proved to be revolutionising in practice.

To return to the Great Commandment as nucleus of Christian ethics, and in particular the commandment to love one's neighbour. We have seen above how this notion expanded under eschatological influence from neighbour and compatriot, c.q. fellow-religionist, to fellow-man. From this notion emerges the peculiar fact that Christendom interpreted the commandment about love as one that is known to all mankind. Consequently the Ten Commandments could be interpreted as the "natural" code of morals, and this greatly facilitated the accommodation of the Christian ethos in the non-Christian world. This interpretation was developed already in ancient days, and so little effort is needed to accommodate the validity of a *locus communis* from non-Christian ethics, namely the doctrine of the four principal virtues of patience, prudence, justice and courage to the Christian ethics. The fundamental proposition of Thomas Aquinas is that Christianity does not wish to abolish, but to complete the existing order of creation. Thus the so-called cardinal virtues are added to the so-called theological virtues of faith, hope and charity.

But in what sequence are these moral values ranked? In a scheme in which mercy does not abolish but completes nature, it is axiomatic that the "theological" virtues are superior to the "natural" virtues. Moreover the future is the direction in which the believer moves. He is on his way to the city of God, to the eschaton. That will be a kingdom where righteousness prevails. But if man, who is a member of Christ's body, helps to realise it, then he must know that the volition and work are of God. For Christ's kingdom is not of this world. It is not the product of human labour, which is always encumbered with iniquity, and it is not judged by the standards of the old world. It derives from God, who has sent the king of that realm, and it is judged by the demands which God makes of his servants. Admittedly that kingdom was originally conceived of as one which would be actualised on earth: the Holy Jerusalem descends from heaven (Revel. 21, 2-10). But the apocalyptical metaphor suggested the conception of a *Jenseitigkeit* which took root in the non-Jewish world in which Christianity expanded. There the principal thought concerned the passage of human life from matter to eternity and the immutability of the divine world.

And so the believer comes to look upon his life as a path leading to heaven. The eschaton is transposed to a reality beyond this earthly and temporal life. Then, however, the renouncement of earthly possessions becomes a primary goal of the Christian way of life, and an image is created in which the value of man is judged by the degree to which he has distantiated himself from earthly life. This fundamentally ascetic conviction leads to an evaluation that can be termed hierarchical, because the one who has progressed further along the road to heaven is bound by love to ensure that those lagging behind him are brought nearer heaven. This is emphatically stated in the very influential works of DIONYSIUS THE AREOPAGITE. In this way the priests are assigned the role of intermediary—they form the link between the laymen and heaven. But also in this way is created a kind of holy space, a holy reality, between the earthly reality and heaven. God can only be approached through this intermediary space and through this intermediation.

This conception was strongly opposed by the Reformation. It accepted the belief that man is the instrument of God's work, but refused to acknowledge any man as intermediary alongside of Jesus Christ. Every believer is a priest, for at his baptism he is endowed with the Holy Ghost, the association with Christ which admits him to God the Father. Here a hierarchy of intermediaries and of intermediary stages between heaven and earth is refuted. Every man in his faith serves the Lord with equal completeness, no matter whether he fulfils a wordly or a spiritual office—an office is the same thing as a function.

Now the remarkable thing is that this did not put an end to the *Jenseitigkeit* of the Christian ethos in the history of Protestantism. In certain forms of Lutheranism, for example, the idea that every function should be a priestly one led to a division between the work of the church and of the governing authorities: they are two instruments in God's hand to realise his aims. The wordly authorities are responsible for maintaining order on earth in obedience to God, the spiritual authorities for reconciliation with heaven, preaching and performing the sacraments, and may not interfere with the work of the wordly authorities. The Calvinist groups took a different view. There every work done in obedience to God is likewise considered pleasing to God, but the church administration, chosen from God's people, is not looked upon as such a separate function and it considers itself much more responsible for worldly activities.

The principal issue in Christian ethics remains the commandment to love God and one's neighbour. Here love must be understood as righteousness in the biblical meaning of the word, as faithfulness regarding God's commandment to preserve this creation, or in modern terms, making the world a fit place to live in. The tenor of the Christian message implies that God is the one who orders this and who shall realise it through the incarnation of his Word. In this manner the first and great commandment of complete love in devotion to God acquires automatically an ethic significance. For in faithfulness to God lies the commandment of faithfulness to His creature, the neighbour.

Mention was made above of the paradox that Christian ethics often have a conservative character and at the same time a revolutionising tenor. As pointed out above, both sides and possibilities can find inspiration in the biblical structure of Christian ethics. There were periods when the conservative trait was too dominant. Then the Christian pattern of life, originating in the will to obey God's commandment, became static, and the rules of Christian life were interpreted as eternal commandmends or—even more dangerous—as laws governing the structure of human nature. Thus aberration became a sin. Up till now, however, Christianity has proved flexible enough, because the other element, the notion of the transitoriness and of being on the road to the revelation of the future of rightenousness, has likewise remained active. Consequently there is created what might be called interim ethics. The rules governing Christian conduct acquire a provisional character, they serve as guiding lines for the obedience imposed on Christian freedom. In a vastly changed world it then appears that the Great Commandment must not be interpreted so much as a short summary of diverse rules and regulations which contain the necessary explanation, but as the compass that must determine the course and position at every moment and in every human situation.

C. *The doctrine*

When mention is made of Christian doctrine, it should be ret membered that what actually is intended is Christian teaching abouthe message of Christ's work. Even if the content of that message is formulated in the terms of the philosophical milieu in which Christianity develops, this does not mean that the Christian doctrine really is philosophical. The tenor of education in the Christian message is the proclamation of Jesus the Lord, the Messiah sent by God, and this is done by means of the story of his work, as laid down in the Scriptures of the Old and the New Testament.

The essence of that teaching is contained in the classical confession of faith, of which the Nicene Creed is the only one common to all of Christendom. The Apostles' Creed is a development of the rule of faith current in Rome since about 200 and is only used in the west. As for the Nicene Creed, it is an eastern symbol (here "symbol" simply means a creed) which was probably in use in Palestine about 300. It was expanded with certain dogmatic additions drawn up at Nicaea in 325 and once more confirmed and further expanded at Constantinople in 381, thus acquiring its present form. Since the sixth century (in Rome, however, only since the beginning of the eleventh century) the western formula has contained an insertion in the article on the Holy Ghost which was rejected mainly on liturgical grounds by the east. This addition speaks of the Holy Ghost which proceeds from the Father *and the Son* (the so-called *filioque*), and has since remained a cause of dissension between the two parts of Christendom.

The doctrine of God has already been dealt with in the section on the conception of God. But church teaching centres on the proclamation of Jesus' appearance. He is God's Word, which is with the Father since time without end and which was made flesh through the Holy Ghost and the Virgin Mary for our sake and for our salvation. The virginity of Mary has become very significant, especially its devotional aspect. For centuries the ascetic ideal of virginity was inspired by it. However it is questionable whether this was the real intention. It is perhaps best to assume that this conception is used to accentuate God's interference in the history of mankind by means of the incarnation of his Son. God and man are brought together in the birth of Christ. The creed passes on at once to Christ's suffering, death and resurrection, in keeping with the structure of the Gospels, which do not narrate the life history of Jesus of Nazareth so much as the redeeming action of the Messiah and which offer little or no information about the biographical-psychological development of this man. Thereafter follows the statement about his ascension to heaven, his place of victory on the right hand of the Father and the promise of his coming to judge. The data of the New Testament tradition are arranged to form this scheme: the work of salvation and the testimonial of the Messianic rulership are concentrated precisely on the death on the cross and the miracle of the resurrection, which is the victory over the last enemy—death. An additional factor of importance is that in all creeds the series of redeeming events is fixed in time; they occur under Pontius Pilate, the Roman procurator of Judea at that time. This makes its clear that the primal story of the Christian message is not an event that can be repeated arbitrarily. For that matter it is entirely in accordance with the apocalyptic view developed in late Judaism, which looks forward to a point in time when all shall change; when men of the old age of distress shall pass into the new eon of salvation. Pontius Pilate is mentioned in order to indicate that the expected change has begun totake place. In a like manner mention is made in the Gospel of Luke about Christ's birth under Augustus (Luke 2, 1) and the preaching of St. John the Baptist, which introduced Jesus' appearance as the Messiah under Tiberius (Luke 3, 1). That the interpretation must indeed be sought in the direction of apocalyptics and not in the urge to write history also appears from the additional words "according to the Scriptures" in connexion with the resurrection: the Lord has risen again "according to the Scriptures" is a formula which, via I Cor. 15, 3 et seq. refers back to the study of the Scriptures in the style of the Jewish apocalyptics. Here the Scriptures are the prophets, whose words were thought to be fulfilled by the resurrection.

The resurrection is the central theme in Christian teaching. Its historical and physical possibilities have seldom given rise to much fuss. For that matter they were more easily acceptable to a world in which most intellectuals considered reality a combination of mysterious forces than they are for us. The resurrection of Christ signified the confirmation of his sovereignty. Within this framework, death and resurrection could be defined in various ways: as sign of the obedience of God's Righteous One, as atonement for the sins of mankind, as ransom for the prisoners of the Evil One, as justification of the godless, as death of our death and life of our life. But the resurrection of Christ, a fundamental element of the Christian faith, has a further future, an extension in time. The Christian proclamation has always stressed that the fulfilment has come, but the fulness of time is till ahead. Already Christ rules over the believers through the Holy Ghost, Who works through the sacraments and through the proclamation of the message of Christ recorded in the Holy Scripture, but also through the conduct of believers as instruments of Christ's will for salvation in the world that is not Christian.

Christian teaching is focussed on this message concerning Christ, who as Lord of the believers forms his community (church). This church must be understood to be the community of those devoted to

Christ and sanctified by Him for his service. Since, however, this takes place by and in the visible world, the church can also be termed the community in which the sacred acts, the sacraments, are performed. It is a community of people who are transposed from the death of guilt and sin to the new life. The community of Christ's followers is one comprising those whose sins have been forgiven and who may expect to inherit everlasting life. It has been pointed out above that this eternal life should not be interpreted primarily as a substantial immortality, but as an existence in which death, man's last enemy, is overcome. Further reference must be made to this point in the section on anthropology.

In Christendom opinions about the significance of the priestly caste differ. The picture of the earliest organisation to be found in the epistles of Paul is not clear in all respects. Nevertheless, within the vague contours given it can be discerned that a special position is attributed to the apostles, the disciples appointed by Christ to continue his work. They possess the Holy Ghost and with them rests the final decision about doctrine and life. It is questionable whether they and their successors can really be called priests in the sense of priests of the temple worship in Jerusalem or of non-Christian religions. True, the comparison is an obvious one and it is sometimes drawn. But the customary terms indicative of a priest are almost entirely lacking. The actual leader of the congregation is the *episkopos*, the man entrusted with supervision over the congregation. Next to him are the *presbuteroi*, the elders, and the *diakonoi*, literally servants. Other dignitaries are mentioned in the New Testament, prophets, teachers, etc., but they did not fulfil proper priestly functions, and this could not be expected in a religious community with a synagogal character. One might say that the emphasis with which Christ is called the true high-priest in the Epistle to the Hebrews indicates rather that the officials of the community were scarcely thought to be priests. The normal qualification of the bishop, the leading official, is shepherd and teacher and not, or at least not at first, priest. But there was an increasing tendency to regard the celebrant of the sacrament of Holy Communion, that is the bishop in the first place and then, too, his representative the presbyter, as a priestly official. The reason for this was the fact that Holy Communion gradually acquired the character of an offering, because of the emphasis placed on the presence of the crucified Christ and of His offering on the cross.

Thus in the course of time a hierarchical caste of priests came into being, and by the end of the ancient period this development was completed. Nevertheless it is at the same time realised that the true priestly body is formed by all the baptised. They are the body of the Lord and because of Christ's high-priesthood they must be considered priests as people who perform the service of atonement and sanctification for the world. This conviction was posited as early as the second century and prevailed right up to the end of the ancient period. However, the development of a Christian society has added a strong priestly relief to the special ecclesiastical office. The church is the sacral department of Christian society, and its servants fulfil the service of atonement and laudation. HUGO OF ST. VICTOR (d. 1141) e.g. defined the ecclesiastical and the secular authorities as the two sides of Christ's single body, the Christian world. During the Reformation opposition was raised to this isolation of a separate priestly caste and the general priesthood of the believers was accentuated, though there was no movement to abolish special office for the various church services (services of the Word and of the sacraments, service of administration, service of diaconal work, etc.). What did take place was that smaller groups of a sectarian character did not appoint institutional officials, but accepted those specially gifted with the Holy Spirit as preachers of God's will and fulfillers of His deeds.

The Catholic doctrine pertaining to the church also includes the doctrine of the primacy of the Bishop of Rome. As successor of Peter, prince of apostles, supported by Christ's promise that his faith shall never fail, charged with the task of guarding Christ's sheep, he has occupied the highest position in the Christian church from of old, and he is recognised as primas. The interpretation of this position, however, has given rise to difficulties. Is he first among equals, the bishops or the other patriarchs of Constantinople, Alexandria, Antioch and Jerusalem, or is he their superior? Protestants have on the whole held a different view about the apostolic tradition of the episcopal dignity and have assumed that with the fixation of the doctrine of the apostles in the New Testament the actual tradition ended. They therefore neither wished nor were able to consider the pope of Rome as more than the ecclesiastical leader of a certain congregation, and they viewed his opposition to the Reformation as usurpation of power and demoniacism. The church is preserved by the doctrine handed down by the apostles and not by what was considered human tradition.

In Christian teaching the church is conceived of as the new people who must carry the message of their Lord to the ends of the earth. In other words, the doctrine of the church also includes missionary work. Indeed, now that God's kingdom has come and God's truth has been revealed in Christ, they must be made to prevail everywhere. Admittedly this has often led to severe aberrations. Certainly at the beginning of the Middle Ages and also during the Iberian occupation of Central and South America, the missionaries often came with the superior feeling of being the enlightened possessors of the truth as compared with the unenlightened heathens. Moreover they were often convinced that the Christian conquerors did godly work with their expeditions. It is also true that the consciousness of being sent by Christ to rid the world of demons and to help the people also prevailed at times. In any case missionary activity should be looked upon as a consequence of the doctrine of the eschata. The eschatology will be further discussed below.

V. The Conception of Man

In the first section of this summary of the Christian religion it was pointed out that man is conceived of as *persona*. He is first and foremost the servant of God the Lord. It is this conviction which influences various aspects of Christian anthropology, including those in which such notions as friend or child of God receive considerable attention. Man was created to serve God. His nature can be conceived of in various ways according to the cultural and philosophical context in which the Christian view of man is placed. Always, however, the function of that nature will finally prove to be the true determinant of the conception, and that function is the service of God. His destiny is seen as the admittance to the glory of Christ's heavenly Father as a reward for faithful service.

A. *Creation and nature*

Man is conceived of as a living creature who was created of the clay of the earth and inspired to life by God. The story about the creation in the first chapter of Genesis was naturally accepted, for it belonged to the Christian Holy Scriptures. But it was accepted in a certain interpretation which was mainly dependent on the way Genesis 1,26 et seq. was understood. God created man in His image and likeness. In the New Testament little attention is paid to the creation of man, and this passage from Genesis is scarcely mentioned. There the prevailing image is the renewal of man according to God's original intention (cf. Col, 3, 10). The real image of God is Christ. He is the new man, the second Adam, the countenance of the Father, and insofar as the people believe in him and share in him, they are renewed after that image. Later, however, Christian thought had need of a more elaborate anthropology and therefore more emphatically questioned what exactly the likeness of God implied. In itself the conception of that likeness in the non-Christian world wherein Christianity acquired its classical form was not unusual: because of his immortal soul and his reason, man resembles and is akin to the divine. That kinship, however, was a conception which Christianity could not readily accept, for one thing above all was certain, man was not a divine being but a creature. There are no other Gods besides God. Man has no inherent divine substance, even though he owes his existence to the being God granted him. Only by adoption is man the child of God, whereas Christ, as God's son, is a true son of the heavenly Father and in essence one with Him. The likeness between God and man therefore does not rest on essential kinship, but on the fact that God has placed on him the mark of his creative work. The Maker can be recognised in His product. That definitely obtains for all that is created, but the designation of man as image of God is of a special quality. Often man's reason has been taken to be the faculty which manifests his likeness to God. The cosmos is the result of God's creative Logos. This Greek word, which is used in the Johannean writings in the New Testament especially to designate the Son, is ambiguous. It means both "word" and "reason". This provided the starting point for this line of thought. Christ, God's Logos, is the new man. In this way a link was found with certain philosophical-anthropological notions. Man's reason is able to discern the structure of reality, and that structure is determined by the process of divine thought itself. Hence, by using his faculty of reason, man can find the path to God, provided he is renewed in Christ, God's own Logos. In other words, as a rational being man is the image of God. Now already in the greek philosophical anthropology man's reason was accounted the seat of man's freedom, while his corporality fettered his mind. But the mind and the reason in it are the truly human essence of man. Hence the now classical Christian anthropology was able to emphasise the fact that man is a creature that manifests a likeness to God because of his mind and reason and consequently his freedom or faculty of freedom.

This concept of freedom, or human will to use the psychological term, constitutes the barrier which enables the createdness of man to be retained in a Christian anthropology. He is neither an automatic executor of God's purpose nor an incarnated thought of God. He is a being of flesh and blood, appointed to obey, to listen and choose in favour of the fulfilment of God's commandments. Admittedly his materiality is usually regarded as the animal aspect of his existence which must be controlled by his reasoning mind, but it is only objectionable if it becomes "disorderly," that is disobedient to man's reason. Man is therefore constructed "hierarchically," with "higher" and "lower" parts, but the materiality is not merely the prison of humanness, the body is an essential part of humanness. As we shall see below, this has consequences for the eschatology, both in the doctrine of the resurrection of the flesh and in that of the kingdom of God. It should be noted that in the very idea of the incarnation of God's Word in Jesus Christ the created materiality is designated a good thing. This viewpoint is further reflected in the conception of the resurrection: Christ rises bodily from the grave, he shows the disciples the scars of his suffering, he speaks to them and shares their meal. Matter is not the counter-force of divine activity and as such the limitation of God's omnipotence, but is God's own work. Hence the doctrine, generally accepted in classical Christianity, of a creation out of nothingness, a formula found in the second book of Maccabees (7, 28) which is aimed at vindicating God's omnipotence over the creation.

In this context the view of life and death merits special attention. Here again the fundamental factor is the relationship between God the Lord and man His servant. Death is where man refuses to obey the Lord, life is where man is obedient. Consequently eternal life means primarily that the age of disobedience is past forever. Christ, the obedient and righteous servant of the Lord has, by accepting man, overthrown the sovereignty of death and opened up the path to eternal life, for which Paul used the word "immortality" in one passage (I Cor. 15, 53). But according to I Tim. 6, 16, only God has immortality. Substantially man has not an immortal soul, but his life and death lie in the judgment of the Lord. Hence eternal life does not mean that the soul continues to exist after the body has died and decayed, but the prospect of man's resurrection as a living creature with body and soul. It was only rather late—at the beginning of the third century—that the idea that immortality is an inherent quality of the soul began to gain ground under the influence of non-Christian conceptions. Then there evolved the view that the statement in Gen. 2, 7 in which God is said to have formed man of the dust of the ground and breathed into his nostrils the breath of life signifies that man is composed of transient matter and an immortal soul. Even then, however, this doctrine is characterised by obedience and freedom, or in other words by God's judgment. After death man can expect either eternal felicity (perhaps after a period of purification) or eternal pain.

The relationship between God and man as Lord and servant, mentioned several times already, has a fundamental significance for the conception of man and the Fall. The Paulinian idea that all have sinned and come short of the glory of God (Rom. 3, 23) was elaborated into a scheme, especially by Augustine, according to which the first people fell from grace because of disobedience and so the road to paradise is closed to all posterity. There is a general state of sinfulness from which man cannot effect his own escape. He remains responsible for the state of death in which he exists even during his lifetime. The human situation is judged wholly as man's entanglement in his guilt and death, and in this situation only Christ can bring righteousness and life. For disobedience is in essence nothing other than death: the concealment of man from the countenance of God and hence of God from man. Life is the same as obedience and faith (cf. John 11, 25 et seq.).

Man is therefore responsible for the state of death, but rescue comes from without. The life-centre of man is not in himself but in God, who accepts him and fulfils his promise of salvation. For that matter man is created out of nothingness, as we have seen, and therefore has in him no lasting substance. But he exists through obedience to God, and his restitution is therefore possible only because the new man Jesus Christ is obedient and taken disobedient man unto himself. Now these thoughts contain another important element of Christian anthropology: man is not an isolated being. Christianity views man as a people and looks upon Adam not so much as the sinful individual nor even the prototype of the sinner, but as the ancestor who passes on the heritage of his curse to succeeding generations. What was said above about history being an essential element in Christian faith also obtains here. The issue is not the history of one man as specimen of all mankind, but rather the history of a race of accomplices together with their ancestor. The same holds good in the doctrine of salvation. There, too, Christ as the new and obedient Adam is not merely the prototype of the redeemed man, but the first-fruit, the Righteous One who as second ancestor leads the people constrained by death to life. Here again it is a question of history as an essential fact of Christian religion. After what has been said of the church as the body of Christ, this does not need to be discussed further. Man is first of all *persona* for God in his encounter with his fellow-man. This quality of being a fellow-man forms the basis of his existence for God. The central issue is not the individual man's appropriation of salvation, but the finding of salvation in Christ in the midst of the people living for the Messiah. This does not mean that man is only a component of a collectivity and that he owes his individuality, his "name," solely to membership of that collectivity. On the contrary, the most important thing is his personal aspect, his *persona*, his own being. This can be discerned, for instance, in baptism, which incorporates man in the body of Christ. The phrasing is: N.N., I baptise you in the name of the Father and the Son and the Holy Ghost, N.N. standing for the proper name of the recipient who is addressed personally in the second person. But he only becomes a person, an individual existence, by acting as servant of God among the servants of God, as one sent into the world to reveal the truth of the gospel. There is a mutual involvement of individual and community, which is understandable enough in the light of the structure of the Christian belief, with its conception of *persona* as the nucleus of the God-man relationship.

B. *Destiny and the path of salvation*

The destiny which God allots his creatures is the kingdom of God, the kingdom of heaven. The background to this conception is the Jewish prophetic-apocalyptic view of the liberation of the people of Israel according to the promise of their God. This kingdom of heaven will appear on earth, but it is not a kingdom founded by an earthly prince, but by the King sent from heaven. In that sense it is not "of this world," it cannot be compared with any human society in the existing state of sin and death. In it there will be no more unrighteousness, but it will be a kingdom in which there is peace in heaven and earth and where righteousness dwells—a kingdom of God's future.

Within this framework, the human life of the faithful is thought to be an active waiting for the revelation of the fullness of time, during which period this activity is aimed firstly at man's avoidance of falling back into darkness now that in Christ the light has appeared, into unrighteousness now that God's righteousness has been revealed in the work of Jesus Christ. The second purpose is, as it were, that man cultivates the soil of the world so that God can make his kingdom grow. In other words the destination of the faithful for the kingdom of God implies that he must look upon his life as a continuous struggle to acquire and preserve righteousness.

Now the idea that God's kingdom is not of this world was soon understood to mean that it is to be found in heaven. This conception was understandable in ancient cosmology. However it brought about a shift in the view of man's destiny. Life was then thought to be a journey to the afterlife, and the accompaniment of man on his way to the kingdom of God—e.g. pastoral care, communion at the Lord's table, education in the Scriptures—tended to become a strengthening of man. The old teaching of righteousness was not forgotten, but increasing emphasis was placed on the distribution of powers of grace through the medium of the sacraments. Man's path of life, menaced by demons of temptation and destruction, developed into a path mapped out along the sacraments: baptism at the beginning, the eucharist as nourishment en route, penance for man's purification, confirmation to equip him with the Holy Ghost, ordination for the priest or marriage for the layman, extreme unction. But Protestantism, influenced partly by pietism, also conceived of life as a path which leads to sanctification through the effect of God's mercy. There came into being the conception—already present in the Protestant orthodoxy—of an *ordo salutis*, an order of salvation, in which the granting of salvation by Christ is separated into a number of stages through which man must pass on his way to an ever greater community with God. The idea that life is a path leading to heaven is even more strongly developed in true pietism. Because of the stress it places on personal conversion and acquiantance with mercy in personal religious experience, the idea that the kingdom of God is formed on earth is either dropped or placed so far beyond the horizon of time that it threatens to become unattainable for the Christian ethical notion of righteousness on earth. This does not mean that the pietist withdraws from the world into an inner experience and falls prey to a sort of religious egoism. On the contrary, the pietists were the ones who took upon themselves the care of those in need, just as the Roman Catholics were the ones who expressed definite opinions on the constitutional and social realities in the nineteenth century, notwithstanding their *Jenseitigkeit* and philosophy of life focussed on a supramundane perspective. But these concerns with the world were based on a religious conception of God's kingdom in which it is detached from the world.

Little wonder, then, that within this framework of thought the original opinion about what the church is changed, at least emotionally. Originally a group which, as body of Christ, was conscious of being an outpost of God's kingdom in a world that had not yet seen it, a community which thought of itself as being on its way to the point where the Lord would fully reveal His glory on earth, the church became on the one hand an institution which distributes the means of salvation needed on the road to heaven, and on the other—especially in Protestant pietism—a vague structure which can be left at will, since it is not a community of people sharing the same religious experience. The church is even felt to be a hindrance because it demands obedience to its doctrine and pattern of life; it is sometimes rejected as a wordly entity. A contrast is created between heaven and earth which no longer accords with the contrast between the old and the new eon as laid down in the orginal Christian preaching, that is life in the unrighteousness of the broken covenant and life under the new covenant of the obedient servant of the Lord. In the eighteenth but especially in the nineteeneth century there evolved in pietism certain groups which were organised and operated independently of the church. Some consider themselves guardians of the true church, and then the creed and church order from the classical period of Protestantism, the seventeenth century, are accounted the tokens of solidarity, the mottos under which the members unite against the big officials churches rather than the proper expression of personal faith. Some, however, are communities united under a certain religious idea and inspired to observe a certain code of moral, liturgical and dogmatic customs, and in them strong religious personalities are followed as honoured leaders.

But there is another way of following the path of salvation leading to man's destination. The community of ascetics resembles the free religious groups to some extent, namely in their aim to sanctify personal life by practice and to withdraw from the world. However it should be noted that classical monasticism, with its church ties, did experience the struggle to preserve the world against the snares of the devil. The objective of winning the world for the kingdom of God was especially effective among the mendicant orders of the thirteenth century and equally among the Jesuits since the second half of the the sixteenth century. This brought them face to face with the spiritual movements of their age, but not to an aversion of them. In various respects they became the pioneers of culture in their day precisely because they found man's destiny in the realisation of Christ's kingdom on earth, possibly in preparation for the coming heavenly bliss.

A somewhat similar phenomenon occurred in Protestantism in the eighteenth century in the so-called neology, a theological school which aimed at bedding the Christian faith in the current of the Enlightenment. Its successor, Modernism or Liberalism, was mainly of importance in the nineteenth century, when man's self-development to his utmost possibilities was seen to be his destiny. In the light of later developments, it was highly significant that the former conception of human life as a journey to heaven was rejected. There was little room any more for the dualism of heaven and earth, God and matter. Various factors influenced the monistic conception of world and life. Not only was there the romanticism and the idealistic philosophy of the opening decades of the nineteenth century, but also, on the one hand, Schleiermacher's view of Christian belief as the activity of religious consciousness, and on the other, the far-reaching experience of a rapidly industrialising world in which man seemed capable of securing a place and which, moreover, could no longer take account of a supranatural reality.

Here in Modernism there evolved a remarkable optimism, though repeatedly there are indications of how strongly the old eschatological seriousness of the Christian faith remained present even in the feeling of progress. As the nineteenth century passed into the twentieth, this optimism began to manifest symptoms of paralysis. Not only was Modernism attacked as half-heartedness by groups that were no longer Christian—it was unacceptable in any case to orthodoxy—it also appeared that the age itself was confronted with greater problems than was suspected. Modernism was largely the faith of the well-to-do class, of the progressive rulers of society. There are very good grounds for linking up Modernism in religion with liberalism in social politics. But industrialisation created an enormous class of have-nots, who became pauperised economically, socially and culturally and were practically out of the reach of Christianity. Tensions in state, society and culture proved too great to be dealt with by an optimistically inclined Modernism. Hence we see that doubt arose about the path of salvation as it had been imagined. Man is not capable of finding his destiny on his own; he is in the power of sin and needs God's mercy. At the same time and following on the very important social work done by pietistic groups there awoke the realisation that Christians were responsible for what was going on in the world. It was not a question of paternalism, but of an attempt to bridge the gap between Christ's commandment and the world's need. On the whole this effort was undertaken by people who were bound to the church but did not act on the orders of the official church leaders. In the youth and student movements, in the labour organisations and suchlike, Protestant and Catholic circles sought international means of bearing the aforesaid responsibility. Obviously then, the majority of the leading promotors of the oecumenical movement and of international missionary work came from the youth movement. In this respect their actions resemble those of the early pietists, insofar as they were not primarily inspired by the existing churches. But to a much greater degree than the pietists they felt they were responsible for the necessity of revitalising the church as a whole. Their aim was to restore the apostolate to the church.

All this had very important effects on modern-day views of man's destiny and the path to salvation. In retrospect, what was thought and done in the period between the First and the Second World Wars often seems uncertain, romantic and even too optimistic. However it is important that in this period the philosophical and unhistorical idealism of the nineteenth century was unambiguously set aside. This is discernible in the development of dialectic theology, of which Karl Barth is the most important exponent. With christology as starting point, man is conceived of as the servant of God, who is faced with the task of preserving God's sovereignty—righteousness, token of true humanness—in all spheres of life. Here we find the distinction that has become so very important in the latest theology and the corresponding feeling about life: the distinction between religion and faith, in which religion is concerned with the subjectivism of piety, focussed on the inner, the personally pious subject, the *Jenseitigkeit* which too much ignored the creed that Christ is Lord of the *world* and not just of the church or the pious mind. And faith is conceived of as obedience to the Word of God which does not proceed from the human spirit, which subjects all human actions, including religiousness, to the judgment of God and which sends man abroad into the world. Dietrich Bonhoeffer, victim of the national-socialist terror and one of the great inspirers of contemporary theological thought has given a new meaning to the distinction between religion and faith, *Jenseitigkeit* and *Diesseitigkeit*, questions about personal salvation and the search for the world's salvation, religious tutelage with respect to divine powers and secular emancipation, *sacrificium intellectus* made for the sake of religious perplexity and rational thinking. This distinction had a clearly radicalising effect on opinions about the church, faith and path of salvation. Christianity is not a religion with its own sacral territory. The structure of the church is objectionable if it applies itself to maintaining such a sanctuary-preserve. The main issue is the possibility of living in a secularised community that has no more room for religious or sacral forms which it considers obsolete. In our world God's kingdom can be nothing but a secular community of righteousness, and the path to it is not indicated by the traditional religious media, but by the secular media of science, economics, politics. Furthermore, it shall be the task of Christianity to criticise social and political structures from the viewpoint of what, in the light of Gods word, humanity should be. *Diesseitigkeit* is the important factor for the destiny of man and theology's task is to think profoundly and consistently on this.

Certainly, no view has as yet been evolved of man, his destiny and his path which is perfectly clear on all points. There is still a good deal of antithesis to be discerned in particulars and sometimes too on points of principle. But the force of these opinions cannot be denied, partly because they manifest themselves in both Catholicism and Protestantism. It is equally true that they give rise to opposition in both groups. Nevertheless it has become unmistakably clear that, in a reality in which, on the one hand, the organ for supranatural reality has been weakened and on the other the modern means of communication bring the reality of elsewhere within our immediate vicinity and which therefore can disturb our conscience to a much greater extent, the view of the earthly character of man's destiny and of his path has a greater power of conviction than was formerly possible.

C. *Personal and general eschatology*

It was said above that according to the Christian religion man's destiny is the kingdom of God. This implies that the eschatological perspective is a community, a conception derived from the Jewish notion of God's people. "Blessed be the Lord God of Israel; for he has visited and redeemed his people" are the eulogising words used by Zacharias in Luke 1,68. The fact that this view of the community is essential to the Christian faith has already appeared in the discussion of its ethics, in which the love of God also refers the believer to his neighbour. The missionary notion that the message of the Messianic reality of Christ's peace, life and salvation must be preached to all mankind is a special aspect of this view. In a religion in which the concept *persona* is so fundamentally significant one can hardly expect anything different. *Persona* always means a counterpart, an other, for only in a relationship is God recognisable and is man really man, namely the servant of God. The *eschaton* is the community of a new heaven and a new earth in which righteousness dwells. In other words the covenant of God and His people has become indissoluble and thus the salvation intended by God is realised.

Though conceived of as a community, the eschaton is nevertheless a kingdom of people who are accepted individually by the Lord and placed in a communal relationship. Man's name, the thing most peculiar to him, must be recorded in the Book of Life (Revel. 7, 8). He derives his name from the Lord (Revel. 22, 4) and this makes him a person, an individual, and enables him to see God. The connexion is clearly revealed in the sacrament of baptism. It is performed in the church community, which shares the responsibility of the recipient's faith (in many churches witnesses, godfathers and godmothers, must therefore attend the baptism of a child), but as name-giving it is performed separately for each recipient of baptism, who is named in the name of the triune God and by name. This ceremony places the recipient in an immediate, and in the case of infant-baptism in a future position of responsibility, for he is placed in the new life by the name of his Lord and with his own name. This duality—the baptism as a sacrament performed for the beatitude of the individual and as communal rite—has manifested itself repeatedly in the history of baptism, and to such an extent that one finds the opposing customs of highly individualised baptism on the one hand and mass baptism on the other. In the individual custom, baptism serves primarily to reveal to the individual the path to his peculiar salvation. Hence the now obsolete custom of performing the baptism of a baby or yound child outside the actual context of the congregation and even of granting non-believers the right to baptise when a life is in danger, which gives rise to the impression that the baptism is an *opus operatum*, an act of which the performance in itself has the power of salvation. The mass custom was sometimes applied during the christianisation of the Middle Ages when a large number of people from one village or a whole tribe was baptised simultaneously. The fact that both extremes are possible shows how both the individual and the community require attention in the Christian sense of religion.

Consequently it is not surprising that both the personal and the universal aspect of Christianity are accentuated in its eschatology. For the perspective of God's kingdom implies a community of people who have individual names and are personally recognised.

The concrete ideas put forward concerning the eschaton are widely divergent. They are generally strongly influenced by the cosmological conviction of the period in which they were operative. In Revelation a city is mentioned; the heavenly Jerusalem, which is described explicitly as a city on the river of paradise, descends from heaven. In it the idea of a community is very prominent and the issue is citizenship in The kingdom of Christ. Similarily in the great work of Augustine "The City of God," which took up old motives and passed them on to posterity, heaven is first and foremost an urban community, a civitas, inhabited by angels and redeemed people under Christ's sovereignty. In another conception, heavenly life is thought to be a table companionship. In this conception the notion of the sacrament of the Eucharist is no doubt present. Dionysius the Areopagite (ca. 500) conceived of blessedness as the vision of God in a mathematically determined circumambulation. But in these cases the cosmological or mathematical ideas are not so essential as the idea of a community. Even in ancient days this community was thought to be structured. There is a larger or smaller degree of bliss depending on man's merits on earth. Scriptural documentation for this idea was found in the parable of the talents distributed unequally among God's servants and also in the motif of this parable: what is important is not what man has received, but what he has done with it. Man receives his due reward. Dante's Divine Comedy is the classical document, at least for western Christianity, containing such a structure of the Afterlife.

The Divine Comedy is composed of three parts, heaven, purgatory and hell. This is in accordance with the mature medieval eschatology which obtained for all, including eastern, Christendom. Already in the earliest Christian tradition the underworld had become a place of punishment for sinners, the doomed. This underworld was the ancient realm of departed spirits long thought to be the residence of the impotent dead by a large section of the eastern Mediterranean region. Hell was conceived of as fire and also as a place where the worm, symbol of death's decay, never ends (cf. Isaiah 66, 24). In ancient days one finds already the idea, based on data interpreted correctly or not from the New Testament, of an intermediate stage between heaven and hell, where some souls go after death. This is the place of purification, which in the west was also thought to be a fire. The word "purgatory" does indeed occur in ancient Christian literature; the notion that it refers to fire was widespread in the west. The east was not so certain of this, since in that part of Christianity the prevailing idea was that the fate of the individual soul would not be finally decided until the Last Judgment. Hence less psychological emphasis was placed on the purification of the soul before it passed on to heaven. There the general conception was a sort of soul-sleep while awaiting the Last Judgment.

Blessedness is eternal, but is hell also eternal? The west always answered this question in the affirmative, and so did the east too on the whole, though there were more doubts there. If God is the omnipotent causer of the cosmos and if all that exists is in His hands, can then an anti-divine power of evil hold out against him? Or, if God's love encompasses all that exists, can anything escape that power and be somewhere out of reach of the divine love? In this context the existence of evil is not denied nor that man can be capable of sin and guilt. The drama of salvation is unfolded to save him. But this can mean that all that is not yet subject to the power of love, that is deficient in goodness, will nevertheless at some time be drawn into the seething dephths of divine goodness, into the momentum speeding on its way to God. Eternal tortures of hell, eternal damnation, a deathless death would seem to contradict this, and such is inacceptable on the grounds of the said premise of God's almighty goodness. So the idea of apocatastasis began to gain ground. This term meaning the restitution of all things and derived from Acts 3, 21, was used by Origen to signify that all that was lost, hence also the host of fallen angels and the doomed ones held prisoner by them, will return to God. Although this idea was rejected by the official church leaders, it continually influenced eastern thought concerning the eschaton. But the feeling that once Christ shall adjudge man's conduct in his earthly existence towards God and his neighbour was more in favour of the idea of an unending place of damnation: hell lasts forever, the lost one will never see the beatifying countenance of God. The material of the New Testament points in this direction. Moreover, it must be realised that an anthropology in which so much emphasis is placed on man's freedom and responsibility and in which man is judged by his merits because of the fundamental idea of servitude to God and its corollary of reward and punishment which is also important in the New Testament, man's conduct was soon placed against the background of eternal beatitude and eternal rejection.

Furthermore if human life is viewed as a struggle for purity required of man by God and consequently life is seen as a process of evolution, it is understandable that the idea of an intermediary stage between heaven and hell should arise. For heaven and hell are quantities just as absolute as old and new world, and God's judgment is thought to be absolute. But when conceived of as an evolution, a growth in the direction of God's righteousness, human life proves incapable of conforming to this absolute criterion. According to the notion of Christian religion, this life is never without sin, and this notion is greatly amplified in ascetic religiousness. Hence he who is judged by God will seldom or never be accounted absolutely righteous. He will have to undergo purification before he can be accounted worthy of tasting the joy of God's vision. This place of purification was found in I Peter 3, 18-20, where Christ is said to have preached to the spirits in prison which sometimes were disobedient, when once the longsuffering of God waited. From I Cor, 3, 15 it could be inferred that purgatory was fire, which was particularly important for late medieval eschatology.

The Reformation rejected this eschatology of an intermediary state between heaven and hell where man had to undergo further purification after death. The idea of an individual righteousness of man was rejected in the reformed doctrine of righteousness. Man is the rejected one, his righteousness is the righteousness of Christ in which he is absorbed. Even as Christian, man himself remains the rejected one in this life if he is judged without Christ. But in Christ he is the glorified, the righteous one who can enter the joy of his Lord because of the merit of Christ, God's righteous servant. Thus the doctrine of purgatory not only lost all meaning, it became a sign of an aberration in the doctrine of justification.

Regarding the moment of God's judgment, originally the prevailing conception was that in the Judgment the dead will arise and hear the heavenly Judge's pronouncement on their works. Until then the dead are at rest. With the dawning of the Lord's day, the coming of the Lord in glory, they will arise from their graves in bodies roused to life. Here the creed speaks of the resurrection of the flesh. But quite soon motifs from another type of religiousness began to prevail. In a world in which the body is considered the material, transient element of man and his soul the bearer of life and the immortal element, there can evolve the idea that after death the soul sleeps, or is already judged in heaven, while the body still must arise on the Day of the Lord. As early as Paul (cf. I Cor. 15) we can perceive that the conception of the resurrection of the flesh was giving rise to difficulties. The latter became all the more urgent as the originally short perspective of the imminent appearance of the Lord in glory became longer. The image of a separation between body and soul then became increasingly clearer, and such a prophetic vision as that of Ezekiel 37, 1-14 became metaphysically applicable. The bodies are once more joined to the souls to appear thus before God's judgment seat.

Speculations about the details of an eschaton can be passed over, though they were very general, e.g. the millenium, the restriction of the devil, the signs of the times. They are deeply rooted religiously and psychologically in man's notion of death, but are of secondary importance as regards the specifically Christian character of the eschatology. However they can be said to have proven ever more difficult to apply in a critical-scientific framework of philosophy concerning man and the world. Ever since the eighteenth century there developed a realisation of the principle of the conversability of all matter, and increasing emphasis was placed on the immortality of the soul, possibly even without any belief in a personal immortality in the sense of an immutable and eternal identity of the ego. The soul forces go on, but they are part of a universum conceived of as spiritual and idealistic. It is difficult to determine what value a personal eschatology still has for the average Christian. Recent opinion polls suggest that this question is becoming less and less important, and in this connexion it is remarkable that belief in hell is relinquished sooner than belief in heaven. The greatest attention is paid to personal fate after death in such marginal groups of Christianity as Jehovah's Witnesses etc. In this respect a very clear shift has taken place in Christianity. As late as the Reformation the fate of the soul after death was still one of the main issues in the belief in justification through faith alone.

Nevertheless the eschatology has remained essential to Christianity, insofar as it concerns the preaching of the future of God's kingdom. In apocalyptic movements the expectation that God's kingdom was at hand appears to have had great inspirational power for life in ancient and medieval times. In contemporary theology the question of personal fate after death has dropped into the background. Now the prime question is, how can the righteousness and peace of God's kingdom be made visible to the entire world? The righteous peace of God is thought to be a much more material thing than formerly. The issue is the salvation of the entire man, of what is called "flesh and blood" in the Bible; hence it is his material conditions as well as his intellectual and psychical development. The same tendencies can be discerned here as noted in the discussion on man's destiny and the path of salvation. Here, too, the decisive factor of contemporary eschatology is the notion that Christ is our real fellow-man and that in Him all people are our fellow-men.

VI. The Religious Situation Today

It is impossible to give in brief anything approaching a complete description of the present state of a world religion, whose cultural and dogmatic history is so complicated and which occurs in such a variety of situations as the Christian religion. For example, can the Christianity of the Dutch Remonstrants, who on the whole are of a higher social and cultural level than the average Christians of the Netherlands, be compared with that of the Thomas Christians of the Malabar coast or the Catholics somewhere in the hinterland of Peru? Can the Unitarianism of certain radical, latitudinarian groups in England of America be weighed against the monophysitism of Ethiopia? Or, to keep to one cultural sphere, can the world of thought of the Salvation Army be compared with that of the Anglican High Church? This imposes to the drawing of an overall picture a restriction that can scarcely be termed acceptable. If account is also taken of the fact that Christianity reveals inner tensions, referred to several times above, which sometimes turn into contradictions in practice, then one realises that the word "scarcely" in the last sentence could more properly be replaced by "not."

There are statistics of the number of Christians in their distinctive forms. The reason why figures are not given here is that the criteria on which they are based differ too much one from the other to produce an acceptable picture. Indeed they must differ, considering the difference in norms applied by the distinctive denominations in deciding who can and who cannot be termed a member. As religion Christianity is still the greatest in the world, comprising 36% of the world population (Islam's percentage is about 16%, Buddhism's 12% and Hinduism's about the same). Needless to say these figures are given with all due reserve.

As for Christianity, there are said to be about 500 million Roman Catholics, more than half that number of Protestants and 185 million Eastern Christians. Here, too, these figures must be read with great reserve, but they can serve as a very rough approximation of the ratios.

Regarding the present state of the largest group, that of the Roman Catholics, it can be said that their church has experienced quite an upheaval since the action taken by Pope John XXIII and particularly since the second Vatican Council. That the "aggiornamento" initiated there would give rise to tensions was predictable. In the first place these tensions became manifest even in the Roman Curia. This central body had great difficulty in maintaining its position against the church leaders of the various ecclesiastical provinces (the bishops) and definitely was forced to give way to some extent. But of at least equal importance was the attendance of non-Roman Catholics as observers at the Council, which contributed a very great deal to a good understanding of what took place there and particularly to a better understanding of Catholicism. Meanwhile steps are being taken in the world church to effectuate the intended "aggiornamento." This is causing further tension. In the first place the differences between the various Roman Catholic churches are so great that a uniform implementation of the Council's intentions must be considered impossible. For that they are too widely divergent as regards spiritual development, religious tendencies and also cultural position. But even within the various countries themselves there are tensions between the conservatives and the progressives. However this may be, the Roman Catholic church has become involved in what is happening in the world today in a way that seemed inconceivable after the conservatism of Pope Pius IX in the last century, and this church has also clearly made itself accessible to other Christians. A brief summary of what the Roman Catholic is aiming at might be phrased as follows—to be no longer the stronghold of a given religion but the people of God who are on their way to expose to the world God's message of peace. In a religious community that is in such a state of ferment it is only natural that there are also strong opposing forces bent on adhering especially to the old values and truths and that these forces manifest themselves in the world episcopacy, the Curia and among the laymen.

In Protestantism the history of the oecumenical movement is half a century old. Its work similarily comprises much more than the organisation of ecclesiastical fusion. Its task is, indeed, to discuss questions of belief and church order, but equally of missionary work, Christian life and work in the world. Its main organ is the World Council of Churches, but there have also been formed denominational organisations which cooperate with the World Council, e.g. Lutheran, Presbyterian (mainly Reformed), Baptist, Unitarian and other groups. The Fundamentalists have taken a stand against the World Council and have founded their own organisation of orthodox cooperation known as the International Council of Christian Churches. Obviously a parallel can be drawn with what has happened in the Roman Catholic church. The same also holds good for the way in which many Protestants view the task of the church and Christians: the church is at most a means or instrument, not so much for the christianisation of the world as for the realisation of the neighbourliness inherent in Christ's person and His message. This thought also has its counterpart in contemporary Catholicism.

Regarding the eastern churches, the majority are members of the World Council of Churches. The largest group of eastern Christians, the orthodox Russians, became split up after the Russian revolution. An intellectually and spiritually important, but rapidly diminishing group has emigrated, while the church in Russia itself can act freely within the limits imposed by the state. But work abroad, missionary and propaganda, is impossible for it, and hence an essential element is excluded.

More important, however, than all these relatively external matters is the fact that Christianity is taking a position in the present world which is different from any it ever had before. In the first place a manifest de-christianisation is discernible in the modern processes of urbanisation and industrialisation. The old social structures of the church, with their local ties and foundation on a different type of society than is generally known today, are admittedly able to provide shelter for a number of people, but in an ever diminishing degree for all. Thus there arises the phenomenon of the so-called marginal or non-membership of a church. Since the time when church and state became independent of one another and the social necessity of the Christian faith became obscure, Christianity has not been an inevitability in the world once thought of as a Christian entity. Moreover it is no longer an inevitability within the circle of those who are bound in some way to a church. As regards the structure of the church, the boundaries between the old church forms and the secular forms of community are fading. All this compels Christianity to ponder anew on its message, and in particular the tenor of the Lord as Lord of the world and not merely of the church must be studied. Connected with this is another question which has appeared to be highly significant, the "enfranchisement" ("Mündigkeit") of the world, a term added to the theological apparatus since Bonhoeffer. The world cannot be approached heteronomously, it has its autonomy and holds on to it. It is the duty of the Christians to accept this. In a certain sense a like train of thought can be found in Paul Tillich: it is the task of theology to answer the questions philosophy poses on behalf of the world. From other quarters, but closely related to contemporary theological problems, comes the question of de-mythologisation. The New Testament presents the message about Christ in a context that has become mythological for us. If the Scriptures are to speak again, if the church is to bring an understandable message, this mythological context must be removed. The central figure in this field of problems is Rudolf Bultmann.

In this summary even an abridged exposition of these problems cannot be aimed at. Reference to them must suffice. Just how actual they are—actual in the sense that they are concerned with the present fundamental questions of the church's existence—is also evidenced in the new programming of apostolate, evangelisation and missionary work, in which the message of God's peace, which is Christ, is more and more understood to be neighbourliness, development aid, social work, etc. That this evokes reaction is understandable, not only because the speed with which changes take place in the work of the churches evokes opposition and cannot be followed by some (psychological reaction), but also because the Christian faith itself evidences, as said repeatedly above, an inner tension between the advent of the new age in Christ and the fulness of time that has yet to come, between the resurrection of the Lord and the martyrium of his followers, who can only discern Christ's triumph in the imitation and bearing of Christ's cross, between the truth which has revealed itself and the expectation that it must still be revealed. But Christianity has always progressed because of the interaction of the forces inherent in this tension and because it has developed an enormous capacity for adaptation, thus enabling it to keep pace with the changing times.

VII. Short History of the Study of Christianity

A religion which considers history such an essential factor in the acts of its God becomes concerned with its own history at a very early stage. Although the Gospels and the Acts of the apostles included in the canon of the New Testament certainly do not describe history in the usual sense of the word, they do interpret historical events and facts, or ones that are considered history. This view of history was in line with the Jewish apocalyptics, which likewise interpreted past events for the present day.

The circumstances under which Christianity evolved have given rise to questions about the true character of this religion. This can be discerned in the works of the second-century apologists and equally in those of the late apocalypticist Hippolyte of Rome (d. 235), among many others.

The first church historian was Eusebius of Caesarea (d. 339). He aimed at demonstrating that the victory of Christianity under Emperor Constantine the Great was proof of divine power and that Constantine was the emperor beloved by God. Augustine placed Christianity within the framework of world history in order to show that it was not the rhythm of the secular powers but of God's kingdom that determined history. By doing so he took what was in fact an apologetic-polemic stand: Christianity was studied in order to refute its opponents.

Medieval Christian historiography was usually in the form of chronicles written about certain monasteries, cities or the papacy (the so-called *Liber pontificalis*). But the scientific study of the Christian doctrine and ethics got under way particularly in scholastics from the thirteenth century onward. The crisis caused by the Reformation in the sixteenth century provided a new impulse to study the Christian message and the history of Christianity. Then appeared such apologetic historical works as the *Magdenburger Centuriae* which was inspired and to a large extent also written by the Lutheran Matthias Flacius Illyricus (d. 1575) .Its purpose was to demonstrate how the church of Rome fell into decline. For the other side Cardinal Baronius (d. 1607) wrote his *Annales ecclesiasticae*. An attempt was also made by the Spiritualists to view Christianity from a certain perspective, namely that of the Spirit, and of these authors Sebastian Franck (d. 1542) deserves particular mention.

The multiplicity of creeds gave rise to the study of the content of truth, the characterisation of the various denominations and equally of the non-Christian religions. Here JEAN BODIN (d. 1596) was the precursor. The diverse churches offered resistance to the teaching of dissenters, and in consequence the study of what Christianity is maintained a mainly apologetic and polemic character. Now such works were usually the fruits of the labours of theologians who bore the stamp of a church. Christianity is ecclesiasticism, the history of Christianity is ecclesiastical history. Obviously this meant that a one-sided viewpoint was taken and certain sectarian or sectarian-like groups were not placed in their proper perspective. The pietistic-inclined GOTTFRIED ARNOLD (d. 1714) tried to remedy this in his *Unpartheiische Kirchen- und Ketzergeschichte*, in which at least in principle he tried to survey Christianity as a whole. Although it cannot be claimed that Arnold himself worked without non-scientific assumptions, the old apriori was broken.

In the nineteenth century Christianity was looked upon as a human religious phenomenon. Then, at least in principle, the universally accepted, historical and critical methods were applied to the material of the Bible, church history, Christian dogmatics and Christian doctrine. It was only to be expected that this historical approach and this relativism met with opposition. The question of Christianity's "absoluteness" is now being raised. For some time this question was not so very actual, but Christianity's encounter with modern culture and with other religions in the development countries, where the missionary fields lie, has brought it once more to the fore. It is also an important question for Catholic theology, with its accentuation of traces of the knowledge of God also occurring outside the circle of biblical religions. Sociological and psychological studies are beginning to deepen our knowledge of Christianity as a religious phenomenon, just as certain historical insights, including such non-Christian ones as those of the Marxists, can provide further help. However Christianity is still a much too living phenomenon for the drawing up of anything but a very provisional survey.

SHORT BIBLIOGRAPHY

It is impossible to chart even sketchily the ocean of literature published on Christianity, though remarkable lacunae still exist. For instance there is nothing approaching a complete or even satisfactory phenomenology of the Christian religion. Whether it can already be written is doubtful. A further handicap is the fact that there are few commentaries available from non-Christian quarters. For most research workers on the subject Christianity is their own religion or the one they are most concerned within their own culture. Hence in the scientific study of Christianity as a religious phenomenon it is almost impossible to test one's opinions against those of members of different religions. This seriously handicaps the methodology of this science.

The best orientation is given in the large encyclopedias and manuals on religion and/or Christianity. For the history of the church mention might be made of the work of FLICHE-MARTIN, *Histoire de l'Eglise depuis les origines jusqu'a nos jours* (24 vols., 1938 et seq.); P. FARGUES, *Histoire du Christianisme* (5 vols. 1928 et seq.); K. S. LATOURETTE, *A History of the Expansion of Christianity* (7 vols., 1938-1945); G. KRÜGER, *Handbuch der Kirchengeschichte* (4 vols., 1923-1931). For the history of the doctrine reference might be made to the work, admittedly outdated on various points, of AD. HARNACK, *Lehrbuch der Dogmengeschichte*, (3 vols., 1909).

ISLAM

BY

ANNEMARIE SCHIMMEL
Cambridge, Mass. U.S.A.

I. What is Islam?

"This day I have perfected your religion for you, and completed my favour unto you, and have choosen for you as a religion Islam" says Sura 5/3.

Thus the name Islam is given in the Quran itself as the name of the most perfect religion and of the ideal state of man—of that man who submits to the will of Allah (*muslim*, participle of the root *aslama*, of which *Islām* is the noun) and performs the duties which He has prescribed in His revelations. Modern theology might call it "commitment." Islam is, thus, a rather large and so-to-say all-embracing concept: the true religion which has existed since the creation of man, has been preached by the Prophets to all peoples, and has been restored to its pristine purity by Muhammad, the messenger of God.

Occidental writers have become accustomed to the use of the name Islam for the religion concerned only comparatively late, as W. C. Smith has shown in a thought-provoking passage. In the middle-ages Islam was called the "Heresy of the Sarrazens"; from the 16th century onwards, the term "Religion of the Sarrazens" is used, later it is called "Muhammadan Religion," "Muhammadanism," whereas the term Islam was generally accepted—though used earlier—in our time when the Muslims themselves insisted on not being called Muhammadans, since this would imply their being followers and adorers of Muhammad in the sense as Christians are followers of Christ. H. A. R. Gibb, however, has defended the current term Muhammadanism by underlining the fact that the "first article of faith—that there is no God but God—may be assented to by many besides Muslims, whereas it is the second (i.e. the witness that Muhammad is the messenger of God) which distinguishes Islam from all other faiths."

A spokesman of this larger meaning of Islam—as a religion which embraces not only those who verbally confess that faith but also mankind "from Indus to the Pole" — is Goethe in his famous lines:

> Wenn Islam Ergebung in Gottes Willen heisst,
> In Islam leben und sterben wir alle.

But as the two parts of the creed are inseparable the two aspects of Islam—complete surrender to God's will and acceptance of the truth of Muhammad's message—are inseparable as well.

Western scholarship and—in earlier times—Western heresiography have tried to explain Islam for themselves for nearly thirteen centuries; it is our duty to investigate into its meaning for its believers. Is Islam "The Straight Path" and/or the way of "schlechthinnige Abhängigkeit" according to Schleiermacher's classical definition of religion? Is it the religion of God's Majesty and Power, and consequently that of man's obedience and humility? Is it a way of preparing man for the end of the world when he is to meet, as the early eschatological *sūras* of the Quran have announced so forcefully, the decision about his eternal life in either Paradise or Hell according to his actions, or is it a method of salvation whose details are organized according to the binding word of the revelation, the model of the Prophet, and elaborated by theologians and lawyer divines into a perfect code in both private and public affairs? Or are the Muslims right who combine, like M. A. Draz, the word Islam with the word *salām*, "peace," which belongs to the same root, thus attesting that "Islam is external and internal peace"? Is L. Massignon right in classifying Islam as the "Religion of Faith," compared to Judaism as the Religion of Hope, and Christianity as the Religion of Love, thus combining the three "Abrahamic religions" under the words of I. Corinthians 13.?

Islam had changed, in a surprisingly short time, from an eschatological preaching into a religious and cultural, social and political system, combining the different spheres of life under a single figurehead. Both the inner values of life—personal piety—and the external rules of behaviour—socio-political questions, legal decisions—are regulated essentially by the same God-given laws which have been revealed in the Quran, and the Muslims still boast that Islam does not know the bifurcation of life into "worldly" and "religious, spiritual" sphere, and understand to-day the Quranic expression that they are "a central people" (2/137) as defining their position in the golden mean between atheistic materialism and exaggerated spiritualism. Every act—as profane as it may seem to the outsider—is done in the immediate presence of God; the Muslim should always be aware of his responsibility towards the Creator of his life who will judge him at the end of time.

On the foundations of the Quranic preaching and the "Prophet's example," a vaste system of jurisprudence, theology, mysticism, but also an immense amount of literature, and marvellous fine arts, came into existence. Greek and Roman, Iranian and Babylonian, Indian and Turkish influences stimulated the genesis of this civilisation which developed into a coherent system which has been maintained for centuries. The question is, in how far Islam without this system—especially its legal and political parts, which have been associated with it for more than a thousand years, can still be called Islam? Is reformed Islam still Islam? That is the question which is posed to the reformers in the Muslim world—a world which comprises now about one seventh of mankind and is growing both through its rather rapid spread in Africa and its comparatively high birth-rate.

II. Historical Development

The cradle of Islam is the Arabian Peninsula. Here, among the nomadic tribes and the inhabitants of the few oases, a rather primitive polydemonism and worship of stones, stars, caves and trees were prevalent. The central sanctuary was the Ka'ba in Mecca. Soothsayers and inspired poets whose word was charged with supernatural power played a distinct role in the life of the Arabs.

The borders of Arabia had long been under foreign rule. Yemen, noted since time immemorial for its fertility and its higher culture (barrages, organisation of worship) became involved in the struggle between Christian Abyssinia and Iran in the 6th century; the ruler Dhū Nuwās (525) adopted the Jewish faith. At the Syrian border, the Nabatean state of Petra had been incorporated into the Roman Empire as Provincia Arabia in 106 A.D.; Palmyra was destroyed in 273. The dynasty of the Ghassanides in Eastern Syria constituted a buffer between the Bedouins of the Peninsula and the Romans; similar in relation to Iran was the function of the Lakhmides in Hira, where Nestorian Christianity was mainly confessed. Small Jewish and Christian groups were dispersed in Arabia, and the monk whose lamp shone from his hermitage in the desert is a well-known topic of pre-islamic poetry. A few persons,—called *ḥanīf*—seem to have sought for a purer faith than that of the pagan Arabs and may have reached a kind of monotheistic concept.

The poetry of the Arabs in the time of *jāhilīya*, the "time of ignorance" before Islam, rarely treats religious subjects; it reflects a certain fatalism and praises the Bedouin virtues of braveness, hospitality, friendship, and revenge. The poems were composed in a language common to all the different tribes that was of amazing expressiveness, and they are rightly considered the perfect exemplars of the complicated Arabic language. This rich, strong and flexible language was the most precious good which the new religion that was to emerge in Arabia could inherit from its maternal soil. —

Muhammad was born about 570 in a cadet branch of the Quraish, the ruling tribe of Mecca, the trade-center of Arabia. Being an orphan he was brought up by his uncle Abū Ṭālib; later the young caravan-leader married his employer, the elderly widow Khadīja who bore him six children of whom four daughters survived. Muhammad who used to retire into a cave in Mount Hira received, at the age of forty, the first revelations which caused a deep shock in him; but his faithful wife helped him to realize the religious importance of his experience. When the revelations continued to visit him he started preaching in public the idea of a judgment in which Allah will punish those who treat their slaves badly, do not care for orphans, widows and the poor, and will reward those who do good. Indeed the social unjustice between the ruling class of rich merchants and the large number of the poor in Mecca was lamentable. The idea of the One God Who has created, sustains, and will summon mankind before Him gains more and more momentum in Muhammad's preaching, and the Meccans, mocking the concept of corporeal resurrection, were afraid lest their idols, and with them the main source of their income, the pilgrimage to Mecca, should be jeopardized by the new message of Allah's dominant rule. Muhammad, though faced with their enmity, found consolation in the revelations which told about the prophets of old who had, like him, suffered persecution but had been marvellously rescued by God.

A group of the new believers who mostly came from lower social strata migrated to Abyssinia to enjoy the protection of the Christian Negus, since Muhammad was sure that his teachings corresponded to the revelations received and preached by Moses and Jesus. After the death of his wife and his uncle in 619, the situation grew more difficult for the Prophet. He was, some time later, invited by the inhabitants of

Yathrib, to arbitrate in a long-standing feud between the two main tribes of the town. Thus, after the departure his friends, he left his home-town in 622 and settled in Yathrib which was soon called *madīnat an-nabī*, Town of the Prophet: i.e. Madina. This *hijra*, or migration, is the turning point in the history of early Islam, since it meant the complete break-up of the bonds of relations, an action nearly unheard of in the clan-conscious society of Arabia. Muhammad now proved his political ability by moulding the different groups in Madina into a single community of faithful, no longer clinging to the inherited Arabic ideals of tribal honor etc. but declaring Allah, the One God, the real ruler of His community (*umma*) and himself as the organ of His supreme will. That is why the Madinan revelations become more and more concerned with the practical needs of the society.

Muhammad's former sympathy for the Jews got a severe set-back since they accused him of having distorted the biblical stories. Now he became convinced that the faith which he was sent to preach in Arabia was the unpolluted faith of the former prophets which had been perverted by Jews and Christians—the faith of Abraham, the ancestor of the Arabs through Ismāʿīl (Ishmael), and builder of the central sanctuary of the Kaʿba. Thus, Mecca and the Kaʿba gained a new importance for Muhammad: the direction of the prayer-service which had been towards Jerusalem, was changed towards the Kaʿba (2/136ff.), and the reconquest of his home-town became imperative for him. In smaller battles the Muslims of Madina met the Meccans; they gained their first victory at Badr (624). The Jewish tribes in the environment of Madina were extinguished.

The revelations contain rules for the war which is allowed first only for defensive purposes (22/39); then this *jihād*—as "Holy War" the most quoted and least understood feature of Islam—becomes a means of extending the realm of Muslim influence (9/29; cf. 3/73 ff., etc.). "Fight against those who do not believe in Allah nor in the Last Day..." This fighting "in the way of Allah" is the only legal war in Islam; it is "duty of the community." The unbelievers should, however, first to be asked to embrace Islam, and be attacked only in case of resistance. If Muslims rebel against the legitimate power it is likewise allowed to fight them. The idea that the world consists of a *dār al-ḥarb*, abode of war, and *dār al-Islām*, abode of Islam, is a later distinction.

In 628 Muhammad concluded an armistice with the Meccans which resulted in the reconquest of Mecca in 630. Most of the tribes in the peninsula embraced Islam; the first attacks on Byzantine territory followed. In February 632 Muhammad performed, for the last time, the pilgrimage to Mecca; the pure lunar year without intercalary months was introduced. Non-Muslims had been excluded from the rites of the pilgrimage already in 631.

When Muhammad died on June 8, 632, in the room of his most beloved young wife A'isha (he had married a number of wives after Khadīja's death) nearly the whole Arabia confessed Islam.

After his death the pious Abū Bakr was made leader of the community, and despite of cases of apostasy among the tribes the Muslims increased in power. Under the reign of Muhammad's second successor (caliph), the energetic 'Omar (634-644) Syria, Egypt, and parts of Iran were conquered. Their inhabitants were by no means converted by force; for those who had been granted a divinely inspired book (Jews, Christians, Sabians)—the *ahl al-kitāb*—enjoyed the protection (*dhimma*) of the Muslims by paying the *jizya*; and formed one of the major sources of income for the budget of the enlarging state; they were exempt from military service and were governed by their own religious leaders (bishop, rabbi). In later time these so-called *dhimmis* sometimes occupied high positions in the administration, as physicians, translators, bankers; their situation deteriorated as a corollary to the political decline of the Muslim states. Forced conversions are rare, for "there is no compulsion in religion" (2/257).

'Omar was killed in 644; his successor 'Othmān, a member of the old Meccan aristocracy, was, in spite of his importance as redactor of the revelations of the Quran, made a target of attacks by several groups. The adversaries were headed by 'Alī ibn Abī Ṭālib, Muhammad's cousin and son-in-law who, after 'Othmān's murder in 656, secured the caliphate for himself with the help of the Iraqian Muslims, but had to cope with the attacks of 'Othmān's cousin Mu'āwiya, the governor of Syria. Though the victory in the longlasting battle of Ṣiffīn, 657, seemed to be his, he was unwise enough to accept an arbitration which decided in neither party's favour. A group of his followers, pretending that the judgment in such cases belongs only to God, left him; these Khārijites (from *kharaja*, secede) were the first to kindle the discussion about the right leader of the community: they laid stress only on his ethical qualities notwithstanding his origin, and elaborated a theology of ethical maximalism according to which they considered nearly all the other Muslims infidels. 'Alī defeated the Khārijites at Nahrawān in 658, but was killed by one of them in 661. Their influence in the theological discussions was great in spite of their small number. Moderate Khārijite groups are still existant in North-Africa (Ibadites) and Zanzibar.

With ʿAlī the time of the Four Righteous Caliphs, later glorified as the ideal period of Islam, had reached its end. Muʿāwiya declared himself caliph; the capital was shifted to Damascus. The Omayyad rule which he inaugurated (661-750) has been criticized by later Muslim historians as *mulk*, kingship, since the rulers did not live up to the ideals of Islamic piety (except ʿOmar II 717-720). Yet they ruled the widening Empire with skill and developed a splendid cultural activity (Great Mosque in Damaskus, desert castles of Syria). North Africa was conquered, the Atlantic reached in 681; in 711 Arab troups crossed the straits of Gibraltar and laid the foundations of Muslim rule in Spain; in the same year they reached Transoxiana and the lower Indus Valley where they founded a state that comprised the southern part of the present West-Pakistan. In 732, the Muslims were defeated as far north as Tours and Poitiers.

Home politics, however, were rather disturbed. Muʿāwiya, dying in 680, designated his son Yazīd as his successor. His governors killed ʿAlī's cadet son Husain who fought for re-establishing the rule of the family of the Prophet. Husain's death at Kerbela, Iraq, on Muḥarram 10 (October 10) 680 is considered the greatest tragic event in history by those who constitute the party of the Alides (*shīʿat ʿAlī*, Shia). The feelings of the Shia were still more incited by Mukhtār who fought the Omayyads in Iraq 685 to 687 and whose candidate was a son of ʿAlī from a wife other than Muhammad's daughter Fāṭima. He proclaimed that this Muhammad ibn al-Ḥanafīya would live in concealment in a mountain until he would come back to instal justice in the world of Islam—this idea of the "hidden imām" was adopted by the different branches of the Shia (cf. p. 138). And not only in the Iraq, which was always ruled by the most energetic governors, but in Arabia itself rebellions against the Omayyads arose: ʿAbdallāh, the son of Muhammad's companion Zubair, ruled as caliph in Mecca for nine years (683-692). The newly converted Non-Arabs who had to attach themselves as *mawālī*, clients, to any Arab tribe in order to get full rights of citizenship defended, against this discrimination, the Islamic ideal of equal rights for all faithful. The common efforts of the Shia propagandists and the *mawālī* eventually opened the way for a new dynasty which stemmed from Muhammad's and ʿAlī's cousin ʿAbdallāh ibn ʿAbbās. The Abbasids overthrew the Omayyads in 750; the last Omayyad prince escaped to Spain where he founded a new dynasty under which Spain was to reach a cultural climax and which lasted till 1031; afterwards, smaller Hispano-Arabic kingdoms—though important cultural centers—twice invited Berber tribes of strong Muslim bias (Almoravides, Almohads) into their countries, asking for help against the Christians, and were subsequently crushed not as much by their Christian neighbours as by their North-African fellow-Muslims. The last moorish kingdom in Spain, Granada of the Nasrides, was conquered by the Catholic kings only in 1492. Ibn Rushd (Averroes) who was court-physician of the Almohades (d. 1198), and Ibn Khaldūn (d. 1406 in Cairo), the first philosopher to apply socio-psychological criteria to the course of history are the two representatives of Western Islam to whom Europe owes the most.

The Abbasides settled in Iraq, built Bagdad and resided for some years in Samarra (836-863); they tried to manifest in their empire the essential unity of Islam, and, at least outwardly, the rule of Islamic law. Persian influences are visible in culture and government; Turkish military slaves soon gained powerful positions which they enlarged into nearly independent kingdoms. Scholars from Syria and the Indus valley frequented the court of Bagdad, and under Ma'mūn (813-833) the Golden Age of Islamic science started: whatever was available of Greek works—be it philosophy, mathematics, medicine, physics etc.—was translated into Arabic. The Muslim scholars enlarged these works, elaborated them and made them more practically applicable; the introduction of the zero which they had learned from Indian mathematics enabled them to develop mathematics to hitherto unknown heights.

The 8th to 10th centuries are the formative period of Islamic thought—philosophy, though despised by the theologians, developed out of the interest in the Aristotelian works which were transmitted in neoplatonic disguise. Al-Kindī (d. after 870), al-Fārābī (d. 950), and Ibn Sīnā (Avicenna, d. 1037) were not only philosophers of high rank but also firstclass scientists.

The discussion of the first problems in theology which had started in the Omayyad period (difference of Islam and faith, ethical qualities of the ruler, free will and predestination) were continued by the Mu'tazila which became, under Ma'mūn, the official theology of the Empire. The Mu'talizites had developed their main tenets against dualist views which seemed, under Iranian influence, to affect the pure monotheism in the late 8th century; thus they emphazised God's absolute unity, without accepting His co-eternal attributes (vd. § II) and held, therefore, that the Quran be created, and, against predestination, they defended His perfect justice. Moreover they introduced methods of Greek philosophy into the theological discussion, attributing to reason an important role. They tried to bridge the gap between the hellenistic culture with which Islam was confronted and the simple "piety of the old women"; neither their method of arguing nor the contents of their teachings which deprived Allah of every imaginability were in the reach of normal understanding. Their doctrines were officially banned in 1029. In the meantime, al-Ashʿarī, a former Muʿtazilite (d. 935) had developed a mediating theology, using the intellectual tools of the Muʿtazila and yet remaining as close as possible to the piety of the traditionalists.

—Every movement inside Islam took its roots from the Quranic revelation. In case the Quran which was considered by the orthodox the uncreated word of Allah did not give a solution to a problem, one had recourse to the example of the Prophet. Since to obey him meant to obey God, traditions (*ḥadīth*) about his customary behaviour (*sunna*) were collected carefully; the majority of the Muslims are proud of calling themselves "the people of the Book and the *sunna*"—hence the term Sunnite. Each group in early Islam tried to support its own views by the authority of the Prophet; hence the number of *ḥadīth* attributed to him grew quickly, reflecting the living tradition of the community. The collecting and sifting of *ḥadīth* became a science in its own right; the chain of transmittors was carefully examined. From the immense number of traditions six collections became regarded as canonical in the late 9th century, of which that of Bukhārī (d. 870) and Muslim (d. 875) enjoyed highest respect.

Quran and tradition are also the main sources for jurisprudence which was also worked out in detail: the *sharīʿa*, comprising ritual, cultic, political, social, and legal precepts (cf. § IV) is the completeness of God's injunctions concerning human actions; the science which is concerned with the *sharīʿa* is *fiqh*. The jurists still had to solve many problems which were not covered by a clear statement in Quran and tradition; in such cases "the majority of the jurists had recourse to analogy (*qiyās*) i.e. the application to a new problem of the principles underlying an existing devision on some other point which could be regarded as on all fours with the new problem" (Gibb).

The different interpretation of the sources of law led to the formation of four main schools (*madhhab*) of thought which are, however, regarded as equally orthodox and differ only in details. A unification of the different views was never tried; smaller differences in legal and ritual matters were explained as a sign of divine mercy. The school of Abū Ḥanīfa, exponent of the Iraqian current (d. 767), giving a certain freedom to *ra'y*, personal interpretation of the facts, is the favorite school of Turkish peoples; the school of Mālik ibn Anās (d. 795) strongly influenced by the classical Madinan tradition, is widely spread in North- and West-Africa; the *madhhab* of ash-Shāfiʿī (d. 820), the founder of the science of jurisprudence, prevails in Egypt, East Africa and Indonesia, and that of Ibn Ḥanbal, the brave defender of orthodox traditionalism (d. 855) is to-day mainly found in Saudi-Arabia; in the middle-ages it was an important agent in the formation of Muslim thought, and has produced some of the greatest theologians of Islam, like Ibn Taimīya (d. 1328). Other *madhhabs*—like the intellectually interesting Ẓāhirites who clung to the outward meaning of the Revealed Book—disappeared after a while. Innovations could be silently accepted as long as the lawyer-divines did not reject them, for "my community will never agree upon an error" (*ḥadīth*). *Ijmāʿ*, "consensus" "the unanimous opinion of the Sunnite community in any generation on a religious matter, constitutes an authority and is to be accepted by all Muslims in later times" (Hourani). *Ijmāʿ*, thus, had binding force, and free investigation into the sources (*ijtihād*) was no longer permitted wherever a point of consensus had been attained. Hence the principle of *ijmāʿ*, first guaranteeing the adaptibility of the *sharīʿa* to new developments, became, from the 10th century onwards, a fetter which hampered further free development and overlaid Islam with a crust of medieval practices and ideas.

The Islamic Empire soon lost its essential unity. Both in the West and in the East independent or nearly independent states emerged. In 929 the Omayyad ruler of Spain adopted the title of caliph, and a few years later a Shiite movement in North Africa, called Fatimides, according to their alleged descent from Muhammad's daughter Fāṭima, claimed the right of caliphate and succeeded in ruling Egypt from 969 to 1171. Smaller dynasties in Syria, the Qarmathians in Central Arabia, Bahrain and Multan, and the Iranian family of the Buwaihids who gained the factual rule in the central parts of the Abbasid Empire likewise professed the Shiʿa doctrine. The Buwaihids left the caliphate intact but assumed the title *Sulṭān* for their own ruler (945). In the the East, Maḥmūd of Ghazna, famous as the destroyer of the Hindu idols, had extinguished some Iranian kingdoms, and invaded India several times after the year 1000. Lahore became a center of Muslim power whence the conquest of North-Western India was carried on; from 1200 till 1857, Delhi was the capital of the most important Muslim state in the Subcontinent; shortly after 1300, Muslims ruled in East Bengal. Most of the Indo-Muslim kingdoms were founded by rulers of turko-mongolian origin; but the Islamization of the country was not due to their military activities but rather to the work of the mystical fraternities who preached the simple faith of Islam, unity of God and equality of men, thus winning over many of those who had been bound in the close caste system of Hinduism.

In the center, a new impetus of orthodoxy had saved the Abbasid caliphate once more—the Sunnite Turkish tribe of the Seljukides gained power over Iran, and 1055 their leader Togrilbeg became the Sultan, the actual ruler of those parts of the Abbasid Empire which were still dependent on Bagdad. During the Seljukid restoration of Sunnite faith the Shiʿa in its most terrible form, that of the Assassins, was fought both by weapon and by theological treatises: Ghazzālī, the most outstanding theologian of the Islam (d. 1111) in the Middle Ages, tried to revive Islamic piety by uniting orthodoxy and moderate mysticism; his numerous works are of paramount importance for the development of spiritual life in Islam. The Seljukids also opened the way for the conquest of Anatolia in 1071, and laid the foundations of a splendid culture whose monuments in Konya, Sivas etc. belong to the finest specimens of Islamic art—the same helds true of the Persian poetry which was written during their time in Iran and Turkey. The Seldjukid's reconquest of Jerusalem from the Fatimids was one of the reasons for the Crusades. The noted hero of the late Crusades, Saladin (d. 1193), from the Kurdish family of the Ayyubites, won over Egypt in 1171 and replaced the Fatimid rule by that of the Ayyubites. In 1250 the reign of the Mamluks (military slaves) was established in Egypt and Syria after the murder of the Ayyubite queen Shajarat ad-Durr.

At the same time the central and Eastern parts of the Abbasid Empire were threatened by Chingiz Khan, who had reached, in 1221, the Indus at Attock, in pursuit of the insurgent prince of Khwarizm; he captured Balkh, and the hordes of his descendents overran Asia and Eastern Europe. In 1258 his grandson Hulagu captured Bagdad; the Abbasid caliph and his family were killed. This event marks the end of the classical period of Islamic history.

In spite of the weakness of the later Abbasid caliphs the importance of this dynasty cannot be overrated. It is typical of the inseparability of religion and state in Islam that the first religious discussions started from the problem of the right caliph. Between the Khārijites, who wanted to elect the member of the community with the highest ethical standard, and be it a "black slave," and the legitimist Shiʿa who claimed the caliphate exclusively for the descendants of Muhammad through Ali, the majority accepted a ruler who should belong to the Quraish, and be free of defects. He has to act as leader of the community in prayer and war, must defend the faith and protect the Islamic countries, but he is subject, like any of his fellow Muslims, to the Divine law (not being endowed with spiritual right of explaining the law, as the Shiʿite *imām*). He should be elected by a committee, but was often designated by his father. When the caliphate became weaker, almost the only sign of his sovereignty was that his name was mentioned in the sermon during the Friday-prayer and was stamped on coins. However the legal theories about the caliphate remained valid as counteracting the centrifugal forces in the Islamic world though the jurists had enough commonsense to admit that obedience to an unlawful ruler is, in any case, preferable to anarchy.—After the fall of Bagdad an alleged member of the Abbasid family came to Cairo and was welcomed by the Mamluk rulers for legitimating their government; the fiction of a caliphal jurisdiction over Muslims who live outside his own territory was invented in the treaty of Küçük Kaynarja (1774) when the Ottoman Sultan was granted "spiritual power" over the Muslims in Russian Crimea. This spiritualistic caliphate inspired the pan-islamic dreams of Sultan ʿAbdul Ḥamīd II. A strange adherence to the Ottoman "caliph" in India led even to the Khilafat-movement after World War I which broke down when Mustafa Kemal (Atatürk) abolished the caliphate in 1924, thus terminating an anomalous situation.

The few countries which were spared from the Mongol invasion, like Egypt, were able to preserve their cultural continuity and became the refugie of many scholars. Egypt turned, likewise, into the economic pivot of the Near East. Bagdad never recovered from the fatal blow, and in Iran the political development under Hulagu's successors and other rulers resulted in nearly incessant wars. In Anatolia, out of the ashes of the Seldjukid kingdom smaller principalities emerged among whom the family of the Ottomans in the North West was destined to play the decisive role in Near Eastern history. Growing steadily, their well-organized army captured Adrianople in 1356, large parts of the Balkans in 1389, and attained the goal which had inspired the dreams of Muslims since the time of the Prophet: to conquer Constantinople (1453). The Ottomans eventually extended their authority in 1517 over the Mamluk region including the holy places Mecca and Madina, and thus became the leading Muslim power, and spokesmen of the faithful for nearly four centuries to come.

In the second half of the 14th century, the conquests of Timur (d. 1405), who devastated the countries between Delhi and Ankara (again with exception of Egypt) mark the next disaster for Muslim civilisation; but Timur, contrary to the pagan Chingiz Khan, was an orthodox Muslim, and his descendants created new centers of art and culture in the Eastern metropoles (Herat, Samarkand etc.) though they ruined themselves in fratricidal feuds. In Iran proper the struggle of two Turkoman tribes lasted for decades. The tribe of the White Sheep, whose ruler Uzun Hasan cultivated relations with Venice and was married with a Christian princess of Trebizond had close connections with the saintly Shiʿite family of Ardebil. From this family came Ismāʿīl, the Safawide, who, at the age of fourteen, succeeded in uniting Iran in 1501, and made the Shiʿa in its moderate form (Imāmīya, ithnāʿashariya) the state religion of Iran. Thus he created a religio-political trench between the sunnite Ottomans in the West and the likewise sunnite Empire of the Moghuls in the East—an Empire which, after Bābur's victory in 1526, expanded until it embraced nearly the whole subcontinent plus parts of Afghanistan.

The political situation of the first quarter of the 16th century—the Ottoman Empire as the Western pillar of Islam, the Moghul Empire as its Eastern pillar, separated by Shiʿite Iran (each of them representing, at times, highest cultural achievements)—this situation remained, with slight changes, characteristic of the map of Asia up to the 19th century.

The sunnite group of Muslims, though sometimes involved in fiery theological discussions, was, on the whole, a rather homogenous community, from which nobody was excommunicated for purely religion reasons; the few executions of "religious" leaders, e.g. some mystics, were due to political motives. Gibb has pointed out rightly:

> "The Sunni principle has been to extend the limits of toleration as widely as possible. No great religious community has ever possessed more fully the catholic spirit or been more ready to allow the widest freedom to its members provided only that they accepted, at least outwardly, the minimum obligations of the faith."

Among those who were excluded from this community since "they desired exclusion and, as it were, excluded themselves" (Gibb) were the two early "religiös-politische Oppositionsparteien," the Khārijites, and the Shiʿites. The Shiʿites have, on the whole, no distinctive theology and religious practice and acknowledge the Prophetic *sunna* as well; their characteristic feature, as developed in the first centuries, is the faith in the *imām* (from ʿAlī's house) as infallible leader of the community. The Shiʿa sees in the living, later in the hidden *imām* the only person endowed with the right of Quranic exegesis and sanctification of traditions; none of their groups accepts the principle of *ijmāʿ*; legal and theological problems are solved by the *mujtahids* who act as representatives of the Hidden Imām in whose name—even today—laws are promulgated. In law, they permit temporal marriage; they also are allowed to practise *taqiya*, dissimulation of opinion, which is a relic from the times of persecution.

The Shiʿa, stemming from different roots and after a purely Arabic beginning, then turning into a cover for manifold foreign ideas which entered Islam—especially Iranian legitimism and gnostic light-mysticism—divided soon into several branches who are called after the Imām whom they revere. The Zaidīya, related to the fifth Imām Zaid, Ḥusain's grandson (d. 724) are closest to puritan sunnite groups; they accept imāms both from Ḥusain's and his brother Ḥasan's offspring and do not ascribe them supernatural qualities. They had a state in Tabaristan till 1126, and succeeded in ruling Yemen from the 10th century up to our days.

The majority of the Shiʿa called Imāmīya or *ithnāʿasharīya* recognize twelve imāms the last of whom disappeared in 873.

The most differenciated group is the Ismāʿīlīya. After the death of Jaʿfar aṣ-Ṣādiq (well-known in alchemy, d. 765) they did not accept his son Mūsā whose descendants are acknowledged by the Imamite group but Mūsā's brother Ismāʿīl. Common to the different branches —the Qarmathians, the Fatimids—is the way of introducing the adept by seven degrees into the mysteries of faith (hence their name Bāṭinīya, the people of the inner meaning), reducing gradually the meaning of the *sharīʿa*; the leaders exerted absolute authority. Gnostic and neoplatonic ideas were amalgamated into a system of philosophical *Weltanschauung* which was made popular by the group of the *Ikhwān aṣ-ṣafā* "The Brethren of Purity" in Basra in the 9th and 10th centuries. The general Shiʿite idea that a Divine light was inherited through the prophets since Adam and then through ʿAlī's descendants was, in some of the Ismāʿīlīya groups, exaggerated to the point of regarding the imāms as incarnations of the Godhead. A typical example of this idea is the Fatimid caliph al-Ḥākim, mysteriously disappearing in 1021, whose adherents saw in him a manifestation of the Divinity; still today the Druzes adhere to this faith. The Fatimid dynasty split up in 1094; the prince Nizār was brought to Iran where Ḥasan-i Sabbāḥ had formed an organisation of absolutely obedient disciples who could be used for every goal, and are known in the West, with which they came in touch during the Crusades, as Assassins. No longer politically active after the Mongol invasion, this branch of the Ismāʿīlīya now flourishes, under the Agha Khan, in Indo-Pakistan and East Africa; the followers of Nizār's brother Mustaʿlī later formed the group of the Bohora in India. The Indian Shiʿites of the different branches now fully cooperate with the Sunnites; one of them, M. A. Jinnah, is the founder of Pakistan. Other—heterodox—offsprings of these movements are the Nusairians in Syria who maintain the emanationist theories of the classical Bāṭinīya, and consider ʿAlī as superior to Muhammad, a tendency which is fully developed with the ʿAlī-Ilāhī who have deified ʿAlī but are rejected even by the other Shiʿite groups.

One can admit that Shiʿa doctrines have influenced also some theories of the great spiritual movement inside Islam which is known as Sufism.

During the period of far-flung conquests in early Islam which were followed by a life of luxury that scandalized the pious some of them started concentrating upon the ascetic interpretation of Islam, insisting upon the meticulous fulfillment of the religious duties. Weeping over their sins, fear of the Doomsday, and repentance were their characteristics. Their woolen (*ṣūf*) frock made them known as *Ṣūfī.* This name was later applied to the whole system of mysticism which developed out of the early ascetism, inheriting the principle of constant struggle with the lower self, abstaining from everything doubtful through which the pious might be led to patience, forbearance, trust in God and gratitude. The notion of pure love was introduced by Rābiʿa of Basra (d. 801), a woman who preached and practised pure love of God without asking for Paradise or fearing hellfire. This notion of love—though not accepted by the orthodox (for them love is obedience to His laws)—was elaborated in the next centuries. The central theme of the Sufis—as of the theologians—was God's unity: be it expressed in the prayers of Dhū'n-Nūn (d. 859) who experienced the revelation of God's beauty in nature, or in the concept of *fanā* (annihilation of the human qualities in the Divine qualities—understood first ethically, then metaphysically), the negative way of union with God as realized by the Iranian Bāyezīd Bisṭāmī (d. 874). The Bagdadian school was represented especially by the sober Muḥāsibī (d. 857) with his careful methods of self-examination, and Junaid (d. 910), the great master to whom the later currents have recourse. His former disciple Ḥallāj was executed in 922; his theories culminated in the expression *anā'l-ḥaqq*—"I am the absolute Truth" which means the unification in the moment of ecstasy of the created soul with the uncreated Divine Spirit. Ḥallāj, "absorbed in serving the will of God" in suffering has become, in later Sufism, the prototype of the suffering lover who dies in love.

Sufism—once defined as "the way that God should cause thee to die from thyself and to live in Him" —was suspect to orthodoxy because of some of its practices, like listening to music, dancing, reciting the Divine names, and because of the danger inherent in the notion of "love of God." A number of writers—Sarrāj (d. 988) and Qushairī (d. 1074) are especially worth mentioning—tried a systematization of the path of mysticism and its reconciliation with orthodoxy by leading it back to Quran and tradition. Others, like the Malāmatīya, deliberately attracted public contempt by committing outrageous sins in order to hide their inner life from the people. The reconciliation between mysticism and orthodoxy is largely due to Ghazzālī, who had studied scholastic theology, knew well the philosophical trends and had, eventually, found the truth by personal mystical experience. This process enabled him to speak authoritatively about the problems of the soul who is between fear and hope, and "he succeeded in assuring the mystical or introspective attitude a place within official Islam side by side with the legalism of the lawyers and the intellectualism of the theologians" (Wensinck) thus quickening the personal religious life.

The late 12th and the 13th centuries is the high time of Sufism. After Suhrawardī Maqtūl (d. 1191), the initiator of the "Wisdom of Illumination," the Spanish-born Ibn ʿArabī (d. 1240) moulded the different trends (gnosticism, neoplatonism etc.) into a formidable theosophical system which he laid down in hundreds of works and which teaches *waḥdat al-wujūd*, the essential Unity of Being. He was, like his contemporary Ibn al-Fāriḍ (d. 1235), a poet of high rank. Ibn ʿArabī's ideas became widely accepted, and the mystical poets made them accessible to large parts of the population who may not have been aware of their logical consequences. Mystical poetry—love poetry in the highest sense—was cultivated especially in Iran in both lyrics and the didactic *mathnawī* (Sanā'ī, d. 1141; 'Aṭṭār, d. 1220). Jalāluddīn Rūmī's (1207 in Balkh, d. 1273 in Konya) oft-commented *mathnawī* is an encyclopedia of all mystical currents of early Islam, and his lyrics are overflowing with boundless love of the Divine Beauty revealed in human form. This mystical poetry influenced Turkey and Muslim India, and the deliberate play with mystical symbols, its charming ambiguity has made it attractive for millions. At the same time, mystical orders and fraternities grew out of the small circles of disciples. The first of them, the Qādirīya, founded by 'Abdulqādir al-Gīlānī (d. 1166), has adherents in almost every Muslim country, other fraternities—like the Suhrawardīya, the Chishtīya, the Rifā'īya—influenced popular life and carried out missionary work by attracting people through their more emotionally tinged piety. They have often played important roles in politics, like the rustic order of Bektashis with strong Shi'ite inclinations, who were associated with the Janissaries, or, in the 19th century, the Tījānīya and Sanūsīya in Africa. The Naqshbandīya, whose founder died in Central Asia in 1389, became in India a defender of the orthodox wing by rejecting the philosophy of essential monism. The ethical importance of the orders, and their useful role in developing the emotional faculties is being counterweighted by its negative: the absolute rule of the *shaykh* over his disciples. The veneration of the mystical leader, living or dead, became part and parcel of popular Islam, as well as the overstressed concept of *tawakkul*, trust in God which may hamper free activity as much as the meticulous clinging to the letter of the law.

III. Conception of the Deity

The Muslim confession of faith starts with the assertion *lā ilāha illā Allāh*: "there is no Deity but Allah." Perhaps no religion is as theocentric as Islam. The formula of the creed is found at every time and in every place, and "this particular set of words when written out is strikingly patterned" (W. C. Smith) and has inspired the calligraphers as much as it has become one of the keywords of the mystics glorifying by their witness (*shahāda*) God the One who has no companions.

The pre-Islamic Arabs had known the concept of a high-God above the numerous idols, who was called *Allāh* (al-Ilāh, "the God"). In Muhammad's revelations this God made Himself known as the

Creator and the Judge. He has created from nothing the whole cosmos, nature and man, and He will summon humanity before Him at the Last Day in order to judge them with perfect justice. This God who is Creator, Sustainer, and Judge, cannot be but one besides Whom nothing else and nobody else is to be worshipped. This pure monotheism is maintained first in the struggle against the Arabic pagan polytheism, then against the Christian doctrine of Christ as God's innate son and the Trinity—Sura 112, the logical end of the Quran, proclaims that:

> "Say: He is Allah, One; Allah, the Eternal; He brought not forth nor hath He been brought forth; Co-equal with Him there hath never been anyone."

This God is the wise Creator (*al-Khāliq*, 6/102) who has created the world in six days (25/60) or in a single moment (54/50). He has arranged everything in the most excellent way, and His wisdom and power are visible both in nature and in the course of history. His knowledge embraces everything and everybody from the moment of his creation, and His mercy (cf. 6/11) is likewise extended to those who acknowledge Him as the Sovereign besides Whom there are no false gods, Whose will is higher than the will of human rulers, and Whose judgment is perfectly just. It is He in Whose name every work is being begun (*bismillāh*), and upon His will depends every future action so that one has to add "*inshā Allāh*" "if God willeth" to every sentence that refers to a future act or a new direction of thought.

The Quran abounds in words which try to give an integral description of the indescribable God and to hint at His mysterious being by encircling Him with the so-called "Most beautiful Names" (cf. 7/179, 17/11, 20/7, 59/24) which might be characterized as "attributes of glorification." God is the First and the Last, the Inward and the Outward (57/3); He exists through Himself (*al-qayyūm*); He is called the Merciful and the Compassionate in the first *sūra*, the *Fātiḥa*, and at the beginning of every Quranic recitation. But He is as well "the Best of Intriguers" since His ways are more inscrutable and wise than all human inventions and plots. And though He may be called the All-Holy (*al-quddūs*) or the Peace (*as-salām*) *par excellence* He is also the Light of Heaven and Earth (24/35)—which means, essentially, a guiding light like the lamp in the monk's cell in the desert which leads the wandering Bedouin through the dark night; later, this epithet was interpreted as the all-embracing universal light, or the inner light in the heart. Modern theology has understood it as synonymous with "absolute" (taken from velocity of light as absolute measure!). He who is completely transcendent so that "the sight reaches Him not" (6/101) is yet closer to man than his jugular vein (50/16)—and "wherever ye turn, there is the Face of God" (2/115). This expression "face of God" occurs several times in the Quran, and has probably denoted the essence of God Himself (cf.: "Whoever is on earth is passing away—only the face of God will remain for ever," 55/31).

The exclusiveness of the formula of creed, that "prophetic No" as Söderblom calls it: "there is no God but Allah" has never been forgotten. This No is the wall against the greatest sin which the Muslim can think of, the sin which can never been forgiven: that of *shirk*, "association," i.e. association of other objects of worship with God. This No, first directed against pagan idolatry, was, in mysticism, overstressed to the extent that nothing besides God possesses real existence. Modernists sometimes use the concept of *shirk* to denounce the ideologies which are taken as substitutes for religion—capitalism, communism, nationalism—and are, in orthodox view, equal to the false gods of paganism and may convert man from the adoration of the One matchless sovereign Power.

Muhammad was not a dogmatic theologian but a prophet overwhelmed by Allah. Thus, after his death, different interpretations of the concept of the Deity came into existence, each of them taking its proofs from the partly contradictory statements of the Quran. Orthodoxy clung to the verbal meaning of the description of Allah (His face, hands, etc.) and was in danger of committing the error of anthropomorphism, *tashbīh*. Due to the first contacts with the methods of Hellenistic philosophy this tendency was counteracted by the theological system of the Muʿtazila who defended the absolute Unity of God even at the cost of His imaginability. They tended towards *tanzīh*, the complete withdrawal from descriptions, emphasizing that God is different from everything created. They regarded the doctrine of the Attributes of God (Hearing, Sight, Speech etc.) as "endangering if not actually contradicting His Unity" (Gibb), and since they held that His attributes have no independent existence they were accused by the Orthodox as "those who deny the attributes." The denial of coeternal attributes led them to maintaining that the Quran is created, and not, as Orthodoxy defended, the Uncreated Word of God. The Muʿtazila—*ahl al-ʿadl waʾt-tauḥīd*, "the People of Justice and Unification"—saw in God, the One, the "God of Justice," the perfectly just Ruler (Who is, according to many of them, not the author of evil), not the arbitrary sovereign Who can do with His creation whatever He pleases but one who *must* bring the pious to Paradise and the sinner to Hell whereas man is free to act according his will. This restriction of God's power, and the stress laid upon the intellectual approach to the Divine made Muʿtazizile theology nearly inaccessible for the broad masses. In some modern circles, the idea of God's absolute Justice against His "arbitrary Omnipotence" is highlighted once more.

A compromising formula between the orthodox point of view and the Muʿtazilite way of arguing was developed by al-Ashʿarī (d. 935) who attested that God is such and such, but *bilā kaifa*, without "how". *tashbīh*, anthropomorphism, and *taʿṭīl*, "depriving God of all imaginable attributes" are both considered grave sins. Slightly different in expression is the argumentation of al-Maturīdī (d. 944). The *mutakallimūn*, using philosophical methods, had still to struggle against the "people of the tradition" but were established officially in 1065. Their ideas about the Highest Being can be summarized in the words of A. T. Tritton:

> "God is eternal, without beginning and without end, unique, for nothing is like Him. He knows by knowledge, lives by life, wills by will, sees by sight, and speaks by His word. These attributes are eternal, inhere in His essence, are not He and not other than He, yet they do not detract from the unity of His essence. He is the absolute Lord of what He has created and none can call Him to account for what He does; should He send all creatures to Hell, it is not injustice, should He take them all to paradise, it is not wrong. "Must" does not apply to Him. The worship and gratitude of man do not profit Him nor does the unbelief of the infidel hurt Him, for all things are His. He willed all that exists, both good and bad, useful and harmful. Right is right and wrong is wrong because God has decreed that they are so."

God has created the world once from nothing and does not cease creating it every moment—this idea of atomism was developed in ashʿarite circles: secondary causes are eliminated, and whatever happens happens through the direct action of God: fire does not burn by its inherent quality but because it is God's custom to connect burning with fire. This *sunnat Allāh*, "God's custom," is visible both in nature and in the course of history; logically a miracle is called the *khāriq ul-ʿāda* "what disrupts the custom." This theory has influenced Islamic thought to a considerable extent.

From the definitions of the scholastic theologians, catechisms were compiled whose contents the faithful were supposed to know and to understand—the most famous booklet of this kind is the so-called *Sanūsīya* from the 15th century in which God's forty-one qualities are enumerated according to twenty qualities of necessity, twenty of impossibility, and one of possibility. The qualities of necessity are: existence, preeternity, eternity, difference from everything created in time, existence through himself, unity, power, will, knowledge, life, hearing, sight, speech, being powerful, being willing, being knowing, being living, being hearing, being seeing, being speaking. The qualities of impossibility comprise the contrary, like non-existence, being created in time, blindness etc. The last quality is, that God has the possibility of doing everything possible and impossible. The orthodox Muslim is proud of having this description of a rationally comprehensible God.

In the meantime the philosophers had developed their own speculations about the Divine Being, and had conceived of God mostly as a *prima causa* from which, in different stages, the First Intellect and the individual souls emerge —thus al-Kindī (d. after 870). The gnostic group of the *Ikhwān aṣ-Ṣafā* of Basra (9th century) likewise believed in an emanation of spiritual beings from the Divine Being. Fārābī (d. 950) held that God, whose Existence is absolutely necessary, creates the world by His thought, and Ibn Sīnā (Avicenna, d. 1037) describes God as *prima causa*, Whose Being is pure Existence. Whatever possibly may exist is already existent in God's knowledge—i.e. actual and potential being are clearly distinguished—; that means, like the theories of the other philosophers, the eternity of the world, since God is prior to the world in grade, not in time—He thinks the world, and thus it is. With Ibn Rushd, however, the distinction is made that God is eternal and without cause whereas the world is eternal but due to a creating and moving power. The Quranic doctrine of *creatio ex nihilo* is thus denied which caused the attacks of the orthodox against the philosophers' position. The voluntaristic God was in danger to be converted into a more or less impersonal source of being.

Against the scholastic interpretation of the Divine qualities and the speculation of the Philosophers, Sufism relied on the personal experience of the Divine. God is found not through reasoning but through intuition (*kashf*), and is obeyed out of love—an attitude which was rejected by the orthodox who did not accept any relation between Creator and creature but that of obedience.

To the early Sufis, God revealed Himself first as the Judge, and their meditations are born from the feeling of their own weakness and His immense power. The fear of the Judgement and the hope for forgiveness alternate in the prayers of early mystics, and they have always loved to iuxtapose the aspects of *tremendum* and *fascinans*, God's *jamāl* and *jalāl* (Beauty and Majesty), or His Mercy and Wrath—being well aware of the dialectic process of life. They also stressed the confession of God's Unity to such an extent that they might even refuse to look at nature, or to love anything created, be it their own family—and even the Prophet—out of fear that they might be led to *shirk*, association, by such an act. However, others, relying upon the Quranic dicta that everything created is proof of His power, and praises Him in its own language, have described in colourful prayers —like Dhū'n-Nūn (d. 859)—the revelation of His greatness and beauty in nature, and in everything beautiful. Ghazzālī has expressed the classical position of moderate Sufism quite adequately:

> "Who looks at the world because it is God's work, and recognizes it because it is God's work, and loves it because it is God's creation does not look at anything else but God, does not know but God, does not love but Him. He is, thus, the real confessor of Divine Unity who sees nothing but God. He also does not look upon himself for his own sake but because he is God's servant, and concerning such a person it is said that he is annihilated in the *tauḥīd* and annihilated from himself."

The interpretation of the *tauḥīd*, the acknowledgment of God's unity and unicity, is dominant in the mystic movement, as Ghazzālī has shown in the above-mentioned passage. *Tauḥīd* could mean, for the Sufis, that Allah is the only Being with real existence, everything else having only a secondary or accidental existence, and it could be stressed to declare that "there is no existent but Allah" which might lead—and has indeed—to a monistic concept of the Deity.

In mystic theories of old which have been elaborated by the poets of all Islamic countries God becomes the Beloved *par excellence*, and the idea that He has manifested His eternal Beauty through creation—expressed in the oft-quoted *ḥadīth qudsī* "I was a hidden treasure and I wanted to be known, thus I created the world"—or that He reflects it in the mirror of the human heart in order to be recognized or loved, was elaborated by the later mystics until they reached the point of saying "Whatever I see, I see Thee in it"—taking their Quranic support from the words "Wherever ye turn there is the Face of God" (2/115).

In the systematization of the mystical theories about Allah influences of the philosophers are visible. The neoplatonic speculations about the pre-eternal Being from Which every thing emanates and into Which it will return, through stages of purification, became one of the main tenets of Sufism, expressed in mystical poetry by the symbol of the drop which is re-united with the Ocean of Being from which it once turned away; and in the system of Ibn ʿArabī (d. 1240) God and world were reduced to two aspects of each other, just as ice and water are essentially the same substance in different states. "God is Absolute Being, and is the source of all existence; in Him alone Being and Existence are inseparable" (Arberry). The duty of the seeker is, then, to find the way into his heart and realize that there the Divine spark is hidden, according to the *ḥadīth qudsī*: "Heaven and earth do not contain Me, but the heart of My faithful servant contains Me." This feeling of God's immanence finds its most typical expression in the alledged *ḥadīth* "Who knows himself knows his Lord."

It is sometimes difficult to discern the different aspects of God the Beloved, the All-Embracing, the Heart of the Heart, in mystical poetry; but one can say that the so-called essential monism which contains Ibn ʿArabi's doctrine about the Unity of Being (*waḥdat al-wujūd*) covered very quickly great parts of the Islamic world, though orthodoxy clearly saw its danger for the Quranic concept of the Transcendent, Willing and Judging Lord. The Indian scholar Aḥmad Sirhindī (d. 1624) tried to go back to the classical interpretation of the Divine in his theory of *waḥdat ash-shuhūd* (unity of testimony) which means that the seeker realizes his unity with God in the moment of ecstasy but understands it as personal experience after his returning to normal levels of conscience.

The search for and meditation of "Allah's Greatest Name" has come down from high mystical speculations into sorcery of which it forms an important part. And one should not forget the role of the constant repetition of the creed, or of the word Allah, or of the numinous syllable *hū* "He" in the assemblies of the mystics who will repeat it until they become enraptured.

Orthodoxy has attacked the idea of the static God of the philosophers Whose creation is not product of His will, and has likewise rejected the ideas of monistic mysticism which leave no room for the personal and active Allah announced in the Quran. Modernist theologians have resumed the orthodox position, and though not clinging to the scholastic definition of Allah's qualities and attributes have tried to go back once more to the Quranic assertation about God: for them

He is active, is a person (which is asserted by His name Allah, and by His promise to answer man's prayer); He is the most perfect—since all-embracing—person, and man can meet Him as the faithful servant meets His All-wise and Powerful, yet Compassionate Lord in a person-to-person encounter. Iqbal (d. 1938) has, in this respect, given a highly interesting picture of God—with him God's life is permanent creativeness; and without denying His Love and Compassion, the modern thinker helds that He is, according to our experiences in history, better revealed under the aspect of Power.

Other modernists go back to the Mu'tazilite concept of *'adl*, the absolute Justice of God, and build their system upon the assertion of God's justice, showing the God of the Quran as a perfectly moral Being whose perfection in justice has been veiled by the deliberate and indiscriminate use of the Most Comely Names (thus D. RAHBAR). Again another group emphazises the words of the Quran according to which God has manifested His Power and Wisdom in everything created, especially in the marvels of nature—words which enable them to accept without hesitation even the most recent discoveries of science which are, then, nothing but proofs of God's creative omnipotence.

IV. A. WORSHIP

a. *Cult*

Islam does not know any sacraments. H. A. R. GIBB has pointed out that in Islam we should speak rather of orthopraxis than of orthodoxy, since in the frame of the confession of faith (vd. § 4, 3) everybody can imagine God, the One, as he believes it provided he maintains His unity; he has, however, to obey the injunctions of the Divine Law concerning the regulations of the religious praxis.

The "five pillars of faith" are:

1) the *shahāda*, confession of faith (vd. IV C) which is the essential condition of the other obligations

Each of the *'ibādāt* (acts of worship) begins with the formulation of *niya* (intention) without which they are invalid. The jurists have prescribed exactly who is *mukallaf*, "bound to fulfil" a certain duty; e.g. a boy of seven is able to pray; after he reaches maturity fasting becomes obligatory for him. Men and women have to fulfil the obligations of *'ibādāt*.

2) Prayer (*ṣalāt*, pers.-turk. *namāz*)

Ritual prayer is prescribed five times a day and must be performed on a clean place (hence prayer-rugs!) in a state of ritual purity (*ṭahāra*) (5/4), i.e. after small pollutions which are caused by everything which goes out of the body *wuḍū'* is prescribed: the Muslim has to wash his face, hands up to the elbow, feet, ears, sucks water into the nostrils, passes the wet hand over the head. After a great pollution (menstruation, sexual intercourse, childbirth) a bath in which no part of the body is allowed to remain dry is obligatory. If no water is available the ablution may be performed with dust (*tayyamum*). During prayer the private parts of the body and the head have to be covered; women have face and hands unveiled, but must be decently dressed. After having heard the call to prayer (*adhān*) the Muslim turns towards Mecca and recites in standing position the formula *Allāhu Akbar* (*takbīr al-iḥrām*), then the *Fātiḥa*, kneels (*rukū'*), stands again, prostrates, squats, prostrates once more, always reciting the prescribed verses of the Quran. The unit of movements and recitations from the first *rukū'* to the last *sujūd* (prostration) forms one *rak'a*; the *ṣalāt* ends by the recitation of the *shahāda*, blessings on the Prophet, and greetings to the left and right, in a sitting position. Each part of the *rak'a* can be prolonged through additional recitations.

The morning prayer (*fajr*) (from first dawn to sunrise) consists of two *rak'a*, the noon prayer (*ẓuhr*) of four, the *'aṣr* (from mid-afternoon to sunset) of four, the prayer after sunset (*maghrib*) of three, the *'ishā'* (after complete darkness) of four *rak'a*. The Quran mentions only three of these prayers (*fajr*, *'ishā'* and *al-wusṭā*, the middle one) explicitely. Each prayer must be said in proper time. Travellers may postpone their prayers; in the battle-field half of the army may worship, half of them watch the enemy. It is meritorious to add supererogative *rak'a*; at the end of the *ṣalāt* one may utter personal petitions.

Prayer may be performed alone or in community; in this case the faithful need an *imām* to lead the prayer; every muslim (in female congregations also a woman) can act as *imām*. On Friday—choosen in contrast to the Christian Sunday and Jewish Sabbath—a service is held in the mosque attend to which is obligatory for men (at least forty persons should be present); women mostly pray at home. At this occasion, a short sermon of two parts is read, in the end of which the preacher prays for the government.

The five prayers are connected in Islamic tradition with Muhammad's ascension to Heaven, and he is reported to have said whenever he longed for the immediate presence of God: "O Bilāl, refresh us with the call to prayer!" Indeed ritual prayer without the presence of the heart is considered meaningless.—Through *ṣalāt* man should learn modesty, and praise God together with all creatures (23/3). Prayer is the usual occupation of the angels who are imagined to remain always in one special position; it "is the key of Paradise." The pious have especially practiced the nightprayer which is mentioned in the Quran but not prescribed. Orthodoxy saw in the ritual prayer a symbol of the servant's obedience towards his Lord, mystics have interpreted it, in a word-play, as *ṣila*, connection and close communication, with the Divine Beloved; others have stressed its importance for self-discipline.

Besides the five daily services we find special forms of *ṣalāt* at burials, and in the morning of the two great festivals; there are formulae for prayer at solar and lunar eclipses, and for the *istisqā*, the rain-prayer which is—even in our days—performed not in the mosque but outside the town in simple clothes. A *ṣalāt al-istikhāra* is performed before taking a grave decision, and on the whole the Muslim may offer a *ṣalāt* of two *rakʿa* at almost every occasion: when entering a mosque, when putting on new clothes, or hearing good news, etc.

The *ṣalāt* has deeply influenced the whole structure of Islamic culture; for the common prayer mosques (*masjid*, from *sajada*, prostrate) were built in which Islamic art reached its zenith. Their only decoration is calligraphy and arabesque-work; their *miḥrāb*, the prayer-niche, is oriented towards the sanctuary in Mecca. A pulpit (*minbar*) is erected for the friday-sermon, sometimes a special place for the ruler is fixed. The mosque in its different forms—court-mosque in the early ages which gave room for tens of thousands of the faithful, the high domes of Turkish mosques, the combination of mosque and theological school under Iranian influence—reflects the different cultural individualities of the Islamic countries. Glass industry has shown its best in manufacturing beautiful mosque-lamps, the *miḥrāb* was decorated with marble, glass, enamelled mosaic, colourful tiles, artistically cut wood, etc.

Besides ritual prayer Islam knows the free prayer (*duʿā*) as well, since God has said: "Call upon Me, and I shall answer you" (40/62). The number of popular devotional books and pamphlets is beyond limit. The term *munājāt* describes the private talk between the Lord and His servant, the lover and the Beloved. Islamic literature in all languages is abundant with most beautiful poetical prayers, each work of literature starting with a praise of God and a laudation of His messenger, which gives, in prayer form, the key-note of the book in question.

Sufism has developed the *dhikr*, recollection of God—based upon the Quranic prescription "Recollect God often" (33/41) and the promise: "Remember Me, and I shall remember you" (2/147), and especially on the verse: "In the remembrance of Allah should not the hearts be at peace?" (13/28).

Hence the mystics repeat the Most Beautiful names of God (vd. § 3), either all the ninetynine, or a single one is chosen for a special purpose. Prayer formulae, the confession of faith etc. also belong to the repertoire of *dhikr* which differs according to the fraternities. There is the *dhikr jalī*, in which the formula is uttered with loud voice until the participants become enraptured, and the *dhikr khafī* in which the sacred words are repeated inside the heart and become so-to-say a part of life. A help in counting the Divine names or the formulae was the rosary which has been used in Islam since the 9th century. To-day the rosary has often degenerated into a simple toy.

Sufi circles invented litanies, *ḥizb*, which are recited either regularly or at special times, and to which great virtues are sometimes attributed; thus, the *ḥizb al-baḥr*, invented by ash-Shādhilī (d. 1258) is used by travellers.

The relation between man and God which the mystic feels in his *dhikr* is expressed in a *ḥadīth qudsī*:

> "When My servant recollects Me in his soul I recollect him in My soul, and when he recollects Me in the crowd I mention him in a crowd which is better than his crowd; and when he draws hear to Me a span I draw nearer to him a yard, and when he draws near to Me a yard, I draw near to him a fathom until I become his hand with which he works, and his feet with which he walks, and his eyes with which he sees..."

Dhikr becomes, thus, a means of realizing the Unity of man and God: until there remains no difference between the recollecting subject, the Recollected, and the recollection.

Muslims have also expressed the secret of the *oratio infusa*—already in early Sufism it was discovered that it is not man who prays but the Divine Spirit in him. The classical locus for this theory is Maulānā Rūmī's *Mathnawi* (where, by the way, this idea has been laid down several times) in the story III 189 ff.:

"That 'Allah' of thine is My 'Here am I' ...
Beneath every 'O Lord' of thine is many a 'Here am I' from Me"

(transl. R. A. NICHOLSON).

3) Legal Alms (*zakāt*)

After a period of free charity, the Quran (2/215, 9/60) ordered a certain amount of "legal alms" or religious tax for each member of the Muslim community; its revenues were for the poor, the destitute, the tax-collectors, those "whose hearts are to be won over," the ransom of slaves, debtors, expenditure in the way of Allah, travellers.

The amount of *zakāt* which everybody had to pay was fixed according to detailed rules, e.g. from fruits of the fields, grapes, dates and similar products 10% had to be given after the harvest; in case of artificial irrigation 5%, from cattle, gold, silver and trade good after one year of possession $2\frac{1}{2}$%. *Zakāt* is frequently mentioned in the Quran together with *ṣalāt*: one being the duty of man towards God, the other his duty toward the community. Modern interpreters hold that the legal alms cover essentially the whole budget of the state; likewise it has been said that *zakāt* would prove the best protection against both capitalism and communism. The government has, from early times, always levied non-Quranic taxes (*mukūs*); then—thus today—*zakāt* is paid besides the regular state taxes.

At the end of Ramaḍān, the *zakāt al-fiṭr*, an offering of food, is usual in addition to the prescribed *zakāt*. Besides, alms (*ṣadaqāt*) are given the amount of which depends on personal reasons.

4) Fasting (*ṣaum*)

In Quran 2/179 the month of Ramaḍān is prescribed for fasting, since in Ramaḍān—the 9th lunar month of the Muslim year—the first revelation of the Quran was sent: the *lailat ul-qadr* (Sūra 97) is considered to be one of the last nights in Ramaḍān.

The fasting begins and ends at the appearence of the new moon which must have been seen by two reliable witnesses. Only in few countries the dates are now regulated according to the calendar.

During Ramaḍān, the Muslim has to abstain from eating, drinking, smoking and carnal intercourse from that moment in the early morning when a black thread can be distinguished from a white one, until sunset is completed. In some countries eating during daytime is still liable to punishment. Pious Muslims would even object to get an injection or to smell a flower during day-time.

The after-sunset meal should start with some water and small eatables like olives; afterwards the evening prayer should be offered, and then the real meal eaten. The performance of the *tarāwīḥ*-prayers (33 *rakʿa*) after dinner is recommended. The night can be spent in pleasure, and shortly before dawn a second meal can be offered. Intentional eating and drinking during day-time breaks the fast; only if it is caused by forgetfulness is it excusable.—Fasting is forbidden for women during menstruction; certain facilities are granted the sick, and pregnant and suckling women, and also during journey and war. The fasting has, however, either to be made up on other days of the year, or, in certain cases, be substituted by feeding a poor person during a corresponding number of days.

Fasting outside Ramaḍān can be a *kaffāra*, expiation, for some sins. It is, however, forbidden to fast on the two great festivals, and disliked on Fridays, Saturdays, Sundays and in the end of the month of Shaʿbān which precedes Ramaḍān. On other days fasting is recommended: thus on ʿAshūrā-day (10. Muḥarram) in remembrance of Ḥusain's death in Kerbela, the day preceding the night of Muhammad's ascension (27. Rajab), etc.

Fasting is partly an ascetic practice and was, therefore, performed by the pious often during long periods; orthodoxy however, objects prolonged fasting because it weakens the body. *Ṣaum Dāʾūdī* means fasting and eating on alternating days. Fasting has sometimes been given an ethical meaning, "since it teaches the rich the feeling of the hungry"; it has been called a method of discipline, which is surely true; in modern time its medical effects have been mentioned.

5) Pilgrimage (*ḥajj*)

Every Muslim has to perform once in his—or her—life the pilgrimage to Mecca (3/91). Here, in Muhammad's hometown, the Kaʿba is located, a building of 12 m by 10 m, with a height of 15 m; in its south-east corner a black stone, probably a meteor, is incorporated at an altitude of appr. 1½ m. The door lies at the north-east of the building which was used as central Arabian sanctuary long before Muhammad; it has been repaired several times.

Sūra 2/119 considers the Kaʿba the place which was built by Abraham and his son Ismāʿīl, and the pilgrimage was connected with the memory of Ismāʿīl's proposed offering.

The last pilgrimage which Muhammad performed in 632 was taken as a model for the correct execution of the different duties during the *ḥajj*. Since 631, non-Muslims are not allowed to participate in the *ḥajj*.

The *ḥajj* in its present form connects the rites of the *ʿumra* (2/192), a circumambulation of the Kaʿba which was, in pre-Islamic times, preferably executed in the month of Rajab, with the rites of visiting ʿArafāt and Minā in the last lunar month, the Dhū'l-ḥijja. The two parts of the ceremony can be connected, or interrupted, according to the *niya* of the pilgrim when he puts on the dress of pilgrimage, the *iḥrām*. This is done on special places in the environment of Mecca; the *iḥrām* consists of two unsewn white sheets which are put around the hips and over the shoulder. Women who should travel with a male relation wear the veil. During the state of *iḥrām*, sexual intercourse, cutting of hair and nails, hunting etc. is prohibited. On the first day (7. Dhū'l-ḥijja) the pilgrims perform the *ʿumra* by circumambulating the Kaʿba seven times and kissing the black stone; then they run seven times between the slight eminences named Ṣafā and Marwā, listen to a sermon in the mosque of the Kaʿba; on 8th Dhū'l-ḥijja they visit Minā, wait a while at Muzdalifa and on the hill of ʿArafāt; the next day they listen to two sermons in Minā, and throw three times seven stones on the "cursed Satan" in Minā; after sunset they run to Muzdalifa. On the 10th Dhū'l-ḥijja, sheep or camels are offered: it is the day of the *ʿīd al-aḍḥā* in which everybody in the Muslim world who can afford it offers an animal. Afterwards the pilgrims can take off the *iḥrām*, and shave, it is recommended to spend the next days in Mina; then to put on *iḥrām* once more and perform the last circumambulation of the Kaʿba on the 13th.

According to the law only those who have enough to live and do not leave their families in debts or poverty should perform the *ḥajj*; but these rules are not always followed. It is licit to delegate somebody else if one cannot go on pilgrimage.

The caravans of the pilgrims came and still come (though in modern times journey by special pilgrim-planes is organized) from all parts of the Islamic world; the journey was often dangerous, the pilgrims threatened by robbers, famines, and epidemies, which finds its expression in the idea that somebody who dies on the *ḥajj* is considered a martyr, *shahīd*, with all his privileges.

Many pilgrims connect their pilgrimage with a visit of the Prophet's tomb in Madina; on their return they will probably bring some water from the holy well of Zamzam which had once sprung up at Hagar's prayer, or a rosary made of Meccan clay.

The mightiest ruler in the Middle-Ages, the Egyptian Sultan, would send the *maḥmal*, a palanquin, covered with precious cloth. The fact that in Mecca tens of thousands, and often hundreds of thousands of faithful from all over the world are united in the same worship wearing the same indiscernible humble dress, makes the *ḥajj* a kind of symbol of Muslim unity and brotherhood.

The mystics have spiritualized the *ḥajj*, and spoken of the importance of the "inner pilgrimage," but most of them have performed this duty not only once, but many times. Some of them lived for a certain period in the sacred environment, so that Mecca was always a center where scholars from every part of the Muslim world could meet.

b. *Magic* (*siḥr*)

Magical practices are widespred in Islamic countries. The Quran teaches that the two angels Hārūt and Mārūt have taught the people of Babylonia magic (2/96), and accordingly theologians and philosophers have discussed magic and partly explained its results as psychological facts. Popular belief has counted many of the philosophers of yore among the great sorcerers: thus Avicenna and Plato; even al-Ghazzālī has become in later traditions a master of white magic.

Different practices from old oriental lore, and from hellenistic sources have been combined with Islamic elements. White and black magic are theoretically carefully distinguished, but do differ rather in their aim than in their practices. Jugglery, too, is classified among magical operations.

It is believed that the spirits, who play a prominent role in the Quran, obey the magician who knows the necessary formulae for conjuring the respective *jinn* or angel, just as the *jinn* obeyed Solomon and carried out his orders (21/78-82; 27/15 ff.; 38/29 ff.). Thus the names of fabulous angels and of different *jinns* are frequently mentioned in the literature; each of them has peculiar features and is called for special purposes; the may appear under the shape of animals; thus friendly spirits manifest themselves in Egypt as cats ... In many cases fumigation with prescribed varieties of incense or wood is considered necessary for calling the spirits; ritual purity, and careful preparation through abstinence or purifications was considered necessary at least according to the classical sources. The sorcerers should write amulets —here, as in many cases the borders between mysticism and magic are not precisely defined; since white magic, too, can be successful only when Allah permits it. Amulets should be handwritten, but nowadays printed specimens—with pictures of the Kaʿba, surrounded by pious sentences and prayers—are even sold near to the sanctuaries. Most amulets contain Quranic verses—chosen according to the aim of the magician or the petitioner—, very frequently magical quadrates are formed of one of Allah's names, and often signs like Solomon's seal. They often consist of detached letters and numbers. A special importance is given the Greatest Name of God (cf. the works attributed to the Egyptian magician al-Būnī—d. 1225) which appears in different forms, from the simple "Allah" up to the combination of Quranic verses, letters, and the Most Comely Names.

Great is the belief in the evil eye whose power may be diverted by the use of the word *māshāʾ Allāh* "what God willeth" when admiring something, by binding blue beads to the object or person for which the evil eye is feared, or by the use of the *yad Fāṭima*, a sign or amulet made of different materials in the shape of a hand. Children are sometimes given ugly names in order to divert evil spirits from them.

Belief in astrology was current, and many scholars in the Middle Ages were experts in this science. The Quran serves for predicting future events; one may open it and decide according to the first verse one reads, or elucidate its secret meaning by a kind of kabbalistic interpretation of the letters and their numerical value. In Iran the Dīvān of Hafiz is used for telling fortunes. Other practices for these purposes are reading coffee-grounds, oil-oracle, palmistry; the magical mirror is sometimes used for finding lost things or persons. The sorcerer will prefer immature children for assisting him in his preparations, and will welcome a "sign" of the person for or against whom his magic shall be used (a handkerchief, or anything else belonging to him).

c. *Sacrifice*

The Muslim immolates an animal—preferably a sheep—at the Day of Slaughtering during the pilgrimage to Mecca; at that day not only the pilgrims but everybody who can afford it will kill a sheep at home, remembering the act of Abraham's obedience when God ordered him to sacrifice his son Ishmael.

Besides, votive offerings are made at sacred places, like tombs of saints. Every animal can be offered here; preferred are cocks and sheep. Pious Muslims may also immolate a sheep or a goat when they start building a house, at a child's birthday or for the sake of expiation.

The meat is usually distributed to the poor, or to the people living at the sacred place where the votive offering is made. In all cases the animal has to be slaughtered ritually by cutting its jugular vein and trachea with one cut.

d. *Holy Persons*

Islam does not accept any mediator between man and God. Yet, in the course of time the Prophet Muhammad has gained an extraordinary place in Muslim piety (vd. § 4, 3b). Besides him—the leader of his community in this world and the other—the members of his family (*sayyid*) enjoy special privileges. The veneration of his cousin and son-in-law ʿAlī ibn Abī Ṭālib who was considered his real heir started during ʿAlī's lifetime, though he did not care for the aura with which his admirers encircled him. He became the paramount example of heroism and wisdom; collections of verses and sentences were collected in his name, miracles ascribed to him. Some Shiʿa extremist sects, like the Nusairis and the ʿAlī-Ilāhī exaggerated his veneration to the point of endowing him with nearly Divine powers and placing him above the Prophet.—In the Shiʿite form of the *shahāda* the words "ʿAlī is the friend of God" (*ʿAlī walī Ullāh*) are added; he and his descendants, the *Imāms*, are the spiritual leaders of the community and only legitimate interpreters of the Quran. The last *imām*, though in concealment (vd. § II, p. 138) is the ruler of the age, and will return at the end of the world to fill the earth with justice as it is now filled with unjustice. In his name in Iran the laws are promulgated.

Among ʿAlī's numerous children Husain has played the most prominent role. He was killed on Muḥarram 10 (October 10) 680 at Kerbela, and this day is still a mourning day throughout the Shiʿa world; it is celebrated with processions, flagellations, even with dramatic plays representing his sad fate, and numerous poems have been written in honour of Husain's martyrdom; weeping for him opens the gates of Paradise.

The tombs of Husain and his family members in Kerbela, Najaf, Mashhad etc. are hold in highest respect by the Shiʿites; to be buried near them is the pious wish of every member of the Shiʿite ommunity.

The word *walī*, in Shiʿite circles used exclusively for ʿAlī, is the common term for "saint" in Sunnite Islam. The Quran asserts: "Verily upon the friends of Allah rests no fear, nor do they grieve" (10/63).

The word signifies originally a person who is in a cliental relation to a mightier person; according to the Mu'tazila—and also strictest orthodoxy—every one of the faithful who does his duty to God is comprised in this Quranic promise. But *walī* came soon to designate those who know God, and already in the late 9th century Tirmidhī composed his book *khatm al-wilāya* "Seal of Saintliness" which contains the theories about the mystics which were then elaborated. One speaks of a whole hierarchy of saints that has either seven or five grades: 300 *akhyār* (the best ones), forty *abdāl* (substitutes), seven *abrār* (the pious), four *autād* (the pillars, i.e. of the four corners of the world) and the *quṭb* (the Pole or axis); in the other list the *ghauth* (help) is located even higher than the *quṭb* who is the interior ruler of the world's affairs. These saints are not known to the people but know each other. If one of them dies, the member next in virtues is promoted to his place. Yet, even if the saint reaches the degree of the Pole, he cannot reach the stage of prophethood: saints are, according to the orthodox doctrine, inferior to prophets. Muhammad, however, is not only the last and greatest prophet but also the greatest saint.

The mystical leaders have been considered the most outstanding manifestations of this hierarchy of saints; several of them have even claimed to be the *ghauth* or the *quṭb*. The founders of fraternities who have influenced their disciples already during their lifetime have been made centers of public veneration after their death. They have excelled by their thaumaturgic gifts; they performed cardiagnosy, or could live at several places in the same moment, some could mysteriously produce food and drink, or convert infidels by a glance, others predict the future—innumerable are the miracles which are told about them. But these miracles are not *mu'jizat*, like those worked by the prophets, but *karāmāt*, charismata. Still in our days the reverence shown to the mystical leaders through all the strata of population is, in some parts of the Islamic world, astonishing, and the faithful still obey every hint of the master and would never contradict him, even when the teacher claims to have reached such a close relation with God that, for him, the rules of reverence are no longer valid, and he talks ruthlessly with God.

Sometimes not only the qualities of mystical leadership, the working of miracles, or the gift of winning the hearts have made a person a saint in the eyes of the people—but poor simple souls, harmless lunatics have, for some reason or the other, also often been counted among the enraptured (*majdhūb*). A large number of pious women belong, likewise, to the category of saints; in many places their shrines can be visited only by women. They have also performed miracles, but rarely played a leading political role as some of the male saints did who, thanks to their influence, sometimes inaugurated rebellious movements, or resisted the government successfully.

The most famous names among the Muslim saints from the early period are perhaps those of ʿAbdulqādir al-Gīlānī (d. 1166) in Bagdad, Aḥmad ar-Rifāʿī (d. 1175) ibid., Aḥmad al-Badawī (d. 1276) in Egypt, Maulānā Jalāluddīn Rūmī (d. 1273) in Konya, Muʿīnaddīn Chishtī (d. 1236) in Ajmer, India; but local saints enjoy likewise great popularity. The tombs of the saints, especially of the leaders of mystical orders, have become holy shrines where thousands come to beseech their blessings in time and eternity; the existence of the tomb of a deceased saint or a *sayyid*, a member of Muhammad's family, was, in some parts of the Islamic world, considered nearly indispensable for the spiritual welfare of the village.

Some saints have become famous for curing this or that disease, others are approached by barren women, again others for spiritual help, or for getting a daughter married, for passing an examination, etc. The rites which are performed here are similar to those in other religions: one lites candles (sometimes now sustituted by electric bulbs), vows certain things, like offering an animal for the poor or feeding the sacred animals which may be found near the sanctuary (fishes, tortoises, pigeons, cats, crocodiles, etc.); pieces of cloth are tied to the windows, the lattices or trees near the shrine; or a child which is born through the saint's intercession, is "sold" to the sanctuary and called with a specific name. The celebration of the *ʿurs*, the anniversary of the saint's death, is a grand popular festival in which sometimes tens of thousands of pilgrims participate. The veneration due to the deceased saint is transferred also to those who "sit on his mat" (the family who cares for the tomb), and members of saintly families still enjoy considerable privileges though orthodoxy—and especially the Wahhabites—have always refused the possibility of human intervention between man and God, and have considered the rites performed at holy shrines repugnant to the true religion.

In saint-worship—the veneration of both living and dead saintly persons—not only Muslims but also non-Muslims may partake; in India and Pakistan a number of Hindus share the love of certain mystics with the Muslims. Muslim sanctuaries have often been erected on localities which were considered sacred by the former religions, and many a Christian or Hindu religious place has been converted into the alleged tomb of a Muslim hero.

Theoretically this common worship could be defended with the excuse that the perfect mystic should have reached a stage beyond the outward forms of religion (—Islam is considered, anyway, the last and most perfect religion and comprises the others in itself—) so that the true saint is no longer confined to a particular creed. Jalāluddīn Rumi, himself the beloved saint of Turkey, has expressed this constantly repeated idea in oft-quoted lines:

> The man of God is made wise by the truth,
> The man of God is not learned from books,
> The man of God is beyond infidelity and faith,
> For the man of God right and wrong are alike.

But the fact that the saint, as close he may be to God, always remains His creature, has been summarized in the Persian couplet:

> The men of God never become God,
> But they are never separated from God.

IV. B. Ethics (*akhlāq*)

The Prophet is reported to have said: "Ethics consists in serving God as if you see Him, for even if you do not see Him, He sees you." The Quran contains a new system of ethics as contrasted to that of the pre-Islamic period, and built upon the threefold belief: in Allah, in His Judgment, and in the necessity of virtuous deeds. The pagan ideals were substituted by the ideals which God had set before the Muslim: fraternity of the faithful instead of blood-relationship; chastity instead of the indecency of which the pagans were accused (chastity does not cover the Christian meaning of the word but means a certain restriction in sexual matters); that wrong notions about Divine and semi-divine powers should give way to the certainty of belief in Allah's all-embracing power. Humility, charity towards orphans, widows and the poor, justice towards the neighbour—these are "duties to Allah" for He sees and hears and knows everything that men and women do (2/233, 237; 24/28). General exhortations in the field of ethics in the Meccan period when the threat and the promise of otherworldly life constituted the center of Muhammad's message, are found especially in Sūra 17/23-40, Sūra 25/64-75, and in the words ascribed to the wise Luqmān (Sura 31/11-17). The injunctions of the Madinan period are more concrete and give legal orders for certain cases of ethical behaviour towards one's fellow-creatures.

Even if we admit that the starting point of the Quranic ethical system was the duty to address the Arab nation in their peculiar way of life, the main aim of the Prophet was to form a new, Quranic, way of behaviour, in contrast to pre-Islamic customs.

Since the Quranic sketch of man's ideal behaviour did not contain sufficient material for a perfect code of conduct but left many questions open, the example of the Prophet was used to integrate the contents of the Quran, and the traditions about his actions and decisions were considered as a code of the standard model of ethics according to which the faithful formed their ethical behaviour. The sunna of the Prophet became the leading principle for the Muslim in every aspect of life: "Good is what the Prophet has sanctioned by his behaviour"—Western critics have put the question: "Can purely imitative conduct be ethical?"

For the first generations a discussion of the ethical qualities of the Muslim seemed necessary. Their problem was: who will be saved at Doomsday? The Khārijites, in their search for the qualities of the right leader of the community, raised the question of faith and work, and declared every Muslim who commits a grave sin an unbeliever. The Murjites, representatives of the moderate general trend in Islam, left the decision of the state of the grave sinner to God's own judgment; the Muʿtazila granted him an intermediate state: he is *fāsiq*, "wicked", neither believer nor unbeliever. Thus the question of the relation between *islām* and *īmān*, "faith", posed itself. *Islām* has sometimes been defined as the acceptance of the duties of a Muslim by confessing the words of the *shahāda*, whereas *īmān* is the acceptance of the intellectual contents of the faith and must be practised through works. The grave sinner, then, is a muslim, since he has pronounced once the confession of faith, but is not a *muʾmin*, "believer," since he does not act like one who has *īmān*. The problem whether faith can grow by actions has been discussed through centuries; the Ashʿarites answer it in the affirmative, the Ḥanafites in the negative.

On the whole the difference between grave and small sins is maintained, but "to continue in light sins makes them grave," and "no sin is grave if man asks forgiveness for it." Repentance involves the feeling of guilt, regret, and the decision not to repeat the sin. God is free to accept repentance; He need not do it but will forgive out of His immeasurable mercy.

From the ethical principles of Quran and tradition, and the legal injunctions contained therein, a legal system was developed which covered almost every aspect of human life. The *sharīʿa* reflects the ideal state as things should be, but it has never been practised in all details—the Quran says: "God wishes to make it easy for you" (2/181) which enables the jurisconsults to invent facilities in certain cases. The most typical aspect of the *sharīʿa* is that it gives every moment and every act a religious value—man must always feel himself in the presence of Allah, Who has revealed Himself through the Quranic Law.

The *sharīʿa* has never been codified; the rules and former decisions of each of the four *madhhabs* (vd. § II, p. 134) are collected, and the lawyers are bound to judge according to them. These religious judges are the *qāḍīs*; others administrated the worldly jurisdiction which sometimes was quite different from the religious law. In cases of doubt the lawyer divines (*muftī*) had to issue a decision (*fatwā*) clarifying the point in question.

The *sharīʿa* classifies every act according to five categories: commanded, approved or recommended, indifferent, disliked or condemned, and forbidden. Besides, it judges whether an act is valid or invalid. The duties can be duties of the individual (like prayer) or of the community (like attending the Friday-service). It is explicitely stated who is bound to fulfil the respective duty (*mukallaf*.)

One distinguishes between the right of God and the right of man. In cases where the right of God has been violated the judge should show as much mercy as possible. For certain crimes (adultery, murder, theft etc.) punishments are prescribed in the Quran (e.g. cutting off the hand of the thief); otherwise the penalty is left to the discretion of the judge. The talio which was usual in pre-Islamic times can be executed under governmental supervision; it is, however, preferable to pay the *diya*, blood-money.

Family law and personal law is complex. Women have been granted in the Quran a much better position than they enjoyed before; marriage is considered necessary; "it belongs to my (the Prophet's) sunna." Celibacy is not recommended; Muhammad who could satisfy his nine wives and still receive Divine revelations is higher than Jesus, the only celibate among the prophets. Polygamy is still allowed up to four wives (4/2-3) in case they are treated equally. The marriage is contracted in the name of the bride by her representative (*walī*); she has the right to refuse the proposed marriage. Certain grades of re-relationship exclude marriage. The groom has to pay a dowry in full or partly before cohabitation; if he pays only an advance the rest is to be paid at divorce; it belongs to the wife. She can also keep the money and estates which she has brought into wedlock. According to many authorities *'azl* (*interruptio coitus*) may be practised in certain cases. For divorcing his wife the man has only to pronounce the formula of *ṭalāq*. He can, however, take her back after a certain period; but after the third *ṭalāq* the woman must have been married to another man before her first husband can remarry her. Women can ask for divorce under certain circumstances; reconciliation is recommended (2/8; 128). The rules of maintaining the wife, the period of suckling and weaning in case there are small children are exactly limited.

The seclusion of women or the veil cannot be deduced from the Quran where only decent dress and behaviour are prescribed and special rules for the wives of the Prophet given; the wife has, however, to obey her husband who may punish her, and must always be at his disposal.

Adultery—i.e. sexual intercourse between persons between whom no legal bonds of marriage exist—is forbidden (4/15; 24/2 etc.); but the evidence of four male witnesses is required for punishment. If a husband kills his wife and her lover *in flagranti delicto* he is not punishable. Sodomy is likewise forbidden (though often practised in a society which excluded women largely from daily life. The object of Persian and Turkish love poetry is generally masculine).

Slavery is taken for granted in the Quran, but the human treatment of slaves is ordered, and it is highly recommended to free slaves or help them to gain money for ransoming themselves. Only prisoners of war of non-Muslim origin may legally become slaves. The situation of the slaves both in houses and in the army was, with the exception of the slave-colonies in the saltmarshes of the Iraq in the 9th century, comparatively good. A number of the later caliphs were sons of concubines; many former slaves have ruled Muslim states (Slave Kings of Delhi, Mamluks in Egypt). A difference between black and white slaves was rarely made; discrimination because of colour and race was forbidden through the Quranic order to treat every one of the faithful as a brother, notwithstanding his origin. Still, some racial prejudices are also found in Islamic history.

The complicated law of inheritance (built upon 4/8-11, 14) gives preference to the male members of the family, daughters inheriting only half of a son's share. The dying Muslim can dispose of one third of his property by bequeathing it to other than the legal heirs; during his lifetime he can distribute his property freely but not for a purpose unpleasing to God. Thus pious foundations (*waqf*) have spread over the Islamic world which are exempt from taxes and whose usufruct can remain in the family of the founder. The first regulation of debts and accounts is given in the Quran (2/281, 283). Trade law is highly developed though the taking of interest is forbidden in the Quran (2/276 ff.), nevertheless the lawyers have invented many tricks (*ḥiyal*) to evade this and similar prescriptions under the cloak of legality—typical are e.g. the hairsplitting discussions about the Quranic prohibition of wine.

The *sharīʿa* comprises also political ethics—regulation of the situation of the non-Muslims and the apostate—and of *jihād*, the only legitimate kind of war in Islam (§ II, p. 129). The problem of the right government is likewise treated in full.

The rapid change from a prophetic message to a rather narrow legalistic system is, for the outsider, surprising. He will be inclined to disdain ethics which rely upon the strict imitation of the Prophet's example and a meticulous observation of the religious law. But

> "however seriously the political and military strength of the vast Empire might have been weakened through exterior influences, the moral authority of the law was but the more enhanced and held the social fabric of Islam compact and secure through all the fluctuations of political fortune" (GIBB).

Islamic literature contains a special branch of books and treatises on ethical problems. The science of morals is considered part of practical philosophy. The term *adab*, which comprises a large literary genre describes "the noble and human tendency in the character and its manifestation in the conduct of life and social intercourse" (GOLDZIHER), and has, therefore, been connected with the representatives of various professions (secretary, physicians etc.). Ethical treatises have been translated from the Greek of Plato and Aristotle, and have been elaborated according to classical ideals by the Muslim philosophers. They hold—beginning with al-Fārābī (d. 950)—that the rules of conduct are taught by reason, and many of them describe the vices as diseases which have to be cured by proper moral treatment. The problem was discussed whether a change of character be possible at all. Ibn Sīnā (d. 1037) and his contemporary Ibn Miskawayh (d. 1030) are the most famous early authors on ethics; the handbook of the latter, *tahdhīb al-akhlāq*, has become the standard-work of its kind. He discusses the three faculties of the soul, the four cardinal virtues—wisdom, purity, courage, righteousness—with their opposites, and shows how man is to prove himself superior to the animal stage by attaining to that high type of existence for which he has potential capacity, and thus to reach perfect happiness. Similar ideas are found in the *akhlāq an-nāṣirī* written by the Shi'ite scholar Naṣīraddin Ṭūsī (d. 1233), and in the *akhlāq al-ejalālī* by Dawwānī (d. 1501), to mention only the most famous works of this kind.

Popular advice in pleasant style were written under the titles *waṣiya* (testament) or *naṣīḥat* (counsel), and the genus of *Fürstenspiegel* was a favorite type of literature. These collections often contain stories about Iranian kings, who are represented as possessing examplary qualities. The most charming combination of ethics and fine literature in Persian is perhaps Sa'dī's (d. 1292) *Gulistān*.

Other works relied upon the alleged sayings of the Prophet who had, according to them, claimed: "I have been sent to fulfil the virtues which go with nobility of character." A typical collection of such sayings is the *kanz al-'ummāl*, composed in the 16th century. Likewise the sayings and exhortations which are attributed to 'Alī ibn Abī Ṭālib and have been collected under the title *nahj al-balāgha* in the 10th century, have edified millions of Muslims since they give in most beautiful Arabic, which has made many of them proverbial, the gist of Muslim ethics: the ideals of clemency, trust in God, patience, gratitude, and it warns of lies, envy, wrath and intemperance, and excess. The right middle way between overdoing and negligence has always formed the ethical behaviour of the Muslim.

The *sharī'a* reached its final point of development about 1000, and the whole life of Muslims seemed to be bound to mechanical observance of the law. In this time the mystics, though mostly very careful in observing the God-given law, tried to revive and to deepen personal piety. The first virtue they taught their disciples was *wara'*, abstinence from everything unlawful or dubious. They tried to annihilate the bad qualities and replace them by good ones, according to the tradition "Adopt for yourselves the qualities of God." Their main aim was to act out of love, not of sheer obedience: the law is fulfilled by the heart, not by the limbs. Though some of the Sufis claimed to have reached a station where the injunctions of the *sharī'a* were no longer valid, or even sought the people's blame, they mostly clung to the word of God and the example of the Prophet as a sign of love and gratitude which they felt towards the Creator and His messenger.

Ghazzālī (d. 1111), who was trained as a theologian and philosopher, has combined orthodox legalism, philosophical argumentation and mystical experience in his work. He gives a fine psychological distinction of sins, and teaches once more the faithful to live every moment in the presence of God, and in the feeling that this world is only a preparation for the meeting of the Lord. The goal is the perfection of the soul. The *sharīʿa* orders that every act should start with the formulation of the *niya*, the intention, and this concept of *niya* has been interiorized in Sufism and is explained as the intention of the heart, an ethical concept. Thus obedience to the law was given a deeper and more ethical meaning.

Modern theologians have underlined the ethical commandments of the Quran instead of the legal ones. The responsibility of the individual, as maintained in the early sūras of the Quran, is emphasized once more, and a revaluation of human endeavour is attempted. The religious impetus, the intention in its widest sense, is now sometimes given priority over clinging to the smallest details of ritual and law which developed only in later times. For: "Legalism is inadequate to vice-gerency" (D. M. Donaldson).

Goldziher's judgment that Islamic ethics are dangerous since they tend to humilate man—be it by placing him into a narrow circle of legal prescriptions, or by teaching him the fatalistic acceptance of God's inscrutable will—seems to be too one-sided and neglects the values of the concept of intention and the practical realities of Muslim life; Tritton is right by closing his study on Islam with the words of a Hanbalite scholar:

> "(Man) sees the defects of his own character and his failures to do his duty; and this knowledge, joined to his knowledge of the Divine blessings, forbids him to hold up his head so that he comes humbly to God, begging for forgiveness."

IV. C. Doctrine

One becomes a Muslim by pronouncing the *shahāda*, i.e. by witnessing "There is no God but Allah, and Muhammad is His Messenger."

Only elements of a creed are found in the Quran, e.g. Sūra 4/135:

> "O ye who have believed in Allah and His messenger and the Book which He hath sent down to His messenger and the Book which He

sent down before; whoever disbelieves in Allah and His angels and His Books and His messengers and the Last Day, has strayed into error far."

The different formulae of creed were elaborated from the 8th century onwards in order to eliminate and restrict influences which seemed dangerous for the faith.

Man has different ways of recognizing the supernatural power: the Prophets are granted *waḥy*, revelation, either direct from God or through the mediation of an angel (mostly Gabriel); it seems that sometimes the *rūḥ al-quds*, "spirit of holiness," or simply *rūḥ* is the spirit of revelation (in case it is not to be identified with Gabriel). The most lucid description of a vision is Sūra 53 (cf. 81/23). More frequently than visions auditions occured (cf. 75/16). *Ilhām*, inspiration, is given pious and saintly persons; it is an influx of supernatural knowledge but refers only to the recipient personally and is not meant to be proclaimed. Mystics claim to discover Divine truth through *kashf*, intuition, and immediate vision, i.e. not through reason but through the "heart."—Even dreams are ascribed a certain content of truth; they are equal to one forty-sixth of Prophecy. Man has, however, to be awake to the danger of satanic or demonic insinuations (*waswās*) which may lead him astray.

According to the philosophers, revelation and philosophy were fostersisters; Ibn Ṭufail (d. 1185) has tried to show in his novel *Ḥayy ibn Yaqẓān* that naturally acquired knowledge is in perfect tune with the contents of Quranic revelation, an idea further elaborated by his successor Averroes.

a) *Angels*

The belief in angels is essential in Islam; tradition holds that they are created from light. The Quran stresses the fact that they are neither children of Allah (10/67) nor female beings (43/18). They are endowed with intelligence and can become visible; the angel-pictures in Persian miniatures show them like traditional Christian angels. Some of them are mentioned by name, like Gabriel, the angel of revelation, the "faithful spirit," or Mīkā'īl (32/11) and Israfil who will blow the trumpet at Doomsday. 'Azrā'īl is the popular name of the angel of death who is sent to everybody.

They are called armies of God (9/26, 33/9 etc.) or function as messengers. They are God's creatures and servants, praising Him day and night; some of them carry God's throne (40/7, 69/17, 4/170), nineteen of them watch over Hell (74/30 f.).—A man is always accompanied by two angels who note down his deeds (82/11, 43/80), and is protected by his guardian angels (6/61, 13/12, 50/16) who also will assist the Muslims in their battles (8/9). After the angel of death has taken a man's soul, two angels, Munkar and Nakīr, will question him in his tomb about his creed.

Man is higher than the angels, since God ordered them to prostrate before Adam which they did, except Iblīs. He, the fallen angel (in this case comparable to Hārūt and Mārūt, the two angels who taught mankind witchcraft and were seduced by a beautiful woman and then imprisoned in a well in Babylon; 2/96)—or perhaps a fire-created *jinn*—is the enemy of man whom he seduced at the beginning of time; he will be punished at the end of time (26/95; 7/178).

Some mystics have invented a strange interpretation of Satan's disobedience: he, not prostrating before anybody but God has proved the only true monotheist, the true lover of God. In modern times M. Iqbal has developed a highly interesting satanology but maintains the Quranic idea that Satan is only a servant of God who, in his turn, makes man forget his duties (6/67) or seduces him to different vices (5/92); but he has no power over the faithful (58/11, 16/102). At the beginning of a recitation of the Quran one takes refuge from him in God.

Besides the angels, Islam has different spirits, *jinn*, who are created from fire, and among whom infidels and muslims are found (Sura 72); even the problem of marriage between man and *jinn* could be discussed. *Jinn*, as well as numerous angelic beings, play an important role in Muslim folklore. Modernists, on their part, have tried to interpret the *jinn* of the Quran as bad powers, as microbes etc., and to transform the angels into spiritual powers.

b) *Revealed Books*

NATHAN SÖDERBLOM has pointed out that in the history of religions Muhammad was the first to introduce the concept of a book-religion—a differentiation of great importance for religious typology.

The Muslims accept the revelation of sacred books to some former peoples. Though the Quran itself mentions only the Tora, the Psalms, and the New Testament as divinely inspired scriptures and those who possess them as *ahl al-kitāb*, People of the Book, who must be granted protection, later generations have interpreted the Avesta and, in India, partly the Hindu scriptures in the same sense.

Muhammad was first of the opinion that he was sent to preach his people the same message as was contained in the scriptures of the Jews and the Christians, but when he discerned the differences between their scriptures and his revelations he could attribute them, according to his conception of verbal inspiration of the Quran, only to a corruption of the scriptures of those communities and their wrong interpretation. Thus the revelation which he received had to restore the pristine meaning of the Divine word; it is final and contains the most perfect solution of all questions of human life. The first revelation of the *Qur'ān* (recitation) which came to Muhammad in a cave of Mount Hira, about 610, was probably the verses which form the beginning of Sūra 96: "Recite, in the name of thy Lord..."

In short, rhyming, rhythmical expressions with strange forms of oaths and impressive imagery, the terrors of judgment were announced; then the stories of former prophets as models for Muhammad's behaviour became more elaborated in the later Meccan period. The Meccan revelations generally centre on the human qualities which are to be developed, on Divine mercy and judgment, on the marvels which God the Creator has performed and which man should acknowledge gratefully. After the *hijra* the content of the Quran becomes more practical, questions of personal status law, of international law, of ritual are touched on.

The revelations continued until shortly before Muhammad's death. Each of the verses was considered a marvellous sign (*āya*) which proved Muhammad's prophethood. The faithful learned them by heart, and partly scribbled them on whatever was at hand—papyrus, bones, pottery etc.

After the Islamic Empire had spread to the boundaries of Asia and Africa and many of the companions who knew the holy words by heart had lost their lives in battles, the third caliph 'Othmān had collected and written down the complete material; this is the form in which the Quran has been preserved without change since then. The principle was to arrange the *sūras* (chapters) according to their length, starting with the longest chapters of Madinan origin. The logical end is Sūra 112, the confession of God's unity. The first *sūra*, al-Fātiḥa, the Opening, is a kind of prayer-introduction to the whole book; its rôle in Muslim piety is even greater than that of the Paternoster in Christianity. The last two *sūras*, 113 and 114, are protecting prayers against the evil powers; they were not contained in the old redaction of Ibn Masʿūd. In spite of the official redaction produced by ʿOthmān, seven canonical ways of recitation, with very small differences, were in use during the first centuries. Since the Arabic script had, at that time, no diacritical marks for discerning among a number of consonants, the preservation of the correct text was not easy, but its authenticity was guaranteed by the oral tradition which was alive since the days of the Prophet without interruption. GOLDZIHER has shown how the constitution of the text formed in itself the first step into the interpretation the Quran.

Since the Quran is not written down according to the original sequence of revelations, the interpreters had to find out the reason for the revelation of each verse or chapter, thus locating it in approximately the correct period, which is of special importance for the question of the *nāsikh* and *mansūkh*, the verses which were cancelled by new revelations.

In Europe THEODOR NÖLDEKE has undertaken in the last century the monumental work of writing the *Geschichte des Korans*, and upon his work almost every orientalist and Quran-specialist relies. The non-Muslim asks how a change is compatible with the pre-eternity of the Divine word. Muslims often interpret it (e.g. in the verses of wine-drinking which show a more and more negative attitude towards alcoholics) as a way of slowly educating the faithful. Another problem is that of the *mutashābihāt*, the "ambiguous" verses whose meaning is understood by God alone (Sūra 3/6) which are contrasted with the obvious verses. Unsolved is also the problem of the detached letters which are prefixed to 29 *sūras*, and which have been interpreted partly as signs of the person who had written down the respective *sūra*, or to whom a collection had belonged, as abbreviations, or attributed mystical meanings. *Ṭaha*, the letters and name of Sūra 20, and *Yāsīn*, Sūra 36 (which is called the Heart of the Quran) are even used as personal names.

For Muhammad, the Quran was the word of God, the Arabic expression of what had been written since pre-eternity on the well-preserved tablet. The *umm al-kitāb* is the heavenly book which contains every Divine wisdom. It was revealed to Muhammad in visions and auditions through Gabriel. Since it is God's own word, it cannot be translated into any other language—only "integral versions" are allowed, and it must be recited in its original Arabic for ritual purposes. The attempt of introducing Turkish recitation in Turkey in 1931 proved abortive. Its stylistic beauty is unsurpassable; numerous books have been composed on the theory of *iʿjāz ul-Qurʾān*: the real miracle is that men have been prevented from imitating the Quran. Since God had revealed Himself in the words of the Quran, in Arabic tongue, everybody who embraced Islam had to learn at least enough Arabic for reciting his prayers correctly, and the Arabic script was, therefore, accepted from West Africa to Indonesia. The unifying character of the "letters of the Quran" (as a movement for writing Bengali in Arabic script is called) cannot be overrated for the development of a rather homogeneous Muslim culture.

Problems of exegesis of the sometimes contradictory passages of the Quran kindled the first theological discussions in Islam, and when the Muslims came into closer contact with Christianity the position of their Holy Book had to be clarified. The Muʿtazila, in their desire to maintain God's unity without any coeternal attributes declared the Quran created though pre-eternal. Orthodoxy, represented in this struggle by Aḥmad ibn Ḥanbal (d. 855), defended the thesis that the Quran is uncreated and co-eternal with God. This was commonly accepted, the general formula being: "What is between the two covers of the book is the uncreated Divine word." According to al-Ashʿarī the Quran is pre-existent and eternal, but its recitation is created; Bāqillānī adds to this formulation that the present arrangement of the Sūras is human work. The extreme mystical school of the Sālimīya maintained that God reads on the tongue of every reciting Muslim, and Ibn Ḥazm (d. 1054), representative of the Ẓāhirite school of thought, considered the Quran, whether written or recited, always God's own word, but paper and voice are created. I know of contemporary mystics who even think the present printed form which is in use in Turkey divinely inspired and therefore fit for kabbalistic interpretations, and others who deny that the Quran can be treated according to the rules of Arabic grammar...

The Quran was interpreted from early times. The careful collecting of all available informations about every act and fact mentioned in the Quran, and the philological analysis of its words and expressions led to a large science of its own. Ṭabarī's commentary, in 30 volumes, comprises the whole knowledge of the first three centuries. The Muʿtazila tried to explain away the anthropomorphisms of the Quranic text; the *tafsīr* of Zamakhsharī (d. 1144), though of Muʿtazilite inclinations, has been considered one of the most important commentaries of the Holy Book. Those of ar-Rāzī (d. 1209) and al-Baiḍāwī (d. 1291) are indispensable for research. Still the number of commentaries, representing the different currents inside Islam, is growing.

The Shiʿa has always maintained that the correct interpretation of the Quran can be given exclusively by the Imām of the time, and in the Bāṭinīya group inside the Shiʿa, the Qarmathians, Ismāʿīlīya etc. a special introduction into the different esoteric meaning of each verse, according to the spiritual capacity of the adept, was practised.

We may assume with L. Massignon that early Sufism developed from an intense meditation of the Quran, and it is among the mystics that the veneration of the Quran reached its first summit, though their methods of spiritual interpretation sometimes yielded strange results. Already Sahl at-Tustarī (d. 896) was sure that the Quran is *dhū wujūh*, "having many facets" and is, essentially, inexhaustible—

> "just as God has no end, thus the understanding of His word has no end; the word of God is uncreated and the reason of created beings is not capable of understanding it completely"—

the same idea is found to-day with M. Iqbal when he praises the "world of Quran with its always newly unfolding possibilities": the Quran rules the times, and has medicine for every time and every need.

Massignon is thus perfectly right in saying that

> "this religious codex is the only lexicon which is given to the faithful in Islamic countries, the fundamental textbook of his sciences, the key of his *Weltanschauung*."

Out of the study of the Quran the different sciences—like history and geography, and especially philology—emerged; its meditation was an important factor in the growth of Sufism; in order to write it in a way worthy of the Divine word the calligraphers invented the finest styles: from the Kufic Qurans of old to the magnificent large Qurans of the Middle Ages or the intricate laces of Quranic verses in religious buildings we find everywhere signs of the reverence which was shown to this book which must not be touched, or recited, by a person in state of pollution (56/79). As a sign of respect the Quran is put on the highest place in the house. The faith in its power often manifests itself in the use of Quranic verses as protecting spells, as charms—small tablets with Quranic verses are hung over the conjugal bed, placed into motorcars for protection. To recite certain verses brings heavenly reward: whoever repeats the throne-verse (2/256) every evening three times will gain a house in Paradise. The Quran is used as an oracle book as well.

Every recitation of the Quran is started with the words "I take refuge in God from the "stoned" Satan," and the formula "In the name of God the Merciful the Misericordious" which is written at the beginning of each *sūra*. To learn the Quran by heart, to become a *ḥāfiẓ*, is most meritorious; children (girls as well), when intelligent enough, begin at the age of five or seven with learning the Quran. For facilitating the memorization, the Quran has been divided into 30 parts (*juz'*); the pupil starts with the last *juz'* (called *juz' 'ammā* according to the first word of Sūra 78, the last *sūra* of this part) which contains the shortest *sūras* which are needed for prayer, and then proceeds towards the longer *sūras*. Its recitation according to the rules of *tajwīd* requires special skill. In non-Arabic countries literal understanding is not required; the word in itself is holy, and the recitation of the Quran is the real—and essentially only!—means of getting into immediate contact with God—"Who reads the Quran is as if he talks with Me and I talk with him" says a *ḥadīth qudsī*.

Typical of the high estimation of the Quran is a prayer spoken at the end of the recitation of the whole Quran (which is often completed during the Ramaḍān, or at other religious occasions, for the welfare of a deceased person, in fulfilling a vow etc.):

> "O God, make us enter Paradise through the intercession of the Quran, and heal us from every affliction of the world and the pain of the other world through the honour of the Quran. O God, make the Quran a friend in this world and a companion in the grave, an intercessor at Doomsday and a light on the Bridge, a companion in Paradise and a veil and cover before the Fire, and a leader and *imām* towards everything good ..." etc.

We may compare the place of the Quran in the religious system of Islam to that of Christ in Christianity: it is the revelation of God in time and space.

Besides the Quran, some words ascribed to Allah are found in the so-called *ḥadīth qudsī*, not to be confused with the normal *ḥadīth* about the words and actions of the Prophet which became, as a kind of integration of the Quran, binding to a very large extent on the community. Bukhārī's (d. 870) collection of 7 000 traditions—chosen out of 60 000—was considered second only to the Quran.

c. *Prophets*

God has never left mankind without prophets—to proclaim His unity and urge people to act righteously; it is His custom to send messengers (16/38). The stories of 28 of them are told or alluded to in the Quran, and in detail worked out by popular piety and pious writers like Thaʿlabī (d. 1035) in his *qiṣaṣ al-anbiyā*ʾ. Orthodoxy endows every prophet with four necessary qualities—truthfulness, fidelity, the propagation of his message, and intelligence; it is impossible that he should lie, falsify his message or hide it, nor can he be stupid. He can, however, be exposed to human accidents. Part of the prophets introduced new laws, others have repeated the message of their predecessors. They are to a greater or lesser extent endowed with *ʿiṣma*, immunity from error and sin.

The number of prophets is known only to God; that is why in modern theology historical founders of religions not mentioned in the Quran—like the Buddha, Zoroaster, Laotse—can be acknowleged as divinely inspired messengers to their respective peoples.

The line of the prophets starts with Adam (vd. § V, A). The island of Ceylon and Mt. ʿArafāt near Mecca are connected in legends with his earthly life.

Noah (Nūḥ) and his family are mentioned among the prophets; Abraham (Ibrāhīm) son of Azar discovered through his contemplation of nature the One Creator: "I do not love those who disappear," i.e. the natural phenomena (6/76); in the Medinan period he is predominantly the destroyer of the idols, the builder of the Kaʿba, the ancestor of the Arabs (2/118, 3/60 etc.). His son who was to be offered is, according to the Quran, Ishmael, not Isaac (2/130); Joseph, whose story—"the most beautiful story"—fills the whole of Sūra 12 is the model of wisdom (interpreter of dreams) and beauty; the story of Potiphar's wife's love for him forms a favorite subject of Islamic poetry.—

Moses (Mūsā), the man to whom God spoke (*kalīmullāh*), who showed the miracle of the White Hand, who led his people through the Red Sea, is frequently mentioned in the Quran as the examplary religious and political leader. To him a strange story is attributed—he wandered with an unknown wise man who is identified by later tradition with Khiḍr, the immortal saint of wandering and seafaring people, and was blamed for his indecent questions.—David, famous for his beautiful voice, and Sulaimān (Solomon), the wise ruler who knew the language of the animals and was served by the *jinn*, are prophets. Yūnus (Jonah), swallowed by the fish and mysteriously saved, is a consoling example for Muhammad midst of his unbelieving people. Essentially almost all the stories about prophets of old, included the non-biblical names of Ṣāliḥ of the Thamūd and Hūd of the ʿĀd, tend to strengthen Muhammad by telling him that his predecessors in the prophetic duty had been likewise denounced by their peoples who, in their turn, had to suffer painful punishment for their disobedience. "The persons derive their value and function from their place in the kerygma of Muhammad's preaching" (BAKKER)—that is a typical aspect of the Quranic picture of history.

Jesus (ʿIsā) is given a special place in the Quran. His story and that of his mother—who has not been touched by Satan, and is considered one of the four best women in the world—is told several times (3/31, 42; 19). The virgin birth is accepted; ʿIsā is called the *masīḥ* "Christos," and is "a spirit from Allah" since God breathed from His breath into Mary. But he is not God's son, which would be incompatible with God's unicity; the dogma of the Trinity is rejected with full energy (in 5/116 Mary seems to be considered the third person of the Trinity). He performed miracles, like quickening the dead and healing the sick, and is portrayed in later traditions as an ascetic who wanders through the world without having a place to lay his head. The Quran denies his crucifixion; rather somebody "was made in his likeness" (4/156) and he himself was taken up by God immediately, and will return shortly before Doomsday (43/61). According to the Ahmadiya sect, ʿIsā migrated to Kashmir and is buried in Srinagar.—Since Islam rejects the concept of aboriginal sin, there is no necessity of Christ's redeeming death.

The Muslim can accept messengers to different peoples provided they have taught before Muhammad, who is the last prophet in the long line, the "Seal of Prophecy", after whom no other messenger will be sent. He has completed the religion (9/6), and has once more preached the pure doctrine which all his prophetic predecessors had promulgated before. He did not claim any divine qualities but is a human being who proclaimed what was revealed to him. Likewise he denied possession of miraculous powers—his only miracle is the Quran which he has received and transferred to his Arabic countrymen.

The Quran itself tells the Prophet "Did we not find thee in error and led thee?" (93/7)—a verse which caused controversy: how could he be in error even before being called to his prophethood? Later theology defends his *ʿiṣma* as a sign of divine blessing (in Shiʿa doctrine: his attribute). Similarly Sūra 94/1: "Did we not open thy breast..." which seemingly alludes to the moment of inspiration was, later on, sometimes interpreted in a literally sense, angels taking out the heart of the child Muhammad and washing it...

In course of time, the person of Muhammad gains more and more momentum in the Quran. He was sent *raḥmatan lil'ālamīn* (21/107), as a mercy for the world: that would imply the all-embracing character of his message. The assertion that God and His angels repeat blessings over Muhammad (33/56) has led the Muslims to pronounce a formula of blessing whenever his name is mentioned or written as well as at the end of the ritual prayer. This is meritorious and protective: "God prays ten times for him who says once the blessings over Muhammad," runs a later tradition.

Since to obey Muhammad means to obey God (8/20), the example of the Prophet has become binding for the Muslims, even in the most insignificant details of outward behaviour. That is why many customs, like wearing a beard, using only the right hand in eating, or the preference for certain food, the abstention from certain colours, the minutiae of ritual, are faithfully modelled among the orthodox even today according to Muhammad's example. The *imitatio Muhammadi* is the ideal for the Muslim because it makes him feel secure—but it is an imitation of work and actions contrary to the *imitatio Christi* which consists in the acceptance of suffering, as A. Abel has shown.

No doubt that Muhammad, prophet and statesman, never considered himself anything but a servant of God. But the pious did not hesitate in attributing him higher faculties. Already the traditionist Tirmidhī (d. 883) collected the *shamā'il al-muṣṭafā*, traditions about the good and marvellous qualities of the Prophet. The literary category *dalā'il an-nubuwwa*, about miracles and high qualities of the Prophet, was especially cultivated in the 11th century. In many a Muslim home one still finds a nicely written *ḥilya*, the description of the Prophet's qualities— standing for what would be in a Christian house a picture of Christ.

The few Quranic allusions to miraculous advents in Muhammad's life were soon worked out in detail. The Night-journey (17/1)—probably a visionary flight to Jerusalem—and the Prophet's *mi'rāj*, his ascension into the Divine presence (celebrated on Rajab 27) were described in detail and became models for numerous mystical works in which the mystics took the Prophet's ascension as prototype of their own spiritual experiences.

Many legends have been woven around his birth—details are similar to the legends of the birth of the Buddha or Christ—and the art of composing touching poems in honour of Muhammad's birthday has been popular since at least the 11th century in all Islamic languages. The simple *maulūd* of Suleyman Çelebi (d. 1429 in Bursa) is still frequently recited all over Turkey, moving the listeners often to tears. The story of Muhammad's birth tells that a light was shining on his father's forehead—a hint to the doctrine of the *nūr Muḥammadī*, the pre-eternal light of Muhammad which illuminated the chain of prophets. Mystics and Shiʿite groups have elaborated this idea which is now a common place in mystical folk-poetry.

Muhammad was, then, considered the *insān kāmil*, the Perfect Man, and turned into a kind of mediator between the human and the Divine, partaking of both "as twilight partakes in day and night." The tradition "I was a Prophet when Adam was still between water and clay" is, with the mystics, as popular as the *ḥadīth qudsī* in which God addresses His beloved Prophet saying "If thou werest not I would not have created the spheres." Mystical poetry has praised his wonderful qualities, from Būṣīrī's (d. 1295) oft-commented and translated *burda* to the simple folksongs in Indian regional languages. In his love peasant, scholar, and mystic are united.

In later mystical fraternities the goal of the mystic becomes the unification with the Prophet, and a whole scale of prophetic levels which the adept has to pass before reaching the last one, that of Muhammad, has been elaborated. The superior qualities of the Prophet are as well contained in his name which is full of power (*baraka*), and it has been discussed whether a child should be called by this name (for the sake of *baraka*) or whether the name is too holy for being given to ordinary men; the former convinction, however, has prevailed.

For the common people, who imbibe from childhood the stories about the marvellous Prophet, Muhammad is still, above all, the *shafīʿ*, the intercessor at Doomsday who will intercede for his community and will save the faithful from hellfire. This intercession—though not completely compatible with the Quranic teaching—has been, for centuries, Muhammad's most important aspect for many simple souls.

The fact that Muhammad's real historical personality had been covered during the ages by a veil of legends, and the critical attitude of Western writers towards the founder of Islam incited the Muslims during the last century to rewrite once more the biography of Muhammad. His life was investigated according to early Muslim sources, and since AMEER ALI's *Spirit of Islam*, 1892, numerous new biographies have been written in all parts of the Muslim world, partly by using modern psychological analysis for explaining miracles like the Ascension. Now Muhammad gains not only religious but political or social importance as well; he is the first to organize his community, to introduce just social measures, to create international law, to promulgate the equality of races, etc. He is, further, the symbol of Muslim unity whose veneration all believers share. Even the slightest attempt not to recognize him as the final messenger would bring a group outside the pale of orthodox Islam—that is why the Ahmadiya has been attacked so vehemently by the Orthodox.

The statement of W. C. SMITH that the second half of the *shahāda—Muḥammadun rasūl Allāh*—is "a statement about God's activity and Muhammad's function" is true—; even to-day the person of the Prophet is considered by the faithful the expression of God's greatest mercy towards mankind: i.e. to send His messenger with the final revelation of His will.

d. *About the belief in the Day of Judgment vd. V D* 4

e. Later creeds add that belief is also required of the fact that good and evil come both from God.

V. CONCEPTION OF MAN

A. *Creation*

According to the Quran, the world was created at a certain moment. This creation was, as is commonly accepted, due to Allah's inscrutable will; according to the Mu'tazila, due to His wisdom; according to earlier, respective later, mystics due to His love, or His wish for self-manifestation: "I was a hidden treasure and wanted to be known, so I created the world". The philosophers assumed that the world is a product of pure thought, eternally existent with God, and creation the actualization of the potentially existent.

Sometimes the difference between *amr* (Commandment) for the creation of spiritual substances, and *khalq* for the creation of material substances is made (vf. 17/85).

It seems that the last being to be created in this world was man.

The Quran tells the creation of the first man, Adam, in a comparatively late period after having described several times the creation of the individual from a sperm— "a drop of liquid"—in the mother's womb. The first revelation, Sūra 96, highlights this marvellous event.

Meditation of the fact that God is the creator of every child and watches, from the moment of its conception, each of its movements, and forms it, should make man thankful to this wise and mighty Creator.

According to some descriptions in the Quran one may gain the impression that everything on earth has been created for serving mankind—*lakum* "for you": the soil produces herbs, crops, animals, the sea carries the ships, camels and sheeps bring forth their offspring so that man may use them. One has even spoken of an anthropocentric *Weltbild* of the Quran (D. BAKKER). The high rank of man which is evident from these expressions, is alluded to, in a mythological form, in the story about Adam's creation (2/28; 15/29; 32/8; 48/71 etc.). The angels objected to Adam's creation, but God formed him from clay and water in a most beautiful form (64/3) and breathed from His spirit (*rūḥ*) into him; then He made the angels bow down before this creature which, endowed with this spirit, was to become Allah's vice-gerent, *khalīfa*, on earth, and has, in this capacity, to carry out His orders in time and space.—God has complete authority over man since without Him he would be non-existent (53/45). Man is given and taught everything by this Creator—when the Quran says "He taught Adam the names" (2/31) it means that he gave him power over the things, since to know the name of something means to possess power over it. Since God is the wise, merciful and powerful Creator of man, the most important duty of humanity is to show gratitude to Him, not only in words of praise but in absolute obedience to His commandments. As the Quran says "We have created men and *jinn* only for adoration" (51/51).

The famous verse (7/171) when God addresses the human race asking them "Am I not your Lord" (*alastu birabbikum*) and they answer "Yes, we witness it!" has been explained by most of the commentators, and especially the mystics, as an allusion to a pre-eternal covenant of God with the future generations who will, at Doomsday, be reminded of having accepted already before their creation in time the absolute sovereignty of their Lord.

B. *Nature of man*

The human being is considered as consisting of body and a spiritual element; however theologians, mystics and philosophers have given different definitions. The *nafs*, soul, is mostly defined as the animal soul, that lower spiritual part which incites evil, with the mystics often comparable to the Christian notion of the "flesh"; but it can as well denote man's self. The Quran speaks of the *nafs ammāra bi'ṣ-sū'* (12/53) "the soul which incites evil," the *nafs lawwāma* (77/2) the "blaming soul" (which may roughly correspond to the conscience) and the *nafs muṭma'inna* (89/72), the "soul at peace" which is the highest spiritual stage man can reach on earth.—The *rūḥ*, translated generally as "spirit," originating with Allah and animating the human body (15/29; 38/72 a.o.), is thought to be a subtle body located somewhere in the gross body or penetrating it completely. That it is a body is maintained by orthodox and mystics. Sometimes the term is exchangeable with *nafs*.

'Aql, "reason" (intellect) is an other important spiritual factor in man. Through reason man can know what is right and wrong; it is an incorporeal and incorruptible substance different in kind from the soul.—The mystics have ascribed more importance to the *qalb*, "heart," the medium of attaining direct knowledge of God, and have sometimes juxtaposed "satanic" reason and loving heart. The *sirr* is, with them, the innermost core of the heart. The ideas of the most important philosopher, Ibn Rushd, about the human faculties have been summarized by TRITTON as follows:

> "The intellect is distinguished from the soul, it is abstract and exists only when it is united with the Universal Active Intellect; in man it is only a possibility of receiving ideas from the active intellect. The soul is the motive power which causes life and growth; it is the form to the matter of the body. It remains as an individual after the death of the body."

Sufism has seen in man the most beloved creation of God, formed "in God's image" (*'alā ṣūratihi*), as the tradition says. From neoplatonic speculations the idea was borrowed that the soul had fallen from its eternal home into a world of wilderness and must strive to become re-united with the eternal source of its existence. Later mysticism has developed the idea of the *insān kāmil*, the Perfect Man (who is represented by the Prophet Muhammad) who constitutes not only the reflection of Divine Beauty but a microcosmos in which all the Divine attributes are united, according to Ibn 'Arabī: "We ourselves are the attributes through which we describe God." The human heart corresponds to the Divine Throne, his reason to the Pen, his spirit to the well-preserved Tablet. Still, the feeling that Lord remains Lord and servant remains servant was always alive even among the mystics.

Islamic modernism has again emphazised the high rank of man which had partly fallen into oblivion under the influence of political, theological, and mystical stagnation and overstressed fatalism (vd. § V C).

C. *Destiny*, *Path of salvation*

Man—even the Prophet—is, in the Quran, called *ʿabd*, servant; however this servantship is a high rank since it means a close connection with the wise and omnipotent Lord, submission to Whose will (*islām*) is the meaning and end of human life. The numerous personal names consisting of *ʿabd* plus one of the Most Beautiful Names (ʿAbdulkarīm, ʿAbdulmalik etc.) hint at this idea.

Man is, according to an oft-quoted tradition, distinguished as the *ashraf ul-makhlūqāt*, the noblest of creatures; everybody is born as a Muslim, and only the parents may turn the child away by making him a Jew or Christian. Though Adam and Eve lent their ear to the temptation of Satan and ate from the forbidden fruit and were consequently expelled from Paradise, their sin is not contagious; thus Islam knows no need for redemption. But man is forgetful of the goodness of His Lord, and often wrongs himself by evil deeds (6/22, 27/45), of which he can, however, repent (vd. § II, 2).

Men and women are created likewise, and though man is considered more responsible than woman, both have to fulfil the same ritual obligations. The Quran often speaks of faithful and believing men and women (*muʾminūn wa muʾmināt*), and in the Medinan period *al-muḥsināt min an-nisāʾ* (the well-doing women) are mentioned several times. Only later the situation of women deteriorated.

Both sexes are bound to offer "prayer and alms" which double obligation marks, in the Quran, the essentials of the Muslim community, besides the *shahāda*.

Though the question of the relation between faith and actions was discussed (cf. § II, 2) in early Islam, the common view was expressed by calling the Muslims *ahl al-qibla*, those who pray in direction towards Mecca. Membership in this community, according to the nonextremist theologians, leads man to Paradise. Even if a Muslim commits a sin he can still be forgiven; but he ceases to belong to the community in a spiritual sense as soon as he denies that the injunctions of the Quran are of Divine origin and therefore eternally binding. As long as he recognizes this binding character of the Divine Law he must be recognized as Muslim.

The Shiʿa theology requests from the faithful to acknowledge the *imām* of his time; otherwise he will die an unbeliever. The Ismāʿīlīya instruct the soul to become united with the Hidden Imam and thus partake in salvation.

In how far outward signs—like circumcision, which is not mentioned in the Quran—are necessary for the real membership in the Muslim community is open to dispute.

The normal path of salvation for the Muslim is, thus, to follow the commands of God and the example of His messenger, and to obey the laws which have been integrated in the *sharīʿa*—the "highway."

Beside the broad street of the *sharīʿa* leads the Path (*ṭarīqa*) of mysticism which aims at educating the adepts by psychological methods teaching them the *itinerarium mentis ad Deum*. Here the adept is taken into the order by a special initiation which has effected the ritual of the guilds and other corporations, and may have been influenced, in its turn, by the initiation rites of the esoteric Shiʿa sects. The mystical leader is sometimes compared to the physician who helps the affected soul by leading it through the different grades (patience, trust in God, gratitude) of subduing the lower faculties to the heights of mystical knowledge or love—so that the heart, being polished by exercises from the stain of lower qualities can reflect the Divine beauty. The mystical leader (*shaykh*, *pīr*) is indispensable for the process of purification; who has no guide, is led astray by the Satan. Complete surrender "like the dead in the hand of the washer" under the leader is required. Though the possibility of enrapturement was admitted an orderly process in the Path was preferred which might lead the adept through the different stages of the prophets—thus following the example set by Muhammad in his ascension to Heaven—until he becomes united with the *ḥaqīqa Muḥammadīya*, or he may go through the illumination of the names, the illumination of the attributes until he reaches, perhaps, the illumination of the Essence. He may experience on his path vision of lights, and be able to perform miracles but should not be tempted by them to remain on his present station.

The permanent control through the mystical leader of the soul's progress proved helpful also for the many who did not attempt at higher mystical stages.

The main problem for the Muslim is, however, the compatibility of Allah's will and human freedom, of predestination and responsibility. Could the obedience to the *sharīʿa*, even if executed with utmost scrupulosity, or the adherence to a spiritual path, or the intercession of his beloved Prophet save the believer—if God is free to do whatever He willeth? The problem of will and predestination has been discussed since the first century of Islamic history.

The Quran takes, in its earlier parts, freedom of will for granted—otherwise there would be no meaning in man's being summoned at Doomsday when his deeds will become apparent. Other Quranic verses, especially in the later revelations, speak rather of God's omnipotence which could even be interpreted as arbitrary power. Does God indeed lead astray mankind, or does He rather leave them without guidance in the desert of error when they turn their ears from His repeated call? Is He going to judge everybody according to his actions, as the Quran has asserted frequently, or will He punish and reward man according to His will and whim, or to a pre-eternal decree, notwithstanding his present attitude? The ambiguity of the Quranic expressions gave room, in the Omayyad period, both for the strict predestinarian attitude of the Jabrīya, and for the defense of human responsibility by the Qadarīya. The Muʿtazila defended human free will and God's perfect justice, whereas the mediating formula was pronounced by al-Ashʿarī (d. 935): God creates in man the will to act and the act, and man acquires the act by performing it (*iktisāb*).

Nevertheless the notion of the overwhelming Majesty of God Whose power is visible even in afflictions, and Whose wisdom cannot be questioned, made man feel so insignificant before Him that he no longer attributed any free activity to himself; in monistic mysticism, on the other hand, there was no room for independent human action left. The virtue of trust in God was overstressed and led to a deeply fatalist attitude in Muslim countries—which was, in a time of political disasters, perhaps the only way of surviving. The Muslim's belief in *qismat* "what has been allotted," should, however, not be confused with a purely passive acceptance of a blind impersonal fate; the faithful have always the feeling that God, Who knows best what is good for His creatures, has ordered this or that event according to His eternal wisdom, and "Praised be He whatever happens."

Modernists have rediscovered the idea of responsibility which is required in the modern active world. Again Muhammad Iqbal has, in his theory of higher fatalism, emphazised the role of man as vice-gerent of God; he is called to work as God's collaborator in ameliorating the world, and should develop his spiritual capacities to the utmost limits. The verse Sūra 33/72 which speaks of the burden which God offered heaven and earth and the mountains and they refused to carry it, but man accepted it (which former generations have interpreted as the burden of obedience, or burden of Love) is, with Iqbal, the burden of individuation with all its possibilities and inherent dangers. Man's spiritual life should be developed to such an extent that his will becomes uniform with God's will, that he may feel he has changed God's decree since he himself has been changed through the Divine power.

The essentials of the anthropology of Islam can, perhaps, be condensed in the simple sentence: man has been created by the wise and omnipotent Lord, and, in acknowledging this truth, he has to prove his gratitude by obeying the God-given laws—then he will not go astray and will follow the right path for which he prays many times a day by reciting the first Sūra:

> "Guide us to the straight path, the path of those upon Thou hast bestowed good, not of those upon whom anger falls, or those who go astray."

D. *Personal and General Eschatology*

The belief in the Day of Judgment is considered essential for the Muslim (4/135).

Muhammad was, in the beginning, overwhelmed by the idea of a judgment which was expected any day, and his preaching is, in the first period, almost exclusively concerned with eschatological problems. The horrible day when everybody will have to face God, the Judge, and will see what he has done, is called by different names. To neglect preparation for death (*ghafla*) is considered a grave sin.

The attitude of moderate orthodoxy seems to be condensed best in the last book of al-Ghazzālī's *Iḥyā 'ulūm ad-dīn* about the signs of death and resurrection. This whole work can be considered a *vademecum* for the right way of life, and that means the right preparation for the day when man will be summoned to the presence of his Lord. For "a this world is only the sowing-field for the other world" where its harvest will be reaped.

Muhammad's fellow-citizens mocked at the possibility of a corporeal resurrection. In order to clarify this problem the Quran brought forth different proofs for the resurrection: 1) God Who has created the world from nothing can easily bring together the scattered parts of men for judging them; 2) the desert which looks completely barren and dead in summer is quickened by the rain—thus the bodies which have become dust will be quickened; 3) the growing of each individual from a single drop of sperm in his mother's womb is not less wonderful than the resurrection. Further: the smaller judgments which have afflicted former peoples who distrusted their messengers hint at the horrible end the unbelievers will find.

The Quranic sayings about the Last Things have been commented upon and enlarged both by theologians and by popular preachers so that a whole literature of more or less mythological character has developed around the question of death, resurrection, and Doomsday.

When a person dies, i.e. when ʿAzraʾīl, the angel of death who is sometimes imagined with 4000 wings, is about taking his soul (softly from the believer, cruelly from the infidel) (8/52), the *shahāda* (confession of faith) is whispered into the dying person's ears because one believes—without Quranic support—that the dead are questioned in their tombs about their faith by Munkar and Nakīr, two terrible angels of blackish colour. Only martyrs (*shahīd*) will enter Paradise immediately (3/163); their corpses are, contrary to the general use, not washed before burial. The category of martyrs which comprised in the beginning only those who have been killed for the sake of religion has been enlarged in later times. According to later traditions they are living in the craws of green birds around the Divine throne—green being the paradisiacal colour.

The Quran gives no details about man's situation in the tomb; the expression *barzakh*, barrier, which occurs several times (25/55; 55/19; 23/102) has been interpreted as both temporal and local, a kind of barrier between the corporeal world and the spiritual world which hinders the dead from returning. It was, later on, sometimes considered a kind of purgatory.—According to the ruling opinion both the faithful and sinners have in their graves already a foretaste of the eternal joy or pain which they will feel after the Day of Judgment, and a tradition says "The grave is one of the pleasure grounds of Paradise or one of the caves of fire." The question how far children are punished or rewarded, (and, if they are able to answer the questions of Munkar and Nakīr), has been answered differently, but mostly the children of Muslims are thought to be taken immediately to a pleasant station of the other world.

Before the Last Day the powerful giants Yajūj and Majūj will appear (18/99; 21/96); later traditions describe the one-eyed Dajjāl whose arrival will bring terror and fear over the people of the earth.

The Christ will appear once more on earth (developed from 43/61), clean the world and kill the swine. The Mahdī, the Guided One, not mentioned in the Quran, has played during Islamic history a very important role, especially in Shiʿa environment: though some people consider Jesus the Mahdi most of the theologians held that he must come from the family of the Prophet. In Shiʿa creed it will be the last of the Imāms who is now in hiding. Under the pretext of being the promised Mahdi, many political leaders have tried to gain power; suffice it to mention the Mahdī of Jawnpur who incited an eschatological movement in India in the end of the 15th century, and, more commonly known, the Mahdī of the Sudan who was defeated by Lord Kitchener (1885). The figure of the Mahdī has, however, never been as prominent in orthodox theology as it was in popular piety.

At the moment of the beginning of Doomsday, Israfil will blow his trumpet, and everybody will die, and then be revived. The excitement, the fear and trembling and the complete confusion of this moment has become proverbial in Islamic languages. Allah comes down with His angels (2/106), and mankind will be gathered in front of Him and the angels (25/24).—The eschatological scenes are shown in different order, though it is the duty of the faithful to believe in all of them as being real. Man's deeds are judged according to the books (17/15); this seems to be the book in which the two angels have noted down man's good and bad deeds, and which is given into man's right hand if he was righteous, or it is hung around his neck.

Of equal importance are the balances—"And just balances will We set up for the day of the resurrection" (21/48; cf. 18/105 7/7, 23/105); but there are some differences of opinion whether the persons themselves, the book of their deeds or the deeds are being weighed.

The bridge which leads over the Fire is mentioned only twice in the Quran (37/23; 7/44); tradition has described it as sharper than a sword and thinner than a hair so that the infidels who have to pass it will immediately fall into the fire, whereas the faithful will passit with ease.

After the judgment has taken place the infidels will be dragged away by their feet and "the lying sinful forelock" (55/41), putting on garments of pitch (14/51) or of fire (22/20) to be punished in Hell.

Hell, sometimes imagined as a terrible monster, is described as filled with fire and stinking water, and awful trees with poisonous fruits grow there. Angels are made its supervisors. Tradition and popular tales have stuffed the Quranic information with rich mythological material.

Paradise is the place of joy and bliss, of lovely gardens with streams of milk and wine (47/16; 55/54; 56/15), with beautiful tents where charming damsels (*ḥūr*, "black-eyed") who always remain virgins abide. The blessed are dressed in silken garments (18/30; 22/38; 35/30; 76/21). The Quran speaks of the *kauthar* (108/1), which is sometimes interpreted as abundance, or as a well in Paradise; besides, there is the *salsabīl* (76/18), again a stream or fountain of heavenly bliss. The commentators have made many attempts of locating these places and the different stages of Heaven and Hell whose names occur without apparant order in the Quran, and even in our days a complete topography of Heaven and Hell has been produced in Turkey.

Paradise is the abode of every faithful Muslim, man, woman, or child (4/123; 9/73; 43/70); as to the ḥūrīs whose charm and beauty popular phantasy has described with never-ending repetition, they are considered in an old Prophetic tradition "the old pious blear-eyed women" who have turned young once more. The idea that women are almost completely excluded from Paradise belongs to the later theological development. The educated classes have been interested in the spiritual side of Paradise: there will be no idle talk, but the highest bliss will be the *visio beatifica*: "that faces beamed with light looking towards their Lord" (75/22). The Muʿtazila has rejected the possibility of the *visio beatifica* in Paradise relying upon Sura 6/103 "Sight reacheth Him not," whereas orthodoxy has not hesitated even to give details of this hoped-for vision of the Almighty.

The question was posed whether or not the punishments of Hell are eternal. According to several verses of the Quran (2/76, 11/108) they are, and thus the orthodox creed (cf. Fiqh Akbar II) has acknowledged. Heaven and Hell are created, but they will never cease to exist. The Muʿtazila agreed with this view but Ibn Taimīya denied the eternity of Hell, reasoning from Sūra 11/109: "those who are damned come in to Hellfire therein to abide as long as the heaven and the earth remain except as the Lord pleaseth" that God's decree and His will can finish the existence of Hell and release the damned. Against the Muʿtazila for whom Hell was the necessary expression of God's justice the Ashʿarīya believed in the possible working of Divine mercy. Qastallānī relied upon the Quranic word that "everyone upon it (in the world) is passing away but the face of God" (55/16). Thus a tradition could be invented "Verily a time will come when the gates of Hell will be slippery, and cress will grow on its floor."

Nevertheless the general conviction was that the infidels will be eternally in Hell (2/75, 214). But what would happen to a sinner from among the Muslim community? According to Sūra 19/60 everybody must go to Hell, which is interpreted in the sense that every soul has at least to pass by, but no believer will remain there for ever. The verses in Sūra 7/44 ff., which describe *al-aʿrāf* as a kind of wall or purgatory where a certain group of persons abids who will enter neither Paradise nor Hell, could suggest that there were a special place for the sinners from Muhammad's community, but the interpretations are not clear about this point.

About the final destiny of man contradictory sayings are found in tradition and theology. Orthodoxy would claim that God is free to punish the faithful whether they be guilty of sins or not, or to grant them forgiveness. The exact counterpart of this idea is the Muʿtazilite view that God "must" even give animals which have suffered here an otherworldly compensation.

The community gained hope and trust through the idea of intercession at Doomsday. Essentially the Quran does not accept this concept (2/45; cf. 10/19, 39/45); but in a later period of revelation Muhammad was mentioned as intercessor of his community, and in orthodox creeds his intercession was accepted as an undoubtable reality and a part of faith. Once in the Quran angels are thought to be intercessors (40/7); the general view is that Muhammad may intercede for his community, and the other prophets for their respective communities; in Shiʿa circles it is the imām, among the mystics the great saints or mystical leaders who may intercede for those who believe in them; we also find the personified Quran, the martyrs, and at last every faithful Muslim may intercede for his friends—which is far from the Quranic statement that at that day no soul will carry another's burden. Anyhow, the famous throne-verse (2/256) with the words "Who will intercede before Him except by His permission?" opened the doors to these later developments. Nowadays in popular piety Muhammad is in the first place loved and venerated as *shafīʿ*, intercessor.

The concept of Heaven and Hell, so phantastically embellished by popular mythology, has been considerably spiritualized by the mystics and the philosophers who thought the descriptions of the Quran parables for the simple people. The philosophers mostly denied the corporeal resurrection; they held that the eternal life of the soul would be fulfilled either in spiritual delight or in pain of different degrees. The *Ikhwān aṣ-ṣafā* located the soul after death either in the sphere of purity or the unhappy souls below the moonsphere. Some sects even defended the idea of transmigration of the soul which is essentially alien to the preaching of the Quran—the Bāṭinīya considered the soul who has not been perfected through the knowledge given by the Imāms liable to purification through transmigration. Sunni Islam, however, has always rejected these ideas.

The Sufis of old had seen in God first the Lord of Judgment whom they adored in fear and trembling, but during the development of the concept of love in Islamic mysticism they realized that the *liqā Allāh*, the meeting with God without any veils would be possible only in the other world. Death, then, was considered the bridge which leads the lover towards the Beloved. The poems and prayers of al-Ḥallāj (d. 922) express the longing for death as the means of unification in the most touching way. The mystic would laugh at the popular ideas of Paradise—"what shall I do with a couple of ḥūrīs who are thousands of years old?" asks Yunus Emre (d. 1321) with an expression common to the mystics since the 9th century. The word "Die before ye die," attributed to the Prophet, was one of the maxims of the mystics, implying the feeling that he who had died from his worldly vices and wishes, has not to fear the Last Judgment or the moment of death. Though contemplation of Divine Beauty was, for them, the goal of Paradise, some of them would even prefer to stay in Hell if they were sure that God willed that. Ghazzālī—whose descriptions of the other world otherwise do not lack sensual colours—says appropriately:

> "What we fear is not the fire of Hell, and what we hope for are not the ḥūrīs, we do not seek but the *liqā' Allāh* and do not fear but being separated from Him ... For the fire of separation is the fire burning from God that concerns the spirits, whereas the fire of Hell does not affect but the bodies, and bodily pain is of lesser importance than spiritual pain" (transl. Wensinck).

For the mystics a general judgment, a Doomsday, so central in the Quranic preaching, is not as essential as the idea of preparing one's own death. For death—as Jalāluddīn Rūmī says—is the mirror of the faithful and of the sinner, is "of the same colour" with man (*Mathnawī* III 3431), is brought up in man's lap. Life has been considered by many of them only a shadowy dream—the tradition: "Men are asleep, and when they die they awake" is found already in very early times though it is not in tune with the Quranic teaching which gives this world a special importance as a field of action. But the "real" spiritual life, the never-ending way into the fathomless depths of the Deity begins only after death. Only through death can union with the Beloved be achieved—that is the tenor of most of the mystical poems in Muslim countries. Muhammad Iqbal has once more stressed the dynamic character of what the faithful call Paradise:—"Heaven is no holiday" —and underlined the possibility of further spiritual development if man has prepared himself on earth for these future tasks.

Modern Quran-interpretation is scarcely interested in the eschatological parts of the Quran. Attempts of a kind of de-mythologization have been made (e.g. by the Ahmadīya). It thus lacks an important aspect of Quranic teaching: the idea that man's life gains its real value only *sub specie aeternitatis*, the outspoken conviction that God has created everything to a certain end. It is this teleological thinking and the firm belief in the power and wisdom of Allah Who is both the Just Judge and the Merciful Forgiving which gives Islam its peculiar character.

VI. The Situation of Islam in Modern Time

Islam passed through a period of stagnation in the later Middle Ages. The danger inherent in dry scholasticism, in the meticulous obedience of the smallest details of the *sharīʿa* in personal life, overstressed *tawakkul* (trust in God), degenerated into passivity, fatalism, and in mysticism, the nearly absolute rule of the "mystic" leaders over great parts of the community resulted in a lack of creativeness; the educational system, too, was continued according to the inherited models by memorizing religious texts without any attempt of interpretating them afresh. People did not know much about the real teachings of the Quran, besides the few sūras which they had learned by rote for their prayers, nor of the real life of the Prophet but accepted whatever they were offered by the *ʿulamāʾ* and *shaykhs*, as nobody was allowed to use *ijtihād*. In spite of the glory of the Ottoman Empire, the Safawid Kingdom in Iran, and the Moghul Empire in India the number of creative scholars in their time was comparatively much smaller than it had been in the Middle Ages, though some outstanding philosophers (Mullā Ṣadrā, Hādī Sabzawārī in Iran), historians and a large number of mystical writers are known.

In the time of anarchy in Muslim India that followed the death of Aurangzeb (d. 1707) and was characterized by the frequent attacks of Western neighbours (Nādir Shāh, Aḥmad Shāh Durrānī) and when Hindus and Sikhs, too, took advantage of the weakness of the regime,

Shāh Walīullāh of Delhi (1703-1762), who combined wide learning and mystical experience, tried to revive the religious conscience through numerous books. By translating the Quran into Persian, the language of the educated class in India, he gave his co-religionists the possibility of going back to the real meaning of the Holy Book; his sons continued his work by translating the Quran into Urdu.

At the same time the Wahhābī movement in Central Arabia—called after the Ḥanbalite theologian ʿAbdul Wahhāb (d. 1787) started fighting against the superstitious innovations which were alien to the spirit of the Quran—just as Ibn Taimīya (d. 1328) had fought, nearly single-handed, against them. They banned mysticism, especially saint-worship and visits of graves in order to obtain blessings, and preached return to the simple commandments of the Quran and the early traditions, rejecting the large amount of innovations which had been introduced by consensus through the centuries. Thanks to their connections with the Saʿūd family the Wahhabites got hold of great parts of the Arabian peninsula, and conquered, 1803-1806, Mecca and Madina, not even sparing the tomb of the Prophet from their reformatory wrath. They were later defeated by Egyptian-Turkish troups but continued to exist in Central Arabia until the house of Saʿūd came into power after World War I, so that to-day the puritan Wahhabite form of Islam is accepted in the whole of Saudi Arabia, and in spite of some very medieval trends in its publications the possibility of the emergence of a new orthodox theology must be admitted.

The first contacts of the Islamic world with the European powers—especially England and France—caused some new developments both in India and in the Near East. Besides a very small group who welcomed European civilisation, the majority wanted to defend Islam against the Western intruders. The feeling of uneasiness before the technically more advanced powers who, to the greatest horror of the Muslims, would slander the Prophet and despise Islam and claimed the superiority of Christian culture over Muslim culture, engendered movements that aimed at proving the superiority of the Muslims. The only possibility of regaining the once so splendid power of Islam seemed to be a thorough re-Islamisation, and a new interpretation of the truths of faith. This was attempted in different forms according to the political and social situation of the respective countries.

The reformist movements in Turkey were first headed by men like Namik Kemal (d. 1888) who saw in Islam the best way of life, and later Mehmet Akif (d. 1936) whose powerful poetry announced a new Islamic feeling. But more influential than Akif (who, though the author of the Turkish National Anthem, left his country shortly after the Revolution in 1923) proved the ideology worked out by Ziya Gök Alp (d. 1924), who was the first to advocate Westernization, Islamisation and Turkisation of the decaying Ottoman Empire, and who is responsible for the introduction in Turkey of the idea of separation of "State and Church" which is alien to Islamic ideology, thus paving the way for a more or less "Western" understanding of the "religion" of Islam. This attitude led, eventually, to the complete laicism of Atatürk's reforms—who, however, did not restrain the individual religious life which remained alive under the surface and became more intense again in the fifties. Typical of the Turkish situation is the admiration for Martin Luther who is considered the prototype of a reformer and whose name is more familiar to the modern Turks than that of Ash'arī or Ghazzālī. Atatürk's abolition of the Arabic script in 1928 meant a complete break with the Islamic heritage and the neighbouring Muslim countries.

In India, the conquest of large parts of the country by the British after the battle of Plassey in 1757 had made many members of the orthodox wing emigrate to Mecca or the Ottoman Empire. Both the followers of Shāh Walīullāh, who supported Syed Aḥmad of Bareilly's "holy war" against the Sikhs in which he was killed in the Peshawar area, in 1831, and the followers of so-called Farā'iḍī-movement among the poor peasants of East Bengal fought relentlessly against the British; for the idea that the infidels should rule a country which had been *dār al-Islām* for centuries was intolerable to them. The tradition of Shāh Walīullāh, though less mystically tinged, is living even to-day in the school of Deoband which has produced some of the leading orthodox theologians of modern India. The fact that the Macauley Scheme for Education in 1835 abolished the traditional methods and Persian as official language made it nearly impossible for pious Muslims to partake in the English educational system. Only Sir Sayyid Aḥmad Khān (d. 1898) found that the Muslims had the duty of acquiring Western knowledge; he founded, therefore, the Anglo-Muslim College in Aligarh (1875) where education in British style was available to Muslim students. Similar institutions were created in different parts of India, in spite of the protest of the orthodox who suspected the danger of complete Westernization—yet the anglophilia of the Aligarh students changed after World War I when Aligarh turned into one of the centers of the Indian Freedom Movement against the British.

Sir Sayyid had maintained that Islam is compatible with modern life, that neither the Quran nor the prophetic tradition prevent a Muslim from eating with fork and knife (to cite a well-known example) or to shave. Other reformers went further and held that Islam is in itself development. Immense is the number of books which were written, since the last quarter of the 19th century, in order to show the superiority of Islamic civilisation, and especially the greatness of the Prophet whose honour had been so sorely offended by Western writers. By showing that Europe had received the foundations of its own scientific culture, during the Middle Ages, from the Muslims they proved that the use of modern technical means was a legitimate reclamation of the faithfuls' capital which had, in the meantime, yielded interest by the works of European scientists.

The ideas of Jamāluddīn Afghānī, who roamed through the different Muslim and non-Muslim countries as a preacher of Islamic revival and unification (d. 1897 in Istanbul after having inspired Sultan ʿAbdul Ḥamīd's pan-Islamic ideas), stirred the hearts of the Muslims; it was he who first formulated the contrast between East and West in words which are still echoed in our times in the Muslim world. Well-known is his controversy with ERNEST RENAN about "Islam and Science."

Afghānī's work was settled in Egypt by his pupil and friend Muhammad ʿAbdūh (d. 1905) whose noble personality has deeply influenced the following generations. In 1884 ʿAbdūh proclaimed the tenets of the creed of the modernist theologians from Paris in his short-lived paper *al-ʿurwat al-wuthqā*:

> "Oh people of the Quran, you will not be anything as long as you do not practise the Quran, and not act according to its orders and prohibitions and as long as you do not take them as the directing rule of all your actions, watching to follow its commands as your ancestors *(salaf)* did it."

Here the central position of the Divine revelation for the modern Muslim is announced, and ʿAbduh and his pupil Muhammad Rashīd Riḍā have, in their magazine *al-Manār*, laid down their ideas of modern life in the light of the Quran, showing the compatibility of the Holy Book with every aspect of modern life and science. The term *salaf*, used by ʿAbduh in the above cited passage, gave his movement the name of *salafiya*, "acting as the first generations of Muslims had done."

From ʿAbduh's time up to our time many commentaries of the Quran have been composed in the different Muslim countries, and translations—though for informative purposes only, not for ritual use—have been published everywhere. Some of the commentaries attempt to prove with more or less ingenious methods that the Quran contains in itself the complete textbook of modern science—there are commentaries which show the A-bomb, the sputnik etc. in the words of the Holy Book. It is a typical trend of all modern commentaries that the eschatological parts are not given much importance; one finds a tendency towards de-mythologization.

One of the most urgent problems in modern Islam is the question of *ijtihād*, the "going back to the sources" of Islamic legislation. *Ijtihād* had been considered impossible since the 4th century of the *hijra*; the jurist and the theologian was bound to the decisions of the former leaders of his *madhhab*, and only the great scholars of the Hanbalite school like Ibn Taimīya had claimed for themselves this right of free investigation in Quran and tradition. The *salafiya* thinks *ijtihād* necessary in modern times, in order to go back behind the petty differences of the four *madhhabs*, and to break through the crust of medieval customs and second-hand interpretations which have turned Islam into an immovable, nearly fossilized, religio-cultural system. The question has been raised in orthodox circles as to how far this *ijtihād* in the field of theology and jurisprudence can, if at all, be exercised by people who do not have traditional training in Islamic sciences. And even if the possibility of *ijtihād* is granted, the question remains how far the modern theologian and jurisconsult should make use of the material contained in the traditions, how far the Muslim community should rely upon *ḥadīth* whose authenticity is mostly doubtful. Scholars like G. Parwez in Pakistan reject *ḥadīth* completely and develop their ideology exclusively from the Quran, whereas most of the modernists hold that the careful use of traditional material is, in many cases, the only way of understanding how the early community has interpreted this or that word of the Quran, and even if *ḥadith* may not contain the true words of the Prophet and his companions it can show how the young community used to act in the true spirit of the Prophet—Dr. Fazlur Rahman has defined *ḥadīth* as an expression of the living *sunna*, which shows the inner dynamics of Islam, and may, thus, be used for reaching a modern interpretation of the Quran.

Another urgent question is the attitude of modern Islam towards mysticism and the Sufi orders. A number of orders—e.g. the *ṭarīqa*

Muḥammadīya of Ibn Idrīs, or the Sanūsīya both of which were founded in the beginning of the 19th century in North Africa, have played an important rôle in the struggle against the foreign powers; the Tījānīya was succesful in founding whole kingdoms in West Africa in the early 19th century. The Qādirīya, too, was influential in political affairs in some parts of Indo-Pakistan. In the Ottoman Empire the importance of the Mevlevīya (Dancing Derwishes) for the formation of cultural life, and of the Bektashis in connection with the corps of Jannissaries is well-known. As indispensable as the orders had been in the Middle Ages for the preaching of Islam and spreading its doctrines into the remotest parts of India or Africa, they, too, had often degenerated, and their leaders sometimes badly misused the faith of their simple followers. That is why Atatürk had the *ṭarīqas* abolished in Turkey as early as in 1925, and the political leaders and reformers almost everywhere tried to break their influence (at present in North Africa). Nevertheless there can be no doubt that a mystically tinged piety, and especially its manifestations in poetry and music, still helds its spell over many people, primarily in the countries from Turkey to India. In our days, some mystical leaders have tried, once more, to teach the Muslim a spiritualisation of religious life—it was necessary to underline the "religious" values of Islam in countries like Turkey which boast of their laicism and perhaps likewise among the Indian Muslims who, in contrast to their Pakistani brethren, have chosen the attitude which the Moghul Prince Dārā Shikōh (d. 1659) and his ancestor Akbar had once practised: to admit the relativity of outward religious forms and acknowledge each religion as true in its own place.

An interesting example of the ambiguous attitude towards mysticism in modern Islam is that of Muhammad Iqbal (d. 1938) who has attacked in his poetry and prose the Sufi *shaykhs* and the lawyer divines alike and is yet comparatively close to the classical type of Sufism: he emphasizes the impulse of love for the religious life, but rejects the later monistic type of Sufism and its quietistic philosophy.—Iqbal himself is, no doubt, one of the most interesting personalities among the modernists—combining a thorough study of European philosophy and poetry with strong Islamic feeling, he has reminded his fellow-Muslims in both Indo-Pakistan and the Persian-speaking countries of the great duties which man, who was called to act as the vice-gerent of God, has to realize in a person-to-person encounter with Him in prayer and has to develop his individuality and his spiritual faculties to a fuller realization of his inner possibilities which will continue even after death. A never-resting dynamism, influenced partly by German vitalist philosophy, partly by his conception of the Quranic revelation, combined with breadth of vision and the gift of expressing his thought in fine, even enrapturing Persian and Urdu verses makes Iqbal's work very attractive for his countrymen and Western readers. In spite of his belief in the all-embracing Islamic brotherhood his feeling that the Muslim minority in the Subcontinent needed a place to be free in worship and religio-social life has led to the foundation of Pakistan as an Islamic Republic.—Islamic modernists have also had to cope with movements that were considered heterodox—not to mention the Babi-Bahai-Movement which developed out of Shiʿa doctrines into an independent religious system at the beginning of the 19th century—;but the Ahmadīya still disturbs the minds of many Muslims. The founder of this movement, Ghulām Aḥmad of Qādiān in the Panjab, declared himself Mahdī in 1880. The movement was split up in 1914 into two branches, but their main teachings are the same—denial of the duty of *jihād*, the claim that Jesus has died in Kashmir, and that the founder of the sect was blessed with Divine inspiration. The Ahmadīya is the only group inside Islam that organized a well-established missionary activity, and founded mosques and teaching centers all over the world, translating the Quran, accompanied by their commentaries, into many languages. The tension between this group and the orthodoxy stems from the fact that their teachings seem contradictory to one of the central dogmas of Islam: that of the finalty of Muhammad's prophethood, by claiming a semi-prophetic status for their founder. In the Panjab riots of 1953 Pakistani orthodoxy made them a target of their hatred. But the proceedings which were instituted against the inspiring forces of the riots, and whose results have been published in the Munīr-Report, have shown another, even more regrettable fact: namely the large gap between the mentality of the Western-trained lawyers of Pakistan and that of the traditional Muslim orthodoxy whose aim is to make their country a model of Islamic life.

The problem of Islam and the modern national State which was treated so lucidly by E. J. Rosenthal is most complicated, since it is nearly impossible to define the different shades of influence Islam enjoys between West Africa and Indonesia in the theories and, quite different from that, in the practice of the countries with Muslim majorities. Nationalism developed soon after the breakdown of the Ottoman Empire in 1918, but only with the withdrawal of the colonial powers from the Near and Middle East after World War II did many Muslim countries gain freedom and have to find a way for preserving their Islamic character without loosing their connection with modern politics. Orthodox circles have always denounced narrow nationalism—though not patriotism, for "love of the country is part of faith"—and have stated that "all Muslims belong to the same nationality" (H. AL-BANNĀ', leader of the Muslim Brethren), that "Islam has made the whole world a vast sanctuary in which God ought to be worshipped in every action and in every moment" (S. RAMAḌĀN). Nationalism has been rejected also by Iqbal as a modern form of *shirk*, i.e. showing reverence to something besides God whereas Islam means "loyalty to God, not to thrones." The Arabs, however, have at times stressed—even when attacking nationalism in general—their own peculiar rôle as the backbone of the Muslim world, in whose language the word of God has been revealed in its definitive form.

The question of the right form of government which had been discussed through the Middle Ages became, once more, of paramount importance for a country like Pakistan which came into existence as a homeland for the Muslims of the Subcontinent, and for whose existence Islam was the only raison d'être. The prolonged discussions about the constitution in this country show some of the difficulties with which the jurisprudents were confronted—a crucial problem was, for example, in how far the minorities should be treated as *dhimmīs* according to Islamic law, or given full rights of citizens, whether or not they should be represented in the parliament, and how women should be treated concerning their political rights. During the last election campaign the question even arose whether or not a woman can be head of a Muslim state; though it was mostly answered in the negative since the *imām* has to be male and free, Miss Fāṭima Jinnah had the support of many pious Muslims.

Should an Islamic state be a theocracy in which the power is delegated to the representatives of the people? Who is the real ruler in a modern Islamic state? Since the caliphate was abolished by Atatürk in 1924 a spiritual head of the whole Muslim community was no longer conceivable. Is the leader of the state indeed still the *imām* who leads the community in prayer and war? Or is not democracy the right form of government? The word *shūrā* in Sūra 44/36 is taken as a proof for the democratic character of the government—

but how to introduce democracy in the Western sense in a country with a large majority of illiterates? Or should "State and Church," the two inseparable aspects of Islamic life, be separated and should the religious affairs be left to the discretion of the individual, as it is the case in Turkey and, to a certain extent, in India: the Muslims of this country having—at least in theory—the opportunity of living neither as rulers nor as ruled but as equal partners with other religions.

Another problem: how can a modern state exist without breaking the laws of the Quran which forbid, e.g. the taking of interest? Already Muhammad ʿAbduh had issued a *fatwā* to the result that governmental institutions, but not private persons, are allowed to take interests; banking can be permitted. Other problems are those of social justice—many modernists maintain that Islam is, in itself, the most perfect system of socialism, the Quran having prescribed exactly the social duties by imposing upon the faithful the *zakāt* with its rules of application. In some countries the Prophet himself is depicted as the Imām of socialism,—yet there are others who doubt that "scientific socialism" in the Marxist sense is compatible with the belief in God and His Book.

The breaking up of the family, once the central unit of life, in the modern industrialized society has created other problems, and though in some of the Muslim countries polygamy is still allowed the rôle of women is considerably improved, so that women are found even in leading political positions, in spite of the violent protests of some orthodox circles. Modern life needs social insurance—in former times secured by the duty of the members of the family to support each other,—and the pious ask themselves in how far a centrally administered insurance (which was classified under the forbidden games of hazard) with its rates of interest is advisable for the Muslim. Industrialisation and more intense methods of agriculture entail difficulties in performing the prayers at the prescribed moment (yet one may combine two of them in one prayer service!), and mean difficulty in keeping the fast during Ramaḍān: that is why in Tunesia *fatwās* have declared hard work a war against hunger and thus conceded the worker the exemption from fasting.—Strange enough that the Islamic Republic of Pakistan keeps the Christian Sunday as the weekly holiday, while others—like Saudi Arabia, Iran, Afghanistan—celebrate the Friday.—The introduction of broadcasting and television into many hitherto untouched parts of the Muslim world created even graver problems by showing the Muslims a picture of the Western world which, in some cases, perfectly justifies the bitter criticism of orthodoxy. The belief in the marvels of technology which is so typical of the younger generation often leads to a dangerous alienation not only from their own religious tradition but from any religion at all—here arises the difficulty of combining modern technical science with the old Ash'arite theory of atomism which did not allow secondary causes but sees in everything the direct action of God and hinders, thus, a real scientific approach to modern problems.

The difficulties in interpreting Islam for the modern world would be less confusing if the Muslim world formed a homogenous whole on comparative cultural levels. But besides the heart of classical Islam, the Arabo-Persian world, and, as cultural provinces of highest importance, Turkey and Indo-Pakistan who are proud of their magnificent traditions, all of whom in their attempt at an accelerated modernisation have to struggle with petrified models of thinking, we have to consider the completely different situation in the recently islamized countries in Africa; these are gaining more weight in the community of the faithful, but their interpretation of the new religion which gave them a higher cultural status must necessarily differ from that of a Turkish or Iranian, Lebanese or Pakistani Muslim scholar—though the common faith in the Quran still exists.

The struggle against *taqlīd*, blind imitation of what former generations have said, which was opened by the modernists, has a second target: they now warn as well of blind imitation of Western values and standards, and of aping the outward manifestations of Western civilisation without entering into its depths. The clinging to the traditional values of their religion is for many faithful Muslim perhaps the only shield against the dangers of a modern "godless" technical civilisation. Thus we can well understand the fundamentalist groups, like the Muslim Brethren or the Jamaat-i Islami of Maulānā Maudūdī in Pakistan in their attempts to preserving an Islamic way of life as they understand it. They have the great advantage of bringing a precise program which the simple Muslim can understand, whereas Islamic liberalism in its different shades—useful as it may be—has never produced a formulated program or a strict line of conduct and thus can attract only a part of the intellectuals, not the masses. And the leaders of the mystical undercurrents in present-day Islam have never formulated any rules of outward behaviour, of political or social importance but lay stress upon the realization of the ethical values of love of God and love of the brother.—For the fundamentalists, like the Muslim Brethren, Islam is "faith and worship, fatherland and nationality, religion and government, spirituality and activity, Quran and sword," i.e. it comprises, according to the classical ideal, all spheres of life without differentiation.

Should the future of Islam really be guaranteed by an adjustment to European culture by the Muslims (C. H. BECKER) or by "going back to the Greeks" (H. H. SCHAEDER)? It is typical that almost every modernist thinker and theologian has underlined the "anticlassical" dynamic character of Islam, the "prophetic" element in it, and that the Quranic verse which they quote with preference since the days of Jamāluddīn Afghānī, and which Iqbal has made the pivot of his thinking, is Sūra 13/12: "Verily God altereth not what is in a people until they alter what is in themselves," i.e. the call to repentance in the widest sense of the word; the call to get out of the state of petrification and then start a new life with the help of God Whose word, revealed in the Quran, is capable of ever new interpretations. The unity of God which is revealed in the one all-embracing Divine Law should be reflected in the essential unity of the community of believers, who, how ever they interpret the Islamic doctrines, will not cease turning their faces towards Mecca in their daily prayers. Iqbal has surely expressed the feeling of many modern Muslims when he wrote in his diary: "We are still indispensable to the world as the only testimony to the Absolute Unity of God."

VII. Short History of the Discipline

In 1590 a *Disputatio de duobus Antichristis primariis, Mahomete et pontifice Romano*, was held in Marburg—Islam had been considered, for centuries, the manifestation of the Antichrist. As the only high religion that had originated after Christianity and formed at the same time a considerable political threat to both Western Europe from 711 (conquest of Spain) to 1683 (second siege of Vienna) it was the most dangerous enemy of the Christian world:—Muhammad's distorted name—Mahound—designs in Scotland the Devil. DANTE, by depicting Muhammad close to Judas as head of the schismatics expressed the feeling of many medieval Christians, and the idea that Islam is but a heresy of Christianity (JOHN OF DAMASCUS) has been repeated even by A. VON HARNACK. Even a wild confusion of the strictly monotheistic Islam with polytheistic paganism is visible.

In Spain the knowledge of Islam and of Arabic was more advanced than elsewhere. The first Latin translation of the Quran was completed in 1143 by ROBERTUS KETENENSIS under the auspices of PETRUS VENERABILIS of Cluny; its author added a short treatise on Islamic history. At the same time many translations from Arabic scientific works were brought to the notice of the West, and a century later Averroes (Ibn Rushd) was made the target of discussions by Christian theologians who sometimes even used the arguments of Islamic theology against this common enemy of revealed religion. Muslim theology was studied in the 13th century with the aim of converting the Sarrazens; the best expert in this field is RAMON LULL (killed 1316 in Tunis) whose works prove his knowledge of Islamic mysticism. The Crusades had brought Christians and Muslim nobles into a certain amount of contact, and the travels of the Franciscan monks after the fall of Bagdad into the Mongol Empire where they hoped to win allies against the Muslims resulted, at least, in some useful information about Eastern life.

In the 15th century, NICOLAS CUSANUS gave a detailed "*Sifting of the Quran*" (cribatio) for, as usual, missionary purposes, and the conquest of Constantinopel and the extension of the Ottoman Empire resulted once more in a new wave of hatred and fear against the Muslim; the ideas about "the Turkish religion" as reflected in German folksongs of the 16th and 17th centuries are rather absurd. LUTHER wrote against "des Papstes und Türken Mord," and for MELANCHTHON Muhammad was the organ of Satan, "the little horn" mentioned in Book Daniel. He wrote the foreword when the old KETENENSIS' Latin translation of the Quran was printed in Basel in 1543, 400 years after its completion. This print became the source of the oldest Italian translation 1547 which was translated into German in 1616 and hence into Dutch in 1641.

The interest in Arabic studies in Europe goes back to the 16th century. After the rather fantastic W. POSTEL (d. 1581) it was his pupil J. SCALIGER (d. 1609) who—without missionary interest!—studied Arabic and discovered the meaning of the *hijra* era which he explained, with many other calendarial systems, in his book *De emendatione temporum*, thus giving the clue to understanding Islamic historical sources. But in general the anti-Islamic literature in Europe continued.—Pope Alexander VII had forbidden publication or translation of the Quran; however an edition was brought forth in 1694 by the Lutheran priest HINCKELMANN in Hamburg, and another one together with a Latin translation in 1698 by MARACCI who used a number of Arabic sources and added his *Prodromus ad refutationem Alcorani.*

Real scholarly interest in Arabic was cultivated in Holland; TH. ERPENIUS (d. 1624) edited for the first time Arabic classical texts and understood the hitherto unknown importance of the *sunna* for Muslim life and thought. His grammar was in use for nearly 200 years, and his successor GOLIUS (d. 1667) compiled the first Arabic lexicon. Historical research was carried on by the Swiss scholar HOTTINGER in his *Historia Orientalis*, and E. POCOCK, the first professor of Arabic in Oxford, filled the short text of the Barhebraeus in his *Specimen Historiae Arabum* with many useful notes about the pre-Islamic Arabs and Islamic religion. His son and successor produced 1671 a translation of Ibn Ṭufail's philosophical novel *Ḥayy ibn Yaqẓān*, *Philosophus autodidactus.* BARTHOLOMÉ D'HERBELOT (d. 1695) though still considering Muhammad an impostor, collected the valuable encyclopedia *Bibliothèque Orientale.*

Only in the Age of Enlightenment a new understanding of Islam was approached. The travel accounts of merchants, missionaries and adventurers to the East had provided the public with some more sensible information about the Muslim world, and the unclerical attitude of the philosophers, their interest in giving the East its true place in the history of the world led to new attempts to understanding Islam and its founder. Muhammad was highly praised in the book of BOULAINVILLIERS which was published posthumously in 1730; H. RELAND— inspite of officially declaring that he detested Islam—maintained in *De religione Muhammedanica* that it was not as absurd as Christians use to believe. GAGNIER translated, in 1723, a rather recent biography of the Prophet into Latin because he wanted to show what the Muslims believe of their Prophet. Typical is the ambiguous attitude of VOLTAIRE who praises Muhammad in his *Essai sur les moeurs* as ruler, legislator, and priest, but makes him in *Mahomet ou le Fanatisme* 1741 a model of shameless priestcraft and hypocrisy.

S. SALE's translation of the Quran 1734 with its *Preliminary Discourse* is much more sober than the previous works, and has influenced the literature of the 18th century considerably. German translations were issued in 1772 by D. F. MEGERLIN and 1773 by F. E. BOYSEN. Still for many authors who wrote about Islam the word of REIMARUS was true:

> "I am sure that among those who accuse the Turkish religion of this or that fault only very few have read the Alcoran, and that even among

those who have read it only the fewest have had the intention of attributing to the words the sound meaning of which they are capable."

The practical study of Islamic subjects in the Oriental Seminaries in Paris and Vienna resulted in a sounder knowledge of Islamic languages and customs. It was J. J. REISKE (d. 1774) who, thanks to the unprejudiced research into the Arabic sources as far as they were available in Europe, placed, for the first time, the history of Islam into the frame of universal history.

It is surprising how excellently GOETHE, in the *Noten und Abhandlungen zum West-Östlichen Divan*, has characterized the Prophet and his mission, in spite of the lack of reliable sources. His words on Islamic poetry are still valid. He was greatly indebted to J. VON HAMMER-PURGSTALL (d. 1856), the indefatigable translator and compilator who opened new vista in almost every field of Islamic studies without giving a scholarly critical foundation to his innumerable publications. —This foundation was laid, at the same time, by SILVESTRE DE SACY (d. 1838) and his pupils, who applied the standard of classical philology to the edition of Arabic, Turkish, and Persian texts, and made Islamics an independent field of studies.

The 19th century scholarship produced a large number of most important sources for the history of Islam, so that the historians slowly got a firmer footing in historical facts. Light was shed upon the life of the Prophet—the new trends started with G. WEIL, *Leben des Propheten*, in 1843. In his *Geschichte der Kalifen* WEIL gave a detailed account of the most important institution in Islam up to the fall of Bagdad, based on Arabic sources, and added another volume about the development in later centuries (1846-62). The new state of knowledge of the sources is reflected in MUIR's biography of Muhammad (1858) where, however, "satanic" influences on the Prophet are maintained. A. SPRENGER (1861-65) laid stress on Muhammad's human weaknesses and interpreted the origin of Islam with social and psychological necessities, but added much new material and personal knowledge, and recognized the importance of Islamic culture for the West. L. KREHL (1884) mostly relied in his study upon the traditions, whereas MARGOLIOUTH still showed Muhammad as an impostor, and tried to explain some facts in his life by means of parapsychology. H. GRIMME, on the other hand, saw in Muhammad primarily a politician and social reformer whose religious system strongly relied upon that of later Judaism (1892-95). The classical biography which closes this period is the well-balanced work by F. BUHL (1903) with an objective and manysided view on Muhammad's life and environment.

In the meantime the study of the development of the Quranic revelations had opened new vista in Islamic history. A. VON KREMER in Austria has given the first Cultural History of Islam which is still worth reading. TH. NÖLDEKE's epoch-making work *Geschichte des Koran* (1860), enlarged in its later edition by A. SCHWALLY 1909, and continued, then, by G. BERGSTRÄSSER and O. PRETZL, aimed at showing the historical development of the Quran, the arrangement of the sūras etc. At the same time J. WELLHAUSEN, with the ingenious eye of the critical historian, contributed important studies to the early history of Islam: he showed which relics of paganism are known in early Islamic times; his masterly study about the rise of the first schism inside Islam, the development of the Kharijites and the Shiʿa is as indispensable as the history of the Omayyads (1902).—Dutch scholars, under the able leadership of M. J. DE GOEJE (d. 1909) edited historical texts; the *ṭabaqāt* of Ibn Saʿd were sponsored by the Academy of Sciences at Berlin from 1904 onwards.

With NÖLDEKE (d. 1930), the great discoverer of Quranic history, and scholar of Semitic languages as well as of Persian, with the ingenious historian WELLHAUSEN who applied the critical method to the history of early Islam (besides his rôle in Bible studies), Islamic studies had made considerable progress. But the greatest representative of Oriental scholarship was I. GOLDZIHER who, in 1890, published his *Muhammedanische Studien* in which he critically sifted the immense material of early Islamic tradition and discovered that the *ḥadīth* material shows the inner development of the early Muslim community rather than Muhammad's own ideas. GOLDZIHER's book on *Die Richtungen der islamischen Koranauslegung* (1920) is essential for the history of Quranic interpretation (it was, on a smaller scale, continued for our time by J. M. F. BALJON); his early book of the Ẓāhirite school of Law is as fundamental as his later work on Ghazzālī and his refutation of the Bāṭinīya. The gist of his immense studies which are reflected also in numerous small but weighty articles is given in his *Vorlesungen über den Islam* (1910) which can be considered the classical introduction into the new science called Islamkunde. Besides GOLDZIHER and NÖLDEKE, the Dutch scholar SNOUCK HURGRONJE (d. 1936) contributed most to Islamkunde—his study about the origins of the *ḥajj*, in *Het Mekkaansche Feest*, as well as his contributions to Islamic law which he knew practically from his activities in Indonesia, and his articles on modern developments inside Islam are of great importance. His countrymen contributed a number of studies into the legal aspects of Islam and about Islam in Indonesia.

GOLDZIHER's criticism of *ḥadīth* was generally accepted, though some scholars, like H. LAMMENS, reached the radical conclusion that the tradition is not to be used at all, and treated the Prophet and his family supercritically.—The interest in the spiritual history of Islam grew likewise. D. MACDONALD has devoted a fine study to the *Religious Attitude and Life in Islam* 1909, and the study of Islamic mysticism which had started in 1822 with THOLUCK's *Ssufismus sive theosophia Persarum Pantheistica* became the special subject of R. A. NICHOLSON's work who devoted his whole life to the investigation of the history of Sufism and mystical literature. From his first work—*Selected Poems from the Dīvān-i Shams-i Tabrīz* 1898—over many editions of Arabic and Persian texts, small but important studies into detail problems, to his monumental edition, translation and commentary of Rūmī's *Mathnawī* leads an uninterrupted line.—L. MASSIGNON's works on Ḥallāj, one of the key-figures of Sufism, opened a new era in the understanding of mystical experience, and showed a deep personal concern with the subject. Following his path, a number of French scholars have, during the last years, contributed most important works about the development of mysticism but also of Islamic theology—thus L. GARDET and G. ANAWATI; the activity of the catholic scholars not only in Cairo but also in Beirut and in other parts of the world and their new approach towards a more sympathetic understanding of the inner values of Islam is one of the most prominent aspects of modern Islamology (the work of P. STIEGLECKER, *Glaubenslehren des Islam*, belongs to this category).—MASSIGNON's disciple, H. CORBIN, has taken up the most difficult problem of Shiʿite gnosticism, and has deeply penetrated, in different books and editions, into the sometimes confusing mysteries of esoteric interpretation; Shiʿa problems were also being studied, after having been unduly neglected, by M. HODGSON; in Germany the tradition of R. STROTHMANN, the specialist in Zaidīya-problems, will probably be continued; the Ismāʿīlīya has been, for decades, the special domain of I. IVANOW, whereas the Indian Ismāʿīlī lawyer A. A. A. FYZEE attempts a new approach to Islamic law from his peculiar point of view.

Among the scholars who contributed to a greater understanding of Islam and especially of the Prophet is TOR ANDRAE, the Swedish historian of religion. He has shown, in his fundamental work *Die*

Person Muhammads in Glaube und Lehre seiner Gemeinde the development of the veneration of the Prophet which is so essential for mystics and in popular piety, and his small book "Muhammad" (1932) is "the most readable and sympathetic biography." Likewise are his studies *Der Ursprung des Islams und das Christentum* (1926) an important step forward—the Jewish sources of Islam having been studied especially by TORREY and, later, by KATSH; ANDRAE's booklet on early Sufism, published posthumously 1947, shows the same positive understanding of religious life in early Islam as his other publications.

British Islamology can boast of the fine works of SIR THOMAS ARNOLD about the *Preaching of Islam*, *The Caliphate*, his studies in Muslim Painting, the *Legacy of Islam* which he edited with A. GUILLAUME, a specialist in early Muslim history; besides the numerous studies of A. J. ARBERRY who is continuing the tradition of R. A. NICHOLSON in his books about Sufism and his translations, and of E. G. BROWNE, the great historian of Persian literature, the penetrating and comprehensive works of SIR HAMILTON GIBB form an important contribution to a modern understanding of problems of Islamic general and cultural history; B. LEWIS has shifted from his first studies into the *Origins of Ismailism* to illuminating studies into Arabic, Turkish, and Persian history. The problems of Islamic theology—treated in full by A. TRITTON—have been taken up, in recent years, by W. MONTGOMERY WATT of Edinburgh, who, after a first analysis of the problem of *Predestination and Free Will in Early Islam* has concentrated upon the biography of the Prophet, and shows deep insight into the religious, economic, and social currents which were at work at the time of the Prophet whom he judges with sympathy.

The study of *ḥadīth* and of theological formation has been treated by A. J. WENSINCK who has given a fine introduction into the growing of *The Muslim Creed*, and whose concordance and handbook of *ḥadīth* are indispensable to every scholar of Islam. His booklet on Ghazzālī is one of the best in the large literature on this subject. New translations of the Quran have been produced in almost every language during recent years; we may mention the English translation of R. BELL with its critical re-arrangement of the sūras according to NÖLDEKE's principles, though even more detailed, and, again in English, ARBERRY's translation which aims at giving an impression of the stylistic beauty of the Holy Book. R. BLACHÈRE's French translation —we owe him too a fine study about the problem of Muhammad— is considered one of the best; another French translation, from the pen of a pious Muslim, M. Hamidullah, is important from the point of view of orthodox Muslim interpretation (as contrasted to the translations given by the Ahmadiyya-Mission); M. Hamidullah has published, with his *Le Prophète de l'Islam*, an interesting and carefully written biography of the Prophet as the modern Muslim sees him. The manysided Italian scholar A. Bausani whose interpretations of Persian literature and Urdu poetry are quite inspiring, has also translated the Quran into his mothertongue; the German translation by R. Paret is very careful and shows the learned author's painstaking scrupulosity. As a corollary to these studies during the last years several scholars—among them Muslims and even a Japanese orientalist, Izutsu—have started analysing the contents of the Quran, its concepts and words by means of linguistic methods, a way which seems to yield quite interesting results.

The discovery of many hitherto unknown manuscripts in the libraries of the East, especially in Istanbul, is due, to a large extent, to the tremendous work of H. Ritter who has not only edited many works of primary importance for the spiritual history of Islam but has, to mention only his most comprehensive book, *Das Meer der Seele*, given a wonderful account of Persian mystical poetry and thought. Islamic mysticism is being thoroughly studied by the Swiss scholar Fritz Meier whose commented editions of Persian texts are indispensable for the investigation into the history of Sufism. The study of the mystical fraternities, though still in its beginnings, has been carried on by J. K. Birge, R. Brunel, H. J. Kissling and others.

On the other hand, our knowledge of the origin and early development of Islamic law has, after the first studies of Th. W. Juynboll, E. Sachau, and then D. Santillana been enlarged by the studies of J. Schacht whose *Origins of Muhammadan Jurisprudence* (1950) form a new starting point for the understanding of Muhammadan law. The application of this law in modern society is being studied nowadays especially by J. N. D. Anderson.

The problems of modern Islam have attracted many scholars in our days, from W. C. Smith whose *Islam in Modern India* is still in spite of some transitional strange views, a standard book on this subject, and who has likewise studied *Islam in Modern History*. E. J. I. Rosenthal, P. Jomier and P. Rondot give interesting accounts of the problems of modern Islam, whereas E. G. von Grunebaum, endowed with an immense knowledge of classical and modern Islam and its expressions in literature has several times dwelt upon the intertwined strands of thought and practices in to-day's Islamic thought.

From quite a different point of view should be judged K. CRAGG's books which reveal, in spite of their missionary tendencies, a rare insight into the religious life of the Muslims. Special mention deserves the study of Constance E. PADWICK into *Muslim Devotions* which treats with warm sympathy a nearly unknown field, the popular devotions in Islamic countries.

The interest in the social and economic history of Islam as well as in its contribution to science and medicine, to philosophy is growing. One should not forget the remarkable contributions of Muslim scholars, in recent years, to the serious study of their own culture and to the understanding of their religious traditions, unbiassed by religious prejudices and none can overlook in this picture of Islam the different attempts of self-interpretation written by Muslims from different parts of the world.

History of religions proper has rather neglected Islam—which was judged as merely receptive and without attractive originality, and the categories of *Religionswissenschaft*, like Phenomenology of Religion, have practically never been applied to this religion, the number of whose followers is second only to that of Christianity.

SELECT BIBLIOGRAPHY

A. AFFIFI, *The Mystical Philosophy of Muhyi'd Din Ibnu'l-Arabi.* Cambridge 1939.
AMEER ALI, *Syed, The Spirit of Islam.* London ²1922.
T. ANDRAE, *Muhammad.* Leipzig 1932.
— —, *Die Person Muhammads in Glaube und Lehre seiner Gemeinde,* Stockholm 1918.
— —, *Der Ursprung des Islams und das Christentums. Kyrkohistorisk Årsskrift* 1923-25. Uppsala 1926.
— —, *I Myrtenträdgården.* Stockholm 1947 (German translation: *Islamische Mystiker.* Stuttgart 1960).
J. N. D. ANDERSON, *Islamic Law in the Modern World.* London 1959.
TH. ARNOLD, *The Preaching of Islam,* London ²1913, Lahore ³1956.
— —, *The Caliphate,* Oxford 1924.
— —, *Painting in Islam,* Oxford 1928,
and A. GUILLAUME (editors), *The Legacy of Islam,* Oxford 1937.
A. J. ARBERRY, *The Doctrine of the Sufis,* Cambridge 1933.
— —, *Introduction to the History of Sufism,* London 1943.
— —, *Sufism,* London 1950.
D. BAKKER, *Man in the Quran.* Amsterdam 1965.
J. M. S. BALJON, *Modern Muslim Koran Interpretation* 1880-1960. Leiden 1961.
H. BAUER, *Islamische Ethik.* Nach den Hauptquellen übersetzt und erläutert, Halle 1916, 1917, 1922.
C. H. BECKER, *Islamstudien.* Leipzig 1924, 1932.
J. K. BIRGE, *The Bektashi Order of Dervishes.* London 1937.

R. Blachère, *Le Problème de Mahomet*. Paris 1952.
Th. J. de Boer, *The History of Philosophy in Islam*, London 1903, [2]1961.
C. Brockelmann, *Geschichte der islamischen Völker*, München-Berlin 1943.
——, *Geschichte der arabischen Literatur*, mit Supplementbänden, 1937-1942, 1943 ff.
F. Buhl, *Das Leben Muhammads*. Kopenhagen 1903 (German translation by H. H. Schaeder, Heidelberg 1929, [2]1955).
R. Brunel, *Le Monachisme errant dans l'Islam*. Paris 1955.
K. Cragg, *The Call of the Minaret*. New York 1956.
N. Daniel, *Islam and the West*. Edinburgh 1960.
J. Fück, *Die arabischen Studien in Europa*. Berlin 1955.
A. A. A. Fyzee, *Outlines of Muhammadan Law*. London-New York-Bombay [2]1955.
L. Gardet et G. Anawati, *Introduction a la théologie musulmane*. Paris 1948
——, *Mystique musulmane*. Paris 1961.
H. A. R. Gibb, *Modern Trends in Islam*. Chicago 1947.
——, *Mohammedanism. A historical survey*. London 1950.
——, *Studies on the Civilisation of Islam*. Boston 1962.
S. D. Goitein, *Studies in Islamic History and Institutions*. Leiden 1966.
I. Goldziher, *Muhammedanische Studien* I. II. Halle 1888/90.
——, *Die Richtungen der islamischen Koranauslegung*. Leiden 1920.
——, *Vorlesungen über den Islam*. Heidelberg [2]1925.
E. G. von Grunebaum, *Islam. Essays in the Nature and Growth of a Cultural Tradition*. Wisconsin 1955.
——, *Der Islam im Mittelalter*. Zürich-Stuttgart 1963.
H. Haas, *Das Bild Muhammads im Wandel der Zeiten. ZMR* Leipzig 1916.
M. Hamidullah, *Introduction to Islam*. Paris 1959.
——, *Le Prophète de l'Islam*, 2 vols. Paris 1955.
R. Hartmann, *al-Kuschairis Darstellung des Sufitums*. Berlin 1914.
——, *Die Religion des Islam*. Berlin 1944.
Ph. K. Hitti, *History of the Arabs*. London [5]1953.
M. Iqbal, *Six Lectures on the Reconstruction of Religious Thought in Islam*, Lahore 1932 and often.
W. Ivanov, *Brief Survey of the Evolution of Ismailism*. Leiden 1952.
J. Jomier, *Le commentaire coranique du Manār*. Paris 1954.
——, *Introduction a l'Islam actuel*. Paris 1964.
Th. A. Juynboll, *Handbuch des islamischen Gesetzes nach der Lehre der schafiitischen Schule*. Leiden 1910.
J. Kraemer, *Das Problem der islamischen Kulturgeschichte*. Tübingen 1959.
H. Laoust, *Les Schismes dans l'Islam*, Paris 1965.
R. Levy, *The Social Structure of Islam*. Cambridge [2]1957.
B. Lewis, *The Origins of Ismailism*. Cambridge 1940.
The Arabs in History. London 1954.
D. B. Macdonald, *Religious Attitude and Life in Islam*. Chicago 1909.
L. Massignon, *Husain ibn Mansur al-Hallaj, martyre mystique de l'Islam*. Paris 1922.
——, *Essai sur les origines du lexique technique de la mystique musulmane*. Paris 1922.
F. Meier, *Die fawā'iḥ al-ǧamāl wa fawātiḥ al-ǧalāl des Naǧm ad-dīn al-Kubrā*. Wiesbaden 1957.
K. Morgan, *Islam—The Straight Path*. New York 1958.
R. A. Nicholson, *The Mystics of Islam*. London 1914.
——, *Studies in Islamic Mysticism*. Cambridge 1921.[2]
Th. Nöldeke, *Geschichte des Korans*, 2. rev. edition by A. Schwally, Leipzig 1901 new combined edition Hildesheim 1961.
H. S. Nyberg, *Kleinere Schriften des Ibn'Arabi*. Leiden 1919.

C. E. Padwick, *Muslim Devotions*. London 1961.
F. M. Pareja, *Islamologia*, Rom 1951.
G. Pfannmüller, *Handbuch der Islamliteratur*. Berlin-Leipzig 1923.
D. Rahbar, *God of Justice*. Leiden 1960.
H. Ritter, *Das Meer der Seele*. Leiden 1955.
E. J. I. Rosenthal, *Islam in the Modern National State*, Cambridge 1965.
P. Rondot, *L'Islam et les Musulmans d'aujourd'hui*. Paris 1958. 1960.
D. Santillana, *Istituzioni di diritto Musulmane Malichite*. Roma 1926-38.
J. Schacht, *The Origins of Muhammadan Jurisprudence*. Oxford 1950.
A. Schimmel, *Gabriel's Wing. A Study into the religious ideas of Sir Muhammad Iqbal*. Leiden 1963.
W. C. Smith, *Modern Islam in India*. London 1946.
——,*Islam in Modern History*. Princeton 1957.
Ch. Snouck Hurgronje, *Verspreide Geschriften*. Bonn-Leipzig 1923.
——,Mekka, Den Haag 1888/89.
H. Stieglecker, *Die Glaubenslehren des Islam*. Paderborn 1962.
A. S. Tritton, *Islam. Belief and Practices*. London 1954.
——,*Muslim Theology*. London 1947.
W. Montgomery Watt, *Free Will and Predestination in Early Islam*. London 1948.
——,*Muhammad at Mecca*. Oxford 1953.
——,*Muhammad at Medina*. Oxford 1956.
A. J. Wensinck, *A Handbook of early Muhammadan Tradition*. Leiden 1927.
——,*The Muslim Creed*. Cambridge 1932.
——,*La Pensée de Gazali*. Paris 1940.
J. Wellhausen, *Reste arabischen Heidentums*. Berlin ²1927.
——,*Die religiös-politischen Oppositionsparteien im alten Islam*. Berlin 1901.
——,*Das arabische Reich und sein Sturz*. Berlin 1902.

Reference works

The Encyclopedia of Islam, 2. ed. since 1954.
J. D. Pearson and J. Ashton, Index Islamicus, Cambridge 1958; Supplement 1962.
Handbuch der Orientalistik. Herausgegeben von B. Spuler. Leiden, since 1955.
Religion in the Middle East, General Editor A. J. Arberry, Vol. 2, Cambridge 1969.

Important Journals

Zeitschrift der Deutschen Morgenländischen Gesellschaft (ZDMG Leipzig; Wiesbaden), *Der Islam*, *Die Welt des Islam; The Muslim World* (MW, Hartford), *Studia Islamica* (Paris), *Oriens* (Leiden), *Oriente Moderno* (Rome), *Islamic Studies* (Karachi, Rawalpindi).

About the translations of the Quran vd. § VIII.

The quotations given in the text are mostly taken from R. Bell's translation (Edinburgh 1937-1939).

ZOROASTRIANISM

BY

MARY BOYCE

London, England

I. The Essence of the Religion

Zoroastrianism is characterised by immense conservatism. Essentially and in details, therefore, the later religion is unchanged from that of ancient Iran. There is worship of one supreme God, Ohrmazd; veneration of lesser divine beings, the *yazads*; and constant vigilance against the active powers of evil, led by Ahriman. The struggle against evil is carried on both ethically and ritually, and a strong sense of personal responsibility is inculcated. The sacred Fire remains the chief object of cult. Tangible offerings are made, to God, the *yazads*, Fire, and the spirits of the dead. The cult of ancestral spirits remains prominent, and an orthodox Zoroastrian is highly conscious of the hereafter. In theology there is a strong sense also of Time, that is, of three periods: the original one, of perfect goodness; the present one, in which evil is present and active; and a future one, of restored perfect goodness. In the living faith it is naturally the second and third periods which are most vividly apprehended.

Zoroastrianism is an active religion, in which a threefold virtue of good thoughts, words and deeds, is inculcated. The fact that for centuries it was preserved by those reduced to poverty, or at least of very modest means, has probably strengthened its practical nature. There was neither wealth nor leisure for the pursuit of theology. Yet though preserved through hardship and oppression, Zoroastrianism has maintained an optimistic character. The ultimate triumph of righteousness is an article of faith, and sorrow and pessimism are held to be among the creations of the Devil, fashioned to undermine the good. Man has therefore a duty to enlist his feelings on the side of serenity, if possible of happiness. There is no virtue for the Zoroastrian in grieving, whether over his own sorrows or those of others. His religion teaches rather the soldierly qualities of discipline, endurance and courage. He is to worship Ohrmazd in gladness, as the Creator of all that is good; to enjoy and further his works; and to defy Ahriman and his counter-creations with vigour and a stout heart, in order to help bring about his ultimate defeat. This is the essence of the religion; and the many rituals, inherited from a remote past, are held to be among the means to achieve these ends.

II. Historical Development

In the 7th century A.D. Persia succumbed to the Arabs, who established Islam as the state religion in place of Zoroastrianism. In the following centuries preaching, persecution, and steady social and political pressures gradually made Muslims of all but the most devoted adherents of the old faith. These forsook wealth, security and worldly advantage to preserve their religion; and preserve it they did, so effectively, that there appears little difference between orthodox Zoroastrianism now and in Sasanian times. The creed, ceremonies and observances have been maintained unaltered in their essentials, although the religion has been shorn of the temporal splendour which must have attended it in old days.

Two groups of Zoroastrians survive: the descendants of those who held out against Islam in their native land of Iran (also called Pars or Persia), who are termed the Iranis; and the descendants of those who left Iran to preserve their faith and settled in India, where they are called the Parsis or Persians.

In Iran the old royal province of Pars remained strongly Zoroastrian till the 10th century A.D., and there was considerable literary activity in the community there in the 9th century. In the north, especially in Khorasan, there were Zoroastrians down to the Timurid invasions of the 15th century; but from the 16th century onwards there were only two strongholds of Zoroastrianism in the land, namely Yazd and Kerman. Both cities are situated in the centre of Iran, far from frontiers and royal courts, and on the outskirts of deserts, where a harsh climate breeds hardy and resolute men. Here the Zoroastrians held out, a small minority even in these places, living in enforced poverty and precariousness of life, but able to practice their religion. Since they were forbidden to follow any skilled trade or craft which brought them into contact with Muslims, the laymen were mostly farmers, drovers or weavers. The priests too had sometimes to eke out a livelihood by working the land; and down the centuries many lost any claim to learning, contenting themselves with preserving the essential rituals. Learning was maintained, however, by the leading priests, who preserved a knowledge of Pahlavi (the 'Middle Persian' language of Sasanian Iran, into which their sacred book, the Avesta, had been translated). To the laymen this, like Avestan, was incomprehensible, at least in its written form. The learned priests also had a good knowledge of standard Persian and Arabic. Among themselves all Irani Zoroastrians came to speak a local dialect of Persian, not understood by their Muslim neighbours. The community, thus isolated in nearly every respect, maintained not only the observances, but also the high moral standards of their faith.

There was no supreme head of the Zoroastrians in Iran, Yazd and Kerman forming two separate communities, each with its own 'cathedral' Fire, or *Atash Bahram*, and its own hereditary religious leader, the *Dastir-mas* or 'Great Dastur', who had considerable authority, tempered by the deliberations of the whole body of priests in council. Until the 19th century there were two or three lesser priestly centres in the villages surrounding Yazd and Kerman, which had their own lesser sacred Fires.

In the early 16th century the great Safavid king, Shah Abbas, settled a number of Zoroastrians in a suburb of his new capital, Isfahan. Europeans who visited his court left accounts of the 'gabrs', as they were called by Muslims, which agree on the poverty and simplicity of their lives, but tell us little of the practice of their religion. Later this colony fell victim to the fanaticism of Shah Abbas' successors, and the Zoroastrians were either slaughtered or fled to Yazd, where some families trace descent from them to this day.

In the 18th century the Zoroastrians of Kerman suffered greatly. First the city was taken in the Afghan invasions, and many Zoroastrians were among those alain. Then it was captured by the Qajar prince Muhammad Agha, and vast numbers of its inhabitants were put to the sword. The old Zoroastrian quarter outside the walls was wholly destroyed; and in the early 19th century the surviving Kermani community numbered little over 1,000 souls. Yazd had been more fortunate, and there were some 7,000 to 8,000 Zoroastrians in the city and its villages at this time. Their larger numbers enabled them to preserve traditions better, and from then on Yazd was the acknowledged centre of Irani Zoroastrianism. Material conditions remained wretched there too until the late 19th century, the chief tool of oppression being the *jizya* or poll-tax exacted from them annually, often with extreme ruthlessness. Meantime their co-religionists in India had prospered, and their concern for their Irani brethren was roused by individual refugees, who made their escape to Bombay despite laws forbidding Zoroastrians to travel. In 1854 a Parsi agent, Manekji Limji Hataria, was sent to Iran to help the community; and in 1882, largely through his efforts, the *jizya* was abolished, and by royal decree Zoroastrians became equal with Muslims under Persian law. The small community took swift advantage, with Parsi help, of its new freedoms. Schools were founded in which a modern education was given. Zoroastrians entered commerce, banking and the professions, their reputation for honesty standing them in good stead. Many moved to the new Qajar capital of Tehran; and when Muhammad Reza overthrew the Qajars and established the Pahlavi dynasty in 1920, this movement was accelerated, for his attempts to curb the influence of Islam were most effective in the capital, where a new religious tolerance was felt. At the present day there are nearly 10,000 Zoroastrians in Tehran, whereas at the beginning of the century there were only two or three hundred. In Yazd and its villages there are just over 5,000, and in Kerman some 2,000, according to a census of 1963, which gave the total number of Zoroastrians in Iran as 17,296. (With the entry of Zoroastrians into trade, small communities have grown up again in such places as Shiraz and Zahidan). Yazd remains the religious centre, but the greatest stronghold of orthodoxy is now the village of Sharifabad, some 60 km. to the north of the city.

The Parsis, who by the 19th century were thus able to extend help to the Iranis, had themselves undergone many hardships previously. The history of their community has long gaps, and its origins may well be various. Persia had old trading-links with India, and it is suggested that there may have been Persian Zoroastrians already in India, engaged in commerce, when the Sasanian Empire fell. Others probably made their way east overland in the years following the Arab conquest. For the history of the religion, however, the important group is one whose story, preserved in priestly tradition, was written down in A.D. 1600 by a priest of Surat, in a poem called the *Qisseh-i Sanjan*. There are no precise dates given in this, but its general indications, which agree with other scraps of evidence, suggest that it was in the 8th century A.D. that a group of Zoroastrians, men, women and children, set sail in 3 ships from the Persian Gulf, and made landfall in the Indian island of Diu, off the coast of Kathiawar. (Attempts to assign this event to the 10th century seem less convincing.) After 17 years in Diu, they sailed on again to land at Sanjan, in S. Gujarat, where they obtained leave to settle from the local Hindu rajah. After a few years they established there an *Atash Bahram*, called the *Iranshah*, or '(Fire of) the King of Persia.' This remained the only perpetually-burning consecrated Fire of the Parsis until the 18th century, and is the object of their deep veneration. The settlers earned their living from the land, and prospered; and gradually groups spread out to other towns and villages in Gujarat, where they lived mainly as farmers, weavers and petty traders. Wherever laymen established themselves in fair numbers, they asked priests to come; and it was probably in the 13th century A.D. that Gujarat was divided by agreement into 5 *panths* or areas of priestly jurisdiction, according to the families of priests who served them. These *panths* were called by the names of their chief Zoroastrian centres, namely Sanjan, Navsari (whose priests are known as Bhagarias or 'sharers'), Godavra, Broach and Cambay. Little is known of the community at large during these centuries, except that there was a steady increase in numbers (added to by occasional new refugees from Iran), and in prosperity, with some disasters such as the Variav massacre, when a settlement of Zoroastrians was wiped out. In the late 13th century Muslim and Zoroastrian came into contact again, with the conquest of Gujarat and its annexation to the Delhi Sultanate. Either then, or in the 15th century under Sultan Mahmud Bigarha, the small Hindu kingdom of Sanjan was invaded. The Parsis fought valiantly beside the Hindus, but were overwhelmed. Priests managed to carry away the sacred Fire to Bahrut in the mountains, and after guarding it there for some years transferred it to Bansda, in the hills about 50 miles north-east of Navsari. Then, probably in A.D. 1516, at the instance of a noted layman, Changa Asa, the *Iranshah* was brought to Navsari itself, which thus became, for the next two centuries, the religious centre of the Parsis, with Sanjana priests serving the Fire, and Bhagarias performing all other duties.

In the late 16th century Gujarat was incorporated by Akbar into Mogul India; and Surat developed as a prosperous port, trading with the west. The enterprising Parsis flocked there; and it was here, in the early 17th century, that Europeans made their first contacts with the community. Meantime Akbar, exploring different faiths, summoned in 1578 a notable Bhagaria priest, Meherji Rana, to his court to expound Zoroastrianism. (Subsequently, at Akbar's request, Shah Abbas sent to him also a Persian *dastur* from Kerman.) Meherji found favour with Akbar, who incorporated some elements of Zoroastrian observance into his own eclectic worship. In mark of his esteem Akbar made a grant of land in Navsari to Meherji; and the Bhagarias themselves did him the signal honour of making him Dastur or head of their priestly body, the *anjoman,* and further of establishing this position as hereditary in his family. His descendants hold the office still. There had been no such dastursship previously in India, and it is probable that in creating it the Bhagarias were influenced by knowledge of the hereditary dasturships of Yazd and Kerman, being by this time in contact with those cities. The title accorded to Meherji Rana was in fact 'Great Dastur', *Wada Dastur*, rendering Irani *Dastir-mas*. Subsequently other *panths* created their own hereditary dasturships; but pre-eminence is accorded to that of Navsari. The Bhagaria *anjoman*, known as 'the *Great Anjoman*' is also held in especial respect as the guardian of traditions.

Gujarat suffered from Maratha depredations in the 18th century, and from 1733 to 1736 the sacred Fire was taken to the safety of fortified Surat. Subsequently, disputes having arisen between the Bhagarias and Sanjanas in Navsari, the sacred Fire was finally removed by the Sanjanas to the little town of Udwada, where it burns to this day. In 1765 the Bhagarias consecrated their own *Atash Bahram* in Navsari, and others have since been established in Bombay and Surat.

Meantime the British had acquired the island of Bombay and from the late 17th century the Parsis began to settle there, contributing greatly to the city's development. In the course of the next two centuries Bombay grew to be the largest centre of Zoroastrianism in the world, with many places of worship. Navsari and Udwada remained, however, the chief places of religious authority. According to a census taken in 1951, there were then 97,573 Zoroastrians in Bombay and Gujarat, and 13,744 in the rest of India, with just over 5,000 in Pakistan.

Europeans made further contacts with the Parsis in Bombay during the 19th century, not only in commerce, but seeking also to learn more of their ancient religion and scriptures. The Parsis themselves profited to some extent from this encounter with western scholarship. Libraries for religious mss. were founded in Bombay and Navsari, and Pahlavi mss. were edited by Parsi scholars. That these mss. exist at all is due originally to the devotion of the Irani community, which preserved them during the dark centuries after the Islamic conquest. During the early hard years in India the Parsi priests, it seems, were chiefly concerned to preserve the oral tradition of their liturgy, and the rituals. From the 13th century, however, there was occasional contact with the Irani community, and from the 15th century fairly regular intercourse developed on the initiative of the Parsis, whose messengers were joyfully greeted in Yazd and Kerman, where there had been no previous knowledge of their co-religionists. The Parsis gradually acquired mss. of their sacred books from Iran. They also received answers to many questions on observances which they put to the Iranis. These answers are preserved by them as the Persian *Rivayats*, and contain much interesting information. The Parsis were thus to some extent the pupils of the Iranis in the 15th to 17th centuries, instruction being given them with fraternal affection. It is plain, however, that they did not accept all answers to their questions, preferring in some matters to adhere to their own traditions. The Persian troubles of the 18th century reduced contact to a minimum again, although it was in this century that a learned Kermani priest, Dastur Jamasp Vilayati came to Surat to advise the priests there. Jamasp made the disturbing discovery that the religious calendar of the Parsis was one month behind that of the Iranis. This was a matter of considerable importance to the community, since the many rituals are tied to the calendar. In due course some priests in Surat adopted the Irani calendar, and a learned priest of Broach, Mulla Kawas, was sent to Persia for further enlightenment. Soon after his return in 1780 there was founded in Bombay the Qadmi sect, which adheres to the 'ancient' or Irani calendar. The rest of the Parsis, who were at first bitterly hostile to the Qadmis, adopted the name Shahanshahis or 'royalists', maintaining that theirs was the calendar of the Persian kings. A Qadmi *Atash Bahram* was established both in Bombay and Surat, the Qadmis having adopted not only the Irani calendar, but also to a large extent Irani rituals (which differ from Parsi ones in a number of small points). The outstanding priest among the Qadmis was the son of Mulla Kawas, Mulla Firoz, who died in 1830. Qadmis are found only in Bombay and Surat, the old Parsi strongholds of Gujarat having remained solidly loyal to their own traditions.

A Qadmi of Bombay, Dadiseth, established a minor fire-temple there to be served solely by Irani priests; and with freedom to travel accorded to the Zoroastrians of Iran, contact between the two communities became again close. But the relationship was subtly altered. The Parsis had by now acquired not only wealth and influence, but also religious learning. They were the custodians of most of the surviving religious mss., and had produced scholars to study them. Moreover, the dispute with the Qadmis had made the Shahanshahis proudly conscious of their own traditions, and unwilling to acknowledge in any way the authority of the Irani community. On the other hand the Iranis, deeply indebted to the Parsis for their benefactions, and impressed by the wealth and splendours of Bombay, were very ready to accord the Indian community respect as well as gratitude. From this time therefore the old tendency was reversed, and some Parsi practices came to be adopted in Iran. The influence of the Parsis in religious matters has increased during the present century.

Further disputes over the calendar have troubled both communities in the present century, with a movement to adopt a fixed calendar (known in India as *fasli* or 'seasonal'). This movement has only a small following among Parsis; but in Iran the Zoroastrians of both Kerman and Tehran have adopted this calendar (which agrees fairly closely with the present national calendar of Persia), whereas the Yazdis adhere in the main to the old one.

In India, apart from these calendar differences, which in no way affect doctrine, there have been two other developments. One is a 'reform' movement, which can broadly be described as seeking to 'restore' the religion to a hypothetical original state by doing away with many of the rituals. The other movement, called *Ilm-i Khshnoom*, is inspired by an ever-growing mass of esoteric and semi-mystical teachings. Its founder, Bahramshah Naoroji Shroff, was an uneducated layman of Surat, who in 1875-6 experienced spiritual enlightenment at Mt. Demavand in Persia. He returned to India, and 27 years later began preaching eloquently and reinterpreting the scriptures on a more 'elevated' plane. At the same time he urged strict adherence to ritual and tradition. A number of the Sanjana priests of Udwada accepted his teachings, and there is now an *Ilm-i Khshnoomist* fire-temple there, and another in Bombay. In general, however, the differences separating *Ilm-i Khshnoom* from orthodox ways are small, and its adherents are generally respected, even by the orthodox, for their piety and orthopraxy. It seems probable that the position of the Zurvanites in the Sasanian church was somewhat similar. (There is no trace of Zurvanite beliefs themselves in later Zoroastrianism.)

In both Iran and India one has to allow for some slight influences from the majority-religions by which Zoroastrianism was surrounded. In Iran these influences appear to be less, because of the implacable hostility of Islam. What was taken over there by Zoroastrians from Muslims seems largely matters of terminology, sometimes adopted protectively. In India the Zoroastrians had in the main a grateful regard for their kindly, tolerant Hindu hosts, and so were more open to their influences, which show in the abandoning of animal-sacrifice, as well as in such minor matters as wedding-customs. Individual Parsis have also sometimes adopted ascetic Hindu practices, such as meagre diet and abstention from meats, especially beef.

III. Conception of the Deity

Parsis and Iranis are at one in considering their religion to be monotheistic, in that they worship one supreme God, Ohrmazd, conceived as wholly just and good, the Creator of all good things; a transcendental Lord, whose kingdom will one day prevail over evil. To please Him and further His creation should be the object of every man.

Below Ohrmazd, like courtiers below their King, are a number of lesser divine beings, the *yazads*, 'worshipped' ones, whose concern for the world is more particular, and who are invoked for aid in specific things. In Iran there are many small shrines to the chief *yazads*, but none to Ohrmazd, who is held to be too exalted to be honoured in this way. In the mountains round Yazd there are, however, ancient shrines, the objects of annual pilgrimage, with altars of bare natural rock; and here, it seems, the supreme God has been reverenced from the remote past in the lofty places of His own creation.

The chief *yazad* under Ohrmazd is Mihr, judge and protector, and mighty foe of demons. (European scholars have tended to think that Mithra was rejected by Zoroaster, but the testimony of the Zoroastrian church is wholly against this assumption.) The fire-temples are called *Dar-i Mihr*, 'Court of Mihr', and the services celebrated there are under this *yazad's* protection. Sarosh, *yazad* of Discipline, is Mihr's lieutenant, and the special guardian of men, in life and at death. Among other *yazads* who are much invoked are Varahram-Bahram, god of Victory and protector of travellers and those in peril, to whom the chief sacred Fires are dedicated; Vahman-Bahman, who has special care of cattle; Spendarmad, *yazad* of the Earth; Tir, who brings rain; and Ashtad, embodiment of Justice and a powerful helper of just men. Anahid Ardvisur, *yazad* of waters and fertility, is invoked by sea and river, and women petition her to grant them children. The *yazads* are reverenced as great and powerful beings, whose concern for man is nevertheless close and immediate; but their subordination to the Creator, Ohrmazd, is never forgotten.

IV. Priesthood and Laity

The Zoroastrian community is divided into two groups, the hereditary priests (called individually in Iran *mobad*, in India *ervad*, and often in both communities by the courtesy-title *dastur*), and the laity or *behdins*, 'those of the Good Religion'. The primary duty of the priests is to pray and perform rituals on behalf of the whole community, although laymen also have a religious obligation to say their own daily prayers, and to conduct household observances. There are no mysteries within the Zoroastrian faith, and no rituals, however sacred, that the laity may not attend. The Zoroastrian believes, however, that rituals are only efficacious if performed and attended by those who are 'clean' (*pāk*), by which term is implied both moral uprightness and physical cleanliness, actual and ritual. For this reason no non-Zoroastrian is allowed to attend Zoroastrian ceremonies, since he does not observe the rules of cleanliness prescribed by the religion. The laity look to their priests to keep themselves the 'cleanest of the clean' (*pāk-i pāk*), so that their prayers may be the more acceptable. The true Zoroastrian priest lives therefore a dedicated life. This does not impose self-mortification, since he may enjoy in moderation all things which are in accord with the good creation of Ohrmazd; but it does require of him a constant self-discipline.

The first steps in the religious life are common to all. A child early becomes familiar with family observances, and if his home is near the fire-temple, he may be encouraged when very small to toddle there and make his first clumsy obeisances to the Fire. At the age usually of 7 (although often later among the Irani laity) he or she is formally initiated into the religion. The child is first taught a few of the essential prayers, in Avestan, and is then invested by a priest, at a solemn family ceremony, with the sacred shirt of cotton (the *sudre-sedre*), and the sacred thread of fine lambswool (the *kusti*), of 72 threads, wound thrice round the waist and tied with 3 knots. The orthodox Zoroastrian thereafter lays aside *sudre* and *kusti* only for ablutions. This initiation-ceremony, called by Parsis *naojot*, by Iranis *sedre-pushun*, is an occasion for rejoicing. The child, who has undergone a ritual bath before the ceremony, receives all new clothes, so that he enters the religious life wholly 'clean'; and relatives and friends often give him other presents as well, and share in a feast to celebrate the occasion.

This ceremony makes the individual a full member of the religious community, and it is only priests who undergo further initiations.

Formerly a priest's son was set, after this, to learn the Avestan liturgical texts, and from 7 to about 14 years of age attended a priests' school daily. The memorising, in a language he did not understand, was monotonous; and the teaching was often stern, with beatings to aid application. Some boys failed to master the mass of texts, and turned perforce to lay occupations; but many priests' sons inherited phenomenal memories, and a strong sense of vocation. Since the late 19th century the tendency has increased for these religious studies to be pursued in early-morning school only, followed by attendance at a secular school later in the day. Accordingly it takes longer now for a priest to become qualified.

The initiation into the priesthood (called by Parsis *navar*, by Iranis *nozud*) is undergone from about 12 years of age upward. In Yazd a candidate had to appear before the entire company of initiated priests. After the Great Dastur had questioned him, any priest present was entitled to ask him to recite some liturgical passage. (A similar practice is known in India among the Sanjanas.) If the candidate passed this examination, he was allowed to undergo the actual initiation. For this he must pass twice in succession (in Kerman thrice) through the *barashnom* of the 9 nights (i.e. a ritual purification followed by 9 days in retreat). Then two qualified priests, themselves having undergone *barashnom*, conduct him through the 4 days of the initiation-ceremony itself, on each of which he, as officiating priest, celebrates the major liturgical ceremony of the *yasna*, with accompanying *baj* and *afrinagan*. On each day the ceremonies are offered to a different divine being. On the fourth day, the initiation complete, the new priest is robed in full ceremonial garments, and takes in his hand the ox-headed mace which has lain before him during all the ceremonies. This mace is the symbol of Mihr, under whom he has now taken up a lifetime's fight against evil. He then, in India, presents himself to the Dastur, is greeted by him, and returns to celebrations held by his own family. In Yazd the whole company of priests used to share in the rejoicings.

After this the young priest is qualified to perform the 'outer' liturgical ceremonies, i.e. those celebrated outside the fire-temple. If he wishes to become a *yojdathragar* or 'purifier', he is further instructed, often by his own father, in the full ritual of the 'inner' liturgical ceremonies, including the long night-office of the *Vendidad*. Then, usually after about 2 years of such instruction, he undergoes the second priestly initiation of *martab*, and is fully-qualified.

The life of the priests is bound up with the fire-temple; and since no major ceremony is ever performed by a single priest, they also have need of one another. It is general, therefore, in all old Zoroastrian communities, to have what are called in Iran *dastur-nishin*, i.e. groups of priests living closely around a fire-temple. In villages, there is usually a single priest who performs minor ceremonies by himself, but refers the major rituals to his colleagues in the priestly community. Yazd and Kerman, and their villages, were divided into *hushts* or parishes, each with a priest in charge; and these *hushts* were redistributed by lot every two years. In India the group of lay families served by a priest constitute his *panthak*; and a *panthak* (which need not be strictly geographical) is hereditary. As well as the *panthakis* or family-priests, there are the *atash-bands*, fully-qualified priests who serve the sacred Fires; other *yojdathragars* who devote themselves almost exclusively to high rituals; and less-qualified priests who help the *panthakis* as required. A priest does not necessarily accept with his office a moral responsibility for the laity. His chief task is the strictly professional one of keeping himself in a state of purity in order to celebrate, exactly and reverently, the intricate rituals and services in which he has been trained.

V. Worship

The Zoroastrians divide the 24-hour day into 5 periods or *gahs*, and religious observances are governed by these. Every Zoroastrian is in strict orthodoxy required to recite certain fixed prayers during each *gah*. These obligatory prayers are called *bandagi* ('service' of God) or *farziyat* ('duty'). They always include untying and retying the *kusti*, with the appropriate prayer to Ohrmazd (this is an essential part of every Zoroastrian act of worship). The recital of the 5 daily *farziyat* is now generally observed only by practising priests, the devout *behdin* usually contenting himself with morning or evening prayers. The Zoroastrian prays standing, facing a source of light (sun, moon, or a lamp); but often ends his prayers by stooping to touch the ground at his feet, in obeisance to God. The *farziyat* are in Avestan; but the pious may supplement them with prayers in the colloquial (Persian or Gujarati). Individual *behdins* sometimes choose to learn considerably more Avestan than is comprised in their *farziyat* (the *yasht* or hymn to Bahram is for example often memorised, at least in part); on the other hand there are simple souls who master little more than the *kusti* and the two great prayers (*ahunvar* and *ashem vohu*, as essential to Zoroastrianism as the Lord's Prayer to Christianity), and who make their private devotions by repeating these many times over.

The chief object of cult is the sacred Fire. This is evidently an ancient element in Indo-Iranian religion, invested in Zoroastrianism with profound moral significance. Fire, the prophet taught, is the living symbol of righteousness. In making it the object of his care and devotion man reminds himself therefore of the power of righteousness and the need to cherish it. Fire, learned Zoroastrians maintain, is thus no more an object of worship than the Muslim *qibla* or Christian cross. Yet since fire is a living thing, which dies if not tended, it is readily personified, and its cult takes on a deep significance. There are 3 grades of sacred Fire. The highest is the *Atash Bahram*, which is consecrated, with great cost and difficulty, from 16 kinds of fire (including that kindled by lightning). There are 2 *Atash Bahrams* in Persia (Yazd and Tehran), and 8 in India (1 each Udwada and Navsari, 4 in Bombay and 2 in Surat). An *Atash Bahram* is kept always burning brightly, even by night, and is served with elaborate ritual, sweet-smelling woods being offered it at the beginning of each of the 5 *gahs*. Only the fully-initiated priests who serve it may enter its sanctuary, and only prayers in its own honour may be offered there. The Fire is to be seen, however, through open grilles in the sanctuary-walls; and other priests and the laity come there at will to offer prayers, and sandalwood or other fragrant things for the Fire.

There are many sacred Fires of the two lesser grades, namely the *Atash-Adaran* and the *Dadgah*. The first must likewise be served by priests, though with less elaborate ritual. The *Dadgah*, though consecrated by priests, may be served by laymen; and occasionally a wealthy Zoroastrian family will have a *Dadgah* Fire in their own house.

The Zoroastrian year has many feast-days, and on these the laity throng to the fire-temples and shrines, to pray and make offerings. Individuals go there also on days of private rejoicing, or to offer private devotions. A priest living near an *Atash Bahram* will seek to go to it daily, and devout laymen may also say daily prayers at their local fire-temple.

In every fire-temple there is a place known as the *urvis-gah* or *yazishn-gah*, where 'inner' liturgical ceremonies are performed. These are usually celebrated in the *Havan Gah*, which is under the protection of Mihr, and lasts from dawn till noon. The *Vendidad* is, exceptionally, a night-office, being specifically against demons, the inhabitants of darkness. The laity have no part in these services, apart from paying for their performance; but may attend them at will. The priests themselves must be fully-qualified *yojdathragars* with *barashnom*. For the services they wear simple clothing (*sudre*, close-fitting trousers, and turban with mouth-veil or *padan*), so that there is no danger of a flowing garment, or even the breath, touching a consecrated object. All utensils and ritual objects used in these services are cleaned, purified and then consecrated, and the priest washes, purifies and then consecrates his own hands. Moreover, the place of each separate act of worship, isolated by hollow lines or furrows (*pavi* or *kash*), is itself subject to the threefold process of washing, purifying and consecrating before the service begins. There is no element of pomp or show in these 'inner' ceremonies, which are strictly ritual acts of worship and consecration, performed for their own sake with a disciplined rigour.

At the core of the services are what appear to be very ancient rituals, designed to consecrate and so further the elements of the good creation of Ohrmazd. Thus each of the 'inner' liturgical ceremonies includes the consecration of bread and animal-products, water and plant-life, and the ritual consumption of these by the officiating priest, who himself derives power therefrom, and who through the ritual confers new force on the elements thus represented, the sources of life for man. Fire also is always present, and becomes itself consecrated through the recital of the liturgy. (In later as in early Zoroastrianism immense power is attributed to the recital of sacred texts in the holy Avestan language.)

The major office of the Zoroastrian church is the *yasna* of 72 chapters, whose liturgy embodies Zoroaster's own hymns or *Gathas*. This office, whose celebration takes usually from 2 to 3 hours, may be dedicated to Ohrmazd Himself, or to any of the lesser divine beings. The daily celebration of the *yasna* is a duty incumbent on the priesthood; and in religious centres such as Udwada or Navsari many *yasnas* are performed each day. In order to obtain power to prepare the *yasna*, the serving priest, the *raspi*, must first perform a lesser ritual, which also embodies the blessing of the means of life. This is called the *panj-tay* '5 twigs', because the priest in celebrating it holds a bundle (*barsom*) of 5 twigs. The *panj-tay*, whose liturgy consists basically of chapters 3-8 of the *yasna*, is the foundation and necessary preliminary for all higher services, and is offered on behalf of 'the whole community' (*hame anjoman*). For performing the most exalted rituals, both officiating and serving priests (*zot* and *raspi*) must qualify themselves by first performing the 'great worship' (*yasht-i meh* or *moti khub*) which consists of the whole *yasna*, devoted to *Mino Navar* (the Spirit of *Navar*, possibly the tutelary spirit of the priesthood). For less exalted ceremonies, they may perform an abbreviated *yasna*, with the same dedication, abridged to those portions of the liturgy which are accompanied by ritual. When both priests need to possess the same power, they perform the *gewra*, that is, they celebrate 6 *yasnas*, on successive days, alternating as *zot* and *raspi*; for it is only the *zot* who acquires full power from the service.

The long liturgy of the *yasna* contains invocations of various divine beings and of natural phenomena, with praise and worship. The ritual centres round a double expressing of the pith from dried twigs of the sacred *hom*-plant (an *ephedra*), and its mixture, at the first expressing, with the sap of crushed pomegranate twigs and consecrated water. The celebrant, having first partaken ritually of consecrated bread (*darun*), drinks the liquid thus prepared, the *parahom*. Milk forms an ingredient in the second *parahom*, otherwise similarly prepared; and during the second part of the service milk and water are used to lave the tie of the *barsom*-twigs, which is made of leaves (palm or tamarisk or oleaster). This act is held to symbolise rain and nourishment for plants. Up to the 18th century, and later, a fat-offering from a sacrificial animal was made to the Fire, but this practice is now abandoned. At the end of the service a part of the second *parahom* is carried out and poured ceremonially into a source of pure water (well or running stream). What remains may be drunk by the celebrant and the serving priest, or by any Zoroastrian present, priest or layman, who wishes to communicate; or reserved for later administration in this way; or poured at the roots of fruit-trees growing in the garden of the fire-temple.

The *yasna* of 72 chapters is further embodied in two longer services. One is the *Visperad*, which is now always offered to Ohrmazd Himself. In this service, which lasts from 4½ to 5 hours, a number of additional liturgical passages are interpolated. The *Visperad* is celebrated especially at the *gahambars*, the 6 seasonal festivals which are held to mark the 6 acts of creation by Ohrmazd (of air, water, earth, plants, animals and man).

The other long service is the *Vendidad*, which lasts from midnight until about 7 a.m. (This is the only service which may begin one day and end the next, the Zoroastrian day being reckoned from dawn.) During this service the whole of the sacred prose work "against demons", the *Vendidad*, is read during the celebration of the *yasna*. (The *yasna* itself is recited wholly from memory; and small variations, according to the dedication of the service, make this an exacting task, however often repeated).

The longest ritual of all is the consecration of urine (*gomez*) from the sacred bull, which is used, with ash from the *Atash Bahram*, in purificatory rituals. This observance, carried out by 2 priests with *barashnom* who have performed the *gewra*, culminates in a *Vendidad* ceremony during which the *gomez* is actually consecrated. It is then reserved, as *nirang*, in the fire-temple for use as needed.

The shortest of the 'inner' liturgical ceremonies, lasting some 15 minutes, centres on the consecration and offering of bread, with animal-products, fruit and water. This ceremony is called briefly either *darun* or *baj*. The *panj-tay* already referred to is a *darun* ceremony; but ordinarily this office is celebrated with a *barsom* of 7 twigs. Whenever a *yasna* is performed, a *darun-baj* is also celebrated with the same dedication.

There are a number of offices which may be celebrated outside the *yazishn-gah*. The most impressive of these 'outer' ceremonies is the *afrinagan*, an office of praise and blessing, with a ritual performed with flowers and fruit, milk and wine. The service is regularly made up of 3 similar parts, the first part being offered to a chosen divine being, the other two to Dahman Afrin (the spirit of Worship) and to Sarosh. For this ceremony the priests wear their stately formal dress, with full-skirted, long-sleeved white robe, and broad white sash, and seat themselves upon a carpet. An *afrinagan* may be celebrated by one priest alone, in a private house, or, on a day of high festival, by the whole assembled priestly *anjoman* in a hall of the fire-temple. The usual number of celebrants is four. An *afrinagan* is a short ceremony, lasting about half-an-hour; it is frequently performed, and is usually attended by the laity.

All Zoroastrian services are offered to a particular divine being on behalf of a person or persons, living or dead, at the behest of someone. A communal ceremony is offered on behalf of the whole community at the injunction of its religious leader, the Dastur; other ceremonies are performed at the behest of a private individual, priest or *behdin*, either on behalf of himself, or for some other living person (in which case the ceremony is said to be for *zinde ravan*, the 'living spirit') or, more often, on behalf of a departed member of his family (when it is said to be for *anaoshah ruwan-asho ravan*, the 'immortal' or 'just spirit').

The Zoroastrians have a strong awareness of the spirits of the dead (the *fravashis*), which leads to many observances on their behalf. Apart from specific ceremonies offered for the individual departed soul, the *ravan*, the great company of the *fravashis* is invoked at all religious observances, and no festival is celebrated without their presence being invited. Many of the specific ceremonies are accompanied by offerings of food, which are afterwards partaken of by the living in communion with the dead, the soul being invited back to join its kinsmen in companionable happiness. Some of the offerings are always given to the poor, for Zoroastrianism is imbued with a deeply charitable spirit.

The Zoroastrians believe that the soul stays on earth for 3 days after death. During these days many ceremonies are performed on its behalf. Each day a *yasna* is celebrated, dedicated to Sarosh, and in each *gah* a *baj* to the same *yazad*. The hymn to the *fravashis*, the *Farvardin Yasht*, is recited daily, as is a *patet* (a formal confession of sins) on behalf of the deceased. A *Vendidad* is often celebrated on one of the 3 nights. 4 *baj* are recited during the 3rd night, and during the one devoted to *Arda Fravash* (the personification of the *fravashis*) a full suit of clothes is consecrated for the departed soul. Just before dawn there is a ceremony of farewell to the spirit, and during the Havan Gah of the 4th day there are further observances to aid it as it undergoes its individual judgment. In Yazd a sheep or goat is sacrificed and ritually roasted on the 3rd night; an oblation of its fat used to be made to the sacred Fire on the 4th morning. In India an offering of sandalwood is now made at this time instead. During the first year ceremonies are held each month, with a major observance on the first anniversary day. In Yazd a sheep is sacrificed again on the first month-day and the first anniversary-day. The family continue to observe the anniversary, with religious observances and offerings of cooked food, for 30 years, approximately the time a son remains alive to remember his parents. After this the soul is held to have become one of the great company of the *fravashis*.

Most 'inner' liturgical services are celebrated on behalf of a departed person, for the soul's comfort and joy. The 'outer' services are quite often performed on behalf of the living, in propitiation, thanksgiving, or simply as an act of worship. No service is ever dedicated to anyone who has lived on earth, for the Zoroastrians do not deify men. The favour of a departed person of great righteousness may, however, be sought through a service celebrated on his behalf, as an *asho ravan*.

All Zoroastrian services are in the sacred language, Avestan. Since

Avestan, as the holy word, is held to have power in itself, Avestan texts are often recited against specific ills, such as sickness, drought or the dangers of travel. Occasionally among simple villagers one finds such usages verging on magic, and even, rarely, on black magic, when no priest is invited to be present, and iron and salt are banished from among the accompanying offerings. Such practices are strongly opposed by both priests and orthodox laymen.

A. *Festivals*

The Zoroastrians have a great bent towards merry-making, and their religious year, down to the 19th century, was studded with festivals, occasions for worship, meeting together and feasting, when only necessary work was done. There was a festival each month, devoted to the *yazad* who presided over that month. The great festivals, which are still celebrated, are: the 6 seasonal *gahambars*, each lasting 5 days; the 5-day festival of *Farvardagan* (devoted to the spirits of the dead); the *Mihragan* (dedicated to Mihr), also lasting 5 days; *Noruz*, dedicated to *Rapithwin*, which celebrates the return of Spring, with its promise of the Resurrection; and *Khordad-i Salin*, the birthday of Zoroaster and anniversary of other great events. Formerly there were major festivals also devoted to Tir, Anahid, Spendarmad and Bahman; but the Zoroastrians are now largely city-dwellers, and their present position as minority communities in mainly urban societies makes the keeping of their own traditional festivals increasingly difficult.

B. *Purification*

The world, in Zoroastrian doctrine, is full of demonaic forces, and a man can readily become unclean through contact with their products (such as dead matter). There are various forms, therefore, of purification. In the simplest a 'clean' person pours water over the 'unclean' from head to foot. Ritual cleansing, administered by a priest, involves also 1) recitation of Avesta; 2) an inward cleansing by drinking *nirang* (consecrated bull's urine) with a pinch of ash from the sacred Fire; 3) a threefold outward cleansing with *gomez* (unconsecrated bull's urine), sand and water. This purification, in its basic form, is administered generally before the *kusti*-initiation, and to the laity before marriage and high festivals. The *si-shur* or '30 washings' is an elaborate form of the threefold cleansing, administered to remove some particular, serious contamination. In the Yazdi area the *si-shur* is still undergone, most often by women who have given birth to a still-born child. The greatest purification of all is the *barashnom* of 9 nights, in which an elaborate threefold initial cleansing is followed by a retreat, under strict rules, lasting 9 days and nights, which are devoted largely to prayer, stillness and more purifications. In India this rite is now undergone only by priests, who often perform it many times in their lives, both to fit themselves for their own high calling and, vicariously, on behalf of members of the laity. In Iran until the beginning of the present century the rite was undergone, in person or vicariously, by almost all members of the community at least once in their life-times, to free themselves from pollution. This is still the practice in the most conservative Yazdi villages.

VI. Ethics

The Zoroastrian virtues are those which forward the good creation of Ohrmazd, and help defeat that of Ahriman. Self-discipline is one of the foremost, since man is a soldier for righteousness. The positive virtues pursued are truthfulness, honest dealing, hard work and thrift (idleness and waste aid the Devil), good temper, cheerfulness (grief is to be controlled if it cannot be banished), charity and helpfulness to all good persons. Moderation (*paiman*) is much urged, so that one may not turn virtue into vice by excess. To marry and have children is better than a barren celibacy, but physical desire should be controlled. Food and drink are to be enjoyed, but temperately. On the other hand, though thrift is good, the demon parsimony lurks beyond it. The worship of God is excellent, but even in this to spend beyond one's means, or to neglect for it one's other duties, is not right. The Zoroastrian has the exacting task of pursuing the golden mean. He may not abandon God's creation to devote himself wholly to the veneration of God, nor flee the temptations of the flesh to take refuge in abstinence. He remains a constant combatant, who, if he strays from virtue through either excess or deficiency, gives increased strength to the enemy.

Although there exist formularies for the confession of sins, Zoroastrianism places the responsibility for his own soul on the individual. All that he does 'goes to the Bridge', i.e. will be weighed in the scales at his judgment on the 4th day after death. If he sins greatly, the only atonement lies in performing even greater good acts (which may include acts of worship), to outweigh the wickedness. One of the leading ethical characteristics of Zoroastrianism is that according to its teachings account is taken, not only of actions, but also of words and intentions. Actions weigh most; but an angry thought adds a little to the burden of a man's sins, and a kindly word increases his treasure in heaven.

VII. Doctrine

The doctrines of Zoroastrianism remain unchanged from the orthodox teachings of Achaemenian and Sasanian times, embodied in the Avestan and Pahlavi books; but these books are in languages incomprehensible to all but the most learned priests. There is no preaching at Zoroastrian acts of worship, and until recently, no medium for the popular exposition of doctrine. Moreover, the surviving church has concerned itself with the practice of religion, rather than with theology. Doctrine therefore has been taught only in broad outline.

The basic teaching, familiar to all, is that although Ohrmazd, Himself wholly good and just, has created the world and everything in it which is good, there exist things which are fashioned not by Him, but by his implacable opponent, Ahriman, who is not subject to His will; and that the world is therefore the scene of a constant struggle, day and night, between the *yazads* and innumerable demons, the one seeking to advance, the other to destroy, the creation of Ohrmazd.

We have already seen something of how good and evil are defined on the ethical plane. On the physical one, the interpretation is wholly anthropocentric. Natural phenomena, such as rain and drought, thunder, and lightning, seed-time and harvest, are seen as the work of *yazad* or demon according to whether they help or hinder man. Dirt, stench, disorder, famine, sickness and death are obvious evils. Cattle, being beneficial to man, are good, and beasts of prey wicked, as are all creatures of the night. The cock, whose call puts darkness to flight, is sacred to Sarosh. Most insects and reptiles, whether actually harmful or merely repugnant to man, are classified as evil, *khrafstars*; and until the 19th century the Zoroastrians of Kerman held an annual festival, on which they went into the desert to kill as many of them as possible, from venomous snake to harmless lizard. Such action is rare nowadays, when stress is on moral combat, and positive attacks are rather upon such things as poverty, disease and ignorance.

The fight against evil is taught, and felt, to be pervasive and constant; but the doctrine is clear that in the end Ohrmazd will prevail.

VIII. The Conception of Man

A. *Creation*

The ancient doctrines about the origin of man have no currency among later Zoroastrians. Mashya and Mashyanag are not familiar figures of reference, as are Adam and Eve to Jew or Christian. The only teachings which are generally known are that man belongs to the good creation, that he was the last of this creation to be made by Ohrmazd, and that by nature and choice he is bound to fight for Him against evil. This doctrine is both proud and humble. Man is the crowning work of Ohrmazd, but at the same time he is linked in fellowship with other creatures of the good creation, such as ox and ass and sheep. The dog especially is held in esteem as just below man in the scale of being. There seem to be some very ancient doctrines exerting influence here; but one factor undoubtedly is that the dog too, through its virtues of faithfulness, obedience and courage, can be regarded as having a moral nature.

B. *Nature*

One of the striking characteristics of Zoroastrianism is the closeness, in its doctrines, of material and immaterial, spiritual and physical. Thus according to Zoroastrian teachings a virtuous man in the state of bodily well-being intended for him by Ohrmazd is the best thing that there is in the created world; but he is open, not only to a moral attack by demons, but also to their physical assault, bringing sickness, deformity, and, in the end, death. The ancient belief that deformity is diabolical brings it about that no deformed person may be a priest; and in sickness there is resort to reciting Avesta to ward off evil. But however it may have been in the past, at present there is no shrinking from the deformed or sick, as unclean. This feeling exists strongly, however, with regard to an effusion of blood, which again is a breach in bodily health, and therefore Ahrimanic. If a priest has a cut from which blood flows, he may not perform rituals; and in strict orthodoxy of the 16th and 17th centuries, if a man even swallowed his own blood from an extracted tooth, he became unclean. Nowadays the belief persists chiefly with regard to menstruation; and in orthodox families a woman in her monthly courses is strictly isolated.

The other great uncleanness is death itself. Even dead matter from the living body, i.e. cut hair and nails, is regarded as impure, and disposed of with care; and a corpse is grossly unclean. According to orthodoxy the better a man has been, the more polluting is his corpse, since the more demons must have gathered to destroy him. The Zoroastrian, who has such reverence for the departed soul, feels none at all for its abandoned body, which is regarded as *nasa* "putrefying matter". The observances which attend its disposal are designed therefore ritually to limit and contain the contamination. They include the repeated gazing at the corpse by a dog, whose look is a deterrent to the powers of evil. The body is never, by orthodox practice, laid in the earth to pollute it, but is exposed on a stone platform in a tower (*dakhma*) at a barren place, to be devoured by birds. This, in Persia and India, is a practical procedure, and has various advantages, other than the doctrinal ones. It is democratic and cheap, and no good ground is wasted. Pressure, however, from other communities, which regard visible vultures with more horror than invisible worms, has led to graveyards being established since 1920 in Tehran and Kerman. Yazd and its villages, and the Parsi community, abide by the old way, and see in it, not the ugliness with which it is invested by non-Zoroastrians, but the beauty of a quick end to corrupting flesh, with bare bones lying clean and exposed to sun and moon and wind. The distaste which an orthodox Zoroastrian feels for burial under ground is very strong.

C. *Destiny and path of salvation*

Man's proper destiny is to remain good, to further the kingdom of Ohrmazd in every way that he can on earth and so, after death, to win a place in heaven, whence he can watch over his descendants, returning as a spirit to receive their offerings and share in their joys. If he fails, and the demons drive him to do more evil than good, his fate will be in hell; and if his good and evil actions exactly counterbalance, then his soul goes to a middle place, a sort of limbo. The performance (either personally or vicariously) of the sacred ceremonies of the Zoroastrian faith is accounted a good act in itself, which weighs in the favourable balance with moral achievements. Negligence of essential observances is added to one's sins.

D. *Personal eschatology*

The old teachings about personal eschatology remain perhaps the most vivid doctrines of later Zoroastrianism. It is held that for 3 days the Soul remains at the place of death, even after the body's removal; and a Zoroastrian coming there to pay his last respects makes to this invisible Soul the profound obeisance accorded to God but never to living men. During this time, if the due rituals are performed, Sarosh protects the Soul, which otherwise is naked to the taunts and threats of the gathered demons. Offerings of food are made for the soul thrice a day, and these are given to a dog to eat. (There is a link between the dog and death going back evidently to the remote Indo-Iranian past.)

At the dawn of the 4th day the Soul goes to the Chinvad Bridge. Here its deeds are weighed before the *yazads* Mihr, Rashn and Ashtad. If the good deeds outweigh the bad, it crosses the broad Bridge to Heaven; if the bad are heavier, the Bridge contracts to a hair's breadth, and the Soul plunges off it into the abyss of Hell. Rituals are performed to support the Soul at this crucial time, which is vividly present to the minds of true Zoroastrians.

E. *General eschatology*

There is a generally-held belief in a final overthrow of Ahriman and the demons, and a resurrection of the body for all men, to be followed by the Last Judgment and the final restoration of the world of good. No details of this general eschatology are current in later popular belief; but there is a yearly festival, that of Rapithwin, which as the old Pahlavi books record, celebrates in the return of spring an annual foreshadowing of the resurrection of the body, through the symbolism of new life springing in seemingly dead twigs. This spring festival of the resurrection is evidently at least as old as the Achaemenian period. Its observance is incumbent on every Zoroastrian; and although its doctrinal significance is now largely forgotten, it remains one of the chief holy festivals, celebrated with solemnity and joy each year.

IX. Present Religious Situation

The present position of Zoroastrianism is complex. There is the orthodox group, which includes priest and layman, rich and poor, learned and simple, who hold by the old faith and observances. The

Ilm-i kshnoom school is closely associated with this orthodoxy, being among the strictest in maintaining rituals. Then there is the reform movement, whose members seek to preserve the ethical teachings while curtailing rituals. Some reformists blend their own beliefs with teachings from Hinduism or theosophy. Certain reformist priests will accept converts and invest children of mixed marriages with the *kusti*. These questions have hardly arisen in Iran, but orthodox Parsi priests are sternly opposed to both practices. Then, as in any faith, there are nominal believers, vague as to both practice and doctrine, who seek the priests chiefly at times of initiation, marriage and death; and, finally, agnostics and atheists, who nevertheless keep their links with the community, since Zoroastrians are bound by religion and blood, and if one tie fails the other holds. Even they, at the wish of their families, often have the last rites of the faith performed for them at death.

The great period of prosperity for the religion was the second half of the 19th century, when it benefited from the community's new wealth, and before the secularising influences of the 20th century began to erode it. This erosion came most swiftly in Iran, where the sudden change in the community's fortunes, with the introduction of secular education, led to the wholesale abandoning of their calling by the sons of priests. There are now hardly a score of practising priests in the whole of Iran. Some are well versed in rituals and observances; but knowledge of the religious books (other than the liturgical ones) has been lost. There are no new entrants to the priesthood, and little inducement for future ones. The priests still receive no stipends, and though the pious lavish money on other religious causes, they cannot bring themselves to the revolutionary step of providing them. As the number of ceremonies asked for dwindles, so the priests' incomes sink. Nor are they any longer respected as the only learned members of the community. The likelihood is, therefore, that the priesthood in Iran will die out with the present generation.

In India the situation is a little less bleak. There communications with European scholars stimulated the Parsi priests to new studies of their own religious books; and with their learning they kept something of their old authority. But the new secular sciences have tempted the majority of priests' sons away in India also. Formerly it was the clever sons of a priest who followed their father's calling. Now the ablest boys go into secular life unless, exceptionally, one of them has a strong sense of religious vocation. The priesthood is therefore declining steadily in India also, although there priests are still to be numbered in their hundreds; but those who are prepared to follow the arduous life of the full-qualified *yojdathragar* grow ever fewer. Though the religious life of the community appears to be thriving, with the priesthood diminishing the future cannot be said to be hopeful for Zoroastrianism even in India.

There are a number of small Zoroastrian communities scattered round the world, mainly in ports of the former British Empire, several of which have fire-temple and priest; but in these isolated outposts secularising influences are prevalent. The chief centres of orthodoxy are Navsari in India, with still a relatively large number of priests, a library of religious mss., and staunchly guarded traditions; and Sharifabad in Iran, where the villagers with their one priest, unsupported by book-learning, maintain traditional observances in a remarkable way.

X. Short History of the Study of the Religion

The existence of Zoroastrianism as a living religion remained unknown to Europe until the 17th century, when a number of first-hand reports of both Irani and Parsi Zoroastrians were made by travellers. Their ancient scriptures were first studied in Surat by Anquetil-Duperron, who read them with a Parsi priest, Dastur Darab, and made a French translation based on the traditional Zoroastrian interpretation. This he published in 1771, with valuable notes on actual observances. The study of the Avesta advanced rapidly in Europe with the discovery in the 19th century of the close kinship between the Avestan language and Sanskrit. Since then the study of Zoroastrianism has been promoted in Europe by two groups of scholars. In the first are many distinguished men who have concerned themselves with the texts, often primarily for their linguistic interest, without seeking help from the living religion. In the second are a smaller number who have supplemented their work by inquiry among the Parsis. The outstanding names here, after Anquetil himself, are J. Darmesteter (whose French translation of the Avesta contains invaluable notes on Parsi usages), M. Haug and E. W. West. The two latter scholars devoted themselves to Pahlavi (the language of Sasanian Persia and of many religious books), and collaborated with Parsi priests in publishing texts.

The Parsis themselves have not made any notable original contribution to Avestan studies since the 18th century; but they have done valuable work in Pahlavi. Most editions of Pahlavi texts have been published in Bombay by Parsis, the leading names among many being TEHMURAS ANKLESARIA and his son BEHRAMGORE, PESHOTAN SANJANA, M. R. UNVALA and his son JEHANGIR, E. K. ANTIA, J. JAMASPASANA, and outstandingly, B. N. DHABHAR. UNVALA and DHABHAR published also the texts and translations of a number of the Persian *Rivayats*, which give valuable information about Zoroastrianism in the 16th and 17th centuries. Other Parsis, in particular J. J. MODI, have made many contributions to the knowledge of observances; in this Europeans have been wholly dependent on Zoroastrian exposition, since no non-Zoroastrian may attend religious ceremonies. A good deal of such work has been published by Parsis in Gujarati, for the enlightenment of their own community.

There were no scholars in the Irani community until recently, when J. SORUSHIAN, a leading Kermani layman, published in Tehran in 1956 his *Farhang-i behdinan*, a dictionary of the Zoroastrian dialect, containing much valuable information on Irani customs, which till then had remained unknown. The contribution of Irani Zoroastrians in preserving old observances which did not cross the sea to India is just coming to be appreciated.

SELECT BIBLIOGRAPHY

for general works on the Zoroastrian religion see Volume I, bibliography of the article by J. Duchesne-Guillemin on 'Religion of ancient Iran')

(a) *The Parsis*

M. HAUG, *Essays on the sacred language, writings and religion of the Parsis*, 3rd ed., ed. E. W. WEST, Bombay, 1884.

D. F. KARAKA, *History of the Parsis*, 2 volumes, Bombay, 1884.

D. MENANT, *Les Parsis: histoire des communautés zoroastriennes de l'Inde*, Part I (Annales du Musée Guimet, Bibl. d'Études 7), Paris, 1898 [The second part was never published]. *Une sacerdoce zoroastrien à Naosari*, Paris, 1911.

K. N. SEERVAI and B. B. PATEL, *Parsis*, in *Gazetteer of the Bombay Presidency*, IX i, 1899, pp. 183-288.

M. M. MURZBAN, *The Parsis in India*, 2 volumes, Bombay, 1917 (an enlarged English edition of Mlle MENANT's book).

S. H. HODIVALA, *Studies in Parsi history*, Bombay, 1920.

J. J. MODI, *The religious ceremonies and customs of the Parsees*, Bombay, 2nd ed., 1937.

b) *The Iranis*

A. V. W. JACKSON, *Persia past and present*, New York, 1909, chapters XXIII-XXV.

E. G. BROWNE, *A year amongst the Persians*, Cambridge, 2nd ed., 1926, p. 394ff.

D. MENANT, article on 'Gabars' in *ERE*.

B. N. DHABHAR, *The Persian Rivayats of Hormazyar Framarz and others*, Bombay, 1932.

M. BOYCE, articles in *Acta Orientalia* 1966, *JRAS* 1966, *BSOAS* 1967-1969, *Festschrift F. B. J. Kuiper*, 1969.

HINDUISM

BY

R. N. DANDEKAR

Poona, India

I. Prologue

Hinduism is, in many respects, a unique phenomenon in the history of religions. Indeed, Hinduism can hardly be called a religion in the popularly understood sense of the term. Unlike most religions, Hinduism does not regard the concept of god as being central to it. Hinduism is not a system of theology—it does not make any dogmatic affirmation regarding the nature of god. And yet—and this is rather confusing—the Hindus are often seen to worship many gods, and that too when most of them may be actually believing in only one god as the single ultimate reality. Similarly, Hinduism does not venerate any particular person as its sole prophet or as its founder. It does not also recognize any particular book as its absolutely authoritative scripture. Further, Hinduism does not insist on any particular religious practice as being obligatory, nor does it accept any doctrine as its dogma. Hinduism can also not be identified with a specific moral code. Hinduism, as a religion, does not convey any definite or unitary idea. There is no dogma or practice which can be said to be either universal or essential to Hinduism as a whole. Indeed, those who call themselves Hindus may not necessarily have much in common as regards faith or worship. What is essential for one section of the Hindu community may not be necessarily so for another. And, yet, Hinduism has persisted through centuries as a distinct religious entity.

The Hindus are usually believed to be rather excessively obsessed with religion—they are said to be sharing this trait of being inordinately occupied with religion with most Asians—but, strange as it may seem, they themselves do not betray any self-consciousness in that behalf. They do not look upon religion as something essentially separate from the other activities of life. For a Hindu, religion is neither an extraneously imposed duty to be specially attended to nor a particular problem to be deliberately pondered over. He views life as an integrated whole and its various aspects as being intrinsically interdependent. This may account for there being no word in Sanskrit to denote religion as it is popularly understood. The word *dharma*, which is usually employed as a synonym for religion, has a far wider connotation. Broadly speaking, it implies the whole complex of theories and practices relating to the actualities and aspirations of the material and spiritual life of the individual and the society. *Dharma*, to a Hindu, is, accordingly, co-extensive with life. It may be said to signify the entire way of life, which, however, is not necessarily and in all respects identical in the case of all those who call themselves Hindus.

Hinduism is, in a sense, an ethnic religion. It was not revealed to a prophet and then either propagated among or imposed upon the people. The Hindus are verily born and grow in Hinduism; and this condition of birth is so compulsive that many persons who are born of Hindu parents have generally to conform to Hinduism though they may not believe in many of its doctrines and practices. It has now almost become a truism to say that Hinduism defies all attempts at definition. One can hardly assert that a person is entitled to be called a Hindu only if he believes in certain doctrines and follows certain practices or that he forfeits his claim to be called a Hindu if he does not believe in certain doctrines and follow certain practices.

Attempts have no doubt been made, from time to time, to lay down some criteria of Hinduism. Belief in the absolute validity of the Veda is, for instance, often mentioned as a distinctive attribute of a Hindu. Actually, however, one can be a good and devout Hindu without having to profess such a belief. The various schools of Tantrism may be referred to as an instance in point. Moreover, such a definition ultimately proves to be singularly vague and nebulous. For, the Veda, as we know it, being a collection of essentially heterogeneous and, in some cases, even self-contradictory texts, one would indeed find it difficult to accept the whole of it as being equally valid and binding. One of the *Upaniṣads* itself characterises the *Ṛgveda*, etc., as embodying "lower knowledge" (*aparā vidyā*). The Veda is also open to a variety of interpretations, no one of which can be said to be invested with absolute authority. Observance of caste-rules is certainly a more potent criterion. It is neither the disavowal of any particular doctrine nor the deviation from any particular religious practice that has been regarded as a serious lapse on the part of a Hindu; it is rather the non-conformity to the caste-rules which has been regarded as such. But even this latter may entail the loss of one's caste-status; it does not necest sarily entail the loss of Hinduism. It may also be pointed out tha-

caste-rules are scripturally and conventionally believed to be non-operative in respect of certain classes of Hindus, such as ascetics and *sannyāsins*. Strictly speaking, Hinduism as a religion must needs be distinguished from Hinduism as a social organization. In this connection, it is significant that, in recent times, responsible Hindu thinkers, who are keen on the preservation and promotion of Hinduism as religion, regard caste-system as a veritable curse and openly advocate its abolition. Incidentally, it may also be noted that conditions of modern life have actually tended to remove the caste-barriers among the Hindus to a large extent. Thus, observance of traditional caste-rules cannot any longer be regarded as a universally valid criterion of Hinduism. The belief in the sanctity of the cow and the Brāhmana is too superficial a feature to be considered seriously in this context. One cannot also speak of any sacraments being obligatory to all the Hindus. Doctrines regarding *ātman*, *karma*, *saṁsāra*, and *mokṣa* may perhaps be regarded as axiomatic in many schools of Hindu philosophy, but they are by no means either universal or essential so far as Hindu religion is concerned. For, a person can claim to be a good Hindu without believing in any or all of these doctrines, while a person is not entitled to be called a Hindu only because he accepts any or all of these doctrines.

The word "Hindu", it must be remembered, is of a foreign origin. It is also of a fairly late origin. Actually, most of what is usually understood by the term "Hinduism" or "Hindu religion" had been in existence since very much long before that term came into vogue. Indeed, the term "Hinduism" came to acquire its specific and complex socio-religious significance only in comparatively recent times. Originally, the term "Hindu" seems to have had a purely geographical connotation. The people who lived on the other side (that is, on the eastern side) of the river Indus were loosely called Hindus. And, even after that name had, as it were, become naturalised, it was for a long time understood in a more or less negative sense. Whoever was born in India and was not a Muslim or a Christian or a Parsi, etc., was called a Hindu. Obviously, such a negative description can hardly be made to serve any useful purpose. It is sometimes suggested that the term "Hindu" is an essentially juricical term, and that a Hindu may be most conveniently defined as a person to whom the Hindu law becomes applicable in the law courts of India. But this would amount to arguing in a circle, for Hindu law itself cannot be defined except as the law which is generally made applicable to the Hindus. Moreover, the Hindu law does not become applicable to all the Hindus in the same manner and to the same extent. Conversely, it is seen that all those who are today governed by the Hindu law do not necessarily profess Hindu religion. Such, for instance, are the Sikhs, the Jainas, and the Buddhists. The relationship between Hinduism and the Hindu law is by no means comparable with that between Islam and the Muslim civil law.

Hinduism cannot thus be said to be amenable to any theological definition or sociological test or juridical characterisation. One has, therefore, inevitably to fall back upon the very simple definition, namely, that a Hindu is one who is born of Hindu parents and who has not *openly* abjured Hinduism. This definition also, no doubt, involves the defect of *petitio principii*; but, in view of the great antiquity of Hinduism, that defect may be treated as more apparent than real and may not be regarded as seriously vitiating the definition. However, the real difficulty here would be in respect of recent converts to Hindu religion. Moreover, the term Hinduism itself would still remain undefined.

By the very nature of its origin and growth, Hinduism has been exceedingly tolerant—tolerant towards other religions and tolerant towards itself. Hinduism has, by and large, always tended to incorporate and assimilate rather than to choose and eliminate. Hinduism is also a remarkably free religion—a religion which is untramelled by any fixed creeds, dogmas, or rituals. In the course of its long history, it has manifested a unique capacity for almost infinite expansion. One of its basic assumptions seems to have been that, though religious practices and beliefs were bound to change according to different times and different climes, they could all be comprehended within a larger unity. Accordingly, Hinduism has always been variable, elastic, and receptive. Unlike many religions, which are prophetic or creedal and which, therefore, necessarily tend to remain static, it has exhibited, throughout history, a remarkable resilience and responsiveness to the needs of different communities and to the demands of different ages and regions. It has never hesitated to sponsor newer scriptures, newer gods, and newer institutions. It has rejected none; it has welcomed within its fold all those who have sought its spiritual leadership and social protection and sustenance. It thus represents different levels of religious belief and practice and different stages of cultural development, and offers almost endless grades of spiritual possibilities. Indeed, the two great merits of Hinduism have been its concern for the specific spiritual competence of a person (*adhikāra*) and its readiness to allow him freedom of worshipping his chosen divinity (*iṣṭadevatā*). A reference may be made in this very context to another feature of Hinduism, namely, that Hindu worship is personal rather than congregational in character. A Hindu feels as uninhibited in adopting any particular religious practice as in subscribing to any particular doctrine.

The result of all this has been manifold. It is true that Hinduism has rarely been guilty of religious persecution. It is also true that this tendency of Hinduism to absorb and sanctify whatever it came across has been to a large extent responsible for the fact that it spread all over India rapidly and without resorting to any active proselytisation. It may be further pointed out to the credit of Hinduism that the religious absorption which it promoted was invariably accompanied by a social absorption and readjustment. But on the debit side it must be mentioned that the over-tolerant and absorptive attitude of Hinduism has resulted in lowering the average level of its doctrines and ritual. And, what is perhaps still more serious, Hinduism has, on account of this trait, all along been deprived of the compactness and distinct characterisation which normally invest a religion with a peculiar strength. It should, therefore, not be surprising that Hinduism had never encouraged a theocratic state or that it had hardly ever become a state religion.

If one might at all speak of any distinctive features of Hinduism, one could mention the belief in the ideological complex of *karma-saṁsāra-mokṣa* on the metaphysico-ethical plane and the acceptance of caste-system on the socio-ethical plane. As the result of his original ignorance, man gets involved in a whole cycle of existences which has been revolving since eternity (*saṁsāra*)—his doings in the course of one life inexorably governing the nature and conditions of his next life in a perpetual chain of causality (*karma*). His religio-philosophical *summum bonum* lies in *mokṣa* or his becoming free from this involvement through the realisation of his true nature, that is to say, of his essential identity with the one absolute reality. A Hindu is, accordingly, ever obsessed with the quest for *mokṣa*, and his attitude towards life is generally determined by his conviction that a single life in a whole cycle of existences is valueless from the ultimate point of view. On the other hand, however, a Hindu does not altogether ignore his individual mundane life—he makes it serve as the ground for his efforts to attain *mokṣa*. He believes that the existence in flux holds a promise for the existence in essence. He further believes—and this is perhaps far more important—that the manner in which he lives his life vitally affects the security and solidarity of the society to which he belongs. A proper co-ordination between the philosophico-ethical ideal of *mokṣa* and the socio-ethical ideal of *dharma*, which latter is believed to have found its most typical expression in the form of *varṇāśrama-dharma* and which is regarded as investing the phenomenal existence with a meaning and a purpose, may be said to constitute the most central problem of Hinduism. *Mokṣa*, it is realised, is theoretically attainable by any individual by himself, but *dharma* has to adjust itself with a given social situation.

Another problem, which has often figured prominently in the history of Hinduism and which, in the ultimate analysis, is just a reflection of the problem referred to above, relates to the conflict between the traditional *dharma* or the way of life prescribed in scriptural texts and the eternal or absolute *dharma* which reveals itself to the enlightened one and to which the traditional *dharma* attempts to give but a practical expression. It is something like a conflict between 'law' and 'justice'. The attitude of Hinduism in this respect is ambivalent—on the one hand, it insists on the subordination of the sense of right to the sense of duty, while, on the other, it unequivocally states that, at a certain stage in his spiritual advancement, the true seeker may set aside the injunctions of the traditional *dharma*.

It needs to be remembered that Hinduism is not a unitary concept or phenomenon nor a monolithic structure. It is, therefore, hardly possible to make any statement which can become applicable, without exception, to Hinduism as a whole. Hinduism is, indeed, as unpredictable as human nature. In the last analysis, a study of Hinduism would invariably amount to a study of the various Hindu castes and sects. The Hindu society is cut up horizontally into castes and vertically into religious sects—the horizontal stratification having been originally more rigid and more exclusive than the vertical one.

Hinduism appears to be marked by several paradoxes and polarities. For instance, it emphasizes religious equality among all men and at the same time not only connives at but actually promotes a rigorous social hierarchy. It allows complete freedom in the matter of belief but insists on a rigid conformity to caste-rules. And what is particularly striking is that, though the lower castes suffer from many disabilities both in the religious and social spheres, one finds that the lower the caste is in the social hierarchy the more religiously conservative and conformistic it usually happens to be. Hinduism does not insist on any set form of worship, but this fact itself has given rise to a veritable plethora of religious practices. Similarly, on the one hand, Hinduism regards god as a superfluity, while, on the other, it sponsors a deeply emotional theism as the noblest form of religion. On the one hand, it lays down rigorous austerities and penances for the sake of religious discipline, while, on the other, it seems to permit various orgiastic and sensualistic rites. On the one hand, it extols *mokṣa*, *jñāna*, and *saṁnyāsa* as the highest religious ideals, while, on the other, it also prescribes elaborate rituals which are believed to win *svarga* for their punctilious performer. Hinduism does not countenance any dichotomy of religion and philosophy. Philosophy is believed to involve man in a very profound manner. It is, indeed, understood to be essentially an applied —and not merely a theoretical or contemplative—discipline. It aims at concrete, tangible results. It is certainly significant that the *Upaniṣads* and similar texts often speak of *vidyās* (pragmatic philosophical doctrines) rather than of *jñāna* (pure, academic knowledge). Philosophy is thus regarded as an integral part of religion. This would also account, in some measure, for the paradoxes and polarities mentioned above. But the true glory of Hinduism consists in presenting all these polarities and paradoxes as also the various levels of doctrine and practice as constituting a single well-coordinated religious system.

II. Historical Survey

Hinduism has in no sense been revealed to or founded by any prophet or messiah. It is, therefore, not possible to speak in terms of the specific origin of that religion. All that we may do in this connection is to go back to the earliest period in the history of India when some of the distinctive features of the Hindu religion as we know it today had already become manifest. Not many years ago, the spade of the archaeologist unearthed a whole civilization in the valley of the river Indus—first centering round Mohenjo Daro and then primarily round Harappa—and thereby gave quite a new orientation to the history of India. The age of the newly discovered Indus valley civilization —which is now more popularly known as the Harappa civilization—is generally believed to have extended from 4000 B.C. to 2200 B.C. A considerable amount of material has become available from the excavations carried out at Mohenjo Daro, Harappa, and other related sites which throws ample light on the various aspects of that civilization, including religion. Indeed, the Indus valley religion is perhaps the earliest form of religion in India about which one may make some statement which is supportable by a more or less tangible evidence. Even on a cursory examination, the Indus religion is seen to display certain traits which, on the one hand, conspicuously differentiate it from the Vedic Aryan religion, which, incidentally, had for a long time been looked upon—of course, erroneously—as the fountain-head of Hinduism but which can now be shown to have exercised but a formal and superficial influence on that religion, and, on the other, establish close and direct affiliations with what may be called classical or historical Hinduism whose many ramifications continue to become evident even to this day. Thus, essentially, the Indus religion is a form of Hinduism and may, in contradistinction to classical or historical Hinduism, be styled as protohistoric Hinduism. It may, accordingly, be said to represent the first period of the history of Hinduism.

Naturally enough, the sources for the reconstruction of the Indus religion are rather limited. We do not have any literature or popular tradition relating to it. We have to depend mainly on such objects as seals, sealings, figurines, and stone images discovered at the various archaeological sites which have laid open different phases of the Indus civilization. But all this material is quite illuminating and can be fruitfully exploited if worked upon with 'scientific imagination'. The first thing which would strike even a casual observer is that, unlike the Vedic religion, the Indus religion was essentially iconolatrous, which feature, incidentally, is seen to have been shared with it by the Hinduism of the later periods. One of the most important objects derived from the excavations in the Indus valley, which may be presumed to throw much useful light on the religion of the period, is the seal, discovered at Mohenjo Daro, depicting a three-faced nude male deity with horns, seated on a stool, with *penis erectus* and with his heels pressed closely together in what is obviously some specific yogic posture. This god is shown with an elephant, a tiger, a rhinoceros, and a buffalo surrounding him and with antelopes under his seat. He is seen to be wearing a large number of bangles on each arm and a pectoral round his neck, and a fan-shaped head-dress rises between the horns. The inscription of six or seven letters appearing at the top of the seal is not yet satisfactorily deciphered—indeed, none of the pictographs from the Indus valley has been so deciphered—and cannot accordingly enlighten us on the true character of the figure. But the cummulative evidence of the various details depicted on the seal would seem to lead to only one conclusion, namely, that the Mohenjo Daro god was akin to—or even identical with—the Śiva of classical Hinduism. The three faces clearly suggest the *trimukha* Śiva and would remind one of the *triśīrṣa* Maheśamūrti of Elephanta. The nudity and ithyphallicism, which characterise the Mohenjo Daro figure, are the distinctive features also of classical Śiva. Śiva is Yogīśvara or the lord of *yoga*-practitioners. This characteristic is adumbrated in the yogic posture of the Indus god, who is represented as seated in something like a *padmāsana* with his eyes apparently directed to the tip of the nose.

The headgear of the Indus god is made up of two horns and a fan-like thing protruding in the middle of those horns. The prevalence of bulls and bull-like animals among the Indus seal-symbols would suggest that the bull was connected with the Indus god in some special way—presumably as his vehicle. The bull is the vehicle also of the classical Śiva. In many primitive religious cults, a god was often represented by his vehicle; or certain distinctive features of the vehicle, such as the bull's horns in the present case, were transferred to the god. The two horns of the Mohenjo Daro god do reappear in classical Hindu mythology—but in a more sophisticated and poetic form, namely, of the crescent moon which is believed to be adorning the forehead of Śiva. And the fan-like protrusion between the two horns, which is seen on the Indus seal, may be regarded as the precursor either of the peculiar head-dress of Śiva in his role as hunter or of the matted hair of the ascetic Śiva, which is so arranged as to form a crest.

The fact that the Indus god is shown with different animals surrounding him establishes a direct connection between him and the classical Śiva in his aspect of Paśupati or lord of animals. It may also be pointed out that classical Śiva is associated, in some special way, with the specific animals seen on the Mohenjo Daro seal. On another terracotta sealing discovered in the Indus valley, the Indus god is shown with the three symbols, namely, the bull, the trident, and the phallus, which are also the special symbols of Śiva. That the phallus-cult must have been a significant constituent of the Indus religion becomes evident from the large number of conical or cylindrical stones (representing *liṅga* or male organ) and rings (representing *yoni* or female organ) discovered in the Indus valley. It is likely that the *liṅga-yoni*-cult had originated and developed independently, but it must have been merged into the larger religious complex centering round the god of Mohenjo Daro who was represented anthropomorphically. Another feature which is common to the Indus god and Śiva is their association with the Mother Goddess cult, the fertility cult, and the serpent cult. Like the phallus cult, the Mother Goddess cult also must have had an independent origin, but, in one of the phases of its development, namely, as the cult of "mothers", it must have become organically associated with the Indus valley religion. The large number of terracotta or faience female figurines, which have been discovered at different sites in the Indus valley, would seem to substantiate such an assumption. The character of the Indus god as a fertility-vegetation god is indicated by his representation, on two seals, with a sprig of flowers or leaves rising from his head. Similarly, on a copper sealing, the same horned god in yogic posture is shown with two devotees kneeling on his two sides with hands joined in prayer and two coiling serpents both facing the god. It is not known by what name the Indus people called their god, but, from the point of view of the history of Hinduism, he may be safely referred to as proto-Śiva.

The worship of proto-Śiva must be said to have constituted a prominent feature of the Indus religion. Indeed, sufficient evidence is available to warrant the supposition that the religion of proto-Śiva had spread far and wide in pre-Vedic India—different aspects of the personality and character of that god having been emphasized in different parts of the country. In his proto-Dravidian aspect, for instance, the god of this religion was celebrated as a 'red' god and was actually called Śiva (which word in proto-Dravidian means 'red'). The religious practices relating to Śiva consisted mainly of *pūjā* (which word, derived from proto-Dravidian, originally signified the besmearing of the god's icon presumably with the offerings of blood, thus confirming the 'redness' of the god) and *bali* (which originally meant the offering of raw oblations like uncooked flesh). Apart from the crude icons reddened with blood, the god of the proto-Dravidians seems to have been worshipped also in two other forms, namely, the phallus and the bull. It may also be presumed that in ancient South India it was the cult of the "mothers" rather than that of the Mother Goddess which had prevailed. Indeed, the religion, which could be characterised as specifically South Indian, concerned these *grāmadevatās* or the female-divinities of the village.

As has been shown above, in the Indus valley version of this pre-Vedic non-Aryan religion, prominence was given to the anthropomorphic figure of the god, his lordship over animals, his mastery over yoga, his character as a wild hunter, and his association with the serpent cult and the fertility cult and with the bull. The Indus version of proto-Śiva was vitally connected also with the cults of the Mother Goddess and the phallus.

Two other aspects of proto-Śiva seem to have been referred to in a Vedic text, namely, the *Śatapatha-Brāhmaṇa*. According to that *Brāhmaṇa*, proto-Śiva was celebrated as Śarva by the Prācyas or the people of Eastern India and as Bhava by the Vāhikas or the Bāhlīkas in the North-West.

The religion of proto-Śiva, which had thus taken deep roots in various parts of India, seems to have been temporarily overshadowed during the interlude when the Vedic Aryan religion had been firmly and rapidly extending its influence. But that pre-Vedic non-Aryan religion could not be altogether smothered or even ignored. Actually, the Vedic religion adapted—or, rather, was constrained to adapt—within itself some of the features of that religion, though with evident hesitancy and reluctance. The Vedic Rudra represents, both in name and character, an aryanised version of the protohistoric Śiva. Some other features of the religion of proto-Śiva also are reflected in some Vedic hymns such as the hymns relating to the *muni* (that is, the ascetic in ecstasy: *Ṛgveda* X. 136), the *brahmacārin* (that is, the observer of the rigorous vows: *Atharvaveda* XI.5), and the *vrātyas* (that is, the followers of the cult of wandering mendicancy: *Atharvaveda* XV). At the same time, some Vedic texts suggest, in quite unequivocal terms, the antagonism of the Vedic Aryans towards the followers of the religion of proto-Śiva, who are variously represented as *śivas* (those having Śiva as their chief god) and *viṣāṇins* (horned head-dress wearers) (*Ṛgveda* VII. 18.6), *śiśnadevas* (phallus-worshippers: *Ṛgveda* VII. 21.5; X. 99.3), and *yatis* (ascetics practising penance, as against *ṛṣis* or householder-sages of the Veda: *Taittirīya-Saṁhitā* VI. 2.7.5; *Aitareya-Brāhmaṇa* VII. 28.1).

The evidence of the seals and sealings unearthed in the Indus valley excavations further points to the prevalence in the protohistoric period of religious cults associated with trees, animals, and water. These cults, on the one hand, isolate the Indus religion from the Vedic religion, and, on the other, represent that religion as the direct ancestor of the historical Hindu religion. In this very context may be mentioned the Indus valley religious practice of burning oil or incense which is suggested by the smoke-stained cup-like objects held by the female figurines. The Vedic Aryan religion does not know of any such practice, while it forms a significant feature of the classical Hindu way of worship. It is true that no temples as such have been unearthed in the Mohenjo Daro or Harappa excavations. But it is not unlikely that the ground-plans of shrines, which were presumably scattered, are now not distinguishable from those of ordinary houses. Evidence for the existence of public places for worship, ritual, and ritual congregation is perhaps available in the form of the fortified citadels at Mohenjo Daro and Harappa. These may have, indeed, been something like tower-temples provided with such accessory arrangements as those for ceremonial ablution and communal lustration. The facts that no idols of gods as such have been found and that many figurines and statuettes possessing religious significance have been considerably damaged would suggest the possibility of this having been the result of the iconoclastic activities of some non-idolatrous antagonistic tribes.

As has been pointed out earlier, the reconstruction of the religious complex in the pre-Vedic non-Aryan India is bound to be largely hypothetical. But two points in this connection may be presumed to be beyond doubt, namely,

(1) that, in most of its essential features, the protohistoric religion was different from the Vedic Aryan religion, and

(2) that its similarities with the classical Hindu religion, particularly with that aspect of it which celebrated god Śiva, were quite unmistakable.

A direct line of relationship is thus established between that religion and the classical or historical Hinduism, so that that religion may be quite justifiably characterised as protohistoric Hinduism.

From the point of view of the history of Hinduism as a whole, the Vedic Aryan period may be said to have occurred more or less as an interlude. It was no doubt an eventful and highly significant period but the religious ideology of that period did not certainly exercise on the formation and character of historical Hinduism as vital and far-reaching an influence as it is usually believed to have done. In a sense, historical Hinduism arose as a kind of reaction against the peculiar religio-philosophical conditions which had been engendered by Vedism—particularly by its later phases. However, the attitude of the sponsors of historical Hinduism was thoroughly realistic and pragmatic. They had fully realised the extent and profundity of the influence of the Vedic way of life and thought and, therefore, decided, as a practical measure, not to alienate themselves completely from it. Hinduism, accordingly, not only did not turn its back on Vedic beliefs and practices, but it actually professed an allegiance to the Veda. It was rightly anticipated that such an allegiance, howsoever formal and tenuous it might prove in actual practice, would help Hinduism in its encounter with the so-called heretic religious movements of the early post-Vedic period.

The Vedic religion, it needs to be remembered, was essentially exotic on the Indian soil, and, in the vigour of this very exoticness, it succeeded in rapidly overwhelming the religious complex of the pre-Vedic non-Aryan India. But, as has been pointed out earlier, it could not obliterate the latter completely. Vedism itself was constrained to assimilate some of its features, albeit reluctantly, while many of its other features remained generally dormant—but quite viable among certain strata of society—until they were resuscitated with the rise of Hinduism.

Unlike the protohistoric Hinduism, the Vedic religion can boast of an ample and varied literature relating to it, namely, the Veda. The term Veda is not to be understood as referring to any single book—it, indeed, implies a whole complex of literature, whose authorship extends over many generations and provenance over widely separated geographical regions and which represents different phases of thought-content and different modes of literary style. It was claimed that the Veda was *apauruṣeya*, that is to say, it was not the work of any human agency. The Veda was eternal, and all that the Vedic seers did in respect of it was just to discover it. It may, however, be incidentally pointed out that the Veda hardly ever specifically referred to itself as the word of god. Consequent upon the claim of the *apauruṣeya* character of the Veda was the claim of its absolute validity. Indeed, for a considerably long time in the history of India, the Veda occupied the most supreme position—a position which was infinitely higher than that of god. As has been already indicated, even historical Hinduism had acquiesced—may be only outwardly—in the absolute validity claimed for the Veda. It was also claimed that the Veda was the fountain-head of the entire Indian thought and culture. Obviously, this claim is historically quite unfounded. The protohistorical Hinduism did not owe anything to the Veda, while its influence on the historical Hinduism was only formal and skin-deep.

Though the Veda is a collection of texts which are essentially varied from the point of view of literary forms and contents, it is also characterised by that great hall-mark of Indian culture, namely, unity in diversity. For the sake of the convenience of proper understanding, the cultural age represented by the Veda is usually divided into three distinct periods, namely, the Saṁhitā-period, the Brāhmaṇa-period, and the Upaniṣad-period. It may be emphasised that these three periods constitute not only a chronological sequence but also a remarkable logical sequence. It is, verily, this logical sequence which invests the multifarious Veda with a kind of unity. Broadly speaking, the Saṁhitās, the Brāhmaṇas, and the Upaniṣads respectively reflect the three phases of the Vedic religion, namely, mythology and magic, ritualism, and spiritualism. Of course, such a stratification of religious ideology must by no means be regarded as exclusive. It has a reference only to the main tendencies.

As for the first literary period of the Veda, namely, the Saṁhitā-period, the tradition speaks of four Saṁhitās—the *Ṛgveda-Saṁhitā*, the *Atharvaveda-Saṁhitā*, the *Sāmaveda-Saṁhitā*, and the *Yajurveda-Saṁhitā*. Out of these four Saṁhitās, the *Sāmaveda* is essentially of a secondary character—it being largely a collection of some verses derived from the *Ṛgveda*, which have been set to music for being ceremonially chanted at a Soma-sacrifice, while the *Yajurveda* mainly consists of formulas and other details connected with various ritual practices. Therefore, in view of their purpose and the religious tendencies reflected in them, these two Saṁhitās may be said to belong conceptually to the Brāhmaṇa-period or the period of Vedic ritualism. Thus, from the points of view both of the history of literature and the history of religion, only the *Ṛgveda* and the *Atharvaveda* are to be regarded as properly belonging to the Saṁhitā-period.

The Vedic religious ideology, like the Vedic language, seems to have received its initial characterisation while the early ancestors of the Vedic Aryans, who may be designated as proto-Aryans, had been living together, presumably in the region round about Balkh, before their three further migrations—namely, towards the Mitanni region in ancient Near East, towards Iran, and towards Saptasindhu or the land of seven rivers in the region of North-Western India. These people lived in close proximity with nature—indeed, they regarded themselves as part and parcel of nature. In conformity with such conditions of life, they developed a kind of cosmic religion, which had two main aspects. On the one hand, they were overwhelmed by the vastness, brilliance, and bounty of nature, as the result of which they sang of the heaven and the earth—Dyāvāpṛthivī—as their cosmic parents, and, on the other—and this may be said to have been a typical Aryan ideological development—they felt deeply impressed by the inexorable regularity of the cosmic phenomena and consequently postulated the religious concepts of the cosmic law Ṛta and the mighty administrator of that law, Varuṇa. The proto-Aryans also seem to have developed a kind of fire-worship and a rudimentary ritual in which the juice of the Soma-plant presumably played a prominent role. As has been already suggested, in course of time, some tribes from among the proto-Aryans—and, in view of the later history, these may be said to have been the tribes of the immediate ancestors of the Vedic Aryans—started on their migratory march towards Saptasindhu. Their progress from Balkh to Saptasindhu was, however, not quite smooth. They had to encounter various impediments (*vṛtrāṇi*) in the form of natural obstacles, and perhaps more particularly in the form of human antagonists. Naturally enough, they now needed a different kind of religion to meet the demands of their changed way of life. The character of the religion of a people is, by and large, determined by the kind of life which that people is required to live. The old cosmic religion was obviously not quite adequate for the new warlike conditions. The ancestors of the Vedic Aryans, therefore, sponsored a new religion centering round the victorious hero turned into a war-god, namely, Indra. Thus there were three main aspects of the religion of the Vedic Aryans when they reached the Indian soil—the cosmic aspect represented by Dyāvāpṛthivī and Varuṇa-Ṛta, the fire-worship aspect represented by Agni, and the hero-wargod aspect represented by Indra. The Vedic religion was essentially an uniconic religion. It comprised principally of prayers which were addressed to the various divinities and the mythological traditions which had developed round them as also of the simple offerings made to them in a rudimentary sacrificial ritual. Several generations of poet-priests must have occupied themselves with creating the myths and composing the prayers. Indeed, this activity must have extended from the time when the early ancestors of the Vedic Aryans lived in the region of Balkh to the time when they eventually settled down in Saptasindhu and even after.

Besides the cosmic religion, the fire-religion, and the hero-religion, which belonged to the "classes" within the Vedic Aryan community, there must have existed among the "masses" of the Vedic Aryan community—as, indeed, is the case with all primitive people—a religious ideology characterised by magic, witchraft, sorcery, etc. Several generations of Vedic magician-priests must have been producing magical formulas and incantations relating to this religion of the masses. After the Vedic Aryans had ultimately established themselves in Saptasindhu and had acquired a sense of comparative stability, security, and prosperity, a major activity which they undertook in the field of religion was to collect together, revise, amplify, and organize their mythological traditions, prayers, magical formulas, etc. Naturally enough, all this material must have remained in a stray and scattered condition throughout their early settlement in Balkh and consequent migration to Saptasindhu. It is, surely, this condition which is presupposed by the term *saṁhitā*, which means collection and planned arrangement. As a result of this activity, two Saṁhitās took shape—the one, namely, the *Ṛgveda*, mostly embodying the mythological traditions and prayers relating to the religion of the classes, and the other, namely, the *Atharvaveda*, mostly containing the formulas and incantations relating to the religion of the masses. By and large, therefore, the central theme of the *Ṛgveda* may be said to be mythology, and that of the *Atharvaveda* to be magic.

It was once generally believed that Vedic mythology was naturalistic in character—that it mainly symbolised natural powers and phenomena. It is, however, now realised that the narrow frame-work of naturalism is quite inadequate to contain the rich variety of Vedic mythology. It was, of course, inevitable that the overwhelming phenomena of nature, with which the Vedic Aryans must have become habituated, should have deeply influenced their mythology, ritual, and poetry. But those phenomena cannot be said to have constituted the exclusive basis—or even the essential factor—of Vedic mythology. Other approaches to Vedic mythology, such as 'philological', 'ethno-sociological', or 'mystic-psychological', are also now found to be quite inadequate by themselves. Similarly, generalisations, such as that Vedic mythology is a mythology in decay or that it is a mythology in the making, are hardly pertinent. Vedic mythology is essentially an evolutionary mythology. Its general character has changed in accordance with the vicissitudes in the cultural life of the Vedic people. For instance, it would be seen that a certain specific god was regarded as supreme and sovereign in a certain specific period. The reason for this was that the character and personality of that god were in full conformity with what may be called the ethos of that period. This is one aspect of evolutionary mythology. The other aspect of it is that, though the basic character of a divinity was determined by the peculiar environments in which it had come into being, that character did not remain static and stagnant throughout. It underwent various modifications in accordance with the changing conditions of the life of the Vedic Aryans. In the course of its evolution, many new features gradually accumulated round that divinity so that the total personality which it finally presented was highly complex. It is, however, not altogether impossible to analyse the complex character and personality of a Vedic god, generally isolate from one another the various elements in that character, and then broadly mark out the different stages in the evolution of that god.

As has been already indicated, cosmic mythology represented one of the earliest phases of the religious ideology of the Vedic Aryans. They generally celebrated the divine parents, Dyauḥ and Pṛthivī, but the normal growth of these divinities into full-fledged Father Sky and Mother Earth respectively seems to have been arrested in the Veda. On the other hand, Vedic mythology emphasised another significant feature in this connection, namely, that the universe, vast as it was, was not a chaos, but that it was a cosmos. An inexorable law (Ṛta) governed, in a subtle manner, the working of both macrocosm and microcosm. The concept of the cosmic law or Ṛta became the centre of a whole mythological complex involving Varuṇa, Mitra, Ādityas, and Aditi. Varuṇa, the "binder" god, held together the entire universe by means of his fetters (*pāśas*) and thereby enforced its regular operation. He also punished the transgressors of his law with those very *pāśas*. Varuṇa's *pāśas* thus possessed a double significance—cosmological and ethical. Varuṇa could exercise his authority over the universe as supreme ruler (*saṁrāṭ*) because he was *asura* or the possessor of *asu*. The concept of *asu* is perhaps most central in Vedic religious ideology. Indeed, it is seen to have vitally influenced the whole religio-philosophical thought of ancient India. It was believed that an all-pervading magical potence-substance penetrated through the universe and thereby invested it, so to say, with existence and life. This magical potence served as the essential basis of the various aspects of creation such as gods, men, animals, trees, etc. There was, accordingly, an essential qualitative unity throughout the universe. It was the varying quantity of this somatic magical potence, which the different aspects of creation such as gods, men, animals, trees, etc., possessed, that made them different from one another. The Vedic Aryans designated this all-penetrating magical potence as *asu*. The larger the quantity of *asu* one possessed, the greater was the magical power which he could wield. Varuṇa could effectively enforce the cosmic law Ṛta because he was believed to have possessed the largest quantity of *asu*-because he was *asura*. It may be incidentally pointed out that the godhead of the Vedic gods depended mainly upon their participation in the magic potence *asu*. Mitra was just a kind of alter ego of Varuṇa. What Varuṇa was in respect of cosmic ethics, Mitra was in respect of human morality. The word *mitra* also is to be derived from a root meaning 'to bind'. Indeed, "organization and regulation through bondage" was the central motif of this entire mythological complex.

The conditions of life of the Vedic Aryans changed substantially when they started on their migratory march towards Saptasindhu, and, true to its evolutionary character, the Vedic mythology also changed its main aspect from the cosmic to the heroic. Indra, the war-god, now came to occupy the supreme position which had been held by the cosmic sovereign Varuṇa. Apart from this manifestation of the evolutionary character of Vedic mythology as a whole, that character becomes particularly evident in the development of the mythological personality of Indra. In a sense, Indra is the only god in the Veda with a real mythology associated with him. The starting point of the Indra-mythology is the mythologisation of history. Originally Indra was a human hero who led the Vedic Aryans in their victorious encounters with the antagonistic tribes, which were collectively referred to in the Veda as Vṛtras and Dāsas, and their consequent colonisation and establishment of sovereignty in Saptasindhu. Indra's epithet *puraṁdara* (smasher of fortresses) would suggest that that intrepid war-commander of the nomadic tribes of the Vedic Aryans was mainly responsible for demolishing at least the last vestiges of the fortified settlements of the pre-Vedic non-Aryan Indus civilisation. In this connection, Indra's hostility towards the Yatis and the Śiśnadevas, which has been referred to earlier, gains special significance. It must not, however, be supposed that all the exploits ascribed to Indra in the Veda were achieved by a single individual. Such ascription is obviously the result of the institutionisation of the individual which marks a distinct stage in the process of the mythologisation of history.

Indra, the human hero who was transformed into the national war-god, is seen to dominate the entire mythology of the *Ṛgveda*, because the *Ṛgveda-Saṁhitā*, as we have it today, relates mainly to the period of conquest and colonisation in the history of the Vedic Aryans. Indeed, Indra became the symbol of the hieratic religion of the *Ṛgveda*, and the status of the other Vedic gods in that religion was determined by the nature of the relationship which those gods claimed with Indra. There are indications in the *Ṛgveda* of a kind of rivalry between the ancient Varuṇa-religion and the new Indra-religion, but eventually Indra is represented to have superseded Varuṇa. The latter was consequently reduced to the position of a god of waters. However, at one stage in this process, attempts seem to have been made to bring about a kind of compromise between the two religious cults. It was suggested that the functions of Varuṇa and Indra were mutually complementary and not contradictory, for, Indra 'conquered' and Varuṇa 'ruled'.

With the conquest of the Vṛtras and the Dāsas and the subsequent colonisation by the Vedic Aryans in Saptasindhu, the historical role of Indra came to an end and his mythological role began to be emphasised. This was accomplished by superimposing upon Indra's basic human-historical character certain cosmic features. Indra, the vanquisher of human foes, began to be represented as the vanquisher of Vṛtras in nature—he came to be glorified as a rain-god or a storm-god. The overpowering of constricting forces in nature and the enlivening of cosmic life attributed to Indra was but a cosmicised projection of an authentic socio-political event in the history of the Vedic Aryans. There were still other features which came to be added to the Indra-mythology in the course of its evolution. In almost all ancient mythologies is to be found the primal myth of the conflict between the hero and the dragon, in some form or another. In the course of the evolution of Vedic mythology, Indra came to be represented as the hero and his principal enemy Vṛtra as the dragon.

Incidentally it may be pointed out that the motif of the mythologisation of history can be perceived, to a certain extent, also in the mythology relating to the Maruts, the twins Aśvinau, and the Ṛbhus.

Two other gods who had been prominent in the religion of the *Ṛgveda* were Soma and Agni. The religious concept of Soma had arisen already during the proto-Aryan period, but, then, Soma had been connected with cult rather than with mythology. Originally, Soma was a specific plant, primarily derived from the Mūjavat mountain, whose bitter-astringent juice played a central role in the simple cultic rites of the Aryans. But, while the human hero Indra was evolving into the national war-god, Soma came to be invested with some kind of mythological significance. It was suggested that Indra achieved his many heroic exploits under the invigorating inebriation produced by the offerings of Soma made to him. Agni, like Soma, was mythologically not very significant, but his cultic importance was very great. If Indra was the pivot of Vedic mythology, Agni was the pivot of Vedic ritual. Incidentally, it is necessary to distinguish clearly between the mythological Agni and the ritual fire.

It may be presumed that, side by side with the hieratic religion of the Saṁhitā-period, some glimpses into which have been given above, there had been in existence various forms of what may be called popular tribal religion. Some of these latter, which, incidentally, need to be distinguished from the religion of the masses referred to above, seem to have become quite a force to reckon with in the religious life of the community—indeed, so much so that the Vedic poet-priests were constrained to accommodate them in their mythological scheme. This gave rise to yet another motif in the evolutionary Vedic mythology, namely, hierarchisation of popular cults. The most common procedure adopted by the Vedic poet-priests for admitting a popular divinity into the pantheon of hieratic gods was to associate that divinity—maybe in a forced and artificial manner—with Indra who had become the very symbol of hieratic Vedic religion. However, in the course of such hieratic upgrading of a popular divinity, the Vedic poet-priests, on the one hand, scrupolously suppressed such features of the character of that popular divinity as were disagreeable to the sophisticated hieratic mentality, and, on the other, emphasised such other features of its character as could suggest—however faintly and indirectly—a possible similarity between that divinity and some hieratic god. But, in spite of such tendentious manipulation on the part of the Vedic poet-priests, some significant traits of the basic and essential character of that popular divinity did not fail to lurk in the representation of that divinity in the hieratic Vedic mythology.

A typical example of such hierarchisation is Viṣṇu—an original fertility-god conceived in a bird-form, who, in the process of his upgrading, was artificially associated with Indra and then came to be regarded as a solar divinity, his original bird-form having facilitated the transition from the fertility-bird to the sun-bird and then to the solar divinity. It may be added, in this context, that solarization, that is to say, the superimposition, at some stage and for one reason or another, of the solar character upon the divinities who had originally nothing to do with the sun, was another common motif in the evolution of Vedic mythology. Besides Viṣṇu, Pūṣan, Mitra, and Savitṛ were subjected to such solarization.

In the case of Vedic Rudra, there did not occur a full-fledged hierarchisation. It has been already seen that, in the proto-historic period, the Śiva-religion had prevailed in various parts of India. Though the attitude of the Vedic Aryans towards that religion, as might be gathered from the Vedic references to the Yatis and the Śiśnadevas, was generally antagonistic, the sway of that religion among the people had been so overwhelming that the sponsors of the Vedic religion must have been forced into adapting it to their mythology in some way or the other. The result was the personality of Rudra, who represents the Vedic version of the proto-Śiva. Some other features of the proto-historic Śiva-religion are reflected in such Vedic hymns as those relating to Muni, Brahmacārin, and the Vrātyas. However, unlike Viṣṇu, Rudra is seen to have been deliberately kept isolated in Vedic mythology and religion. In the remarkably long and continuous history of the religious domination of Śiva, this will have to be regarded as just a brief intermission, for, soon after the Vedic period had ended, Śiva almost recovered his original supreme position.

It is true that, by and large, the aspect of the Vedic religion, which was represented in the *Ṛgveda*, comprised mainly of mythological traditions and prayers. There was, however, another item of religio-philosophical significance which seems to have interested the authors of the *Ṛgveda*, and that was cosmology. Several Vedic gods were represented as having been responsible for the creation, organization, and sustenance of the universe. This may be accounted for by the general 'asuistic' trend of the Vedic mythology. Besides such mythological descriptions, however, there are a few typical cosmological theories which have been adumbrated in the *Ṛgveda*. In one of the hymns (*Ṛgveda* X. 121), for instance, the process of creation is said to have started with the emergence of the golden embryo. This hymn is important also from another point of view. It reflects the Vedic poet's feeling of the general inadequacy of the mythological gods and his consequent groping for the true godhead. Another hymn (*Ṛgveda* X. 90), popularly known as the *Puruṣa-sūkta*, describes the universe as resulting from the ritual self-immolation of a hermaphrodite god-man. A similar cosmological concept is suggested through a peculiar mythological allusion relating to Yama (*Ṛgveda* X. 13.4). A third current of cosmological thought is represented by the famous *Nāsadīya-sūkta* (*Ṛgveda* X. 129), which, in a way, anticipates the later Upaniṣadic speculation in this behalf. According to this hymn, the first cause of the universe was undefinable—it could not be described as *sat* or 'being' because it was uncharacterisable, nor as *asat* or 'non-being' because it possessed creative potentiality. The author of this profoundly thought out but rather obscurely worded hymn ultimately concludes on a note of a kind of agnosticism.

The Ṛgvedic religion was uniconic, but it seems to have promoted a kind of domestic worship centering round the family-fire and usually carried out without the intervention of professional priests. The Ṛgvedic ritual, as compared to the later brahmanic ritual, was quite rudimentary in character. The employment of various Ṛgvedic verses in connection with the sacrificial ritual was clearly an after-thought; those verses were originally by no means intended for that purpose. The Ṛgvedic religion was also free from most of the extravagances of the theistic Hindu cults, though, it may be incidentally pointed out, the germs of the *bhakti*-doctrine, which later became almost the hall-mark of classical Hinduism, can be discovered in such hymns as those which refer to the peculiar personal relationship between Varuṇa and Vasiṣṭha.

Philosophising as such was rare in the Ṛgveda, though it cannot be said to have been altogether foreign to it. One of the most significant features of the religious ideology of the *Ṛgveda* is the belief in the magic potence of the *mantra* or the cultically pronounced word. The *mantras* possessed a kind of compelling power, and, if properly uttered and employed, they would never fail to achieve the desired end. There are also to be found in the *Ṛgveda* some indications of religious ecstasy and mystic exaltation, but these are presumably the result of the influence of the religious practices of protohistorical Hinduism. It is to be specially noted that the Ṛgvedic Aryans never thought of this life as being just one in the unending cycle of existences and therefore of little consequence, nor did they believe in its being predestined by the law of Karma and consequently initiative-deterrent. Their general attitude was, therefore, essentially life-affirming, dynamic, free from pessimistic gloom, and full of hearty genial piety and feeling of buoyancy and cheer. A happy, secure, and prosperous family-life had always been the goal of the Ṛgvedic Aryans.

It needs to be emphasised that, from the point of view of the history of religion, the *Ṛgveda* and the *Atharvaveda* have to be regarded as being contemporaneous and as relating to the same community of the Vedic Aryans—the *Ṛgveda* being, by and large, the Veda of the classes and the *Atharvaveda* the Veda of the masses. Naturally enough, in comparison with the *Ṛgveda*, the scope of the *Atharvaveda* is much wider and its contents of a more varied interest. It is free from the sophistication and priestly hierarchy which characterise the *Ṛgveda*. It concerns itself with the common life of the common man from its prenatal to postmortem stage, with all its light and shade, and often reflects obscure human emotions and uncanny human relations.

The basic concepts of the *Atharvaveda* ideology were that all existing entities participated in the same all-pervading somatic magic potence, that, therefore, there was no real scope for such differentiation as between spirit and matter or the living and the life-less or the person and the thing or the abstract and the concrete, and that—and this is of particular significance from the point of view of the religion of the *Atharvaveda*—the magic potence in an entity could be enhanced or diminished or transferred to another entity by means of cultic incantations and action. More than any other Veda, the *Atharvaveda* aimed at achieving some definite practical end, and that too in a direct tangible manner. That Veda was originally known as *Atharvāṅgirasaḥ*, which name indicated the two types of magic employed by it—the white magic sponsored by Atharvan which was intended to promote one's own happiness, security, and prosperity, and the black magic sponsored by Aṅgiras which implied curse, imprecation, and exorcism. The *Atharvaveda* contains charms to cure diseases and possession by evil spirits, to secure prosperity, freedom from danger, and harmony and influence in the family and public assembly, to win the love of the desired woman, and to expiate sin and defilement, prayers for long life and health, and imprecations against demons, sorcerers, and enemies. Another aspect of the *Atharvaveda* magic is represented by the office of the Purohita or royal chaplain, who, as his name suggests, served, through special magic rites, as a protective shield "placed before" the king.

A rather unexpected feature of the *Atharvaveda* is that it contains more matter which can be called philosophical than any other Saṁhitā. The occurrence of such philosophical material in a book of magic need by no means be regarded as the result of a secondary fusion. It should be remembered that the dividing line between magic and 'non-learned' philosophy is very thin. Indeed, much of the later Upaniṣadic philosophy may be described as the ideology of the *Atharvaveda* magic presented in a speculative garb. In the view of early Vedic thinkers, philosophy was as closely connected with a practical purpose as magic. Their basic dictum was that the knowledge of the end to be achieved was the surest means of achieving that end. The polarity of the contents of the *Atharvaveda* is thus more apparent than real.

Towards the end of the Saṁhitā-period, the Vedic Aryans had, by and large, become politically stable, economically secure, and socially organized. The transition from a toilsome, adventurous, nomadic life to a life of household comfort and leisure did not fail to influence their religion—more particularly their religious practices. Out of the simple prayers, fire-worship, and Soma-cult, and primitive magic of the earlier period, there was now evolved a highly complex and complicated system of ritual, which soon assumed the status of the only recognised form of religion. Elaborate rules were prescribed and rigidly enforced in connection with the various details of the ritual, such as the proper time and place for sacrifice, the sacred fires, the officiating priests, the sacrificial materials and implements, the divinities, the oblations, the *mantras*, the *dakṣiṇā*, and the reparation or expiation rites for the errors of commission and omission in the sacrificial procedure. The natural consequence of all this was that the initiative and operative capability in religious matters now passed, for all practical purposes, into the hands of the newly arisen class of professional priests who claimed a certain amount of expertise in ritual practice and could therefore authoritatively guide the people in their sacrificial performances. The need must also have been felt for literary manuals which described and discussed the many details of the theory and practice of this intricately worked out sacrificial system. It was, verily, out of this need that the *Brāhmaṇa*-texts originated. The central theme of the *Brāhmaṇas* is ritual. The *Yajurveda* and the *Sāmaveda*, though traditionally called Saṁhitās, are also ritualistic in character—the former directly and the latter from the point of view of the purpose which it was expected to serve—while the *Śrauta-Sūtras*, which actually belong to the post-Upaniṣadic period, seek to consolidate and systematise the teachings of the *Brāhmaṇas*. All these texts must, therefore, be regarded as conceptually representing the religious ideology of the Brāhmaṇa-period.

A *Brāhmaṇa*-text is normally constituted of two parts, the *vidhi* and the *arthavāda*, which do not necessarily occur sequentially but are usually intermingled. The *vidhi*-part deals with the theory and practice of sacrifice, while the purpose of the *arthavāda* is to justify, glorify, and thereby recommend as it were a particular sacrifice or a part of a sacrifice or any specific feature of a sacrifice which is prescribed in the *vidhi*-part.

The Brahmanic sacrifices were classified in different ways. Some sacrifices, for instance, were regarded as obligatory (*nitya*), while some were regarded as optional (*kāmya*), that is to say, they were to be performed for the fulfilment of certain specific desires. Some sacrifices constituted the norm (*prakṛti*), while some represented only the modifications of that norm (*vikṛti*). Further, in view of the principal oblations to be offered in the sacrifices, one could speak of *havis*-sacrifices (*havis* having been usually understood in the sense of milk or milk-products or sacrificial cakes made of the flour of different kinds of grains and baked on certain specific number of potsherds), animal-sacrifices, and Soma-sacrifices. Among the Soma-sacrifices, again, there were some whose principal rites were completed in one day (*ekāha*), some which extended over from two to twelve days (*ahīna*), and some which lasted for days together (*sattra*).

The sacrificer (*yajamāna*) normally belonged to one of the first three social orders, namely Brāhmaṇa, Kṣatriya, and Vaiśya—the Rathakāra (chariot-maker) also having been mentioned as being entitled to the performance of a sacrifice. The sacrificer himself had but little to do in the actual performance of the sacrifice. Most of the ritual procedure was initiated and actively carried through by professional priests specially appointed for the purpose. The number of priests varied according to the nature of the sacrifice. The four principal ones were: the Adhvaryu who usually belonged to the *Yajurveda* and went through most of the ritual action on behalf of the sacrificer; the Hotṛ who belonged to the *Ṛgveda* and recited, usually at the instance of the Adhvaryu, the prescribed verses from the *Ṛgveda* in connection with such rites as the kindling of the sacred fires and adding fuel to them, the invocation of the divinities, and the offering of oblations to them; the Udgātṛ who belonged to the *Sāmaveda* and whose duty was to chant *sāmans* at the Soma-sacrifice; and the Brahman who belonged to the *Atharvaveda* and generally supervised the entire sacrificial procedure. Each one of these principal priests had three assistants—the Pratiprasthātṛ (attached to the Adhvaryu), the Maitrāvaruṇa (to the Hotṛ), the Subrahmaṇya (to the Udgātṛ), and the Āgnīdhra (to the Brahman) having been the more prominent among them. The formal setting up of the three sacred fires—the *gārhapatya*, the *āhavanīya*, and the *dakṣiṇa*—was the starting point of all *śrauta* ritual. Specific types of utensils, mostly made of wood, were employed, and strange materials (such as, for instance, saline soil, earth dug out of a mole, earth dug out by a hog) were often prescribed to be used for different purposes. The *dakṣinā*, which was not to be regarded merely as fee paid to the officiating priests for their services but which perhaps had a far deeper significance, was different for different sacrifices and consisted mainly of cows.

The Vedic ritual texts have discussed these and numerous other details relating to the sacrificial practice and procedure so minutely and punctiliously (but often without rhyme or reason!) and with such an air of seriousness as to create the impression that there was nothing more important in their world than sacrifice and that no detail of the ritual practice, howsoever minor or trivial it might appear, could afford to be neglected or treated in a cavalier fashion. For, a sacrifice could either be perfect in every single detail and therby prove wholly fruitful, or it could become vitiated on account of even the slightest error or deficiency in its performance and be therby rendered not only ineffectual but also positively harmful.

Unfortunately, the extreme obsession of the ritualists with the complexities of the actual performance of the sacrifice has tended to overshadow the more significant aspects of the ideology underlying the Vedic sacrifice. A Vedic sacrifice was believed to be an autonomous religious system. It operated and became effectual independently of any extraneous factor. The law of sacrifice was at once deterministic and inexorable. Further, a Vedic sacrifice was regarded not as a mere propitiatory rite—it was believed to possess a profound cosmic significance. A cultic act established a magical rapport with the entire cosmos. A sacrifice was not only a representation in miniature of the cosmic order, but it was also a necessary condition for the proper working of the cosmic order. A sacrifice is very aptly compared to clock-work which must be wound up in order that the world should be kept going. It may be noted that the performance of specific cultic rites was made to correspond with the rhythmic course of nature. Several sacrifices can be shown to have been intended as yearly rites for cosmic regeneration.

Another important feature of the philosophy of sacrifice was the doctrine of *bandhutā*, which sought to establish a kind of mystic magic relationship among the various aspects of macrocosm and microcosm. The *Brāhmaṇa*-texts also emphasised that adequate knowledge on the part of the performer and the priests of the true significance of a sacrificial rite was a necessary condition for the efficacious working of that rite. Sociologically, the institution of Vedic sacrifice reflects one of the earliest efforts made in India to invest religious beliefs and practices with a definite and organized form. Moreover, a Vedic sacrifice meant a huge co-operative enterprise, which actively involved the various strata of the community and thereby helped promote—though, perhaps, indirectly—a sense of solidarity among them.

In actual practice, however, the exaggerated glorification of Brahmanic ritual stirred up intellectual and social simmerings against the religion of sacrifice. In the *Brāhmaṇa*-period, sacrifice was exalted so extravagantly that it had come to be regarded not merely as a means to an end but as an end in itself. Not only had sacrifice become the very pivot on which the entire communal life of the Vedic people revolved, but it had also been elevated to the position of the basic motive force of all cosmic phenomena. It was then but natural that the priests, who held the key to the theory and practice of sacrifice in their hands, should have exerted upon the entire community an intellectual and social influence which almost amounted to domination. But such a state of things could obviously not endure for long. There arose a band of free thinkers who resented the attitude of blind acceptance, which the priests had more or less deliberately fostered among the people, and therefore sought to replace it with the attitude of uninhibited inquiry. Many of these free thinkers came from social strata other than those to which the Brahmanic priests had belonged. They began by challenging the two basic claims implied in the *Brāhmaṇa*-texts, namely, that the Veda possessed absolute validity and that the purpose of the Veda was exclusively ritualistic. They asserted that the Veda embodied only a lower kind of knowledge (*aparā vidyā*), and that the Brahmanic sacrifice, which placed inordinately greater emphasis on the 'form' of religion than on its 'spirit', represented an inferior kind of religion (*avaraṁ karma*). Sacrifice, they insisted, was an unsteady boat on which one could ill afford to rely for successfully crossing the perilous ocean of this mundane existence. In fact, this mundane existence, comprising both the microcosm and the macrocosm, was just a figment created by nescience—it was the result of an ignorant superimposition of manifoldness on the underlying supreme reality which was one and without a second. The mystic realisation of one's essential identity with the one ultimate reality—the merging of one's individuality into the cosmic totality—was declared to be the chief goal of all religious practices and philosophical speculations. And every one was presumed to be free—both intellectually and socially—to pursue his own lonely course towards that goal. It is this new trend in religio-philosophical thinking which is reflected in the *Upaniṣads*.

The teachings of the *Upaniṣads* cannot, however, be said to constitute any regular religio-philosophical system as such. For one thing, the *Upaniṣads* do not present any properly argued homogeneous doctrine. The Upaniṣadic speculations may be best characterised as the inspired musings of the newly awakened minds. The Upaniṣadic thinkers indeed start with the conviction that the highest reality cannot be comprehended by means of mere ratiocination. Nor, again, is mere 'knowledge' of the reality to be regarded as the spiritual goal. That knowledge must ultimately lead to a direct mystic realisation of that reality—a state which is variously described as *mokṣa* (liberation), *abhaya* (fearlessness), *amṛtatva* (immortality), etc. And in order to attain this state, the *Upaniṣads* not unoften recommend extra-rational means. In a sense, therefore, the Upaniṣadic philosophy is what may be appropriately called an applied philosophy. Looked at from another point of view, the *Upaniṣads* may be said to aim at the inwardisation and spiritualisation of religion. The religion of the *Upaniṣads*—if we may at all speak of such a one—is constituted of inner contemplation and spiritual experience rather than of any material worship and external physical action. Indeed, in the ultimate analysis, it transcends mere intellectualism and moralism as much it does sheer mythicism and ritualism.

The *Upaniṣads*, which are traditionally also called *Vedānta*, not only mark the chronological end (*anta*) of the Vedic age (*veda*), but they may also be said to represent the high-water mark (*anta*) of Vedic ideology (*veda*). Even against the background of the strikingly creative thought-ferment which characterised the civilised world during the few centuries round about 600 B.C., the grand visions of the Upaniṣadic thinkers do not fail to stand out quite prominently. In the context of the religious history of India, however, what could be considered to be the strong points of the Upaniṣadic speculations from one point of view proved to be their weak points from another point of view. The exalted spiritualism (*brahmavidyā*) of the *Upaniṣads*, for instance, went over the heads of the common people. The adequate comprehension of the monistic-idealistic teachings of the *Upaniṣads* and more particularly the mystic realization of the ultimate reality on which they lay a special emphasis necessarily called for a high intellectual capacity and an austere spiritual discipline. And these an ordinary person could obviously not be expected to command in sufficient measure. Further the fact that the *Upaniṣads* had not set forth any one consistent philosophical doctrine was responsible for their failure to produce a uniform and concentrated—and, therefore, more or less abiding—effect on the minds of the people. In this very context may be mentioned the essentially individualistic character of the Upaniṣadic teachings. The Upaniṣadic thinkers do not seem to have made any effort to build up a kind of spiritual brotherhood among the masses. Indeed, no one among the great Upaniṣadic teachers ever sought to be the spiritual leader of the people at large. The *Upaniṣads* may be said to have ignored more or less completely the practical side of the spiritual urge of the people. They gave to the people a philosophy, or philosophies, which most of them were not competent enough adequately to comprehend, but not a religion, which many of them could have readily practised. The result of all this was that Vedism, of which the *Upaniṣads* represented perhaps the very pinnacle, suffered a set-back. The period following the major *Upaniṣads* saw a veritable ideological ferment and the emergence and interaction of new religio-philosophical trends.

The religious interregnum occasioned by the interruption in the continuity of the Vedic tradition offered a propitious opportunity for the consolidation of the heterodox or non-Vedic beliefs and practices such as were, for instance, represented by Jainism and Buddhism. The beginnings of many of these beliefs and practices may actually be traced back to a common pre-Vedic non-Aryan culture-complex. Jainism and Buddhism took advantage of the atmosphere of free thinking and the attitude of inquiry even with reference to the Veda, which had been promoted by the *Upaniṣads*, and assimilating their strong points but avoiding the weak ones, steadily extended the spheres of their influence. On the other hand, however, Vedism, which had taken deep roots among the people in the course of its fairly long history, had not lost its vitality altogether. The rear-guards of that great religious movement again mustered themselves and made a strong bid to counteract the advance of the non-Vedic religious forces by consolidating, reorganizing, and thereby revitalizing the Vedic way of life and thought. The various branches of Vedic knowledge, such as phonetics, etymology, grammar, metrics, and astronomy, were systematized in the form of Vedāṅga-texts, and—what is far more important from the point of view of the history of religion—the socio-religious life of the community was sought to be regulated through the *Kalpasūtras*—its ritual aspect through the *Śrautasūtras*, individual and domestic aspect through the *Gṛhyasūtras*, and socio-political aspect through the *Dharmasūtras*. However, this revivalistic movement, which does not seem to have become a popular movement in any sense, could not, by itself, succeed in its mission. A reference may be incidentally made in this very context to a third current of thought which had become evident in the period immediately following that of the major *Upaniṣads*. It may be broadly described as a blend of realistic, materialistic, and secular tendencies on the one hand and a new morality, which insisted that the end justified the means, on the other. This new trend, which is best reflected in the *Arthaśāstra* of Kauṭilya, was obviously the result of a reaction against the exaggerated spiritualistic, idealistic, life-negating outlook, promoted by the *Upaniṣads*, and also by Jainism and Buddhism.

The fourth religious trend, which manifested itself during this period, made parhaps the most powerful impact on the future religious history of India. It was classical or historical Hinduism. As has been already pointed out, even from very early times, there had been in vogue, side by side with the hieratic Vedic religion, various popular religious cults, some of which at least had established themselves firmly in the pre-Vedic non-Aryan period of the history of India. When, however, Vedism began to dominate the religious scene in India, these popular religions were naturally relegated to the background, though they did not altogether fail to influence—directly or indirectly—the growth of Vedism itself. The gods and goddesses of these popular religions were different from the divinities of the hieratic Vedic pantheon. Their religious practices also differed fundamentally from the religious practices of the Vedic Aryans. Indeed, these popular tribal religions were clearly non-Vedic in provenance and character. From this point of view at least, they were more akin to the heterodox systems of thought mentioned above. There was, however, one point of essential difference between these two. These popular tribal religions soon came under the spell of Vedism. And, though they did not actually adopt the religious beliefs and practices of Vedism to any appreciable extent, they followed the very practical and realistic course of avowing allegiance to the Veda—howsoever nominal and formal that allegiance might have proved to be in actual practice. Naturally enough, while Vedism had been in ascendancy, the sphere of influence of these popular religions was restricted to the respective tribes among which they had originated. They could not have then emerged as quite the forces to reckon with. But the decline of Vedism afforded them an opportunity to assert themselves. It would, indeed, seem that the rear-guards of Vedism had themselves boosted up these religions to a certain extent. For, they must have soon realised that the challenge of the heterodox movements could not be effectively met by mere revivalist efforts. A common popular front needed to be built up against them. Consequently, most of the popular tribal religions, with the variety of their gods and religious practices, came to be loosely organized into one single but multi-charactered whole, which was held together by means of the thin thread of their allegiance to the Veda.

This is, in broad outline, the genesis of historical Hinduism. It may be noted that Hinduism steered clear, on the one hand, of the extreme orthodoxy of the *Sūtra-Vedāṅga* revivalists, and, on the other, of the extreme heterodoxy of the religious movements like Jainism and Buddhism. While arresting the growth of anti-Vedic ideology, it successfully combated the insularity and exclusiveness of Vedism by bringing together under its banner large masses of people and, at the same time, saved the Vedic tradition from becoming altogether extinct.

The main characteristics of this religious movement may be stated as follows: The principal gods of hieratic Vedism like Indra and Varuṇa came to be superseded by the popular gods like Śiva and Viṣṇu-Kṛṣṇa. The *Purāṇa*-legends, such as that Kṛṣṇa did not recognise the Indra-festival, that he protected the cowherds and their cattle against Indra's fury by lifting up the Govardhana mountain, and that he plundered Indra's garden and snatched away the *pārijāta* tree, are suggestive of such change of religious loyalties. The *Upaniṣads*, which are traditionally believed to have represented the culmination, as it were, of the Vedic way of life and thought (they are significantly called *Vedānta*), had already replaced the gods of the *Saṁhitā* by the supra-personal Absolute or the impersonal Brahman. Hinduism again energetically revived the religion of personal gods—and this it did with a strong monotheistic bias. The god now came to be looked upon essentially as friend and saviour. The elaborate sacrificial ritual promoted by the *Brāhmaṇas* was substituted by *pūjā* which was basically of the nature of individual worship, and the cold and austere metaphysics of the *Upaniṣads* yielded place to *bhakti* or personal emotional relationship between the god and his devotee. The *Upaniṣads* had laid great stress on self-realisation (*ātmajñana*) as the highest goal of man's spiritual quest. The new Hinduism now emphasized *lokasaṁgraha* or the stability, sustenance, and solidarity of society as the true aim of religion. The Upaniṣadic speculations were essentially *mokṣa*-oriented; the Hindu philosophy of life, on the other hand, may be said to have become *dharma*-oriented. As a natural result of this, the new Hindu ideology began to be dominated by the doctrine of *karmayoga* or activism rather than of *saṁnyāsa* or renunciation. True religion, it was now taught, consisted in the pursuit of one's duties as required by one's *dharma* and in accordance with the will of god, with a view to the attainment of *lokasaṁgraha*. Hinduism eschewed all exclusiveness and dogmatism in the matter of religious practices and philosophical teachings, and sought to bring about a grand religio-philosophical synthesis. Such a synthesis might have meant a considerable logical strain, but it did certainly help to weld together large masses of people with different spiritual backgrounds and attitudes. Incidentally it may be added that Hinduism showed a keen sense of realism and robust practical outlook. It seemed to believe that moral precepts were by no means absolute and that, if the end was morally justifiable, it might be achieved by all possible means.

The rise of the dynasty of the Śuṅgas in Magadha, in the second century B.C., gave great impetus to the movement of the resurgence of Hinduism. Buddhism and, to a certain extent, Jainism were actively patronised by the Mauryas. Particularly, under the great Aśoka, Buddhism had reached almost the peak of its glory. However, the deterioration in the Maurya imperial power was accompanied also by the gradual decline of Buddhism and the corresponding consolidation of popular Hinduism. When Puṣyamitra Śuṅga established himself as the ruler of Magadha after having overthrown his Maurya master, he signalised his victory by performing the brahmanic *aśvamedha* sacrifice. It must, however, be remembered that the performance of this brahmanic sacrifice did not by any means mark the revival of Vedic ritual. It was merely symbolic, on the one hand, of the decline of the non-Vedic religions, and, on the other, of the pretext of the allegiance to the Veda which Hinduism always wanted to flaunt. Sacrifices in the right brahmanic fashion were hardly ever performed in Hindu India, and, whenever they were performed, they were intended to assert political power rather than to satisfy any religious urge. Far more significant than this formal resurrection of brahmanic sacrifice were the definition, consolidation, and propagation of Hinduism through the epics, which are appropriately called the Vedas of the masses. Through them, the cult of *bhakti*, which was associated with the gods of the people, reached even the lowest strata of society. This period also saw the beginning of the fragmentation of Hinduism into sects. By way of illustration, a reference may be made in this context to such facts as that the inscription of Heliodorus, the ambassador of Greek king Antialkidas (Antalikhita) in the court of Bhagabhadra of Besnagar (2nd century B.C.), refers to the Bhāgavatas, that the Ghusundi inscription (150 B.C.) mentions the construction of a building to the glory of Vāsudeva and Saṁkarṣaṇa, that Kadphises assumed the title of Maheśvara, and that Gondophares and Vāsudeva issued coinage with the Śaiva symbols. The popular form of Hindu religion and philosophy as presented in the final redactions of the epic, particularly the *Mahābhārata*; the Hindu ideal of social and political organization as taught in the *Manusmṛti*; and the definition of Pāṇinian Sanskrit in relation to Vedic Sanskrit as reflected in the works of Kātyāyana and Patañjali—these may be said to have been the main features of Hinduism as consolidated in the Śuṅga period.

The characteristics of Hinduism as have been set forth above are best represented in the *Bhagavadgītā* and in the character of Kṛṣṇa as portrayed in the *Mahābhārata*. It is hardly necessary to emphasize that the *Mahābhārata*, as we know it today, is the outcome of a long process of expansion, assimilation, revision, and redaction. Presumably, it originated as a bardic-historical poem, called *Jaya*, which had the eventful Bhārata-war as its central theme. In course of time, a large amount of material belonging to the literary tradition of the Sūtas, which had been developing, since very early times, side by side with the *mantra*-tradition embodied in the Vedic literature, came to be added to the historical poem, so that the latter was transformed into the epic *Bhārata*. But this transformation of the *Jaya* into the *Bhārata* received added momentum from another, and, from our present point of view, more significant factor, namely, the rise of Kṛṣṇite Hinduism. The protagonists of this religion realised that the bardic poem, which had been enjoying wide currency, would serve as the most efficient vehicle for the propagation of their ideology. They, therefore, redacted that poem in such a way that the *Bhagavadgītā* became the cornerstone of the new epic superstructure and Kṛṣṇa its central character. Upon this new literary product, called *Bhārata*, which had derived its bardic-historical elements from the ancient Sūta-tradition and its religio-ethical elements from Kṛṣṇite Hinduism, there came to be gradually superimposed elements derived from the brahmanic learning and culture as also from the other aspects of Hinduism. The result was that the *Bhārata* became the *Mahābhārata*.

Kṛṣṇaism was one of the major constituents of historical Hinduism. It will not be an exaggeration to say that no other Hindu god has captured the popular imagination so thoroughly and is treated in literature and arts so profusely as Kṛṣṇa. It is easy to realise the syncretic character of Kṛṣṇa's personality, but not so easy to separate its various components. Vāsudeva-Kṛṣṇa, a Vṛṣṇi prince, who was presumably also a religious leader, had been elevated to godhead already in the 5th century B.C. He taught a religio-ethical doctrine, which was later embodied in the *Bhagavadgītā* and included in the *Mahābhārata*. There was probably another Kṛṣṇa, who sponsored a new morality to supersede the ancient ideal of chivalry. A Kṛṣṇa, son of Devakī, is mentioned in the *Chāndogya-Upaniṣad* as having learnt from Ghora Āṅgirasa the doctrine of man's life as a sacrifice. The cowherd Kṛṣṇa was obviously the god of a pastoral community, which had abjured the Indra-dominated Vedic religion. His cult aimed at a religious sublimation of sensuous love. The Kṛṣṇa, who emerged from the blending of these various religio-ethical trends, was ultimately identified with the All-god, Viṣṇu-Nārāyaṇa.

The *Bhagavadgītā* may be said to constitute the gospel of Kṛṣṇaism. Indeed, it is the most seminal of all Hindu scriptures. The *Bhagavadgītā* teaches that man's chief duty is *lokasaṁgraha*, that is to say, the stability, solidarity, and progress of the society. The society can function properly only on the principle of the ethical interdependence of its various constituents. Man must, therefore, see to it that, as an essential constituent of society, he furthers the process of *lokasaṁgraha* through an active awareness of his social obligations. The *Bhagavadgītā* has thus invested its teaching with positive social values. The *svadharma* or the special socio-ethical obligations of different types of men are, according to the *Bhagavadgītā*, best embodied in the doctrine of *cāturvarṇya* or the scheme of four social orders. However, it needs to be noted that, unlike the avowedly brahmanic texts, the *Bhagavadgītā* never refers to the superiority of one social order to another. It consistently emphasizes only the socio-ethical significance of that scheme. It would, indeed, seem that the main insistence of the *Bhagavadgītā* was on man's active recognition of his *svadharma* or social obligations, the *cāturvarṇya* having been referred to—almost by way of an example—as a scheme, which, in the context of the contemporary conditions, best ensured the recognition by men of their respective *svadharmas*.

The promotion of *lokasaṁgraha*, through the fulfilment of one's *svadharma*, necessarily implies an activistic way of life. The *Bhagavadgītā* has accordingly discussed, at some length, the why and the how of this *karmayoga*. Verily, that is the main theme of the poem. It seeks to reconcile its ideal of *lokasaṁgraha* with the Upaniṣadic ideal of *mokṣa* through its teaching of *anāsaktiyoga*, that is, renunciation *in* action and not *of* action. The *karmayoga* of the *Bhagavadgītā* is not to be confused with the *karmakāṇḍa* of the ritualistic texts. Kṛṣṇa fully realised that the elaborate and highly complex system of sacrifice could never become the religion of the people. He, therefore, sponsored a way of spiritual life in which everybody—irrespective of caste, creed, and sex—could participate. It was the way of *bhakti* or devotion. Some faint traces of the doctrine of *bhakti*, which involves such items as consciousness of guilt on the part of the devotee, his complete self-surrender before god, his earnest longing for a close personal communion with god, and the mystic experiences which he enjoys in the companionship of god, can be discovered even in certain hymns of the *Ṛgveda*, particularly those addressed to Varuṇa by Vasiṣṭha (VII. 86-88); but it is only in historical Hinduism that devotion to a personal god has been represented as one of the most essential features of religion. In his teaching of *bhakti*, however, Kṛṣṇa has stressed one very significant point. He has insisted that a true *karmayogin*, that is to say, one who adopts the activism as taught in the *Bhagavadgītā* as his creed, can alone become a true *bhakta*, for, by pursuing his *svadharma*, the *karmayogin* actually subserves the will of god and participates in the divine project. Among other features of the teaching of the *Bhagavadgītā* may be mentioned the ethical idealization of sacrifice and the promulgation of a positive religio-philosophical synthesis.

If the *Bhagavadgītā* was, in a sense, the basic text of Hindu religion and ethics, the *Smṛtis* must be said to have been the basic texts governing a Hindu's personal, domestic, and social behaviour. Though the term *Smṛti* was sometimes used to denote almost the entire religious literature of early classical Hinduism in contradistinction with the term *Śruti* which denoted the religious literature of Vedism (or Brahmanism), that term denoted, more specially, the versified texts on Dharmaśāstra. Easily the best known work of this type is the *Manusmṛti*, which may be presumed to have belonged to the period when the *Mahābhārata* was undergoing its final redaction. The *Manusmṛti* begins with a statement on cosmology, and then proceeds to lay down, in the next few chapters which may be said to constitute the very kernel of the work, the rules of conduct of persons belonging to the different social orders (*varṇadharma*) and the different stages of life (*āśramadharma*). Indeed, in course of time, the *varṇāśramadharma* as formulated in the *Manusmṛti* came to be almost identified with Hinduism as a whole. The *Manusmṛti* then goes on to discuss matters relating to polity (*rājadharma*), whereby in connection with the administration of justice, it deals at some length with the eighteen titles of law. It ends with the mention of some expiatory rites (*prāyaścittas*) and a desultory discussion of a few topics of a metaphysical character.

It was also during this period of the definition and consolidation of Hinduism as a socio-religious system that typical concepts such as those of *pravṛtti* and *nivṛtti*, the three *ṛṇas*, the four *puruṣārthas*, and more particularly of Karma and *saṁsāra*, which, incidentally, may be regarded as perhaps the only dogmas (if at all any) of Hinduism, came to be specially emphasised. It may be pointed out in this context that, though, in ancient and medieval India, religion and philosophy were not always sharply demarcated, the various systems of Hindu philosophy seem to have developed almost independently of religion. In the course of the first few centuries before Christ, what may be called the Hindu philosophical thought seems to have been, for the first time, crystallized in the form of regular orthodox philosophical systems. These systems were characterised as orthodox or *āstika*, not because they believed in the existence of god—indeed, for most of them, god was quite superfluous—, but because, unlike Buddhism and Jainism, they claimed to have been derived from and owed allegiance to the Veda. Actually, however, out of the six established orthodox systems, only two, namely, the Pūrvamīmāṁsā (as represented in the *sūtras* of Jaimini) and the Uttaramīmāṁsā (as represented in the *sūtras* of Bādarāyaṇa) can be said to have been directly related to the Veda, while the remaining four, namely, the Sāṁkhya of Kapila, the Yoga of Patañjali, the Vaiśeṣika of Kaṇāda, and the Nyāya of Gautama, were connected with the Veda (if they could be said to have been at all so connected) only in a forced, tenuous, and essentially formal manner. Similarly all these six systems cannot be said to have been 'philosophical' in the strictest sense of the term. The Pūrvamīmāṁsā, for instance, mainly dealt with the methodology of interpretation of Vedic texts, particularly those relating to ritual; the Yoga taught the theory and practice of mental and spiritual discipline; and the Nyāya constituted a system of logic and epistemology. It was only the Uttaramīmāṁsā or Vedānta, the Sāṁkhya, and the Vaiśeṣika, which treated of metaphysics as such. However, all the six systems had a few points in common, such as the doctrine of the soul, the doctrine of Karma, and the doctrine of *mokṣa*.

The Vedānta sought to represent the apparently inconsistent and contradictory philosophical teachings of the *Upaniṣads* as a harmonious system of thought, by emphasizing, in one way or another, their monistic-idealistic trend. The Sāṁkhya was relatively realistic, and taught a metaphysical dualism by positing the original existence of two independent entities, namely, Prakṛti and Puruṣa, though, in view of its assumption of many Puruṣas, its teaching could be actually characterised as pluralistic. The Vaiśeṣika was essentially realistic and propounded the doctrine of atomic pluralism, which doctrine, incidentally, could not be even remotely traced back to the Vedic thought-complex. It is accordingly quite understandable that the Vaiśeṣika did not enjoy any wide currency in Hindu religious thought and literature. Between the Sāṁkhya and the Vedānta, the appeal of the former seems to have been greater so far as classical Hinduism was concerned, as the epics and the *Purāṇas* testify. The Sāṁkhya offered (in contrast to the Vedānta) a more or less rational scheme of the evolution of the phenomenal world out of the twenty-four *tattvas*; it supplied a metaphysical basis for the Yoga which was becoming increasingly popular; and it stressed that *mokṣa* did not imply the merging of the soul into the impersonal *brahman* (as suggested by the Vedānta) but that it implied a state of isolation of the soul from Prakṛti and other Puruṣas. However, in its grand philosophical synthesis, the *Bhagavadgītā* has shrewdly attempted to superimpose the Vedāntic monism upon the Sāṁkhya dualism-pluralism.

The fall of the Śuṅgas marked the beginning of a period of a kind of uncertainty in the fortunes of Hinduism. Various circumstances may be said to have been responsible for bringing about this state of things. For one thing, there was at that time no single paramount political power which could have promoted the advancement of Hinduism. It was a period of great social upheaval and unsettled political conditions. Adequate impetus could not, therefore, be given to the momentous upsurge of Hinduism which had started in the post-Maurya era, though some efforts in that direction are known to have been made by the Kāṇvas, the Āndhras, the Bhāraśivas, and the early Vākāṭakas. The religious affiliations of the foreign tribes like the Bactrian Greeks, the Śakas, the Pahlavas, and the Kuṣāṇas, who made inroads in India during this period and eventually settled down in this country, were divided between Buddhism and Hinduism. Most of these foreign tribes had sojourned in Serindia before they came over to India and had, accordingly, already come under the influence of Buddhism, which had spread far and wide in that region. In course of time, however, many of them seem to have been converted to one or the other sect of Hinduism. Another significant factor which must have seriously affected the growth of Hinduism was the rise, during this period, of a strong rival to that religion in the form of Mahāyāna Buddhism. The Hīnayāna, which represented an earlier scholastic formulation of the original teachings of the Buddha, did not concern itself very much with metaphysical speculations and logical subtleties. It rather put an emphasis on a life of rigorous self-discipline and supramundane contemplation. As against the Hīnayāna, the Mahāyāna was a more popular religion. In the words of Eliot, "it was less monastic than the older Buddhism, and more emotional, warmer in charity, more personal in devotion, more ornate in art, literature and ritual, more disposed to evolution and development." The Mahāyāna, richer in mythology and teaching selfless devotion, thus substantially resembled the popular Hinduism of the epics. In a sense, the Mahāyāna was in relation to the Hīnayāna what Hinduism was in relation to Upaniṣadic Vedism. It, therefore, wielded among the masses an influence more or less similar to that of Hinduism. When, however, in the early fourth century A.D., the Guptas came to power, Hinduism attained a truly classical efflorescence.

One of the foremost religio-literary activities of the age of the Guptas was the final redaction of the *Purāṇas*. *Purāṇas* as legends of antiquity had been in existence from very early times, but they had not been given any fixed literary form for a long time. The term *itihāsa-purāṇa*, which occurs in different contexts in the Vedic literature, seems to have denoted the floating and dynamic literary tradition of the *Purāṇas* and not any specific literary works. It would appear from the available epigraphic and literary evidence that what may be called the first draft of the *Purāṇas* had become ready in the early centuries of the Christian era. This first draft itself must have been the result of a long process of editing and revision. The *Purāṇas* themselves define a *Purāṇa* as comprising five main topics, namely, *sarga* (creation), *prati-sarga* (dissolution and re-creation), *vaṁśa* (divine genealogies), *manvantara* (ages of Manu), and *vaṁśānucarita* (genealogies of kings). However, none of the existing *Purāṇas* can be said to adhere to this definition. It may, therefore, be assumed that the *pañcalakṣaṇa Purāṇas* belonged to an earlier stage in the development of this literature. Many topics not covered by the *pañcalakṣaṇa* definition [or even the *daśalakṣaṇa* definition which adds *vṛtti* (means of livelihood), *rakṣā* (incarnations), *mukti* (final emancipation), *hetu* (*jīva* unmanifest), and *apāśraya* (*brahman*)] came to be incorporated in the *Purāṇas* during the course of their growth. A critical study of these additions clearly shows that this process of revision and amplification must have continued till the early Gupta period. The beliefs and practices of the Hinduism of the age of the Guptas are accordingly best represented in these "scriptures of the common man." The *Purāṇas* reflect not only the culmination of the process of the classicalization of Hinduism but also the beginnings of the proliferation of Hinduism. A clear indication of this latter tendency is to be found in the rise of the various sects which were essentially monotheistic in character. Indeed, hereafter, one can speak of the history of Hinduism only in the sense of the history of the Hindu sects, for, apart from these sects, Hinduism as such hardly had any independent entity. In this context, it should be remembered that sects can arise easily only in such religions as have no clearly defined dogmas. Otherwise, there is the risk of the sects becoming heresies.

A reference has already been made to Kṛṣṇaism or the Bhāgavata sect, which was but an aspect of Vaiṣṇavism. Vaiṣṇavism, as a sect, developed round the single god Viṣṇu, who was believed to have revealed himself through various *avatāras* or incarnations. It may, however, be incidentally added that Vaiṣṇavism had not been always associated with the idea of *avatāras*. Just as Vaiṣṇavism developed round the figure of Viṣṇu, who cannot be said to have belonged to the hieratic Vedic pantheon, Śaivism developed round the pre-Vedic non-Aryan god Śiva. It is, indeed, remarkable that an austere and ascetic god like Śiva should have been made the object of an emotional and emancipatory love. It would seem that the *Śvetāśvatara-Upaniṣad*, which had sought to elevate the personal god over and above the impersonal *brahman*, had played the same role in respect of early Śaiva theism as the *Bhagavadgītā* had done in respect of the early Bhāgavata theism. History shows that these two major sects of Hinduism lived and grew side by side without generating any feeling of mutual ill-will. Epigraphic and numismatic evidence indicates that most of the Gupta sovereigns were devout Vaiṣṇavas or Bhāgavatas. Candra Gupta II, Kumāra Gupta I, and Skanda Gupta style themselves as *paramabhāgavatas* on their coins. The emblems normally used for the personal and official seals of the Gupta monarchs, such as *śaṁkha*, *cakra*, *lakṣmī*, *garuḍa*, etc., also point to their Vaiṣṇava inclinations. But they were singularly free from any kind of sectarian insularity. The facts that some of the Gupta emperors, who styled themselves as *paramabhāgavatas*, had their own personal names, such as Kumāra and Skanda, derived from the Śaiva sect and that they patronised with commendable impartiality both Vaiṣṇava and Śaiva religious establishments would provide a sufficient testimony in this regard.

Apart from Vaiṣṇavism and Śaivism, the emergence, during the period of classical Hinduism, of several other minor sects, is evidenced in history and literature. Some of the Gupta inscriptions, for instance, point to the prevalence of the worship of the sun-god during the period. Similarly, the remains of the Gupta temples at Padmāvatī and Rajgir are suggestive respectively of the Yakṣa-cult and the Nāga-cult. As for the literary evidence, the different *Purāṇas* have, indeed, to be regarded as constituting the specific religious texts pertaining to different sects of Hinduism.

Another very significant aspect of the development of Hindu sects is to be seen in the *Tantras*. *Tantra* is a generic term denoting the literature of certain religious cults, whose beginnings have to be traced back perhaps even to the pre-Vedic times but which were systematised and began to become prominent within Hinduism (and, for that matter, also within Buddhism) from about the 5th century A.D. This literature cannot be said to have necessarily arisen to oppose the Vedas which claimed some kind of formal authority in respect of Hinduism. It was only averred that the Vedas had been all right for the earlier ages, but that their teachings and practices had lost their appeal in the Kaliyuga. The *Tantras*, therefore, took the place of the Vedas as the authoritative religious literature of the new age. Tantrism also opened its doors to all social orders and women. Paradoxically, however, while the *Tantras*, on the one hand, sought to democratise Hinduism by removing the barriers of sex and caste in religious matters, on the other hand, they laid down such strict rules for the initiation of the *sādhakas* into their secret practices that they thereby tended to become an exclusive esoteric cult. The dogmatics and ethics of the *Tantras* were more or less similar to those of Brahmanic Hinduism; but their distinctive feature was their mystic-magical practices which comprised such items as *mantra* (magically potent formula), *bīja* (mystical letter forming the essential part of a *mantra*), *yantra* (magic-mystic diagrams), *nyāsa* (placing of the hands on different parts of the body), *mudrā* (gesture which sought to preserve the form of the *mantra* intact), etc. The *Tantras* also dealt with the various details of *pūjā* and orgiastic rites as also of temple-architecture and iconography. Many of the late sectarian *Upaniṣads* are of the nature of *Tantras*, while the influence of the *Tantras* on some of the *Purāṇas* is quite unmistakable.

Unlike the Vedas, the *Tantras*, whose number is fairly large, are emphatically sectarian in character. They relate mainly to the three sects—Śaiva, Vaiṣṇava, and Śākta—and the Tantric texts belonging to these three sects are respectively called *Āgamas*, *Saṁhitās*, and *Tantras*. It is generally believed that the *Āgamas* originated in Kashmir, the *Tantras* in Bengal and Eastern and North-Eastern India, and the *Saṁhitās* in various parts of this country, particularly Bengal and South India. There are 28 Śaiva *Āgamas* which are traditionally believed to have originated from the five mouths of Śiva. The time of the final redaction of the *Āgamas* is uncertain, but they have been profusely used by Tirumular and other Tamil writers and must have accordingly belonged to a period not later than the 7th century A.D. The principal Tantric Vaiṣṇava cult is known as Pāñcarātra. Traditionally 108 *Saṁhitās* of the Pāñcarātra are mentioned, though their number is sometimes given as 215 or even 290. Side by side with the Pāñcarātra, there also developed the Tantric Vaiṣṇava cult known as Vaikhānasa. The chronology of the Śākta *Tantras* is difficult to determine, but there are indications of their influence even in the *Mahābhārata* and some of their elements have been epigraphically documented since 424 A.D.

The age of the Guptas thus witnessed a solid, opulent, and many-sided expansion of Hinduism. A brief reference may be made here to some of the characteristic features of this grand cultural movement. Firstly, it becomes clear from the study of epigraphic and literary records of the Gupta period that classical Hinduism had generally developed a remarkable spirit of tolerance vis-a-vis other religions as also among its various sects. Secondly, this new, vigorous Hinduism is seen to have given a great fillip to Sanskrit language and literature. It may be noted, in this connection, that classical Sanskrit was widely—and perhaps deliberately—used even for popular and secular purposes and that even the Jainas and the Buddhists thought it necessary to write their religio-philosophical works in Sanskrit. Thirdly, thanks to the activities of the peripatetic minstrels, who visited the distant parts of the country under the pretext of the various pilgrimages recommended by the popular scriptures and thus carried the message of Hinduism directly to the masses by means of the *Purāṇa*-recitations, Hinduism proved in that period a significant force in unifying the heterogeneous elements of the population in a common bond of religion. And, finally, Hinduism had then assumed a positive missionary role. The movement of the spread of Hinduism in foreign lands had already begun in the earlier period, and there is ample evidence of its expansion over the whole of South-East Asia, from Burma to Java and Bali, from at least the second century onwards, though many indications in this connection have been partially obscured by Buddhism which had preceded and then again followed Hinduism. Indeed, a Hindu mission is known to have penetrated into the Hellenistic world and to have advanced as far as Egypt at a very early date. This activity as well as that of the Hinduisation of foreign tribes which came to

India continued with equal zeal even in the classical period of the history of Hinduism.

The next millennium, that is roughly from 700 A.D. to 1700 A.D., was characterized by the vigorously continued proliferation of Hinduism in various directions. Hinduism came to be further fragmented into more sects and sub-sects. This resulted in the creation of a kind of dichotomy between the *smārta* Hinduism and sectarian Hinduism. It must, however, be remembered that, howsoever radical a sect might have been, it made it a point not to abjure the parent creed, though some of the sects had obviously arisen under the inspiration of non-Hindu religious ideologies. The emergence of these sects usually followed a certain set pattern. Some religious leader started a movement with a view either to reforming the existing vulgarised religious practices or to widening the appeal of Hinduism by claiming equal religious privileges for all castes and classes. It may, however, be incidentally added that most of the movements started for the purpose of the democratization or popularization of religion eventually tended to become exclusive and esoteric. The newly arisen sects and sub-sects centred round specific divinities, and adopted as their gospels the sayings and sermons of their promoters (or of the immediate disciples of those promoters), which were usually delivered not in Sanskrit but in the languages of the people and which were preserved either in oral or written form. They were also, not unoften, marked out from one another on account of their distinctive apparel or emblems. Thus, though Hinduism as such did not swear by any Prophet or any Book or any Church, the sects of Hinduism may, in a sense, be said to have done so.

A notable feature of these sects was that they had arisen not so much to sponsor any specific philosophical tenets as to establish and popularize particular types of theism and ways of *bhakti*. Proper religious experience, it was now fully realised, could be had neither through mechanical ritualism nor through abstract philosophical contemplation; it could be had only through *bhakti* which, according to Renou, implied "an affective participation of the soul in the divine." It is true that Hinduism has never been able to isolate itself completely from the deeper pantheistic trends inherited from the *Upaniṣads*. Nevertheless, it is equally true that from the 9th-10th centuries onwards "all that is most vital in Hinduism has manifested itself in the form of *bhakti*." This renaissance of *bhakti* is known to have received its main impulse from South India. And it was presumably this fact which initiated the tradition preserved in the *Padmapurāṇa*, namely, that *bhakti* was born in the Draviḍa country. In South India, there were the Naināṛs, who, in the first half of the ninth century, developed a kind of sensuous mysticism for Śiva, and the Āḷvārs, who, a few years later, expressed in their Tamil songs a deeply emotional and intensely personal devotion for Viṣṇu.

But the Vaiṣṇava *bhakti*-cult underwent a truly exuberant ramification in Northern and Central India from the 13th to the 17th century. Two main currents of devotional worship could be distinguished in this connection—one relating to Rāma and the other to Kṛṣṇa. In the case of the latter, again, there were to be seen two distinct lines of development—one centring round Kṛṣṇa and his spouse (as generally sponsored by the saints of Maharashtra) and the other round Kṛṣṇa and his beloved Rādhā (as popularized, among others, by Nimbārka, Caitanya, and Jayadeva). So far as Śaivism is concerned, a reference may be made to the Trika or the Tantric-metaphysical aspect of Śaivism which had become established in Kashmir round about the ninth century A.D., the elaboration and systematization of the Śaiva siddhānta in South India, and the rise of the various Śaiva sects like the Kāpālika, the Kālamukh, the Vīraśaiva, and the Liṅgāyata.

Besides this proliferation of sects and cults there was also in evidence a fairly active proliferation in respect of the orthodox philosophical systems. For instance, the *Vedānta-Sūtras* of Bādarāyaṇa, which constituted perhaps the most important basic text of the Uttaramīmāṁsā or Vedānta, were interpreted differently by different commentators and were thereby made to yield different sub-systems of Vedānta. Certainly the most prominent among these commentators was Śaṁkara (8th-9th century A.D.). But the qualified monism (*viśiṣṭādvaita*) of Rāmānuja (11th century A.D.) seems to have enjoyed a wider appeal outside the learned circles than Śaṁkara's absolute monism (*kevalādvaita*), for, the former furnished a kind of philosophical basis to the doctorine of *bhakti*. Indeed, one of the pioneers of the renaissance of *bhakti*, namely, Rāmānanda, belonged to the school of Rāmānuja. Nimbārka (11th century A.D.), who, like Bhāskara (circa 900 A.D.), derived a dualistic non-dualism from the *Vedānta-sūtras*, may be said to have been the first to grant philosophical recognition to the cult of Rādhā, while Vallabha (14th-15th century A.D.) emphasised the doctrine of god's grace. Madhva (13th century A.D.) struck a distinctive note by insisting that the triad of the orthodox Vedānta philosophy (*prasthāna-trayī*) taught dualism.

A survey of the history of Hinduism during this long period, would bring out two prominent facts. Firstly, the influences on Hinduism of non-Hindu religious ideologies have been quite superficial and therefore almost negligible. And, secondly, for its length, this history must be said to have been marred but seldom by religious persecution either by or of or within Hinduism. The missionary activities of Buddhism and Jainism were generally pacific, and with the Hindu theistic-philosophical renaissance in South India they had become more or less subdued. Islam was more aggressive—on the negative side it sought to exterminate Hinduism and on the positive side it aimed at the conversion of the Hindu population. The encounter between Islam and Hinduism, on the one hand, evoked a religio-political solidarity such as was evidenced in the Maratha and Sikh reaction, and, on the other hand, it inspired efforts to bring about a spiritual rapprochement between the two faiths.

The eighteenth century was a period of stagnation for Hinduism. Not much activity was evident either in respect of doctrine or of literature. But, roughly with the advent of the British rule in India, traditional Hinduism had to face quite a new problem—the problem arising from its confrontation with modern culture (in the early stages of its evolution). The educated classes among the Hindus reacted to this phenomenon, which was fraught with serious and far-reaching consequences, in three typical ways. The remarkable achievements of science and technology in the West and the new philosophies of life to which they gave rise made a tremendous impact on one section of the Hindu intelligentsia. They critically studied the situation in India and concluded from this self-examination that the root-cause of the material and the spiritual poverty of India—yes, even the spiritual poverty, for, the much-flaunted Hindu spirituality was, according to them, to be found neither in books nor in practice—was the kind of religion which she traditionally professed. They, therefore, felt that this root-cause needed to be removed, that is to say, religion had to be rejected. Such rejection of religion took two forms. Firstly it meant the rejection of traditional Hinduism in favour of a religion which was considered to be more amenable to modern developments, particularly of Christianity. The other variety of rejection was far more radical. It cannot, of course, be said to have been restricted only to India. Indeed it was a common intellectual attitude which had been engendered by the multiple material forces in most parts of the civilized world. This variety of rejection insisted on religion as such being entirely banished from human affairs. But the rejectionists of neither of these two varieties could command any extensive support in India.

The second kind of reaction was represented by the equally strongly expressed tendency towards the preservation—either wholesale or selective—of the beliefs and practices of Hinduism. It was claimed that traditional Hinduism could not and must not be banished, for, it had efficaciously served and would continue to serve as the perennial source of inspiration and the one beacon light for the Hindu millions. The traditional Hindu spirituality, it was insisted, was the only rampart which could successfully withstand the cursed onslaught of the degrading Western materialism. Three principal manifestations of this tendency have become particularly evident in recent times.

(1) There are, first of all, the obscurantists like the Varṇāśrama-dharma-Saṁgha and the Rāṁarājya-Pariṣad, who insist that the traditional Hinduism with all its religious and socio-ethical implications must be preserved at all cost. They believe that any kind of change in that regard will jeopardise the very existence of Hinduism.

(2) The second group representing the preservationist attitude consists of the Hindu Mahāsabhā and the Rāṣṭriya-Svayaṁsevaka-Saṁgha. The followers of these two organizations may be characterised as Hindu nationalists. They are not necessarily in sympathy with the extreme obscurantists. Their one and principal claim is that Hinduism is the national religion of India. According to them, the preservation of Hinduism amounts to the maintenance of the national solidarity of the country. In principle, they are not averse to suitable reforms in Hindu society. Indeed, many of them entertain the vision of a strong, socially reconstructed Hinduism. Naturally enough, the Hindu nationalists are anti-conversion and pro-reconversion. They firmly believe that, without the basic spiritual and social values of traditional Hinduism, India will lose her essential personality. They are quite unwilling to separate Hinduism from the larger national life of the country. For them, Hinduism is the flag of patriotism.

(3) Finally, there are the fundamentalists like the Āryasamāja whose main slogan is: "Back to the Veda." The fundamentalists believe that the Aryan religion in its purest form is presented only in the Veda. The weakness and the degradation of Hinduism are due to the non-Vedic elements which have, in course of time, accumulated round the Vedic kernel. Hinduism must be drastically shorn of all its non-Vedic excrescences, and the Vedic Aryan religion must thereby be made to assert itself in its pristine purity and splendour. The Āryasamāja

further claims that the Vedic Aryan religion has nothing to fear from the so-called modern sciences. For, the Veda distinctly anticipates most of these sciences and technological inventions.

The third kind of reaction resulting from the confrontation of traditional Hinduism with modern culture was reflected in the attempts to restate Hinduism in the light of the newly arisen complex situation in India and the world. This tendency may be said to be the ruling tendency of the present times. It has its origin in the firm conviction that Hinduism possesses the innate character of what may be called the eternal religion, *sanātana dharma*, and that it can adequately satisfy the religious urge of any age. The past history of Hinduism, as RADHAKRISHNAN points out, encourages one to believe that it will be found "equal to any emergency that the future may throw up, whether on the field of thought or of history." All that needs to be done is to reinterpret Hinduism to suit the changing conditions—and this, it is believed, can be done without any serious violence to the basic character of Hinduism—or to isolate and emphasize such characteristics of Hinduism as are universal and perennial in their appeal and thereby relate its teachings suitably to modern developments. This tendency towards restatement, reinterpretation, or revision of Hinduism has manifested itself in various ways, but a reference may be made here only to three of these manifestations.

Firstly, there were attempts made, mostly under the inspiration of Christianity, to liberalize, humanize, and rationalize traditional Hinduism. The Brāhma Samāja of Calcutta represented one such attempt. This movement sought to overcome the formidable contradictions inherent in the traditional Hindu way of life and thought—contradictions, for instance, such as those between renunciation on the one hand and sordid sensuality on the other, between unnatural insistence on chastity on the one hand and exaggerated sex-obsession on the other, and between morbid respect for animal life on the one hand and beastly cruelty to fellow human beings on the other. Among other things, it lay stress on monotheism, which was supposed to be more rational, and, from the practical point of view, more conducive to the intensity of religious feeling; it discouraged idolatry, which was regarded as being reminiscent of primitive totemism and as a morbid growth on the original religion; it promoted congregational worship which was believed to engender a sense of religious integration in the community; and it exalted the human values in religion above other values. The Brāhma Samāja, however, never became an all-India movement. Its influence was mostly restricted to Bengal and that too only to certain sections of the community. Of course, religious and social movements similar to the Brāhma Samāja, such as the Prārthanā Samāja in Bombay, were started in other parts of the country as well, but they too cannot be said to have caught the imagination of the people as a whole.

The second religious movement, which undertook to reinterpret Hinduism in the light of modern developments in thought and life, was that of the Ramakrishna Mission. Under the inspiration of the mystic sage RAMAKRISHNA PARAMAHAṀSA and with the fervour derived from the Vedāntic Karmayogin missionary Swami VIVEKANANDA, the Mission has, through its many branches manned by devoted Swamis, done quite remarkable work in different parts of the country and also at some centres established outside India. The Mission lays special emphasis on the universality of the fundamental teachings of Hinduism, such as the divinity of man, the non-duality and spiritual character of the ultimate reality, the basic solidarity of all existence, the character of religion as realization and not as mere creed, and the essential harmony of all religions. The humanatarian activities of the Ramakrishna Mission and its social service particularly in the field of education and medical and other relief need special mention.

It is, however, the third kind of manifestation of the tendency of restatement and reinterpretation of Hinduism which seems to appeal most to the Hindu intellectuals today. Surprisingly enough, this kind of manifestation has not taken the form of any organized religious movement like the Brāhma Samāja or the Ramakrishna Mission. It is largely the result of the endeavours—which are mostly academic in character—of individual thinkers (a leading figure among them is RADHAKRISHNAN), who having become "conscious of many of the imperfections and disabilities of the historical faith, seek to find within it, by some kind of rationalization, a faith adequate to meet the demands of Indian life in the present age." Their re-evaluation of Hinduism is rational, critical, and essentially philosophically oriented. Their attitude is one of constructive criticism tempered by trust. Traditional Hinduism, they are convinced, is by no means free from mistaken concepts, excesses, and abuses; but these are but excrescences to be gotten rid of. Underneath these are solid, universal principles to be held to without hesitation. "Our times", says RADHAKRISHNAN, "require not a surrender of the basic principles of Hinduism, but a restatement of them with special reference to the needs of a more complex and mobile social order." "The great ideals of our culture," he says elsewhere, "cannot be discarded; but their embodiment in forms and institutions we must get beyond. There is no reversing history." Change in religion is inevitable, but tradition must grow. Indeed, RADHAKRISHNAN has a larger vision of Hinduism. He does not regard it merely as a faith fit for a section of the people of India. He entertains the hope that, if the Hindu religious thought and practice were suitably reorganized, Hinduism would "recover its conquering force and power to advance, penetrate, and fertilise the world."

One must, however, hasten to add here, by way of a postscript, that whatever has been said above about the impact of modernity on Hinduism pertains but to the narrow upper fringe of the Hindu community. The nationalised or liberalised or rationalised or philosophised version of traditional Hinduism is not likely to percolate easily to the Hindu masses, much less to exert any appreciable influence on them. Indeed, the masses do not feel the need to do any deliberate thinking about religion. They seem to be content to be able to practise their traditional religion in the form in which and to the extent to which it is possible for them to do so, and to derive from it whatever solace they are capable of deriving.

III. Conception of the Deity

It is generally assumed that belief in god constitutes one of the essentials of religion. Such an assumption cannot, however, be said to hold good in respect of Hinduism as a whole. A survey of the conception of godhead in the various periods of the history of Hinduism would amply substantiate this statement. To begin with the proto-historical Hinduism, it has been already pointed out that the sources of our knowledge regarding the religious situation prevailing in the pre-Vedic non-Aryan period of the history of India are quite limited. It is no doubt possible to derive from the archaeological and allied evidence relating to that period a few glimpses in what may be called the externals of the religion of that period. But, in the absence of any literature or mythological tradition, one is not in a position to say anything significant about the doctrines or ideology of that religion. All that we are entitled to presume is that, if one could visualize the later Śiva-religion as an essentially monotheistic religion, one might thereby get some idea about the theology of the proto-historical Hinduism. With the advent of Vedism, a new religious ideology makes its appearance on the Indian scene. Fortunately, from this period onwards, we have a rich and almost unbroken tradition of religious literature which enables us to study, in a fairly detailed manner, the various topics which are connected with the concept of god, such as the nature of the deity, the relation of the deity to the world, and the relation of the deity to the finite self in its three principal conditions, namely, the condition prior to its involvement in the phenomenal world, the embodied condition, and the condition following emancipation.

So far as the *Ṛgveda* is concerned, it may be suggested that Veda is primarily occupied with mythology rather than with theology. To put it in other words, most of the Ṛgvedic gods appear to have been created for the myths and not the myths to have been created for the gods. For the Vedic poet-priests, the myth is the primary mode of apprehending reality. The myth, indeed, is the thing, while the divinities are conceived more or less as mere actors in the mythological drama. It is generally agreed that the Vedic gods are not amenable to being reduced to any kind of set pattern. The character of these gods, as imagined by the Vedic poets in different contexts, is too fluid and intangible. And this feature of their character gets more and more confirmed on account of the absence, during that period, of any attempt to represent them in a plastic or graphic form. A sculpture or a painting certainly tends to invest a god with a kind of characterisation. Normally, a Vedic god cannot be said to be represented as a god in the spiritual, moral, or mystical sense. He is usually projected through the medium of conventionalised epithets and functions. Whatever theism there is in the Veda is little more than glorified anthropomorphism, which latter, again, is highly variable. Vedic gods would seem to defy any classification—whether regionwise, ritualistic, or functional. They are too vague and impersonal for any kind of characterisation and classification.

Notwithstanding all this, attempts have been made, even from early times, to discover some norm or derive some system in this connection. The *Nirukta* of Yāska (circa 6th century B.C.), for instance, refers to the theories of scholiasts like the Nairuktas, who, depending mainly on the etymologies of the names of Vedic gods, regarded them as personifying different natural powers and phenomena, the Aitihāsikas, according to whom the Veda sought to present actual history in the form of mythology, and the Yājñikas, who saw in Vedic mythology little more than a reflection of Vedic ritual. The etymological-naturalistic interpretation of Vedic mythology, which Yāska himself has sponsored, found a large following among the modern Vedists, particularly in the initial stages. They were content to look upon the Vedic myths as a sort of paraphrase of natural phenomena. It is, however, hardly necessary to emphasize the inherent inadequacy of such a view. As pointed out elsewhere, it was but inevitable that the religious thinking of the Vedic people, who lived in close communion with nature, should have been profoundly influenced by naturalistic concepts, but those concepts cannot be said to have constituted the basic foundation of their religious thinking. Natural phenomena do not generally create myths and legends; the similarity with a natural phenomenon may only help to reinforce mythologically a story which often has a real historical happening for its basis.

Some scholars have gone a little deeper into the question of the significance of Vedic religion and mythology. BERGAIGNE, for instance, begins with the assumption of a strict interdependence of Vedic mythology and Vedic cult. The sacrificial ritual is, according to him, the true reproduction on earth of the cosmic phenomena. These phenomena are of two kinds:

(1) those which accompany the rising of the sun (solar phenomena), and

(2) those which accompany the falling of rain after a long drought (meteorological phenomena).

In both these kinds of phenomena, Vedic mythology differentiates between male and female elements; and these different elements are represented differently in the frame-work of mythological anthropomorphism and zoomorphism. Even this bare sketch of BERGAIGNE's theory will suffice to show that BERGAIGNE, who sought to present Vedic religion and mythology as a simple system consisting of a few easily intelligible formulas, has actually ended by producing a highly complicated and schematic pattern.

In recent years, another French scholar, DUMÉZIL, following the lead of DURKHEIM who emphasises the functional relationship between social and sacred phenomena, has arrived at the tripartite division of the Indo-European social organization into priests, warriors, and food-producers (that is, peasants and artisans), as the keystone of a common religio-mythological ideology. DUMÉZIL further goes on to point out that, so far as the Vedic religion and mythology are concerned, the two antithetical yet complementary divine rulers Mitra and Varuṇa are the representatives of the class of priests, Indra (or Vāyu) of that of warriors, and Aśvins of that of food-producers. It will, however, be agreed that Vedic mythology is too complex, comprehensive, and free to be squeezed into such a narrow frame-work.

The primary and the most basic religious concept of the early Vedic period may be characterized as Asuism. As has been pointed out elsewhere, the Vedic man believed that a somatic magic potence permeated through nature and the human world and thereby constituted the essential basis of their existence and functioning. This magic potence was shared alike by gods, human beings, animals, trees, etc.—of course in varying proportions. The Vedic man further believed that, through his *mantra* and cultic action, new magic potence could be created in an entity and the magic potence already existing in an entity either enhanced or reduced or transferred to another entity. The concept of an all-pervading somatic magic potence such as this is, indeed, common to the religious ideologies of many primitive peoples, and anthropologists have designated that potence differently. The Vedic poet-priests seem to have denoted this potence with the word *asu*, and it is from that word that the term Asuism has been coined. The essential nature of the Vedic gods is that they are *asuras* or possessors, in a special sense, of the *asu*-potence. Varuṇa is *asura* par excellence, and is often celebrated in the *Ṛgveda* as the *saṁrāṭ* or world-sovereign, who, by virtue of his binding power arising from his character as *asura* establishes the cosmic order *ṛta* in this vast and complex universe. This may be said to be the norm of the cosmic myth which is presented in the Veda in different forms and as connected with different gods in different contexts. The Vedic poet-priest speaks of several other aspects of this essential magic potence, to the operation of which man is believed to be subjected either positively or negatively. The Vedic poet-priest further emphasizes the fact that, while man is dependent for his existence and activity on the *asuras* or the bearers of the magic *asu*-potence, the latter too are dependent for their proper functioning on man's *mantra* and cultic action. This, in brief, is perhaps the only theology that can be derived from the *Ṛgveda*; everything else is mythology.

Thus, theologically, the religion of the *Ṛgveda* may be characterised as "pan-asuism"; but, mythologically, that religion is distinctly polytheistic. The Ṛgvedic polytheism is anthropomorphic in character, and, as has been indicated above, the anthropomorphism of the Vedic gods is often variable. Again, there is hardly any hierarchy among these gods. No clear and well-defined functions in connection with the world-process and world-rule are seen to have been assigned to the various members of the Vedic pantheon. It is rightly pointed out that the Vedic gods do not have any recognised undisputed leader like Zeus or Jupiter, and that they generally present a picture of 'interminable variety of ranks and confusing interchange of characters'. The Ṛgvedic polytheism is, accordingly, a diffuse polytheism. It is suggested that one may discover in the *Ṛgveda* a distinct trend towards polytheism gradually making way for monotheism. For instance, one notices in that Veda an increasing tendency to identify one god with another. The frequent grouping of gods also points in the same direction. Further, the mythological concept of Viśve-Devāḥ (All-gods) is regarded as reflecting a collective godhead, while a few Ṛgvedic passages are said to be indicative of a kind of "integral multiplicity" in the divine world. In spite of all this, however, it must be clearly stated that monotheism in the sense of a belief in a single ethical god, who, while being intimately involved in the world-process, is yet transcendental in character had not developed in the Vedic period.

In his treatment of Vedic religion, MAX MÜLLER has emphasized one significant tendency of the Vedic poets, namely, to celebrate individual gods successively as the highest. The Vedic poets are often seen to address either Indra or Agni or Varuṇa as, for the time being, the only god in existence with an entire forgetfulness of all other gods. To this successive belief in single supreme gods MAX MÜLLER has given the name of henotheism or kathenotheism. He further adds that henotheism marks a stage between the original polytheism and the later monotheism of the *Ṛgveda*. As against this it is suggested that such successive glorification of the Vedic gods has a reference only to different sacrificial contexts and thus has little theological value. The protagonists of urmonotheism, on the other hand, are inclined to regard henotheism as deteriorating monotheism. Some scholars, again, are inclined to think that henotheism is only another name for several 'tribal' or 'regional' monotheisms. A mental attitude similar to the one which has inspired the *dānastuti*-hymns (eulogies of patrons) in the *Ṛgveda* is also sometimes said to have been responsible for the henotheistic passages in that Veda. It would rather seem that henotheism represented a distinct religious attitude, namely, that of eclecticism (as against absolutism or exclusivism) which has characterised Hinduism almost throughout its history. Its further development may be traced to the concept of *iṣṭadevatā* which implies a complete freedom of choosing one's special god and mode of worship, without, however, that freedom being allowed to become in any way detrimental to other gods and other modes of worship. Monotheism often tends to be exclusive in character. From this point of view, henotheism is not only not a stage leading towards monotheism, but it implies, in a sense, an opposition to it. One may claim that one's god is supreme, but one must not claim that that god is unique.

Two main tendencies are noticeable in what may be presumed to be the last stages in the evolution of the Ṛgvedic religion. A feeling seems to have been gradually growing among the Ṛgvedic poets that the mythological gods were quite inadequate to satisfy their religious instinct. They were, as it were, groping for a real god, and, therefore, asked in great anguish: "Unto which god may we offer service with oblation?" (*ṚV* X.121). The other tendency was to reduce the perplexing multiplicity in the divine world to some kind of unity.

The basic foundation of the Atharvanic religion of magic is no other than the "pan-asuism" of the *Ṛgveda*. This latter is also at the root of the Vedic ritual such as has been developed in the *Brāhmaṇas*. The *Brāhmaṇas* seem to give some prominence to the new god Prajāpati. But Prajāpati is by no means a mythological or a theological deity. He does not possess any individuality; he mostly appears as the central figure in the ritual of creative self-immolation. The Vedic ritual is conceived as an autonomous phenomenon; it operates automatically, that is, independently of god or man. Accordingly, in the ideology of the Vedic ritual gods do not play any important role. On the contrary, sacrifice itself is believed to bestow godhead on gods.

If the Brahmanic ritualism had, in a sense, divested the mythological gods of their individualities and functions, the Upaniṣadic spiritualism negatived more or less completely their importance and influence in connection with the world-process. The early *Upaniṣads* taught the doctrine of the ultimate identity of the *brahman*, the universe, and the individual self. This utter monism allowed no scope whatsoever for theism. It was, however, obviously not possible that such a rigorous metaphysical position could be maintained for long. Popular religious sentiment is not satisfied with an abstract impersonal entity; it craves for a personal deity. Besides, there must have been pressures—both of a positive and a negative character—from the non-Vedic religious ideologies. Consequently there began to appear, in the *Upaniṣads*, more or less clear-cut theistic tendencies which are seen to have reached their culmination in the *Śvetāśvatara-Upaniṣad*. Already in the *Chāndogya-Upaniṣad* (III. 14), Sāṇḍilya speaks of the *ātman* in terms which are reminiscent of a personal god. The doctrine of the "inner controller" (*antaryāmin*) in the *Bṛhadāraṇyaka-Upaniṣad* (III. 7,8), and the characterisation by that *Upaniṣad* of the "great unborn self" as the "controller of all", the "lord of all", the "ruler of all", the "ruler of all beings", the "protector of all beings", etc., may also be regarded as a step in the theistic direction. Elsewhere (I. 4.7), that *Upaniṣad* seems to think of the supreme being as something external to the world.

But the transition from monism to theism becomes evident in the later *Upaniṣads*, such as the *Muṇḍaka-Upaniṣad* and more particularly the *Śvetāṣvatara-Upaniṣad*. The *Śvetāśvatara-Upaniṣad* (I.12) unequivocally distinguishes *bhoktā* (the individual self), *bhogya* (the phenomenal world), and *preritā* (the god) from one another, and then speaks of these three as forming the threefold reality (*trividhaṁ brahma*). The supreme being is referred to in that *Upaniṣad* (IV. 11-13) by terms denoting a personal god, such as the "lord", the "bestower of blessing", the "adorable god", and the "ruler of all". He is Rudra, the source and origin of the gods and the supporter of all this which is a combination of mutable and immutable. He is not identical with the individual self, but pervades it without sharing its imperfections and actions. There is also a suggestion in that *Upaniṣad* of a *bhakti*-like personal relationship between the supreme being and the individual self. The god in his immanent aspect is to be realised through yoga; the god in his transcendent aspect is to be worshipped with loving devotion. Further, the *Śvetāśvatara-Upaniṣad* emphasizes the necessity of moral conduct and the possibility of the grace of god. The *Śvetāśvatara-Upaniṣad* may thus be regarded as presenting perhaps the earliest full-fledged statement of theism in historical Hinduism. And the fact that the great god according to that statement is Rudra is historically significant, for, it may have been a direct result of the influence of the proto-historical Hindu monotheism centering round proto-Śiva.

The history of classical Hinduism presents a strange phenomenon. While, on the one hand, Hinduism sought to substitute the impersonal absolute of the *Upaniṣads* with a personal god, the various philosophical systems, which it adopted as its own, were, by and large, basically atheistic. The Sāṁkhya system, for instance, had originally no place for god in its metaphysics. The process of the evolution of the material and the psychological world from the Prakṛti was believed to be autonomous. It was only at a later stage in the development of the Sāṁkhya doctrine that god came to be posited as being instrumental in bringing Prakṛti and Puruṣa into contact with each other and thereby initiating the world-process. The Hinduism of the epics and the *Purāṇas* has mostly sponsored this latter kind of Sāṁkhya, namely, the *seśvara* Sāṁkhya. The Yoga system, which concerns itself essentially with mental and spiritual discipline but which has generally adopted the Sāṁkhya doctrine as its metaphysical basis, does accept god. God, according to that system, is after all a Puruṣa or soul; but he is a distinctive kind of soul. He is different from other souls in that, unlike other Puruṣas, he ever remains unaffected by the ramifications of Prakṛti. He is also said to be responsible for the maintenance of the cosmic order, but he is never specifically represented as the cause of the universe. He is thus redeemed of any liability for the inequality and cruelty in the world. Not only this, but he is said to be positively compassionate. But the most outstanding feature of god's personality which the Yoga system seems to emphasise is that he is the ideal object of contemplation. Yogic concentration, it is suggested, is facilitated through devotion to god. The Yoga system may, accordingly, be said to reflect the beginnings of the theistic ideal of religio-ethical godhead.

The Vaiśeṣikas, like the Sāṁkhyas, generally seem to hold that the world-process is in no way dependent on god, though, it may be added, the *Vaiśeṣika-Sūtras* proper do not contain any direct passage bearing on the creation and the dissolution of the universe. The Vaiśeṣika system maintains that reason cannot prove the existence of god. However, the attitude of that system towards god cannot be said to be as uncompromising as that of the original Sāṁkhya. The later Vaiśeṣika theory such as is, for instance, developed in the *bhāṣya* of Praśastapāda, presumably under the growing theistic influence, speaks of god as being actively instrumental in the evolution and dissolution of the universe. The metaphysical basis of the Nyāya system is derived largely from the Vaiśeṣika atomism. It mentions god mainly as the sentient administrator of the law of Karma. It is god who ensures that that law does not operate promiscuously. Some Naiyāyikas, like Vācaspati and Udayana, offer logical proof for the existence of a primal cause possessing intelligence of the highest order. God is believed to initiate the creative process. He is the operative cause of the universe, but he does not get himself involved in the workings of the universe. It, however, needs to be underlined that the god of the Nyāya system is hardly comparable to the personal god of the proper theistic ideology.

The Pūrvamīmāṁsā treats god with scant respect. For, according to it, the Vedic ritual, which is its chief concern, operates automatically and autonomously. God is subservient to the ritual performance and is often regarded as even superfluous. Indeed, for the Pūrvamīmāṁsā, which essentially deals with the technique of interpreting the Vedic texts, the subject of god is almost irrelevant. It, therefore, often ignores god. It has been well said that, according to the Mīmāṁsā, gods can be regarded only as hypothetical entities which one has to assume because they are essential for the ritual act.

A characteristic feature of the Vedānta as represented by Śaṁkara is the assumption of two levels of reality—transcendental or absolute and phenomenal or empirical. The ultimate and the only reality is, no doubt, the *brahman* in its transcendental aspect. Naturally enough, this immutable *brahman* cannot be made liable for any kind of activity like that of creating the universe. The universe may have only relative reality, but its creation has nonetheless to be explained. It is in this context that god is posited by Śaṁkara. In other words, god is real on the same level as the individual self and the universe. The conception of god is, after all, a hypothesis which right knowledge eventually discards. But, as long as that right philosophical knowledge does not dawn upon a person, he has to accept god seriously and with adequate zeal. Thus Śaṁkara does not deny the existence of god on the empirical level. However, on this level, the individual self is not to be identified with god. For, the ways in which the *māyā* operates with reference to god on the one hand and to the individual self on the other are essentially different. Of course, when the *māyā* ceases to operate, there is neither god nor individual self.

A brief mention may now be made of the attitude of some of the avowedly theistic schools. The *Bhagavadgītā* seems to oscillate between pantheistic monism on the one hand and fervent theism relating to a personal god on the other. It sometimes represents god as an aspect of the *brahman*—as a personalized version of the *brahman*—it being thus suggested that the *brahman* is the supreme being, but it ultimately proclaims as its *guhyatama*—most esoteric—teaching that, beyond the undifferentiated unity of the *brahman*, there is the god, who is the Supreme Person characterised by numberless perfections, who is the ethical lord, who is actively involved in the world-process but who nevertheless remains eternally changeless in his essence, and who, above all, bears deep affection and love for his devotees. The teaching of the *Bhagavadgītā* regarding the nature of god continues to dominate the later religio-philosophical texts of the Bhāgavatas, such as the *Nārāyaṇīya* and the *Anugītā* in the *Mahābhārata*, the *Viṣṇu-Purāṇa*, the

Pāñcarātra-Saṁhitās, and the *Bhāgavata-Purāṇa*. The only noteworthy modification in the basic teaching of the *Bhagavadgītā* is the doctrine of *vyūhas*, which is adumbrated in the *Nārāyaṇīya* and fully developed in the *Pāñcarātra-Saṁhitās*. According to this doctrine, the true nature of Vāsudeva, the supreme god, is constituted of the *ṣāḍguṇya* or six qualities, namely, *jñāna* or absolute consciousness with its five characteristics, namely, *śakti* (which enables Vāsudeva to become the material cause of the universe), *aiśvarya* (or independent spontaneous power of action), *bala* (or inexhaustible power of sustaining the world), *vīrya* (or the ability to remain unchanged despite being the material cause), and *tejas* (or prestige and authority with which he brings forth the universe without any extraneous help). These six *guṇas* are represented, on the one hand, as forming Vāsudeva's body, and, on the other, as serving, through the three *vyūhas* called Saṁkarṣaṇa, Pradyumna, and Aniruddha—in each of these three *vyūhas* only two out of the six *guṇas* being specially attested—as the instruments of his creative activity.

By far the ablest statement of what may be called philosophical theism we owe to Rāmānuja. Rāmānuja's personality often betrays an inner conflict between a philosopher and a theologian—the latter usually having the upper hand. Rāmānuja was not only a metaphysician, he was also—and perhaps more essentially—a founder of a religious sect. According to him, the existence of god cannot be established by means of logic. For instance, one cannot argue, as on the empirical plane, that just as a living body presupposes the existence of the soul or intelligent agent, even so does the world-process presuppose the existence of an intelligent motive principle like god. For, the analogy here is not perfect, the soul not being ever assumed as the creator of the body. Nor can the analogy of potter-clay-pitcher be regarded as strong enough to establish in connection with the universe the existence of god as the agent possessing the knowledge of the material cause. For, as Rāmānuja seems to suggest, even a lesser being than god as he has conceived of him would be quite adequate for the purpose. On the other hand, though the scriptures constitute for Rāmānuja the only authoritative source for the knowledge of god, his peculiar attitude towards the *Upaniṣads* tends to show that he has realised that the *Upaniṣads* do not support the doctrine sponsored by him.

God, according to Rāmānuja, has for his attributes the six *guṇas* namely, *jñāna*, etc., mentioned by the Pāñcarātra texts. He is characterised by all perfections. He is the supreme divinity which creates this world of manifold experience which is essentially real. The world, consisting of souls and matter, is dependent on god; it is, indeed, god's body. Rāmānuja further says that the world is related to god as modes or attributes are related to substance. Incidentally it may be noted that, according to Rāmānuja, god exists in five different modes—as Para or the entire supreme spirit, as the four *vyūhas*, as an *avatāra* like Rāma or Kṛṣṇa, as the *antaryāmin*, and as a duly consecrated image.

Madhva may be said to be teaching a sort of an almost undiluted monotheism. He unequivocally recognizes the dualism between god and the creation, both of which are real, though he does not fail to add that god alone is absolute and independent. Madhva emphasizes the fivefold difference, namely, between god and soul, between god and matter, between soul and matter, between one soul and another, and between one atom of matter and another. Indeed, he is so uncompromising in this respect that he is not unoften seen to be twisting the patently pantheistic texts to yield monotheistic-dualistic sense. As for the theism of Vallabha and Caitanya it may be pointed out that emotional, passionate—almost erotic—love for a personal god is its most outstanding feature.

Various views have been put forth regarding the nature of god and the ultimate reality in modern Hindu thought. The Arya Samaj, for instance, seems to sponsor a kind of monotheism as against Vedāntic monism. It believes in three fundamental realities, namely, god, soul, and the universe. On the other hand, Śrī Aurobindo speaks of integral advaitism—of one Brahman with positive and negative aspects. But the general trend in Neo-Hinduism may be said to be towards some kind of reconciliation between the absolute and the god. Swami Vivekananda regards god as the dynamic aspect of the highest reality. Tagore thinks of the reality as being both impersonal and personal, as changeless and evolving, as being and becoming. And to Radhakrishnan, the god is the absolute from the cosmic point of view and the absolute represents the precosmic nature of god.

It may be specially pointed out here that, in whatever forms theism developed in classical Hinduism and Neo-Hinduism, it always had a pantheistic tinge. Hindu temperament and Hindu logic must be said to be particularly conducive to a pantheistic religion. Indeed, India, as a whole, has come to be recognised as the classic land of pantheism, and the various Indian religions are regarded as representing but different stages of pantheism. There is, however, often perceptible a tendency to suggest that even pantheism is not the ultimate truth. Actually, Hindu thought is not inclined to make any sharp distinction between philosophical monism and religious pantheism. It is, therefore, not infrequently that this monism-pantheism tends to be represented either as acosmism or as polite atheism.

The two main questions relating to god and the world-process are: (i) How did god create the world? and (ii) why did god create the world? Various views have been expressed in connection with the first question. To begin with, there are some schools of Hindu thought which do not at all regard the world as the handiwork of god. One extreme view is that the phenomenal world is basically an illusion, a false presentment of god or the ultimate reality, an imagined transformation of the supreme being. The usual analogy in this respect is that of the rope which, under certain circumstances, appears as serpent. It is pointed out that so long as the world appears it is in the *brahman* which is the only reality. This does not, however, affect the transcendent character of the ultimate reality, *brahman*, in the same way as the "ropeness" of the rope is in no way affected by the illusory character of the serpent. From the ultimate point of view, there does not exist any god as such apart from the impersonal, absolute *brahman*. However, in view of the essential immutability of *brahman*, the existence of god may be temporarily posited as a kind of connecting link between the immutable *brahman* and the temporary illusion of the world. For, as long as the illusion of the world is not recognized as an illusion, it does possess what may be called relative reality. So, god, according to this view, stands on the same level of reality as the world and the individual self.

The *Brāhmaṇas* and the early *Upaniṣads* often mention a cosmological theory according to which creation amounts to some kind of emenation or rather discharge (*sṛṣṭi*) which is not dependent either on the will or the activity of a divine person. In other words, creation is there represented as a purely materialistic process. Another cosmological theory, which is atheistic and materialistic, presupposes the timeless co-existence of two essentially contradictory and mutually independent entities, namely, Prakṛti or the undifferentiated matter, which, however, possesses the potentiality of evolving, and Puruṣa or the multiplicity of souls, which is capable of seeing but incapable of acting. These two come into a relation with each other—one cannot say how—and the process of the evolution of the cosmological and psychological world is thereby started. The Vaiśeṣika cosmology, which involves a specific kind of conglomeration of eternally existing atoms, is, like the original Sāṁkhya Prakṛti-Puruṣa cosmology, also atheistic.

Side by side with such atheistic-materialistic theories of creation, there have developed in Indian thought, even from very early times, different kinds of personalistic-theistic theories of creation. The descriptions of Vedic gods as having been responsible for the creation and sustenance of the universe have to be understood rather as poetical exercises intended to emphasize the power and greatness of those gods than as any deliberate cosmological speculations. But a reference must be made in this connection to the view suggested in the *Puruṣasūkta* (*ṚV* X.90) that the universe is the result of the ritual self-immolation of a hermaphrodite man-god. Some Upaniṣadic accounts, however, represent cosmology with a more specific personalistic bias. For instance, the *Praśna-Upaniṣad* (I.3-13) tells us that, at the beginning of creation, Prajāpati the creator, having become desirous of creation, practised penance, and, after having practised penance, produced the pristine couple, *rayi* and *prāṇa*, who eventually created all existence. Elsewhere (*Taittirīya-Upaniṣad* II.6), Prajāpati is said to have become tired of his solitude and, by way of a relief from that solitude, to have emitted whatever existed. The ideas underlying these two theories seem to have merged together to give rise to a third theory. Ātman, who alone existed in the beginning of things in the form of man, with a view to getting rid of his loneliness, divided himself into two halves —one male and another female—and then procreated the various species in the organic world (*Bṛhadāraṇyaka-Upaniṣad* I.4.1-4). These and similar other theories are no doubt more or less personalistic (in contrast to the purely impersonalistic theories referred to above), but they can by no means be characterized as theistic in the strictest sense of the term.

A mention has already been made of the inclusion of god in some cosmological theories as a demiurge or a secondary creator. It may be added that the demiurge is sometimes represented also as the power (*māyā*, *śakti*) or the manifestation (*vyūha*) of the ultimate reality which alone must be regarded as the absolute substratum and source of the universe. In this context must be mentioned also the imagery of the golden embryo, in which the first personal creative being is represented as having himself proceeded from a material substratum. In the mythical form, this being is called Hiraṇyagarbha or Nārāyaṇa (*ṚV* X.121; also *Ch.-Up.* III.19.1-3; *Nṛsiṁhatāpanīya-Upaniṣad* I.1). Such cosmological ideologies, however, are basically pantheistic and seem to have later developed in the direction of a pale and shallow theism which Hinduism is said to have often "confessed with lips but which has never won the homage of its heart." In a more distinctly theistic theory, the creation is represented as a process of manifestation or evolution starting from god. The world-process is, indeed, regarded as a rhythmic movement consisting of alternate emissions and reabsorptions of the world by the supreme being. It is this form of cosmology which usually figures in the Purāṇic Hinduism. Another cosmological theory which is popular with the *Purāṇas* is a modification of the original Sāṁkhya doctrine. At a later stage in the development of the Sāṁkhya doctrine, god came to be superimposed on the Prakṛti-Puruṣa dualism (pluralism?) as having been responsible for bringing Prakṛti and Puruṣa into relation with each other and thereby initiating the world-process. Prakṛti and Puruṣa came to be regarded as just the two aspects of the supreme lord who, through his guiding and controlling will, gave the first impulse to Prakṛti to shake off its equilibrium. It may be added that, like this theistic Sāṁkhya doctrine, we also have a theistic Vaiśeṣika doctrine which postulates a god who is responsible for switching on the process of the conglomeration of the eternally existing atoms. Thus, by and large, the role of god in Hindu cosmological speculations may be said to have been thought of as being only secondary, and its scope to have been regarded as very much limited.

Assuming that god did create the world, one might ask as to what could have been god's motive for doing so. This motive cannot have been 'love', for, love normally implies the craving for sympathy and fellowship from an entity other than oneself and god is believed to transcend all kinds of craving. Nor can it have been the impulse to 'work', for, work normally aims at getting one's needs satisfied or one's insufficiencies recouped and god is regarded as being free from all needs and insufficiencies. Similarly, the world cannot have been created by god for his own benefit, because god is perfect; it cannot have also been created for the benefit of man, because it is characterized by innate inequality and cruelty. Again, in creating the universe, god cannot be said to have felt urged to execute any specific plan. Indeed, in connection with god's relation to the world, Hindu thinkers have hardly ever thought in terms of the design, plan, or object of the world. It is sometimes suggested that god created the world because he was moved by some reproductive impulse, by an instinctive urge to multiply himself; or that it was just a passing whim of god. But this would seem to go against the rationality of god. Another assumption is that god himself, as much as man, is subject to some universal law which constrains him to create the world. Obviously, such an assumption would negate the omnipotence of god. According to still another view, god has created the world with a view to affording man the opportunity to redeem himself of his liabilities under the moral law of Karma (though, it must be added, the law of Karma is believed to be operating independently of god and god in no way predestinates the conditions of man's life). This would, on the one hand, account for the inequality and cruelty in the world without making the creator responsible for them and would, on the other, emphasize god's solicitude for man in hastening his journey on the road to *mokṣa*.

But the theory which seems to have been found generally acceptable by various schools of thought is that the world-process is but the sport—*līlā*—of god. This *līlā*, which provides an outlet for the exuberant spirit of god, is to be thought of just as play for the sake of play. Essentially it amounts to the release of energy for the sake of release of energy. The assumption of *līlā* alone can explain why one who is perfect and self-sufficient does do anything. Actually to impute any motive to god's activity would mean denying his very god-head. *Līlā* constitutes a motive which is indeed no motive at all. The assumption of *līlā* is significant from yet another point of view. Metaphorically, the word *līlā* would very well bring out the sense of the miracle of the 'one' appearing as 'many'. It would further suggest the temporal character of the world whose reality is not to be taken with absolute seriousness. Again, the concept of *līlā*, in its sexual connotation, may be related to the concept of god and his consort Śakti being responsible for the creation of the universe. Of course, it must be conceded that the concept of *līlā* does not explain away all the difficulties in connection with the question of god's motive for the creation of the world. For instance, it fails to rationalize the inequality and cruelty in the world. It would seem as if god's sportive instinct was governed by the universal moral law of Karma. At any rate, the concept of *līlā* cannot be said to constitute any serious philosophical doctrine; it only serves as a fairly satisfactory analogy.

Unlike many other religions, Hinduism is hardly ever represented as a system of ethics. Indeed, ethics occupies a minor place in Hindu religious ideology. By and large, Hindu thought does not make any sharp distinction between spirit and matter; it thereby discards the very basis of morality. The pantheistic overtone of Hinduism must also be said to have been responsible for its amoralism. In Hindu thought, god is rarely conceived as a moral lord and governor. Hindu morality, accordingly, does not mean obedience to the will of god. Profound speculativeness is a distinctive mark of Hindu temperament, and this is reflected in the fact that Hindu religio-philosophical ideology has raised knowledge to a higher pedestal than either morality or devotional worship of god. Virtue is, no doubt, desirable, but without true knowledge it is rendered futile. For a Hindu thinker the real sin is ignorance; it is man's understanding which is involved in sin and not his will. According to the Hindu thought, salvation does not mean deliverance from sin against god; it rather means freedom from *avidyā*. The consciousness of moral guilt becomes manifest relatively seldom, and the prayer is usually intended for vision rather than for pardon. The attitude of Hinduism in respect of morality is essentially polar. On the one hand, morality as such is believed to be in no way related either to religion or to god. An immoral act, for instance, is not regarded as being necessarily irreligious. Even the Thugs could claim that their nefarious activities were a part of their religion. A saint may be morally extravagant but he is nevertheless religiously much esteemed. For, it is through his rigorous asceticism, which may not be necessarily compatible with the conventional code of moral conduct, that the saint is believed to attain a direct insight into the divine mystery. At best, morality may be looked upon as an instrument of social adjustment. At the same time, Hinduism is seen to have gone to the other extreme in that it has elevated the doctrine of Karma, which is intensely ethical, to the position of an irrefragable cosmic law.

In the course of the development of various views regarding the gods of Hinduism, some landmarks are clearly noticeable. As has been already pointed out, in the early Vedic period, people celebrated many gods—most of them anthropomorphic in character and most of them embodying the "asuistic" ideology—but no one god in the monotheistic sense. In the *Upaniṣads*, the supreme being, which was emphatically asserted to be one and without a second, was more or less completely impersonalised. The classical Hinduism, which must be said to have largely inherited the religious ideology and practice of the proto-historical Hinduism, manifested itself, in its initial stages, in the form of the two major sects, namely, Vaiṣṇavism and Śaivism. These sects were almost monotheistic in character-they represented a kind of modified monotheism. Viṣṇu and Śiva were regarded as having, as it were, transcended the hierarchy of mythological gods, who were quite numerous and were headed by Indra, the king of gods, and his regents, the *dikpālas*. Besides Vaiṣṇavism and Śaivism, there also emerged sects centering round other divinities like Śakti, Sūrya, and Gaṇeśa—each of these sects again representing a kind of modified monotheism. It must, however, be stressed that these sects, howsoevermuch they differed from one another in respect of their strength and the extent of their influence, hardly ever sought to extinguish one another. On the other hand, in course of time and in conformity with the usual trend of development in Hinduism, the five cults, respectively centering round Sūrya, Gaṇeśa, Viṣṇu, Śiva, and Śakti, instead of each of them having been regarded as absolute and independent, came to be regarded as constituting the five steps in a single religious echelon.

A brief note on the female divinities in Hinduism would be quite apropos at this stage. So far as the proto-historical Hinduism is concerned, it is overwhelmingly dominated by the three-headed horned male god-proto-Śiva. But, as pointed out elsewhere, the worship of "mothers" also seems to have constituted a significant feature of that religion. As against this, in the hieratic Vedic religion, not much importance is attached to female divinities. Aditi in the *Ṛgveda*, for instance, is hardly ever invested with the personality and character of the Mother-Goddess as such, while the character of Uṣas—as also of Pṛthivī—has been conceived by the Vedic poets as being little more than transperently naturalistic. Some of the other female divinities in the Veda are either mere colourless female counterparts or wives of male gods, or otherwise they represent the late deification of some abstract concepts. It would, indeed, seem that the distinctive religious ideology centering round the female divinities was essentially indigenous and that it forced itself into the Vedic ideology—though not to any large extent—as the inevitable result of the contact of the Vedic Aryans with the indigenous population of India. Two aspects of this ideology deserve to be specially noticed here. For one thing, these female divinities are mainly worshipped by the common folk. A mention may be made in this context of the *grāmadevatās*—the mothers—like Mariamman and Koṭṭavai of the Tamil country as also of the divinities like Śitalā and Manasā. They are regarded specifically as "negative" divinities in the sense that they are prayed to not so much that they may bestow any positive good on the worshipper as that they may forestall the evils which are likely to befall him. Nirṛti, Sinīvālī, Kuhū, and Guṅgū are presumably the Vedic reflections of some of such indigenous female divinities. It would also be seen that, in the *Atharvaveda*, spirits with feminine names were usually associated with diseases and disasters. Such "negative" female divinities are, indeed, quite numerous in popular Hinduism.

The second aspect of the religious ideology relating to the female divinities is far more significant from the theological point of view. In this context, one may speak of one goddess rather than of many female divinities. This goddess usually represents the personification of the "power" of the great god and is often regarded as his consort. The great god is, indeed, the self-sufficient, static aspect of the ultimate, but he is believed to have a consort, who is both one with and subordinate to him and who alone serves as the motive force behind the world-process. It is only through her that the supreme being becomes involved in the cosmic activity. Such goddess, for instance, is Śakti. On the one hand, she personifies the creative as well as the destructive power of the great god Śiva, while, on the other, she is the great goddess—the Mother Goddess—in her own right and has an independent religious cult developed round her. In the Pāñcarātra texts and the *Purāṇas*, Lakṣmī is sometimes represented as the *śakti* —both from the formal and the material points of view—of Nārāyaṇa. It is through her that Nārāyaṇa passes from his transcendental and undifferentiated form to a form characterised by the six qualities of *aiśvarya*. The proto-historical counterpart of Śakti is not as distinctly represented as that of Śiva, but the extent of her influence, even in the pre-Vedic times, may very well be judged from such of her reflections in the Vedic literature as Vāk (*ṚV* X.125) and Umā (*Kena-Upaniṣad* 25). Incidentally, it may be added that the two aspects of the religious ideology concerning the female divinities, which have been referred to above, are sometimes seen to mingle with each other in a loose manner.

In Hindu religious thought, the concept of Satan or Devil or Prince of Darkness as such hardly ever occurs with any prominence. The sharp duality of superhuman powers with opposite moral qualities—the duality, that is to say, of powers of light and powers of darkness—as, for instance, in the Zoroastrian ditheism, has never been the basis of Hindu religious ideology. The character of Vṛtra or Ahi of the *Ṛgveda* whom Indra vanquishes is essentially different from that of the Devil. He can by no means be said to represent evil personified in a single figure. The same thing may be said of Rāvaṇa, the adversary of

Rāma in the *Rāmāyaṇa*. Indeed, Rāvaṇa is often represented as a pious and learned Brāhmaṇa. Many demoniac antagonists of the divine powers have, no doubt, been mentioned in the *Purāṇas*. But they are often shown to possess several good features of character, and they are either quickly overpowered by the gods or actually become the worshippers of gods. Many of them have originally been great and noble persons, who, for some minor lapses, are cursed to be temporarily transformed into demons.

The doctrine of *avatāra* or descent of god on the earth marks a new and fairly well-defined phase in the development of Hinduism. God is believed to appear on this earth in various forms at various times to fulfil certain specific purposes. Of course, in this incarnations, god does not appear in his highest form, which is indeed incomprehensible to the mortal eye. He assumes a mortal form (either human or animal), but, even in that form, his transcendental power becomes unmistakably manifest. The *avatāra* is not to be understood merely as transitory manifestation of the deity; it represents a mystic but real presence of the supreme being in a mortal body. The anthropomorphism (or, in a few cases, the zoomorphism) is complete in every respect, but there becomes clearly evident a union of infinite divinity on the one hand and finite individuality on the other.

The *avatāras* must be said to be a special characteristic of Vaiṣṇavism. However, the classical theory in this respect does not seem to have been formulated in the epic period. The *Mahābhārata*, for instance, does not contain any systematic account of the *avatāras*. It is in the *Purāṇas* that the scheme of ten *avatāras* is fully developed. Indeed, the treatment of this subject in some Purāṇic passages is quite diversified and they give lists of *avatāras* other than the classical ten. The ten incarnations, in which Viṣṇu is, according to the normal classical tradition, believed to have appeared on this earth, are: Fish (*Matsya*), Tortoise (*Kūrma*), Boar (*Varāha*), Man-Lion (*Narasiṁha*), Vāmana, Paraśurāma, Rāma, Kṛṣṇa, the Buddha, and Kalki. Rāma is sometimes regarded as only a partial *avatāra*—one half of the divinity having been divided among his brothers. As against Rāma, Kṛṣṇa is celebrated as a full incarnation or *pūrṇāvatāra*. As a matter of fact, in some accounts, Balarāma (Kṛṣṇa's elder brother) is substituted for Kṛṣṇa as *avatāra*, for, the latter is believed to be god himself and not his *avatāra*. In some other *avatāra*-lists, Kṛṣṇa is mentioned after Balarāma or in the place of Balarāma or in the place of the Buddha. In the Buddha-incarnation, Viṣṇu is supposed to have been born as the "Deluder" in order to mislead the demons with false doctrine and thereby bring about their undoing. That *avatāra* may also be regarded as being intended for recognizing the personal greatness of the Buddha while, at the same time, deprecating his teachings. The tenth and last *avatāra*, namely, Kalki, is to appear at the end of the present *kali*-epoch. Riding a horse called Devadatta, Kalki will overrun the earth, put an end to all evil powers, and re-establish moral order.

The Hindu theory of *avatāras* is significant from various points of view. It was always asserted that the main purpose for which Viṣṇu appeared in his various incarnations was to establish moral order in a world which had become spiritually dissolute. As the *Bhagavadgītā* (IV. 7) says: Whenever righteousness languishes and unrighteousness thrives, then does god incarnate himself. This moral aspect of the *avatāra*-theory was emphasized in another way as well, namely, by suggesting that god, appearing in his *avatāra*, placed before man a norm which might help the latter in properly orienting his spiritual quest. God was believed to have come to man in order that man might become god by following his example. The *avatāra*-theory also facilitated the transcendent being brought into direct relation with the phenomenal world. It was suggested that from his eternal existence as an incomprehensible undivided unity god descended into the existence characterised by time and history and thereby invested with some meaning the otherwise meaningless cycles of time. The *avatāra*-theory was a grand attempt by the religionist at personalizing the impersonal reality of the philosopher, not only conceptually but also empirically. It afforded the unique experience of the One co-existing with the many, and thereby helped the consolidation of the doctrine of *bhakti*. For, the motive for the *avatāras* which was stressed as strongly and as often as the establishment of Dharma was god's desire to show grace and do good to those who were devoted to him and whom he loved. Psychologically, a single god manifesting himself in various forms must have adequately met the fancies of different kinds of people. The *avatāra*-theory also served, from time to time, as an assurance, which was perhaps psychologically much needed, that god did not remain merely an indifferent and uninterested spectator of the world-process but that he duly recognized his role of responsible involvement in it. From the point of view of the history of Hinduism the *avatāra*-theory may be regarded as a major factor in the religious synthesis brought about by that religion. Originally, the different divinities like Rāma, Kṛṣṇa, Paraśurāma, etc., seem to have been the gods of different religious cults. When, in the course of the religious history of India, these cults federated themselves to form what came to be known as Hinduism, some kind of unity of godhead was sought to be achieved by those gods being represented as the incarnations of one single god Viṣṇu. On the other hand, this also helped to elevate the status of the objects of worship of certain primitive cults. Incidentally, a reference may be here made to the suggestion made by some modern writers that the sequence of the *avatāras* reflects the various stages in the evolution of man himself.

One of the striking features of popular Hinduism, as against Vedism which may, in a sense, be said to have culminated in Upaniṣadic spiritualism, is that it seeks to substitute a religion as contemplation by a religion as practice. It is in this context that a study of the Hindu concept of worship becomes relevant. The Vedic Aryan religious practice was mainly of the nature of *homa*, that is, of the offering of oblations to gods, who were not directly present before the sacrificer in the form of idols or images, on the sacred fires in the accompaniment of Vedic *mantras*. With the advent of historical Hinduism, Vedic *homa* or ritual came to be more or less superseded by a form of worship popularly known as *pūjā*. The centre of the entire procedure of *pūjā* was the idol or the image or some other concrete symbol of the divinity, which was ceremonially bathed and anointed with sandalwood-paste or coloured powder and to which offerings of flowers, food, milk, sweets, etc., were made in the accompaniment of the recital of *mantras* and prayers, the ringing of bells, and the burning of lights and incense. Actually, the pre-Vedic non-Aryan religion—that is to say, proto-historical Hinduism—also seems to have been characterised by some kind of religious practice akin to *pūjā*. Naturally enough, during the Vedic interlude, *homa* or Vedic ritual came to be generally recognised as the representative religious practice. But in classical Hinduism, *pūjā* was again revived in a highly developed and complex form. A third kind of religious practice which may be referred to here consisted of Tantric ritual and worship, many features of which were, in course of time, incorporated in the hieratic Hindu ritual and worship.

A distinctive characteristic of Hindu *pūjā* is that, in essence, it is a personal activity rather than a congregational or communal performance. For a Hindu, *pūjā* is an individual experience; it is an act of private devotion. Temple-worship is, of course, not uncommon, but it cannot be said to be an essential constituent of Hindu religious practice. The piety of a Hindu is by no means dependent on his visiting a temple and offering worship there. Indeed, many devout Hindus prefer home-worship to temple-worship. It may, however, be noted that the basic pattern of temple-worship is more or less the same as the one indicated above. Naturally enough, in temple-worship, the devotees have usually to be content with being mere spectators of rather than active participants in the procedure of worship. Even in the case of home-worship it is only one member of the family who offers worship for the whole family. Thus, in the ultimate analysis, the individual's part in worship is limited mainly to his own contemplation of and prayer to the divinity. In this connection a special mention must be made of *japa* or the repeated murmuring of the name of god which is believed to possess deep religio-magical significance. As for prayer, the religious man seeks to establish, by means of it, a living communion with god conceived as personal and present in experience. It implies on the one hand an unflinching faith in god's grace and on the other one's complete surrender to his mercy.

Such individual worship is perhaps of greater spiritual value; but there is no doubt that the absence of any obligatory worship of a congregational type has, to a certain extent, adversely affected the religio-social cohesion and integration among the Hindus. Hinduism certainly provides for such religious affairs of a communal nature as the recital and exposition of epic and Purāṇic texts and works of religio-philosophical import, seasonal festivals, and pilgrimages to sacred places. But these can by no means be said to constitute the essentials of religious practice. Nor are they, in any sense, obligatory.

Though, as has been pointed out above, the basic pattern of Hindu worship is more or less fixed, there are often made in it numerous and minute variations in accordance with the different cults, different divinities, and different occasions. Indeed, one often wonders whether the diversity of Hindu worship does not actually exceed the diversity of Hindu doctrine. A reference to the ritual and worship sponsored by the Tantra schools would be quite relevant in this context. The Tantric ritual and worship are more rigorously organized than the normal Hindu ritual and worship. The Tantras do not make any distinction on the basis of caste and sex in the matter of religious practice. Their ritual is essentially of an esoteric character and its knowledge is usually transmitted and preserved through a strict teacher-pupil tradition. It comprises of various sexual, orgiastic, and bloody rites. One of the basic assumptions of the Tantras relates to the almost organic correspondence between man and the universe; and, on the strength of this assumption, the practitioner of Tantric rites seeks to control the universe through the control of his own body. The Tantras also emphasise the religio-magical potence of such items of worship as *mantra*, *yantra*, *bīja*, etc. Indeed, the Tantras believe in magically compelling the divine powers rather than religiously propitiating them.

It has been stated elsewhere that, from the strict philosophical point of view, god is only relatively real; that is to say, he is real only on the phenomenal plane. Worship of god cannot, accordingly, be regarded as possessing any ultimate spiritual value. The *Bṛhadāraṇyaka-Upaniṣad* (I. 4.10), for instance, says: "Whoever worships another divinity (than his self) thinking that he (= god) is one and he himself another, he knows not." Actually the same Upaniṣadic passage further suggests that gods do not like that men should know the ultimate truth of transcendental unity, for, then they would know gods to hold but a subordinate position and so cease offering worship to them. Notwithstanding this predominating philosophical attitude which tends to look upon all rules, rites, and creeds as being part of a lower and temporal order of things, a Hindu is normally not half-hearted in respect of his worldly obligations. His devotion to god and his zeal and earnestness in the matter of worship cannot be called in question. The worship of god reflects his genuine response to the supreme reality as conceived on the empirical plane—a response of fear, hope, and trust. Hindu worship is also regarded as an efficacious means of moral discipline and spiritual fortification which human life so badly needs. Indeed, Hindu worship has a very wide connotation. It does not necessarily imply some deliberate act of devotion. As the *Bhagavadgītā* proclaims, one who performs his prescribed duties exclusively for the sake of *lokasaṁgraha* and without being selfishly attached to their fruits must be deemed to be offering the most devout and the most agreeable worship to god. Whatever one does in the spirit of true *anāsakti-yoga* is in essence an act of worship.

The doctrine of grace must, indeed, be regarded as an essential constituent of theistic ideology. Some intimation of this doctrine may be discovered in such Ṛgvedic references as that Varuṇa chose Vasiṣṭha for his exclusive companionship and, through his majesty, made him a true seer (VII. 88.4); but it makes its appearance in a fairly developed form, for the first time, only in the later religiously oriented *Upaniṣads*. Already in the *Kaṭha-Upaniṣad* (I. 2.23) we are told that this supreme self 'cannot be attained by instruction, nor by intellectual power, nor even through much hearing. He is to be attained only by the one whom he chooses.' The *Muṇḍaka-Upaniṣad* (III. 2.3) repeats the same view. But the *Śvetāśvatara-Upaniṣad* is perhaps more explicit on this point. At one place (I.6), for instance, it says that the self blessed by the Lord, the Mover (*preritā*), gains life eternal, while, at another (III.20), it actually speaks of *dhātuḥ prasāda* or the grace of the creator.

The doctrine of grace forms an integral part of the teaching of the *Bhagavadgītā*. One of the principal attributes of god in the *Bhagavadgītā* is love for his devotee. Indeed, god is said to be the friend of all beings (V. 29) and to be actively helping man in freeing himself from the *saṁsāra*. Several times in the poem is Lord Kṛṣṇa seen to have assured Arjuna that 'for whomsoever attains to him there does not remain any rebirth' (VII. 16). Mainly through god's grace does one win the eternal immutable realm. So, almost by way of his final precept, Kṛṣṇa urges Arjuna to relinquish all other religious duties and betake himself only to him. He alone shall deliver him from all sins whatsoever (XVIII. 66).

In the epics, and more particularly in the *Purāṇas*, divine grace is a frequently occurring religious motif. God is said to have assumed finite forms for the sake of love for his worshippers and in order to free them from the shackles of this worldly existence. In the Pāñcarātra scriptures, this function of freeing the devotee from *saṁsāra* is ascribed to the *sudarśana* portion of Lakṣmī, the transcendent character of the supreme lord himself being thereby scrupulously maintained. The *sudarśana* is represented as operating like god's grace and as gradually leading the self on the way to *mokṣa* or deliverance. Incidentally, however, it may be added that just as god is endowed with the attribute of *anugraha* or grace he is also endowed with the attribute of *nigraha* or the power of obstruction by means of which he keeps man bound down to *saṁsāra*. In the course of the further development of the Vaiṣṇava theism, the doctrine of grace became so basic a theme of its teaching that it came to be unequivocally claimed, as, for instance, in the *Nārāyaṇīya* (349. 75.76), that one could attain religious enlightenment not through penance or knowledge or the like but only as the result of the compassion of Nārāyaṇa. The *Bhāgavata-Purāṇa* glorifies the grace of god as the very crown and consummation of religion. The Āḷvars sing of god as being condescendingly merciful even to the lowliest among men and bestowing on him his grace.

Rāmānuja, who seeks to give a philosophical foundation to the theistic ideology, has to encounter the problem of the coordination of the two concepts, namely, the grace of god and the law of Karma. With reference to the statement in the *Kauṣītaki-Upaniṣad* (III. 8) that 'this one (that is, the supreme being), truly, causes him, whom he wishes to lead up from these worlds, to perform good actions; this one, indeed, also causes him, whom he wishes to lead downward, to perform bad action,' he seems to suggest that god's grace does not operate arbitrarily but that it does so in accordance with the law of Karma. This does not, however, imply that the law of Karma is something external to or independent of god. It is itself the expression of god's mode of action. God is the source and substratum of both grace and law of Karma. There is, therefore, no question of one of these two being subservient to the other. God often employs the law of Karma as a kind of testing exercise for one to whom grace is to be ultimately shown. As hinted in the *Bhagavadgītā* (VI. 41-43), the *saṁsāra*, which is the inevitable consequence of the law of Karma, is intended to afford to man an opportunity to qualify himself for god's grace, for *mokṣa*. In other words, man is subjected to the law of Karma because of god's desire to show him grace and not in spite of it. A reference may be made, in this very context, to the two major schools of the Vaiṣṇava theology propounded by Rāmānuja. The southern school or the Tengalais insisted that *prapatti* or complete surrender by the self to god was the only way for obtaining god's grace. This school is credited with having explained the devotee's relationship with god in this connection by the *mārjāranyāya* or the cat-analogy. Just as the kitten remained passive and self-surrendering while its mother carried it about in her mouth, in the same way the devotee was required to do nothing for his salvation except completely giving himself up to the mercy of god. The northern school or the Vaḍgalais, on the other hand, took recourse to the *markaṭanyāya* or the monkey-analogy in order to explain the relationship between the worshipper and god. The young one of a monkey had to exert itself to some extent to stay clinging to its mother while being carried about. Likewise the devotee could not depend on mere passive submission to god for his emancipation, but was required to resort also to other ways of salvation prescribed by the scriptures.

Incidentally, it may be added that, even in the Śaiva theism, the greatest attribute of Śiva is believed to be love, and the soul (*paśu*) is said to be dependent for its liberation from the threefold fetter (*pāśa*) of *māyā*, *karman*, and *āṇava* (the atomic impurity or human ignorance) entirely on the grace of Śiva.

While speaking of liberation (*mokṣa*), one must clearly realise the distinction between its theistic concept and its metaphysical concept. From the strictly advaitic point of view, *mokṣa* does not imply any new state of being to be attained by the soul. Indeed, it denotes its original state of being—the state of what, in a catching phrase, is called the 'pre-biographical unity'—which it temporarily forfeits as the result of ignorance but which it is entitled to regain through true knowledge. In this state, the soul transcends time, space, and causality which characterise the phenomenal world. It fuses into the absolute and is thus freed from any further possibility of rebirth. *Mokṣa*, in this sense, has hardly anything to do with god. But religious theism does not countenance the illusion of the individual self implied by advaitic absolutism. *Mokṣa*, according to theism, represents a specific kind of relationship between god and the soul. The world-process, as has been already pointed out, is an unending cycle of emanations and reabsorptions, and the aim of religion is some kind of union or close association of the soul with god beyond that cycle. It is also suggested that, through deep contemplation of god, one actually becomes either god or like god. But, generally, in Hindu theism, *mokṣa* is not understood either as union with or fusion into or identification with god. It rather means isolation—the isolation of the self from all other things such as the world and the other selves. It is, indeed, the isolation of the soul in its essence. This kind of liberation is believed to be more desirable than either the annihilation of the soul or its absorption into the vaster spirituality of Brahman. The soul is eternal; it has its true being beyond time and space. It is just in this sense that the soul is said to participate in divine nature. And, thus participating in divine nature, it 'persists' even in the state of liberation. Freed from evil of all kind and having attained all desires through the grace of god, the soul becomes isolated from the associations of the manifested world, and yet continues to experience the unending and ever-increasing love of god.

All Hindu mysticism aims at the transcendence of personality by the soul, either through the realisation of complete unity with the universal spirituality or through the total isolation of the eternal in the soul from the temporal in it. There has, however, been often mentioned still another type of mysticism, namely, loving communion with god even during the state of embodied existence. It is in view of this that one speaks of 'impersonal' mysticism and 'personal' mysticism. But, in the ultimate analysis, the experience of mysticism is essentially uniform, though that experience is expressed in different ways, such as, through silence or negation or contradiction or superlation. Hindu mysticism transcends the tyranny of words usually encouraged by philosophical dogmas or religious doctrines. It is, indeed, from its mysticism that Hinduism has derived its unique attitude of tolerance.

In the history of Hinduism, man's attitude towards god has undergone many changes. However, three principal landmarks may be specially noted in this connection. In the early Vedic period, man sought to exert on gods a kind of magically compulsive influence by means of his word (*brahman* or *mantra*) and action (*yajña* or ritual). In the Upaniṣadic period, knowledge of god—or, to be more precise, of the supreme being—came to be regarded as the only source of salvation and eternal bliss—though, incidentally, even then, the magic potence of knowledge was duly emphasised. To know was to attain—indeed, to know was to become. Desire for knowledge, respect for knowledge, and trust in the practical religio-philosophical efficacy of knowledge—these continued to be the distinctive features of Hinduism throughout its history. This knowledge-partial attitude of the Hindu was often carried to such an extreme that he could logically posit and substantiate a religion without a god and persist in regarding ignorance as a more grievous sin than even the most serious moral lapse. It is, indeed, on account of this that Hinduism is frequently —though not always justifiably—characterised as 'wisdom' rather than 'spirituality'.

With popular Hinduism, *bhakti* or passionate devotion to god became the watchword of religion. *Bhakti* necessarily presupposes the belief in a personal god, who is often a divinity of a popular cult elevated to the status of the supreme being. Before this personal god, man experiences the feeling of moral inferiority, spiritual imperfection, helplessness, and humility. He, however, has unquestioned faith in the grace of god, and, therefore, surrenders before him in a completely self-oblivious manner, hoping thereby to achieve a direct mystic communion with him, which, for a *bhakta*, constitutes the ultimate spiritual goal. Some traces of this emotional theism may be discovered in a few hymns of the *Ṛgveda*, particularly those addressed by Vasiṣṭha to Varuṇa, but it is in the *Śvetāśvatara-Upaniṣad* that it seems to have been first formulated into a religious doctrine. The rise of various Hindu sects gave a fillip to the growth of *bhakti*; and the Purāṇic tradition that *bhakti* was born in the Dravidian country gets historical confirmation from the fact that the two principal and more or less parallel currents of early medieval theism, namely Vaiṣṇavism and Śaivism, had their main spring in southern India.

The religion of *bhakti* generally substituted theology for mythology, but its most outstanding achievement was that it sought to establish the equality of all persons, irrespective of caste, creed, and sex, in the sight of god. Of course, both mythology and social distinctions proved too tenacious to be so easily stifled. The role of *bhakti* in the history of Hinduism may be said to have been self-contradictory. On the one hand, the doctrine of *bhakti* served as a unifying force among the Hindu masses who were rallied together, under the banner of religious equality and brotherhood, to counteract the exclusivism of Vedism-Brahmanism, while, on the other hand, the various sects which sponsored that doctrine, each in its own way, tended, in course of time, to consolidate themselves into exclusive groups and thereby encourage the fissiparous trends in the Hindu society.

And now to revert to the question which was posed at the beginning of this section, namely, whether belief in god could be regarded as constituting a primary principle of Hinduism. Hindu thinkers, it will have been seen, generally did not start with the certainty of god. They seem to have accepted god only as a workable hypothesis. The historical process of the phenomenal world and man were not essentially dependent on god; on the contrary, gods themselves were believed to be subject to some universal law like the law of Karma. The concept of god can be thus said to be by no means central to Hinduism. The Hindu thinker showed greater ardour for the experience which was most immediate to him, namely, the self.

IV. Conception of Man

The Hindu thinker, as suggested above, set out on his spiritual quest with the examination of the question relating to his own self rather than with that of the question relating to god. This did not, however, result in his ideology becoming anthropocentric. He hardly ever acquiesced in the dictum that man was the measure of all things. On the contrary, the "asuistic" tendencies, which, incidentally, had become evident in Vedic mythology, ritualism, and spiritualism, tended to give the speculative wisdom of the Hindus a distinctly cosmic orientation. One of the major *Upaniṣads* very graphically says that the vital essence in man is the same as that in ant or gnat or elephant or the three worlds or the whole universe. This essential qualitative identity among the various aspects of existence precluded any possibility of "man" being fundamentally differentiated from "things". It was recognised that mutual coordination—and not subordination of one to another—was the principle which governed the relationship among the various entities. This cosmic-asuistic outlook is seen to have deeply influenced the Hindu concept of man in its three aspects, namely, of man in relation to himself, of man in relation to god, and of man in relation to his fellow-beings and the external world in general.

One of the basic tenets of Hinduism is that the "real" man is different from the man who moves about, acts, and has various experiences —who, in short, "lives"—in this phenomenal world. In other words, the essential or real self of man (*ātman*) is different from his empirical self (*jīva*). It is often emphasised that the true philosophical knowledge consists in not confusing the one with the other. This is, indeed, the moral of a famous parable in the *Chāndogya-Upaniṣad* (VIII. 7-12). The gods and demons, we are told, once became anxious to learn the nature of the essential self, for, it was made known that whosoever comprehended that self, 'which is free from sin, free from old age, free from death and grief, and free from hunger and thirst, and which desires nothing and imagines nothing', would win all the worlds. So gods deputed Indra and the demons Virocana to acquire its knowledge from Prajāpati. They both lived with Prajāpati as his pupils for a period of thirty-two years. On the termination of this period, Prajāpati told Indra and Virocana that the essential self was in no way different from 'the image that we see in our eye'—that is to say, the essential self was identical with the embodied self in the condition of wakefulness when it was conscious of external objects and enjoyed gross things. Complacent in the belief that he had understood the true nature of the essential self, Virocana hurried back to the demons and proclaimed that he had succeeded in his mission. Indra, on the other hand, was not satisfied with this teaching of Prajāpati, namely, that the essential self was identical with the bodily consciousness—the teaching which the *Upaniṣad* slyly characterises as the "gospel of the demons" because the representative of the demons had found it quite adequate. Indra thought to himself that, if this body were really identical with the essential self, the characteristics of that self which had been generally made known, namely, that it was free from fear, sin, old age, death, etc., would be invalidated. For, the body was actually subject to fear, old age, etc. He, therefore, again went back to

Prajāpati in his search for the essential self. Instead of communicating forthwith the final truth in the matter, Prajāpati led Indra one step further each time. He told Indra, on the conclusion of the second term of his studentship, that the essential self was identical with the self in the condition of dream, when that self was not affected by the limitations and characteristics of the body, and when, because only the mind was active, it was conscious only of internal objects and enjoyed subtle things. But even this teaching, though it represented some advance over the first, could not satisfy Indra. In the dream-condition, the self might not suffer from the limitations and characteristics of the body but it still remained subjected to the limitations and characteristics of the mind. It did not become free from fear, pain, etc.

Even the next stage in Prajāpati's teaching, namely, that the essential self was identical with the self in the condition of deep-sleep, when neither the body nor the mind affected the self and when it 'desired no desire and dreamt no dream', could carry conviction to Indra. In the deep-sleep condition, thought Indra, one might be free from fear and pain but one was actually conscious of nothing, neither of oneself nor of external objects. That state of rest and repose was,indeed, comparable with the rest and repose of a 'log of wood'. Moreover, this condition of deep-sleep was only transient. So Indra lived another term of studentship under Prajāpati. On the completion of that term, Prajāpati imparted to Indra the knowledge of the ultimate truth about the self. The essential self was not to be regarded as being identical either with the bodily consciousness or with the dream-consciousness. It transcended even the deep-sleep condition though some intimations of its nature were available in that condition. The essential self was really of the nature of pure and abiding self-consciousness (*cit*) and ever remained unaffected by all bodily and mental conditions. It was free from all the limitations, mutations, and experiences to which the body and the mind were subjected. It was eternal and immutable (*sat*). The essential self was neither the subject nor the object nor the act—it was neither the knower nor the known nor the knowing. In the expression "I know", for instance, the essential self was not denoted by the word "I" nor was it represented by the act of knowing. At the same time, however, the "I" and the "knowing" were impossible without the existence and the direct awareness of the essential self.

Thus the essential self does exist—it is *sat*—but not as any particular individual conditioned by the limitations of body, mind, intellect, and ego, and is, therefore, not subject to any mutations. It is also conscious

—*cit*—but not of any particular object, external or internal; nor is it to be identified with the consciousness in any particular state. One cannot realise the true nature of the essential self in any of the three states, namely, wakefulness, dream, and deep-sleep. It is in a state, which transcends these three—the state in which body and senses, mind, intellect, and ego cease to function, 'when there is no knowledge of internal objects nor of external ones nor of the two together, when the self is not a mass of intelligence or knowledge, transcending as it does both consciousness and unconsciousness, when it is invisible, uncommunicable, incomprehensible, and indefinable'—that the nature of the essential self as pure self-consciousness becomes realisable.

Besides being of the nature of pure *sat* and pure *cit*, the essential self is something more. There is another interesting attempt in the *Upaniṣads* to analyse the human personality and thereby attain to its very core or essence. In this attempt, the sage of the *Taittirīya-Upaniṣad* proceeds from the grosser and more external forms of the human personality to its subtler and more internal forms—it being clearly implied that the subtler and more internal the form the more real and essential it is. First of all there is the physical body, which is said to be made of food or matter (*anna*). This can obviously not be the ultimate or real essence of the human personality. For, within this physical form, there is 'another form which is made up of vital air (*prāṇa*)'. More internal—and, therefore, subtler and more real—than the form made of vital air is another form made of mind (*manas*). More internal still than the mental form is another form made of intelligence or consciousness (*vijñāna*); and within this form of intelligence or consciousness is the most internal and central of all the forms, namely, the form of bliss (*ānanda*). This last is the subtlest and, therefore, the most real and essential of all the other forms. What is intended to be suggested here is that the essential self in man transcends the physical, vital, mental, and intellectual "forms" of the human personality, and is to be identified with its innermost and subtlest form, namely, the beatific form. Thus the ultimate nature of the real or essential self is pure existence (*sat*), pure self-consciousness (*cit*), and pure bliss (*ānanda*).

Side by side with the analysis of man, the Upaniṣadic thinkers also attempted an analysis of the external world and thereby came to the conclusion that, at the basis of this multifarious and gross phenomenal world, which was of a changing and fleeting nature and which was, in the ultimate analysis, a mere bundle of names (*nāma*) and forms (*rūpa*), there lay but one eternal, immutable, sentient reality. Thus this ultimate cosmic reality, or the cosmic self, which, it was frequently reiterated, was one and without a second, was also *sat* and *cit*. It, therefore, naturally followed that the essential self in man (*ātman*) and the ultimate cosmic reality (*brahman*) were one and the same. This grand philosophical doctrine emphasised the fact that neither the empirical self nor the tangible phenomenal world with which the empirical self seemed to come into contact possessed any reality from the ultimate point of view.

The foregoing statement gives the most representative view in Hinduism about the nature of man's essential self. But it is by no means the only view. There are, for instance, some thinkers who regard the self as being finite and atomic. There are others who believe that man's essential self is identical with the cosmic self or the supreme being only in essence but not in form. There are still others who assert that the essential self is distinct from the supreme being both in form and essence. It is not necessary to elaborate all these different views at any length. It may only be pointed out that, in spite of such differences in details, there is general agreement that man's real self is distinct from the body-mind-complex.

According to the Hindu view, as the result of the operation of original ignorance or nescience (*avidyā*), the ultimate identity between the essential self and the supreme reality becomes, as it were, shrouded,—the essential self thereby falls off from its pedestal of serene aloofness and self-luminiscence and gets involved in the phenomenal world which itself is a fiction created by the self under the influence of *avidyā*. Incidentally, it is claimed that the question as to how and why the original nescience becomes operative is, by its very nature, logically inadmissible. For, logical thinking—or, for the matter of that, any thinking—can, strictly speaking, relate only to the conditions subsequent to the operation of *avidyā*. So, under the influence of *avidyā*, the assumption of the operation of which is philosophically necessary, the essential self becomes conditioned by the limitations of individuality. Some aspects of the nature of the individual or the empirical self will have already become evident from the foregoing discussion regarding the nature of the essential self. The most distinctive characteristic of an individual is the assumption by him of a body. In Hindu thought, the term "body" (*deha* or *śarīra*) is understood in a very comprehensive sense and is made to denote various kinds of limitations which are produced by *avidyā*. The empirical self or the individual (*jīva*) is, accordingly, also called the embodied self (*śārīra ātman*).

The body to which the essential self is supposed to be attached as the result of the operation of *avidyā* is, according to the most representative Hindu view, of three kinds. There is first of all the gross physical body (*sthūla śarīra*), which is produced out of the five elements, namely, earth, water, light, wind, and ether, and which serves as the ground for all the experiences relating to the external world. At the death of an individual only his physical body is believed to perish. It actually dissolves into the five elements out of which it is produced.

The second body is known as the subtle body, because it is constituted of elements for subtler than the five elements. The constituents of the subtle body are seventeen in number—five vital breaths, five organs of action, five organs of knowledge, mind, and intellect. This body serves as the basis of the dream-consciousness. But the more important role of the subtle body is the one which it plays in connection with the transmigration of the self from one physical body to another. It has been already pointed out that, at the death of an individual, only his physical body perishes. Death, however, does not mark the end of individuality. This latter comes about only with the realisation by the self of its essential identity with the ultimate reality, in other words, with *mokṣa*. Till then the journey of the self (or its individuality) continues through one body or another. What is called death is not the terminus; it is only a junction where the self changes the body and also perhaps the route of its journey. It is believed that the medium by means of which the self passes from one physical body into another is the subtle body. Such an assumption is, indeed, philosophically necessary. For, firstly, at death, the self cannot be assumed to be leaving both the physical and the subtle bodies simultaneously; that would amount to the termination of individuality, that is to say, to *mokṣa*. Secondly, it is the subtle body, which, in a sense, determines the type of the physical body to be taken by the self for the next lap of its journey. According to the doctrine of Karma, which will be dealt with in the sequel, the body to be assumed by the individual in each of his rebirths is conditioned by the moral consequences of the deeds done by him in the preceding life. It is believed that the subtle body serves as a repository of these moral consequences —direct (*phala*) as well as indirect (*saṁskāras*)—until they have their effect in respect of the individual's rebirth. The direct moral consequences of the past deeds determine the actual kind of physical body to be taken at rebirth as well as the other environments relating to the rebirth, while the indirect moral consequences produce in the individual certain innate tendencies which prompt him to act in a particular way in his new life. Thus the subtle body constitutes one of the basic factors in the operation of the inexorable law of Karma.

The third body, which the empirical self is believed to assume, is known as the causal (*kāraṇa*) body. The *kāraṇa śarīra* becomes manifest in that state of the existence of the individual in which both the physical and the subtle bodies cease to function temporarily, as, for instance, in the condition of deep-sleep. The gross and the subtle bodies seem to arise from this body—that is why it is called causal body. They also seem to dissolve into it, wherefore it is called the *laya-sthāna*.

The idea of rebirth is common to several ancient religions of the world. But the distinctive contribution of Hinduism is that it has attempted to invest that idea with a metaphysical and ethical rationalisation. Four main principles may be said to be involved in the Hindu theory of rebirth or transmigration (*saṁsāra*), namely, the permanence of the essential self, the operation of *avidyā*, the possibility of *mokṣa*, and the doctrine of Karma. Perhaps the most fundamental of these principles is the Hindu concept of the permanence of the essential self. It is quite obvious that, without the assumption of a permanent entity, any talk of rebirth or transmigration would become meaningless. The second principle, namely, the operation of *avidyā*, is also quite basic. For, *avidyā*, by causing the essential self to assume an individuality, may be said to start the very process of transmigration. Further, according to the Hindu view, the *saṁsāra* is not an idle or unmotivated journey; nor is it a wild-goose chase. It has been invested with a definite meaning and purpose. This is where the third principle, namely, the possibility of *mokṣa*, becomes relevant. In a sense, *mokṣa* represents the answer to the eternal question: Whither man?

In connection with *mokṣa*, it must be made clear that, though, in common parlance, one speaks of "attaining" *mokṣa*, the state of *mokṣa* does not denote anything different from the state in which one realises the essential nature of his self. *Mokṣa*, it is claimed, is not *prāpya* (to be reached) nor *utpādya* (to be created) nor *vikārya* (to be got as the result of some modification or change) nor finally *saṁskārya* (to be got as the result of some operation for refinement or perfection). It is native and not derivative. *Mokṣa* does not imply that the self acquires something which does not belong to it, or, to be more precise, something which it is not. It is ever there though one becomes temporarily blind to it under the influence of *avidyā*. This being so, *mokṣa* is to be regarded as the birth-right of every individual. Hindu thinkers speak of three kinds of "liberation" from individuality (*mokṣa* or *mukti*)—liberation attained forthwith at death (*sadyo-mukti*), liberation by stages (*krama-mukti*), and liberation while living (*jīvan-mukti*).

As for the fourth principle involved in the theory of transmigration, it may be pointed out that, if the operation of *avidyā* is the cause of the "birth" of an individual, the operation of the law of Karma is the cause of his "rebirths". It may be further pointed out that, out of the four principles involved in the theory of transmigration, the first two are metaphysical, the third is significant both from the metaphysical and ethical points of view, and the last, namely, the doctrine of Karma, is primarily ethical. The doctrine of Karma is one of the most distinctive features of Hinduism. It has vitally influenced most of the important Hindu—nay, Indian—beliefs and practices. The faiths of India differ widely, being at some points, the very poles asunder. But all of them—orthodox as well as heterodox (with the exception of the materialists like Cārvāka)—accept this doctrine as one of their cardinal tenets.

The doctrine of Karma may be said to constitute the solution offered by Hinduism for the great riddle of the suffering and inequalities in this world. According to the Hindu view, the law of causation operates not only in the physical world, but it operates, in an equally invariable and inviolable manner, also in the moral world. One cannot think of any acts which fizzle out without producing results (*kṛtapraṇāśa*), nor of any results which have no antecedents in the form of some acts (*akṛtābhyupagama*). Further, morally good acts are believed necessarily to produce good results and morally bad acts to produce bad results. It is, however, often seen that all the acts of an individual do not fructify within the brief span of a single life. And, according to the inexorable law of Karma, that is to say, of the law of actions and their retribution, no actions may remain barren. It, therefore, becomes necessary to postulate another life for that individual, during which he may reap whatever had not already ripened and been reaped in his preceding life. Indeed, by a logical extension of this postulation, one has to assume the existence of a series of lives terminating only when all the acts of an individual become exhausted in one way or another. This is the theory of *saṁsāra*, which constitutes a necessary corollary to the law of Karma.

The present life of an individual is conditioned by such of the acts done by him in the preceding life as had not attained their fructification during the course of that life. The moral consequences of those acts are, so to say, conserved and have their effect in the present life. For instance, his past acts determine the kind of body which he may assume, the family, society, and position in which he may be born, and the kind of acts which he may feel prompted to do in his present life. Thus, in a sense, every creature is the creation of his own past deeds. In this way, the otherwise inexplicable suffering and inequalities among human beings are rationalized by the doctrine of Karma. Nothing in this world—physical or moral—happens as the result of mere caprice or blind chance. Every happening is to be seen as resulting from the operation of an immutable law.

The doctrine of Karma must, however, not be confused with fatalism. Nor must it be supposed that it denies man his initiative as a free agent. At the very outset it should be clearly understood that this doctrine does not imply the operation of any extraneous factors in man's life and doings. No external power, such as fate or destiny, is assumed to shape the life of man. On the contrary, the doctrine of Karma teaches that man himself is, in a sense, the architect of his own life. What he has done in the past life is entirely responsible for what he is in the present life. So viewed this doctrine represents the very antithesis of fatalism. It rejects caprice or chance and discountenances the working of an overriding providence. The causes of the nature of an individual's life and doings are to be ultimately traced back to the individual himself.

Two main objections are generally raised against this position. Even assuming that, in this *saṁsāra*, an individual's present life is conditioned by his actions in the preceding life, one may ask: What about that individual's "first" birth in the process of transmigration? There is no possibility of the assumption of any anterior actions and their retribution in respect of that birth. Therefore the law of Karma cannot be supposed to operate so far as that birth is concerned. What is it, then, that conditions the individual's life and actions at that stage? Such a question, however, is logically inadmissible. For, according to the Hindu view, the *saṁsāra* is beginningless. It is, indeed, impossible to visualise an individual without antecedents. Strictly speaking, individuality itself is a product of antecedents.

The other objection is perhaps more pertinent. One may accept that, in the beginningless series of rebirths, an individual's actions in the preceding life condition his present life. One may also accept that the individual himself—and not any extraneous factors—is accountable for what he is in the present life. But do an individual's "past" actions not become, in a sense, extraneous forces so far as his "present" life is concerned? What control does he *now* have over his past actions which are supposed to govern his present life? The past, although it is *his* past, is already an accomplished fact; and it is this that determines his present, thereby leaving him no freedom to shape it as he likes. Such an objection is met by the Hindu thinkers by postulating a twofold fructification of all actions. Firstly, every action produces its direct result (*phala*). The *phala* of one's unexhausted past deeds determines the nature of his present body and the conditions directly relating to and consequent upon his birth. In respect of these he has no choice. But his past deeds also produce what may be called their indirect result in the form of his innate tendencies (*saṁskāras*). It is these *saṁskāras*, produced in him by his past deeds, which prompt him to act one way or another. It is, however, necessary to emphasise that the *saṁskāras* only *prompt* but do not *force* him to act in a particular manner. This fact affords ample freedom for initiative and self-determination to an individual. He can, if he will, control and properly direct his *saṁskāras*. Though, therefore, an individual's birth and initial environments are predetermined, he has before him the gratifying prospect of mastering his *saṁskāras*, which, indeed, are the main springs of all his actions. The doctrine of Karma thus includes within itself also the possibility of moral progress. It does not imply fatalism, nor does it preclude the operation of free will which is the very basis of ethical conduct. Since it emphasises that, in the ultimate analysis, an individual is himself the architect of his own life, this doctrine does not countenance any such thing as cruel fate or an unjust god.

How can the inexorable law of Karma be reconciled with *mokṣa* which is generally regarded by the Hindus as their spiritual goal? Are Karma and *mokṣa* not essentially antithetical? Would even morally good actions not continue to keep an individual involved in life, howsoever ethically elevated that life might be? The *Bhagavadgītā* seeks to provide an answer to such questions by teaching that a man's actions attain their fructification in the form of *phala* and *saṁskāras* affecting him only if he performs those actions with a feeling of attachment for their results. If, however, he acts—as, indeed, he must, in obedience to the law of Karma—but, while doing so, controls and directs his *saṁskāras* in such a manner as to produce in himself an attitude of passionless detachment in respect of the fruits of his actions, he will, while doing his *svadharma*, still leave the road open for his progress towards *mokṣa*. The *anāsaktiyoga* of the *Bhagavadgītā* may be said to bridge, as it were, the gap between the doctrine of Karma and the ideal of *mokṣa*.

If the philosophical approach to the study of man in Hindu thought gives rise to the dualism between the essential self and the empirical self, the religious or theistic approach presupposes the dualism between man and god. It may, however, be pointed out that, from the ultimate point of view, the concepts of man and god do not possess absolute validity. They belong to the realm of the phenomenal world. This may account for the fact that many philosophical systems in India are essentially atheistic. They are not required to posit the existence of a personal god for being able to answer the various cosmological, psychological, metaphysical, and even ethical questions which arise in the course of their discussions. All this does not, however, mean that Hinduism has nothing to do with god. On the contrary, Hinduism, particularly popular Hinduism, is certainly god-conscious—perhaps very much so. In Hinduism, absolute monistic idealism and emotional theism abide side by side and without much conflict. Hinduism seeks to reconcile this apparent incompatibility by means of the assumption of two points of view in spiritual-philosophical matters—the absolute (*pāramārthika*) point of view and the relative or phenomenal (*vyāvahārika*) point of view, each of the two having relevance and validity in its own way. One need not, therefore, feel shocked to find that a staunch monistic idealist like Śaṁkara has composed some of the most poetic and stirring hymns in praise of personal divinities.

To put it in broad—but logically not quite precise—terms, god stands in the same relationship with the ultimate reality or the supreme being as the individual does with the essential self. So the relationship between god and man is in many ways influenced by the relationship between the supreme being and the essential self. Theistically, the ultimate goal sought after by man is either to live in the same world as god (*salokatā*) or to be near to god (*samīpatā*) or to assume the same form as god (*sarūpatā*) or, finally, to achieve intimate union with god (*sāyujyatā*). It will be seen that, while the first three goals may be understood to represent the stages leading to the final goal, the final goal is but a theistic version of the philosophical goal of the realisation of the ultimate identity of the essential self with the supreme being. The philosophically accepted identity between the supreme being and the essential self is sometimes qualified in theism—it being suggested that god and man are identical in essence but distinct in form. For instance, what sparks are in relation to fire, man is said to be in relation to god. Another line of development of this partial differentiation of man from god is to regard god as being not really external to man but as being the inner controller (*antaryāmin*) of man. God is looked upon as the efficient directive cause (*prayojaka-kartā*) in man's life.

The philosophical doctrine of the perfect identity between the supreme being and the essential self is thus modified into the doctrine of qualified identity or partial separateness between god and man. This latter doctrine is still further extended in the direction of complete dualism between god and man. God is then conceived as the creator and moral governor of man and the universe. Particularly in relation to man, he is often represented as playing the role of the dispenser of the law of Karma. It may, however, be noted in this connection that, even accepting the complete separateness and the awe-inspiring distance between man and god, a Hindu seeks to achieve a direct personal communion with god through a perfect surrender of his whole being to god. This is the ideal of a Hindu devotee. True devotion (*bhakti*), according to the *Bhagavadgītā*, implies, firstly, dedicating all one's actions—physical, mental, and spiritual—to god, rendering service to him, and meditating on him in single-pointed concentration; it further implies ridding oneself of all consciousness of "I"ness and "my"ness, and developing in oneself an attitude of being the same to all god's beings—whether friendly or otherwise; and, finally, it implies creating in oneself a peculiar mystic power through self-surrender, humility, and faith. Prayer, worship, ritual, religious vows and observances (*vratas*), etc., do have a place in Hindu religious practice. But *bhakti* must be regarded as the most potent factor, which, in Hinduism, governs the relationship of man with god.

So far as the relationship of man with the world in general and his fellow-beings in particular is concerned, it needs to be remembered that, according to the higher philosophical thought of the Hindus, the essential self of man is never involved in the doings of this phenomenal world. From the ultimate point of view, therefore, the question about the role of man—the 'real' man—in this world has no relevance whatsoever. Even with reference to the empirical self the consideration of such a question has but little intrinsic value. For, the highest spiritual goal of a Hindu is to transcend the limitations of his individuality, which binds him to this phenomenal world, and so to realise his identity with the supreme being which is, indeed, his native character. Life in this world is accordingly to be looked upon as a bridge, over which one has, of necessity, to pass in order to reach one's destination but on which it would be unwise to build one's house. The question of man's role in this world thus belongs to a very much lower order, and is generally treated as such by the Hindu thinkers. The usual complaint that, in Hindu thought, ethics is regarded just as an "aside" from the serious business of philosophy—a concession, as it were, to the contingency of man's contact with the phenomenal world—cannot, therefore, be said to be quite unjustified.

This does not, however, mean that the Hindus have altogether ignored this aspect of the role of man. Hinduism does offer man adequate guidance for a safe and speedy passage over the bridge of life. Its most significant contribution in this respect is the concept of *dharma*. *Dharma* is, indeed, a very elusive term, and denotes different things in different contexts. It may mean Vedic ritual, or religion and ethics in general, or caste-rules, or civil and criminal law. But the underlying idea is everywhere the same. *Dharma* seeks to resolve the inevitable conflict between the real and the phenomenal, the spiritual and the material, the eternal and the temporal. It recognises that, while striving after the ideal, man cannot afford to neglect the actual. *Dharma*, therefore, lays down a way of life which aims at securing the material and spiritual sustenance and growth of the individual and the society.

The basic question which arises in this context is: How is it possible to get over the obvious contradiction between the individual good and individual ends on the one hand and the social good and social ends on the other? The ultimate goal of the individual, namely, *mokṣa*, presupposes that his constant endeavour should be to isolate himself, as far as possible, from this world. In other words, the individual is expected to follow the path of resignation and actionlessness (*nivṛtti-mārga*). The goal of social stability and progress, on the other hand, requires for its realisation positive efforts on the part of every member of the society. Unless, therefore, every individual were to play his part in this world with active interest and a sense of responsibility—unless, in other words, he were to follow the path of action (*pravṛtti-mārga*)—the society would disintegrate. The usual tendency is to regard these two ways of life—the way of action (*karma*) and the way of renunciation (*saṁnyāsa*)—as mutually exclusive, and to extol one at the expense of the other. The Hindu view of life, however, is governed by an implicit faith in the efficacy and validity of both these ways and in the possibility of reconciling the claims of action and renunciation. In a sense, this faith is the very motive force of Hindu *dharma*. It is fully realised that the life of actionless contemplation is as much fraught with evil as the life of attachment and bare activity. The ideal set forth in this connection is to synthesise these two ways of life in such a manner that one does not prove an impediment to the other, and both together facilitate the realisation of *mokṣa* for the individual and solidarity and progress of the society. It is not action *per se* which entangles man in the turmoil of this phenomenal world thereby rendering his chances of liberation remote. The root cause of this entanglement is not action, but the passion and attachment which accompany that action. What, therefore, is really needed is the annihilation of such passion and attachment, and not the abandoment of action itself. This is the *anāsaktiyoga* of the *Bhagavadgītā*; it implies renunciation *in* action and not *of* action.

One of the most typical results of this ideal of life is the Hindu doctrine of the four ends of man (*puruṣārthas*). The Hindu thinkers have recognised that man possesses a complex personality which seeks fulfilment mainly through four channels—his instincts and natural desires, his craving for power and property, his solicitude for social security and progress, and his urge for spiritual emancipation. They have related these four channels respectively with the four ends of man, namely, *kāma* (enjoyment of the pleasures of personal life), *artha* (material prosperity), *dharma* (maintenance of religious and socio-ethical laws), and *mokṣa* (liberation from the involvement in *saṁsāra*). It is emphasised that these four *puruṣārthas* are by no means mutually contradictory. On the contrary, it is possible, through their proper correlation—that is to say, by so regulating *kāma* and *artha* that they do not hinder but promote *dharma*, and by properly subordinating these three to the ultimate end of *mokṣa*—to build up a truly integrated personality and to live an essentially full life. The doctrine of the four *puruṣārthas*, indeed, serves as the psychical-moral basis of man's role in this world.

Though the general pattern of the organization of man's individual life and social existence is thus more or less fixed, its details vary in accordance with the different "types" of men, as also with the different physico-psychical stages in an individual's life. It is this principle which is at the bottom of the concepts of *varṇadharma* and *āśrama-*

dharma. The *āśramadharma* aims at an ethical organization of an individual's personal life with a view to a fruitful synthesis of the way of action and the way of renunciation as also to the realisation by him of the four *puruṣārthas*. The word *āśrama* literally means exertion or the place where such exertion is practised. By an extension of this meaning, the *āśramas* came to denote the main stages in an individual's life, which, if properly organized, itself becomes a planned exertion. Presumably, the origin of the scheme of the *āśramas* is to be traced back to the impact between the Aryans and the indigenous communities of India. Another factor which must have helped the formulation and consolidation of the *āśramadharma* was the ethical concept of the three debts. Every individual, it is declared, is born with the liability of three debts which he is expected to requite during his life. There is, first of all, the debt which he owes to god (*deva-ṛṇa*). Of this he can redeem himself by dedicating his life to the service of god and to the proper promotion of the scheme of things as laid down by him. Then there is the debt owed to the seers (*ṛṣi-ṛṇa*) which a man can repay by preserving and enriching the cultural heritage handed down to him from age to age. Lastly there is the debt which he owes to his ancestors (*pitṛ-ṛṇa*). This he can discharge by procreating good progeny and thereby ensuring the continuity of the race. The *āśramadharma* organizes the life of an individual in such a manner that he remains ever mindful of these sacred obligations of his and is also given adequate opportunities for their redemption. According to the Hindu view, there are four *āśramas* or stages in an individual's life which follow one another in succession—*brahmacarya* (life of a student), *gṛhasthāśrama* (life of a householder), *vānaprasthāśrama* (life of a hermit), and *saṁnyāsa* (life of an ascetic).

After the rite of initiation (*upanayana*), which was significantly characterised as his second birth, a boy commenced his life as a student. He approached his teacher with the sacred fuel in hand—a gesture which was symbolic of his willingness to obey and to serve. For the next few years—the normal period of *brahmacarya* extended over twelve years, though it varied in some cases—he had to live in the house of the teacher devoting himself fully to the achievement of the three main goals of studentship, namely, the acquisition of knowledge, the building up of character, and preparing himself for shouldering the responsibilities which were to devolve on him in future life. Normally, a student lived by begging and was not required to pay any fixed fees to the teacher.

It may be incidentally pointed out here that the practice of *brahmacarya* in the traditional manner is now rare. Indeed, this is more or less true in respect of the working, in the present time, of the entire ideal scheme of the *āśramas*. The whole system of education in India has undergone vital changes in consonance with the changed conditions. Some stray attempts are, however, being made even today to preserve as far as possible the spirit and the practice of the old *brahmacarya*.

The end of studentship was marked by a ceremonial bath (*samāvartana*). Fully equipped—physically, mentally, and morally—a person now prepared himself to face with confidence the cares and responsibilities of the life of householder. This stage in an individual's life is frequently and with full justification glorified in Hindu literature. *Gṛhasthāśrama* is described as the sacred ground for all achievements and is said to offer the greatest scope for the realisation of the first three ends of man. Indeed, this *āśrama* is regarded as the foundation and support of all other *āśramas*. The starting point of the life of a householder was, of course, marriage. The Hindu marriage is regarded as a sacrament and a religious duty, and not a contract. According to the *Manusmṛti*, the relationship between the husband and the wife was governed by the sentiments of loyalty and devotion to each other until death. The Hindu law-givers have also often emphasised the social purpose of marriage, namely, procreation of progeny (*prajanana*) and continuation of the line (*santāna*). Marriage, it was pointed out, laid the foundation of family, which was the most fundamental of all the social institutions of the Hindus. A Hindu householder was enjoined to look upon his home (*gṛha*) as a trust, which had come down to him from his forefathers and which it was his duty to carry forward to posterity without any dimunition. A householder thus helped to maintain also a kind of spiritual continuity, the outward visible symbol of which was the sacred fire which was often kept burning in the house.

Among the duties of a householder, great emphasis was put on the daily performance by him of the five great sacrifices (*mahāyajñas*). Firstly, there was the *brahmayajña* which was intended mainly for the preservation, through constant study, of the sacred lore which one had acquired during the stage of studentship. It consisted of the daily revision of the Vedic texts—partly actual and partly symbolical. The second *yajña* (*pitṛyajña*) was dedicated to the ancestors, and comprised of daily offering of waters to the manes (*tarpaṇa*). The sacrifice to gods (*devayajña*) was accomplished by means of devotional offering, even of a stick of fuel, in the sacred fire. The sacrifice to creatures (*bhūtayajña*), which consisted of offering food to them, and the sacrifice to men (*nṛyajña*), which was only another name for the proverbial hospitality of the Hindus, implied a kind of deprecation of selfish tendencies in man and emphasised his obligation to share his possessions with his less fortunate fellow-beings.

Though, in the matter of religious practices and social duties, a householder depended on the cooperation and help of his wife, various limitations were placed on a woman's own initiative and activity in that respect. Of course, some of these limitations related to the details rather than to the spirit of religious practice. For instance, some of the sacraments were performed in the case of a woman in the same way as in the case of a man, but without the relevant sacred *mantras*. Normally, a woman was not regarded as eligible for a full observance of the *āśramadharma*. She was not entitled to the rite of initiation, which marked the commencement of studentship. It may, however, be added that ancient writers have expressed contrary views on this point. The most important landmark in the life of a woman was marriage. And, after marriage, she was generally considered to have no existence apart from her husband's—particularly so far as religious practices were concerned. The husband was her true preceptor (*guru*), and in all spiritual matters she was dependent on him. According to the *Manusmṛti*, the conscientious performance of household duties constituted her proper ritual. At the same time, a man's religious life was regarded as incomplete without his wife's active participation in it. It may also be pointed out that, though various restrictions had been placed on a woman's role in connection with what might be called Brahmanic rites, in popular Hinduism, she was allowed greater freedom in the matter of worship (*pūjā*) and religious observances (*vratas*).

But if the Hindus could be said to have made the most correct estimate of a woman in respect of anything, it was in respect of her role in the family. As the *Mahābhārata* put it, a home was not really a home unless a woman presided over it. As the mistress of the house, it was she who was responsible for the stability and solidarity of the family. A Vedic text says that, without a wife, the psychological and moral personality of a man attains only half its normal stature. Then there was the woman's role as mother. A mother was always regarded as more divine than divinity—she was to be respected ten times as much as the father. The great philosopher Śaṁkara paid perhaps the highest compliment to a mother when he declared that a bad son might be born, but there could never be a bad mother.

After having lived a full and fruitful life as householder, a man began to think of freeing himself from the ties of family and society. This was the stage of withdrawing from active life and taking over the life of a forest-hermit (*vānaprastha*). In this *āśrama*, a man could be accompanied by his wife, who too was expected to dissociate herself from all family and social bonds. A man's role as a recluse consisted not in service or leadership but in disinterested counsel. Without imposing himself upon the community in any way, he placed at its disposal the rich experience which he had gathered during a long and active life. But a man was not expected to continue for long even this partial and passive contact with the affairs of the world. He, therefore, soon entered into the last stage of life—the stage of complete renunciation and solitude (*saṁnyāsa*). His one and only aim now was the realisation of *mokṣa*. An ascetic (*saṁnyāsī*) drowned his consciousness of "I"ness (*ahaṁkāra*) and "my"ness (*mamakāra*)—he cut himself loose from the limitations of individuality—and so got ready to attain the goal for which he had been, as it were, serving, during the first three *āśramas*, a well-planned apprenticeship.

As if to make the broad scheme of the *āśramas* more tangible and definite, the Hindu thinkers have correlated it with the more minute scheme of sacraments (*saṁskāras*). A sacrament may be generally understood as a religious rite which is intended to mark the creation in an individual of some inward spiritual grace and strength. Among the various items which played a prominent role in the Hindu *saṁskāras* were the sacred fire, prayers and formulas (*mantras*), sacrifice, lustration, orientation, symbolism, taboos, and magic. Each important juncture in the journey of life was sanctified by means of a sacrament. As a matter of fact, sacraments touched the life of a Hindu from before his birth up to after his death. For, the first sacrament in the series related to the conception by the mother (*garbhādhāna*) and the last to the funeral (*antyeṣṭi*), while some of the important intervening sacraments related to the name-giving (*nāmakaraṇa*), the tonsure (*cūdākarma*), the initiation (*upanayana*), the end of studentship (*samāvartana*), and the marriage (*vivāha*).

If the scheme of the four *āśramas* represented a kind of ethical organization of an individual's personal life, the scheme of the four *varṇas* or social orders could be regarded as representing a kind of ethical organization of the social life of the Hindus. There is an indication in the *Puruṣasūkta* of the *Ṛgveda* that the society, even in those early days, had been organized into four distinct orders, namely, Brāhmaṇa (the poet-priest), Rājanya (the warrior-ruler), Vaiśya (the trader-agriculturist), and Śūdra (the servant-labourer). In later literature these social orders were frequently referred to as *varṇas*. The scheme of the *varṇas* is often erroneously equated with the caste-system of the later times. It must, however, be emphasised that the original nature of *varṇa* was essentially different from that of caste as understood today. Strictly speaking, the word which denotes caste is not *varṇa*; it is *jāti*. The word *varṇa* literally means "colour", and there can be little doubt that, in such passages in the *Ṛgveda* where that word is used in connection with the antagonism between the Aryan invaders (*ārya-varṇa*) and the tribes conquered by them (*dāsa-varṇa*), it denotes the colour of the skin. It thus seems to emphasise the racial distinction between the early Aryan immigrants on the one hand and all other tribes—collectively—whom they encountered and vanquished on the other. When, however, the word *varṇa* is used to denote the four social orders mentioned in the *Puruṣasūkta*, it does not possess any racial connotation whatsoever. As a matter of fact, the four social orders, namely, the Brāhmaṇa, the Rājanya (or the Kṣatriya), the Vaiśya, and the Śūdra—which, incidentally, are described in that *sūkta* as constituting respectively the mouth, the arms, the thighs, and the feet of the Cosmic Being (*Puruṣa*)—are not even called *varṇas* in the *Ṛgveda*. It was only in the later Vedic literature that the word *varṇa* came to be employed with reference to them.

Originally the *varṇas* seem to have represented the four main classes in which the Vedic society was segmented presumably for certain magic-ritual purposes. This segmentation was intended for properly distributing throughout the community the various duties connected with the communal ritual and thereby ensuring that those duties were performed by persons duly qualified by heredity, by purity preserved by means of taboos etc., and by the knowledge of the special functions connected with the ritual. It would appear that, in order that the ritual character and functions of the four orders should be clearly distinguished, four distinct colours had been assigned to them—white to the Brāhmaṇa, red to the Kṣatriya, yellow to the Vaiśya, and black to the Śūdra. This would explain the significance of the name *varṇa* by which those orders had come to be eventually known. The magic-ritual character of the *varṇas* is further confirmed by the concept of the ceremonial re-birth of persons belonging to the first three among them. They were accordingly called *dvijas* or twice-born. It was only after the sacrament of initiation that they became qualified for their respective ritual functions. In their early phase, the *varṇas* seem to have been fluid in character, and instances of the assumption by persons belonging to one *varṇa* of the character and duties of another *varṇa*, though rare, were not altogether wanting. This was perhaps in keeping with the magic-ritual ideology, according to which a person could effect an alteration in his magic-ritual potence and thus qualify himself for functions different from those of his own order.

This deliberate hierarchical organization of the Vedic society contained within itself certain factors, which, on account of the interaction of certain other factors, must have so developed as to transform that organization gradually into the caste-system. Indeed, one of the most significant features of the social history of ancient India may be said to have been the evolution of the various castes (*jātis*) out of the four original *varṇas*. It is now wellnigh impossible to mark out the different stages in that process. It may, however, be added that the drift of the evolution had been in the direction of hardening and secularization. Presumably, among the indigenous communities of India also, there existed certain distinctive concepts of taboo, pollution, purification, etc. Further, there is sufficient ground to assume that their social life was organized on the basis of graded functional guilds. The impact of the social organizations of the Aryans and the indigenous Indian communities on each other must have helped the growth of castes. And, besides the factors implied by these two social organizations, such as the ideas relating to *asu*, taboo, pollution, and ceremonial purity, the belief in magic associated with different crafts and functions, the anxiety for guarding the secrets of trade, etc., several other factors, such as the geographical isolation of the Indian subcontinent, the enforcement of deliberate economic and administrative policies, the clash of cultures, the fusion of races, the shrewd application of the doctrine of Karma, and the natural tendency towards religious and social exploitation, must have further led to the consolidation of these castes into a full-fledged rigorous system. Except on the assumption of such multiple origin, it is indeed, impossible to account for the extreme complexity of the nature and form of the caste-system.

Varṇadharma thus originally implied the duties and obligations of the four social orders—of the Brāhmaṇa: study, teaching, performing sacrifices, officiating at sacrifices, charity, and accepting gifts; of the

Kṣatriya: protection of the subjects, charity, performing sacrifice, study, and non-attachment to sensuous pleasures; of the Vaiśya: tending cattle, charity, performing sacrifice, study, trade, usury, and agriculture; and of the Śūdra: service of the first three orders. Later on, however, when the various castes (*jātis*) had evolved out of the ancient social orders (*varṇas*), the term *varṇadharma* came to denote, more or less loosely, the body of rules governing the functioning of the caste-system. It would seem that, in the initial stages of the social pattern of the *varṇas*, the preeminence among the four social orders of the Kṣatriya or Rājanya was traditionally acknowledged, presumably because a representative of that order played the central role in the communal sacrifice. However, in the Vedic literature, which is mainly the creation of poet-priests, a conscious effort seems to have been made to glorify the function of the Brāhmaṇa. The function of the Vaiśya was not clearly defined, and the Śūdra, who was regarded as untouchable so far as sacrifice was concerned, participated only indirectly in it. In addition to these four orders, mention is made in the Vedic literature also of certain occupations like those of the chariot-maker, the barber, the potter, etc., all of which seem to have originated in a scheme for distributing throughout the community the various duties connected with the ritual. There were also classes, like the Cāṇḍālas, who seem to have been entirely debarred from participation in the communal ritual and who eventually formed the fifth *varṇa*.

There are clear indications in the brahmanic literature of the post-Vedic period that various closed groups were being formed in the society though they were all still included within the scheme of the four ancient orders. The earlier gradation among the social orders tended to harden into general social inequality, in which process a man's birth played the most vital role. The position of the Brāhmaṇas as the specially privileged class was confirmed, and, correspondingly, the Śūdras came to be degraded and suffered from many disabilities in religious and secular matters. The Kṣatriyas were struggling to retain their original position of preeminence, while the Vaiśyas were slowly but surely sinking in the social scale. The various occupational groups were generally assigned either to the Vaiśya *varṇa* or to the Śūdra *varṇa*. This stratification of society became so rigid that, in course of time, in every single matter, big or small—from scales of taxation to mode of address and salutation, and from the age of initiation to location of cremation-grounds—the distinction of one *varṇa* from another and the gradation in their status were emphatically brought out. The most complete and detailed picture of this social pattern with all its ramifications is to be found in the *Manusmṛti* (cir. second century B.C.), which lays down that obedience to caste rules (*varṇadharma*) is the very essence of *dharma*.

A reference may be made in this very context to a kind of ethical idealization of the scheme of *varṇas* implied in the *Bhagavadgītā*. There the emphasis is put not so much on the differences and the gradation among the *varṇas*. What, according to the *Bhagavadgītā*, is really important is the principle of ethical interdependence involved in that scheme. Society as an integrated whole can be held together and progress only if its various components carry out the functions assigned to them with a sense of social awareness. The consideration whether any particular function is high or low, or whether it is to one's liking or not, is not of any real value. The *Bhagavadgītā* teaches that the feeling that, by faithfully following one's *varṇadharma*, one is actively promoting the solidarity, stability, and progress of the society is in itself a reward greater than any other to be sought after in this world.

Though caste is universally looked upon as one of the most distinctive features of Hinduism, it is indeed very difficult to define it precisely. All that one can do is to indicate certain essential features of the caste-system as it operates in India. The first thing to be noted in this connection is that a man's caste is determined by his birth. Further, the caste normally regulates marriage, diet, and occupation of the persons belonging to it. For instance, a caste is an endogamous group so that its members are forbidden to marry outside that caste. In most cases a caste is further subdivided into smaller exogamous groups, the members of which must necessarily marry outside those groups. Similarly, restrictions are placed by different castes on the kind of food which may be taken by their members. For most castes, again, the occupations are fixed. Further, since birth invests an individual with a particular caste for life, change of caste is generally not possible. An important feature of the caste-system is that there is some social gradation among castes, according to which the Brāhmaṇas are generally assigned a position at the top. Even the normal social intercourse among the various castes is governed by certain set regulations, many of which are based on ideas regarding pollution through direct contact or otherwise. Caste in India also implies the denial of certain civil and religious rights to a large number of people. It may also be added that certain castes have special rights to wear certain ornaments or garments and that the kind of language to be used by one caste with reference to another is sometimes determined by the status of those castes in the hierarchy. Verily, caste affects all the relations and events of the life of a Hindu. It has influenced the social process in India to such an extent that the caste of a Hindu seems to persist even after he changes his religion.

A few other points regarding the functioning of the caste-system need to be noted here. Firstly, it will be seen that each caste represents an independent social unit. The different and exclusive customs of a particular caste, in a sense, isolate it from other castes. Indeed, each caste seeks to guard its own special customs so jealously that it has given rise to the dictum that caste is custom. But the Hindu society has integrated several such independent units into an organic whole. This social organism, called caste-system, is so built up that it can easily accommodate within itself any new unit that may come into existence. Similarly, if one unit breaks up into smaller units, each one of the latter, instead of falling out, becomes naturally integrated into the bigger organism as an independently functioning cell.

The exclusiveness and independence of a caste as a social unit are further confirmed by its essentially autonomous character. Each caste makes its own rules and establishes its own customs. It also commands the power to enforce those rules and customs on its members through its council or *panchāyat*. The main—or, perhaps, the only—sanction behind caste rules and customs is excommunication from the caste—a contingency which a Hindu is anxious to avoid more avidly than any other. In actual practice it is observed that the lower the caste is in the social scale the more efficient are the organization and functioning of its council. This autonomous character of castes was sometimes vitiated by the fact that the king or the state sought to assume the ultimate authority in respect of them. What, however, the Hindu *dharmaśāstra* called upon a king to do was to see that the rules and customs of a caste were being properly observed by its members. It further required him to take care that his own laws were as far as possible compatible with the rules and customs of the various castes.

In their original magic-ritual character, the varying status of the four social orders was perhaps not so very keenly felt. All sense of inequality must have been drowned into the ritual ceremonial through which they sought to achieve the common weal of the community and in which each of them had a distinct and necessary part to play. But with the secularization and hardening of the *varṇas* into castes, such gradation became more complex and pronounced. Attempts were, therefore, made to palliate the sense of inequality among the castes and to rationalize the difference in the privileges and prerogatives enjoyed by persons belonging to different castes. On the one hand it was argued that castes were divine in origin, and, therefore, beyond the control of man. On the other hand, the responsibility for the particular caste in which a person was born was thrown on the person himself by suggesting that the actions done by an individual in the preceding life determined his lineage—and therefore his caste—for the next life. Caste was thus regarded as a matter to be decided exclusively according to the inexorable law of Karma. Further, with a view to extenuating the sense of inequality among the various castes, it was argued that if the privileges of a higher caste were greater its responsibilities also were greater. A reference may also be made, in this context, to the fact that the allocation of a caste in the social hierarchy was not necessarily rigid. There was always the possibility—and there have actually been instances—of a caste rising in the social scale by means of its own efforts.

In the course of history, voices were occasionally raised against the rigid social stratification engendered by the caste-system, but without any tangible result. Neither the rise of Buddhism nor the advent of Islam can be said to have been effective in the matter of the extermination of castes in India. In more recent times, religious leaders like Kapilar, Vemana, Basava, Kabir, and Nanak—among others—strongly opposed caste, but their protests ultimately proved sterile. The sponsors of the reformist movements in modern India have made caste the main target of their attack. Many of them do recognise that caste has played a useful role in the social history of India. For instance, it is the institution of caste which has enabled diverse elements of population in India to live together in a more or less organized form. It has proved to be an effective integrating and stabilising force. The caste has also provided its members with a kind of social and economic security. Further, it has served as an agency by means of which several arts and crafts were adequately preserved. But these social reformers sincerely believe that, in the final accounting relating to the caste-system, the debit side shows itself to be heavier than the credit side. For one thing, the concept of caste represents the very antithesis of the principle of the essential equality of all men. Again, by accepting birth as the only criterion which determines one's caste, caste-system generally blocks the way to an individual's rise in social status. Caste-system also implies the denial of certain civil and religious rights to a large number of people. History shows that, having created and stabilised social inequality which was usually accompanied by oppression and exploitation of one class by another, the caste-system has proved a constant source of discontent and unrest, and, consequently, a perennial obstruction to social progress. The extreme social segmentation naturally prevented the growth of the sentiment of national unity. Patriotism was not unoften equated with the loyalty to one's caste, and the interests of the caste—rather than those of the community as a whole—became the motive force in social life. True morality was superseded by the demands of caste observances, and sin came to mean no more than breach of caste rules. It is generally believed that the caste-system, as it has operated through centuries, cannot be mended—it will have to be ended.

It may, however, be added in this connection that conditions in modern India are changing rapidly. The very pressure of the new set of circumstances has helped to minimise the rigidity of many features of the caste-system. The present economic set-up, for instance, is slowly but surely frustrating the occupational significance of castes. The increasing compulsiveness of and the growing facilities for communication among persons belonging to different castes have effectively neutralised the restrictions regarding commensality and social intercourse. The observance of the rigid rules relating to pollution through contact etc. is now wellnigh impracticable in the ordinary day-to-day life. These rules may—if at all—be enforced only in ritual situations. Incidentally, it may be pointed out that the various *bhakti*-movements in the history of Hinduism have done much to unite different castes into a kind of religious democracy. There is, however, one feature of the caste-system which seems to die hard, namely, its control over marriage. But the present trend in connection with the question of castes is very well reflected in the constitution of the Republic of India which lays down that "the State shall not discriminate against any citizen on grounds only of religion, race, caste, sex, place of birth or any of them" and that "untouchability is abolished and its practice in any form is forbidden."

Besides the *āśramadharma* and the *varṇadharma*, the Hindu theorists speak of four other kinds of *dharma*: the *varṇāśramadharma* or the *dharma* applicable to an individual of a particular social order at a particular stage in his personal life; the *guṇadharma* which concerns some distinct office or position which an individual holds; the *nimittadharma* which refers to certain special circumstances; and the *sāmānyadharma* or general ethics. As for this last kind of *dharma*, it may be pointed out that Hindu ethics or morality cannot be said to have been reduced to any regular code as such. For, as in metaphysics so in ethics, the Hindu thinker seems to place greater emphasis on the inculcation of a right attitude of mind rather than on the postulation of any elaborate theories. For instance, the theoretical question regarding the freedom of will does not seem to have bothered him much. For him, the neutralisation of will constituted the very essence of morality.

Speaking of what may be called the practical side of Hindu ethics one may, first of all, refer to the three cardinal virtues enumerated in an interesting parable in the *Bṛhadāraṇyaka-Upaniṣad* (V.2.1-3), namely, self-control (*dama*), charity (*dāna*), and compassion (*dayā*). It may be added that, in this context, the word 'charity' is not used in the sense of merely giving alms etc.; it rather implies sharing what one has with one's fellow-beings, not being selfish, and, therefore loving one's fellow-beings. The *Bhagavadgītā* has mentioned, in different contexts, quite a large number of other virtues, such as, for instance, fearlessness, purity of mind, sacrifice, uprightness, non-violence, truth, freedom from anger and covetousness, gentleness, modesty, and steadiness. It also enjoins on man the avoidance of certain vices—more particularly of lust, anger, and greed, which are characterised as the "triple gate of hell" leading to the ruin of the soul.

It will be thus seen that the general practical ethics of the Hindus is much the same as that of the most of the civilised peoples. What, however, distinguishes it is the special emphasis put by the Hindus on truth (*satya*), non-violence (*ahiṁsā*), sacrifice (*yajña*), and renunciation (*saṁnyāsa*). The parable of Satyakāma Jābāla occurring in the *Chāndogya-Upaniṣad* (IV.4) teaches very tellingly that undaunted truthfulness is to be recognised as the only real criterion of a man's character and worth. The positive aspect of *ahiṁsā* is to respect all life—indeed, all god's creation. Closely allied to the teaching of *ahiṁsā* is that regarding *ātmaupamya* or seeing with equality everything in the image of one's self and *sarvabhūtahita* or doing good to all creatures. The concept of *yajña* must be said to be dominating the entire Hindu view of life. The form and extent of sacrifice may have varied from age to age, but its underlying spirit expressed by the *Bhagavadgītā* in the words, "fostering each other you shall attain to the supreme good," has endured throughout. The *Bhagavadgītā*, indeed, describes the whole universe as a "wheel of sacrifice" which operates on the principle of ethical interdependence among its constituents. No one could afford to be remiss in playing his appointed part in that sacrifice, lest the proper functioning of the world would be brought in jeopardy. The concept of *saṁnyāsa* in Hinduism is very much misunderstood. It is often suggested that *saṁnyāsa* is a negative virtue, that it is not a social value, and that a *saṁnyāsī* has no social personality. It cannot be denied that the actual practice of *saṁnyāsa* in popular Hinduism does give sufficient ground for such an estimate. But the true ideal in this respect may be said to have been laid down in the *Bhagavadgītā* which seeks to reconcile *saṁnyāsa* with the ideal of *lokasaṁgraha* (solidarity of the society and sustenance of the universe) and the doctrine of *yajña*. A true *saṁnyāsī* practises renunciation *in* action and not *of* action. The *Bhagavadgītā*, indeed, sets forth, in the following words, the dictum, which, according to Hinduism, should govern the role of man in relation to the world: "Therefore, without attachment, perform always the work that *has* to be done, for, man attains to the highest by doing work without attachment."

Not much need be said about the eschatological speculations of the Hindus. The Ṛgvedic people concerned themselves with the stability, security, and affluence of life on this earth so thoroughly that they do not seem to have bothered much about the life after death. There is, however, an indication in one of the funeral hymns of that Veda (X. 14.8) that, after his death, a person, as the result of the good deeds which he has done during his life, leaves behind his earthly taint, assumes another resplendent form, and goes to the highest heaven to become united with his "fathers" and with Yama who, incidentally, is often celebrated as the lord of the blessed dead. The *Atharvaveda* (IV. 34) specifically refers to *svarga* or heaven where the deserving dead enjoy all kinds of material pleasures which represent but a manifold magnified replica of the earthly pleasures. But such allusions in the early Veda are few and fortuitous. References to hell are still more vague, such as, for instance, those where the Ṛgvedic poet speaks of the lap (X.18.10) or the realm (VII.58.1) of Nirṛti, the goddess of perdition. In the *Brāhmaṇas* and other ritualistic texts, the *svarga* is mentioned particularly prominently as the fruit accruing from the performance of sacrifices. As a matter of fact, the desire for winning the *svarga* is regarded as the principal motive force behind Vedic ritual. But even here one can hardly see any strictly eschatological concept.

Naturally enough, the *Upaniṣads* could not avoid dealing with eschatological questions at some length. According to the ultimate philosophical point of view represented in those texts, the facts of life and death possess only relative reality. The *Upaniṣads* often speak of immortality (*amṛtatva*)—not in the sense that man's individuality persists for all time, but in the sense that man is destined to realise the identity of his essential self with the ultimate reality which is eternal and immutable. This beatific condition of man is variously described as "becoming free from the reach of day and night" (*Bṛ-Up*. III.1.4) or "having the self as one's only desire" (*Bṛ.-Up*. IV.4.6) or "sinking one's deeds and understanding in the supreme immutable being" (*Muṇḍaka-Up*. III.2.7). Elsewhere, the *Bṛhadāraṇyaka-Upaniṣad* (VI.2. 15-16) posits three eschatological alternatives: (1) those who realise the true nature of the self proceed along the path of the gods (*devayāna*) and ultimately attain to the *brahmaloka*, never to return; (2) those who perform sacrifices and practise charity and penance proceed along the path of the manes (*pitṛyāṇa*) and attain to the world of the moon; there, they become food; 'gods feed upon them, and, when that passes away from them, they start on the return journey to be reborn as human beings; thus do they rotate'; and (3) those who do not belong to either of the foregoing two categories become 'insects, moths, and whatever there is here that bites.' The *Kauṣītaki-Upaniṣad* (I.2) says that those who depart from this world go to the moon, which, verily, is the door of heaven. There they are questioned by the moon as to their true nature; 'whoever answers it properly, him it sets free to go to the higher worlds; but whoever answers it not, him, having become rain, it rains down here.' The *Upaniṣad* further (I.3-6) goes on to describe in highly picturesque details the soul's journey to the *brahmaloka* along the path of the gods. Of those 'deluded men who regard sacrifices and works of merits as most important and who do not know any other good,' the *Muṇḍaka-Upaniṣad* (I.2.10) says that they, 'having enjoyed in the high place of heaven won by good deeds, enter again this world or a still lower one.' With the proliferation of classical Hinduism there also occurred a proliferation of ideas regarding the heaven and the hell. The *Mahābhārata* and the *Purāṇas*, for instance, speak of different kinds of heavens and hells which are intended for different kinds of holy men and sinners respectively.

By and large, Hinduism does not countenance the possibility of the complete annihilation of human personality, for, it goes against the universal law of moral causality. Nor does it believe in eternal happiness in heaven or irrevocable damnation in hell, for, in the ultimate analysis, life in heaven or in hell is as unreal and transitory as the life on this earth. Hinduism emphasises that *mokṣa* is the birth-right and the true destiny of the human soul.

V. Epilogue

The modern age has thrown out a serious challenge to all traditional religions. However, in the course of the long period of its evolution, Hinduism may be said to have acquired adequate strength to meet any new challenge and to respond to the demands of any new set of conditions more or less successfully and without allowing its essential character to be vitiated in any way. History bears abundant testimony to this kind of strength of Hinduism. But there are also other valid reasons which would support the belief that Hinduism can adjust itself with modern culture without much conflict.

In this connection, it needs to be, first of all, noted that many of the claims of modern culture, which seem to imply the futility of religion in modern times, have been proved to be inherently untenable. For instance, the apotheosis of formal logic by modern rationalism, which, incidentally, is seen to have actually tended to crush out life, can hardly stand a critical examination. It seems to have been forgotten that, after all, life is larger than logic. Modern intellectualism, which discountenances faith because it is said to breed fanaticism, has completely failed to realise the true nature of faith and the significance of the role which faith plays in the life of man. It must be emphasised that, particularly in the realm of morality, reason is incomplete and arrested in growth if not allowed to blossom into faith. It may be further pointed out that intuition, which is so much exalted in the Hindu tradition but which is generally anathematized by modern rigorous rationalism, is not a-logical, but that it is supra-logical. Faith and intuition have proved to be veritable sources of strength to man. It is well and truly said that the attitude of mind which sterilizes fanaticism at the cost of extinguishing faith constitutes a supreme danger to the spiritual health. It seems as if, while combating one kind of fanaticism, modern intellectualism has fomented another kind of fanaticism, namely, the fanaticism regarding the invulnerability of reason. Actually, however, never before had man lost, so completely as now, his faith in reason as the final arbiter in metaphysics, aesthetics, and ethics. Moreover, is a wholly rational individual not a myth? Has not the new psychology unravelled the dark forces of the unconscious and also exposed the incapacity of reason to deal with them?

Modern science claims to have established that reality is ordered, that man's reason is capable of discerning this order as it manifests itself in the laws of nature, and that the path to human fulfilment consists primarily in discovering these laws, utilizing them where this is possible, and complying with them where it is not. It is further claimed that the ever-increasing fund of scientific knowledge has delimited—and, in some cases, entirely negatived—the scope and the purpose of religion. Science has, for instance, unravelled the mystery of the origin of the world and of man, and has thereby rendered religious cosmology and anthropology quite nugatory. These and similar claims of modern science have, however, now been proved to be wholly unwarranted by what has been called "post-modern" science. Modern science, it is suggested, showed us a world at odds with our senses; post-modern science is showing us one which is at odds with our imagination. Scientists now confess that the structure of nature has eluded them. They are confronted with something which is truly ineffable. It is also now generally agreed that science by itself does not constitute a value. On the contrary, the scientist has to accept without question the system of ethical values current in his time and in his society. The limitations of science vis-a-vis the physical world and human life are thus being more and more emphatically pressed in. Human life, it is now realised, is "too broad, deep, subtle, and rich to be exhausted by anything that the scientist would find out in his own field."

It may also be added that several features of modern culture have been found to be not very desirable—indeed, they have been instrumental in stirring up serious crises in the life of man. Modern technology, it will be seen, has thoroughly changed the structure and character of traditional society. The caste-system, which had enjoyed, through the ages, a kind of religious sanction, is now inevitably required to soften its rigours and to connive at the transgression of many of its laws. New social relationships are now evolving—relationships which are entirely unrelated to religion. Modern technology has also brought about a clearly noticeable rise in the standard of the material and physical life of man. This, in its turn, has given rise to the changed concept of human needs—and to the belief that religion is, by its very nature, not competent to satisfy these needs. There is perhaps not much in all this that may be complained against. But many of the other consequences of modern technology are distinctly undesirable. For instance, technology has tended to promote a social organization which is essentially impersonal in character. This new social organization does not inspire a sense of belonging. The large-scale introduction of machinery has reduced man himself to the position of a machine. It has dehumanized man. Technology has also led to the concentration of authority, power, and wealth—and, what is worse, by its very nature, it does not possess the capacity to lay down the norms in the matter of the use of that authority, power, and wealth. Again, the rush of the machine-age has disturbed the equilibrium in human life; it has created a kind of imbalance. Similarly, man can no longer hope to enjoy the personal solitude which is so very essential for his spiritual health. It has also to be emphasised that the persisting conditions of war have revealed technology in a grave and dangerous perspective. Of course, science and technology by themselves are not to be condemned. Indeed, man cannot now do without them. All that is intended to be suggested is that the employment of science and technology needs to be governed by a proper sense of values.

As regards the emphasis laid by modern culture on the freedom of the individual, it may be borne in mind that a wholly free individual is as much a myth as a wholly rational individual. Even the materialistic view, which is one of the most dominant views of the present age, looks upon man as "a passive creature moulded and pushed from behind by mechanical forces, a slave of physical energy he can never control." The two ideals of modern culture, namely, individual freedom and socialism, have remained incompatible. Indeed, the socialization of the individual is threatening to develop into a major crisis of the modern times.

The untenability of certain claims of modern culture and the undesirability of several of its features may be said to have actually created in India—as, perhaps, in many other countries—a propitious atmosphere for a fresh rethinking about the need for religion. Such rethinking in respect of Hinduism is, indeed, now seen to be engaging the attention of Hindu intellectuals.

Secondly, certain characteristics of Hinduism, arising from the very nature of its origin and growth, render it capable of adequately meeting the challenge of any new set of circumstances. As has been pointed out elsewhere, Hinduism has generally remained free from any kind of institutional rigidity. This is surely the secret of its remarkable responsiveness to the changing conditions of life and thought. This is also why Hinduism has continued to be a "growing" religion. As RADHAKRISHNAN points out, "Hinduism is a movement, not a position; a process, not a result; a growing tradition, not a fixed revelation." There is, accordingly, no possibility of any serious conflict arising from the confrontation of Hinduism with modernity. Indeed, one need not be surprised if, in course of time, modernity itself becomes an organic part of the Hindu tradition. It is interesting to recall, in this context, that Hinduism is often picturesquely compared to a snow-ball. Tolerance, which is rightly mentioned as one of the most outstanding characteristics of Hinduism, is another factor which has operated as an effective deterrent of insular and exclusivist tendencies in the matter of belief and practice. It is, however, complained that Hindu tolerance is not rationalistic, but that it is the expression of an amazing nonchalance on the part of the Hindus. Another complaint that is usually made against Hindu tolerance is that, in most cases, it actually amounts to abject and uncritical submission to the other's point of view, or that—and this is perhaps worse—it represents a tendency to make virtue of necessity. But the history of Hinduism would show that such complaints were generally unfounded and that Hindu tolerance was deliberate, positive, and realistic. As GANDHIJI has said, it is not necessary for tolerance that one must invariably approve of what one tolerates. But one must be always willing and prepared for intellectual and social accommodation. This represents just elementary good manners in civilized life. In the matter of religion, Hindu tolerance implies a kind of sublimation of religious feelings—a recognition that religion is polymorphic.

A third reason why Hinduism will be able to meet the challenge of modern culture adequately is that Hinduism either already possessed several of the elements of modernity or it has steadily assimilated them in the course of its evolution. Rationalism as such, for instance, is by no means new to the Hindu tradition. It is well known that Hindu thought can boast of a fairly well-developed epistemology. Indeed, Nyāya (Hindu system of logic and epistemology) has played a significant role in the development of almost every branch of Hindu knowledge. As for the *Veda-prāmāṇya* or the acceptance of the ultimate validity of the Veda, it has been pointed out elsewhere that, in actual history, that doctrine had only a formal, nominal, and essentially practical significance in that it served merely as a thin thread binding together various systems of thought and practice. And, even when the Veda was regarded as the final authority, complete freedom was allowed in the matter of its interpretation. Have not systems of various shades of thought, ranging from absolute monism to dualism and pluralism, claimed to have the full and exclusive sanction of the Veda? The spirit of inquiry has always been a ruling passion with Hindu thinkers. They are seen to have devoted themselves to a fearless and uninhibited pursuit of truth regardless of where it led. A Cārvāka or a Kauṭilya is not unknown to Hindu intellectual history. At the same time, it is verily a strong point of Hindu thinkers that they have duly recognised the limitations of human intellect. But they refuse to stop at the inevitable intellectual indeterminism. *Śraddhā* or faith, which they have glorified, is actually an indication of their epistemological optimism.

Like modern scientists, the Hindus also tested their knowledge, limited in scope and variety though it might have been, pragmatically, that is, by the quality of personal experience which it made possible. For instance, immediate experience of reality, and not merely its mediate knowledge, is the goal towards which all the religio-philosophical activities of the Hindus are directed. This accounts for the fact that Hindu seekers after truth often have recourse to supra-intellectualistic disciplines like yoga. In a sense, Hindu philosophy is an "applied" philosophy; it looks upon human life as a laboratory for experiments with truth.

It further needs to be pointed out that, for a Hindu thinker, the "attitudinal" aspect a philosophy has been more important than the "cognitional" aspect. What really matters is not what one "knows" but what one "becomes"! All this makes Hinduism an essentially mystic-personal religion. It need not, therefore, come into any serious conflict with modern culture. As claimed by the modernists, the theologic aspect of religion may have lost its *raison d'être* after the rise of modern science and secular ethics, but its mystic-personal aspect, as all protagonists of modernity are now generally inclined to admit, will ever remain coeval with man. As for the inherent incompatibility of the two ideals of individual freedom and socialism, which poses a serious problem in modern times, the Hindus can get over it without much difficulty because their ultimate world-view is cosmic and not anthropocentric.

Today, India, like the rest of the civilized world, is witnessing a major conflict of values. In India, as elsewhere, there is a distinct shift of interest. Interest in politics and economics is becoming more and more predominant and the tendency is becoming evident to subordinate all other values to this single value. Toynbee regards this state of things as marking the decay of civilization. Particularly on the background of the religion-oriented past history of India, this shift of interest strikes one in a very pronounced manner. In the matter of religion, the Hindu intellectuals have now generally become listless.

They are merely drifting. It is clear that the kind of equilibrium which traditional Hinduism had established has now been seriously disturbed by modernisation. But it is equally clear that, for the sake of national solidarity, a new kind of equilibrium must be substituted, and that Hinduism, as indicated above, does possess the capacity to meet this challenging situation in quite an adequate manner. Man is essentially a religious creature. Constituted as he is, he cannot live without some kind of religion; religion is for him a psychological and a sociological necessity. This being so, irreligion or rejection of religion is positively unnatural. The secularism, which is now accepted by the Indian people as an article of faith, does not imply irreligion or antitranscendentalism or non-spirituality. Indian secularism is a positive-negative concept. On the one hand, it implies positive good will and respect for all religions; and, on the other, it insists that institutionalized religion shall not, under any circumstances, be employed to influence adversely the civic life of the people and the normal functioning of the State. In a country like India which is characterized by religious pluralism, this doctrine of secularism is fully justified. In the India of today, communities professing different religious faiths and practices have not only to live together in harmony, but they have also to work together in a spirit of active and responsible collaboration. Under these circumstances, secularism, properly understood, can alone operate as a positive force in the proper development of the country. Secularism, which seeks to subordinate the theologic, creedal, institutional, ritualistic aspect of religion to its mystic, personal, spiritual aspect, does not contemplate an outright reversal of the spiritual tradition of the country. It rather promotes a healthy evolution of that tradition so that it may suitably respond to the changing conditions. History would show that Hinduism could not have anything intrinsically against such secularism.

SELECT BIBLIOGRAPHY

Bergaigne, A., *La religion védique d'après les hymnes du Rig-Veda*, 3 volumes, Paris 1878-83.

Dumézil, G., *L'idéologie tripartite des Indo-Européens*, Bruxelles 1958.

Eliot, C., *Hinduism and Buddhism*, 3 volumes, London 1921; (Second Edition, 1954).

Gonda, J., *Die Religionen Indiens* I: *Veda und älterer Hinduismus*, Stuttgart 1960; II: *Der jüngere Hinduismus*, Stuttgart 1963.

Güntert, H., *Der arische Weltkönig und Heiland*, Halle (S) 1923.

KONOW, S. and TUXEN, P., *Religions of India*, Copenhagen 1949.
MAX MÜLLER, F., *Hibbert Lectures on the Origin and Growth of Religion as illustrated by the Religions of India*, London 1880.
MORGAN, K. (Ed.), *The Religion of the Hindus*, New York 1953.
RADHAKRISHNAN, S., *The Hindu View of Life*, London 1927; (Seventh Impression, 1948); *Religion and Society*, London 1947.
RENOU, L., *Religions of Ancient India*, London 1953.
WHEELER, M., *The Indus Civilization*, Cambridge 1960.
ZAEHNER, R. C., *Hinduism* ,London 1962.

JAINISM

BY

CARLO DELLA CASA

Palermo, Italy

I. The Essence of Jainism

The religion of the followers of Jina, "the Victorious", is called Jainism. It is a doctrine of salvation from the cycle of existences. Jainism appeared more then two thousand five hundred years ago, and is still alive and flourishing in India, although in very fixed social classes. Through the centuries it has preserved many of its original doctrinal characteristics, unlike other Indian religions, which have undergone even fundamental changes in conception and ritual.

Jainism attributes a soul to every manifestation of nature, including plants, stones and drops of water: with its hylozoism or rather panpsychism it seems to reflect extremely archaic currents of thought. On the other hand, it aims at overcoming the impermanence and transitoriness inexorably linked with earthly life. Thus it accords fully with the atmosphere of the late Vedic period in which it originated or at least assumed its definitive formulation. Jainism resembles the various *mārga*, or "ways to salvation", in that actions produce consequences, the effects of which go beyond the limits of a life, and determine an endless succession of existences. So the ancient optimism has disappeared. Man no longer aspires to the lengthening or the glorification of the earthly life, but recognises as his goal the overcoming of the human condition through the exaltation now of one, now of another of his own activities or abilities.

The negation of a validity proper to existence itself is expressed in the practice of asceticism. This is one of the most marked features of Jainism. It is probably of pre-Aryan origin and is common to many of the Brahmanic and Hindu currents which use different theoretical foundations as a base for the mortification of the flesh which so strikes a foreign visitor to India. But, while asceticism is the last and indispensable stage on the way to liberation, not less important is the personal striving for moral perfection, which prepares one for asceticism and is expressed above all in the absolute observance of the principle of *ahiṃsā*. This means, first of all, the "not harming" of any living being, but is then extended in its positive aspect to resemble *dayā*, active "compassion" for all living beings.

In its ethical imposition Jainism is closely related to Buddhism, with which it is roughly contemporary. Indeed, for some time it was confused with Buddhism. Effectively, just like primitive Buddhism, Jainism is, at first, an essentially monastic religion and atheistic and heterodox with respect to the Vedic-Brahmanic tradition, being repelled by its cruel sacrifices and the supremacy claimed by the Brahmans. In both religions however, the existence of a laity leads to a re-evaluation of social life, with the practical acceptance of the caste system. It leads also to the forming of a ritual, which is often inspired by the Hindu world. But there are much deeper and more irreconcileable differences between Buddhism and Jainism not only in tradition and organisation, but also in theory and practice: for example, the Buddhists believe that there is nothing permanent, and reject asceticism as "unseemly and useless".

Centuries of contact and reciprocal influences have attenuated the differences between Jainas and Hindus, but some attitudes of the former have remained constant. This is the case with a certain materialistic and mechanical quality in the conception of action, which gives rise to precepts aiming more at renouncement than morality. In any case, the assertion that a conscious withdrawal from action leads to a more favourable destiny is canonical. Attention is directed, mainly if not wholly, to the perfectioning of the individual; for instance, birth control is today advocated because family preoccupations distract one from meditation; moreover vegetarianism would be very difficult in an overpopulated world. Finally the adversion to soaring metaphysical flights is typical. The Jainas are faithful to a sort of archaic realism firmly based on common sense. They accept the surrounding world in its immediate appearance and analyse with minute pedantry every fact of mythological constructions and experience (hence the enumerations, the subdivisions and distinctions typical of their systematic works.) So they arrive at the assertion of the indeterminateness of being (*anekāntavāda*), according to which it is possible to formulate many judgements on one object, all of them true but all partial, in that they consider only one of the many aspects of a mutable reality, which is in a continual state of becoming.

For the upholders of Jainism, the doctrine of the relative pluralism of the aspects of reality constitutes the best proof of its scientific attitude towards life. I think it reveals an attitude similar to that which induces primitive Buddhism to shun any ontological enquiry in that it does not serve the purpose of the salvation of man. Indeed man and his destiny are at the centre of Jaina doctrine. Man may be guided onto the right path by doctrine, but, in a last analysis, he must rely on himself alone to carry out that striving for moral elevation which will rescue him for ever from the dominion of matter.

II. History of the Jaina Church

For Jainas, doctrine, which comprehends the eternal law of the eternal truth, is immutable. However it may be obscured by superstitions and heresies, as the various cosmic epochs are subject to a gradual and continuous mutation in the conditions of physical and moral life. To restore the integral knowledge of doctrine to its pristine condition therefore, from time to time there appear twenty-four Tīrthaṃkaras, "builders of the ford" which enables one to pass beyond the ocean of existences. Of these, only the last two, Pārśva and Mahāvīra, are considered to be historical personages. The other prophets completely lack individuality and are millions of years distant in the past. This fact seems to lend substance to the conviction that the church organisation and doctrine, which we know in the form imparted by the ascetic Mahāvīra about 500 B.C., in fact originate in an antiquity lost in the world of myth. Pārśva was born into a warrior family of Benares two and a half century before Mahāvīra, and fasted to death at the age of a hundred. He founded a community of monks and laymen bound by four vows: not to harm, not to lie, not to steal and not to possess. Traditional information about Pārśva seems quite credible. His existence appears to be further confirmed by the fact that Jaina writings distinguish the followers of Pārśva from those of Mahāvīra. Perhaps the former may be identified with the Nirgranthas, the "released" from all earthly cares, who were already known and widerspread at the time of Buddha, Mahāvīra's contemporary. On the other hand, the claim that church and doctrine have been immutable at all times is evidently confuted, if, two hundred and fifty years after their foundation, they had to be reformed to escape a rapid and inglorious end.

Vardhamāna Mahāvīra belonged to the tribe of the Jñātṛ (hence the epithet of Jñātṛputra or Nātaputta by which he is known in Buddhist texts). He was the son of Siddhārtha, the king of a small aristocratic republic and was born at Kuṇḍagrāma, a suburb of Vaiśālī (the modern Besārh) in Magadha (Bihar). According to tradition, he lived between 599 and 527 B.C., but it is more probable that his life lasted from 549 (or 540) to 477 (or 468) B.C. (Hemacandra, basing himself on ancient material, places his death a hundred and fifty-five years before the accession to the throne of Candragupta Maurya. This took place in 322 or in 313 B.C.). He soon became the subject of a literary tradition, which contains numerous analogies with the history of other personages, divine or deified, and bears witness to the substantial unity of the milieu. As is narrated for Kṛṣṇa, he was transferred from the womb of a brahman's wife to the womb of the consort of Siddhārtha, as a Tirthaṁkara must be born into "families which are noble, elevated, and of royal origin". The name Vardhamāna is interpreted as "the Augmenter" (more exactly "he who augments"), because of the benefits he caused in his father's kingdom, even before being born. From his youth he was conscious of the transitoriness of human things, but he was able to begin a monastic life only at the age of thirty. At that age, he left his wife and daughter, tore out his hair, and began to wear a cassock. However, after thirteen months he ceased wearing even that. For twelve years he practised a harsh asceticism and exposed himself to the mercy of the elements and to the maltreatment of hostile peoples. Finally, after long meditations and after having extirpated in himself love and hate, desire and repugnance, he attained absolute knowledge, the revelation of a method for escaping from universal suffering. From that moment, he became a *Jina*, "conqueror" of the world and his own passions, a *Kevalin*, "omniscient", an *Arhat*, "venerable", and a *Mahāvīra*, "a great hero". For thirty years he dedicated himself to preaching, wandering around Magadha. He never ceased, except during the rainy seasons. These he spent in a different place each year, and was honourably received by the members of the warrior aristocracy to which he himself belonged. The places he stayed at are listed in the canonical texts. He never met Buddha who was active at the same time and in the same places. He disputed with his erstwhile disciple, Gośāla Maskariputra. The latter had left him to become the head of the ancient, deterministic and fatalistic sect of the Ājīvikas, from which some particulars of the doctrine and practice of Jainism may derive.

Mahāvīra died at the age of seventy-two, probably shortly after Buddha. Canonical writings claim that he left a community of more than a half a million people. This figure is undoubtedly exaggerated, but Mahāvīra's preaching must have been succesful. How else could one explain the lively and continual polemics of the Buddhist texts against the followers of Nātaputta? In spite of his rigid character and his upholding of the most extreme asceticism, Mahāvīra was nevertheless disposed to share his achieved omniscience with everyone. He used the dialects of the people, and could avail himself of a spellbinding eloquence, scanty traces of which remain in the canonical literature. As the heir and reformer of the church of Pārśva, he established a fifth vow, the explicit obligation of chastity, and confirmed the distinction between monks and laymen, the latter being bound to less intense vows. He was aware of human necessities and weaknesses, and so turned his attention above all to a system of rules, with minute prescriptions regarding duties, customs and offices, which anticipate the casuistry of the mediaeval *śrāvakācāras*, "rules for laymen".

The attribute of omniscience which enabled the prophet to acquire sacred knowledge directly, disappeared with Mahāvīra's second successor. There began then the transmission of the sacred texts. At first this was oral; the texts were first written, in what was already a mutilated form, at the time of Bhadrabāhu, who died about 300 B.C. This age also saw the beginning of the schism between the Śvetāmbaras, the "white-dressed", and the Digambaras, the "air-dressed". It became definitive about 80 A.D., and still exists today. The latter were the descendants of those who had emigrated into Mysore under the leadership of Bhadrabāhu, driven by a famine. They did not recognize the canon established at the council of Pāṭaliputra by their fellow-believers who had remained in Magadha. They also wanted to perform a vow of nudity, which had been observed but not imposed by Mahāvīra. Their intransigence is shown also by the fact that they deny the possibility of salvation to women, who are not allowed to practice nudity. In addition, they reject the tradition of Mahāvīra's marriage, and of any contact of his with the Brahmanic world.

The information given in the religious writings is partly confirmed by the dedicatory inscriptions in grottos and monasteries (such as the edicts of Aśoka cut in the rock at Toprā in Punjab and the epigraph at Hāthigumphā of king Khāra Vela, who reigned in Orissa perhaps towards the end of 2nd century B.C.), by archeological evidence (such as the tablets of the second century B.C. found around Mathurā, which are important for the history of the cult), and by the remains of later monuments. The writings list among the faithful Candragupta Maurya, Aśoka and Samprati (about 200 B.C.). Samprati is said to have sent the first missions to southern India. The names of many other sovereigns who reigned in the first millennium A.D. in Gujarat, Deccan and in Dravidic India are also given. However, if one bears in mind the impartial tolerance in religious matters practised by Indian monarchs, it seems probable that they felt a mild sympathy rather than true conviction and adhesion to the principles of the faith, a sympathy prompted also by a desire to be on good terms with the economically powerful Jaina communities.

Both the Digambaras, whose main centre was at Śravaṇa Beḷgoḷa in Mysore, and the Śvetāmbaras, who flourished in Western India, divided into dioceses in the course of the centuries. These were called by the former, *saṃgha*, and by the latter, *gaccha*, and were characterised by different customs and tendencies. The Digambaras recognized as authoritative for their sect the works of certain patriarchs, such as Vaṭṭakera and Kundakunda (2nd century A.D.), Samantabhadra (5th century) and Akalaṅka (9th century). On the contrary the Śvetāmbaras established their canon at the council of Valabhī in Gujarat (980 or 993 years after the death of Mahāvīra). This canon (*Āgama* or *Siddhānta*) comprehends 11 *aṅgas*, "members", 12 *uvaṅgas*, "secondary limbs", 10 *paiṇṇas*, "scattered" passages, 6 *cheyasuttas*, "rules of discipline"?, 5 *mūlasuttas*, "fundamental rules"?, and 2 isolated texts. The first, second, and fifth *aṅga*, respectively *Āyāra*, *Sūyagaḍa* and *Viyāhapannatti*, are among the most important works. The *Āyāra* contains "the norms for behaviour", the *Sūyagaḍa*, "information on the various doctrines", the *Viyāhapannatti*, "the announcement of the explanations". Also important are the so-called *Kalpasūtra*, "norms of discipline", which is part of the *cheyasuttas* and is attributed to Bhadrabāhu, and the first *mūlasutta*, *Uttarajjhāyā*, "the continuation of the exposition", a sort of anthology on the ideal of the ascetic life. Some parts of the canon are very ancient. Its internal contradictions (e.g. the mention of the vow of nudity) lead one to suppose an absolute respect for texts of venerable tradition. The prakrit used is based on the spoken dialect of Magadha, with more or less evident elements of the māhārāṣṭrī, the later western dialect preferred by the Jaina authors. The canon, which is tiring and monotonous to read, is intended to be a systematic and definitive encyclopaedia of sacred knowledge, and also of profane. It should therefore be the object of interpretation, and not of completion. However, an increased speculative maturity and polemical necessities imposed an adaptation and deepening of the texts. Very full commentaries were produced both in prakrit and in sanskrit, together with independent treatises, almost always in sanskrit. Umāsvāti,

Siddhasena Divākara, Haribhadra, Hemacandra and Malliṣeṇa are worthy of mention. Umāsvāti is claimed by both the Digambaras and the Śvetāmbaras. He may have lived in the third century A.D., i.e. before the establishment of the canon. Using the style of the Brahmanic *sūtras* he wrote and commented on the *Tattvārthādhigamasūtra*, "the aphorisms to attain knowledge of the truths". Siddhasena Divākara (7th century) was the first to systematize the logic, which from that time on was largely cultivated together with epistemology. Both Haribhadra (8th century) and Hemacandra (1088-1172) produced abundant writings. The former was of Brahmanic origin and education; the latter was active in every branch of knowledge. A short work by Hemacandra in praise of the last Tīrthaṃkara was commented on by Malliṣeṇa Sūri (13th century). He enlarged his own commentary, *Syādvādamañjarī*, "The flower-spray of the Quodammodo doctrine", into a complete treatise, which, among other things, is interesting for its closely-reasoned confutation of opposing systems. Hemacandra enjoyed great prestige in public life. He converted Kumārapāla, the sovereign of Gujarat, who was led to create a model Jaina state, in which the principle of *ahiṃsā* was strictly observed.

Jainism continued to receive the protection of some princes. The faithful continued to give imposing manifestations of their zeal, building splendid temples. But the greatest prosperity of Jainism was in twelfth century already drawing to an end. There were bloody but isolated persecutions, especially at the hands of the Vīraśaivas, but the decline of Jainism was due more to the success of the Brahmanic counter-reformation, which succeeded in reconciling philosophical speculations with myths and intuitions of the peoples of various origins, and also to the increased sway of emotional and mystic currents based on the *bhakti*, or devotion and trust in Viṣṇu, Śiva and their hypostases. Finally, the violent entry into Indian life of the rigid Islamic monotheism destroyed monasteries and enforced conversion without distinction between Hindus, Jainas and Buddhists. The Buddhists suffered a mortal blow with the destruction of their universities and monasteries. Jainism, however, although very restricted, managed to endure and even underwent occasional revivals, for example under Akbar, whom the Jainas consider as belonging to their faith.

The reasons for the different fates in India of the sister-religions are certainly many and various. Among them was the economic power which had always belonged to the Jainas, and the substantial immobility of doctrine through the centuries. Indian Buddhism lacked both these attributes. However, what decided the issue seems to have been the different organisation of the two communities. In contrast to the Buddhists, the Jaina laity always felt themselves closely linked to their monks, whom they acknowledged as indispensable guides for the preservation of the faith necessary for salvation. Thus, there was never lacking an active solidarity which enabled the Jainas to endure the greatest trials.

Another indubitable sign of the vitality of the Jaina religion are the reform movements. These aimed at removing various abuses, or at rejecting cult practices which derived from Hinduism and were considered unworthy. Sometimes they assumed the character of veritable schisms, within the two great divisions of Śvetāmbaras and Digambaras. The latter had to give up nudity, in public at least. Among the Śvetāmbaras, one may note the Āgamikas, the Sthānakavāsīs and the Saṃvegīs. The first of these arose in the twelfth century and are hostile to the cult of Śrutadevatā, the personification of the holy scriptures. The Sthānakavāsīs, "dwellers in private houses," or Ḍhuṇḍhiyās, "seekers" of the truth, arose in the fifteenth century, and were in turn reformed in the seventeenth. They reject a part of the canon. In their iconoclasm (possibly influenced by analogous Islamic conceptions) they resemble the Terāpanthīs, "the followers of the system of the first thirteen supporters of the reform." The Terāpanthīs arose in 1761, and desired a return to the severity of ancient times. The Sthānakavāsīs also oppose worship in temples. Finally the Saṃvegīs, "the agitated ones," who wear a yellow robe, and count among their founders the famous and prolific philosopher Yaśovijaya (17th century), are respected even today for the purity of their lives and their great culture.

We shall speak of the present situation later on.

III. Eternal Cosmic Law and Transitory Divinities

The existence of a supreme divinity, unique, purely spiritual, omniscient and omnipotent, creator and ruler of wordly things, is resolutely denied by the Jainas. Indeed, the attempt to show the futility of every traditional conception of the divine has been an important part of Jaina polemical writing of every age down to the modern apologists and advocates of the ancient faith.

The universe was not created and is eternal. Just as it is impossible to show rationally that the universe will one day be destroyed, so the concepts of a creation *ex nihilo* and of emanation are equally obscure. The former, indeed, reveals a contradiction in terms at once, when it affirms that the non-existent becomes existent. As far as regards emanation, one should have to suppose a passage from the pure, perfect spirit to impure, defective matter. Let us grant for a moment the existence of a creator who has not himself been created (but the postulated eternity of such a being is not a valid argument for excluding the eternal existence of many substances). What motives could have induced this completely perfect being to create the universe? There could obviously have been no desire, as he would have attained all his ends previously. He could not have been moved by compassion for creatures unable otherwise to achieve liberation, as, before the creation, neither suffering nor sufferers existed. If this god had created the world to amuse himself, then he would be like a child.

If other substances existed side by side with the divinity, they could not be inert, as the mode of being of substances lies in the accomplishment of their own function. Furthermore, as god is a pure light, there lacks any material device to serve as the base of the activity of the divine thought and will, directed not towards creation but solely towards the dominion of things. Finally, if the universe is an illusion, then either this illusion constitutes, in a sense, a second reality, or, if it is not real, it cannot produce concrete effects.

Although this world is not the worst possible, joys rapidly give way to endless unhappiness, cruelty and injustice. Every creature is at times the cause or the victim of such things, from the animals, who kill and are killed cruelly, to man, exposed to the dark terrors of a destiny he cannot foresee. If one believes that sufferings is a test of behaviour and thus of the capacity for salvation of individuals, then neither the means nor the purpose seem worthy of an omniscient and merciful god. If one considers that everything is determined by the previous actions of the creatures themselves, then the function of a god, who oversees the ineluctable process of just reward, does not appear indispensable, and autonomous even less.

So the Jainas deny the existence of god through logical considerations; or rather, they reject that mystical impulse which alone permits the intuition of god, beyond any rationality. Nevertheless, they are equally convinced that the problem of the universe and of the dwellers thereon transcends the ambit of any single life. They hold that the reason for the continuous becoming of the cosmos is to be found in the characteristics of its increate, constituent elements. This becoming is determined by *karman*, the law of the just reward for actions effected. *Karman* is enough to explain the fate of individuals, the reality of evil and suffering, and is necessary and inexorable like all laws of nature.

Only souls that have attained their essential perfection, which excludes any contact with matter, are freed from *karman*. The Siddhas, "the Perfect Ones," are the true divinities for the Jainas, and serve as psychologically valid examples of the possibility of obtaining liberation. Prayer, in the sense of a request for help in need, or as an expression of trusting self abandonment and hope, cannot be directed towards them, as they are completely detached from all earthly contingencies, and can only be objects for meditation. However, the human need to have help and consolation from acknowledgedly superior forces has led to a compromise solution, which is similar to the Buddhist position and is codified in the canon. Thus there is conceded the existence of a myriad of transient divinities. These are souls whose past actions have permitted them to enjoy happiness and the possession of superhuman possibilities, but this state is by no means definitive. They are honoured in Jaina temples, and requests for purely material favours are made to them. Yet these gods are subject to the law of *karman* and can achieve emancipation only through the human condition. This is therefore rescued from the impermanence which distinguishes it because of the possibility, which it alone possesses, of realizing the potential divinity in the innermost nature of every man.

IV. Religious Activity

Religion is a total mode for the interpreting and living of life. Its subject is man, who is an indivisible whole of thoughts, feelings and volitive impulses which determine actions. Thus, the religious fact will reveal itself in the intellectual field, as an attempt to explain the origin and purpose of the various appearances which surround us, in the emotive-sentimental field, as the expression of a reaction before superior forces, however they may be considered, and in the practical field, as conduct conforming to a determinate conception of life. Doctrine, cult and ethics are the three components on which every religion is based.

A. *Doctrine*

The systematic treatises (e.g. *Tattvārthādhigamasūtra*, which is even today considered extremely authoritative by all Jainas) catalogue the entire contents of the doctrine in seven "fundamental truths", which are: 1) *jīva*, "spiritual substance", 2) *ajīva*, "inanimate substances", 3) *āsrava*, "afflux" of matter into the spirit, 4) *bandha*, "slavery", 5) *saṃvara*, "halting" of the afflux of matter, 6) *nirjarā*, "elimination" of the matter accumulated in the soul, 7) *mokṣa*, "liberation".

Everything which exists falls into six classes of substances (*dravya*), which are divided into *jīva* and *ajīva*, and are elementary and eternal, the permanent subject of mutable chance. Even their name (from the root *dru*, "to flow") seems to place the idea of "becoming" within the idea of "being". Continual evolution (*pariṇāma*) with all its logical consequences, is, in fact, typical of archaic Jaina substantialism, according to which everything exists and everything becomes, just like gold in a crucible, which may change state, but never ceases to exist even for an instant. Substances are space (*ākāśa*), the necessary conditions for movement and rest (*dharma* and *adharma*), time (*kāla*), matter (*pudgala*) and souls (*jīva*). They are all incorporeal, except matter, and all inanimate, except the souls. These latter are infinite in number. They are all the same, when they are metaphysically pure. They pervade every apparition, and are conceived of as being a sort of fine substance and as being able to expand or contract and receive or reject the influx of matter. Time determines chronological evolution; space and the necessary conditions for movement and rest allow localisation, motion and stasis, and fill the whole universe, with which, however, they are not identical. They fill it as the flames of a thousand candles fill a room, but are not the room itself. Matter is made up of an infinity of atoms, possessing sense, smell, taste and colour. They aggregate among themselves, and are eternally united with the incorporeal souls, to which they adhere like grains of dust on an oil-sprinkled surface. From them, all the phenomena of the empirical world originate, which are destined to dissolution and death like all composite products.

Fortytwo different channels conduct the afflux (*āsrava*) into souls of particles of matter, or rather of energy impulses of material nature, which are transformed into *karman*, the mysterious determinant of every condition of life. Souls lose the four perfections proper to their nature (sight, consciousness, happiness, and infinite possibilities of action), and they acquire others, as happens in nature with water for example, which is composed of two gaseous elements. Thus the new empirical creature which arises from the union of soul and matter finds itself immersed in the limitations, in the continual becoming, and in the differentiations, which are proper to matter, that is, in a state of slavery (*bandha*) which lasts until the bond which keeps the soul in symbiosis and synergy with elements extraneous to its true nature is broken. Souls are no longer undifferentiated, but classified (in a way similar to the Ājīvikas, from which the archaic conception may derive) according to the *leśyā*, which is a sign revealed above all in the coloration, and otherwise imperceptible to our senses, and which continually varies from black to azure, to grey, yellow, pink and white. They are also endowed with a varying number of bodies. In these we may see the development of the primitive belief in the existence of many souls. Besides the "material body", the only visible one, there may exist the "transformation body", which can be varied at will by the possessor, the "body of transposition" to inaccessible regions, the "igneous body", made up of condensed energy and believed by the mass to be the cause of digestion. Finally there is the "body of the *karman*".

The ancient conception which holds that action infects the soul with a determinate substance, that produces effects appropriate to it, until it is repelled by a suitable procedure, finds a methodical exposition in the doctrine of *karman*, as formulated by the Jainas. *Karman*, which is of a material nature, binds the spirit to the material world, i.e. to the *saṃsāra*. It carries out its action in eight ways which, in turn, are divided into one hundred and forty-eight categories. It is consumed only when the effects, good or bad, which its quality has conditioned, are no more. Although *karman* determines the psychic qualities of the individual, and thus forms predispositions, it does not completely annul the aspiration to be happy and the ability to distinguish between good and evil, which are considered innate in man, albeit this belief is not shown to be true by demonstration. They are regarded as the residue and glow of original perfections in the incarnate soul. In this way the principle of free-will is saved. Indeed, the conviction that man may decide his own destiny, and may never flee from his own responsibilities is insisted upon, and is one of the most noble features of Jainism.

Karman has no beginning (as the soul, if once it had been pure, would never have descended into the sansaric becoming). It is also endless, if we consider the way of its production. It is produced by five causes: error, the failure to observe precepts, negligence, passions, and *yoga*, which is taken by Jainas to be "the activity of the body, the mind and the word." The strength of the hold of *karman* is in direct proportion to the intensity of the passions (*kaṣāya*, properly "resin"). *Yoga* cannot be eliminated for the very reason that the soul is associated with matter, and takes part, albeit passively, in objective reality. The soul is agitated by objective reality in a way which can be compared to the expectation of a man who has some food placed before him. Thus, in the natural order of things, it is not possible to detach oneself from matter and attain liberation (*mokṣa*).

The halting (*saṃvara*) of the causes of the arising of *karman* and the expulsion (*nirjarā*) of the *karman* accumulated, constitute the specific object of the doctrine of salvation preached by the Tīrthaṃkaras. It obliges one to accept totally the "three jewels", in order for the soul, the only conscious element, to return or better still to ascend to natural purity. This reveals its dogmatic character, which, in any case, is inevitable in a doctrine which founds its validity on the presumption of omniscience attained by the Tīrthaṃkaras. "Right faith, right knowledge and right conduct are the way to liberation" (*Tattvārthādhigamasūtra*, I, 1). Right faith is the full adhesion to the fundamental truths according to the preaching of Mahāvīra. One attains it through right knowledge, which is peculiar to the omniscient, who may transmit it to the faithful. Finally, right conduct depends on the observation of the precepts enunciated by Mahāvīra, and gathered together in the canonic writings.

The soul ascends a flight of fourteen steps arranged logically according to the degree of increasing purity. So doing, it frees itself little by little from error and acquires the right faith, accompanied by an ever increasing degree of control, renunciation, and of inward concentration. Finally, by means of the "way of the ascetic, the destroyer of *karman*," the soul achieves its metaphysical purity, recovers its original perfections, and is eternally free and blessed.

B. *Ethics*

The mechanism which brings about the slavery of the soul might lead one to think that the only means of liberation would be the complete abstention from action, i.e. suicide. In fact, suicide is still admitted today, but only as the last step in the process of purification. Otherwise it is condemned as a flight from responsibility, and in any case would not solve the problem of the destruction of the *karman* already accumulated. Life cannot be avoided, but only death is inertia. Therefore, Jaina doctrine, like other ways to salvation, is also concerned, one might say, with the re-evaluation of the morally pure action. This is chosen by a natural disposition of the soul, and produces a smaller quantity of *karman*, which lacks the adhesive strength deriving from passions. But in their generally negative formulation, the moral precepts well express the tendency towards renunciation which is a part of all Indian doctrines. "Abstention from harming other creatures, abstention from falsity, from appropriating other people's things, from sexual union, from cupidity of possession, from wrath, from pride, from fallacy, avidity, love and hate, abstention from strife, from denigration, from delation, from slander, from pleasure and from repugnance, from deceit and falsehood, and finally the keeping distant from error, which is like a thorn, enable souls to elevate themselves" (*Viyāhapannatti*, I, 9).

Having obtained *saṃvara*, one must achieve *nirjarā*. The maturing of *karman* which awaits the production of its effect must be made quicker, or else it will recede farther and farther in time making a new rebirth necessary. Just like the mango fruit exposed to the heat of the sun, so the fruit of action, the *karman*, by means of the heat of asceticism (*tapas*) is brought to an earlier ripening, its effects are exhausted and it is eliminated. As *karman* is material, one realizes how Jaina asceticism accomplishes inhuman practices, even arriving at suicide through inanition (*saṃlekhanā*), in order to cleanse (*saṃlikh*) the soul of everything linked with matter. After this event, the soul lacks the body, but still has dimensions. However, these are immaterial and are equal to two thirds of the dimensions it had in its last existence (this is in proportion to the shrinking of the body after death). The soul ascends in a straight line to the highest point of the universe. There, in company with other liberated souls, it is completely detached from the world and its vicissitudes, and enjoys all the perfections which the *Upaniṣads* attribute to the Absolute, with the exception of oneness: thus the divine is multiplied into an infinity of autonomous monads.

Only the monk may practice asceticism and thus hope to attain emancipation. Those whose faith is firmly rooted, but who are not induced to renounce the world, may still become lay adherents of the doctrine. The merits they acquire will perhaps allow them to become monks in a future existence. Thus the Jaina church is composed of four "dignities" (*tīrtha*): male and female monks and male and female members of the laity, with bonds and rules varying in intensity of observance according to the condition chosen.

The five great vows (1st not to harm any living being, 2nd not to lie, 3rd not to steal, 4th chastity, 5th the renunciation of any possession) are pronounced at the moment of the consecration after the novitiate, which generally lasts four months. From that moment on, the monk can own only a robe, a wooden bowl to gather food, a water filter, a handkerchief for his mouth (both the filter and the handkerchief are to prevent the involuntary swallowing of some microscopic being, while the handkerchief is also to avoid harming the spirit of the air), a walking staff, a broom to clear the road of any creature, and sometimes a book which symbolizes the absent master. The precept of *ahiṃsā* is observed with extreme rigour. It imposes a strictly vegetarian diet, and has led to the building of hospitals for old and sick animals (*panjar poḷ*), with wards for worms and other unclean beasts. Originally this prescription was of a formal and magic character (the most ancient parts of the canon allow the eating of meat or fish, as long as there is no responsibility for the butchering or preparation of these foods). Later *ahiṃsā* is justified with the conviction that everything in the universe is animated. Today *ahiṃsā* is still considered the foundation of any civilised cohabitation.

The five great vows and the recommendation to practice the positive virtues which correspond to them, especially benevolence to everyone and compassion for the afflicted, are accompanied by other explicative precepts: 1) "control" of the sense organs; 2) "scrupolous attention"; 3) observance of the ten "duties", among which there are gentleness, humility, voluntary poverty, and discipline; 4) the twelve "reflections" on the transitoriness of life and on the method for attaining liberation; 5) "endurance" of the twenty-two hardships, sufferings and privations, both physical and moral, to which the monk is exposed; 6) "right conduct", exemplified in the life of Mahāvīra.

Anyone, of any cast or race, as long as they are more than seven and a half years old, and without physical or juridical impediments, can enter the communities of monks. Each of these communities acknowledges the authority of a master (*ācārya*) as competent in disciplinary and doctrinal matters. Each is part of a certain diocese or school. The monk must lead a wandering life, except in the rainy season when air and soil are swarming with animals. At that time he takes shelter in the refuges which serve as gathering places for laymen as well, who are thus able to receive religious teaching. Day and night are carefully divided into periods destined to the asking for alms, feeding, study, meditation, teaching, mortification of the body, and confession. Only from the followers of the faith, the monk may receive boiled water, i.e. without any vitality, and the remnants of food, which he may not preserve. He cannot eat after sunset, when "scrupolous attention" could not exist. He is not to have the slightest care for his body, and must submit from his consecration on to having his head shaven (in ancient times it was customary to tear the hair out, following the example of Mahāvīra). Any inobservance of the rule must be revealed in the morning and evening confession, which lays down schematic formulas of remorse for unconscious transgressions, as these, too, have objectively taken place, and thus produce the contaminating effect. Confession is followed by penitence, which may involve the renouncing of a certain number of meals, the recitation of formulas or hymns, the loss of rank in the hierarchy, and even the temporary or permanent exclusion from the order. This discipline prepares one for the practice of asceticism, both outward and inward, by which one arrives at pure meditation, free from any participation in worldly things. The same rules are valid for nuns, who have always been esteemed for their deeply moral lives, in contrast to the female members of other communities.

The laity have been induced by the exigencies of practical life to temper the precepts with a certain empiricism. The fourth vow is taken to oblige one to be faithful to one's spouse, and the fifth to require moderation in the acquisition of worldly goods. It is also evident that the preparation of food and drink causes the laity to transgress against the precept of *ahiṃsā*, while the monks are able not to do so. No meat or fish may be consumed. The faithful should also avoid the use of certain excitants, such as honey and the alcoholic drinks (furthermore, fermentation leads to the destruction of too many animate beings). They should avoid foods which are held to be the dwelling of many souls, such as the tubers in general, or too rich in seeds, such as the *uḍumbara* (*Ficus Glomerata*). There also exist supplementary vows and supererogatory vows. The layman imposes on himself obligations and limitations which regard nourishment, activity, movement and meditation. In this way he avoids the immediate occasions for sin and perturbation, and approaches the monastic state temporarily, amid conditions which may be more difficult in that he remains exposed to worldly temptations. There is no express prohibition of the practice of agriculture, but it is subject to many restrictions. On the contrary, the digging of wells, traffic in arms and ivory, as well as hunting and fishing are forbidden as they involve the destruction of living beings. Therefore the Jainas have preferred to turn their energies to trading, business and the liberal professions, while the great wealth they have handed down has made them more influential than their scanty number would seem to warrant. The Jaina laity have always been attached to their faith. They have generously maintained the monastic communities, while keeping a control over their regulations and morality. They have profusely spent their wealth on the construction of sanctuaries and the celebration of rites for the edification of believers, and as a testimony to their own prosperity and the strength of their church.

C. *Cult*

Perfectioning and purification are strictly individual. However, the existence of a laity soon made it expedient to take into account the exigencies and customs of the environment from which the proselytes came. They themselves were inclined to seek help and comfort in the face of the difficulties of life in the solidarity of their fellows. Thus the veneration for superhuman personages, the service in the temples, the ceremonies and the processions, the symbology and the so-called sacraments are not very unlike the manifestations of other Indian religious communities. Indeed, in what concerns ritual, Jainism has always been rather tolerant, in contrast with the rigid conservatism of the doctrine. For instance Khāra Vela, who was mentioned above, although he was Jaina, did not refuse to admit sacred Hindu ceremonies. In any case the acceptance of rites from other religions, as long as they do not conflict with the fundamentals of the faith, is justified by Somadeva (10th century) and by Hemacandra, although it is rejected by later writers.

In the most rigorous orthodoxy the cult of the Tīrthaṃkaras and of the Siddhas, who are not accessible to prayer, has a purely subjective value, in that it offers the faithful an example to imitate. It consists in the praising of and meditating on their virtues. The exertion of the believers is aided by the contemplation of images, which have evolved into fixed types (the Digambaras represent Jinas in an erect position, while the Śvetāmbaras show them seated with their legs crossed). These images are opposed by the iconoclastic sects, but must have already existed in the fourth century B.C., according to the inscription of Khāra Vela. They are distinguished only by the animal or symbol peculiar to each Tīrthaṃkara (e.g. the lion for Mahāvīra, the snake for Pārśva), and are placed in houses or in the niches of temples by the side of the figures of the transitory divinities of the Brahmanic tradition. Only to these latter can requests for help and favours be addressed. Before the images of Jinas the monks practice only the "inward honouring", i.e. meditation, while the laymen perform the "honouring of the limbs" and the "supreme honouring". These consist of the care of the statues, the burning of incense, the swinging to and fro of lights, and the offering of vegetables, accompanied by the recitation of hymns and sacred formulas. In order to negate the apparent idolatry of such practices, the offering is considered as the renunciation of what is offered, or as a prompting to elevated meditations (e.g. rice = *akṣata* appears as the symbol of the eternal dwelling = *akṣayapada*).

During the ceremonies the faithful wear the holy triple cord, a symbol of the "three jewels", and they decorate their foreheads with a heart-shaped mark. They frequently use a rosary of a hundred and eight beads, and votive tablets, bearing engraved sacred figures and formulas. The latter are similar to the Brahmanic and Buddhist *mantras* and also derive from a magic vision of life. The symbol of the religion is the *svastika*, surmounted by three dots and a half-moon. The four arms symbolize the four states of rebirth (human, divine, ferine and demoniacal); the three dots represent the "three jewels", and the half-moon recalls the liberation.

There are other actions which, as they are carried out publicly, belong to the ritual as well. They refer rather to the process of personal purification. For example, there are the six *āvaśyakas*, "indispensable" formulas for the confirmation of vows. They are recited one or more times a day. It is thought that certain postures facilitate concentration. Finally the so-called sacraments (*saṃskāra* or *kriyā*) are ritual. These began to be commonly used in the ninth century (when they are described for the first time by Jinasena). They mark the most important events of life, through conception, birth, and adolescence, to the exequies, which are sometimes followed by rites and offerings, which are rejected by the most rigorous Jainas.

There have been found the remains of Jaina *stūpas* or funeral mounds, dating from the centuries before Christ, but there doesn't seem ever to have been a cult of reliquies. Many places, especially hills and mountains, are sacred inasmuch as they are linked with the memory of sacred personages or of celebrated masters. Temples and sanctuaries are quite numerous, and sometimes constitute veritable cities, such as those on the mountains Girnar and Shatrunjaya (Kathiawar) and Abu (Rajputana). The *beṭṭas* in Mysore are characteristic in their sobriety. They are uncovered enclosures around colossal statues.

Pilgrimages are recommended, but ablutions, in ancient times at least, are not granted any purifying value. Ceremonies and processions, accompanied by dances, often coincide with popular Hindu festivals, but are interpreted differently. The cult of the *yakṣas* and of the *yakṣiṇīs* is widespread. These are a sort of semi-god and assist the Tīrthaṃkaras. The concept of the *bhakti* appeared among the laity and a tantrism also developed which degenerated later into forms of white and black magic, of which certain monks were considered the dreaded masters.

However, though there are the inevitable but isolated degenerations, it may be asserted that the ritual is only a concession to the needs of the laity for prestige and emotive satisfaction. This is confirmed by the fact that the ritual is entrusted to the *Pūjārīs*, who are not Jaina as a rule. It is almost as if the ritual were scorned by the monks, who, instead, reserve for themselves the work of teaching, which is imparted in the already mentioned refuges or *upāśrayas*.

The character and also the limit of the Jaina religion, which aims at attaining an exclusively personal purification by means of mortification and renunciation, is in any case evident in the most important religious occasion of the year, the *Paryuṣaṇa*. This takes place at the beginning of the rainy season. For ten days or more the devout pass their time in meditation, in the carrying out of ascetic practices, and in the contemplation of the Perfect Ones, whose aloof clarity, devoid of all perturbation and suffering, but also without any activity and compassion, they hope one day to attain.

V. The Conception of Man

(Nature, Creation, Surroundings and History of Humanity)

Jainism has not a really redemptionist vision, as the innate qualities of the soul were not lost after an initial state of perfection, but realize themselves, one might say, historically, through the dissolution of every particle of matter which has always impugned the soul. But the antinomy between spiritual and material, and the preference given to the former, determine the aspiration to reject the world by overcoming it.

However, one should emphasize that only man can reach liberation.

The gods have no impulses towards perfection, while the animals obey their instincts. This really does place man at the centre of the universe, and confers on him a supremacy based on the free choice of action, not a whit weakened by the predestinationist hints easily definable in the theory of the *bhavyas* and the *abhavyas*, as well as in the essence of the rigid mechanism of the law of *karman*.

Below the souls migrating through the cycle of existences there are the *nigoḍas*, very small beings which are neither developed nor can be perceived. They are a kind of vegetal spirit, which can, however, without any special reason, pass to the sphere of perfectibility. Thus the cosmos will never be deserted. Among the migrating souls, some (*abhavya*) are condemned to remain forever ensnared by erroneous doctrines. Others (*bhavya*) have the innate capacity to save themselves. *Karman* determines their incarnation in immobile beings (*sthāvara*), possessing only the sense of touch, and mobile beings (*trasa*), which can possess 2,3,4,5 senses (taste, smell, sight, hearing). It decides the condition of existence (human, divine, ferine and demoniacal) and thus the mode of birth. In the case of man the birth takes place by means of the conceiving of an embryo.

As well as the five senses and their organs, man also possesses reason, which is a sort of semi-sense, and has, as its organ, the mind, made of a fine matter. By perceiving, by reasoning and through the testimony of others, at least according to the most ancient theory, one obtains indirect knowledge. Immediate knowledge, which is the only absolute kind, is the intuition of the truth, without the mediation of senses. It is inherent in the pure soul, and is therefore restricted to the liberated, omniscient being. As the senses and the reason are not efficient in overcoming the limits of materiality, only the faithfulness of the transmission of absolute knowledge guarantees the possession of the truth, i.e. the simultaneous comprehension of all the "points of view" (*naya*). If one takes any of these in isolation, one is able to perceive only one of the infinite aspects of reality. In fact, an object may be considered without distinguishing between its generic and its specific qualities. One may consider the former or the latter. One may abstain from any concept of evolution. One may refer to things only by hearing their names, or distinguish the meanings on their etymological basis. Finally, one may consider the question of the correspondence between reality and etymology. Thus an object may be judged in various contrasting ways, all of which are valid "in a certain sense" or "relatively" (*syād*). Thus a thing relatively: 1) is; 2) is not;

3) is and is not; 4) is indeterminable; 5) is, and is indeterminable; 6) is not, and is indeterminable; 7) is, is not, and is indeterminable. For example a drink may be hot or not to different people or at different times; but it is indeterminable if one affirms the existence of opposite qualities at the same time. The doctrine of "it could be" (*syādvāda*) was perfected in the verbal controversies so dear to mediaeval India, and began from attitudes deriving from Mahāvīra. It is a logical consequence of the doctrine of the indeterminability of being and of the relative pluralism of the aspects of reality (*anekāntavāda*). With this doctrine the Jainas opposed both the agnosticism and the dogmatism of other religions. They were so proud of it that they called their whole system *syādvāda*; but as this system is redolent of dogmatism, it could easily be exposed to logical attacks of a similar kind.

The universe, uncreated and everlasting, is the stage of the drama of life. Beyond its limits there is space which is absolutely empty. Post-canonic literature often compares the universe to a man or a woman standing with his or her legs apart. This representation underlines the analogy between micro- and macrocosm. The universe has dimensions which transcend any human sense, and comprehends three worlds, the lower, the middle and the upper. Moving creatures live only in a longitudinal section of it. The lower world is formed of seven levels which contain 8,400,000 hells, places of suffering, darkness and terror for all its inhabitants, the damned and the demons, who have a horrible and monstrous appearance, and torment one another. Here they are punished for their sins, but for a limited period of time. Only souls guilty of unpardonable crimes plunge into a bottomless abyss, from which all escape is impossible.

The middle world corresponds to the belt of the cosmic man. It has a circular surface and includes a succession of ringshaped continents and oceans. These surround the Jambudvīpa, "the continent of the rosy apple-tree", which stretches like a disc around Mount Meru. This latter is thus at the centre of the universe. Various systems of suns and moons, accompanied by planets and constellations, revolve around Mount Meru. Two of these systems belong to the Jambudvīpa, which is divided into seven zones; in twenty-four hours they revolve through an arc of 180 degrees and confer the same conditions of light and shade to the southernmost part, the Bhāratavarṣa, as to the corresponding northernmost part, which is identical in every respect. The Bhāratavarṣa is delimited to the north by the chain of the Himālaya. Parallel to the Himālaya there is another chain which, together with two rivers flowing north-south, divide the area into six parts. Only the lower central part is inhabited by civilized men (*Ārya*), and that is India, or, as the modern Jainas have it, the whole of our earth. In certain regions, called *bhoga-bhūmi*, "lands of enjoyment", a continuous prosperity reigns, which, however, excludes the attainment of liberation. Other regions, among them Bhāratavarṣa, are *karma-bhūmi*. Here the life is subject to the law of *karman*, men must work and suffer, but at certain periods there exists the prospect of achieving the condition of the Perfect Ones.

Above the celestial vault, in the upper world, disposed on various levels shining with the purest lights, there live the gods, who are always young and very beautiful. They are arranged in a hierarchy, which assigns pleasures that are increasingly detached from materiality and the senses the higher the position reached. However, this is the transient reward of merits which have not yet gone beyond the sphere of earthly interests.

"Unlimited, incomparable, endless beatitude" is possessed only by the Perfect Ones, who enjoy the perfections of the pure soul in the "region of the gentle slope." It resembles the diadem of the cosmic man, and stretches like a parasol above and detached from the world of the gods, thus symbolizing in the mythical cosmic construction the distinct, irrevocable and eternal separation existing between liberated souls and any other human apparition and imagination.

The regions of the middle world, where the law of *karman* rules, are subject to a continual mutation, at times leading to a deterioration, at others to an improvement, which involve the environment and the physical and moral characteristics of its inhabitants. The cosmic periods last an enormously great number of years and repeat themselves to infinity. They are comprised of two phases which follow each other like the two halves of a circumference. Each phase contains six ages of varying duration, defined with the terms *suṣamā*, "happy", and *duḥṣamā*, "unhappy", suitably repeated or combined. From an age of the greatest happiness and prosperity, in which men do not need to work and are spontaneously virtuous, one passes through successive grades of corruption to an epoch of extreme poverty, until terrible cataclysms destroy almost every trace of life on earth. This will be followed by the ascendent phase, in which epochs similar to the others will take place, but in reverse order. The ages of great prosperity and of great misery are not propitious for the attainment of liberation. During them the law and doctrine were either not preached or completely disappeared. The first Tīrthaṃkara, Ṛṣabha, in fact proclaimed the Jaina faith in the third age, divided men into the four casts, and introduced the liberal arts, writing and the various techniques, in anticipation of future necessities. Most of the "great personages" of the mythology appeared in the fourth age. These were the other twenty-three Tīrthaṃkaras, the universal emperors, and the groups of heroes, paradigmatic personages who exemplify the struggle between good and evil and the triumph of justice. The present epoch began shortly after the death of Mahāvīra. It is the fifth of a descending phase, and will last 21,000 years. In it Jainism is destined to disappear, and no one will be able to attain liberation unless they are born at least once in regions more favourably disposed, in that they do not undergo the extremes of happiness and misery.

The Jainas tell of the names, deeds, and prodigies of the "great personages" of the descending and ascending phases of the present cosmic period, as well as of those of personages of other zones in the middle world which are subject to continuous mutations. In this grandiose framework Brahmanic legends, above all of the Kṛṣṇa cycle, combine with the memory of historical personages and real events. However, their historical individuality is lost in the continual and undefined renewal of vicissitudes amid the everlasting stability of the universe.

VI. The Present Situation of Jainism

The Jaina communities accepted many of the usages and customs of the Hindus, including the caste system, in which, however, they attribute pre-eminence to the warrior caste. Therefore, in spite of all the ideological differences, the Hindus habitually consider the Jainas as belonging to a sub-caste or sect within Hinduism. While this has materially benefited the individual communities, it has represented a danger for the preservation of the religion. Although there has never been any lack of learned monks concerned to preserve the authentic tradition, it cannot be doubted that the renewed interest of the Jainas themselves in their own past has been encouraged by the studies of western scholars, who were able to recognize the autonomy and originality of Jainism. From the second half of the last century onwards there have been many concerted actions by Jainas of the various sects to defend the fundamentals of the religion above sectarian divergences, and to spread the knowledge of them. Vijaya Dharma Sūri

(1868-1922) is particularly important for his active collaboration with western scholars. Not only did he study the sacred literature, producing editions of, and commentaries on, canonic texts and rare manuscripts, he also carried out an intense missionary activity, renewed the ancient custom of the wandering teacher, and founded institutions for the education of the young, and for the creation of new teachers. Since that time the work of propaganda has been considerable. The work of the "World Jain Mission" is noteworthy. This mission was founded in 1949 at Aliganj (Etah, U.P.), and publishes a monthly bulletin, "*The Voice of Ahiṃsā*". *Ahiṃsā* was the starting-point for the non-violence of M. K. Gāndhī. In the first place it leads to vegetarianism, which frees one from the lowest instincts and is also warmly recommended as means of solving the problem of hunger in the world. In its positive significance of universal love, it combines with the "doctrine of the relative pluralism of the aspects of reality". Thus it conduces to a toleration of the various faiths, which are not considered as erroneous, but as partial "points of view."

At the present there are about a million and a half Jainas. They are generally convinced of the hoary antiquity of their faith, which, they assert, is much older than *Vedas* themselves.

There are large Śvetāmbara communities in Kathiawar. The main centres of the Digambaras are in Mysore and Deccan. One can also find Jainas and Jaina temples in the great port cities and in the centres of traffic. The Jainas in these places occupy eminent positions in industry and commerce, not so much because the Jaina religion favours the interests of the commercial middle-class, but rather because the caution, sobriety, and reflective capacity required of the laymen are the same qualities which lead to success in business.

Both in Europe and America certain aspects of Jaina religiosity have not failed to arouse interest and to receive a positive evaluation. In 1913, Herbert Warren founded a Mahāvīra Brotherhood in London. It had a very limited success. The followers of the principles and methods of Jainism in Europe and America appear to be equally isolated still in these times.

VII. Short History of the Study of Jainism

Indian ascetics and anchorites are often recalled by Greek and Latin authors, but their summary descriptions do not allow us to distinguish with any certainty to which order or sect they belonged. However, a note by CLEMENS of Alexandria (*Stromata*, III, 7,60) seems to refer in particular to the Jainas, who, perhaps, are also to be identified in the 'εννοί of HESYCH.

After the long silence of the Middle Ages, an ever-increasing quantity of new information on the Jainas appears in the accounts of travellers and in the reports of missionaries. A notable example is the description of the *Vertei* or Śvetāmbara monks (gujarātī *varti* = ascetic) by EMMANUEL PINHEIRO, S.J. (1595), while the name *Zaina* appears for the first time in an anonymous report of the second half of the seventeenth-century.

The truly scientific enquiry into Jainism occurs at the same time as the rise of Indo-Aryan philology. At first the similarities between Buddhism and Jainism induced scholars to think that they were branches of the same tree. Some held that Jainism was anterior (H. T. COLEBROOKE, J. STEVENSON), whereas others considered the Jainas to be a Buddhist sect (H. H. WILSON, E. BURNOUF, TH. BENFEY, CH. LASSEN, A. WEBER). But in 1879, H. JACOBI demonstrated that the two religious traditions were autonomous and independent. The features they had in common were explained by the fact that they had arisen in the same milieu. It was JACOBI himself who, after the pioneer work of WEBER and G. BÜHLER, greatly stimulated the study of the Śvetāmbara canon. Noteworthy in the same field are E. LEUMANN and, later, W. SCHUBRING and his school of textual criticism. There has always been a lively interest in Jainism in Europe. One may recall the acute and brilliant syntheses of H. v. GLASENAPP, W. KIRFEL, L. RENOU-O. LACOMBE, and E. FRAUWALLNER, together with the imposing work of SCHUBRING, while a host of scholars in various countries have dedicated their attention to particular works of the non canonical literature in prakrit and sanskrit, especially in the field of narrative, in which the Jainas have been unusually prolific. Finally I hope my reader will permit me to recall the lively interest in Jainism which was shown at the beginning of this century in Italy by many scholars (PULLÈ, PAVOLINI, BALLINI, BELLONI-FILIPPI, SUALI, TESSITORI, almost all of whom owed allegiance to the school of *Jacobi*).

In India, there are numerous series of Jaina publications, subsidised by munificent patrons, which have brought, and continue to bring, to light a quantity of works by Jaina authors, often very interesting from a literary point of view. A special place is held by A. N. UPADHYE among those who publish editions in prakrit and apabhraṃśa dialects.

The Digambara CHAMPAT RAI JAIN also deserves particular notice.

Around 1930 he published many writings in which he expounded his vision of the function and mission of Jainism in modern society, and sought an accord with Christian principles. Although the modern interpretation given to the ancient texts limits the value of these and similar writings, these are however very significant, inasmuch as they bear witness to the capacity for self-renewal of the ancient, millenary Jaina faith.

BIBLIOGRAPHY

a) *Texts and translations*

The Śvetāmbara canon is repeatedly published in India. Almost all canonical writings are collected in *Suttāgame*, 2 vol., Nirnaya Sagar Press, Bombay, 1952-54.

H. JACOBI, *Ǵaina Sūtras*, Oxford, 1884, 1887 (Sacred Books of East, voll. XXII, XLV). Contents: "Āyāra", "Sūyagaḍa", "Kalpasūtra", "Uttarajjhāyā."

H. JACOBI, "Eine Jaina Dogmatik. Umāsvāti's Tattvārthādhigama Sūtra," in *Zeitschrift der Deutschen Morgenländischen Gesellschaft*, 60 (1906).

W. SCHUBRING, *Das Mahānisīha Sutta.* Abh.d.Preuss.Akad.d.Wiss., Berlin, 1918.

W. SCHUBRING, *Worte Mahāvīras*, Göttingen, 1926.

W. SCHUBRING, "Die Jainas", Tübingen, 1927 (*Religionsgeschichtliches Lesebuch*, 7).

MALLIṢEṆA SŪRI, *Syādvādamañjarī. The flower-spray of the Quodammodo doctrine*, transl. by F. W. THOMAS. Deutsche Akad. d. Wiss., Berlin, 1960.

b) *Selected modern works*

JAGMANDARLĀL JAINĪ, *Outlines of Jainism*, Oxford, 1916 (rev. edit. 1940).

H. v. GLASENAPP, *Der Jainismus*, Berlin, 1925 (repr. 1965).

W. KIRFEL, "Die Religion der Jaina's," Leipzig, 1928. (*Bilderatlas zur Religionsgeschichte*, 12).

CHAMPAT RAI JAIN, *What is Jainism?*, Allahabad, w.y.

M. WINTERNITZ, *History of Indian Literature*, vol. II, Calcutta, 1933.

W. SCHUBRING, *Die Lehre der Jainas nach den alten Quellen dargestellt*, Berlin, 1935. English translation: Dehli, 1962.

K. K. HANDIQUI, *Yaśastilaka and Indian Culture*, Sholapur, 1949.

A. L. BASHAM, *History and Doctrine of the Ājīvikas, a vanished Indian religion*, London, 1951.

L. RENOU-O. LACOMBE-J. FILLIOZAT, "Le Jainisme," in *L'Inde Classique*, vol. II, Paris, 1953.

E. FRAUWALLNER, *Geschichte der indischen Philosophie*, 2 voll., Salzburg, 1953-56.

C. DELLA CASA, *Il Giainismo*, Turin, 1962.

L. ALSDORF, *Beiträge zur Geschichte von Vegetarismus und Rinderverehrung in Indien*, Wiesbaden, 1962 (Akadem.d.Wiss.u d.Liter. in Mainz).

R. WILLIAMS, *Jaina Yoga. A survey of the Mediaeval Śrāvakācāras*, London, 1963.

C. CAILLAR, *Les expiations dans le rituel ancien des religieux Jaina*, Paris 1965.

BUDDHISM

BY

ALEX WAYMAN

New York, U.S.A.

TABLE OF CONTENTS

I. Essence of Buddhism

Buddhism posits a religious goal called *nirvāṇa* to be attained through a path of ethical conduct, mind training, and insight. Early Buddhism and later consistent traditions consider that goal to be a quiescent state contrasting with the phenomenal circling called *saṃsāra* and sometimes described as blissful. In this bifurcation into mundane and supramundane the mundane is the realm of sorrow, inexorably brought about by past nescience and craving, and continued by habits of action in countless lives and transmigrations. The path of escape from the *saṃsāra* of rebirth is indicated in two verses [84]:

> Begin, going forth (into the religious life)! Apply yourselves to the teaching of the Buddha! Destroy death's army like an elephant a reed-hut.

> The one who proceeds with carefulness in this Doctrine and Discipline abandons the circling of rebirth and makes an end to suffering.

This religion involves taking refuge in the Three Jewels—the Buddha, his Doctrine (*dharma*), and the Brotherhood (*saṃgha*)—as the inception of Buddhist faith. The Buddha was enlightened to the Doctrine and revealed it to the Brotherhood in the course of what are conventionally described as twelve acts. The Doctrine is both scripture and its full comprehension, while deeply rooted in myth, as of the three worlds—of desire, of form, and the formless, each full of deities, demons, and incarnate or disincarnate men. Also the Doctrine is profound but not excluded from people. The Doctrine holds that all constructed things are impermanent and suffering, that the personality aggregates of man are void of a self and of what belongs to a self, and that causation is Dependent Origination. The Brotherhood is conventionally the ordinary persons who have entered the religious life and in an absolute sense those who have fulfilled the Buddhist path of eight members, which is the Middle Path avoiding the extremes of indulgence and mortification.

Buddhist ethics treat moral, immoral, and indeterminate conduct by way of body, speech, and chiefly mind, thus the basis for rebirth in good or bad destiny, where good destiny is that of man and gods, bad destiny that of animals, hungry ghosts, and hell beings. Buddhism stresses the rational ground of ethics, namely discrimination of good and evil, while avoiding the speculative use of reason for discourse on metaphysical ultimates. Buddhism is pessimistic regarding the prevalence of suffering and is optimistic concerning blissful states. Some persons, having fully understood the selflessness of personality, avoid both good and bad destiny and achieve *nirvāṇa*. Central to the Buddhist path is the theory of meditation with calming of the mind, clear vision, and the two combined, yielding mundane (supernormal faculties) and supramundane (Nirvana and Buddhahood) fruits. In time, Buddhism presented numerous techniques for the calming and various theories of what constitutes clear vision.

Later Buddhism developed the theory of the Buddha in terms of bodies. An omniscient and omnipresent Buddha Body, the Dharmakāya, ever silent, projects phenomenal Bodies (Saṃbhoga-kāya and Nirmāṇa-kāya) to manifest the Doctrine in words. Buddhism came to stress the beatific vision: by faith or pure heartedness one could see the Apparitional Body (Nirmāṇa-kāya) as the Buddha or Buddhas in front, and the *Sūtrālaṃkāra* is cited [61]:

> As in a broken water-pot the reflection of the moon cannot be seen, in the same way to those that are evil the Buddha does not manifest himself.

The hero of later Buddhism is called the Bodhisattva. He takes a vow of benefit for others and enlightenment for himself, and then in ten sequential Stages perfects the virtuous natures. On the Tenth Stage he becomes tantamount to a Buddha, but not a Complete Buddha is endowed with Buddha natures, some exclusive, and is in the 'Nirvana of no-fixed abode' as described in the lines "thus with knowledge, not fixed in the phenomenal world; and with compassion, not fixed in quiescence."

II. Historical Development

The standard scholarly dates for the Buddha Śākyamuni (all accounts agree on his 80 years) are 563-483 B.C. [27]. These can be shifted a few years either way. The Ceylonese Chronicles led to the Southern Buddhist tradition of the Buddha's birth and death each 60 years earlier, whereby the 2500th anniversary of His passing was celebrated in the years 1956 or 1957 A.D. in the various South Asian countries. Buddhist tradition states that before becoming a Buddha he had the personal name Siddhārtha and the family name Gautama in the Śākya clan, and that he was born to the royal family of King Śuddhodana and Queen Māyā, the latter dying through childbirth. The kingdom was in the Himalayan foothills, approximately the modern southern Nepal, and had Kapilavastu as the capital city.

After marrying and having a son named Rāhula, at the age of 29 years Siddhārtha left the capital to adopt the life of a religious wanderer, of which there were many in those days. He practiced yoga techniques under the teachers Ālāra Kalāma and Udraka Rāmaputra, then decided that their methods did not yield the highest attainment of Complete Enlightenment. He applied himself to severe austerities for six years by the river Nairañjanā (in present-day Bihar State). It was during this time that five mendicants, Kauṇḍinya and others, joined him. But his mortifications proved no more conducive to the goal than his former indulgences as a pampered prince. Therefore he broke off his austerity, partook of moderate food, and proceeded to the terrace of enlightenment, a certain tree of variety *ficus religiosa* at

Bodhgayā. In a memorable night, with remarkable experiences beginning with repulse of evil forces at dusk and ending with Illumination toward dawn, he became a Buddha at the age of 35. [41]

Proceeding to the Deer Park just north of Vārāṇasī (= Benares), he preached his first sermon, the celebrated "Setting into Motion of the Wheel of the Law" to those five disciples, whereupon Kauṇḍinya is reported to have experienced a flash of understanding, and so is thereafter called Ājñātakauṇḍinya ('K. who understood'). Subsequently, Śāriputra and Maudgalyāyana, who after their Vedic training had been followers of the heretic teacher Sañjaya, were converts to the Doctrine and became the two chief disciples of the Buddha, before whom they seem to have passed away. The most famous other disciples were Mahākāśyapa, Upāli, and a cousin Ānanda, the last named becoming the Buddha's constant attendant. In Central Asia and China, the "Ten great disciples" are found in the order: Śāriputra, Mahā-Maudgalyāyana, Mahā-Kāśyapa, Subhūti, Pūrṇa-Maitrāyaṇīputra, Aniruddha, Mahā-Kātyāyana, Upāli, Rāhula, and Ānanda. [41] A list of sixteen is found in ritual [cf. Worship, 1 Cult, B. Ritual]. His aunt and foster mother Mahāprajāpati insisted on joining the order, and thus began the Buddhist nun order.

During the long years of mendicant preaching, the Buddha frequently returned to Rājagṛha, the then capital of Magadha. It was here that the pious king Bimbisāra was overthrown by his son Ajātaśātru, who embarked on the conquest of neighboring states. Another famous site of the Buddha's lectures was Śrāvastī, capital of Kośala State, where he spent most of his time. The city had at least three monasteries, of which the most famous was the Jetavana erected through the generosity of the rich merchant Anāthapiṇḍada. Perhaps because of a princely background of his own, the Buddha easily associated with the kings of his day.

There were rival schools. Deep entrenched was the old Brahmanism, derived from the 1500-1000 B.C. period when the Vedas were first composed. But the spoken language had changed so much in the intervening centuries that the Vedic texts were meaningless except for many years of study, which rendered this religion the rather exclusive prerogative of a priestly class or caste called the Brahmins. This is a reason that the Buddha preached in the vernaculars. Also the Brahminical animal sacrifices were repugnant to many persons such as the Jains, who while constituting a rival sect to the Buddhists, agreed with them on this opposition. The gradual break-up of the old political states due to military incursions apparently made possible by the novel use of iron, contributed to a growing lack of faith in the old religious order. Of course this Brahmanism underwent profound changes and emerged in the form known as Hinduism. Buddhists texts speak of the six heretical teachers, whose doctrines are now difficult to define. But the most troublesome rival seems to have been one of the Buddha's own cousins, Devadatta, who caused the first, and brief schism in Buddhism.

After 45 years of itinerant preaching, the Buddha entrusted his Doctrine to Mahā-Kāśyapa and passed away (referred to as 'his Nirvana') at the town of Kuśināgara. His relics were divided among eight claimants, including kings, cities, and tribes, and deposited in shrines called *stūpa*. In the very next summer (rainy) season, under the sponsorship of King Ajātaśātru, Mahā-Kāśyapa held a meeting at Rājagṛha in a mountain cave. This is known as the 'First Council'. It was attended by some five hundred Elders (Sanskrit *sthavira*, Pāli *thera*) of the Brotherhood. In the Ceylonese tradition, the monks then rehearsed and thereby collected the Doctrine (*dharma*) and Discipline (*vinaya*). [27] Mahā-Kāśyapa first questioned Upāli about the Vinaya, and subsequently questioned Ānanda about the Dharma. In Northern Buddhist tradition, first Ānanda rehearsed the Sūtra collection, then Upāli the Vinaya, and finally Mahā-Kāśyapa the Abhidharma, the three being called the 'three baskets' (*tripiṭaka*). The later Sanskrit tradition of the Mūla-Sarvāstivādin sect centered in Kashmir, and which developed the Vaibhāṣika Abhidharma interpretation, has a lineage preserved in Tibetan texts in this verse: "The powerful one of the *munis* made the [Teaching] well expressed (*subhāśita*); and Kāśyapa, Ānanda, Śāṇavāsa, Upagupta, Dhītika, Kāla (or Kṛṣṇa), and Mahāsudarśana, are the seven hierarchs of the Teaching." [48] This lineage may have referred to the Abhidharma specialists and in the early days nothing more complicated than what we today would consider the authorities on the meaning of Buddhism, who could give the answers to the kind of questions Śāriputra, just prior to his conversion, asked the monk Upasena, including "What is frequently set in motion?" (i.e. what topics are most frequently mentioned). At that time Upasena referred Śāriputra to the Buddha. Immediately after the latter's passing, Mahā-Kāśyapa had this role. In the course of centuries, however, Abhidharma became overloaded with theological technicalities.

A century (Tibetan tradition: 110 years) after the Buddha's Nirvāṇa, the monks at Vaiśālī were committing ten transgressions of the Vinaya code, including an inadmissible confessional and the amassing of wealth. [48] An elder named Yaśas, noticing this, joined with other Buddhist leaders in an attempt to eject the erring monks with the support of the ruling king of Magadha, then Kālāśoka, who had moved the capital to Pāṭaliputra (now Patna). Under the patronage of this king (not to be confused with the more famous King Aśoka), the 'Second Council' reviewed the charges and ejected the transgressing monks. But the orthodox Southern School (Theravādin) records that 10,000 of the heretical monks formed their own school called Mahāsāṃghika (perhaps 'the Numerous Clergy'). It is feasible that these monks allied themselves with the laity who worshipped and maintained the shrines, and then began to make theological justifications for the lay worship with such teachings as 'the Buddhas are supramundane'. [5,27,30]

Once the basic split occurred, the two groups began to subdivide into sects, totalling eighteen by the third century, B.C., and began to hold increasingly disparate and differentiated doctrines. One tradition records that 137 years after the Nirvana, when Nanda and Mahāpadma were reigning, a monk started a 60-year quarrel over five points disputing the Arhat status. Another tradition said that in the course of varying dialectical recitation of the Scripture, 160 years after the Nirvana (hence approximately Candragupta Maurya's accession, circa 321 B.C.) four basic sects had arisen, namely the Sārvāstivādin, Mahāsāṃghika, Sammatīya, and Sthavira, which in turn subdivided to make a total of eighteen. The terminology 'Third Council' means a council with royal patronage to reconcile these disputes, and usually this expression refers to the council supposedly sponsored by King Aśoka (Maurya Dynasty) when it was decided that the Buddha was an Analyzer (Vibhajyavādin). [35,41,48,77]

King Aśoka was consecrated 218 years after the Nirvana and therefore in 265-64 B.C. by the 483 B.C. Nirvana date, hence possibly a few years earlier. After his conversion to Buddhism (as a layman, not a monk) his patronage supported Buddhism as a 'converting' religion, although he was considerate to other religions of India, especially Śaivism. Buddhism began to prosper in Gandhāra and Kashmir and south in the Deccan, as well as in Ceylon. Among the legendary '84,000 shrines' Aśoka built, one should include the great *stūpa* of Amarāvatī in So. India by the Krishna River. [67] The rock and pillar edicts of Aśoka show the influence of Buddhist ethics.

After the death of Aśoka the Maurya Dynasty speedily declined and its fall around 187 B.C. coincides with Puṣyamitra's establishment of the Hindu Śunga Dynasty which lasted over a century. Both the successors of Aśoka and Puṣyamitra persecuted the Buddhists. The Śuṅgas could not control the border areas, and foreign peoples began to spill into the Northwest provinces. The Greek Menandros, ruling around 150 B.C. in Northwest India, became a 'convert' to Buddhism. This episode has its literary remains in the well-known work "The Questions of King Milinda," representing the spirited dialogue between the king and the ingenious monk Nāgasena. The Greek rule there was brought to an end in the first half century B.C. by barbarous hordes of Central Asian provenance, called after the Greek word the Scythians, and distinguished as two groups by the names Yüeh-chih and Śaka. This incursion led to establishment of the Kuṣāṇa empire, of which the crucial date is that of King Kaniṣka's accession; here there are various theories, notably 78 A.D. (1st year of the 'Śaka era') or 125 A.D. Kaniṣka, king of the Yüeh-chih, was a lavish patron of Buddhism, with Kashmir becoming virtually a Buddhist state.

Previously, in the first century, B.C. the Buddhist canon in Pāli had been committed to writing. Now, under the Kuṣāṇas, the more-or-less equivalent Sanskrit canon was presumably committed to writing in the monastery of Jālandhara in Kashmir, where Vaibhāṣika monks prepared the Sanskrit Abhidharma collection in seven sections, and monks and laymen compiled a large commentary under the title of *Mahāvibhāṣa*. Preeminent in this adoption of the Sanskrit language for Buddhist literature is the greatest poet of Buddhism, Aśvaghoṣa, who about the same time composed a religious poem in ornate style (*mahākāvya*) describing the life of the Buddha (the *Buddhacāritā*). [36] Sanskrit was also employed for the Mahāyāna ('Great Vehicle') scriptures, of which the earliest, to wit, the *Aṣṭasāhasrikā Prajñāpāramitā* (Perfection of Insight in 8,000 sections), may have attained its present form at that time. Also during the first century, A.D. the first Buddha image appeared in Gandhāra with Greco-Roman influence. [25]

The great Buddhist teacher Nāgārjuna seems to have lived in 2d cent. A.D. and to have been a native of South India who erected the rail around the Amarāvatī *stūpa* and was a sage advisor to the Śātavāhana king Hala. Nāgārjuna subsequently went north to the Buddhist university Nālandā, the ruins of which are in present Bihar State, and propagated his way, later called the Mādhyamika, of reconciling the new Prajñāpāramitā scriptures with the older Buddhism in opposition to both the Abhidharma theology of Buddhism and the logical school

(Nyāya) of Hinduism. In his declining years he retired to the mountain Śrīparvata in the Āndhra country of South India. Presumably in his memory is the place-name Nāgārjunikoṇḍa for a site by the Krishna River that was for a long time a flourishing center of Buddhist monasteries and art. [67] His chief disciple and worthy successor is named Āryadeva, latter 2d cent. A.D. This teacher (born in Ceylon), besides producing some famous works on the Mādhyamika, converted to Buddhism the heretical teacher Mātṛceṭa, who thereafter composed some celebrated versified praises of the Buddha. [2] At about the same time (3rd cent.) we should place the Āryaśūra who wrote the *Jātakamālā* (Garland of Birth Stories) which ultimately attained such fame as to be represented in the frescoes of Ajaṇṭā (in the Deccan) and at Borobodur (in Java).

The Kuṣāṇa rule was succeeded by the Imperial Guptas, the golden age of Hinduism. This dynasty begins in A.D. 320 with a new Candragupta. Then Candra Gupta II (c. 376-415) is probably the famous Vikramāditya during whose reign is placed Kālidāsa, the great Indian poet-dramatist. Fa-hsien, a Chinese Buddhist pilgrim, noted the peacefulness of India during six years of that reign. [7] A great many works, both Hindu and Buddhist, were composed and attributed to divine authority. The later Mahāyāna scriptures fall around this time, as do the 'revealed' Buddhist Tantras. Certainly the Mahāyāna scripture collections called Ratnakūṭa ('heap of jewels'), Avataṃsaka ('garland ornament'), and Prajñāpāramitā ('perfection of insight') came to approximate their form for later times. Here falls (in Ceylon) the greatest commentator of the Pāli scriptures, Buddhaghosa (4th-5th cent.), a convert from a Magadha Brahminical family. We also find the activity of the brothers (probably half-brothers) Asaṅga and Vasubandhu. Asaṅga (circa 375-430 A.D.) first belonged to the Mahīśāsaka among the 18 sects. Then he received two remarkable summary verse works called the *Madhyānta-vibhāga* and the *Mahāyāna-Sūtrālaṃkāra* of a teacher referred to in Paramārtha's "Life of Vasubandhu" [87] as Maitreya, who may be an historical teacher not to be confused with the future Buddha Maitreya. Asaṅga also came under the influence of a Mahāyāna scripture called *Saṃdhinirmocana*. He composed a ponderous work called the *Yogācārabhūmi* to combine the new Mahāyāna materials with the older Buddhism (the 'Hīnayāna' or Lesser Vehicle) of his Mahīśāsaka leanings and later summarized his position in the *Mahāyānasaṃgraha* and the *Abhidharmasamuccaya*. [87] During the long life of Vasubandhu (c. 400-480 A.D.) the Gupta Dynasty received a severe blow in the Northwest from an invading Central Asian people called 'Hūṇas'. Vasubandhu began in the Abhidharma schools and wrote a popularizing work called the *Abhidharmakośa* ("Treasure of the Abhidharma"). Ignored at first, this treatise did not help the survival of the enormous Vaibhāṣika Abhidharma because it enabled one to study the subject with a minimum of analytical complexities. Converted to the Mahāyāna by his brother Asaṅga, Vasubandhu popularized Asaṅga's school, sooner or later called "Mind Only" (*cittamātra*) or "Representation Only" (*vijñaptimātra*), with his brief works called "Twenty Stanzas (on Representation Only)" and "Thirty Stanzas (on ditto)". Vasubandhu also wrote a number of commentaries on Mahāyāna scriptures and in old age became celebrated. After his death, fresh Hūṇa inroads led to disintegration of the Gupta empire, and in early sixth century Buddhism was fiercely persecuted in Western India by the Hūṇa king Mihirakula. Buddhism was also declining in Kashmir as Śaivism prospered there.

After Vasubandhu the chief Buddhist authors were more specialized. According to a Tibetan tradition, there were four disciples—but not necessarily immediate—of the master Vasubandhu who were more learned than he in their specialized fields, namely Sthiramati in the Abhidharma, Dignāga in Logic, Ārya Vimuktisena in the Prajñāpāramitā texts, and Guṇaprabha in the Vinaya. [48] Dignāga's dates are approximately 480-540 A.D., and there is a lineage of Dignāga, Asvabhāva, Dharmapāla (530-561 A.D.). [29] Sthiramati, whose teacher is Guṇamati, lives in early- and mid-sixth century. [29] According to the Tibetan Tāranātha, Ārya Vimuktisena is linked to Vasubandhu through one intermediate teacher. [15] The variant theories about Guṇaprabha's teacher suggest that also in his case one or two teachers intervene. [48]

Also in the mid-sixth century, we must place two contemporaries who opposed each other's interpretations of the Mādhyamika, Bhāvaviveka and Candrakīrti, as well as the Buddhist grammarian and poet Candragomin. [48,90] Later in the century and probably extending into the seventh is the Buddhist logician Dharmakīrti, even though the Chinese pilgrim Hsüan-tsang's account of his travels (629-645 A.-D.) is silent about Dharmakīrti.

Harṣa ascended his throne in 606 and during a rule of forty-one years gained control of most of Northern India. He partially restored the glory of the Guptas and in the latter part of his reign fell under the influence of Buddhism. Hsüan-tsang visited during his rule and noted the definite decline of Buddhism, but Tantric cults were growing. The confusion that followed the death of Harṣa was resolved by two dynasties dividing the hegemony of Northern India. The Pālas of Bihar and Bengal patronized Buddhism for their three centuries of rule, their greatest power being with the king Dharmapāla (c. 770-810). [7] During the Pāla dynasty, the Buddhist Tantric cults became more public and the Tantric commentarial literature began to flourish. In the late tenth century, Turkish chieftains in Afghanistan began plundering raids on India, and the resulting political situation in Western India was most unfavorable to Buddhism. In South India, both Śaivism and Vaishnavism were pushing out Buddhism, and in Karnatak country (Mysore State) Buddhism was losing to Jainism and to a form of Śaivism that came to be called Lingāyat and which even today recognizes its debt to Buddhism to which it has warm feelings. A number of Buddhist pandits were invited to Tibet, perhaps the most famous being Atīśa, who arrived there in 1042 A.D. from the Vikramaśīla monastery. Thereafter, many Buddhist teachers would migrate as refugees to near-by Buddhist lands, such as Burma, and many settled in Nepal. The final blow to Northern India and also to Buddhism there came with the invasion in the last decade of the twelfth century by Muhammad of Ghor. His soldiers destroyed the great Buddhist university of Nālandā. The Buddhist laity of Northern India was more easily absorbed into Muslim communities than into Hinduism.

There are two kinds of reasons, internal and external, for the disappearance of Buddhism from India. Internal reasons: (a) Buddhist strength lay in the monasteries, and was not deeply imbedded in the village life of the people; (b) Buddhist prosperity depended on steady patronage by royalty and rich merchant classes; (c) Buddhism, while not actively opposed to the social system of India, did not defend it, and often offended it; (d) Buddhist sectarian divisions were wasteful of institutional power; (e) Buddhism, in its Indian form, was nonviolent—had no defense against aggression; (f) the Buddhist doctrine was too profound for the masses. External reasons: (a) Other Indian religions—themselves great—adopted strong points of Buddhism; (b) Hostile kings, ruthless invaders of India, and sometimes incensed mobs, destroyed numerous monasteries and religious monuments of Buddhism and murdered monks; (c) Revived Hinduism gradually squeezed out Buddhism in many areas, undercutting holy places by deliberate placement of their own edifices; (d) Buddhist support by invaders of Northwest India around the beginning of our era and subsequent success in Asian nations may possibly have placed a 'foreign' stamp on Buddhism in Indian eyes. A poor internal reason often advanced is that in its last stages Buddhism had become degenerate by its adoption of Tantrism; however, Hinduism also was colored by Tantrism, and persons who advance that reason do not know the long history of Tantrism and its antecedents and appear not to have studied the Tantric books. A poor external reason is that after the time of Dharmakīrti Buddhist monks were crushed in debate with the great Hindu teacher Śaṅkara; however Śaṅkara's works do not bear out the legend, and Indian Buddhism had its great teachers up to the end, such as Atīśa and Abhayākaragupta, as shown by the works translated into Tibetan.

Modern books on the Indian systems of thought when written by Hindus have usually treated Buddhism as a phase of Brahmanism. It is true that Buddhism arose on the same Brahmanism background as did the orthodox Hinduism, but Buddhism followed a different course and has had a different destiny; and by the very Indian viewpoint that destiny depends on inner nature, Buddhism must accordingly have a different essential nature than Brahmanism or the later Hinduism. Also Buddhism left a permanent impress on other Indian systems, and other Indian systems on it.

B. *Asia generally and the Canons*

a) *Central Asia and the Far East.* It appears that during Aśoka's reign an Indian colony was established in Khotan, but whether this involved any transmissal of Buddhism to that outlying region is a matter of speculation. It is certain that Buddhist texts were disseminated into the Khotan area during the time of the 'Old Silk Road' (100 B.C.-200 A.-D) from China to the Oriental Roman empire through Central Asia, which had a branch extending down into Northwest India where it passed the university town of Taxila (or Takṣaśilā), a great center of East-West learning. The texts were usually not in standard Sanskrit but in a mixture of Sanskrit and Prakrit that Franklin D. Edgerton has called "Buddhist Hybrid Sanskrit." [23] A remarkable text is the equivalent to the Pāli *Dhammapada* by the name *Dharmapada* preserved in the old Central Asian script called Kharoṣṭhī. [9] Among other works with such mixed language perhaps the most well-known is the *Mahāvastu*, an extant text of the Mahāsāṃghika in its Lokottaravādin subsect. Besides such works which came to Central Asia from Northwest India, as Buddhism penetrated into Bactria didactic texts and other documents were written in a dialect of the Śakas or Indo-Scythians, called 'Khotanese' in the series of fragments being published by H. W. Bailey from the remnants of what was once an extensive literature.

Various pious legends grew up concerning the introduction of Buddhism into China. In fact, Buddhism was carried there by foreigners such as merchants, envoys, and immigrants in the first century B.C., and in the middle of the first century A.D. contemporary Chinese sources attest to its existence. In the first two centuries A.D. (the later Han), it became widely disseminated along trade centers, starting with Tunhuang at the Western gateway to China, and at the end of the period Buddhism is represented by some prosperous communities as at the capital Loyang. After the downfall of the Han in 220 A.D., Buddhism rapidly advanced, and from about 300 A.D. had penetrated the high gentry clans in Northern China, while the Buddhist monasteries became prestigious places for escape during dangerous times. [91] The Buddhist ethic, independent of social systems, and the elaborate metaphysical structures were appealing and intriguing. From now on, the influence of Buddhism would be manifested in many fields, and a great Buddhist art type would arise. Buddhism came to share with Taoism and Confucianism a deep-seated affection in the hearts and minds of millions of Chinese, while politically there was a triangular conflict. Toward the mid-millenium Buddhism had serious troubles and became helpless upon cessation of relations between India and China in the eleventh century.

Buddhism had the advantage of flourishing in China when it was introduced into Korea in 372 A.D. The Koreans were mere transmitters, namely, of Buddhism to Japan about 552 A.D. In Japan, Buddhism underwent a native development and modification.

The various catalogs of Buddhist scriptures prepared in China, starting with the lost one by Tao-an in 374 A.D., then the Sui official catalog in 594 A.D., that of the T'ang Canon in 730 A.D., and the 1410 A.D. catalog of the Ming Canon, all place stress on the date of translation and name of translator, when known. Gradually the Mahāyāna scriptures attained precedence, and in the case of multiple translations of a single text certain translations became authoritative. [65] The presently most employed collection of the Chinese Buddhist scriptures is the Japanese edition known popularly as the *Taishô Issaikyô*, published at Tokyo from 1924 to 1929 under the direction of J. Takakusu and K. Watanabe.

b) *Southeast Asia.* During the reign of the great king Aśoka, the mission of his son Mahinda and his daughter Saṃghamittā (her religious name) brought about the conversion of Ceylon to Buddhism, where it has predominated as a cultural factor ever since. The Pāli canon was committed to writing during the reign of Vaṭṭagāmaṇi (c. 29-17 B.C.). Earlier it had come to be called 'Three Baskets'. The Doctrine as scriptures (*sutta*) consist of five collections (*nikāya*): *Dīghanikāya* "Corpus of the long ones", *Majjhimanikāya* "Corpus of the middle-length ones," *Saṃyuttanikāya* "Corpus of those grouped (by subject)," *Anguttaranikāya* "Corpus of numerical passages, progressively higher," and *Khuddakanikāya* "Corpus of minor works" which contains such popular works as the *Dhammapada*. The first four collections are also called *āgama* ('traditional text'), which is the name given to the equivalent four collections in Sanskrit form, preserved for the most part only in Chinese translation. The Pāli disciplinary code named Vinaya is in two chief sections, I. *Suttavibhanga* consisting of the Pātimokkha rules, the major and minor sins; and II. the *Khandhaka* of topics, consisting of 1. *Mahāvagga* (Great Series), the general rules of the order; and 2. *Cullavagga* (Small Series), the special rules including history of the councils. The Vinaya has a kind of appendage called the *Parivāra* containing summaries and classifications. Both the Doctrine and the Discipline canon is roughly equivalent to the Sanskrit canon of the Mūla-Sarvāstivādin school. However, the third Pāli 'basket' of Abhidhamma is quite distinct from the Sanskrit Abhidharma. [65,77]

At the end of the fifth century A.D. it is recorded that both Hinduism and Buddhism were flourishing side by side in Funan (Cambodia). The Great Temple of Angkor is a Brahmanic temple principally of the ninth to eleventh centuries, taken over by Mahayana Buddhists in late twelfth century, and then by Hinayanists in the fourteenth. Except for some festivities, there is scarcely any Brahmanism left in the country. [47]

Buddhism seems to have gained a foothold in Campā, now called Annam or Viet-Nam, by the third century A.D. In the course of time both Hīnayāna, especially the sect called Āryasammitīya, and Mahāyāna came to dominate; and since the fifteenth century, Chinese-type Buddhism has prevailed, especially in the form of Ch'an and Pure Land (Amidism). [4]

Siam also had early penetration of Buddhism, perhaps as early as first century, A.D. Here, as so frequently elsewhere, the early history of the religion is represented by art remains. Perhaps five hundred years of pre-Khmer art is inaugurated by the Gupta style Buddha image going back even to the fifth century A.D., and Siam was also influenced by the Pāla style through the intermediary of Burma. The Khmer era lasts for three centuries beginning about 1000 A.D.; their sculptors preferred sandstone for their realistic portrayal of the human figure. The subsequent Tai people in Siam created more abstract sculpture and in time also introduced a temple architecture akin to Chinese forms. [47]

Burmese Buddhism was apparently fostered by a great Hīnayāna Buddhist center which arose in the fifth century A.D. at Conjeeveram near Madras. In the eleventh century the Burmese kings of Pagān had intimate dealings with Bodhgayā in Bihar and the Burmese art from then on is traceable to the school of Nālandā. Also, in the twelfth century many monk refugees from Nālandā went to Burma, and since Ceylonese Buddhism had likewise fallen in a desperate state, pilgrims from far and wide came to worship at Burmese shrines in Pagān. [47]

Also in Java and Sumatra the influence of the Gupta era is obvious for what has been taken as the earliest Buddha stone image in second half of the fifth century A.D. But Coedès says that Amarāvatī-type images, antedating the Gupta, have been found in the Celebes and in Sumatra. The history of this area is not clear. However, it does seem that the Indian names Suvarṇadvīpa ('Continent of Gold') and Jayabhūmi referred to a powerful kingdom which started at the end of the eighth century A.D. and united Malaysia including the peninsula, Sumatra, and Java into a single kingdom, and which at the end of the ninth century lost control over Java. The life of Atīśa shows that he started a voyage to Suvarṇadvīpa (apparently in 1012 A.D.) to study under Dharmakīrti, the high priest there, considered the greatest Buddhist scholar of his day, and that Atīśa resided for twelve years. [13] Java is the site of the famous Borobodur, the Buddhist super-shrine to which Paul Mus has devoted an elaborate memoire. From the fifteenth century on, Islam became predominant in that area and Indian culture faded out. [47]

c) *Nepal, Tibet, and Mongolia.* Aśoka's visit to Lumbinī (the Buddha's birth spot) in Nepal and his having an inscribed pillar erected there marks the early trace of Buddhism in Nepal; also his daughter Cārumatī is said to have married a Nepalese nobleman who erected some Buddhist shrines. Tibetan history is obscure until the late sixth century A.D., for which time the records mention its king Sroṅ btsan sgam po (born 569 A.D.) as marriyng two princesses, one Nepalese, the other Chinese; and both ladies, being Buddhists, as converting the king to Buddhism. It is obvious that Nepal had already become a strong base for Buddhism. Not having a script for his language, the Tibetan king dispatched Thon-mi Sam-bho-ṭa to India (possibly Kashmir) to learn the Indian language. Upon his return, Thon-mi created the Tibetan alphabet on the model of a late Gupta script, and composed a Tibetan grammar. Then translations into Tibetan were inaugurated in the seventh century, at first both from Sanskrit and from Chinese. The mid-eighth century was a time for strong Nepalese-Tibetan Buddhist associations, such as the activity in Tibet of Padmasambhava and Śāntarakṣita. The Tibetan king Khri sroṅ 1de btsan, by edit of 791, officially adopted Buddhism as the religion of the state; and it was Indian Buddhism. The extensive translation project from Sanskrit originals required standard equivalences for Sanskrit-Tibetan terms, which were made mandatory for the translators. The system is embodied in the Buddhist Sanskrit-Tibetan dictionary *Mahāvyutpatti*, which centuries later would have both Chinese and Mongolian translations, and in modern times (the Sakaki edition) a Japanese translation. Soon after the king's edit, perhaps between 792 and 794, occurred the celebrated 'Council of Lhasa', the debate between the Chinese quietists with an extreme Ch'an Buddhist point of view and the Indian party, headed by Śāntarakṣita's disciple Kamalaśīla, defending the gradual path. As might be expected, the Indian party 'won' the debate. [18] Thereafter, translations were restricted to Sanskrit texts. However, a few of the translations from Chinese were preserved as authoritative in the Tibetan canon as extant up to present times. Preeminent among these is one of the two versions of the *Mahāparinirvāṇa-sūtra*, one of the three versions of the *Suvārṇaprabhāsa-sūtra*, and the great commentary on the *Saṃdhinirmocana-sūtra* by Wen-tsheg. Translations in this first period predominated in Mahāyāna sūtras, the Mūla-Sarvāstivādin Vinaya, Tantras of what would be later classed as Kriyā, Caryā, and Yoga-tantra, along with commentarial literature on the foregoing as well as of the Yogācāra school. Despite the king's edict, the native Bon religion remained strong. In 836 A.D. Glan dar ma was installed on the throne and pressured by Bon partisans soon began persecuting the Buddhists. Monks fled to the outskirts of Tibet carrying the translated books, and in 841 the king was slain by the arrow of a monk who escaped. The kingdom, which had commanded suzereinty over Nepal and extended into Central Asia with a border in common with the Turks, promptly collapsed. The later spread of the Doctrine starts with the life of the great translator Rin chen bzaṅ po (born 958 A.D.). The Sexegenary Cycle was introduced in 1027 A.D., giving a firm foundation for subsequent Tibetan history. In the new period, works on the Anuttarayoga-tantra, Mādhyamika school of philosophy, and Buddhist logic, were enthusiastically translated. A stream of Indian pandits aided the Tibetan translators and introduced the lineages of the texts and tantric practices. Most important is Atīśa, arrived 1042 A.D. When the Indian monastery Vikramaśīla was destroyed, its abbot the Kashmirian pandit Śākyaśrībhadra fled to Tibet, arriving in 1204 A.D., and transmitted another ordination lineage of the Mūla-Sarvāstivādin to Tibet. Under the Mongols, his disciple, the Sā-skya paṇḍita (1182-1251) became a kind of priest-king of Tibet (a prototype of the later Dalai-Lama system), and with him the Tibetan form of Buddhism, often called Lamaism by Westerners, began to penetrate the Mongol court in China. Sā-skya's nephew Ḥphags pa, at the age of 19, participated in Kublai's great religious conference of 1258, and helped gain the victory for the Buddhists in the debate. The Mongols were thus converted to the Tibetan form of Buddhism. By the time of the Sā-skya paṇḍita the second period of translation from Sanskrit had practically come to an end with the downfall of Buddhism in India, and with him the native commentarial tradition begins. Bu-ston was born 1290, ten years after Ḥphags pa's death in 1280; he is the final redactor of the Tibetan canon, called the Kanjur (translation of the word of the Buddha) and the Tanjur (translation of the exegesis), and is the author of many works. Tibetan commentary on the Indian Buddhist works reaches its maturity with Tsoṅ-kha-pa (1357-1419), founder of the Gelugpa reform sect. The later Dalai Lama and Pan chen Lama system arose among the successors to Tsoṅ-kha-pa. [82] During Tsoṅ-kha-pa's lifetime the Mongol Dynasty fell in China, to be succeeded by the Ming; this Dynasty was not hostile to Buddhism, but dropped the courtly religious tie to the Tibetan Sa-skya-pa. Among the Manchu emperors of China, Chien-lung (1736-1796) charged the Mongolian Lama Lcaṅ-skya rol-paḥi rdo-rje to revise all the Mongolian translations from the Kanjur and to translate the Tanjur into Mongolian. Mongolian Buddhism was always completely dependent on the Tibetan forms, and accepted the whole range of deities worshipped by the Tibetans. Tibetan Buddhism in its second diffusion was increasingly different from the Chinese form of the religion. In China the stress was on *sūtras*, the basic scripture held to have been taught by the Buddha; in Tibet the authoritative commentary came to precedence. The strict adherence to the rules of authoritative texts is seen also in Tibetan art, restricted usually to a severely hieratic formalism, whereas in China and Japan Buddhist art was more free to develop by artistic inspiration.

III. Conception of the Deity

A. The Buddha and chief epithets. The name 'Buddha' means 'the awakened one,' i.e. awakened to the incomparable enlightenment. The explanation for the Tibetan translation *saṅs rgyas* is that he is awakened (*saṅs*) from the sleep of nescience and his discriminative faculty (*buddhi*) is expanded (*vibuddha*, *rgyas*). [88] The Buddha is also most frequently referred to as Bhagavat ('The Lord', 'Blessed One'), Jina ('Conqueror'), Tathāgata ('who has come the same way' or 'who has understood the same way'), Sugata ('well gone'), Mahāpuruṣa ('great person'), Mahāmuni ('great capable one'), Mahāśramaṇa ('great ascetic'), Arhat ('who has destroyed the enemy'), and Śāstṛ ('teacher' of gods and men), as also by the stock phrase Tathāgata-Arhat-Samyaksaṃbuddha, where Saṃyaksaṃbuddha means 'rightly completely enlightened'. The arising of a Buddha is considered most rare to see, like the Udumbara flower in a glade.

The old Pāli and Sanskrit sources recognize seven Tathāgata, the historical Buddha and six predecessors: Vipaśyin, Śikhin, Viśvabhū, Krakucchanda, Konākamuni, and Kāśyapa. [65] Mahāyāna works increase the Buddhas to five, who are supramundane: Akṣobhya, Vairocana, Amitābha, Ratnasaṃbhava, and Amoghasiddhi. One tradition holds that Gautama Buddha became completely enlightened as Mahā-Vairocana; another that the highest attainment is to be Mahā-Vajradhara. [48]

Also the Book of Numerical or Gradual Sayings (ii, 37-38) relates that a brahmin named Doṇa saw the mystic marks on the Buddha's feet and concluded that these were not the feet of a human being. In the ensuing dialogue, the Buddha successively denied that he was a god, a gandhabba (S. *gandharva*, celestial musician), a yakkha (S. *yakṣa*, a spirit apparition), a man. "Brahmin, truly I was a god, a Gandhabba, Yakkha, a man as long as I had not purged myself of fluxes. Brahmin, just as a lotus or a water-lily born of the water...remains unstained by the water, even so, brahmin, being born of the world...I remain unstained by the world. Therefore, O brahmin, consider me as the

Enlightened One." [34] In the Buddha's life up to this point, also in the case of his previous lives, he is called a 'bodhisattva' (a being intent on enlightenment).

B. Early Statement of the Enlightenment. In the first sermon, "Setting into Motion the Wheel of the Law," the Buddha explained that when, under the Tree of Enlightenment, he methodically fixed his mind on the thought, "This is suffering" (so also on the other Noble Truths), knowledge (*jñāna*) arose, vision (*cakṣus*) arose, wisdom (*vidyā*) arose, discrimination (*buddhi*) arose, intelligence arose, insight (*prajñā*) arose, light arose. This experience is said to have occurred in the last watch of the night in the full moon night of Vaiśakha month, just as the ruddy dawn was appearing. He *saw* the *dharma* (as the Vedic seers *saw* the Veda). Furthermore, "he who sees the Dhamma sees me, and he who sees me sees the Dhamma" (*S*. iii.120; *It*.91; *Mil*. 73). [16] And "who sees Dependent Origination sees Dhamma; who sees Dhamma sees Dependent Origination" (*Majjhima-nikāya* I, 190-91). Hence, on the day of Gautama's enlightenment the serpent king Kāla addressed him: [77]

> Even as Krakucchanda goes,
> Konākamuni, and Kāśyapa,
> So dost thou go *(tathā gacchasi)*, O great hero,
> Buddha today wilt thou become.

That is to say, like the former Buddhas, so Gautama came, whereby he is called Tathāgata (who came or went the same way)—so also, who *saw* the same and was the same Dhamma (Dhammabhūta, D.iii. 84).

C. Later (Mahāyāna) Statement of the Enlightenment. The early statement of Enlightenment is expanded in the Mahāyāna scripture *Bodhisattva-pitaka* (PTT V.23, p. 19):

> Whatever is the meaning of Dependent Origination, is the meaning of Dharma; whatever is the meaning of Dharma, is the meaning of Tathāgata. Therefore, whoever sees Dependent Origination, sees Dharma; whoever sees Dharma, sees the Tathāgata. Also, seeing that way, and accordingly fully understanding in the sense of Thusness, still one sees scarcely anything. What is that 'scarcely anything'? It is the Signless and the Non-apprehension; the one who sees in the manner of Signless and Non-apprehension, sees rightly.

In the "Meeting of the Father and Son" (*Pitāputrasamāgama*, last chapter), the Buddha explains to his father, King Śuddhodana:

> Great King, 'Buddha' is an expression for seeing reality. 'Seeing reality' is an expression for real limit *(bhūtakoṭi)*. 'Real limit' is an expression for nature realm *(dharmadhātu)*. Great King, that 'nature realm' is incapable of being explained in another way that pertains to name only, term only, manner of speech only, convention *(saṃvṛti)* only, speech only, or designation only.

That is to say, words fail to explain 'nature realm'. One must see reality: there is no substitute. Furthermore, that is the only way to see the Buddha according to the "Diamond Cutter" (*Vajracchedikā*): [43]

> Those who see me as form, who follow me by voice, those persons, engaged in wayward exertion, do not see me. The Buddhas should be seen as Dharma, for the leaders are the Body of Dharma. Moreover, True Nature being imperceptible, it cannot be discerned.

The Buddhist emphasis on vision as the fruit of the religious exercise gave rise to the use of the word 'eye' in metaphorical ways. Early Buddhism spoke of three eyes: the eye of flesh, the divine eye, the eye of insight. Later Buddhism added two more, the *dharma* eye (= knowledge eye) and Buddha eye; and texts have differing explanations for the various eyes. A complete explanation from the Yogācāra standpoint is in Sthiramati's commentary on the *Mahāyāna-Sūtrālaṃkāra* (Bodhipakṣya chapter) from which the essentials are given here:

(a) The eye of flesh sees forms in present time.

(b) The divine eye is of two kinds, both seeing forms in past and future: (1) that born of past action (*karma*), the eye of the gods; and (2) that born of contemplation (*bhāvanā*) in the *samādhi* of a yogin, and which sees the sentient beings passing away from here and going to various destinies in accordance with past actions.

(c) The eye of insight is the non-discursive knowledge which understands the individual and the general characteristic of the *dharmas*, seeing them in the absolute sense (*paramārthatas*).

(d) The eye of *dharma* understands without impediment all the scripture; understands the stream of consciousness of persons in the sense of discriminating whether it is an ordinary person, or one of the eight classes of disciples (on the four paths or in the fruits of the four paths), or a Bodhisattva and if so then on which of the ten Bodhisattva Stages; and seeing the *dharmas* in the conventional sense (*saṃvṛtitas*).

(e) The eye of a Buddha understands all *dharmas*, whether with or without flux, whether constructed or unconstructed; and realizes directly every knowable field; understands the state of Arhat ensuing from the 'diamond-like *samādhi*' and the freedom from fluxes of the Tathāgatas.

In Mādhyamika tradition, the eye of insight is said to see natures (*dharma*) as arising in a dream, as lacking intrinsic nature, and so on.

D. Theory of Enlightenment (bodhi) as Knowledge.

From the outset, Enlightenment is set forth in terms of knowledge, either by the word *jñāna* (knowing this or that) or the word *vidyā* (Pāli *vijjā*, wisdom). There are three kinds of wisdom (*vijjā*) which the Buddha is held to have experienced respectively in the three 'watches' of the night in which he attained complete enlightenment: (a) In the first 'watch' he directed his mind to the knowledge of his previous births. (b) In the middle 'watch' he directed his mind to the passing away and rebirth of sentient beings, seeing with a divine eye, surpassing the human one, the beings passing from here to various destinies—usually stated as five in number—in accordance with their motivated actions. (c) In the last 'watch' he directed his mind to the destruction of the fluxes (Pāli *āsava*, Sanskrit *āśrava*), the defiling elements. He realized: "This is suffering, this the source of suffering, this the cessation of suffering, and this the way leading to the cessation of suffering." Accordingly he realized: "These are the fluxes, this the source of fluxes, this the cessation of fluxes, and this the way leading to the cessation of fluxes." Thereby his mind was released from the fluxes, and he knew that there was no more rebirth for him, and that the needful had been done. [53] It seems that the description of the third wisdom is the same as given for an Arhat,[6] and a consistent observation is given later [Cult, A. Persons]. Also the Abhidharma explains the knowledge that arose during the experience under the Tree of Enlightenment ('knowledge arose,' etc.) as constituting 'knowledge of destruction' (i.e. knowledge of the Four Noble Truths) as well as the certainty of having exhausted knowledge and cultivation, i.e. 'knowledge of non-arising' (because there is nothing more to know or do in those respects). The three wisdoms are more fully stated as the six 'supernormal faculties' (*abhijñā*), which are actually faculties of knowledge, to wit, divine eye, divine hearing, knowing the make-up of another's mind, recollection of former lives, knowing magical acts, and knowing the destruction of the fluxes. [45]

The theory of his four special knowledges (*pratisaṃvid*) became important. They are explained in the *Bodhisattva-piṭaka* (chapter on Prajñāpāramitā) as follows:

a. Special knowledge of the object (in the sense of relating a special understanding to the object), for example, knowing the past as detached, the future as limitless, the present as all; knowing a dream as a truthless vision, an echo as dependent origination, a reflection as transmigration; and so on. Furthermore, whatever object serves as point of reference, knowing it as void, as signless, as purposeless (the three doors to liberation).

b. Special knowledge of natures (in the sense of knowing which natures), for example, knowing the natures involved in good and evil, in flux and non-flux, in the mundane and the supramundane, in the constructed and the unconstructed, in the corrupted and the purified, in *saṃsāra* and *nirvāṇa*; knowing the sameness of the Dharmadhātu, of enlightenment, and of realms.

c. Special knowledge of language, for example, he preaches the Law to creatures of the five destinies in their own language, whether to gods, serpents, spirits, and so on; he knows the language of men, women, and hermophrodites, the languages of the past, the future, and the present.

d. Special knowledge of eloquence, namely, ability to communicate in attractive and appropriate sounds all the principles of Buddhism. (This special knowledge is expanded, in the case of the Buddha, to the sixty elegant features of his speech).

In Mahāyāna Buddhism, Enlightenment consists of the four or five knowledges or wisdoms, the four being the 'mirror-like' (because devoid of discursive thought), the 'sameness' (of all the *dharmas*), the 'discriminative' (of the individual and general characteristics of all the *dharmas*), and the 'procedure-of-duty' (for the happiness and welfare of sentient beings) kinds of knowledges; and the fifth, the 'pure *dharmadhātu*' knowledge, which is both the object of the other four and their basis. [46]

Asaṅga's *Mahāyānasaṃgraha* (Chap. X) states that the turning around of the 'aggregate of perception' (*vijñāna-skandha*) yields control over the four kinds of knowledge, the 'mirror-like', and so on. [42] The school of Asaṅga and Vasubandhu called Vijñaptimātra develops this idea to show which perceptions from the eightfold set of perceptions correspond, by reversal, to the different knowledges. Thus, the reversal of the store consciousness yields the 'mirror-like' knowledge;

that of the defiled mind, the 'sameness'; that of the mind-based perception, the 'discriminative'; and that of the five outer-sense perceptions, the 'procedure-of-duty'. [46]

E. Bodies of the Buddha. In early Buddhism, the Buddha had a formal body (*rūpa-kāya*) and his Dharma (Doctrine) also was a body (*dharmakāya*) metaphorically. The formal body was the one in which he was born, became enlightened, and so on. The body of *dharma* was the corpus of his teachings, which according to the *Parinirvāṇa-sūtra* should be the authority for the monks after the Buddha's passing. The Mahāsāṅghika tenet that the Buddha is supramundane undoubtedly helped to develop the notion of multiple bodies as found in the Sarvāstivādin Abhidharma. [5] In the fully developed conceptions, the formal body had become two bodies, the Saṃbhoga-kāya (body of enjoyment) and the Nirmāṇa-kāya (apparitional body). The Dharmakāya had become a Cosmical Body, and sometimes this is called the only Svābhāvika-kāya (Self-existent Body).

The Nirmāṇa-kāya is the body in which a Buddha appears on earth, and performs twelve acts as formalized in the *Ratnagotravibhaṅga*: 1. The descent from Tuṣita, 2. Entrance into the womb, 3. Rebirth, 4. Skill in worldly arts, 5. Enjoyment of the harem women, 6. Departure from home, 7. Arduous discipline, 8. Passage to the terrace of Enlightenment, 9. Defeat of the Māra-host, 10. Complete Enlightenment, 11. The Wheel of the Law, 12. Departure into Nirvana. [48] It is also held that the Buddha only seemed to engage in those acts of the Nirmāṇa-kāya; such is the message in the Parable of the Physician in the "Lotus Sūtra".[11]

The Saṃbhoga-kāya is the body in which he becomes fully enlightened in the Akaniṣṭha heaven of the fourth Dhyāna, while his apparition shows on earth the way of becoming a Buddha. The Saṃbhoga-kāya is the body usually attributed the 32 characteristics (a standard list) and 80 minor marks (some differences in various lists), with the latter constituting a commentary on the former in sub-sets. The 32 are here given, grouped accordingly: [88]

1. each hair of the head curled to the right, 2. having the *uṣṇīṣa* protuberance on the head. 3. treasure of hair *(ūrṇā-kośa)* (in middle of forehead). 4. eyes dark blue, 5. eye-lashes bovine. 6. jaws leonine. 7. tongue long and slender, 8. voice pure, 9. teeth very white, 10. teeth without gaps, 11. teeth 40 in number, 12. teeth equal in size, 13. taste perfect. 14. shoulders gently curved. 15. standing, not bending himself,

> 16. hands which hang low, 17. skin delicate, 18. skin of golden hue, 19. upper part of body leonine, 20. broadshouldered, 21. rounded like a Banyan tree, 22. seven mounds on his body. 23. secret of privities drawn into a recess. 24. legs like those of an antelope. 25. each hair of body turning to the right side. 26. fingers and toes long. 27. hands and feet marked by a wheel rim, 28. feet well-planted, 29. hands and feet soft and tender, 30. webs joining (the fingers and toes on) his hands and feet, 31. heels broad, 32. ankle joints inconspicuous.

These characteristics are held in common with the 'universal emperor'.

The Dharmakāya is the incomprehensible realm, and 'profound, most profound'. The Sarvāstivādin school held that the Dharmakāya is quintuple, namely, the five supramundane aggregates devoid of flux, which are 1. morality. 2. concentration, 3. insight, 4. liberation, and 5. knowledge and vision of liberation. [45] In Mahāyāna scriptures the content of the Dharma-kāya is referred to either as 'Buddha natures' or as 'the merits (*guṇa*)', set forth briefly in Asaṅga's *Mahāyānasaṃgraha* (Chap. X) and completely in the Buddhist dictionary *Mahāvyutpatti*. These merits or natures include the four 'Special knowledges' and 'six supernormal faculties' presented above, as well as the ten powers, four confidences, eighteen exclusive natures, the six perfections (see under Path), great compassion (*mahākaruṇā*), and omniscience (*sarvākārajñatā*). The ten powers are as follows:

> 1. power of knowing the right and wrong place, 2. power of knowing the maturation of *karma*, 3. power of knowing the various faiths, 4. power of knowing the various realms, 5. power of knowing what is and is not the best sense organ, 6. power of knowing the paths going in any direction, 7. power of knowing all the meditations, liberations, concentrations *(samādhi)*, equipoises *(samāpatti)* defilements and purifications, 8. power of knowing remembrance of former lives, 9. power of knowing death, transfer, and rebirth. 10. power of knowing the destruction of the fluxes.

Nos. 8-10 are equal to three of the six supernormal faculties. The four confidences are: 1. confidence that he is fully enlightened about all *dharmas*, 2. confidence in knowing the destruction of all defiling fluxes, 3. confidence that he explains exactly and definitely the obstructive conditions (to the religious life), 4. confidence in the correctness of his path of salvation for realizing all (religious) success. [23] The 18 exclusive natures include such ones as 'he is free from error'; 'he never forgets'; 'he has no loss of insight'; 'there is going on in him the unclinging, unhindered knowledge and vision of the past, the future, and the present.' Asaṅga includes in the Dharmakāya the 32 characteristics and 80 minor marks possibly because it is considered the basis or sources of the Saṃbhoga-kāya (usually attributed these signs of the Great Person) as well as of the Nirmāṇa-kāya which appears to, shows and teaches ordinary men.[42]

IV. Worship

1) *Cult*

A. *Persons*

(a) *śramaṇa-brāhmaṇa*. In ancient India, the religieux were generally subsumed by the words, occurring frequently in compound, *samaṇa-brāhmaṇa* in Pāli or *śramaṇa-brāhmaṇa* in the Sanskrit language. While the ancient usage of these words is not entirely clear, it seems that a *brāhmaṇa* was a person leading a religious life while adhering to the orthodox life of social stages, which became standardized as four in Hinduism; and a *śramaṇa* was a person guarding his sanctity while not committed to the orthodox social stages of Brahmanic society. The Buddha was called the 'great *śramaṇa*', or 'great ascetic'. [21]

According to Asaṅga, there are four *śramaṇas*: the one victorious over the path, the teacher of the path, the one who lives by the path, and the one who spoils the path. Among those, any 'well-gone one' (*sugata*) is one victorious over the path. Any 'speaker of the doctrine' is the teacher of the path. Anyone who has entered the stream is the one who lives by the path. Anyone waywardly entered is the one who spoils the path. The expression 'well-gone one' means anyone having achieved, without remainder, the extirpation of lust, hatred, and delusion; and hence this title of the Buddha is equivalent to 'great *śramaṇa*' in Asanga's tradition. [87]

(b) Members of the Buddhist Saṃgha.

In the early Saṃgha, the fully ordained priesthood consisted of the male monk called *bhikṣu* and the nun called *bhikṣuṇī*. Of less advanced degree as regards the priesthood were the learners (*śikṣamāna*) and the male and female novices in *śramaṇa* status (*śrāmaṇera* and *śrāmaṇerikā*). Also there were the words for the male and female Buddhist laymen (*upāsaka* and *upāsikā*), who were also called 'son of the family' and 'daughter of the family'. The ordained monk and nun are the ones who begged. The laymen gave service, namely the four items necessary for existence: clothing, shelter, food, and medicine; and thereby the laymen gained merit (*puṇya*). The monastic instructor was called the *ācārya*, who when especially learned was called *paṇḍita*. The abbot of the monastery is the *upādhyāya*.

(c) The *ārya* and the *pṛthagjana*. The *ārya* is the noble one; the *pṛthagjana* the ordinary person adhering to the notion of separateness. *Saṃyutta-Nikāya*, iii (Khandha-Vagga, 42) explains the vulgar person as the one who has not heard the Doctrine or been disciplined in it, who has not come in contact with the noble ones or illustrious persons; and this vulgar person identifies his self with the five personality aggregates of form and so on. On the other hand, early Buddhism said that the noble one (Pāli *ariya*) is of four kinds as successive attainers of the path, namely, the one who has entered the stream, the one who will return once more to the world, the one who will not return, and the saint (*arhat*) as the fourth path (see Path of Salvation).

(d) The *śrāvaka*, *arhat*, and *sthavira*. A *śrāvaka* ('hearer') is a disciple of the Buddha, and the one who depends on a teacher—whether an instructor (*ācārya*) or a virtuous guide (*kalyāṇamitra*). Generally speaking, the word '*śrāvaka*' is used in Mahāyāna texts for followers of the 'lower vehicle' (*hīnayāna*) and so, in effect, for the first three kinds of '*ārya*'. Also in the *Jātakamālā* (Story of Sutasoma, 69,70): [69]

> Discovering the glory of religious practice by sitting on a lower seat; enjoying the honey of the (sacred) words with eyes joyously transfixed; respectfully bending one's mind serene and pure in single-pointed attention;—so one should listen devoutly to the Doctrine as a sick man to the words of a physician.

Upon becoming a saint through progress on the path he is no longer a disciple and is called *arhat* (P. *arahan*), in its Pāli meaning 'the worthy one' and in its later Sanskrit reinterpretation 'who has destroyed the enemy' where the enemy is the passions. The eighteen Buddhist sects had differing theories about the *arhat* which sometimes were hotly contested. [5]

In further development of the *arhat* notion as a forerunner of the Mahāyāna Bodhisattva, the *arhat* is conceived as able to postpone his entrance into Nirvana by living a prolonged life alongside the four Great Kings to protect the Doctrine until the next Buddha (Maitreya) shall appear, whereupon the *arhat* will be allowed to enter Nirvana. He has all the supernormal powers, including adoption of any form at will. In this role, he is also called a *sthavira* ('elder', Pāli *thera*). In the earliest theory of such Arhats, as in the *Ekottarāgama*, there were four:

1. Mahā-Kāśyapa, 2. Piṇḍola Bhāradvāja, 3. Kuṇḍopadhānīya, 4. Rāhula. There are intermediate lists of eight, and finally the Mahāyāna, as in the *Mahāyānāvatāra*, settled on sixteen: 1. Piṇḍola Bhāradvāja, 2. Kanakavatsa, 3. Kanakaparidhvaja, 4. Subinda, 5. Nakula, 6. Bhadra, 7. Kālika, 8. Vajraputra, 9. Śvapāka, 10. Panthaka, 11. Rāhula, 12. Nāgasena, 13. Iṅgada, 14. Vanavāsi, 15. Ajita, 16. Cūḍapanthaka, [41] possibly because sixteen fit neatly on a 16-petalled lotus for visualization in ritual. The prophecy, iconography, and prayer for the sixteen to appear, is found in a brief Tibetan text simple entitled "Rite of the Sthaviras". [20] Here the verse is included: "May the sixteen *sthaviras*, having abandoned their own aim and applied to the aim of others in the jungle of *saṃsāra*, with the vow to hold uppermost the protection of the Teaching promulgated by the Blessed One, come here by dint of compassion!" In the iconography the layman Dharmatāla (or Dharmatrāta) is added; and, in China, also Hvā-śang or 'Pot-Bellied Buddha', to make a total of eighteen, depicted in Chinese painting as crossing the sea to implant and foster Buddhism in China. [49]

The word 'elder' (*thera*) was also applied to a monk upon his being at least ten years in the Order after the higher ordination as *bhikṣu*. There was a healthy scepticism about the spiritual attainment of monks. The *Dhammapada* (260-261) says: [59]

> He is not therefore an 'elder' merely because his head is grey; ripe is he in age, 'old-in-vain' is he called. In whom are truth, virtue, harmlessness, restraint, and control, that wise man who has cast out impurities is indeed called an elder.

(e) The *pratyekabuddha* and the *muni*. The word *pratyekabuddha* means 'one enlightened by himself', and so contrasts with the *śrāvaka* who depends on a teacher. The word *muni* is understood as 'the capable one' in Tibetan translation. According to Buddhaguhya (PTT V. 76, p. 43), "The *munis* are *pratyekabuddhas*: because they have their own religious practice, pledge, and vow, and are capable by themselves although lacking a master, they are 'the capable ones' (*muni*)." This explanation is consistent with the account about the Sanskrit name Ṛṣipatana (P.: Isipatana), another name of the Deer Park where the Buddha gave his first sermon: [48]

> Formerly when the time approached for the Buddha Kāśyapa to appear in the world, there lived on that hill five hundred Pratyekabuddhas. They learned from a message given by the devas that the Buddha was to manifest himself. By their magical power they soared

> up to the sky and equipoised themselves in the element of fire *(tejo-dhātu)*. The fire that issued from their own bodies burned their material bodies, and the ashes fell to the earth. It was said, 'The Ṛṣis have fallen,' and for this reason the place is called Ṛṣipatana (the falling of the Ṛṣis).

Compare the *Ṛgveda* (X.136, Griffith's translation): "The *munis*, girdled with the wind, wear garments soiled of yellow hue...The muni,... flies through the region of the air." Hence, this meaning of *pratyeka-buddha* in the sense of the *muni* who can fly as the fruit of asceticism agrees with the expression 'seer' (*ṛṣi*) in connection with fire. Buddha-guhya's explanation (PTT V. 76, p. 21) of the Buddha's title Śākyamuni is as follows: "Śākya means the Śākya clan, and also because of taming Māra by power (*śākya*) he is 'Śākya'; he is 'muni' because capable in Body, Speech, and Mind." The statement by the Buddha that he was enlightened without dependence on another master seems consistent with this usage of the word *pratyekabuddha* as synonymous with *muni*. But the Pratyekabuddha came to be looked upon as a selfish renunciant and his attainment inferior to that of a completely enlightened Buddha, who is never called '*pratyekabuddha*'. Asaṅga contrasts two kinds of *pratyekabuddha*, the one like a rhinoceros, i.e. living a lonely life, and the one 'victorious by himself' (*pratyekajina*). Since the *pratyekabuddha* also attains the state of *arhat*, there is some overlap in the use of these two terms.

(f) The Bodhisattva, and the 'son and daughter of the family'. The rise of the Bodhisattva practice around the beginning of our era was meant for a person who would generate the double object—enlightenment for himself, and the benefit of others. A Bodhisattva ('enlightenment-being', or 'a being intent on Enlightenment'), is one who, having experienced suffering in his own stream of consciousness, arouses compassion for all other beings sharing this lot and aspires to allay their suffering. In comparison with the theory of sixteen *sthaviras*, it can be seen that the aim of helping others is shared, while the Bodhisattva is superior in having the aim of Enlightenment, which in this doctrine is distinguished from the passive Nirvana which is the goal of the 'Lesser Vehicle' and instead is aimed at the 'Nirvana of no fixed abode.'

Bodhisattvas are of two kinds: those who have entered the religious life as monks, and householders. The householder type seems especially to have been indicated by the frequent expression in Mahāyāna scriptures 'son of the family' and 'daughter of the family', although in early Buddhist texts the same expressions merely stand for Buddhist laymen. [30]

(g) The *kalyāṇamitra* and the *guru*. The qualities of the virtuous guide (*kalyāṇamitra*) are stated by the *Sūtrālaṃkāra*: [50]

> One should rely on the friend who is restrained, pacified, pacified further, and strives for the remaining merits; is rich with scripture, awakened to the truth, endowed with speech facility, compassionate by nature, and free from weariness.

Wherever Buddhism was firmly entrenched, similar explanations were given of the spiritual guide.

In addition, the development of Tantra in later Buddhism laid great importance on the *guru* or tantric hierophant (*vajrācārya*). The characteristics of the hierophant who confers the tantric initiation are stated in the work "Fifty Stanzas in Praise of the Guru": [48]

> Steadfast (in body), controlled (in speech), intelligent (in mind); forbearing, just, and without deceit; skilled in the praxis of *mantra* and *tantra*, compassionate, and learned in the expository texts; experienced in the ten categories, expert in drawing the *maṇḍala*; who can explain the *mantras*, is devoted and ruler of his senses, so should be the Hierophant.

The ten categories refer to tantric practices.

The *Vajrapāṇyabhiṣeka-mahātantra* says: "Master of the Secret Folk, how should a disciple look upon his preceptor? As though upon the Lord Buddha. The mind of him so disposed incessantly generates merits; he becomes a Buddha bringing benefit to all the worlds...One should hold to the preceptor's virtues, and never hold to his faults. If one holds to virtues, he attains success; if one holds to faults, he attains failure." [80] This is the basis of the Tibetan *guru-pūjā* (worship of the *guru*), in Tibetan the Lama (*bla ma*) in continuation of the Indian tantric hierophant status. It seems that an analogous attitude was held toward the Ch'an (Zen) master or patriarch (*rōshi*), but other Buddhist traditions did not stress such devotion.

B. *Ritual*

(a) Buddhist ritual, generalities. While Buddhism opposed the Vedic ritualism, it was through charging its animal sacrifices to be meaningless and cruel. Buddhism is not opposed to the type of ritual devoid of harm to other beings and which undermines only the psychological defilements. The traditional Buddhist ritual is a mental discipline, restraining the mental wandering in fields of desire and forcing it into certain orientations whereby it may pass to higher levels of consciousness. Later Buddhist ritual borrowed various practices from Vedic praxis, for example, the burnt offering (*homa*) in Tantrism.

In Buddhist countries there have been varying daily, monthly, and yearly rites, in addition to the essential sacraments in the life of an individual. These vary considerably from country to country. The universal festival is to honor the birth and enlightenment of the Buddha in the month of Vaiśākha (April-May). In South and Southeast Asia this worship (on whatever day it be set) is often called "Wesak", and referred to in the West as "Buddha's birthday." In Nepal, where in recent centuries there has been a loose fusion of Hindu and Buddhist rites, the most well-known observance is the worship of the Three Jewels on the third day of the bright fortnight of Vaiśākha. [10]

(b) Priestly ritual. When Gautama fled his father's palace to enter the religious life, he first shaved his head hair. The tonsure appears to symbolize the sacrifice of ordinary human nature, or the newly born, and this became the general practice for the Buddhist monk or nun. There were also several kinds of ordination (*upasaṃpadā*), including the one which the Buddha employed with the words beginning "Come hither, bhikṣus!" The standard ordination rite in later times, as witnessed in Ceylon, begins with the candidate's appearance, together with his tutor, before the abbot. In a most solemn service, the candidate, holding the alms-bowl and robes, first prays for the ordination. The tutor confers upon the candidate the three refuges and the ten moral precepts. For the three refuges the candidate is made to repeat "I put my trust in Buddha; I put my trust in the Dharma, I put my trust in the Samgha." He is made to repeat "Again I put my trust..." and finally to repeat, "Once more I put my trust..." thus a triple recital of each refuge. The ten precepts are "abstinence from destroying life," etc. (see Ethics, below). Now the candidate is qualified for the formal ordination under a named superior. Before the assembly of priests, he is asked various questions concerning possible possession of disqualifying attributes, such as certain diseases. Upon the candidate's answering them properly, one of the tutors asks the assembly to approve the ordination by silence or to object by speech. By keeping silent the assembly expresses its approval, and the candidate is accordingly ordained. [86]

The ancient priesthood held regular meetings called Posatha on certain lunar days, in the waxing phase on the eighth day, the day before the full moon, and the full moon day; in the waning phase on the eighth day, the day before the new moon, and the (dark) new moon day. The priests fasted on those days and confessed their sins against the precepts. The confession took place with the priests retiring in pairs, and kneeling face to face, confessing in whispers. In later times, and in various Buddhist countries, the number of days was reduced to the two days, full moon day and new moon day. [86]

The daily devotions of the monks, as still current in Thailand among other Southern Asia countries, includes the Morning and Evening Chanting. [63]

(c) Lay ritual. To become a lay Buddhist, one simply repeats thrice after any ordained monk the formula of triple refuge and takes from him the five moral precepts (see Ethics). The only departure is the Tibetan addition of a further refuge, that in the Lama or guru.

The Buddha directs in the *Mahāparinirvāṇa-sūtra* (the equivalent Pāli in *Dīgha-Nikāya* II also containing the four holy places): [24]

> O *bhikṣus*, four are the spots on earth to be held in mind during the life of a son of the family or daughter of the family, having faith. What are the four? Here the Bhagavat was born. Here the Bhagavat was completely awakened to the highest right perfected enlightenment. Here the noble wheel of the Law, having three turns in twelve parts, was set in motion by the Bhagavat. Here the Bhagavat entered *parinirvāṇa* in the realm of Nirvana without remainder. *Bhikṣus*, after my passing away, those who go circumambulating shrines, bowing to shrines, are to speak as follows: "Here the Bhagavat..." Among these places, whoever with pure thought will die in my presence, all those belong to heaven *(svarga)*, whoever are with remainder.

The four places are Kapilavastu, Gayā, Sarnath, and Kasia (= Kuśinagara), sanctified in the given order. [21] It seems that pilgrims to the particular place would pick up an appropriate symbolic figure, i.e. a tiny tree at Gayā. Until the first century A.D., representations of the Buddha were aniconic. [25]

Accordingly, it was the laymen who cremated the Buddha's body; worshipped his relics with perfume, flowers, music and dance; erected and administered the shrines (*stūpa*, *caitya*) and adorned them with jewels, canopies, banners, and so on, and lighted oil lamps. It seems that originally the priests disdained such worship, but that during the time of King Aśoka the shrine worship, such as circumambulation, was adopted by the monks in order to keep the Buddhist laity tied to the Samgha in a period when great numbers of shrines were being constructed with imperial patronage. Still, even a later monk sect like the Mahīśāsakas, to which Asanga belonged, held that there is little merit in worshipping shrines. [30]

Mkhas grub rje states that there are three kinds of relics to put into a *stūpa*: the relics of the Dharmakāya of the Tathāgata, which are memorial sentences; the relics of his corporeal substance, even when no bigger than a mustard seed; and the relics of his drapery, which are the icons; and that they are in the given order, highest, middling, and lowest. [48]

Another lay worship of Mahāyāna type (Indo-Nepalese-Tibetan) was in keeping a small shrine in the home dedicated to some Bodhisattva such as Mañjuśrī, with the appropriate icon; and in making offerings and in reciting the 108 names of that particular Bodhisattva. Each of the eight great supramundane Bodhisattvas have 108 names in individual texts translated into Tibetan from Sanskrit. Devout Buddhist everywhere could be expected to have some sort of household shrine, with varying observances.

(d) Bodhisattva ritual. Here there developed what is called the seven-membered rite, or 'supreme worship' (*anuttarapūjā*), as follows: 1. Praising, 2. Offering, 3. Confession of Sins, 4. Sympathetic Delight, 5. Entreaty, 6. Generating the Mind of Enlightenment, 7. Transfer of merit. Among those, the praising is of the deity (see g. below); the offering is of flowers, etc.; the Bodhisattva practice developed the confession of sins before a supramundane Bodhisattva or thirty-five visualized Buddhas; the sympathetic delight is with the merit of Buddhas and Bodhisattvas; the entreaty is for the Buddha to continue to teach in the world; generating the mind of enlightenment is done ritually (see Path of Salvation); and the Bodhisattva contemplatively transfers his merit to the sentient beings. [8, 48]

(e) Tantric rituals. These are basically: generating oneself into deity; generating the deity or deities in front. They operate on three levels: body with symbolic gestures (*mudrā*), speach with incantations (*mantra*), and mind with deep concentration (*samādhi*). Generally such rites are in three phases, preliminary or preparatory, the body of the rite, and concluding acts; and are aimed at mundane fruits, namely, appeasing (of deities), prosperity, and drastic consequence; or at supramundane fruits, especially complete Buddhahood; and are believed to realize such fruits faster than non-Tantric methods. Some of the rituals become very elaborate, as in the case of the *maṇḍala*, evocation of deity (*sādhana*), initiation (*abhiṣeka*), and burnt offering (*homa*). Buddhist Tantra is deeply indebted to the Neo-Upanishads, especially the group called Yoga-Upanishads. Essentially of practical nature rather than of doctrinal speculation, the tantric symbols are usually not accompanied with their rationalizations and so are easily misunderstood when being, for example, sexual symbolism. [48, 73, 82]

(f) Representations of deity. Early representations of the Buddha were in aniconic form: The footprint with mystic 'fortune-telling' marks stands for the prophetic life, the Great Person. The white umbrella stands for the Buddha's royal lineage and the meditating ascetic's protection. The tree means the invariable place of enlightenment. The wheel, from the Wheel of the Law, is the power of conversion, a royal symbol stemming from the chariot wheel of the victorious monarch. The white elephant, the form under which the Buddha descended from Tuṣitā into his mother's womb, the hypostasis of divine essence. The empty throne is the contemplative seat and the site of teaching. The *stūpa* is the incorruptible body of the Buddha, the Parinirvāṇa. The pillar of fire (a stone relief from Amarāvatī) is the magical ascetic power of the Buddha. [25, 67]

Iconographic representations of the Buddha can be traced back no earlier than first century A.D., when they began, especially under Greco-Roman influence, in the region of Gandhāra, Northwest India.

(g) Praises of the deity. Mātṛceṭa's poetical praises of the Buddha cover these topics: reason for praise, the Buddha's attainment of the six perfections, his uniqueness, his wonderful deeds, his form, his compassion, his speech, his teaching, his vow of benefit to the world, adaptability of his path to all kinds and conditions of living creatures, the hardships he bore, his skill in conversion, the discharge of his debt to the world. Mātṛceṭa justifies the praises this way: [2]

> In whom at all times and in all ways all faults are absent and in whom all virtues in every manner are established, in him it is proper for them that have understanding to take refuge, to praise him, to serve him, and to stand fast in his teaching.

The praise of the Buddha himself is especially in terms of the merits of his Body, Speech, and Mind:

> Lord, your beautiful body, the eye ambrosia, is decorated with the characteristics like a cluster of stars in the cloudless autumn sky. Muni, the lovely pious drapery of golden hue which covers you, is like the (yellow-red) cloud which enwraps the peak of the golden mountain (the Himalaya toward sunset). [80]

These words of yours are for all; they please the wise, strengthen the intelligence of the middle sort, and dispel the darkness of the slow-witted. [2]

Oh Buddha, the *dharmas*, the mines which produce all forms, come at all times within the compass of thy intelligence, like a myrobolan berry in the palm of the hand. [3]

(h) Symbolic directions. Buddhist tantric ritual rather thoroughly integrates non-tantric Buddhist concepts with esoteric practices descendent from non-Buddhist origins. For example, the allotment of divine functions to directions descends from the correspondences of the Vedic period, although it is in classical Hinduism that the associations are finally settled with Indra, chief of the gods, in the East; Yama, King of the Law and who showed the path to the other world, in the South; Varuṇa, high priest of cosmic regularity, in the West; and Kubera, guardian of treasures, in the North (non-tantric Buddhism replaces these four with the four Great Kings). In Buddhism, the initial impact of directions occurs when Prince Siddhārtha has his visions through the gates of Kapilavastu: through the East Gate, suffering; South Gate, sickness; West Gate, death; North Gate, a saint (*arhat*). Then the Pāli *Sigalovada Suttanta* tells how an Ariyan disciple should look upon the quarters: parents as the east, teachers as the south, wife and children as the west, friends and companions as the north. [11] In a tantric rite by Buddhaguhya (PTT V. 76, p. 24) of over a millenium afterwards, sixteen of the Buddha's disciples, foremost in some way, were drawn in the cardinal directions:

East:
1. Nanda – his younger (half-)brother
2. Rāhula – son of his body
3. Śāriputra – best in insight
4. Subhūti – who could best answer questions

South:
5. Maudgalyāyana – best in magical power
6. Udāyin – who generated faith in householders such as his father King Śuddhodana
7. Aniruddha – of magical (= clairvoyant) eye
8. Kauṇḍinya – who first heard the holy word from the Teacher

West:
9. Upāli – retainer of the Vinaya
10. Aśvajit – who aroused faith in the chief tempter (Māra)

11. Gavāṃpati – who had power over cessation-*samādhi*
12. Ānanda – his continual attendant

North:
13. Mahānāman – the barber of the Śākyas
14. Bakula – who gave all (medical) prescriptions
15. Pūrṇa – the intrinsic nature of a purified man's qualities
16. Kāśyapa – who served him in the declining years.

The symbolic assignment of directions should be explained. The intention is to parcel the aspects of the historical Buddha by way of his chief disciples. It supposes the Buddha as the Great Person and his directly-realized Doctrine in the East; so the disciples representing the Śākya clan or most profoundly in the Doctrine are there. In the *Sammanaphala Suttanta*, Jīvaka points out the Buddha to the King: "That is he, O king, sitting against the middle pillar, and facing the east, with the brethren around him." [11] Also, the *Aṣṭasāhasrikāprajñāpāramitā* (Chap. 30) contains this: [14]

> Subhūti: How then did the Bodhisattva Sadāprarudita search for the perfection of insight?
>
> The Lord: First of all Sadāprarudita, the Bodhisattva, searched for perfect insight in such a way that he did not care for his body, had no regard for his life; and gain, honour and fame did not interest him. He found himself in the seclusion of a remote forest, and a voice up in the air said to him: "Go East, son of the family! There you shall hear the perfection of insight!...You must not look to the left or right, to the South, East, West or North, upwards or down-wards, or in any intermediate direction.

The correspondences further suppose the Buddha as the teacher and wonder-worker, founder of a new religion, to be in the South; so also the disciples who best carried out that function through their special appeal to the layman.

The Buddha as the irreproachable high priest is intended in the West; so the brotherhood of monks (*saṃgha*), preservers of the orthodoxy, and progressing toward liberation through the Buddhist path, are there. Also it is written in the *Parinirvāṇa-sūtra*: [80]

> Among all ploughings of a field, the best is at the return of autumn;
> Among all tracks, the best is the track of a bullock [cf. 'a cow's donation', Godānīya, name of the Western Continent];
> Also, among all ideas, the ideas of impermanence and death are best.
> These dispel all the lust, ignorance, and pride of the three worlds.

The Buddha, in the sense of having Buddha natures serving the aim of sentient beings, is associated with the North; so those disciples best able to render service are there as well.

2) *Ethics*

(a) Books on Buddhist ethics and generalities. Buddhist ethics are especially represented in the work *Dhammapada*, a text of Pāli Buddhism, extant in an expanded form in Dharmatrāta's compilation in Buddhist Hybrid Sanskrit called *Udānavarga* with classical Asian translations. Simple ethical statements have made the *Dhammapada* beloved and famous in ancient as well as in modern time: [59]

> 1. The natures *(dhamma)* are preceded by the mind, have mind as leader, are made of mind. If one speaks or acts with a wicked mind, sorrow follows him even as the wheel follows the hoof of the draught-animal.
>
> 5. Hatreds never cease by hatred in this world; by love alone they cease. This is an ancient law.
>
> 103. Though he should conquer a thousand men in the battlefield, yet he, indeed, is the noblest victor who would conquer himself.
>
> 121-2. Think not lightly of evil, saying, "It will not come nigh unto me"; even by the falling of drops a water-jar is filled; likewise the fool, gathering little by little, fills himself with evil. Think not lightly of good, saying, "It will not come nigh unto me"; even by the falling of drops a water-jar is filled; likewise the wise man, gathering little by little, fills himself with good.
>
> 202. There is no fire like lust, no crime like hate; no ill like the five personality aggregates, no bliss higher than Nibbāna (= Nirvāṇa).

The implication of Buddhist ethics is drawn out in popular form in the story collections with moralistic coloring or conclusions, namely the *Divyāvadāna* (Divine Tales), *Karmasātaka* (Hundred tales of *karma*), "The Wise and the Fool," and the extensive collection of *Jātaka*. A standard Buddhist narrative (*avadāna*) contains a story of the present, a story of the past, and a moral, showing the strict causation of past act and present fruition. When the hero of the story of the past is the Bodhisattva (the Buddha in a previous life), the *avadāna* is a *Jātaka*. [90] The Buddhist stories generally oppose the ideal of "an eye for an eye," or the reversal of roles. Instead, they indicate specifically in a number of stories, as in the *Mahāvastu*, that the same role is continued through a series of lives. In some Jātakas, the historical life of the Buddha is not the first time that his cousin Devadatta has been ungrateful and envious. Indeed, this has happened before. [37] This is consistent with the Buddhist doctrine that actions remain as tendencies to reactivate those actions.

The various story collections bear out a contrasting emphasis between early and later Buddhism. The early ethics stressed morality (*śīla*), the later ethics generosity (*dāna*). The tales of outstanding gifts (the Buddhist kind of heroic feat) also belong to that part of Hīnayāna which anticipated the full-blown Mahāyāna. The most striking as well as famous legend is the one called "The Buddha as Viśvāntara" (Pāli: Vessantara). [69] In this tale a prince is fantastically extravagant in generosity, relinquishing everything asked for, not only precious materials, but even his own wife and children, and later getting back his family through divine intervention. The later precedence of generosity is indicated by its position as the first of the six Bodhisattva Perfections (*pāramitā*), which are Giving, Morality, Forbearance, Striving, Meditation and Insight. Undoubtedly the reason for the growing preeminence of generosity in the Mahāyāna is that it is the primary factor in the theory of persuasion or conversion to the Buddhist religion. There are four of these 'articles of attraction' (*saṃgraha-vastu*) which are considered to mature the sentient beings. [80] They are (1) giving, equal to the Perfection of Giving; (2) fine, pleasant speech; (3) acts in accordance; (4) oneself serving as an example. By the first one, the subject becomes a fit vessel, psychologically prepared to listen to the Law. By the second one, faith is aroused in him toward the Law that is taught. By the third one, he is made to exercise in accordance with the Teaching. By the fourth one, he is led to continue training his mind accordingly. The first one involves material things, and the last three involve Doctrine (*dharma*). The theory of generosity was enthusiastically represented in story and sculpture, and the doctrinal implications discussed at great length.

In the theory of the Buddhist path, the instruction of morality is the basis for the instructions of meditation and of insight. Atīśa (*Bodhimārgapradīpa-panjikā*, PTT V. 103, p. 37) explains why morality is taught first of all:

> It is this way: the great perfected enlightenment is dependent on the two collections (of merit and knowledge); the two collections are dependent (respectively) on the aim of others and supernormal faculty; supernormal faculty is dependent on calming of the mind (*śamatha*); calming is dependent on morality; therefore first of all, we teach morality.

(b) Lay and monk morality. The moral rules for laymen and monks have much in common since the monastic life adds a multitude of rules to those for the layman. The Buddhist layman pledges to observe the five precepts of not killing, not stealing, not committing adultery, not telling falsehood, and not taking intoxicating things conducing to heedlessness. The monks have ten points of instruction, the first five being the layman's precepts observed more strictly, and 6.-10. being the refraining from eating at the wrong time; from entertainments with dancing, singing and instrumental music; from adornments of garlands, perfumes, and unguents; from high, broad beds; and from accepting gold and silver. This list was variously reduced to eight points, for recitation at the Uposatha. Also, the five precepts are more fully formulated as the 'ten paths of action' as found, for example, in "The Sūtra of 42 Sections," traditionally held to be the first scripture translated into Chinese: [12]

> The Buddha said: "There are ten things by which beings do good and ten by which they do evil. What are they? Three are performed with the body, four with the mouth and three with the mind. The (evils) performed with the body are killing, stealing and unchaste deeds; those with the mouth are duplicity, slandering, lying and idle talk; those with the mind are covetousness, anger and foolishness. These ten are not in keeping with the holy Way and are called the ten evil practices. Putting a stop to all of them is called performing the ten virtuous practices.

The precept usually stated for the layman as 'not committing adultery' is understood generally as refraining from unlawful sexual commerce, and is meant to protect the mother. There are brief treatises on the subject, which set forth the forbidden women, forbidden bodily members or orifices, forbidden places for the act, and forbidden times. [51] In the more strict observance by the monks, one must refrain from all unchaste deeds, including those of the mind.

The kind of precepts stated in Nāgārjuna's "Friendly Epistle" to a king are common to monks and laymen: [89]

> Good and bad action each have five main bases: (1) constancy, (2) addiction, (3) freedom of expression, (4) meritorious domains, and (5) superiors. Exert yourself to practice their good (possibility)!

Likewise in common is the doctrine of five sins of immediate retribution, committing which causes a destiny in the lowest hell called Avīci, namely, matricide, patricide, murder of an Arhat, creating schism in the Brotherhood, and causing the Tathāgata's body to bleed with an evil intention.

The main list of monk observances over and beyond those of the laymen is the Prātimokṣa (Pāli: Pātimokkha), which enumerates the major and minor sins rehearsed at the Uposatha providing occasion for the monk confessional. Each Vinaya code of the various Buddhist sects has some form of Prātimokṣa and is distinguished by its varying number of rules. According to the *Mūlasarvāstivādavinaya* the main categories with their inclusive numbers are as follows: [65]

Class I. The four 'defeats' leading to permanent expulsion from the Order: fornication, murder, theft, and unjustified pretence of having saintly powers.

Class II. Thirteen rules whose violation incurs atonement through temporary expulsion.

Class III. Two equivocal cases of meeting with a woman which might belong to Class I, II, or V.

Class IV. Thirty cases of objects unduly obtained, to be confessed and forfeited.

Class V. Ninety 'stumbles', requiring formal confession.

Class VI. Four 'mentionables', requiring formal confession.

In addition this Vinaya has 106 rules of decorum, and 7 disciplinary procedures.

(c) Bodhisattva ethics. The basis of Bodhisattva ethics is his 'mind of enlightenment' which is his own aim along with his vow on behalf of others (see Path of Salvation). The Bodhisattva praxis consists in combining the 'means' (*upāya*)—consisting of the first five Perfections, Giving, Morality, Forbearance, Striving, and Meditation—with 'insight' (*prajñā*). The Mahāyāna scriptures make some striking claims for this Bodhisattva. Thus Śāntideva quotes the *Ratnarāśi Sūtra*: [8]

> Those beings that belong to the three states of existence, let them all make shrines for each of the Tathāgatas, of such an height, as is Sumeru King of Mountains, and let them pay worship to each of these through as many ages as the sands of the Ganges are: and let a Bodhisattva, with a mind of untrammelled omniscience, put but one flower there, he would produce greater merit than all that merit aforesaid.

Śāntideva explains eight Root Sins or transgressions: 1. discouragement of *śrāvakas* by premature teaching of the profound doctrine, 2. dissuading someone from following the Perfections and suggesting he should be a *śrāvaka* or *pratyekabuddha*, 3. preaching that the Bodhisattva path obviates the adherence to monastic discipline, 4. undue disparagement of the *śrāvaka* vehicle, 5. self-aggrandisement with exaggerated claims for his own group and disparagement of other Bodhisattvas, 6. advertising condescendingly one's profound knowledge, although it be gained just by reading books without direct realization, 7. incitement of princes to assess fines on the Saṃgha or on shrines for personal advantage, 8. submitting to degraded reckless princes, thus abandoning skillful means for the unworthy esteem by the prince and his court. [8] The Bodhisattva must confess these sins to august Akāśagarbha standing before him in a vision of sleep, or confess them to the imagined thirty-five Buddhas of Confession.

Also, Śāntideva quotes the *Ārya-Caturdharmanirdeśa-nāma-mahāyānasūtra*: [8]

> There are four rules, Maitreya, by which the Bodhisattva who is a great being overcomes the accumulated sin. And which four? As follows: resorting (its) condemnation; resorting to (its) antidote; the power of amendment; the power of refuge.

When the Bodhisattva reaches the Eighth Stage, he does not regress from Enlightenment, meaning that he no longer commits such sins. The reason is made clear in the *Vimalakīrtinirdeśa-sūtra*, which has such passages as these: [44]

> Reverend Upāli, the sin neither exists within, without, or between the two. Why is that? Because the Bhagavat has said: "By the corruption of the mind the sentient beings are corrupted; by the purification of the mind they are purified."
>
> The ideas *(vikalpa)* of the impure *(sāsrava)* and of the pure *(anāsrava)* make two. If the Bodhisattva understands the equality of intrinsic nature of all the *dharmas*, he no longer produces the notions of the impure and the pure.

The last is a statement about consciousness rather than about practice; hence the Bodhisattva can still practice virtue by 'second-nature' and refrain from vice while avoiding dualistic distinctions of the sort expressed in speech.

(d) The Tantric code. The Tantric moral code has usually been condemned as degenerate. Indeed, so recent as the appearance of 2500 *Years of Buddhism* (Delhi, 1956), we find it written (p. 358), "For instance, in the Guhyasamāja, murder, falsehood, theft and intercourse with women are recommended. Can the Buddha ever be imagined to have sanctioned such things?" [4] Of course, the Buddha did not sanction the exact opposites of the layman precepts; but also, one would search in vain in old Buddhist scriptures to find the Buddha prohibiting the metaphorical understanding of expressions. It is strange that scholars did not consult the various commentaries on the *Guhyasamāja-tantra* that are extant in Tibetan translation in the canon called the Tanjur to see what would be said about such a passage. Such statements first occur in the *Guhyasamāja*'s Chapter IX, and when we consult the great commentary called *Pradīpodyotana* composed by the tantric writer Candrakīrti, we find the following explanations:

1. Tantra : "He should kill all sentient beings with this secret thunderbolt."

   Comm.: "He should destroy all sentient beings by rendering them into the Void."

2. Tantra : "He should contemplate the stealing of all materials with the triple thunderbolt."

   Comm.: "'Stealing' means he summons the substance of all the Tathāgatas."

3. Tantra : "There he should contemplate the conjunction of all of them to the aspect of a lady."

   Comm.: "'There', in that *maṇḍala*, he should contemplate the conjunction with, i.e. the transformation (of all other male deities) into, the appearance of goddesses."

4. Tantra : "He should contemplate all forms as the diamond expressions which are lying words."

   Comm.: "He should contemplate all forms of sentient beings as lying words, since all *dharmas* are like illusions."

In view of those explanations of the *Pradīpodyotana* (PTT V. 158, pp. 66-67), it is clear that such Tantras had to be esoteric cults: just as not everyone can understand the metaphors of poetry, so not everyone can understand the metaphors of Tantra. But the *Guhyasamāja-tantra* brought to a logical conclusion the teaching of the *Prajñāpāramitā* scriptures that all *dharmas* are an illusion, by recommending that the one who sees things as they really are, stay in the world nevertheless, and so speak 'lying words'.

(e) Buddhist attitude toward suicide and military defense. In the *Milindapañha* (Questions of King Milinda), the King is represented as asking the monk Nāgasena why the Blessed One declared to the priests that no one should destroy himself, when he also taught the extirpation of birth, old age, disease, and death. The monk replied:

> The virtuous and well-conducted man, your majesty, is like a medicine in destroying the poison of human corruption; ... is like the magic jewel in giving all good fortune to men; ... is like the wind in extinguishing the heat of man's threefold fever; ... is like a teacher in training men in the acquirement of merit; ... It was, your majesty, in order that the virtuous man, ... who is such a cause of welfare to men, might not perish, that The Blessed One, your majesty, out of compassion for men, laid down this precept ... [86]

However, the self-sacrificing nature of the Bodhisattva ideal in time served to justify a different attitude toward suicide. The chief scriptural source appears to have been the "Lotus Sūtra" (*Saddharmapuṇḍarīka*), which has the story of how the Bodhisattva Bhaiṣajyarāja in a previous existence showed his gratitude to the Buddha by immolating his body. This story might be interpreted symbolically as indicating the mystic heat, one of the four states preceding the condition of sainthood. In practice, it encouraged suicide by fire, sometimes for political martyrdom. [33]

Again, while early Buddhism interdicted the taking of life, the Buddhist monks in Asian nations from time to time resorted to arms to defend their temples and monasteries. The theological justification for this has been suggested in the "fundamental transgressions" of the Anuttarayoga-tantra, no. 10 among the fourteen: "to have love for the wicked (but one should have compassion for them)." [48] How this compassion operates in a given situation is illustrated by an example in Asanga's *Bodhisattvabhūmi*. If a Bodhisattva sees a bandit about to kill many men or to commit some other crime leading to immediate damnation, he thinks that were he to kill the bandit he himself would go to hell but save the bandit from a worse fate; and so out of compassion for all concerned except himself does the deed which horrifies him. The theological conclusion is that in this he commits no fault, but instead gains much merit. Such a case occurred in Tibet with the assassination of the king Glaṅ dar ma. [19]

(f) Problems of Buddhist ethics. Among various ones that could be cited, certain problems both to the Buddhists and to the Western scholars of Buddhism, can be pointed out.

1. One might observe that Buddhism regards 'craving' (Pāli *taṇhā*, Sanskrit *tṛṣṇā*) as the chief cause of the phenomenal world and subjection to its misery, and then wonder if the desire to attain Nirvana

or Buddhahood is different from this. Buddhism has been forced to use a different word for virtuous desire; it is 'longing' (*chanda*), almost equivalent to 'conviction' (*adhimukti*).

2. The old Buddhism, and continuing today, recommended the cutting off of family ties, and regarded such affections as a hindrance to monastic progress. Indeed, 'regret' (for phenomenal associations left behind) is a principal obstacle in a certain advanced stage of Buddhist meditation. Still, Buddhism always praises the love and gratitude to parents; and in time this becomes a spiritual exercise [see Path of Salvation, (g), (1)].

3. There is a problem in the assurance of retribution for the volitional actions of men, since Buddhism denies a continuing, unchanging 'soul'. Still, Vasubandhu in his commentary *Pratītyasamutpādādi-vibhanga-nirdeśa* (PTT, V. 104, p. 285) states, "It is said in the Sūtras that the equipoise of cessation (*nirodha-samāpatti*) is attended with consciousness,...therefore, there is no perceptual break up to Nirvana without remainder." Of course, it still remains for the proponent of such a viewpoint to show its consistency with the 'momentary' tenet one also finds in the Yogācāra literature.

3) *A. Myth*

The sacred scriptures of Buddhism are pervaded with myth or mythic elements involved with the spirit world, as is also the traditional biography of Gautama, the founder of the Buddhism. Western scholars have noticed considerable solar symbolism in his legendary life. The doctrine of Buddhism takes for granted the mythic structure of the world in three divisions, the realm of desire, of form, and the formless realm, with their various sub-realms inhabited by various classes of deities.

(a) Myths connected with the Buddha's life. The traditional life of the Buddha is probably based on actual historical events overlaid with various mythological elements of which some follow: (1). The Bodhisattva made a vow in a previous life to become completely enlightened, whereupon after numerous rebirths, as king of the fishes, and so on, up to his illustrious life as Viśvāntara when he gave away everything, he was then reborn in the Tuṣitā heaven to abide until the time to descend for his last life. In that heaven he made five investigations to determine the right time, continent, place, social class, and individual family. When the Bodhisattva entered the womb of Queen Māyā, she had a remarkable dream of an elephant descending into her womb, which established the sacred mother-son relation. When the Bodhisattva was born, two streams of water fell from the sky, one of cold and one of hot water, washing the Bodhisattva and his mother. Promptly the Bodhisattva firmly footed took seven long steps towards the north and proclaimed, "I am the chief in the world, I am the best in the world, I am the first in the world. This is my last birth. There is now no existence again." (2). In the case of the four sights which appeared to Gautama outside the gates of his father's palace, it is traditionally stated that the gods created these visions and it is sometimes added—by reason of his stored-up merit of previous lives. (3). The night session at the base of the tree of enlightenment is full of myth, starting with the onslaught at dusk of the forces of Māra and their defeat with the help of the earth goddess, followed by Gautama's visions with the 'divine eye' of sentient beings passing to various destinies. (4). Once, at Kapilavatthu the Buddha surrounded by thousands of Arhats, in order to convince his proud kinsmen the Śākyas, rose in the air and performed the miracle of pairs: flames of fire came from the upper part of his body and streams of water from the lower part. Then the process was reversed. Next fire came from the right side of his body and water from the left, and so on through twenty-two variations of pairs. He then created a jewelled promenade in the sky, and walking along it produced the illusion that he was standing or sitting or lying down, and varied the illusions in a similar way. [78] (5). With the Buddha's 'blessing' (*adhiṣṭhāna*)—a cause often included in the account—his great disciple Maudgalyāyana (Pāli: Mahā-Moggallāna Thera) by means of magical power (P. *iddhi*) ascended to the various heavens and described the deities there, and also descended into the various hells and returned to describe their respective tortures.

(b) Myths prevalent in the scriptures. The gods (*deva*) are frequently introduced near the beginning of *sūtras* as auditors or interlocutors of the Buddha. For example, the very first sermon in the *Saṃyutta-Nikāya*, Part I, begins, in the translation of Mrs. Rhys Davids: [66]

> Thus have I heard:—The Exalted One was once staying near Sāvatthī, at Jeta Grove, in Anāthapiṇḍika's Park. Now a certain deva, when the night was far spent, shedding radiance with his effulgent beauty over the whole Jeta Grove, came into the presence of the Exalted One, and coming, saluted him and stood at one side. So standing he spake thus to the Exalted One—'Tell me, dear sir, how didst thou cross the flood?'

In many of the usually brief scriptures of the same volume, the gods along with the tempter Māra are as likely to be encountered by a monk as would be other monks.

Mahāyāna scriptures continue and expand upon inclusion of deities among the Buddha's retinue. The "Lotus Sūtra" in its remarkable first chapter shows the Blessed One staying at Rājagṛha on the Vulture Peak mountain with an assemblage of twelve hundred monk-Arhats, the great disciples, two thousand other monks, six thousand nuns, the great (celestial) Bodhisattvas, thousands of other Bodhisattvas; also the gods of the quarters and various spirit kings, all with thousands of gods or spirits as their respective retinues; further the four chief demons followed by myriads of demons; the four Garuḍa chiefs (the mythical bird) followed by myriads of Garuḍa; and finally, Ajātaśatru, king of Magadha. The Lord entered a meditation upon infinity, whereupon there fell a great rain of divine flowers, the whole Buddha field shook in six ways, and the vast congregation gazed at the Lord with amazed ecstasy as a ray issued from the 'circle of hair' of the Buddha's forehead which illuminated all the Buddha fields in the eastern quarter and also all beings in the six destinies. The chapter concludes with the great Bodhisattva Mañjuśrī explaining to the future Buddha Maitreya the reasons for the prodigious affair. It is not until the second chapter that the Buddha speaks, addressing a human disciple, Śāriputra. [39]

(c) The mythic structure of the world. [54] The creation myth (see Conception of Man: Creation) assumes the Buddhist classification of animate beings as belonging to one or other of three realms, of desire, etc. and the manifestation of the receptacle worlds. The four formless heavens have no limited abodes and so do not constitute receptacle worlds. The realm of form, divided into the First, Second, Third, and Fourth Dhyānas, is thereunder variously enumerated with sixteen, seventeen, or eighteen heavens, constituting receptacle worlds for named deity classes, yogins who have attained those states, and certain classes of discarnate men. The realm of desire contains abodes for all five destinies—gods and men (good destiny), hungry ghosts, animals, and hell beings (evil destiny). Some traditions add a sixth destiny called *asura* (titan), enemy of the gods. The gods in the realm of desire are in six passion heavens, four above the earth, one on the summit of Mount Meru, and one half-way down its sides. Mankind is on four continents in the cardinal directions. Hungry ghosts (*preta*) are on the earth surface or just underneath. Animals are in the air or on the dry or watery parts of earth. Hell beings are in eight hot hells or eight cold hells. The basic system of abodes (realms of desire and form), and no limited abode (formless realm) in a standard list is as follows: [45]

> Formless Realm: 1. base of boundless space; 2. base of boundless perception; 3. base of nothing-at-all; 4. base of neither ideation nor non-ideation.
>
> Realm of Form: First Dhyāna (1. Brahmā's retainers, 2. Brahmā's ministers, 3. Mahābrahmā); Second Dhyāna (4. Lesser Light, 5. Immeasurable Light, 6. Clear Light); Third Dhyāna (7. Lesser Virtue, 8. Immeasurable Virtue, 9. Total Virtue); Fourth Dhyāna (10. The Cloudless, 11. Meritorious Birth, 12. Great Fruit, and 13-17. five Pure Abodes, with Akaniṣṭha as no. 17).
>
> Realm of Desire: Six 'Passion Gods', Men, Hungry Ghosts, Animals, and Hell Beings—variously located on the complex of the Central Mountain Meru, ranged about by seven mountainous circles, eight great oceans, and four continents (with hells in the outskirts or beneath the southern continent).

In Burmese Buddhism this earth system rests on water twice the thickness, the latter on a mass of air twice the water's thickness. [76]

(d) Mythology of the spirit classes. (1) The *Ārya-Saddharmasmṛtyupasthāna* states the human sin respectfully responsible for birth as one or other of the thirty-six kinds of 'hungry ghost', which are: 1. Limbless-trunk Preta, 2. Needle-mouth P., 3. Vomit-eater P., 4. Ordure-eater P., 5. Foodless P., 6. Odor-eater P., 7. Doctrine-eater P., 8. Water-eater P., 9. Hopeful P., 10. Spittle-eater P., 11. Garland-eater P., 12. Blood-eater P., 13. Flesh-eater P., 14. Incense-eater P., 15. Malevolent-conduct P., 16. P. looking for the opportunity, 17. Underworld P., 18. P. of great magical power. 19. Blazing P., 20. P. looking for the opportunity regarding human infant, 21. Able to assume any form at will, 22. Seashore P., 23. Yama policeman, 24. Child-eater, 25. (Human) vital heat eater P., 26. Brāhman demon, 27. Hearth P. 28. P. of unpleasant street, 29. Wind-eater P., 30. Ember-eater P., 31. Poison-eater P., 32. P. of forest, 33. P. of charnel ground, 34. P. of tree, 35. P. of crossroad, 36. Member of Māra group. [52, 88]

Vinītadeva explains as classes of *preta* the spirits called *Piśāca* (flesh and blood eaters), Kumbhāṇḍa (gourd-shaped), Pūtana (putrid) and Kaṭa-pūtana (body with charnel odor). The Deva (gods) are Indra, and so on; and included here are also the Yakṣa (the sacrificers in the realm of the gods) and the Gandharva (the singers and musicians among the gods). The Nāga is a snake spirit and the Mahoraga is a serpent or large snake spirit and a royal snake (*nāgarāja*). The Kiṃnara ("Is it a man?") are animal-like, i.e. part man and part animal. [85]

(2) The five Buddhas of Mahāyāna Buddhism are regularly explained as the nature of the five knowledges. In the commentarial tradition of the *Mañjuśrī-nāmasaṃgīti* they are also associated respectively with the five eyes, as follows: [68]

Buddha	*Knowledge*	*Eye*
Amitābha	Discriminative	Insight
Amoghasiddhi	Procedure-of-duty	Fleshly
Ratnasambhava	Equality	Divine
Akṣobhya	Mirror-like	Buddha
Vairocana	Dharmadhātu	Dharma

The five Buddhas appear to be personifications of five knowledge-vision aspects of deity (see Conception of Deity).

(3) The great Bodhisattvas might be personifications of biographical elements in the Bodhisattva career of Gautama. Especially likely is the derivation of Avalokiteśvara (the lord who looks down) from the look which Gautama had under the Tree of Enlightenment when he surveyed the sentient beings in the different destinies, as well as shortly after his enlightenment when he compassionately saw the sentient beings as different stages in the rise of a lotus from the mud. Gautama's victory over Māra entitles him, in the Indian tradition, to the post of Indra, who wields the thunderbolt; and so the Bodhisattva Vajrapāṇi (the thunderbolt-handed) may be the personification of this victory. Also the Bodhisattva Mañjuśrī, whose sword cuts down the thicket of nescience and who holds the book of insight, should personify the enlightenment. However, once such Bodhisattvas develop an individual character, partly by absorption of Hindu elements, their cult and iconography depart considerably from the primitive conception. Noteworthy is the shift of Avalokiteśvara's sex to female in Chinese Buddhism. The traditional list of eight Bodhisattvas contains Maitreya, Gaganagañja, Samantabhadra, Vajrapāṇi, Mañjuśrī, Sarvanivaraṇaviṣkambhin, Kṣitigarbha, Ākāśagarbha.

(4) Tantric Buddhism also incorporates major and minor deities. Especially prominent are the three Mothers of the Families, Locanā of the Tathāgata Family, Pāṇḍarā of the Lotus Family, Māmakī of the Thunderbolt Family. When there are four, the green Tārā is the Mother of the Pledge Family. [48]

3) *B. Doctrine*

(a) Generalities. The Buddhist doctrine is one of the three Jewels, the Jewel of *dharma*. It is the 'sublime doctrine' (*saddharma*) and has a stock epithet, 'the well expressed' (*subhāṣita*) of which a fuller form is the frequent description "lovely at the beginning, lovely in the middle, lovely at the end," explained in the *Arthaviniścayaṭīkā* as respectively the instructions of morality, mental training, and insight.

In the *Mahāparinibbāna-sutta* of the Pāli canon (*Dīgha-Nikāya* II, 100) the Buddha states: "Ānanda, the doctrine I have taught is neither 'insider' nor 'outsider'. Since it was prepared that way, the Tathāgatas does not have a teacher's closed fist toward doctrines." This means that the Buddha did not have one doctrine for close disciples as contrasted with Buddhist laymen or with non-Buddhists. The history of Buddhism shows that the first splits in the Buddhist community were not over doctrine, but over practice. Of course, once such splits occurred, a new sect would gradually develop some specialized doctrinal interpretations.

But then there is the 'silence' of the Buddha to certain metaphysical questions such as 'whether the Tathāgata exists after death, or does not, or both, or neither;' 'is the soul identical with the body or different from it?' Apparently, the Buddha refused to answer certain questions, the very answers to which in conceptual or dogmatic terms would arouse misunderstanding in the mind of the questioner, and thus divert him from the religious goal. The Buddha was pointing toward direct realization as the only answer to certain questions. [56]

Also, it does not follow from the Buddha's non-withholding of doctrine that the disciples understood it the same. It is recorded in the Brahmā Suttas of the Pāli canon (*Anguttara-Nikāya*, I, 135, ff.): [66]

> Thus have I heard;—The Blessed One was once staying at Uruvelā, on the banks of the river Nerañjarā, beneath the Goatherd's Banyan, and he had just attained full enlightenment. Now as he was privately meditating, the thought arose in him: 'I have penetrated this Dhamma, deep, hard to see, hard to understand, peaceful and sublime, no mere dialectic, subtle, intelligible only to the wise. ... And now I only might teach the Dhamma, and others might not acknowledge me ... 'Then did Brahmā Sahampati ... vanish from the Brahmā world and appear before the Blessed One ... and he said: 'Lord! Let the Blessed One preach the Dhamma! Let the Blessed One preach the Dhamma! There are beings whose eyes are hardly dimmed by dust ...' ... Then the Blessed One, understanding Brahmā's entreaty, because of his compassion toward all sentient beings, looked down with a Buddha's Eye over the world. The Blessed One saw, with a Buddha's Eye, so looking

> beings whose eyes were scarcely dimmed by dust, and beings whose eyes were sorely dimmed by dust, beings of keen sense and beings of dull sense... ...Seeing Brahmā Sahampati he made response in verse: 'Open for them the doors stand to ambrosia! Let those that hear renounce the faith they hold. Foreseeing hurt I have not preached, Brahmā, the Dhamma sublime and excellent for men.

Even the Buddha's close disciple Ānanda still had some dust in his eyes, as reported in Dīgha-Nikāya (II, 55): Once when the Lord was staying among the Kurus, the venerable Ānanda approached him and said: "It is wonderful, Lord, that while Dependent Origination is so deep and looks so deep, to me it seems perfectly clear." "Do not speak like that, Ānanda. For this Dependent Origination is deep and looks deep too." [31]

While the Pāli editors punctuated the scriptures to begin, "Thus by me it was heard. Once the Buddha was dwelling...," there are indications that the division should be: "Thus by me it was heard upon an occasion. The Buddha was dwelling..." [10] The latter interpretation stresses the personal experience of the narrator, since 'hearing' in the Indian context means that undistracted attention mentioned near the end of the "Lotus Sūtra", where it is also said, "By writing, reciting, studying this Dharmaparyāya, and by treasuring it up in one's mind, young men of good family, one is to acquire innumerable good qualities." [39] Here 'undistracted attention' is a kind of mental calming (*śamatha*) and the 'good qualities' include the 'insight arising from hearing' (*śrutamayī prajñā*). In short, the opening of the Buddhist *sūtras* implies that the scripture which follows is a topic of Buddhist meditation. Consistently, the Abhidharma, which is the exegesis of doctrine, declares that Dharma is of two kinds, the scripture (S. *āgama*, P. *nikāya*) and its higher comprehension (*adhigama*). [45] The scripture can be classed in nine sets according to the Pāli canon: 1. *Sutta*, separate texts of sermons, 2. *Geyya*, mixed prose and verse, 3. *Veyyāṇkara*, solemn exposition and prophecy, 4. *Gāthā*, verses, 5. *Udānā*, joyous utterance, 6. *Itivuttaka*, legend, 7. *Jātaka*, accounts of previous births, 8. *Abbhuta*, accounts of the marvellous, 9. *Vedalla*, (possibly:) teaching by question and answer. [65] In Sanskrit Buddhist texts there is also a classing in twelve sets. The first five, the same as the Pāli ones in equivalent Sanskrit, are explained as the Hīnayāna 'Sūtra basket'. The equivalent ones to 6. and 7., plus the Sanskrit categories of *Nidāna* (occasion for a Vinaya rule due to some person's conduct) and *Avadāna* (narrative with moral), are counted as the 'Vinaya basket' of both

Hīnayāna and Mahāyāna. The equivalent to 8., plus the Sanskrit *Vaipulya* (grand scripture) and *Upadeśa* (explanation) constitute the 'Abhidharma basket' for both vehicles. Mkhas grub rje explains that the Abhidharma arose from compiling the random passages in the canon that deal with specific and general characteristic of *dharmas*. He also mentions Asanga's view that the category of *Upadeśa* is the Abhidharma of both vehicles; and this view might suggest the *Upadeśa* as a development of the old Pāli group called *Vedalla*. [48]

(b) Scriptural doctrine. When ancient Buddhism divided into eighteen sects, naturally there arose discussion of what the basic Buddhist doctrinal position, upon which all sects can agree, however disagreeing on other points. The solution to this problem came to be called the four 'aphorisms' or 'seals' of the Doctrine: (1) All constructed things are impermanent; (2) All constructed things are suffering; (3) All natures are devoid of self; (4) Nirvāṇa is calm. [50]

The doctrine of the Buddha as heard by Śāriputra and which occasioned his conversion to Buddhism is surely the most repeated verse in Buddhism, having been turned countless times in Tibetan prayer-wheels:

> Whatever things have arisen through causes, their cause the Tathāgata has declared and whatever is their cessation—speaking thus is the Great Ascetic *(mahāśramaṇa)*.

This cardinal statement takes two directions in further scriptural passages: (1) the four Noble Truths including the Middle Path which avoids the extremes of indulgence and mortification, and where the point of departure is suffering, a kind of feeling; (2) the twelvefold Dependent Origination avoiding the extremes of existence and non-existence, and where the point of departure is nescience due to discursive thought.

(1) The traditional statement of the four Noble Truths: This is Suffering, a Noble Truth—to be fully experienced; this is the Source of Suffering, a Noble Truth—to be eliminated; this is the Cessation of the Source, a Noble Truth—to be directly realized; this is the Path leading to the Cessation of Suffering, a Noble Truth—to be cultivated (or contemplated).

(2) The traditional list of Dependent Origination, each successive one having the preceding as its condition: 1. nescience, 2. motivations, 3. perceptions, 4. name-and-form, 5. six sense bases, 6. sense contact, 7. feelings, 8. craving, 9. indulgence, 10. gestation, 11. birth, 12. old

age and death. The basic division is always into the first seven and the last five, where the prior group is a passive reflex of the past *karma* or previous life, and the last group shows the development of new *karma*.

From the outset the doctrines of Buddhism are associated with vision and knowledge, for in the first sermon "Setting into Motion the Wheel of the Dhamma," which the Buddha delivered at the Deer Park near Benares, he said, "When, monks, among previously unheard doctrines I thought 'This is Suffering—a Noble Truth,' vision arose, ...knowledge arose..." [35]

The typical doctrines of Buddhism are indicated in Asaṅga's explanation of the category '*Sūtra*': [87]

> Among those, what is *Sūtra*? When the Bhagavat, having begun such and such subjects of discipline and practice in such and such matters, gave an account related to personality aggregates, related to sense bases, related to dependent origination, related to foods, truths, realms, related to Śrāvakas, Pratyekabuddhas, Tathāgatas, related to stations of mindfulness, right elimination-exertions, bases of magical power, organs, powers, branches of enlightenment, limbs of the path, or related to the unpleasant, mindfulness of inbreathing and outbreathing, the points of instruction, faith with understanding; and those who established the canon, having received that account, arranged it in order and connected it in order, as proper, with beautiful sets of terms, sentences, and syllables, namely, so as to indicate such and such meanings and virtues associated with aims and associated with chastity—that is called *Sūtra*.

The topics from 'stations of mindfulness' down through 'limbs of the path' constitute the thirty-seven *bodhipakṣya-dharmas* (for which see Path of Salvation).

(c) Higher comprehension of the Doctrine.

(1) Abhidharma. In the medieval period of India, it was usual to classify the differentiated doctrinal exegesis in four sets of reasoned conclusions, called the four *siddhānta*-s, the Vaibhāṣika, Sautrāntika, Yogācāra, and Mādhyamika. The first two are principally known to Western scholarship from Vasubandhu's *Abhidharmakośa-kārikā* (Vaibhāṣika viewpoint) and his auto-commentary (Sautrāntika viewpoint). The former is based on traditional exegesis in the Kashmir school; the latter on reinterpretation of the scriptures, especially in the Gandhāra school. Vasubandhu's *Abhidharmakośa* arranges the Abhidharma material in eight chapters devoted to the following topics in order: 1. Elements, Realms; 2. Sense organs, natures (*dharma*), 3. Cosmology; 4. Deeds (*karma*); 5. Defiling forces; 6. Noble persons, the Buddhist

paths; 7. Knowledge; 8. Meditative attainments. Vasubandhu appends a section ('Chapter 9') in which he refutes the doctrine of *pudgala* (personal self). [45]

Vasubandhu explains all the elements of the universe—the natures (*dharma*) as amounting to seventy-five according to the realistic Vaibhāṣika position of the 'Sarva-asti-vada' (everything-exists-doctrine), and of which none is a self. The two grand divisions are into the conditioned natures and the unconditioned natures. The unconditioned ones are 73. space, 74. cessation through understanding each case, 75. cessation not through understanding each case (but through meditation). The first seventy-two are all conditioned natures, and fall into these groups: [71, 73]

I. Forms: the sense organs 1. eye, 2. ear, 3. nose, 4. tongue, 5. body; the sense objects 6. form, 7. sound, 8. smell, 9. taste, 10. touch, 11. form without representation.

II. 12. consciousness.

III. Elements combining with consciousness.

A. Universal elements in every consciousness: 13. feelings, 14. ideas, 15. volition, 16. contact, 17. longing, 18. insight, 19. mindfulness, 20. attention, 21. conviction, 22. concentration.

B. Universal virtuous elements in every virtuous consciousness: 23. faith, 24. striving, 25. indifference, 26. modesty, 27. shame of, 28. non-greediness, 29. absence of hatred, 30. non-injury, 31. cathartic, 32. carefulness.

C. Universal defiled elements in every defiled consciousness: 33. delusion, 34. carelessness, 35. laziness, 36. lack of faith, 37. torpor, 38. excitation.

D. Universal unvirtuous elements in every unvirtuous consciousness: 39. lack of modesty, 40. lack of shame.

E. Occasional defiled elements: 41. anger, 42. hypocrisy, 43. envy, 44. jealousy, 45. approving the reproachable, 46. causing harm, 47. enmity, 48. deceit, 49. trickery, 50. arrogance.

F. Indeterminate elements: 51. repentance, 52. sleepiness, 53. general conception. 54. specific conception, 55. love, 56. hostility, 57. pride, 58. doubt.

IV. Elements not combining with forms or with consciousness: 59. reach, 60. non-reach, 61. comparability, 62. condition without ideas, 63. cessation without ideas, 64. cessation-equipoise, 65. life span, 66. birth, 67. subsistence, 68. old age, 69. impermanence, 70. the set of terms, 71. the set of sentences, 72. the set of syllables.

This school holds that the seventy-five elements, although distinct, are found linked in the world by ten causes—six basic causes and four conditional causes. The six basic causes are: the motivating cause, the co-existent cause, the cause of like type, the concomitant cause, the prevalent cause, the maturation-cause. The four conditional causes are: a basic cause as condition, the immediately following condition, and objective support as condition, the governing condition. [73]

The Abhidharma also acutely discusses the doctrine of *karma* (deeds as causation). Karma is volition (the act of mind) and what is produced by it (the verbal and corporeal act). The verbal and corporeal acts are each of the varieties representation and non-representation. [45]

(2) Mādhyamika. Nāgārjuna, celebrated founder of this school, develops his doctrinal exegesis to explain the Middle Path with a dialectical procedure to destroy discursive thought and a visionary procedure to see reality. He uses a theory of two truths, conventional truth established by process (e.g. defilement and purification) and absolute truth established by non-discursive vision. The Tibetan tradition is that he shows the meaning of the Prajñāpāramitā scriptures aimed at the insight which sees the void. His known works stress the doctrine of the void.

His emphasis on the discriminating mind as the key to conventional truth starts with the first verse of his *Madhyamakakārikā*: "Never have any modes-of-being originated from themselves, from another, from both, or from no cause." In line with the old Buddhist doctrine that the third Noble Truth, of Cessation, is realized directly (*sākṣāt*, 'before the eyes'), he says from the standpoint of absolute truth (Ibid., XXV, 19-20): "There is no distinction at all between *nirvāṇa* and *saṃsāra*; there is no distinction at all between *saṃsāra* and *nirvāṇa*. What is the limit of *nirvāṇa* is also the limit of *saṃsāra*. Between the two there is not the slightest difference." Thus, *nirvāṇa* is attained when it is seen; it is seen, according to Nāgārjuna, when *saṃsāra* is seen devoid of origination and destruction.

Furthermore, conventional truth is resorted to in preparation for teaching the supreme meaning, according to his verse (*ibid.*, XXIV. 10): "Without [first] taking recourse to a manner of speech (*here* = convention), the supreme meaning cannot be taught; without [first] understanding the supreme meaning, one does not attain *nirvāṇa*." The great Mādhyamika commentator Candrakīrti, in his discussion of the fifth Bodhisattva stage in his *Madhyamakāvatāra*, explains why the

Truths of Suffering, Source, and Path are conventional truth, while the Truth of Cessation is supreme truth. [56]

Again, Nāgārjuna's verse (*op. cit.*, XXIV, 40), which is stated in terms of 'seeing' the reality in the Buddha's teaching, points to the standpoint of absolute truth, since it means pure imagery free from discursive thought: "The one who sees dependent origination, sees precisely suffering, source, cessation, and the path." Here he presumably alludes to the experience of enlightenment about all the knowable.

Nāgārjuna's Nirvāṇa appears to be the Mahāyāna 'Nirvana of no fixed abode' (*apratiṣṭhita-nirvāṇa*) and not a realm antithetical to phenomenal life (*saṃsāra*) as it was in early Buddhist thought.

While the opponents of his school charged it with an over-stress on Voidness to the point of nihilism, the facts are that Nāgārjuna's powerful writing was enormously influential in India even on non-Buddhist philosophy and that his own Buddhist followers disagreed on his purport to the extent that two Mādhyamika schools arose. The chief writer of the Prāsangika-Mādhyamika is Candrakīrti; this position is that the Mādhyamika does not have independent arguments: its arguments, to the extent of having them, are only to refute the opponent by using speaking techniques on his level of convention. The Svātantrika-Mādhyamika, headed by Bhāvaviveka (or Bhavya), holds that the principles of Buddhism can be defended by independent arguments. Candrakīrti's works became generally authoritative in later Mādhyamika, but Bhāvaviveka's writing also has considerable appeal. [56]

(3) Yogācāra. Āryāsanga, celebrated founder of this school, avoids the Mādhyamika emphasis on Voidness by adhering to the entire Sautrāntika-like edifice of Buddhist categories which fill up his major work, the *Yogācārabhūmi* consisting of seventeen *bhūmis* or 'stages' and of four exegetical collections called *saṃgrahaṇī*. Moreover, Asanga incorporates a judicious selection of Mahāyāna tenets, especially from the *Saṃdhinirmocana-sūtra*, insofar as they do not conflict with his sect of Buddhism, the later Mahīśāsakas. [87]

Asaṅga is not a simple collector, although the *Yogācārabhūmi* is indeed encyclopedic; in accord with his idealistic philosophy, he especially clarifies the Buddhist teaching about 'perception' (*vijñāna*). In early Buddhism there was a standard list of six—the five based on the outer senses and the sixth based on the mind (*manas*) as the sixth sense. Asaṅga decides that various canonical passages, including the different treatment of *vijñāna* as when it is a member (the third) of Dependent Origination and one of the five personality aggregates, make it necessary to distinguish certain *vijñānas*. He keeps the sixth perception based on the mind (having the function to perceive *dharmas* in the mind) and adds a seventh, the 'tainted mind' (*kliṣṭa-manas*) (tainted by ego delusion and so on, and immediately succeeding any of the first six perceptions), and an eighth, the 'store consciousness' (*ālaya-vijñāna*) (the store of impregnated seeds of past volitional actions). The first seven can be grouped as 'evolving perceptions' (*pravṛtti-vijñāna*). Some opponents of this system have unfairly charged that the 'store consciousness' is just a Buddhistic substitute for the Hindu *ātman*. However, in Asaṅga's treatment (*Viniścaya-saṃgrahaṇī*), the 'store consciousness' must cease for Nirvana without remainder and for advanced beings, namely, Arhats, Pratyekabuddhas, Bodhisattvas on the last three Bodhisattva Stages, and Tathāgatas. [46]

Analysis in the Yogācāra school posits three levels of characteristics, Imaginary (*parikalpita*), Dependency (*paratantra*), and Perfect (*pariniṣpanna*).

(4) Buddhist Logic. The early trend of the Mādhyamika school appears to have been anti-logical by destroying the boundaries between the mutually-exclusive categories of common sense, for example, like Nāgārjuna erased the boundaries between the phenomenal world of bondage and the superior realm of release. However, Nāgārjuna's theory of two truths includes 'conventional truth' to salvage something upon which to base ordinary discursive thought. Candrakīrti, in his commentary called the *Prasannapadā*, stresses this 'conventional truth' as permitting all four of the Indian logical school's 'sources of knowledge' (*pramāṇa*): direct perception, inference, trustworthy scripture, and analogy. However, Candrakīrti may well have been forced into this declaration by the powerful thrusts of the Buddhist logicians starting with Dignāga. Buddhist logic in the classical period begins with Asaṅga, who adopts the Indian rules of debate, merely changing certain examples to give a Buddhistic flavour and doing nothing to rationalize this logic in terms of his idealistic philosophy. Asaṅga admits three sources of knowledge: direct perception, inference, and trustworthy scripture. Vasubandhu, who developed the idealistic viewpoint as Vijñaptimātra, expands upon this interest in logic by independent writing on the subject.

The creative period of Buddhist logic begins with Dignāga, whose great work is the *Pramāṇa-samuccaya*, extant in Sanskrit only by fragments but fortunately fully available in Tibetan translation. Dignāga bases his logical reform on the Vijñaptimātra school by his bold opposition to the realistic position that both direct perception and inference rely on the same (external) object. Instead, Dignāga declares that there are actually two different fires, $fire_1$ and $fire_2$; and direct perception has $fire_1$ as object, while inference has $fire_2$ as object. This follows from the idealistic standpoint of the Vijñaptimātra school by which there is no external object independent of consciousness. Indeed, what is said to be the external object cannot be distinguished from the mental image of it. Hence, there are merely two means of cognition, of which direct perception has a particular (such as the particular of a fire) as object, and inference has a universal (such as the fire denomination of an utterance) as object. And Dignāga further insists that the particular has more reality than the universal. [40]

Thus Dignāga accepts only two independent sources of knowledge —direct perception and inference. Also, he is probably the first to distinguish between inference for one's own sake and inference for the sake of others, the former apprehending an object by an inferential mark, and the latter demonstrating that prior inference by the statement of thesis, reason, and example. [29]

Dignāga's great successor Dharmakīrti clarifies and develops Dignāga's system. In Dharmakīrti's works, the most important of which is the *Pramāṇavārttika*, the universal is practically bereft of reality while the particular is the real. Still later Buddhist logicians differentiate Dignāga's philosophical base from that of Asaṅga by claiming that Dignāga is a Yogācārin holding that absolute knowledge is always attended with images (*sākāra*), while Asaṅga is a Yogācārin holding that absolute knowledge is without images (*nirākāra*). [38]

(5) Theory of Voidness. The Buddhist theory of Voidness is well represented in early Buddhism in the *Majjhima-Nikāya* (III, pp. 104-109) by a scripture entitled *Cūlasuññatāsuttaṃ*: "For example, this Migāramātu Assembly Hall is void of elephants, cows, horses, and mares..." This explanation of voidness is repeated in the *Laṅkāvatāra-sūtra* (text p. 75): "Again, Mahāmati, what is relative (or: respective) voidness? As follows: In whatever place something is not present, one says it is void of that thing. For example, Mahāmati, in the Mṛgālamātu Assembly Hall, there are no elephants, cows, sheep, etc., but I affirm it is not devoid of monks: it is said to be void of the former. Besides, Mahāmati, the assembly hall does not lack assembly-hall-hood nor do the monks lack monkhood, nor is it that elephant-cow-sheep-etc. states are not present elsewhere." This passage is referred to by Vasubandhu in his commentary on the *Akṣayamatinirdeśa-*

sūtra (Derge Tanjur, Ci, 120a-5): "Moreover, in whatever place something is lacking, there it is void of that thing. That is also said in the *Laṅkāvatāra*, 'Because this Mṛgālamātu Assembly Hall lacks hogs, sheep, etc., it is void.' Here also, because there is neither self nor what belongs to self in the sensory base of eye, it is 'void'. The same remark applies to the sensory bases of ear, etc." Vasubandhu's comment shows that the 'respective' kind of voidness is probably the oldest Buddhist sense in which word 'voidness' (*śūnyatā*) is employed. It is equivalent to the 'non-self' teaching of Buddhism, that there is neither 'I' nor 'mine' in any of the five personality aggregates, the same as saying that the personality aggregates are void of self.

The Abhidharma adds to the voidness doctrine. Voidness is one of the three gates to liberation, the other two being the gate free from purpose and the signless gate. Vasubandhu's *Abhidharmakośa* (VIII, 25c-d and 26a-b) has the expression 'voidness of voidness' referring to the Arhat's *samādhi* in which the *dharmas* are considered as both void and non-self, or that the voidness (of the voidness gate) is also void of self. [45]

Śāntideva quotes the Mahāyāna-sūtra "Meeting of Father and Son" as asserting that both the convention and the absolute have been well seen and realized directly by the Bhagavat as void, where convention is worldly usage and the absolute is inexpressible. [8] This explanation appears consistent with the Mādhyamika presentation of voidness, where the realization of the convention as void is shown by Nāgārjuna in *Madhyamakakārikā* XXIV, 18,19:

> Whatever has origination in dependence we call the 'voidness'. That is the designation when there is depending. Precisely that is the middle path. Since no *dharma* originates outside of dependence, it follows that there is no *dharma* whatsoever that is not void.

However, Nāgārjuna does not appear to explicitly attribute voidness to the absolute (*paramārtha*).

In the *Madhyāntavibhāga*, a treatise highly authoritative to the Yogācāra school, Voidness is the absolute as the void 'realm of natures' (*dharmadhātu*), the content or material cause of the world. In that Voidness is the Imagination of the Unreal, which is also real and emanates Dependent Origination and the unreal subject-object duality; this Imagination provides the form or formal cause of the world. The philosophy is idealistic as concerns form and realistic as concerns content. [88]

Buddhist tantra texts frequently speak of the yogin's 'entrance into the void' and of imagining in the void a germ syllable *mantra*, such as *Hūṃ*, and then imagining that germ syllable to change into some symbolic form with color and shape, and then the latter to change into the body of a deity. [48,82]

In Mahāyāna Buddhism there are also lists of sixteen, eighteen, and twenty voidnesses. Here is a list of sixteen: 1. voidness of the internal, 2. voidness of the external, 3. voidness of internal and external together, 4. voidness of voidness, 5. voidness of the supreme goal, 6. voidness of the conditioned, 7. voidness of the unconditioned, 8. voidness of the neither prior nor subsequent, 9. voidness of non-elimination, 10. voidness of ground, 11. voidness of all the elements, 12. voidness of individual characteristics, 13. voidness of non-support, 14. voidness of non-substantiality, 15. voidness of self-existence, 16. voidness of non-substantiality and self-existence together. [48] In these cases, just as before, voidness always means that a place is void of something. So, when one sees voidness of the internal, a place is void of the internal and that place is void. Perhaps the most frequently occurring voidness of the list in Mahāyāna texts is 'voidness of self-existence'. Voidness is an objective reference; the subjective factor that 'sees' the Voidness is regularly stated to be 'insight' (*prajñā*).

V. Conception of Man

1) *Creation*

The Buddhist genesis story is very ancient, being found in the Pāli scriptures besides the northern Buddhist accounts. It is mentioned in all three branches of Buddhist scriptures, Sūtra, Vinaya, and Abhidharma; and elements of the story are intimately tied up with Buddhist metaphysics. In the Abhidharma literature the account is given in the description of *vivarta* (differentiation of the beings due to evolution of the inferior worlds) as contrasted with *saṃvarta* (consubstantiation of the beings due to dissolution of the inferior worlds). Thus creation in Buddhism implies a preceding destruction. There are three efficient causes of the periodical destruction of the world systems, *viz.*, fire, water, and wind. Fire brings an eon of evolution to an end by destroying all of the realm of desire (*kāma-dhātu*) and the First Dhyāna heaven of the realm of form. Water destroys all that as well as the Second Dhyāna heaven; and wind destroys all the latter as well as the Third Dhyāna heaven of the realm of form. Only the Fourth Dhyāna of this realm remains intact. The sequence of creation may be summarized as follows: [88]

I. In the next period of evolution, while the lower receptacle worlds are re-evolving pursuant to the destiny of beings, the sentient beings fall to lower planes in a process usually described as starting from the level of the Clear-Light deity class of the Second Dhyāna (after the destruction by fire). They fall from that divine world to this place ('here'), passing through each of the intermediate worlds by a type of birth called 'transformation' (*upapāduka*). Other beings with this type of birth are the hell-beings, the beings of the intermediate state between death and rebirth, and the gods. Those 'men of the first eon' fall through the intermediate worlds with actions described as involved with supernal desire and fruitions experienced immediately. They have a beautiful form, are 'made of mind', are self-luminous, feed on joy, and are wherever they wish to be. While in the First Dhyāna (realm of Brahmā), Brahmā thought, "I have created them;" they thought, "Brahmā has created us." Hence, they have the same idea, while having different bodies, and this idea is delusive.

II. Then, on the surface of the earth which at that time was fluidic there appeared an earth essence which some being disposed to greediness tasted with his finger. It pleased him, he came to eat mouthfuls, and others beings followed suit. Thus these beings became dependent on morsel food, still subtle. They lost their original qualities of feeding on joy, body made of mind, and so on, and their bodies became more substantial. The ones who least indulged, proudly retained their beautiful form. The sun, moon, and year became known. In time this earth essence disappeared and a honey-like excrescence appeared on the surface of the earth. Hell beings, beings in the embryonic states, and the gods involved with desire also have just the subtle kind of food, which does not give rise to excrement or urine.

III. Then, in place of the honey-like earth excrescences, a rice-pap appeared and the beings subsisted on that coarse morsel food. At that time, the distinguishing characteristics of male and female appeared, and the beings had mutual sexual desire with associated acts.

IV. In the last phase of the legend there arose the 'private property' idea with individual rice plots, then stealing with consequent violence. Those beings selected a judge, called the great chosen one (*mahāsammata*), to render decisions on the disputes; he was given one-sixth of the rice crop for his royal services to provide security. Mahāsamatta was the first king, and inaugurated a lineage, of which the most important intermediate name is king Ikṣvāku. During the latter's reign the marriage code was established, and the Śākya clan emerged, to continue down to the birth of Gautama Buddha (and his son Rāhula).

The Buddhist Tantra tradition adds to the above account that the 'men of the first eon' fell because they lacked the 'illusory *samādhi*', the intense concentration in which the natures (*dharma*) are seen as illusion, and so they were trapped by appearances when the 'earth essence' manifested. [88]

2) *Nature of Man*

(a) The personality aggregates and transmigration. There are five constituents of man, called the aggregates (S. *skandha*), which in the standard order are: form (*rūpa*), feelings (*vedanā*), ideas (*saṃjñā*), motivations (*saṃskāra*), and perceptions (or 'consciousness of') (*vijñāna*). The last four are frequently referred to as 'name' (*nāma*), or the four 'names', whereby the five aggregates are called 'name and form' (*nāma-rūpa*). Buddhaghosa, in his *Visuddhimagga*, preserves an ancient tradition that 'name' includes only the three middle aggregates (omitting 'perception'). 'Form' is explained as the elements (fire, air, water, earth) and their evolutes and combinations; in short, 'form' is matter, especially visible matter, since 'form' is the object of the eye sense organ. Sometimes perceptions, the 'consciousness of (objects)', is taken as the leader of the aggregates and to stand for the group of 'names' as in Nāgārjuna's *Ratnāvalī* (Chap. I, 80-81), where a man is said to be a set of six elements, earth, water, fire, wind, space, and consciousness, and therefore not any of these.

Buddhism agrees that in those five personality aggregates no permanent, unchanging entity can be found. Sometimes this thesis is set forth in the form, "There is no 'I' or 'mine' in the personality aggregates." This doctrine is ordinarily understood as opposed to the Hindu Ātman, an immortal soul in the heart which is one with the supreme spirit of the world, the Brahman. Buddhist metaphysics claims that the 'non-self' doctrine fits the equally cardinal doctrine of transmigration with rigid justice of recompense for acts committed. Early Buddhism emphasized *karma* ('action') as what transmigrates. In fact, this *karma* which determines destination after death is explained as the volitional 'act of mind'. The "Story of Sahasodgata" has this verse: [84]

> The acts of the 'indwellers' are not lost even in a myriad of aeons; having reached fullness and death's time—you should know—they come to fruition.

In the Buddhist usage of the word 'indweller' (*dehin*), this refers to a 'stream of consciousness' (*citta-saṃtati*), changing momentarily and full of impressions (*saṃskāra*) impregnated by good and bad actions, which transmigrates to a new abode while the imagined agent who thinks 'I' and 'mine' does not so transmigrate. [80]

(b) Man and the other destinies. According to the Mūlasarvāstivādin *Vinaya-vibhaṅga*, the Buddha recommended that the five different destinies could be clarified for the disciples by pictorical representation. By this tradition, the first such representation during the Buddha's lifetime was presented to King Udrāyaṇa. This came later to be called the "Wheel of Life". In the center are the three 'poisons', lust, hatred, and delusion, represented by the dove, the snake, the pig. Ranged about those are the five destinies. In the outer ring is the twelvefold dependent origination depicted symbolically. [84] Some ways in which man contrasts with the other destinies are shown through the theories of food, pleasure and pain, and Buddhist path possibility. Men differ from the six god classes of the desire realm by living on coarse morsel food, while those gods subsist on subtle food. Also the divine eye surpasses the human eye. Asaṅga (*Vastu-Saṃgrahaṇī*) mentions that the gods of the third Dhyāna have complete (i.e. undiluted) pleasure, the hell-beings complete suffering. Animals, hungry ghosts, men, and gods in the realm of desire, have both pleasure and pain. From the fourth Dhyāna up through the formless realm there is neither pleasure nor pain. Furthermore, men differ from animals in having the trait of compassion (*karuṇā*), the capability of serving the aim of others, according to Candragomin's *Śiṣyalekhā* (verse 101).

Preeminently, the human destiny differs from the others in the matter of following the path. In their view of transmigration, the Buddhists believed that the stream of consciousness could transfer to other destinies besides the human, while entrance upon the path ensured continued rebirth in a human family. These theories are summarized in the doctrine of the eight unfavorable 'moments' (*akṣaṇa*) for hearing the Buddhist Law, listed in Nāgārjuna's Friendly Epistle: 1. adherence to perverse views; 2-4. animal, hungry ghost, and hell modes-of-being; 5. a time when there is no promulgation of the Jina (Buddha); 6. life beyond the borders (i.e. not in the 'Middle Country'); 7. deficiency of sense organs; 8. life among the long-lived gods. [89]

These 'long-lived gods', according to Aśvaghoṣa's *Aṣṭākṣaṇakathā*, are the Great-Fruit gods of the fourth Dhyāna who are 'devoid of ideas' through cessation of consciousness and mental elements. [80]

(c) The embryo of Tathāgata. A group of Mahāyāna scriptures called the Tathāgatagarbha works—one of them has that very title—sets forth a theory that each sentient being has hidden in the stream of consciousness the embryo (*garbha*, sometimes translated 'womb' in this context) or element of the Tathāgata, called the 'jewel lineage'. These theories are summarized and integrated into Buddhist doctrine in the treatise *Ratnagotravibhāga*. [74] The basic idea is that a being could not attain Enlightenment unless he had the possibility of such an attainment: an effect is traceable to a cause. This cause is set forth as an element—the true mind or true nature—that had been obscured by adventitious defilements in the stream of consciousness. Primarily these defilements are lust, hatred, and delusion. The thesis rests upon an ancient disputed doctrine, "The mind is intrinsically pure." [5]

Asaṅga's authority, the *Saṃdhinirmocana-sūtra*, does not use the term Tathāgatagarbha, although the *Lankāvatārasūtra* employs it synonymously with the *ālayavijnāna* so basic to Asaṅga's position; and, interestingly, the *Ratnagotravibhāga* employs the term Tathāgatagarbha but not *ālayavijñāna*. The theory that this embryo of the Tathāgata possesses, even if just in potentiality, the thirty-two characteristics and eighty minor marks of a Buddha, suggests that in this tradition the title 'Tathāgata' belongs to whichever body of the Buddha, usually the Saṃbhoga-kāya, is attributed those corporeal characteristics.

The *Laṅkāvatāra-sūtra* holds that some beings are destitute of Buddha nature; these are called *icchantika*. [72]

3) *Path of Salvation*

(a) The Buddha's Path of Salvation. According to the Buddhist legends, Gautama was successively shown signs outside the four gates of the capital city Kapilavastu, an old man, a sick man, a dead man, a dignified monk; and these signs awakened in the Bodhisattva a longing to emulate that monk. Upon his return to the city in royal pomp, a *kshatriya* maiden named Kisā Gotamī standing on the roof of the palace joyfully viewed his beauty and glory, and spoke out this utterance:

> Happy indeed is the mother,
> Happy indeed is the father,
> Happy indeed is the wife,
> Who has such a husband.

The word for happy in the Pāli text is *nibbuta*. When the prince happened to hear what the maiden said, he understood that word not only in the secular meaning of 'happy' but in the religious meaning of 'extinguished', for it is an adjectival form of the word *nibbāna* (S. *nirvāṇa*), meaning 'extinction'. The Bodhisattva in thought agreed with the maiden, and further asked himself, "Now when what is extinguished, is the heart happy?" He decided, "when the fire of passion is extinguished, it is happy; when the fire of illusion, when pride, false views, and all the lusts and pains are extinguished, it is happy. She has taught me a good lesson, for I am searching for extinguishment (Nirvāṇa). Even today I must reject and renounce a household life, and go forth from the world to seek Nirvana. Let this be her fee for teaching." He sent up to the maiden his precious pearl necklace (a religious act of presentation to the *guru*), which she mistakenly understood to mean the prince was in love with her (a secular interpretation of the act). [78]

After six years of study under teachers and fruitless austerities, he adopted a middle course, and in meditation at the 'terrace of enlightenment', a certain fig tree, he attained the incomparable enlightenment. The traditions agree that the four Meditations (*dhyāna*) were the preparatory phase of the Great Enlightenment. [6] He told his first disciples he had attained that enlightenment without dependence upon another teacher. And his last words were: "And now, O monks, I take my leave of you; all compounded things are transitory; work out your salvation with diligence." Upon passing from this life, he achieved Parinirvāṇa.

(b) The three instructions. Buddhaghosa's celebrated work of Pāli Buddhism, *The Path of Purification* (*Visuddhimagga*), is organized in three sections according to the three instructions set forth in Saṃyutta-Nikāya (I, p. 13):

> The wise man who, firmly standing on morality, cultivates consciousness and insight, he the monk ardent and prudent, may disentangle this tangle.[58]

Asaṅga, in his *Yogācārabhūmi*, section called *Cintāmayī bhūmi*, explains that the first instruction, that of Morality, has six aspects: (the monk) (1) dwells with morality, (2) is restrained by the Prātimokṣa vow, (3) is possessed of good behavior, (4) is possessed of lawful resort, (5) views fearfully even minor sins, (6) takes and learns the point of instruction (*śikṣāpada*). When one has mastered the first instruction, he goes on to the second instruction, that of Consciousness or mental training, summarized by four Meditations—correlated to the mythic four Dhyāna heavens—called 'right dwelling in *samādhi*,' and presented in a traditional statement stemming from ancient Buddhism: [53]

> Having abandoned the main defilements and secondary defilements of mentals as well as well as the five hindrances (sensuous lust, ill-will, torpor and sleepiness, mental wandering and regret, and doubt), then—
>
> (1) Free from desires, free from sinful and unvirtuous natures, with general conception and specific conception, having attained the First Meditation, he abides in the joy and pleasure arising from liberation (from the things mentioned).
>
> (2) After allaying the general and specific conception, purifying himself inwardly, and making the stream of consciousness one-pointed, having attained the Second Meditation, he abides in the joy and pleasure arising from the *samādhi* free from general and specific conception.
>
> (3) After becoming dispassionate toward joy, he abides indifferent. Mindful and aware he experiences pleasure by way of body, just as the one of whom the Noble ones said: "Indifferent and mindful he dwells in pleasure." Having attained the Third Meditation he stays free from joy.
>
> (4) Having eliminated both pleasure and distress, his former satisfaction and dissatisfaction having also vanished, having attained the Fourth Meditation, he abides in the purity of indifference and mindfulness free from both pleasure and distress.

And he goes on to the third instruction, that of Insight, whereby he trains himself to realize each of the four Noble Truths by four aspects, to wit, the Truth of Suffering by the aspects impermanence, suffering, voidness, and non-self; the Truth of Source (of suffering) by the aspects cause, source, production, and condition; the Truth of Cessation (of suffering) by the aspects cessation, calm, excellence, and exit; and the Truth of Path (leading to the cessation of suffering) by the aspects path, method, process of accomplishment, and way of deliverance. [87] Since Asaṅga holds to the doctrines of the later Mahīśāsaka sect, he takes the second instruction as training in the mundane path, and the third instruction as training in the supramundane path; but Buddhist sects had disagreements about application of the terminology 'mundane' (*laukika*) and 'supramundane' (*lokottara*).

The course of mental training was also known from early times as

Calming (P. *samatha*, S. *śamatha*), and the course of insight as Clear Vision (P. *vipassanā*, S. *vipaśyanā*). In time there arose various procedures for Calming the mind, the greatest contrast being between those of the monastic type and those peculiar to Tantrism. There also arose important differences in the procedure of Clear Vision. The earliest form of this seems to have been the contemplation of the five personality aggregates as empty of self and of what belongs to self, or the contemplation of aspects of the four Noble Truths. Among the aspects of the Noble Truth of Suffering, the set of three 'characteristic marks' —impermanence, suffering, and non-self—constitutes a preeminent object of Clear Vision in early Buddhism. [53] Later there arose the various voidness contemplations, especially as in the "Heart Sūtra" (*prajñāpāramitāhṛdaya*), Nāgārjuna's dialectical analysis, and Asaṅga's analysis by intrinsic characteristic and general characteristic (practically the Abhidharma). Also, among the six Perfections of the Bodhisattva path (infra), the training in Meditation (*dhyāna*) and in Insight (*prajñā*) is respectively the course in Calming and Clear Vision.

Certain well-defined meditations were called 'abodes'. The Noble Abode (*ārya-vihāra*) is the voidness abode, the abode free from image, the abode free from purpose, and the abode of cessation equipoise. The first three are well known as the three gates of liberation: [58]

> Whosoever being filled with determination, considers all constructions as impermanent, is one who attains the Imageless Liberation; whosoever being filled with tranquillity, considers all constructions as suffering, is one who attains the purposeless Liberation; whosoever being filled with insight, considers all constructions as void, is one who attains the Voidness Liberation.

Besides the Noble Abode, there is the Divine Abode (*divya-vihāra*), which is the abode of the four Dhyānas and of the formless realm; and there is the Sublime Abode (*brahma-vihāra*), which is the abode in friendship (*maitrī*), compassion (*karuṇā*), sympathetic joy (*muditā*), and indifference (*upekṣā*). [87]

(c) The thirty-seven natures accessory to enlightenment.

Asaṅga, near the beginning of his *Śrāvakabhūmi*, explains the arising of Buddhas as follows:

> Some individuals in this world generate good will and desire of benefit to all sentient beings. After three immeasurable aeons of thousands of difficulties and the equipping with merit *(puṇya)* and knowledge *(jñāna)*, they acquire their last ordinary body and take their seat at the terrace of enlightenment. Eliminating the five hindrances,

> they well stabilize their mind in the four Stations of Mindfulness. They contemplate the thirty-seven natures accessory to enlightenment, and manifestly completely realize the incomparable right complete enlightenment. In that way there is 'arising of Buddhas'. Moreover, in the past, present, and future, that is the only way any Buddha Bhagavat arises.

The Pāli Buddhist tradition also highly regards the thirty-seven natures as an important list comprising all the principle nomenclature of the Buddhist path. However, that and other traditions outside of Asaṅga's do not represent that list as describing the essential elements in Gautama's attainment of enlightenment. They rather constitute directions for the subsequent candidates. The thirty-seven are the four stations of mindfulness, the four right elimination-exertions, the four bases of magical power, the five faculties, the five powers, the seven limbs of enlightenment, and the noble eightfold path. Various of these items overlap each other, and certain ones are of more importance for extended explanation.

(1) Stations of Mindfulness. Generally, mindfulness is the power of tying the mind to a meditative object; and after the fault of mental straying, of bringing the mind back to the same mental object. [80]

In the Abhidharma tradition, the four stations of mindfulness are the antidotes for the four delusions, to wit: mindfulness toward bodies is the antidote for the delusion that the impure is pure; mindfulness toward feelings, the antidote for the delusion that suffering is happiness; mindfulness toward thoughts, the antidote for the delusion that the impermanent is permanent; mindfulness toward mental natures, the antidote for the delusion that non-self is self. [45]

In the Maitreya-Asaṅga tradition of the *Madhyānta-vibhāga* (Chap. IV), the four stations of mindfulness enable one to understand the four Noble Truths, namely, by mindfulness of bodies, feelings, thoughts, and mental natures, one respectively understands the Truth of Suffering, Source of Suffering, Cessation of Source, and Path leading to the Cessation.

(2) Four Right Elimination-Exertions. These are approximately the same as 'Right Effort', the sixth member of the eightfold Noble Path.

(3) Four Bases of Magical Power. According to the *Śrāvakabhūmi*: "...called 'basis of magical power, accompanied with elimination-exertion motivation of longing-*samādhi*; called 'basis of magical power, accompanied with elimination-exertion motivation of striving-, thought-, and analysis-*samādhi*.' [87]

(4) Five Faculties and Five Powers. The list is the same for the faculties and powers. According to the *Sūtrālaṃkāra* commentary tradition, they are first faculties, and then on stages of the path that are still subject to defiling forces they exhibit their power to counteract those defilements. The five are as follows:

1. faith with understanding, four: toward the Buddha, the Dharma, the Samgha, and toward the moral rules dear to the nobles. [45]
2. striving, equivalent to the four right elimination-exertions.
3. mindfulness, equivalent to the four stations of mindfulness.
4. *samādhi*, equivalent to the four Meditations (*dhyāna*).
5. insight (*prajñā*), equivalent to the four Noble Truths.

By assiduous devotion to and repetition of those five faculties and powers, one develops the roots of virtue conducive to penetration, whether weak, middling, or great, as follows: warmth, summits, forbearances consistent with the truth, and supreme mundane natures. [87] There are various explanations of the four degrees conducive to penetration (*nirvedha-bhāgīya*).

According to Vasubandhu's *Abhidharmakośa*, the four degrees can only be practiced by beings in the realm of desire. Warmth comes from prolonged contemplation of the four Noble Truths with their sixteen aspects; summits means the most excellent realization of those sixteen aspects. Forbearance of the *dharmas* (the same sixteen but especially suffering) is promoted by them, while supreme mundane natures are restricted to the four aspects of the first Noble Truth. The *Abhidharmakośa* observes that both men and women can engage in the four degrees conducive to penetration; but that when a woman masters the supreme mundane natures, she loses her female sex attribute and is converted into a 'male'. [45]

The Prajñāpāramitā of '25,000' and its *Abhisamayālaṃkāra* summarization explain the four degrees as follows: When a Bodhisattva dimly realizes that there is no self but only the consciousness apprehending externals, he is in the state of warmth. Continuing, as his understanding increases and the image of the external fades, he is in summits. When the reality of the external world disappears, with 'consciousness only' remaining, he is in Forbearance and is now liberated from rebirth in the three evil destinies. Finally, when the Bodhisattva realizes the unreality of the perceiving consciousness as well, he is in the supreme mundane natures and not yet a saint, but this *samādhi* conducts him without interruption to the state where he can contemplate the supramundane natures whereby he will be a saint. [22, 62]

Sthiramati, in his commentary on Chapter XIV of the *Sūtrālaṃkāra*, explains those four stages of *yoga* as follows: 1. at the time of warmth, one understands names as illusion; 2. at the time of summits, one understands material things as illusion; 3. at the time of forbearance, one understands the objective thing without apprehending (it); 4. at the time of supreme worldly natures, one understands also the (subjective) perceptiveness without apprehending (it).

These four steps are included by Sthiramati in the path of training (*prayoga-mārga*), and they can also be regarded as a symbolic death, preparatory to the embryonic life as a Bodhisattva. [88]

(5) Seven Limbs of Enlightenment. Asaṅga's *Śrāvakabhūmi* states that when one attains the supreme mundane natures, he then proceeds to the supramundane natures, which are the seven limbs of enlightenment, to wit, the cathartic, *samādhi*, and indifference, in the category of calming; analysis of the doctrine, striving, and joy, in the category of clear vision; and mindfulness in the category of both. This is reasonably consistent with the *Abhisamayālaṃkāra* (IV, 8): "By means of the twenty marks of one based in warmth, summits, forbearance, and supreme mundane natures, he does not retreat from enlightenment." Asaṅga goes on to say that upon obtaining the seven limbs, one contemplates the Eightfold Noble Path.

It is of interest that the seven, in the standard order of mindfulness, analysis of the doctrine, striving, joy, cathartic, *samādhi*, and indifference, were recommended by the Teacher to sick monks for getting over their illness.[21]

(6) The Eightfold Noble Path. This is the ancient description of the Path, the fourth Truth, to wit: [60]

1. Right Understanding, especially of the four Noble Truths, of good and bad acts (three of body, four of speech, and three of mind); that the five personality aggregates are void of self and what belongs to self; and of other Buddhist tenets, such as Dependent Origination.

2. Right Conception, which is free from the three bad acts of mind (lust, ill-will, and cruelty).

3. Right Speech, which is free from the four bad acts of speech (lying, tale-bearing, harsh language, vain talk).

4. Right Bodily Action, which is free from the three bad acts of body (killing, stealing, unlawful sexual intercourse).

5. Right Livelihood, which avoids trades prohibited to the disciple —trading in arms, in living beings, in flesh, in intoxicating drinks, and in poison.

6. Right Effort, to avoid or deter the arising of evil things; to overcome the evil already arisen; to cultivate the good or wholesome states not yet arisen; or to guard the wholesome things already arisen.

7. Right Mindfulness, in four stations, namely on bodies, feelings, thoughts, or mental natures.

8. Right Concentration, which is the single area of thought on a virtuous meditative object, and of two kinds—threshold concentration (the state of being almost in one of the stabilization levels of the Realm of Form or Formless Realm) and attainment concentration (the state of being stabilized in one of those levels).

The eightfold Noble Path is also formulated in terms of the three instructions: 1. Theravāda method: The instruction of insight includes Right Understanding and Conception. That of morality, Right Speech, Bodily Action, and Livelihood. That of mental training, Right Effort, Mindfulness, and Concentration. [60] 2. Asaṅga's method: The group of insight includes Right Understanding, Conception, and Effort. That of morality, Right Speech, Bodily Action, and Livelihood. That of mental training, Right Mindfulness and Concentration. [87]

(d) Degrees of Sanctification. Traditional Buddhism considered the path to be a matter of lives, and so classified the noble ones (*ārya*) following this path in four groups with four fruits: 1. The one who has entered the stream, the first path, has as fruit that he will be reborn at most seven times. 2. The one who has one more life ahead, the second path, has as fruit that he will return once more and make an end to suffering. 3. The one who will not again return, the third path, has as fruit, in descending order of his faculty, *parinirvāṇa* in the intermediate state (in the Pure Abode), *parinirvāṇa* after birth, *parinirvāṇa* not requiring instigation, *parinirvāṇa* requiring instigation, or migration upwards (*urdhvaṃsrotāh*) to the Sublime Gods. 4. The one in the fourth path, the state of arhat, has as fruit that he will be liberated by faith (*śraddhādhimukta*) or liberated by insight (*prajñādhimukta*) from the obscuration of defilement (*kleśa-āvaraṇa*), or liberated from both the obscuration of defilement and the obscuration of equipoise (*samāpatti-āvaraṇa*). [58, 87]

(e) The Five Paths and the Ten Bodhisattva Stages. Neither the 'five paths' (*pañcamārga*) nor the 'ten stages' (*daśabhūmi*) terminology is found in Theravada Buddhism. Such explanations were gradually developed in the Buddhist sects rivalling the Theravada and in time were taken over by Mahāyāna Buddhism. In this theory, the Bodhisattva who would become Gautama Buddha had been accumulating merit and knowledge for three incalculable aeons before being born the son of King Śuddhodana. In Mkhas grub rje's summary: "He completed the first incalculable aeons while on the path of equipment and the path of training. He completed the second one between the first and seventh stages. He completed the third incalculable aeon while on the three stages, the eighth, ninth, and tenth." [48]

The paths of equipment (*saṃbhāra-mārga*) and training (*prayoga-mārga*) are the first two of the five paths, of which the remaining three are path of vision (*darśana-mārga*), path of intense contemplation (*bhāvanā-mārga*), and path beyond training (*aśaikṣa-mārga*). These paths were formulated by the Abhidharma schools of Sarvāstivādin and then worked up by the *Abhisamayālaṃkāra* tradition of Prajñāpāramitā Buddhism as applying with somewhat different explanations in each case to the Śrāvakas, Pratyekabuddhas, and Bodhisattvas, who are supposed to belong to three different families (*gotra*) which develop their own enlightenments (*bodhi*). The topic of five paths for the three species is worked out in great detail in the *Abhisamayālaṃkāra* and commentarial literature. [62] The "Lotus Sūtra" denies the diverse families by its doctrine of 'One Vehicle' (*ekayāna*).

The Mahāsāṅghika text *Mahāvastu* contains the 'ten stages' theory. Certain Mahāyāna scriptures, following suit, usually describe a Bodhisattva's progress, not in terms of five paths but in ten stages. The most famous presentation of such a theory is the topic of the *Daśabhūmika-sūtra*; and the ten stages in Nāgārjuna's *Ratnāvalī* are consistent and the apparent basis for Candrakīrti's *Madhyamakāvatāra*. The *Saṃdhinir-mocana-sūtra* presents the theory of ten stages in connection with abodes (*vihāra*), and the brief indications of this *sūtra* are expanded by Asaṅga in his *Bodhisattvabhūmi*. [17]

In later Indian Buddhism, scholastic attempts were made to combine the explanations of the five paths with those of the ten stages. The earliest suggestions along these lines are found in the *Mahāyāna-Sūtrālaṃkāra* (Chap. XIV of the edited Sanskrit text) which assigns the first stage to the path of vision, and the remaining nine stages to the path of intense contemplation. This leaves the last path, that beyond training, to be equivalent to the Buddha stage, sometimes labelled the eleventh stage.

The names of the ten stages according to the *Daśabhūmika-sūtra* are: 1. Joy, 2. Immaculate, 3. Illuminating, 4. Blazing, 5. Unconquerable, 6. Facing, 7. Far-reaching, 8. Motionless, 9. Perfect Wisdom, 10. Cloud of Doctrine. In the theory of Bodhisattva Stages according to this *sūtra* the Bodhisattva practices ten Perfections in each Stage and emphasizes one among the ten in the usual order in each successive Stage. To the well-known six Perfections, Giving, Morality, Forbearance, Striving, Meditation, and Insight, this system adds four more called Skillful Means, Vow, Power, and Knowledge. Hence, Giving is emphasized in the First Stage and Knowledge in the Tenth. Candrakīrti, following this indication in his *Madhyamakāvatāra*, discusses the Perfection of Insight as Mādhyamika philosophy in a large chapter six.

The three most dramatic stages are the First, the Eighth, and the Tenth. The First Stage is important as equivalent to the 'path of vision' among the five paths and as predominating with Giving that begins to mature the sentient beings. The *samādhi* is called 'Lion's Dignified Stretching' (*Siṃhavijṛmbhita*). [1] Now a person is a saint. According to the Bodhipakṣya chapter of the *Sūtrālaṃkāra* (verses 58-61, and Sthiramati's commentary), in this stage the Bodhisattva is equipped with the seven branches of enlightenment which are comparable to the seven jewels of a world emperor (*cakravartin*): 1. mindfulness, to the jewel of wheel; 2. analysis of the doctrine, to the jewel of elephant; 3. striving, to the jewel of horse; 4. joy, to the jewel of the (imperial) gem; 5. the cathartic, to the jewel of woman; 6. concentration, to the jewel of treasurer; 7. indifference, to the jewel of minister of war.

With the Eighth Stage the Bodhisattva is irreversible because he does not retreat from the goal of complete enlightenment. The reason is given by Ārya-Vimuktisena that here he gains the 'Illusory-samādhi' (*māyopama-samādhi*) in which the mental natures are seen as illusion; this is the 'non-falling *samādhi*' which avoids the fall as per the Tantric tradition of genesis (above: Creation). [64] This also explains the passages which say that the Bodhisattva now has 'forbearance of the unoriginated mental natures' (*anutpattikadharmakṣānti*) in the current of *dharma*, instructed by the Buddhas (per the *Daśabhūmika-sūtra*) and dwells there without effort (per the *Bodhisattvabhūmi*). Abhayākaragupta mentions that here the Bodhisattva obtains both the 'Buddha eye' and the six supernormal faculties which are brought to perfection on the 'Buddha Stage'. [1] In texts with Yogācāra terminology, the Bodhisattva lives in a 'body made of mind' upon the turning around (*parāvṛtti*) of the basis of the eightfold set of perceptions. The *Laṅkāvatāra-sūtra* says this wonderful body is like a current of dreams. It is usual to teach that the turning around of the basis of the *ālaya*- or store-consciousness yields the 'mirror-like knowledge' (*ādarśa-jñāna*). The Zen master Shoju Rojin said, "...at the moment you smash open the dark cave of the eighth or Ālaya consciousness, the precious light of the Great Perfect Mirror Wisdom instantly shines forth. But strange to say, the light of the Great Perfect Mirror Wisdom is black like lacquer." [55]

On the Tenth Stage, the Bodhisattva is initiated as 'King of the Law of the Three Worlds'. He is a Buddha although not a Complete Buddha. He is in the retinue of the Saṃbhoga-kāya in the Akaniṣṭha heaven at the top of the 'realm of form'. According to the teachings of the 'Pāramitā School', at the completion of the tenth Bodhisattva stage, there occurs in the stream of consciousness the final knowledge called 'knowledge at end of the stream' as well as the 'diamond-like samādhi'. This is immediately followed by the 'second instant' of realization—the obtaining of both the Dharma-kāya and the Saṃbhoga-kāya. [48]

(f) The Quick and the Gradual Path. The foregoing paths are based on the premise that one should follow a graduated ascetic course, followed by a quick attainment of enlightenment. Also, the 'quick attainment' can be construed in a graded sense. There have been extreme trends of thinking in India during the Buddhist period, in China and Tibet, that the highest attainment must be achieved instantaneously and that, moreover, gradual exercises are in vain because based on the phenomenal illusion that things arise. In India there were some who said that the only Perfection needed was the Perfection of Insight (*prajñāpāramitā*), which 'sees' the voidness (*śūnyatā*) through non-apprehension of natures (*dharma*); and so one could neglect the 'means' (*upāya*) consisting of the other Perfections beginning with Giving. Or they said that both good and bad deeds lead to rebirth in the realm of sorrow; and so one should 'rise above *karma* (action)' by non-action. In China some extreme Ch'an Buddhist sects held to the method of instantaneous entrance into Enlightenment, which to some extent was adopted by the Tibetan Rdzogs chen sect. A clash between Indian 'gradualists' and the Chinese 'instantaneous entrance' party led to the 'Council of Lhasa' (rather, Bsam-yas). [18, 80, 81]

Some of those disputes are certainly based on mutual misunderstanding. Of course, a denial of action towards Enlightenment amounts to discarding the path itself, a basic feature of Buddhism from its inception. However, both non-tantric and tantric Buddhism have their versions of 'quickness'.

In Mahāyāna Buddhism, quickness is in following the supramundane path or the ten Bodhisattva stages beginning with possession of the limbs of enlightenment. Here, quickness is credited to Striving (*vīrya*), comparable to the jewel of horse. This Striving is said to have Longing (*chanda*) as its foundation; and Longing is identified with Faith (*adhimukti*), as Śāntideva writes in the *Bodhicaryāvatāra* (VII, 39-40A):

> Through my lack of longing for (= faith in) the Dharma in the former and in the present life, such a poverty as this arose. Who should abandon longing for the Dharma? Longing (= faith) the Muni has declared to be the root of all virtues. [80]

Also, the Mahāyāna *sūtra* called *Śrīmālādevīsiṃhanāda* sets forth three true disciples of the Buddha, the third one being "that son of the family or daughter of the family who shrinks from gaining the knowledge of the profound Dharma by himself, thinking, 'I cannot possibly know it; this meaning can only be understood by the Tathāgata himself,' and so keeping the Lord in mind, obtains the mental presence of the Lord." The profound humility in terms of faith is indicated as quickly bringing about the presence of the Lord. This idea was highly influential in Sino-Japanese Buddhism.

Tantrism is also a quick path in the sense that it claims to show the way to Complete Buddhahood in one life in contrast to the old 'three incalculable aeons'. The theory here is that when one affiliates with the three 'secrets' of the Buddha, namely his Body, Speech, and Mind, by way of gestures (*mudrā*), incantations (*mantra*), and concentration (*samādhi*), then the principal avenues of man are free from cross-purpose and mutual cancellation, and so the entire being is lent to the purpose of achieving the goal of enlightenment, if this supreme goal, rather than a mundane fruit of occult powers, is the one aimed at. One must find a capable *guru*, called the 'diamond master' (*vajrācārya*), serve him with suitable presents, and petition to be conferred the initiations (*abhiṣeka*) which mature the stream of consciousness along with taking of vows. Through the worship of the deity (*devapūjā*) and worship of the *guru* (*gurupūjā*), the mundane and supramundane fruits are made possible. [48]

The foregoing are stated in terms of techniques of the path. There are also considerations in terms of the persons travelling the path. From early Buddhism persons were divided into two (sometimes still finer) groups, as those with weak sense organs (*mṛdvindriya*) and those with keen sense organs (*tīkṣṇendriya*). The rule is given for those two, that in the case of the weak sense organ, when one has not attained the basic Dhyāna, supernormal faculty is slow and painful, and is slow and pleasant when he has attained that; and in the case of the keen sense organ, when one has not attained the basic Dhyāna, supernormal faculty is speedy and painful, and is speedy and pleasant when he has attained that. [87] In practice, the difference is between the ordinary and the superior candidate. The quick path is laid down for the superior candidate.

(g) The Bodhisattva Vow and Perfections. [80] Essential to the gradual path—even if it be considered quick—of the Bodhisattva stages is that the person generate the Thought of Enlightenment, first as an aspiration and then as a vow. Certain preliminaries are stipulated: The person must have the right circumstances of life, called the four reasons: 1. he should be in this family, 2. taken in hand by spiritual guides ('virtuous friends'), 3. be compassionate toward living beings, 4. have zest of austerities. Also, he should have one or other power to generate that Thought: 1. his own power, whereby he craves the perfect enlightenment through his own force (of character), 2. another's power, whereby he craves it by way of another's power, 3. the power of a (deep-seated) cause, whereby he generates the Thought through the mere hearing in the present life of praises of the Buddha and Bodhisattvas by reason of having formerly cultivated the Great Vehicle, or 4. the power of praxis, in the course of which he has for a long time been following a path of virtue, seeking out high-minded persons, and listening to the Law. If the person has such qualifications, he is given a religious exercise to further put his mind in the right frame. In Tibet one could choose between two exercises, one handed down by Atīśa, and the other found in the texts by Śāntideva, his *Śikṣāsamuccaya* and *Bodhicaryāvatāra*.

(1) Atīśa's precepts of "Seven causes and effects": The candidate 1. reflects on the *kindness* of his 'mother' in tending him when helpless, and that all sentient beings have served as his 'mother' in past lives; 2. this recollection arouses *gratitude*; 3. from gratitude comes *love*; 4. with empathy for the suffering of one's 'mother' and hence for that of all sentient beings, he is colored by *compassion*, expanded into the Boundless State of Compassion; 5. he aspires to relieve these sufferings by *altruistic aspiration*, expanded into the Boundless State of Sympathetic Joy with happiness; 6. that aspiration leads to the *Thought of Enlightenment* with its two aims of enlightenment for oneself and de-

liverance for others; 7. the Thought of Enlightenment in fruition is the basis of *perfect enlightenment.*

(2) Precepts based on Śāntideva's texts. First he reflects on the benefit of changing places with another, holding others as dear in preference to oneself. This is an interchange of feelings, taking on another's suffering, installing in him one's happiness. Finally, even one's worst enemy is so contemplated that his mere absence would cause sadness. Various contemplations are set forth to disprove the usual views of personal ego which militate against such a feeling interchange. Eventually, the meditator abandons a private aim for his various organs of action; his mind, eyes, hands must work for the aim of others, not for his own sake.

The person has already become imbued somewhat with the Aspiration Thought which is technically such a thought as "I shall become a Buddha for the sake of the living beings." In order to have the Entrance or Progressing Thought, he takes the following vow from a good preceptor in ritual manner:

> "All the Buddhas and Bodhisattvas dwelling in the ten directions, pray take cognizance of me! Preceptor, pray take cognizance of me! I, named so-and-so, have the root of virtue of this and other lives, consisting in the self-existence of Giving to others, the self-existence of Morality, and the self-existence of Contemplation; and by means of that root of virtue consisting of what has been done by me, what has been granted to do, and of sympathetic joy with what is done,
>
> "Just as the former Tathāgata-Arhat-Samyaksambuddhas and the great Bodhisattvas dwelling on the great earth were made to generate their heart into the incomparable Right-Perfected Enlightenment.
>
> "In the same way, I, named so-and-so, also holding from this time on, up to reaching the precincts of Enlightenment, shall generate my Thought to the Incomparable Right-Perfected Great Enlightenment; shall rescue the unrescued beings; shall save the unsaved; shall encourage the discouraged; shall bring to Nirvāṇa those who have not attained complete Nirvāṇa."

In the case where it is not possible to find a good *guru* or preceptor, an adjustment is made in the statement and ritual so the person can take it by himself. He must imagine the Buddha in front and take the vow from him; and this is a rationale for the frequent passages of Mahāyāna scriptures where the Buddha appears in front of a person who then takes vows and receives a prophecy from the Buddha. The layman Bodhisattva type would be more likely to take the Bodhisattva vow from the imagined or visualized Buddha. The monk Bodhisattva would ordinarily take the vow from a superior in the order.

With the Aspiration Thought, or preferably the Entrance Thought, the Bodhisattva then practices six Perfections (*pāramitā*) to mature his own 'Buddha natures', of which the Thought of Enlightenment is considered the seed, and at the same time can begin to practice the four methods of Persuasion to mature others' stream of consciousness, for which see Ethics.

The six Perfections are 1. Giving (*dāna*)—giving of the Buddha Law, security, or material things (either imagined or concrete); 2. Morality (*śīla*)—morality of restraints and prohibitions, of gathering virtuous natures, or acting on behalf of others in a sinless manner; 4. Forbearance (*kṣānti*)—forbearance of not retaliating to another's harm-doing, the acceptance of suffering in one's own stream of consciousness, or the unshakeable conviction when presented with the Buddhist Law and the realizable in the Buddhist sense; 4. Striving (*vīrya*)—striving that is armored or heroic, striving for virtuous ends, or striving on behalf of other beings; 5. Meditation (*dhyāna*)—the virtuous one-pointed mind fixed without straying from the meditative object, both mundane and supramundane; 6. Insight (*prajñā*)—the faculty of seeing an entity as it really is, which understands the supreme (*paramārtha*), the conventional (*saṃvṛti*), or serves the benefit of others, and which in the special sense of omniscience is called "Mother of the Buddhas." The six Perfections are also grouped under the three instructions in this manner: Giving, Morality, Forbearance, under the instruction of morality; Meditation under the instruction of mental training; Insight under the instruction of insight; and Striving under all three instructions.

4) *Eschatology*

(a) Death and the Deathless. Buddhism has always emphasized the common lot of mankind to reach death (the 12th member of Dependent Origination), popularly represented as seizure by the Lord of Death (Yama) or his 'messengers'. More technically, Asaṅga (*Vastu-Saṃgrahaṇī*, section 1) explains it as taking place between the transfer of the impregnated *saṃskāras* and the cessation of the life organ in the heart. The *saṃskāras*, so impregnated with the psychological poisons of lust, hatred, and delusion, transfer to various destinies—since Buddhism also emphasizes the difference in death. Even the residents of the higher worlds are subject to the sway of death and rebirth, according to *Saṃyutta-Nikāya* (I, 132-3), and Nāgārjuna in his "Friendly Epistle" states the prognostics announcing death in heaven, similar to the signs portending death to men on earth.

The theory of the four Māras show how man is in bondage to death, and also how he may transcend it. According to Asanga, Māra means 'death' either metaphorically or concretely. There are four Māras: 1. The personality-aggregate Māra is the five grasping aggregates. Man dies among these. 2. The defilement Māra is the defilements present in the three worlds. It is the reason for man's birth; and since what is born must die, it is also the reason for his death. 3. The killing Māra is what fixes the time of death of the various sentient beings in the various destinies by fixing the time for cessation of the life organ. 4. The son-of-the-gods (*devaputra*) Māra obstructs the yogin who is trying to transcend death by transcending the first three kinds of Māra. This kind of Māra is the king of the Paranirmitavaśavartin gods among the six passion-god classes of the realm of desire. According to Vasubandhu, the Buddha defeated the son-of-the-gods Māra by the *samādhi* of love beneath the Tree of Enlightenment when Māra appeared at dusk. More fully, Gautama passed through the four 'sublime abodes' or 'boundless states'—love, compassion, sympathetic joy, and indifference; and in this way removed the impediment for transcending the other three kinds of Māra. At the time of Enlightenment toward dawn, he defeated the defilement Māra; and at the same time, by revolution of the basis of the 'store consciousness', he defeated the personality-aggregate Māra. At Vaiśālī, three months before passing into Nirvana, the Buddha repressed the life motivation by achieving the power over life and thus defeated the killing Māra. [88]

In ancient Buddhism the chief difference in death is in whether the person is disciplined or undisciplined, referred to as having 'carefulness' or 'carelessness' in the *Dhammapada* (21-23): "Carefulness is the path to the deathless; carelessness is the path to death. ... The constantly meditative, the ever earnestly striving ones, realize the bond-free, supreme Nibbāna." This carefulness is also required in the time of experiencing the fruits of the three instructions. It is said that the ten virtues are the path to heaven (*svarga*) as gods in the desire realm intoxicated by sensuous desires. The four *dhyānas* are the path to good destiny as gods in Brahmā's realm and so on, relishing pleasure. The Ārya's Right Conception in the instruction of insight is the path free from evil destiny as gods in the Pure Abode relishing the motive of

Nirvana. Therefore, carefulness requires a status with temptation to carelessness, and it is taught that the formless realm provides no such opportunity. [1]

(b) The Judgment. In popular Buddhist representation, Yama's judgment hall has much in common with the one in Hinduism. Yama has a consort, a city, a doorkeeper, a judgment seat, a register of human actions, a scribe, and servants. There is a tradition that on the seventh day after death one must cross a river (called the Vaitaraṇī) with three currents speeds (the *karma* of the three evil destinies of hell beings, animals, and hungry ghosts); if the deceased can cross the river presumably he goes to one of the good destinies (men and gods). [88] Various Buddhist texts have graphic descriptions of the tortures in the cold and hot hells and the pleasures in the various heavens, to impress upon the faithful the rewards and punishments of good and bad action. [57] The scripture *Sukhāvatī-vyūha* mentions a heaven called the "Western Paradise," or the "Happy Land (*sukhāvatī*), ruled by Amitābha ('Immeasurable Light') who will ensure rebirth in his Paradise if one has true faith in him and calls his name, rightly pronouncing it.

The intermediate state (*antarābhava*) is scarcely described in the Pāli canon, except that the being is headed for a rebirth place and is called a *gandhabba* (S. *gandharva*). The *Ārya-nanda-garbhāvakrānti-nirdeśa* (in the Ratnakūṭa collection) explains that beings headed for an evil destiny have in the intermediate state a displeasing color of personality aggregates, namely hell beings have a color like the burnt stump of a tree; animals, like smoke; hungry ghosts, like water; and that beings headed for a good destiny have a pleasing color in the intermediate state, namely, men and gods (in the realm of desire), like the color of gold; gods in the realm of form, the color of abiding white; while gods in the formless realm are colorless for the very reason that the realm is formless (and therefore lacks both color and shape). [80]

(c) Nirvāṇa and Parinirvāṇa. In the canon (*Saṃyutta-Nikāya*) the realm of release has been referred to this way: [11]

> There is, monks, an unborn, not become, not made, uncompounded, and were it not, monks, for this unborn, not become, not made, uncompounded, no escape could be shown here for what is born, has become, is made, is compounded.

It appears that the early use of the term '*parinirvāṇa*' was to indicate the *nirvāṇa* attained through death. So the famous statement of the Buddha's *parinirvāṇa*: [86]

> Thereupon the Blessed One entered the first Dhyāna; and emerging from the first Dhyāna, he entered the second Dhyāna; and emerging from the second Dhyāna, he entered the third Dhyāna; and emerging from the third Dhyāna, he entered the fourth Dhyāna; and emerging from the fourth Dhyāna, he entered the base of infinite space; and emerging from the base of infinite space, he entered the base of infinite perception; and emerging from the base of infinite perception, he entered the base of nothingness; and emerging from the base of nothingness, he entered the base of neither ideation nor non-ideation; and emerging from the base of neither ideation nor non-ideation, he arrived at the cessation of ideas and feelings.
>
> Thereupon the venerable Ānanda spoke to the venerable Anuruddha as follows: "Reverend Anuruddha, the Blessed One has passed into Nirvāna." "Nay, brother Ānanda, the Blessed One has not passed into Nirvāna; he has arrived at the cessation of ideas and feelings."
>
> Thereupon the Blessed One, emerging from the cessation of ideas and feelings, entered the base of neither ideation nor non-ideation; (and so on, in order, down to) emerging from the second Dhyāna, he entered the first Dhyāna. And emerging from the first Dhyāna, he entered the second Dhyāna; and emerging from the second Dhyāna, he entered the third Dhyāna; and emerging from the third Dhyāna, he entered the fourth Dhyāna; and rising from the fourth Dhyāna, immediately the Blessed One passed into Nirvāṇa.

Thus the Buddha entered *parinirvāṇa* by way of the fourth Dhyāna at the top of the realm of form, understood in later times to be Akaniṣṭha, fifth of the pure abodes.

There were sectarian differences concerning the 'cessation' (*nirodha*) constituting *nirvāṇa*. The Abhidharmists included two kinds of cessation among the unconditioned natures (see Doctrine), the *pratisaṃkhyā-nirodha* (cessation through understanding each case) by the supramundane path, and the *apratisaṃkhyā-nirodha* (cessation not through understanding each case, but through meditation) by the mundane path. These terms are the topics of acute discussion; principally, the *pratisaṃkhyā-nirodha* means an absolute destruction or permanent detachment from defilements and obscuration of the knowable; and *apratisaṃkhyā-nirodha* is a temporary cessation such as is obtained usually by the 'non-moving *samādhi*' (temporary detachment from sorrow and pleasure) and the 'cessation of ideas and feelings' (temporary detachment from consciousness and mental elements). Because Nibbāna (later the Hīnayāna Nirvāṇa) contrasts with the phenomenal world, it is usual to identify it with the *pratisaṃkhyā-nirodha*, which the *Abhidharmakośa* explains as an unconditioned fruit of the ascetic life or human agency. However, besides this negative attribute, there are canonical passages which assign positive attributes, such as happiness, to Nirvāṇa. [21, 46]

Subsequently, as in Asaṅga's *Yogācārabhūmi*, there are two kinds of *nirvāṇa*, that with remainder, and that without remainder. 1. Nirvāṇa with aggregate remainder is free from all defilements (*kleśa*); however, it is not free from certain kinds of suffering such as suffering due to hunger and thirst, and that inflicted by hostile creatures, while free from such suffering as evolving perceptions create. 2. Nirvāṇa without remainder is the cessation of both the evolving perceptions and the store consciousness; it is the unconditioned realm (*asaṃskṛta-dhātu*). It is attained by the Arhat liberated from both the obscuration of defilement and the obscuration of equipoise.

As was shown before (in Doctrine), Nāgārjuna denies the contrast of Nirvāṇa and Saṃsāra. His Nirvāṇa may be the Mahāyāna 'Nirvana of no fixed abode' stated in Bhāvaviveka's *Madhyamakahṛdayakārikā*:

> He leaves phenomenal existence because of its faults.
> He is not fixed in Nirvāṇa because of his compassion.
> Vowed to accomplish the aim of others, he again takes abode in phenomenal existence. [80]

(d) Prophecy.

(1) Prophecy of the Buddhist Doctrine. Buddhist scriptures contain various 'prophecies' about duration of the Buddhist doctrine. A usual figure is 1000 years after the Buddha's Nirvāṇa, of which the first 500 years can be considered "the period of development" and the latter 500 "the period of regress". Such prophecies are sometimes related to relaxation of monk morals leading to decadence of the Samgha. In Tibet these figures were understood to refer to India proper, and "the period of regress" to refer to a time of propagation as Buddhism spread to neighboring countries with corresponding weakening of the India centers. Some Buddhist teachers opined that the highest doctrine of the Buddha Śākyamuni is to exist for five times 500 years, a total interestingly bringing Buddhism up to a crisis in the present generation when the 2500 year of Buddhism was celebrated widely in May 1956. Still more optimistic is the figure of 5000 years, including a prediction "2500 years after I have passed away into Nirvāṇa, the Highest Doctrine will become spread in the country of the red-faced (people)." [61]

(2) Prophecy of Buddhas. In the theory of a series of Buddhas,

someone takes a vow of enlightenment before a particular Buddha and obtains a prediction certifying that person to be a 'future Buddha'. This is legendary for the historical Buddha Śākyamuni. The next Buddha is agreed to be the Messiah Maitreya (the compassionate one), whose epithet is 'the unconquerable' (*ajita*). The devotion to Maitreya (Pāli, Metteyya) was common to Buddhism in the Southern Asian countries such as Ceylon and India, especially the latter's Northwest. Maitreya was thought to abide in the Tuṣitā heaven of the desire realm until he descends to earth. The cult of Maitreya especially flourished in Central Asia up to the ascendency of Islam and consisted almost exclusively of pure devotion (*bhakti*). [41]

(3) Prophecy of other persons. Later Indian Buddhism bolstered the authority of preeminent Buddhist authors and religious leaders by assigning textual prophecy to each. The most celebrated example is that of Nāgārjuna, for whom transparent references are inserted in several Mahāyāna scriptures, especially the *Laṅkāvatāra-sūtra*. The last chapter of the *Mañjuśrī-mūla-kalpa* abounds in such 'prophecies' for famous medieval Buddhists. [61] For Bodhisattva followers generally, the tantric writer Vajravarman quotes the scripture "Fulfilment of the Mahāyāna": "In future times, my sons will be three—one will serve others without stint; one will increase the treasures of the father; one will requite the spiritual lineage of the Lion (= the Buddha)." [83]

(4) Generalities of Prediction. The Buddha discouraged monks from practicing divinatory methods, such as astrology. Nevertheless, Buddhism holds that the divine eye (see 'Conception of Deity') can envision an individual's destiny. It believes that certain dreams are portentious, but also that their indications can be averted by appropriate action. [88]

The *Śūraṃgamasamādhi* scripture claims that only the Tathāgata, not the Śrāvakas or Pratyekabuddhas, knows the four kinds of prediction (*vyākaraṇa*) which it sets forth and explains for Bodhisattvas. These are 1. the prediction concerning the one who has not yet produced the mind of enlightenment; 2. the prediction conferred on the one who has produced the mind of enlightenment; 3. the prediction concealed from the one concerned; 4. the prediction made face-to-face with the one who has obtained the forbearance of the unoriginated natures. [43] Of those, the second kind is ordinarily made to Bodhisattvas in the First Stage, and the fourth to the non-regressing Bodhisattvas in the Eighth and higher Stages.

The scripture "Meeting of Father and Son" (chapter on the Tushitā gods) inquires about the *dharma* for which the Bhagavat prophesied the Incomparable Right Enlightenment, and successively denies that it is any of the five personality aggregates, 'form', and so on. Since in an absolute sense, these aggregates neither arise nor cease, no prophecy can be made for them. But in a conventional sense, these same *dharmas* are said to arise void of self-existence. In this sense of their 'arising', a prophecy can be made for them.

VI. Present Religious Situation of Buddhism

The present situation of Buddhism shares with other religions the challenges of despotic political ascendencies and the modern so-called rational life which gnaws at the mythological roots of religion. Indeed, Buddhism in its Asian setting has experienced in recent years both striking reverses and striking successes. One of the great strengths of Buddhism is the experience garnered in 2500 years of adaptation to varying social and political climates. Another is the perennial and universal appeal of certain of its classics, such as the ethical treatise *Dhammapada*; the remarkable spiritual vitality of such a scripture as the "Lotus Sūtra" or the "Diamond Cutter"; the fascinating character of a wide range of Buddhist texts such as the "Vimalakīrti" to have attracted the unremitting attention of numerous Western scholars of other religious backgrounds, in the study, preparation of editions and translations based on these scriptures. Again, Buddhist psychology, despite the difficulty of translating its technical terms, is based on practical investigation of man's potentialities, the behavior of his mind in the conditions of laxity as well as discipline, neglect as well as meditative cultivation; and, as such, is as valid today as thousands of years ago, if it be granted that man's nature and capabilities have not significantly changed in that time. The calming of the mind attained through Buddhist meditation and exemplary conduct are as capable today of producing at least mental health, and at best the saint, as in centuries past. The symbols of the religion in architectural forms or hieratic painting today arouse the respect and devotion of Buddhists in other lands of the world as they did in countries of origin. The Buddhist goal of enlightenment is as appealing to man's longing as in ancient times. The Buddhist ethic of non-aggression when combined with political control—as in the case of the Mongols—worked for peace, and still has this optimism of saving power. The compassion basic to Mahāyāna Buddhism will ever be an inspiration to humanity, no matter under what banner it appears.

(a) Buddhism in Ceylon and India. After a lethargy and gradual attrition of Buddhist following and influence in Asia for some centuries, striking new developments occurred in this religion starting in the nineteenth century. The beginning of the new period is observable in Ceylon where Buddhism had long been at a gross disadvantage through the successive political domination by European powers. Colonel H. S. Olcott, an American, came to Ceylon in 1880, became himself a Buddhist and founded the Theosophical Society of Colombo which helped to develop several hundred Buddhist educational institutions including some colleges. He encouraged many of the younger generation; the most important of these, named David Hewavitarane, was later called Anagarika Dharmapala (b. 1884; d. 1933). The Venerable Dharmapala helped found hospitals and rest houses and championed social reforms. He founded the Maha Bodhi Society at Colombo in 1891, especially with the purpose of restoring Buddhist control to the Bodh Gaya temple close to the 'Bodhi tree' near Gaya in India. After a long struggle this was partially restored to Buddhist management in 1949. It was the Venerable Dharmapala's idea to erect a temple at Sarnath, and his labors in this direction were realized with the completion of the Mūlagandhakuṭi Vihāra in 1931. He also introduced Pali studies at the University of Calcutta. The revival of Indian interest in Buddhism on a high prestige level is principally due to the efforts of the Venerable Dharmapala who was intimate with the Tagore family. The Maha Bodhi Society of India in Calcutta celebrated his Birth Centenary in 1964-1965. [4]

In India, the country of Buddhist origins, the ancient glory of this religion in architectural and plastic forms are now found among the chief visiting sites, which were renovated and supplied with approach roads and guesthouses by the Indian government beginning with the 2500 year anniversary celebrations. Sarnath with the Deer Park next to Benares; Bodhgaya, Rajgir, and Nālaṇḍā in Bihar; Ajaṇṭā in Mahārashtra, Sanchi in Madhyapradesh, and Nagarjunakoṇḍa in Andhra, are now the chief visiting sites of this nature, approached through natural beauty. Much of the great sculptural remains of Amarāvatī in Madras State are now housed in the Madras Museum. Isolated pieces of Buddhist sculpture from the Kuṣāṇa and Gupta periods are treasured by museums around the world.

Almost simultaneously, three groups of Buddhists sprang up in recent years. As a result of the partition of India with the creation of East Pakistan, a number of old Buddhist families migrated, some as refugees, to the Calcutta area. In the 1950's, under the leadership of the late Dr. Ambedkar, a movement began at Nagpur, Mahārashtra, of converting scheduled classes (the former 'untouchables') to Buddhism. So far, the conversions have been mainly restricted to the group in Mahārashtra called the Mahārs, but great numbers of these have turned to Buddhism, assisted by a series of monks from the Southern Asia Buddhist countries. The principal festivals of this group are 'Buddha's Birthday' and 'Ambedkar's Birthday', or a combined Buddha's and Ambedkar's Birthday celebration. Also in Nagpur, each year at Dasamī (the 'tenth day', Day of Victory) in the autumn, the Buddhists go single file out to the initiation ground. The third group are the refugee Tibetan Buddhists who are principally in the far north, particularly the Punjab, but are found on the East coast in various places, having already established several Tibetan temples; and they also have a monastery in Delhi.

(b) Observations on other Buddhist countries.

Buddhism in some areas has been directly confronted by revolutionary political movements. The Mongolian form of Lamaism suffered apparently irremediable blows from Russia during the 1930's and subsequent years. For the Tibetan form, it has been a different story. The great blows dealt by China during the 1950's to Buddhism in Tibet is a tragedy of the modern age, but after an initial period of adjustment, the refugees in Northern India have been reprinting their sacred scriptures, of which dozens have come off their new presses and the icons are again making their appearance. Tibetan Buddhism is the most tenacious, deep-rooted form of Buddhism in the world. The great works found in this tradition constitute a potential revelation of Buddhism different from, but of magnitude equal to the translation of the entire Pāli canon. Thich Nhat Hanh, the Director, School of Social Work, Vanh Hanh University, Saigon, has explained in 1967-68 public addresses that Vietnamese Buddhism is caught in the middle between two 'ism-s', Communism and Anti-Communism, both of which are alien to Buddhist ways of thinking. He explains that when the soldier kills men for their 'ism', he does not shoot at men but at an idea, his own fear. That monk-poet believes that Buddhism needs more to actualize than to modernize. His statements actualize the Yogācāra teaching of 'mind only' and the first verse of the *Dhammapada*, "The natures are preceded by mind." [75]

Another consideration is the present-day interest by Buddhists in problems that have occupied the attention of Buddhist scholars in all the past centuries. They will still discuss the formula of Dependent Origination and again wonder how it works. Professor Wolfram Eberhard has investigated the texts that are memorized and studied by Chinese Buddhists on Taiwan and ascertained that the same texts, e.g. the "Heart Sūtra", are popular in about the same proportion as in the textual remains of Tun Huang in Western China, a millenium ago. Certainly the religious scepticism that E. Michael Mendelson has observed in modern Burma is paralleled by the remarks preserved in Tibetan books that reduce all the gods to the void.

(c) Lay Buddhist associations and scholarship. Traditionally, Buddhist laity looked upon the Samgha as the chief Buddhist organization, although, as we have seen, from the beginning of the religion laymen were responsible for construction and maintenance of the shrines. In modern times, with the advent of modern scholarship demanding the equivalent of university training, with the spread of Buddhism to the West, as well as with the challenges of modern technology and the ease of communication between nations that have undergone rapid changes in political and social forms—new forms of lay activities have arisen.

The Young Men's Buddhist Association (YMBA) movement began in Ceylon in the late nineteenth century and spread to India and Burma. Then similar groups, usually 'Young Buddhists Association' (YBA), were established in Japan, the United States (especially Hawaii and California), Thailand, Korea, China, Penang, Singapore, and Viet-Nam. [26] In California and presumably elsewhere in the United States as well as in Canada, such groups are mainly formed by descendants of Japanese ancestry and are under the wing of a 'Buddhist church' led by a minister who has been trained in Japan or Hawaii and who ordinarily belongs to the Shin sect of Japanese Buddhism, the ministers of which are usually married. One of the activities of such an association is regular meetings, open to the public, for studying Buddhism.

The other chief development was the partial shifting of Buddhist scholarship to laymen. This came about through the accomplishments of Western scholars whose philological training enabled them to approach Buddhist doctrine in a manner differing from the traditional monasterial study. Eventually the fruits of such scholarship became so outstanding that, almost in self-defense, Buddhist or part-Buddhist countries began to favor the equivalent person who would combine such modern study of Buddhism with his role either as a monk or as a lay Buddhist maintaining loyal relations with the Samgha. This is especially the case in Japan, but it is necessarily a comparable situation in Ceylon and other countries of Southern Asia. There is also the monk who goes abroad to learn the Western approach and is practically a layman for the duration of his studies. However, the scholarly layman has his parallel in ancient times: it seems that during the Buddhist prosperity under King Kaniṣka the laymen were especially active in compiling the Abhidharma into the huge work called the *Mahāvibhāṣa*. Lay Buddhist scholarship may also be indicated less obviously by the expression 'householder Bodhisattva'. Again, convert Buddhism in the West almost entirely consists of laymen.

(d) Convert Buddhism in England, Europe, and the United States. For lack of the traditional monasterial forms of Asia whereby persons can live in self-supporting or in community-supported style while practicing meditation and the like, Buddhists in the West have been principally restricted to the doctrinal side of Buddhism. Nevertheless, some hardy individuals have travelled to Asian countries and gone through rigorous disciplines side by side with Asians. Some have been influential in Buddhist countries, as in the case of some German Buddhists who migrated to Ceylon, and some have returned to be influential in Buddhist movements in their native countries.

The Buddhist Society of England was founded in 1906 and became the Buddhist Society of Great Britain and Ireland with Professor Rhys Davids as President. This was followed by the Buddhist Lodge, started by Christmas Humphreys in 1924 under the auspices of the Theosophical Society from which it seceded in 1926. It publishes the periodical which since 1943 is called *The Middle Way*. A London branch of the Ceylon Mahā Bodhi Society was founded in 1925 by Anagarika Dharmapala. The Paris group 'Les Amis du Bouddhisme' was founded in 1929 by the American-born Miss Constant Lounsbery. Between the two great wars Buddhism was much studied in Germany and Dr. Paul Dahlke built the first Western Vihara (Buddhist temple) near Berlin. [32] Groups have arisen in Holland and many other countries as sketchily reported in the Buddhist magazine *Golden Light*. [28]

Buddhism in the United States, exclusive of the Japanese sectarian centers and some Chinese temples, and also leaving out of account small study groups in some cities, has mostly consisted in enthusiastic listening to eloquent expositions of the doctrine. The most successful teacher so far has been the late Dr. D. T. Suzuki, whose writings fostered a wide-spread cult of Zen Buddhism which appeals to younger persons and whose talks were always eagerly and well attended. There is growing interest in Tibetan Buddhism.

(e) World Buddhist Conferences. Most appropriately, the first World Buddhist Conference was held in Kandy, Ceylon, in May, 1950, with inauguration of the World Federation of Buddhists. Buddhists of 29 countries met there, and began a continuing exchange of cultural missions, with a feeling of solidarity that had not existed previously. Some subsequent Conferences are the ones in Tokyo in 1952, Rangoon 1954, Nepal 1956, and Bangkok 1958. [28]

VII. Short History of the Study of Buddhism

Pāli Buddhist studies began in Europe with the French essay on Pāli in 1826 by E. Burnouf and Christian Lassen. Burnouf's 1844 publication of his *Introduction à la histoire du buddhisme indien* (reprinted 1876) opened up the topic of Sanskrit Buddhism. Here we notice the expressions after M. Hodgson, 'Dhyâni Buddhas' and 'Dhyâni Bodhisattvas,' terms which have been repeated in books up to present times even though not attested by the texts. Burnouf also translated into French (1852) the *Saddharma-puṇḍarīka* ('Lotus of the Law', or the 'Lotus Sūtra'). Tibetan sources were exploited by the Hungarian scholar, Alexander Csoma de Körös, who studied Tibetan in Ladakh and early published his Tibetan grammar and Tibetan dictionary (1834) and 'Analysis of the Kanjur' (*Asiatik Researches*, Vol. 20, 1836). W. Wassiljev published at St. Petersburg (1860) a German translation from his Russian under the title *Der Buddhismus, Dogmen, Geschichte und Literatur*, Erster Theil. He included such data as the story of Asanga's obtaining the five books of Maitreya in the Tuṣitā heaven, and Vasumitra's treatise on the tenets of the eighteen Buddhist sects. A. Schiefner made much historical information accessible by his translation into German from Tibetan of Tāranātha's *History of Buddhism* (1869). Those and other editions early called Mahāyāna and Sanskrit Buddhist materials to the attention of European scholars, and such researches continued with steady progress. [4]

However, the most imposing development during the remainder of the nineteenth century was not in Mahāyāna Buddhism but in Pāli Buddhism. A pioneer in the study of early Buddhism was Ivan P. Minayeff (1840-1890), whose miscellaneous findings were translated from Russian under the title *Recherches sur le Bouddhisme* (Paris, 1894). The *Dictionary of the Pali Language* by ROBERT C. CHILDERS appeared London, 1875. This was quickly followed by V. FAUSBÖLL's edition of the Jātakas (1877-97) and V. TRENCKNER's edition of the *Milinda-pañha* (London, 1880). H. OLDENBERG, well known for his work, *Buddha, sein Leben, seine Lehre, sein Gemeinde*, made an edition in five volumes of the *Vinaya-piṭaka* (London, 1879-83). In 1881, T. W. RHYS DAVIDS (1843-1922) founded the Pāli Text Society. In the subsequent years of the nineteenth and early twentieth centuries this Society published in Roman type the entire canonical Pāli literature and all important non-canonical works such as commentaries. At the same time, translations into the chief European languages were being published of the original texts. MRS. C. A. F. RHYS DAVIDS (1858-1942) made many fine translations into English, and after the death of her husband, energetically led the Society. Her successor, I. B. HORNER, has newly translated and re-translated a number of texts. [4]

The study of Mahāyāna Buddhism in Europe was stimulated by the texts and studies published at St. Petersburg in the series *Bibliotheca Buddhica*, beginning with CECIL BENDALL's edition of the *Śikṣāsamuccaya* (1897-1902). The Russian scholarship of Buddhism in the twentieth century has been dominated by TH. STCHERBATSKY. In his famous *Buddhist Logic* (2 vols., 1932) he sets forth three periods of Buddhist philosophy. The first period, starting with the Buddha, stresses the 'No-Soul' theory, salvation by individual efforts, and reality of the external world which is a flow of innumerable particulars. The second period, at the start of the fifth century after Buddha, replaces the "human Buddha who disappears into a lifeless Nirvāṇa" with "a divine Buddha enthroned in a Nirvāṇa full of life." Pluralism became Monism, with unreality of the separate elements. The third period starts a millenium after the Buddha by the impetus of the brothers Asaṅga and Vasubandhu, who inaugurate the Idealistic system of Buddhist philosophy with a spirited interest in logic. STCHERBATSKY explains the four systems, the Vaibhāṣika, Sautrāntika, Yogācāra, and Mādhyamika, in his work *The Conception of Buddhist Nirvāṇa* (Leningrad, 1927). One of his students, EUGENE OBERMILLER, translated important works from Tibetan; another, OTTO ROSENBERG, utilized Japanese sources. This school is terminated with the death of STCHERBATSKY circa 1942. Collaboration between SYLVAIN LÉVI (Professor at the Collège de France) and J. TAKAKUSU (Honorary Professor at the Imperial University of Tokyo) resulted in three fascicules of a Buddhist encyclopedia project entitled *Hôbôgirin* (Tokyo, 1929-1937), along with an invaluable annex of tables providing access to the individual works of the *Taishô Issaikyô*. The series *Mélanges chinois et bouddhique* has appeared at Brussels starting in 1931-32. The series *Buddhica; documents et travaux pour l'étude du Bouddhisme* (Paris, 1926-1956) was begun under the editorship of JEAN PRZYLUSKI. This contains LOUIS DE LA VALLÉE POUSSIN's learned translation *Vijñaptimātratāsiddhi* (1928-1929); the same scholar is well known for his *L'Abhidharmakośa de Vasubandhu* (Paris, 1923-31). The growing world-wide flood of books and articles on Buddhism led to a series within *Buddhica* called *Bibliographie Bouddhique* (covering Jan. 1928 to May 1958). É. LAMOTTE (Louvain) and A. BAREAU (Paris) are now at the forefront. In Germany, M. WALLESER, J. NOBEL, F. WELLER, and E. WALDSCHMIDT have brought out important editions and translations of Mahāyāna texts; and WALDSCHMIDT, together with his students, have processed the text fragments from Turfan. *Zeitschrift für Buddhismus* appeared at München (1920-1931); *Materialien zur Kunde des Buddhismus*, at Heidelberg (1923-1935). In Italy, G. TUCCI and L. PETECH made great strides in Tibetan Buddhism and history; the brilliant work of ALFONSA FERRARI was cut short by untimely death. *Serie Orientale Roma* has run to many volumes. In England, both J. BROUGH and H. W. BAILEY have studied Central Asian Buddhist texts; and EDWARD CONZE, while settled there, became an authority on Prajñāpāramitā scriptures. Some important Mahāyāna texts have been published in the series *Sacred Books of the Buddhists*, which began with J. S. SPEYER's translation of the *Jātakamālā* (London, 1895). The *Harvard Oriental Series* has published scholarly editions and translations, and the greatest contribution to date by an American is FRANKLIN EDGERTON's *Buddhist Hybrid Sanskrit Grammar and Dictionary* (1953). Columbia University in New York is now publishing a series of Buddhist text translations in line with an Oriental Humanities program. Graduate programs of Buddhist studies have been inaugurated in the 1960's at The University of Wisconsin, the University of Washington, and Columbia University. In Australia J. DE JONG heads such studies.

In India, an early classic was the work *Nepalese Buddhist Literature* (1882) by RAJENDRA LAL MITRA and HARA PRASAD SHASTRI. SARAT CHANDRA DAS was a pioneer in Tibetan Studies and responsible for the *Journal of the Buddhist Text and Anthropological Society* (1893-1906); he prepared a *Tibetan-English Dictionary*. SATISH CHANDRA VIDYABHUSAN and NALINAKSHA DUTT edited important Buddhist Sanskrit texts and wrote survey works. P. C. BAGCHI studied the Chinese canon in his *Le Canon Bouddhique en Chine* (1927-1938). B. BHATTACHARYA edited fundamental Buddhist Tantra works. DHARMANANDA KOSAMBI (1871-1947) wrote influential works on Buddhism in Marathi and Gujarati; his successor at Fergusson College, PROF. P. V. BAPAT utilizes both Pāli and Chinese sources. [4] DR. RAGHU VIRA founded the International Academy of Indian Culture in New Delhi; his son, LOKESH CHANDRA, has been publishing many rare Tibetan manuscripts, such as the collected works of Bu-ston; and has compiled a large Tibetan-Sanskrit dictionary. P. L. VAIDYA tried to restore the Sanskrit text of Āryadeva's *Catuḥśataka* (Chap. 8-16) from its Tibetan translation. He has edited the reprint series of *Buddhist Sanskrit Texts* running into many volumes, and published by The Mithila Institute, Darbhanga, India. BHIKKHU JAGADĪS KASSAPA has edited the main Pāli canon in Devanāgarī script; this is called the Nālandā-Devanāgarī-Pāli-Series, published by the Bihar Government. Important centers for Buddhist studies are Santiniketan in West Bengal and Nalanda in Bihar. Some foreigners while resident in India have advanced Tibetan studies, especially GEORGE N. ROERICH by *The Blue Annals*, Part One (1949), Part Two (1953), published by The Royal Asiatic Society of Bengal; and HERBERT V. GUENTHER by *The Jewel Ornament of Liberation* (London, 1959).

The Ceylonese scholar, G. P. MALALASEKERA prepared the *Dictionary of Pāli Proper Names* (1937-38, reprint London, 1960); and is Editor-in-Chief of the *Encyclopaedia of Buddhism*, which began in 1957. O. H. DE WIJESEKERA has correlated Pāli passages with Vedic literature concerning deities. W. RAHULA's *History of Buddhism in Ceylon* (1956) is based on original Pāli sources.

BUNYIU NANJIO (1849-1927) and JUNJIRO TAKAKUSU (1866-1945) pioneered the introduction and progress in Japan of Western scholarship toward Buddhism. [4] NANJIO published at Oxford in 1883 his *Catalogue of the Chinese translation of the Buddhist Tripiṭaka*, based on the Ming catalog of 1410. UNRAI WOGIHARA (1869-1937) edited Sanskrit works of fundamental importance, such as Asaṅga's *Bodhisattvabhūmi*. CHIZEN AKANUMA (1884-1937) prepared *The Comparative Catalogue of Chinese Āgamas and Pāli Nikāyas* (1929), and *The Dictionary of Proper Names of Indian Buddhism*, 1931. Buddhist scholarly study is mainly centered at Tokyo University, the Toyo Bunko of Tokyo, Kyoto University, and Tohoku University; but there are a number of other centers (sectarian) where Buddhist scholarship is carried on. At Kyoto,

RYOZABURO SAKAKI published his edition of the *Mahāvyutpatti* (1916, reprint 1962), the famous Sanskrit-Tibetan Buddhist dictionary with a late Chinese translation, to which Sakaki has added the Japanese translation; the two volumes include a Sanskrit and a Tibetan index. Both SUSUMU YAMAGUCHI and GADJIN NAGAO have made fine contributions to the Yogācāra study, and NAGAO's students have specialized in Buddhist logic and Yogācāra. At Tokyo, HAKUJU UI (in Yogācāra and lexicography), SHOSON MIYAMOTO (in Mādhyamika), and HAJIME NAKAMURA (in a variety of topics) have been preeminent. NAKAMURA summarizes Japanese studies on Buddhism in *Acta Asiatica* 1 (Tokyo 1960), and surveys the scholarly conclusions about Mahāyāna and esoteric Buddhism in *Acta Asiatica* 6 and 7 (Tokyo, 1964). Remarkable contributions to Tibetan studies have been made with catalogues, such as the Tohoku University's *A Complete Catalogue of the Tibetan Buddhist Canons* (Sendai, 1934) based on the Derge edition; and *A Catalogue of the Tohoku University Collection of Tibetan Works on Buddhism* (Sendai, 1953) of extra-canonical works. The Suzuki Research Foundation (Kyoto-Tokyo) has photographically reproduced in 168 handsome volumes the Peking edition of the Kanjur-Tanjur and included the collected works of Tsoṅ-kha-pa; the Tables of Contents and other indexes are published in a single volume, the *Catalogue and Index to The Tibetan Tripiṭaka* (Tokyo, 1962). The same Foundation has published reprints of important reference works. In a book published at Kyoto in 1959, RYUJO YAMADA has surveyed all the modern Western work on Sanskrit Buddhism. Japanese researches in all aspects of Buddhism are especially known from the *Journal of Indian and Buddhist Studies* (*Indogaku Bukkyogaku Kenkyū*—articles in Japanese and Western languages—which in Vol. XIV:2 (March 1966) contains a valuable report on Indian and Buddhist studies prepared by AKIRA HIRAKAWA.

A general outcome of those numerous researches in various countries is that Pāli Buddhism is certainly the most imposing corpus of early Buddhism, but still does not tell the whole story even for the 'origins'. Mahāyāna Buddhism, particularly its Vinaya texts, preserves important materials bearing on early Buddhism. Pāli Buddhism has had the advantage of a canon available in its 'original' language as preserved in various scripts of South-East Asia. The philological problems in dealing with Sanskrit Buddhism were compounded by the lack of extant Sanskrit for most of the works translated into Chinese and Tibetan.

SELECTED BIBLIOGRAPHY

[1] ABHAYAKARAGUPTA, "Muni-Matālamkāra," *PTT*, V. 101.

[2] BAILEY, D. R. SHACKLETON, *The Satapañcāśatka of Mātṛceṭa* (Cambridge University Press, 1951).

[3] BAILEY, D. R. SHACKLETON, "Varṇārhavarṇe"..., *BOAS*, XIIl, 3, 1950.

[4] BAPAT, P. V., General Editor., *2500 Years of Buddhism* (Government of India, 1959).

[5] BAREAU, ANDRÉ, *Les sectes bouddhiques du Petit Véhicule* (Saïgon, 1955).

——,*Recherches sur la biographie du Buddha dans les Sūtrapiṭaka et les Vinayapiṭaka anciens* (Paris, 1963).

[7] BASHAM, A. L., *The Wonder That Was India* (New York, 1954).

[8] BENDALL, CECIL, and ROUSE, W. H. D., trs., *Śikshā-samuccaya compiled by Śāntideva* (London, 1922).

[9] BROUGH, JOHN, *The Gāndhārī Dharmapada* (London, 1962).

[10] BROUGH, JOHN, Articles in *Bulletin of the School of Oriental and African Studies*, XII:3,4 (1948) and XIII:2 (1950).

[11] BURTT, E. A., ed., *The Teachings of the Compassionate Buddha* (Mentor Book, 1955).

[12] CH'AN CHU, tr., *The Sutra of 42 Sections* (London, 1947).

[13] CHATTOPADHYAYA, ALAKA, *Atīśa and Tibet* (Calcutta, 1967).

[14] CONZE, EDWARD, tr., *Aṣṭasāhasrikā Prajñāpāramitā* (Calcutta, 1958).

[15] CONZE, EDWARD, *The Prajñāpāramitā Literature* ('s-Gravenhage, 1960).

[16] COOMARASWAMY, ANANDA K. and HORNER, I. B., *Gotama the Buddha* (London, 1948).

[17] DAYAL, HAR., *The Bodhisattva Doctrine* (London, 1932).

[18] DEMIÉVILLE, PAUL, *Le concile de Lhasa* (Paris, 1952).

[19] ——,Article in *Mélanges publiés par L'Institut des hautes études chinoises*, Tome Premier (Paris, 1957).

[20] Dge ḥdun rgya mtshoḥi dpal. *Gnas brtan cho ga*, separate block print.

[21] DUTT, NALINAKSHA, *Early Monastic Buddhism* (Calcutta, 1960).

[22] ——,ed., *Pañcaviṃśatisāhasrikā Prajñāpāramitā* (London, 1934).

[23] EDGERTON, FRANKLIN, *Buddhist Hybrid Sanskrit Grammar and Dictionary*, 2 vol. (New Haven, 1953).

[24] EDGERTON, FRANKLIN, ed., *Buddhist Hybrid Sanskrit Reader* (New Haven, 1953).

FILLIOZAT, JEAN. See RENOU, LOUIS.

[25] FOUCHER, A. *The Beginnings of Buddhist Art* (Paris, London, 1917).

[26] GARD, RICHARD A, ed., *Buddhism* (New York, 1961).

[27] GEIGER, WILHELM, *The Mahāvaṃsa or the Great Chronicle of Ceylon* (Colombo 1950).

[28] *The Golden Light* (the Penang Buddhist Association, Malaya), Vol. III:3, Oct. 1960, and IV:1, Jan. 1961.

[29] HATTORI, MASAAKI, tr., "Dignāga on Perception, being the Pratyakṣapariccheda of Dignāga's Pramānasamuccaya," from the Sanskrit fragments and the Tibetan versions (*HOS* 47, Cambridge, Mass., 1968).

[30] HIRAKAWA, AKIRA. "The Rise of Mahāyāna Buddhism and its Relationship to the Worship of Stupas," *Memoirs of the Research Department of The Toyo Bunko*, No. 22 (1963).

[31] HORNER, I. B., "The Teaching of the Elders," in E. CONZE, ed., *Buddhist Texts Through the Ages* (Oxford, 1954).

HORNER, I. B. See COOMARASWAMY, ANANDA K.

[32] HUMPHREYS, CHRISTMAS, *Buddhism* (A Pelican Book, 1951).

[33] JAN, YÜN-HUA, "Buddhist Self-Immolation in Medieval China," *History of Religions* 4:2 (Winter 1965).
[34] JAYASUNDERE, A. D., tr., *The Numerical Sayings: II* (Adyar, Madras, 1925).
[35] JAYATILLEKE, K. N., *Early Buddhist Theory of Knowledge* (London, 1963).
[36] JOHNSTON, E. H., *The Buddhacarita or Acts of the Buddha*, Part II (Calcutta, 1936).
[37] JONES, J. J., tr., *The Mahāvastu*, 3 vols. (London, 1949, 1952, 1956).
[38] KAJIYAMA, YUICHI, *An Introduction to Buddhist Philosophy; An annotated translation of the Tarkabhāṣā of Mokṣākaragupta* (Kyoto, 1966).
[39] KERN, H., tr., *Saddharma-Puṇḍarīka or The Lotus of the True Law* (reprint New York, 1963).
[40] KITAGAWA, HIDENORI, *A Study of Indian Classical Logic-Dignāga's System* [in Japanese] (Tokyo, 1965).
[41] LAMOTTE, ÉTIENNE, *Histoire du Bouddhisme Indien* (Louvain, 1958).
[42] ——,*La Somme du Grand Véhicule d'Asaṅga "Mahāyāna-saṃgraha"*, 2 Tomes (Louvain, 1938-39).
[43] ——,*La Concentration de la Marche Héroïque "Śūraṃgamasamādhisūtra"* (Bruxelles, 1965).
[44] ——,*L'Enseignement de Vimalakīrti "Vimalakīrtinirdeśa"* (Louvain, 1962).
[45] LA VALLÉE POUSSIN, LOUIS DE, *L'Abhidharmakośa de Vasubandhu* (Paris, 1923-31).
[46] ——, *Vijñaptimātratāsiddhi; La Siddhi de Hiuan-Tsang*, 2 Tomes (Paris, 1928-29); Index (Paris, 1948).
[47] LE MAY, REGINALD, *The Culture of South East Asia* (Government of India, 1962).
[48] LESSING, FERDINAND D., and WAYMAN, ALEX., *Mkhas grub rje's Fundamentals of the Buddhist Tantras "Rgyud sde spyiḥi rnam par gẓag pa rgyas par brjod"* (The Hague, Paris, 1968).
[49] LESSING, FERDINAND D., "The Eighteen Worthies Crossing the Sea," *The Sino-Swedish Expedition Publication* 38 (Stockholm, 1954).
[50] LÉVI, S., ed., *Mahāyāna-Sutrālaṃkāra* (Paris, 1907).
[51] LÉVI, SYLVAIN, "Autour d'Aśvaghoṣa," *Journal Asiatique*, CCXV, Oct.-Dec. 1929.
[52] LIN, LI-KOUANG, *L'Aide-Mémoire de la Vraie Loi* (Paris, 1949).
[53] MAHĀTHERA, PARAVAHERA VAJIRAÑĀNA, *Buddhist Meditation in Theory and Practice* (Colombo, 1962).
[54] MCGOVERN, WILLIAM MONTGOMERY, *A Manual of Buddhist Philosophy* (London, 1923).
[55] MIURA, ISSHU, and SASAKI, RUTH FULLER. *Zen Dust* (Kyoto, 1966).
[56] MURTI, T. R. V., *The Central Philosophy of Buddhism* (London, 1955).
[57] MUS, PAUL, *La Lumière sur les Six Voies* (Paris, 1939).
[58] ÑANAMOLI, BHIKKHU, tr., *The Path of Purification "Visuddhimagga"* (Colombo, 1956).
[59] NĀRADA THERA, tr., *The Dhammapada* (London, reprint 1959).
[60] NYANATILOKA, *The Word of the Buddha* (Colombo, 1952).
[61] OBERMILLER, E., tr., *History of Buddhism by Bu-ston*, two parts (Heidelberg, 1931-32).
[62] ——,"The Doctrine of Prajñā-pāramitā as exposed in the Abhisamayālaṃkāra of Maitreya" (in *Acta Orientalia*, Vol. XI, 1932).
[63] *The Pali Chanting Scripture with Thai and English Translation* (distributed in Bangkok, B.E. 2505).
[64] PENSA, CORRADO, ed., *L'Abhisamayālaṃkāravṛtti di Ārya-Vimuktisena*, Primo Abhisamaya (Rome, 1967).

PTT. Abbreviation for *Tibetan Tripitaka*, q.v.

[65] RENOU, LOUIS, and FILLIOZAT, JEAN, *L'Inde Classique* II (Paris, Hanoi, 1953).

ROUSE, W. H. D., See BENDALL, CECIL.

[66] RHYS DAVIDS, Mrs., tr. *The Book of the Kindred Sayings "Saṃyutta-Nikāya"*, Part I (London, 1917).

SASAKI, RUTH. See MIURA, ISSHU.

[67] SIVARAMAMURTI, C., *Amaravati Sculptures in the Madras Government Museum* (Madras, 1956).

[68] SMṚTIJÑĀNAKĪRTI, "Mañjuśrī-nāmasamgīti-lakṣa-bhāṣya" (*PTT* V. 75, p. 46).

[69] SPEYER, J. S., tr., *The Jātakamālā or Garland of Birth-Stories* (London, 1895).

[70] STCHERBATSKY, *Buddhist Logic*, two volumes (Dover ed., New York, 1962).

[71] ——, *The Central Conception of Buddhism* (Calcutta edition, 1961).

[72] SUZUKI, DAISETZ TEITARO, *Studies in the Lankavatara Sutra* (London, 1930).

[73] TAKAKUSU, JUNJIRO, *The Essentials of Buddhist Philosophy* (Honolulu, 2d ed., 1949).

[74] TAKASAKI, JIKIDO, *A Study on the Ratnagotravibhāga "Uttaratantra"* (Rome, 1966).

[75] THICH, NHAT HANH, *Aujourd'hui le bouddhisme* (traduit du Viêtnamien par LE VAN HAO) (Paris, 1964).

[76] THOHEY, GABRIEL, "Burmese Buddhism," *Annali Lateranensi* XXI (1957).

[77] THOMAS, EDWARD J., *The History of Buddhist Thought* (London, reprinted 1963).

[78] ——, *The Life of Buddha as Legend and History* (London, 1952).

[79] *Tibetan Tripiṭaka*. This is the photographic reproduction in 168 vols. (Kyoto-Tokyo, 1959-61) of the Peking edition of the Kanjur-Tanjur and accessory volumes, with abbreviated reference 'PTT'.

[80] TSOṄ-KHA-PA, *Lam rim chen mo* (Tashilunpo blockprint).

[81] TUCCI, GIUSEPPE, *Minor Buddhist Texts* Part II (Rome, 1958).

[82] ——, *Tibetan Painted Scrolls* (Rome, 1949).

[83] VAJRAVARMAN, "Durgatipariśodhana-vyākhyā-sundarālaṃkāra" (*PTT* V. 76, p. 108).

[84] "Vinaya-vibhaṅga" (*PTT* V. 43 on 31st *pātayantika*) and *Sahasodgatāvadāna* in *Divyāvadānam* ed. by Dr. P. L. VAIDYA (Darbhanga, 1959).

[85] VINITADEVA, "Vinaya-vibhaṅga-pada-vyākhyāna" (*PTT* V. 122, on Fourth Defeat, pp. 304-313).

[86] WARREN, HENRY CLARKE, *Buddhism in Translations* (Cambridge, Mass., 1947)

[87] WAYMAN, ALEX., *Analvsis of the Śrāvakabhūmi Manuscript* (Berkeley, 1961).

[88] ——, Articles in *Liebenthal Festschrift* (Visvabharati, 1957); *Journal of the American Oriental Society* 75:4, 1955; *Indo-Iranian Journal*, 3:1-2 (1959); *Journal of Indian and Buddhist Studies* (Tokyo), 7:1 (1960); *Oriens Extremus*, 9:1 (1962); *Philosophy East and West*, XV:1 (Jan. 1965); *History of Religions*, 7:1 (Aug. 1967); *Studies of Esoteric Buddhism and Tantrism* (Koya-san, Japan, 1965).

WAYMAN, ALEX. See LESSING, FERDINAND D.

[89] WENZEL, H., tr., "Bçes pai phrin yig" (Friendly Epistle), *Journal of the Pali Text Society*, 1886.

[90] WINTERNITZ, MAURICE, *A History of Indian Literature*, Vol. II (Buddhist Literature and Jaina Literature) (Calcutta, 1933).

[91] ZURCHER, E., *The Buddhist Conquest of China*, Text (Leiden, 1959).

THE RELIGIONS OF CHINA

BY

HANS STEININGER

Würzburg, Germany

CONFUCIANISM

I. Essence of Confucianism

Since the great revolution of 1911/12 the question has continually been raised as to whether Confucianism has ever been a religion. Among many others the renowned scholars Hu Shih (1891-1962) and Liang Ch'i-Ch'ao (1873-1929) in particular praised the rational agnosticism of this way of thinking; and Liang even expressed the opinion that in China religion had never played that fatal rôle in the official sphere which it had played elsewhere in the world. It was true, and very unfortunate, he stated, that there was also pagan-mythical Taoism which was indigenous to China. However, at no time had it been able to assert itself in Chinese public life, and it had been rejected time and again because it had proved detrimental to peace. All other religions in China, such as Buddhism for example, which were founded upon faith and strove for transmundane goals had been imported into China. It was with such arguments that those young Chinese progressives of that time tried to convey to the modern Western world with its rationalism the idea that thanks to 'rational and agnostic Confucianism' China had at all times been a well-tempered and well-balanced state. By maintaining this, they wished to prove that both their country and they themselves could well match Western ideas and attainments.

Without going into details of the much-discussed question of how to define the concept of "religion" in the narrower or the wider sense of the word, we may discard the above assertions as being tendentious and biassed by their time without, however, wishing to deny at all the doubtlessly strong rationalist features which, together with an ever-reappearing tendency toward agnosticism, can be observed in many eminent Confucians throughout Chinese history.

The essence of Confucianism as a religion or, in other words, the religious elements in Confucianism have their origins in Chinese antiquity, i.e. in the time prior to Confucius. In the *Lun Yü* (VII, 1) Confucius says, "I have transmitted what was taught to me without making up anything of my own. I have been faithful to and loved the Ancients." These words mainly apply to the religious ideas and only to a lesser degree to ethical ideas, which were transformed and developed by Confucius as well as by his disciples and successors and which bear a definite "Confucian" stamp.

Although its essence remained the same through centuries, Confucianism naturally underwent development and changes in the course of history, and in this section we will outline a few essential features many of which will be treated at more length later.

The Chinese people in general have always had a strong feeling of being dependent on uncontrollable powers and spirits, a feeling which nourished fear and piety. And this feeling of dependence finds manifold expressions in the highly esteemed Confucian Book of Rites and in the almanachs, which have played an important rôle at all times up to our days.

Confucius as well as Mencius shared this awareness of man's dependence on inconceivable powers of moral force, which was so deeply rooted in their people. In their time they adopted the traditional belief in Heaven (*T'ien*) which ruled over man and nature. And when at the end these two men, who are generally regarded as the founders of Confucianism, despite their great courage and self-assertion failed in reaching the position and influence they had hoped for, they both accepted the inscrutable judgement of Heaven which they had again and again implored during their lives as a sufficient explanation. Since their time belief in Heaven has remained an established ingredient of Confucianism. In the Five Canonical Books (also called Five Classics) of the *Ju-chia* (Confucian teaching) reference is frequently made to Heaven distributing reward and punishment. A "Heaven religion" is taken for granted in the canonical books, in addition to ancestor worship which soon became a firm component of Confucianism.

Also the belief in predetermination which Confucius appeared to adhere to when, in old age and somewhat resigned, he studied the old Book of Divination, the *I Ching*, seems to indicate a feeling of dependence within which rationalism and religion smoothly tallied with one another—a fact which is true of Confucius as well as of most of the later Confucians.

In addition to the ancient "Heaven religion" and ancestor worship, which gradually came to imply the worship of nature gods and, in the

Han era (206 B.C.-220 A.D.), the worship of heroes, Han Confucianism also took over from the "Weltanschauung" of ancient China the idea of the interplay of forces between *Yang* and *Yin*, the *Wu Hsing* (Five Elements), as well as the concept of *Tao* as that of the predetermined and morally correct way. *Yang* and *Yin* are understood to be the male and the female principle, reflecting the hot and cold, light and darkness, representing Heaven and Earth and governing the behaviour of all creatures. The Five Elements are 'spatio-temporal categories rather than materials': Wood-East, Fire-South, Earth-Centre, Metal-West, Water-North.

The adoption of the proto-sciences (*Yang-Yin* and *Wu Hsing* doctrine) in the 3rd and 2nd centuries B.C. made it possible to assume a world functioning anonymously in which one only had to know the right formulae. Nature and society were mechanistically interrelated. But in actual fact this interrelationship was not based on empirically gained scientific ideas but on symbols which were arbitrarily manipulated according to fixed methods in order to grasp and direct the world. Even Heaven could be conceived of as an abstract function. This possibility of man's being autonomous, which was first established by Tsou Yen (350-270 B.C.) in the school at Chi Hsia and which was taken over into Han Confucianism, was advocated by only very few intellectuals; nevertheless it was important because Confucian agnostics throughout the ages refer to it.

The Confucianism, however, which was effective and successful throughout the centuries is neither fatalistic—insofar as it does not believe in the unrestricted sovereignty of Heaven over man and nature (i.e. without allowing anybody or anything to influence it) nor is it moralistic and deterministic because it does not believe that man's good conduct could force Heaven to be benevolent and distribute blessings and benefits.

The following passages will, it is hoped, elucidate the fact that Confucianism as a religion during the periods when it flourished, i.e. until the beginning of the 20th century, was rooted in the State although it lacked the independent organization or outward form of a church as is the case with Buddhism or Taoism. The belief in Heaven and the confession of this belief, the religious worship of the deceased and, finally, the fight against false doctrines and the acknowledgement of ethical principles all go to prove the religious character of Confucianism. An execllent summing up is given by C.K. YANG in "*Religion in Chinese Society*" (p. 277) where he states, "The Confucians, therefore,

...must be regarded as part of the general pattern of Chinese religious life with only relative differences due to their social and economic position."

The most original and the most lasting achievements of Confucianism, however, lie in its ethics the religious background of which was, so to speak, borrowed from Chinese antiquity. It is these ethics which even today we meet all over East Asia, not only in Taoism and Buddhism, but also in the Shintôism of Japan and in lesser local cults. The deities may change, but Confucian ethics remain the same. The few agnostics among Confucians were well aware of this fact, and by using the religions to serve as vehicles of Confucian ethics they found it easy to gain control over the religious people.

Confucianism replaced nobility of birth by nobility of mind. The *Li* (broadly speaking a hierarchical set-up commanding the respect of the younger for the elder) were a system of observances encompassing the living as well as the dead. Having at one time only been valid for the members of the nobility, the *Li* were used by Confucianism as a means to enable even those who were not born noble to gain access to the nobility of the spirit.

Confucianism does not recognize monks, nuns or an official priesthood. The sacrifices for Master K'ung were performed by state officials. And although from the 12th century onwards the Neoconfucians headed by Chu Hsi attached special importance to the old doctrine which said that Man was good and Heaven was moral, no confession of faith was demanded of the Confucians. Nor do we find any missionary activity in Confucianism, no adoration of relics, no amulets, and very few martyrs.

II. Historical Development

K'ung Ch'iu, who was styled Chung-ni and whose honorary name K'ung Fu-tzu, Master K'ung, was Latinized to Confucius in the 17th century by the Jesuit patres who then lived at the court in Peking, was born about the middle of the 6th century B.C. in the small town of Tsu not far from Ch'üf-u, the place where he spent most of his life and where he also died. Ch'ü-fu was situated in the feudal state of Lu (Province of Shantung). According to tradition he lived from 551-479 B.C.; these dates are, however, of qualitative rather than of quantitative relevance. Seventy-two, the number of years he allegedly lived, is a figure of cosmological and astrological importance (12 times 6). Significantly enough, he is also said to have had seventy-two direct disciples. Even such old sources as the *Tso Chuan*, which tries to establish family ties between the K'ung family and the ancient Shang-Yin dynasty, and the otherwise generally reliable *Shih Chi* provide no dependable information on K'ung's life, but they gave rise to those legends about Confucius which were elaborated on during and after the Warring States period in order to embroider the story of K'ung's modest life. An excellent summary of their contents will be found in J. LEGGE's prolegomena to his *Lun Yü* translation. These honours reached their climax as late as 1907 when the decaying Manchu dynasty equated Master K'ung with "Heaven", perhaps in order to create in the very last minute a Chinese Saviour who could be set against the Western Saviour, Jesus Christ.

The most reliable reports are to be found in the *Lun Yü*, Selected Sayings, which relate the master's talks with his disciples and which were written down by his direct disciples or at least by the direct disciples of the latter. We learn but little about the social position of the Magister Sinarum. His parents are not mentioned in any of the reliable sources. It seems certain that he was married and that he had one son and one daughter. However, in the traditional sources, his family does not play such an important rôle as K'ung's own teachings ascribe to the family. Confucius himself says that he spent his youth in very modest circumstances; and the highest position he ever held was that of a *Shih-shih*, Master of the Rites, who instructed young knights, i.e. members of the lower aristocracy to which he himself belonged but which had already lost most of its privileges by this time.

The high-sounding titles he was awarded in his home state towards the end of his life gave him no influence over public affairs. In those days people of his standing obtained power and influence over the princes by displaying their eloquence. However, throughout his life Master K'ung was deeply sceptical about all forms of glibness. In his opinion the only way out of the dilemma of his age, in which human as well as public relations were in disarray, was the maintenance of the *Li*, which he understood as being the sacred customs and rites in their entirety. However, he did not merely demand the formal observance of the traditional prescriptions designed to guarantee harmony between Heaven, Earth, and the People, but also required people to act in the right way out of moral conviction. Human relations were of the highest importance. Confucius himself was convinced that he was doing nothing more than advocating the Way of the Former Kings and the Way of Goodness which had been followed and practised not only by the founders of the Chou dynasty but also by the mythical emperors Yao and Shun. He set up his doctrine of peace in opposition to the tyranny of his time.

If we read the sources with neither too much credulity nor scepticism we may say that Confucius studied the oldest parts of what later became the *Shu Ching* (Book of Documents) and the oldest parts of the *Shih Ching* (Book of Odes) and the *I Ching* (Book of Change). The very dry and matter-of-fact statements of the *Ch'un Chiu*, the Spring and Autumm Annals of the State of Lu, which, perhaps, he edited himself, served as "hinges" for his political and moral doctrines which he probably only gave orally and which were written down by later authors "in keeping with the Master's views". Historical events were allotted praise or blame in the belief that it was possible in this way to create a thesaurus from which one might learn the "will of Heaven" in similar events of the present and the future. For Confucius history was not a process but a well-balanced permanent state, conditioned by the unswerving harmony in Nature, *Tao*, the correct moral way, which is valid at all times. This way coming from the past continues in the same direction and leads into the future. Thus, Confucius regarded all his teachings as a mere restauration of the old, basic ideas adapted to the times that had changed.

After Confucius had failed in public life and had not succeeded in becoming the prince's counsellor as he had hoped, he devoted himself more and more to classical studies and passed his ideas on to his disciples whom he trained for the civil service.

At the age of sixty he is said to have gone "abroad" in order to win over a prince outside his home state for his plans. Although his propaganda journeys into present-day Shantung and Honan were unsuccessful, his ideas were carried beyond the borders of the state of Lu, and their dissemination in the Chinese world was initiated by the "teacher of ten thousand generations" himself.

After his death, Confucius's teachings were propagated by his disciples a few of whom had succeeded in obtaining high offices in the feudal states. Whereas during Confucius's lifetime feudal thinking still proved a hindrance to the carreers of men trained in the Confucian way of thinking (they were called "*Ju-Chia*" men, i.e. weaklings, because their strength was intellectual rather than physical) the potentates of the Warring States period (480-221 B.C.) were very interested in increasing their reputation and their power by enlisting the help of *Ju-chia* people.

On a lower level, *Ju-chia* people, who wrongfully claimed they were interpreting the Master's teachings, were very popular as specialists in questions of ritual, and on ceremonial occasions (weddings, ancestor worship) they earned nice sums of money. Those of them who were fond of writing wrote the numerous unimportant passages of the *Li Chi*, a manual on the rites, and probably also the appendices to the *I Ching*. By doing this they made the exacting doctrines of the Master, who had attached more importance to the substance of his teachings than to their outward form, more accessible to the people but, at the same time, of course, they made them somewhat trite.

There is no doubt that other thinkers and other schools of thought influenced Confucianism in its early stages. Among such thinkers we today include Mo Ti who was born about the time of Confucius's death. Whereas the *Ju-chia* people believed in Heaven and relied upon the example of the sage kings of antiquity, Mo Ti was opposed to the idea of hereditary monarchy and wanted the most virtuous man to be on the throne. This idea was advocated by later Confucians whenever they desired a change in the existing conditions. Otherwise, they stuck to the dynastic principle just as their Master K'ung had done.

Meng-tzu (Mencius) (372-289 B.C.) gave important impulses to early Confucianism although he did not gain full recognition until the Sung era when he was recognized as the "Second Holy Man" (after Confucius). Like the master, he also wandered through the Chinese world trying to find a prince who would be willing to carry out his ideas. And as in the case of the Master his teachings, attaching as they did more value to the good than to the useful, met with little approval on the part of the princes. They would not believe him when he preached that they ought to make the welfare of the people their sole task in order to obtain the Mandate of Heaven which meant sovereignty over the *T'ien-hsia*, the Chinese world. His words went unheeded when he recommended them to employ *Ju-chia* people as their ministers or officials. (In later times, it is true, *Ju-chia* people were sometimes employed as tutors for young princes who, in compliance with Mencius' demands, treated their former masters like their "fathers" or "elder brothers" even after they had succeeded to the government.)

In spite of having had bad experiences and in contrast to his Confucian adversary Hsün-tzu, Mencius advocated the idea of the good nature of man. And he believed that this moral man was able to know—by means of a kind of introspection (*Liang-chih*)—the morally composed world. Although Mencius' mysticism comes very close to Taoism, he attaches great importance to the study of the canonical books in order to be able to follow the "way" of the ancient model emperors Yao and Shun and also to be able to comply with the virtues of *Jen* (humanity) and *I* (righteousness) in an orthodox way. Although he got into contact with the academicians of the *Chi-hsia* Gate Academy during his stay in Ch'i, this essentially scientific school of the *Wu Hsing* and *Yang-Yin* evidently did not impress him at that time. However, it was perhaps the fact that this science was based on necessity, which brought him to the very unorthodox conviction that it was permissible to revolt against a notoriously bad sovereign and that under certain circumstances it was even admissable to assassinate him. Because of such subversive statements, Mencius was banned from the Confucius temple at the beginning of the Ming era, since the new and still very unstable dynasty detested such doctrines.

Shortly after Mencius' death, Hsün-tzu (298?-238?) studied and taught at the court of the King of Ch'i who was the patron of the *Chi-hsia* Gate Academy. His doctrine that man's nature was essentially bad was in sharp contrast to that of Meng-tzu. For this reason and also because he rejected the old belief in Heaven—seeing Heaven as a principle rather than as a god—Hsün-tzu was regarded as being unorthodox after the Han era. Yet, due to the emphasis he placed on the normative and educational importance of the *Li* for the improvement of man's character, his teachings exerted influence on the development of the school system in the State Confucianism of the Han era. One of his treatises was incorporated in the *Li Chi*, and his rationalism influenced such eminent Chinese historians as Sse-ma Ch'ien and Pan Ku as well as the Confucian philosophers Yang Hsiung and Wang Ch'ung, and others who initiated Confucian agnosticism. The aim of studies was not only to produce a wise man or a teacher but also to educate a virtuous sovereign or an official trained in the *Li* to assist the sovereign.

The most famous of Hsün-tzu's disciples, however, completely abandoned the Confucian ideals. Han Fei-tzu (died 233 B.C.), the philosopher, and Li Szu (died 208 B.C.), the statesman, advocated a kind of Chinese Macchiavellism which in the Han era was given the name of *Fa Chia*, "Legalist school". This *Fa Chia*, which was never really a school in the sense of Confucianism or Mohism (the school of

Mo Ti), and which associated itself in a peculiar way with Taoism, came to be the archenemy of Confucianism during the Ch'in dynasty the first emperor of which, Shih Huang Ti, forced the unification of China into one great empire for the first time. The sovereign was omnipotent while the ministers were mere assistants of minor importance. The traditional morals no longer served as the standard by which everything was judged; now efficiency alone was important. The laws of the State were to be so draconic that nobody would dare to revolt and the Emperor and his state bureaucracy could exercise the Taoist *Wu Wei* (non-action).

The classical books, especially the *Shu Ching* and the *Shih Ching*, were demonstratively burned in order to silence the ideas dating from an ideal antiquity. This "Burning of the Books" (213 B.C.) was exaggerated to such an extent by the Confucians of later times that Master K'ung, who was alleged to have edited the classical books, was adorned with the gloriole of a martyr centuries after his peaceful death.

Yet the continuity of Confucian studies was preserved thanks especially to the *Po Shih*, an assembly of scholars which was given permission by the emperor to continue its work. Out of political prudence he again and again tried to come to an arrangement with the Confucian paragons many of whom survived the "persecution" and eventually slipped into the service of the victorious Han dynasty (207 B.C.-220 A.D.).

In 191 B.C. the Han emperor lifted the ban on the books that had been burned by the Ch'in in 213 B.C., and it apparently proved possible to reconstruct the greater part of their contents. Confucianism increasingly enjoyed the favour of the Han emperors, and by that time the Confucians had learned from the legalists how to govern a centralized empire by means of bureaucracy and yet to place the *Li* above the laws necessary.

It must be mentioned that Han State Confucianism owes the incorporation of the Five Planet Gods (*Wu Ti* = Five Emperors), including the Confucian model emperors Yao and Shun and even Shang-ti, the Supreme God, to the Ch'in era.

However, it was not until the reign of Emperor Han Wu-ti (141-87 B.C.) that Confucianism really became established in state affairs. This mainly came about thanks to the influence of the Confucian Tung Chung-shu who laid the foundations for the setting up of a civil service composed of scholars (literati). Thorough knowledge of the Five Classical Books (*Wu Ching*) opened the way to the civil service. This was completely in accordance with the ideas of the philosopher

Hsün-tzu who demanded the meliorization of man's bad character by instruction in the *Li*. At the same time Confucius legends and the Confucius cult began to flourish to an extent which the Master himself would certainly have disapproved of. The cult, it is true, never attracted the people in general, but it was always connected with Confucian education and the schools from which the state recruited its civil servants. As early as in the Han era Confucianism became a "class religion of the literati", and by the reign of Han Wu-ti Confucian ethics had permeated the whole social life and they enjoyed the same esteem with the educated classes as Christianity did in the Occident. On account of its intimate connection with the state, Confucianism flourished when the state was strong but it also shared the times of crises which the state went through.

During the Liu Ch'ao era (3rd-6th century A.D.) Confucianism suffered periods of decline, Buddhism and Taoism being prevalent. The word *Chün Tzu*, "Confucian gentleman" even became an expression which at times "produced nothing but ribald laughter" (A.F. WRIGHT).

During the Sui era (518-618 A.D.) the school and examination system was developed still tentatively, but then in the T'ang era (618-907 A.D.) it attained its full development, and the Confucian-spirited *Han-Lin* Academy was founded. Censorship was revived, and brave Confucians showed manly pride in accordance with the principle that one has to be more obedient to the Confucian *Tao* than to all men including the sovereign.

Under the influence of Buddhism, beautiful sculptures were erected in the Confucian temples and not only the plain name tablets as before. Han Yü (767-824) not only condemned the emperor's acceptance of a relic of Buddha and the unproductiveness of Buddhist and Taoist monastic life, but he also opposed idolatry in his own Confucian camp.

Whereas most of the T'ang emperors only availed themselves of Confucianism in the interests of the state, being themselves personal devotees of Buddhism or Taoism, the majority of the emperors of the Sung dynasty (960-1279) were Confucian-minded. It must, however, be mentioned that the Chinese are very well able to be adherents of several religions at one and the same time and that what has been said above ought to be interpreted as a shift of emphasis rather than as a question of being exclusively Confucian or Buddhist or Taoist.

In the Han era Tung Chung-shu and others had already silenced the heretics of their time by incorporating the pseudo-sciences (as we would call them) in Confucianism, and now Neoconfucianism or, as it is often called, Sung philosophy, met a further need of the people. Neither in Chou nor in Han Confucianism are metaphysical or dialectic problems to be found; Confucius was in no way concerned with transcendental problems because he was of the opinion that they had already been solved in the sacred books. However, it was precisely this study of metaphysical problems that had been fascinating the educated Chinese already for a long time and that had made them feel particularly attracted to Buddhism. This shortcoming in Confucianism had to be compensated for, and this was by no means just an ideological and religious problem but a political one of the utmost importance: social power, revenue, and court prestige were at stake in the disputes between Confucians, Taoists, and Buddhists. In the struggle against alien Buddhism, the Neoconfucian movement was the last and the most sucessful reaction against the menace of foreign infiltration.

Chuism, as Sung Confucianism is sometimes called after its most eminent representative Chu Hsi (1130-1200), incorporated Buddhist and Taoist ideas into Confucianism by producing commentaries to the old texts in order to give them a metaphysical and philosophical foundation. The ethics were left untouched. If we compare Han Confucianism with Sung Confucianism, we may come to the same conclusion as J.K.Shyrock (which is not widely accepted), namely that the Sung people were closer to the old Confucianism as envisaged by the Master than the Han Confucians who introduced what today we call superstition.

The so-called *Ssu Shu* (Four Books; see below) came to be highly esteemed because, together with the *I Ching*, they were made the subjects of creative interpretations. The basis of the new philosophy was the *T'ai Chi*, the Great Ultimate, the Absolute, which, however, was not meant to supplant Heaven. It was merely intended, so to speak, to create scope for philosophical speculations. The same applies to the expression *Ko Wuh*, Investigation of Things, which was taken from the *Ta Hsüeh*, one of the *Ssu Shu*, and which became the issue over which two Neoconfucian schools diverged. Whereas Chu Hsi understood it to mean—as we, too, do—a kind of scientific examination of things, from which ethical principles could be derived, Lu Hsiang-shan (1139-1193) and later his descendant Wang Yang-ming (1472-1529) were of the opinion that the essence of the things could most clearly be cognized by introspection. Here, too, was room for speculation on the one hand and, on the other, also for meditation and vita contemplativa neither of which had had a place in Confucianism before.

The emphasis placed on phliosophy in Sung and particularly in Ming Confucianism reduced the Confucius cult to ancestor worship again. Earlier, under the influence of Buddhism, Confucius had almost been equated with a Boddhisattva, and there had even been attempts to confer upon him the name of *Ti* (emperor god). However, the Ministry of Rites had always rejected such suggestions.

The era of the Yüan (Mongol) dynasty (1260-1368) was an age of great religious tolerance. The Mongol rulers who soon recognized the state-supporting power of Confucianism began to build the great Confucius temple in Peking in 1273 which was not finished until 1306. Donations of land were made to the K'ung family in Ch'ü-fu and their descendants retained them until 1932/33 when the lands were disappropriated. As had often before happened in history, a new, flamboyant title was bestowed upon the Master. Deserving men of the past or the present were enthroned in the Confucian temples, for example the Han scholar Tung Chung-shu (1330).

During the Ming era (1368-1643) Chu Hsi's Sung Confucianism became fully orthodox. And since it was regarded as thoroughly Chinese it was at the same time regarded as an anti-doctrine against the all too tolerant, foreign Mongols. The philosopher Wang Yang-ming, who has been mentioned above, was not recognized to such a degree as his master Chu Hsi who has—not unjustifiably—been compared to St. Thomas Aquinus. With one of his postulates Wang Yang-ming may be regarded as a forerunner of Mao Tse-tung, in that he demands the unity of theory and practice. Otherwise, however, Chuism was victorious. Even in the examination system it had become absolutely rigid; the "eight-legged essay" decided whether or not the candidate had passed the examination, and the form was more important than the content. The reformation of the Sung era was continued. 1530 is a decisive year, because at that time people wanted to return to the principles and practices of the Chou era. The sculptures were again replaced by the ancestor tablets, and many a fine sculpture was probably smashed during this outbreak of iconoclasm.

During the reign of the three great emperors of the foreign Manchu dynasty (1644-1911) K'ang Hsi, Yung Cheng, and Ch'ien Lung (1622-1796) a form of Confucian programme was put into effect. Above all the educational system was revived, which in traditional China always gave, at the same time, new impetus to Confucianism because the subjects taught were taken from the sacred books. A holy edict expressly placed Confucianism before Taoism and Buddhism. By such measures many of the Confucian literati were won for the new regime; others, the loyal adherents of Ming, joined secret societies which for centuries worked underground and prepared the 1911/12 revolution. During the Ch'ing era the Confucian temples (*Wen Miao* = Temple of Literary Culture) were restored throughout the country and sumptuously furnished. However, the lively Confucian activity, which is reflected in the comprehensive reports in the local gazetteers of those years, declined toward the end of the 19th century.

Confucian "ecclesiastical history" the beginnings of which date back to the Sung era now also included criticism of historical texts and led more and more educated people to doubt the authenticity of the traditional texts and the sacred *Li.* Moreover, Western, effective imperialism awakened the critical, restless young generation to the utter powerlessness of the "Holy Confucian Empire of the Chinese Nation". In 1905 one essential feature of Confucian education, the examination system, had been abandoned. Yet, in 1907 ,when scepticism and uncertainty had already reached their climax, the dying dynasty equated Confucius's cult to that of Heaven and Earth. Thus, in the very last hour the Magister Sinarum was equated with the supreme deities. Yet, this act, trusting, as it were, upon magic, could not save the decaying Empire.

In the sphere of state theory Sun Yat-sen superseded Master K'ung, but he lacked, of course, the religious background which had made Confucianism a state religion.

Before concluding the history of Confucianism I think it necessary to look briefly at the Confucian canon which was the determining influence on the Chinese and the East Asian world for centuries in the same way as the Bible and the ancient writers were the determining factors in the Occident. It is true that Buddhism and Taoism also had a canonical literature. But in contrast to Confucianism, this literature demanded special studies because non-experts could not decipher its secret language.

Time and again the Confucian texts which were currently valid were engraved in stone, and scholars came from afar to take rubbings of the authentic texts. Paper, of course, had long been invented. It seems that such steles were first erected in the year 175 A.D. and the last in 837 A.D. In the 3rd century steles bearing classical texts written in different styles of writing were even erected in order to make comparative studies between earlier and later editions possible. Later those steles became less important because with the invention of wood-block printing scholars could draw their knowledge from books.

THE FIVE CLASSICS (*Wu Ching*)

1. *Shu Ching*, Canon of Historical Documents. No doubt the oldest parts of the work date back to the time around 1000 B.C. Han time forgings have been detected. The book contains speeches and reports on the deeds of the emperors from Yao (allegedly 2nd half of the 3rd millenium B.C.) down to the early Chou era.

2. *Shih Ching*, Canon of Odes. A collection of approximately 300 odes of the catchment area of the Huang-ho, which gave the Confucians an opportunity for moral contemplation. Many a harmless love song was distorted.

3. *I Ching*, Canon of Changes. Most probably the oldest extant book of divination in the world, dating back to 1000 B.C. and before. It does not only belong to Confucianism but even more to Chinese Universism or Sinism.

4. *Ch'un Ch'iu*, Spring and Autumn Annals. It relates the history of the feudal state of Lu during the years 722-484 B.C. Together with three commentaries it presents the historical material by means of which the correctness of the doctrine can be verified. I consider it possible that Confucius himself worked on the text.

5. *Li Ching*, Canon of Ritual and Protocol. It contains three works from different periods: a) The *Chou Li*, which was probably compiled from old sources under Wang Mang (33 B.C.-23 A.D.); b) the *I Li*, which is certainly the oldest book of rites dating from the Chou era whereas c) the *Li Chi* was compiled as late as the Han era.

The following texts are grouped under the heading of *Ssu Shu*, Four Books, and their rôle in Confucianism may be compared to that of the New Testament in Christianity if we dare compare the Five Classics to the Old Testament.

1. *Lun Yü*, The Analects or Selected Sayings. Verbatim quotations of the Master's words.

2. *Chung Yung*, The Doctrine of the Mean. It was originally part of the *Li Chi*, from which Chu Hsi extracted it and added it to the *Ssu Shu*. It contains much "Taoist material".

3. *Ta Hsüeh*, The Great Learning, also extracted from the *Li Chi* by Chu Hsi. It deals with questions concerning the individual in society.

4. *Meng Tzu*, Mencius. It contains detailed supplements and additions to Confucian teaching and dates from the time of Mencius, i.e. between 390 and 305 B.C.

Apart from these standard works, the *Hsiao Ching*, Canon of Filiality, of the Han era also attained great importance.

If in later times (Ch'ing era) we hear of the "Thirteen Classics", these include works and commentaries which are all connected with the books mentioned above.

III. Confucian Conception of God and the Deities

Neither Confucius nor his successors had a conception of their own of the deities and spirits to offer. In Confucius' Analects the gods and spirits are only mentioned in a very respectful and cautious way. His religiosity was ancient and was rooted in the traditional ideas reflected in the Five Classics.

These ancient and most highly esteemed books refer to the God of Heaven (*T'ien*), or the Heavenly Lord (*T'ien Ti*), or the Supreme Ruler (*Shang Ti*). This supreme god is not a creative god in the Christian sense although as the supreme guardian he watches over the morals of mankind and the corresponding morals (laws) of Nature, and he distributes reward and punishment. *T'ien* originally signifies the atmospheric sky, and in this capacity *T'ien Ti* may manifest his indignation at man's ill-conduct by sending disastrous storms and bad omens.

The element *Ti* in the above-mentioned compounds originally meant the ancestor of the governing Shang-Yin dynasty, and *Shang Ti* was most probably understood to be the august ancestor of this dynasty, who was identified for religious, and doubtlessly also for political, reasons with the natural God of Heaven. It is these two identical concepts of ancestor worship and worship of nature which have given rise to the concept of *Shang Ti* which can be interpreted as meaning God the Father. This concept was preserved, mut. mut., through the centuries and has been the theoretical basis of the patriarchical-authoritarian system in Confucian China. There is hardly any doubt nowadays that the expression *T'ien* referred to the ancestors of the reigning dynasty assembled in Heaven from where, as a unit so to speak, they performed their task as guardians over the oecumene, i.e. the *T'ien Hsia*, the Under-the-Heaven, the Chinese world in general. Thus the expression "Son of Heaven" for the universal sovereign as the one who performed the sacrifices was originally meant to be taken literally.

Incidentally, a similar idea can be observed in the case of the feudal lords who identified the gods of nature—the God of the Soil and the God of the Grain (*Shê Chi*), i.e. deities of lesser importance than *Shang Ti*, with their own ancestors.

It is true that such ancient conceptions might have lead to the idea that a dynasty could not be deposed because it was descended from the supreme god in the same way as, for instance, the Tennô in Japan is regarded as the direct descendant of the Goddess of the Sun and can, therefore, never be dethroned. However, even during the Chou dynasty it had already become clear that such a conception of God and the relationship of the sovereign to this God was untenable. The facts, the weak dynasty and later—after the breakdown of the feudal state—the change of dynasties contradicted it.

The Chou dynasty had justified its victory over the "nefarious" Shang-Yin dynasty by pretending that Heaven—here again as an independent phenomenon without any ties to the dynasty—had abandoned the dynasty and that it had even done so at the advice of the dynasty's own ancestors who, just like the ancestors of all dynasties to come, played the rôle, as it were, of Heaven's counsellors. The idea of the divine nature of the sovereign was henceforth abandoned, even under despotic rulers, and it was replaced by the concept of *T'ien Ming*, the Mandate of Heaven, which made the sovereign Heaven's adopted son, an idea which was further elaborated on by Mencius. What Heaven had granted, it could also withdraw again. If a sovereign succeeded in putting down a rebellion, it meant that Heaven had retained him as its mandatory. If the rebel was victorious, the Mandate had been conferred upon him. Thus the power of the sovereign was restricted by the authority of the Confucian canon, and the rebels could—if they were victorious—appeal to the *Ko Ming*, i.e. the change of Mandate, and the *T'ien Ming*, i.e. the renewed conferment of the Mandate of Heaven, unless the principles of Confucian ethics and the cooperation of the Confucian bureaucracy were endangered. Such a conception of God tended to awaken and promote anti-authoritarian thinking which, however, never had any practical effects on the history of imperial China.

Heaven was coupled (*p'ei*) with the Goddess of the Earth, and the pair of them were made the symbolic parents of the emperor who henceforth served his own parents and ancestors by affording them merely the usual ancestor worship that everybody owes to his ancestors. It was his "ancestors", Heaven and Earth, before whom the emperor on ceremonial occasions kotowed nine times calling himself their *Ch'en*, i.e. subject. Heaven and Earth and the Gods of the Soil and the Grain (*Shê Chi*) together with the imperial ancestors and, after 1907, Confucius as well were all regarded as Gods of the First Rank. However, it was the Emperor who was sovereign over all deities—except Heaven and Earth. This meant that he was authorized to admit new gods into the state pantheon. He could appoint, promote, and depose gods, and was advised in making his decision by the Ministry of Rites. Thus, the number of gods varied greatly throughout the ages. In general, there was a strong increase in their number up to the Ch'ing dynasty, although some cults perished. Alien elements—Buddhist and Taoist—infiltrated into the official Confucian cult or came under Confucian control.

The Gods of the Second Rank include: Sun, moon, emperors and kings of the previous dynasties, the patron of agriculture, the patroness of sericulture, the spirits of Heaven and Earth, the Year Star (Jupiter).

The Gods of the Third Rank include the patron saints of medicine, the God of War *Kuan Ti*, the God of Literature *Wen Ch'ang*, the North Star, the East Mountain *T'ai Shan*, the patron saints of the city of Peking (following a Ch'ing decree of the 17th century) etc.

All the Gods of the First and Second Ranks had already been worshipped during the Shang era—with the exception of Confucius himself, of course. Most of the Gods of the Third Rank date from the Han era.

Also gods that distinctively belonged to the Buddho-Taoist folk religion and were worshipped in local cults came under the jurisdiction of the Emperor i.e. the Ministry of Rites (*Li Pu*). A report was given to the emperor who bestowed on them rank and title according to how effective they were and what miracles they had performed, and their communities were allocated certain sums of money for the building and maintenance of temples. In this way the local cults participated in the official Confucian religion. The beginnings of this practice of controlling the religions indirectly can be observed as early as in the Han era, and it was practiced until the overthrow of imperial power in 1911. In doing this the state secured for itself all supernatural assistance which at the same time it held under permanent control.

One particular god that granted power and consolation to the Confucian mandarins in their offices in the district towns all over the country was *Ch'eng Huang*, the Protector of Walls and Moats, who deserves special mention. Whenever a new mandarin was appointed to a district, or in times of tension and distress, he would spend days and nights in the temple of the respective *Ch'eng Huang* in order to obtain consolation, strength, and good advice from his spiritual counterpart, *Ch'eng Huang*, the "spiritual magistrate". In many a difficult criminal case the mandarin would pray for an enlightening dream in the temple of the local god. No doubt, certain features of the folk religion play an important part here. On behalf of the Emperor the mandarin had to worship the State gods as well as the sanctioned local deities (*Hou T'u*) in the local temple, and last but not least the patron saint of his own class of the literati, Master K'ung himself.

It is true that after 1911, when the State had ceased to exert its control over all religions, Confucius was incorporated—as had occasionally been the case previously—in the myriad gods of the folk religion—a fact at which nobody could have been more annoyed than Master K'ung himself.

IV. Worship

The noblest sacrifice in imperial China was perfomed by the emperor himself in the most ceremonial way and according to ancient rites and with the assistance of a great number of officials who were experts in matters of cult. The ceremony was held in the place of sacrifice of Heaven in the south-east corner of the imperial capital during the night of the winter solstice which is the geomantic counterpart of that direction of the compass, because it is there and then that the heavenly *Yang* principle begins its new development.

The preparations, for the sacrificial ceremony took many days; they mainly consisted in carrying out an official inspection of the animals to be sacrificed, in performing ritual purifications in accordance with exact prescriptions, and in observing a fixed period of fasting and abstinence. It was not until all this had been performed that the emperor was allowed to step on the round Terrace of Heaven symbolizing Heaven to make a sacrifice of the offerings which consisted of beef broth, meat, cooked cereals, fish, fruits, cakes, pickled vegetables, etc. It is very likely that these offerings remained the same throughout the centuries.

Without doubt the oldest and noblest offerings, which may date back to the 2nd millennium B.C., are a round jade disk (*P'i*) with a round hole in the middle, which was meant to symbolize Heaven, and a bullock. The twelve pieces of blue silk with the symbols of the zodiac, which corresponded to the imperial robe of the emperor, are of more recent origin. For the duration of the ceremony the ancestor tablets of the dynasty were placed to the right and to the left of the tablet in which the God of Heaven took his place, so that the ancestors, too, might participate in the ceremonial and salutary sacrifice which was now performed in nine solemn acts. It began with the placing of the *P'i* and the pieces of silk on the altar and ended with the dismissal of the imperial ancestors and the burning of the offerings. The purpose of the sacrifice is expressed in the emperor's prayer in which he says, "Thy humble subject (*Ch'en*) has received from thee the order to govern and nourish the ten thousand countries and to strive for a government willing and able to secure peace. ... With his forehead on the ground he implores thee to look down upon us in thy shining virtue so that the seasons may receive rain, light, and heat in appropriate quantities and the hundred fruits of the fields may thereby develop perfectly. Oh, may thou and the souls of the ancestors standing beside thee accept our offerings. ..."

In the northern surburban area of the capital is situated the place of sacrifice for the imperial deity of the Earth. And because traditional ideas claim the earth to be square, the whole sacrificial area and the buildings erected on it are square. When—at the time of the summer solstice—*Yin* becomes active again, a similar sacrifice to that for the more important God of Heaven is performed there for the God of Earth and the deities of many important regional districts. In rural districts these important sacrificial functions were the task of the mandarin who, on behalf of the emperor, as *Fu-Mu*, Father-and-Mother (of the people), had to perform the sacrifices for their districts.

With the collapse of the empire, the sacrifices to Heaven and Earth declined as well, since for better or worse they had been intimately tied up with the idea of the Son of Heaven and the conception of the oecumene. What survived were some local sacrifices to the local deities of the soil (*Hou T'u*) while the universally performed sacrifice to the imperial Deity of Earth (*Huang Ti Ch'i*) perished along with imperial power and the official worship of Heaven. The worship of certain historical personalities who had been elevated to gods of stars (e.g. *Wen Ch'ang*, the God of Literature) cannot be regarded as a modified continuation of the worship of Heaven. Moreover, these deifications which include also the God of War, who was at the same time the very popular God of Trade, *Kuan Ti*, are, strictly speaking, from an orthodox standpoint deities of secondary importance. They were subordinate to the two ancient mythical emperors Yao and Shun, the only two holy persons recognised, who embodied the Confucian idea of the ideal sovereign. According to Confucian thinking no emperor of any other dynasty had ever come up to these two who were already "established" in Confucius's *Lun Yü*.

Even Master K'ung's great example, the Duke of Chou, of whom the Master dreamt at times and who had proved his loyalty by ceding the throne to the young sovereign who had just come of age, although this was directly against traditional practice, was far more a prototype of the loyal and efficient minister (such as Confucius considered himself to be) than a holy person. The fact that all the above-mentioned personalities were, nevertheless, deified by the people in the course of history must be seen in the light of the tendency of the Chinese to apotheosize, a tendency which has continued—though to a lesser degree—up to our days.

It is, therefore, the more suprising that the official Confucius cult again and again succeeded in resisting the attempts made by the people to deify the Master under the influence of Buddhism and Taoist folk religion. In the Ch'ing era the actual performer of sacrifices in the Confucius cult (for Confucius as the patron saint of the literati, not as a god) was the emperor who could delegate this office to his officials, as in the case of the sacrifices to Heaven and Earth. The sacrifices were performed twice a year, namely on the *Ting* day of the second spring and autumn months (*Ting* is a character in the cycle of the Ten Heavenly Stems).

The offerings consist of silk, wine, soup, and—as the noblest offering—an ox. The introit already alludes to the pedagogical and moral influence of the Magister Sinarum when the congregation sings, "Great, indeed, is K'ung-tzu. Above all he possessed knowledge and wisdom. The third is he, together with Heaven and Earth, the Master of centuries. ..."

The old ceremonial dances in the temple of Confucius are also worth mentioning. One of them was performed with pheasant feathers, accompanied by flutes, and it was meant to symbolize the foundation of culture by peaceful actions. Students danced to the music of an orchestra intoning long-drawn semibreves. Together with K'ung-tzu, the whole Chinese culture and civilization was worshipped in his temple, the *Wen Miao*. Judging from all we know about the historical K'ung-tzu, he would by no means have agreed to such ceremonies in honour of his person. Viewed from the standpoint of his age he would have regarded it as some queer form of ancestor worship and would have dismissed it with the words, "To sacrifice to spirits which are not those of one's own dead is mere flattery." (*Lun Yü* I, 24,1). As a matter of fact, ancestor worship, which plays a central part in correct Confucian conduct, was mixed up with Confucius to such an extent that in Hongkong, for example, where the Confucius temple has degenarated into a place of prayer of the folk religions, ancestor sacrifices are still performed today.

The connection between nature worship and ancestor worship was also to play a rôle in the local Confucius cult in his home town of Ch'ü-fu. Confucius was, so to speak, identified with the local god; he was thus raised out of the sphere of mere ancestor worship which only applied to his family and at best to his nearest disciples. On his tours of inspection the emperor never failed to pay homage to the gods of the district, and both Han Kao-tzu, the founder of the Han dynasty, and even Ch'in Shih Huang-ti, the founder of the Ch'in dynasty, honoured Confucius in this capacity. As the Confucian civil service developed, the temple in Ch'ü-fu was furnished more and more splendidly. Master K'ung's descendants were knighted and were officially entrusted with the worship of their ancestor Confucius.

A Confucius cult embracing the whole empire first arose in 59 A.D. when Ming-ti decreed that sacrifices be performed in the Confucius shrines which had to be erected in all schools, and the cult spread along with the development of public education. And although, with the Taoist renaissance and the development of Buddhism in the Chinese Middle Ages, Confucianism became discredited or assimilated into the two other religions, it survived wherever the traditional teaching continued or was revived. Due to the influence of the two other religions, even independent temples were founded near the academies and schools in the capital and in the large cities of the country.

What lies at the bottom of ancestor worship, which had existed before Confucius and which he merely incorporated into his teachings, is actually the fear that the haunting spirits of the dead might take revenge and display ill will if they were not given the appropriate sacrifices. At the same time one hoped that blessings and benefits would emanate from the dead if they were satisfied. The spiritual (*Yang*) part of the deceased, who were believed to live in Heaven, took its seat during ceremonial sacrifices on the house altar in the soul tablets bearing the names of the deceased, whereas their bodily (*Yin*) part had to be taken to the graveyard and laid to rest there in the best possible geomantic position. Whereas blessings and benefits can be expected from the spiritual part (*Shen*), misfortune and distress may emanate from the dead body (*Kuei*). In my opinion such an interpretation of the *Yang-Yin* bipolarity, which originally had nothing to do with ethics nor with the fight of light against darkness, only sprang up when the attempt was made to make the conception of the soul plausible by means of the *Yang-Yin* doctrine. To avert evil and attract good was the significance of ancestor worship, and in late Chou time the gratitude of the living towards the dead became an additional feature. While the belief in the dependence of the deceased on sacrifices and the dependence of the living on the blessings of the dead has remained alive among the common people up to our days, enlightened Confucianism held more rational ideas.

The text *Hsün-tzu* (340-245 B.C.) says, for example, that the Confucian gentleman (*Chün Tzu*) considered ancestor worship to be a human affair whereas the common people were of the opinion that they served the spirits of their ancestors.

Mourning practices are considered very important in the family, because here all those assemble who depend on the blessings of the person who has passed away most recently. The eldest son and his wife play the most important part in all the ceremonies, and the old regulations of the *I Li* are still valid today. And although in the modern world of business the three-year period of mourning can no longer be observed so exactly, other customs such as wearing the white colour of mourning and other sartorial regulations dating back to Han time can be observed even today in Taiwan and in many Chinese communities in South East Asia. Even after the funeral it is the noblest duty of the clan to perform frequent continual sacrifices for the most recently deceased and all other ancestors. This has to be done at home, in the graveyard, and in the clan temple.

Owing to this permanent concern for the deceased, they remained alive in the memory of the living, and were not dead in the sense of being completely neglected. Rich people owned a clan temple where the family would meet at regular intervals in order to perform sacrifices. At the same time family ties were renewed, and the genealogical books were supplemented. Also important business projects of common interest were discussed there in the presence of the ancestors under whose eyes mutual trust was guaranteed. All important events in the family had to be reported to the ancestors in due form. Traditional Chinese society cannot be understood without taking ancestor worship into account, the performance of which was essentially the same in the case of the emperor for his human parents as in the case of lesser persons. In my opinion it is without doubt a religious service and not merely a respectful remembrance of the deceased as the Jesuits argued in the "rites controversy" with Rome when they tried to prevent ancestor worship being branded as heresy.

V. Confucian Ethics

The *Li* (= rites, including etiquette), which in Chinese antiquity had only applied to the feudal aristocracy, were democratized, so to speak, by Confucius who made them the vehicle for his spiritual aristocracy, at the same time giving lesser persons access to higher social ranks. As has been mentioned, the *Li* demanded the respect of the younger for the elder, of the subject for his superior, and regulated their conduct towards one another both in the profane sphere of life and during religious ceremonies. Whereas in ancient times the *Li* had been so intimately linked with the nobility by birth that they were considered to be inborn in a person and to radiate magic power, Confucianism regarded them as the sign of a personality trained in the secularized ethics of Confucianism and, therefore, as a sign of a person of "moral integrity", of a *Chün Tzu*.

The whole, complicated *Li* code which the Confucians took over was held together by *Hsiao*, a virtue that is usually translated as "filial piety". It was *Hsiao* that kept alive ancestor worship and mourning practices. In Confucianism, however, it does not only imply reverent behaviour, thought and action towards the dead; it also applies to the parents who are still alive. *Hsiao* is the very basis of civilization. It begins with serving one's parents and extends to the service of one's prince or superior. Seen in this light, the family is not only a home for the children. On the contrary, the children have been called to life because of their parents, their ancestors, and the deceased; it is their duty to render them services and reverence. Thus, *Hsiao* is the cardinal virtue of the good man and a guaranty that the machinery of state functions well. Recently an attempt has been made in a negative way to trace the conformism of Chinese society back to this long-practiced virtue of *Hsiao*.

On account of its long standing *Hsiao* became so important as a virtue that at times it pressed back the highest Confucian virtue *Jen*, which means being good on the largest possible scale, which implies moral perfection to the utmost degree. This was made much more possible because Confucius himself stated that he had never met any person who had had *Jen*, and he only attributed it to the mythical cultural heroes.

Jen first becomes more humane and more tangible again in the works of Mencius. We find it together with the virtue *I* which means justice and benevolence in the sense of the "suum cuique" within a hierarchical order in which the *Wu Lun*, the Five Relationships, i.e. between sovereign and subject, father and son, elder and younger brother, husband and wife, friend and friend, are regulated to the minutest detail. In this sense *I* can also be understood as "applied" *Jen*, as ethics applied to a specific situation.

Although most of the morals, which proved so stable through centuries, and also the ways of thinking corresponding to them can be traced back to the often simple regulations of a harmonious, well-functioning Chinese family, they were also effective on a broader social basis. And although, on the one hand, Confucian morals strengthen the family and even give rise to family egotism, they continually go beyond the bounds of the family and bring forth in Chinese civilization a genuine "we-consciousness".

Another important ethical principle is the concept of *Tao* in its most comprehensive sense. *Tao* is the only right way, the only good, moral method, of which Confucius himself says, "He who has listened to (my) *Tao* in the morning, may die in the evening witouth remorse." (Lun Yü IV, 8)

And the golden rule in Confucianism, *Shu* (= reciprocity), that goes beyond the family clan, must be seen as a positive feature. By striving for one's own perfection, one is to strive for the perfection of others. In the noble emotions of one's own heart one finds the principle according to which one has to behave in intercourse with other people. Seen in the light of the history of ideas, the transition from ritual and magical thinking to ethical thinking was effected in the Confucian ethics of early times.

The metaphysical basis of Confucian ethics is *Ch'eng*, which can best be translated by "harmony with nature". This preestablished harmony is, indeed, the Confucian faith or ideal which is projected into nature.

VI. Conception of Man

The above-mentioned family virtues, which transgress upon and embrace the state as well as the generally valid standards and ways of behaviour, are best embodied in the ideal figure of the Confucian man, the *Chün Tzu*—the best possible assistant of the sovereign. In ancient, pre-Confucian literature, this expression implies a member of the ruling upper class. The members of the subordinate, lower classes of the people are summed up by expressions like *Hsiao Jen*, small people, *Shu Min*, common people, etc. To the Confucian mind, however, the *Chün Tzu* is independent of his birth and social standing and is only obliged to obey the moral codex. The paradigm of a *Chün Tzu* is depicted in the 10th apocryphal book of the *Lun Yü*, but also in the genuine passages of the same work. The *Chün Tzu* is depicted as a person whose behaviour is in accordance with fixed regulations. He lacks all violence and arrogance; he refrains from all vulgar expressions and avoids speaking dialect. He is always subject to certain rules of the game, which shows that the ritual, outward behaviour was still definitely of predominant importance. The etiquette of ancient times survives; the underlying attitude, however, is now absolutely ethical and no longer magic-ritual. While the *Chün Tzu*, whose noble character is apostrophed in contrast to the selfish *Hsiao Jen*, is through and through a practical man the *Hsien Jen*, the prudent man, and the *T'ung Jen*, the complete educated man, are people who have acquired the necessary intellectual and spiritual equipment for practical life; they have, however, not had the same measure of practice as the *Chün Tzu*.

Higher than all these, however, was the *Sheng Jen*, the Holy Man, an ideal that was aspired to during the Sung era under the influence of Buddhism and Taoism, but which actually goes further than the moral activity of Confucianism. But whereas the Buddhist meditation sect *Ch'an* (nowadays better know in its Japanese form of Zen Buddhism) in particular contends that it is possible to become a Holy Man merely by meditation and enlightenment, without any studies, the Confucian Ch'eng Ming-tao (1032-1085) puts forward a different thesis. He says, "By means of exhaustive studies one can attain saintliness." The "aggiornamento" Confucians of those days allowed themselves to be affected by the Indian doctrine that everybody could become a Buddha.

The only Holy Man who was acknowledged beside the mythical emperors Yao and Shun was Master K'ung .To equal him, however, was only possible by intensive studies. It was claimed in those days that one ought not to spend too much time on studying "what was human" but "what was celestial" (scil. metaphysics). Such speculations which, according to the Confucian Wang Yang-ming of the Ming era, made sudden enlightenment and awakening to the status of a Holy Man possible also in Confucianism, only catered for a religious urge of the homines religiosi of that time but could not assert themselves in the long run against the "practical reason" of the *Chün Tzu.*

VII. The Present Situation of Confucianism

In order to understand the present state of Confucianism in Mainland China, Taiwan, Korea, and South East Asia, we ought to look at a chapter of the history of ideas of the 19th century.

When after the Opium War (1840-1842) it had become clear that traditional China would have to adopt certain innovations from the West, an experiment was made to save the old substance of State Confucianism. Confucians like Li Hung-chang (1823-1901) expounded the idea that it was quite safe to adopt Western science and technology in order to use them for the greater glory of the Confucian State. The so-called "self-strengthening movement" whose exponent was Chang Chih-tung (1836-1909) was of the opinion that the Chinese substance (*T'i*) could remain undamaged in the wrappings of a Western technical function (*Yung*). He derived his concept from Chu Hsi's Neoconfucianism; however, Chu Hsi had wanted the relationship between *T'i* = substance and *Yung* = function to be understood roughly in the same way as basis and superstructure. As was to be expected, the experiment failed, for *T'i* meant—as we have seen—principally Confucian education which, naturally, was soon seized upon by *Yung*, function (of the European science).

It soon became evident that the separation of Chinese substance from subsidiary European scientific functions could not be put into effect in the field of education. The material Western sciences and a leftish line of thought that had developed by the 20th century proved to be more and more useful and effective in the *Yung* field, the field of "subordinate functions", while at the same time the *T'i* field, the Chinese Confucian substance, shrank more and more. Owing to their effectiveness, modern science and technology frustrated the aggiornamento efforts of the traditionalists both before and after the 1911/12 revolution and the 4th May Movement.

About the turn of the century the young critical generation rejected decisively not only antiquated, "feudal" Confucianism but also Christianity and consequently all attempts by the missionaries to carry out a "propagatio fidei per scientias." The young iconoclasts did this all the more gladly since, in their eyes, Christianity was the unscientific, feudal, imperialistic Western counterpart to Confucianism in their own country, and so they concluded that Chinese history was not all that inferior to that of the West. With the fall of the last emperor, Chinese State Confucianism, the essence of which had been sacrifices to Heaven and Earth, together with the whole complicated ritual, collapsed after it had been undermined long before. What, however, survived until the great upheaval of 1949 and what is still alive in Taiwan, Korea, and South East Asia, is the most constant feature of Confucianism, namely Confucian ethics. Apart from that we still find throughout South East and East Asia (except on Mainland China) ancestor worship and family observances, especially in the country and among old people—facets which were at all times encouraged by Confucianism.

In modern times a kind of practical philosophy has been developed from the Confucian cardinal virtues and their exegesis, which finds its teachers and adherents among the intelligentsia of the countries mentioned. The *K'ung Meng Yüeh K'an* (Confucius-Mencius Journal) containing valuable treatises on theology and ecclesiastical history, thereby continuing an old Ch'ing tradition, still appears monthly in Taipei.

In Communist China Confucius has a bad reputation. People still remember very well that many of the war lords claimed to be brave Confucians and pretented to assert Confucian civilization. In practice, however, they proved to be nothing but despots. Even the fact that Sun Yat-sen, the "Father of the Republic", who is still highly esteemed in Communist China today, called Confucius and Mencius exponents of democracy, even the fact that he emphasized that Yao and Shun did not hold the Empire in hereditary possession, and that in his Five-Power Constitution he adopted the censorate as well as the examination system (although it now demanded different, more Western subjects)—all this did not bring the young critical generation back to Confucius. Instead, they turned to Mao Tse-tung who, according to his own words, has hated Confucius from the time he was eight.

When Liu Shao-ch'i wrote his book "*How to Be a Good Communist*" (Peking 1952), he could still afford to given verbatim quotations from Confucian texts in order to lend support to his own opinions by means of the argumentum historicum. Now that, since the Cultural Revolution, Maoism has definitely asserted itself against "Liu-ism", such references would be both abominable and dangerous. Nevertheless, the moral argumentation has remained the same throughout the millennia. Neither Confucianism nor Maoism asks what is objectively right or objectively wrong, but the expressions *shih* and *fei*, right and wrong, imply a judgement as to what is good or bad; thus they distribute praise or blame now as at all times since the days of Confucius in accordance with the practice of Confucian historians. The signs, it is true, have changed. Now one listens to Mao and blames Confucius for having been a supporter of feudalism which, on closer consideration, he personally never was. It was his school which developed into State Confucianism.

Therefore, in Mainland China Confucius and his cult have virtually disappeared. Before the Cultural Revolution some Sinologists were inclined to see a general revaluation of Confucianism in the sumptuous restauration of the Confucius temple in Peking in the late 1950ies. This temple had been of utmost importance for State Confucianism from the Sung era up till the Ch'ing era. However, this was a fallacy. In those years people were of the opinion that Confucianism had degenerated to mere museal significance, just as the deities of Greece and Ancient Rome can be viewed in the Vatican Museum. However, the Cultural Revolution showed that these works of art dating back to feudal and capitalistic times—by means of osmotic pressure, so to speak—could still affect the minds of the Chinese and that, therefore, it had to be made a special concern of the Cultural Revolution to destroy or isolate monuments of historical and artistic value so that their obnoxious radiation could not reach the people who are supposed to become new, Maoist men.

For the same reason one is very much intent on fighting all festive days and the omens that may be connected with them – facets which conform with the customs of Imperial China and which still hold their ground here and there. As late as 1953, the Communist government of the Mainland was very much concerned lest subversive effects might emerge from the "superstition of the people" because at that time a solar eclipse happened to coincide with the first day of the Lunar New Year, a fact which might, according to tradition, have been interpreted as an omen for impending disaster and bad times, a sign of the disapproval of the God of Heaven whom Confucius and Mencius also feared over two thousand years ago.

In the non-Communist countries of South East and East Asia, Confucius is highly esteemed in Chinese communities. He has even found access to the temples of the Chinese syncretistic folk religion which is mainly influenced by Buddhism, and there he is worshipped as "Boddhisattva" and protector of ancestor worship as, for instance, in the *Cheng Hoon Teng* Temple in Malacca and in the *Lung Shan* Temple in Taipei.

The puritan, official Confucianism still survives, above all in National China on the Island of Taiwan. There, especially in the Confucius Temples of Taipei and Tainan, the birthday ceremonies of the Master are celebrated every year in the autumn by the local prominent people in the old manner, but without bloody animal sacrifices. Students of certain schools, in Taipei the students of the China Academy, have the honorary obligation to perform the ancient dances. The common people, however, do not participate in these ceremonies—as of old.

In the Confucius temples we do not meet people burning incense or wrapped in prayer as in all other temples. We will meet them before the Confucius statues in the temples of the folk religion, and most of the worshippers will be students praying for successful examinations.

A certain exception is the Confucian school in Seoul (Korea), the Sung Kjun Kwan Academy, where a kind of State Confucianism is still being taught. Like the Chinese Emperor of ancient times, the President of the State of South Korea is regarded as the supreme sacrificer in the Confucius temple there. This academy, which is intended to produce, above all, loyal civil servants, cultivates in its own small circle the idea of State Confucianism, which has perished everywhere else in East Asia.

One person who has a special position and plays a peculiar rôle in the Confucianism of our days which is so difficult to define precisely is the Duke K'ung, Teh-ch'eng. Since 1233, the head of the K'ung family has held the title of Duke K'ung. Since the abolition of the titles of nobility in the Republic, he is the only person who is allowed to continue to call himself "Duke". As Number 77 in the line of descent from Confucius, he is esteemed everywhere in East Asia as a brilliant interpreter of Confucian philosophy which he himself thinks is, after all, a religion.

VIII. Short History of the Study of Confucianism

The picture of a monolithic China, which is still predominant in many circles and which many China experts like to draw of Imperial China as well as of the China of Mao Tse-tung, can be traced back above all to the reports of the Jesuit missionaries who depicted the uniformity of State Confucianism in the most beautiful colours – reports which went so well with the trend toward enlightenment of those days.

The American Sinologist H.G. Creel devotes a whole chapter of his book "*Confucius and the Chinese Way*"(1949) to the contribution which Confucianism made to the formation of Western democracy, the foundations of which were laid during the age of Enlightenment, i.e. at the time when the first Jesuit reports reached Europe.

The Jesuits, whose reports gave rise to a Sinophily in the Western world which has hardly ever been paralleled again, had only the Chinese Empire in mind. Matteo Ricci (1552-1610) was the first Jesuit trained in orthodox Confucian studies to convey comparatively reliable reports on China to the West. Books written by Athanasius Kircher (1667) and Pater Louis Comte (1696) followed; and a work written by Pater du Halde, "*Description géographique, historique, chronologique, politique et physique de l'empire de la Chine et de la Tartarie chinoise*" (1735), is still being used today. Furthermore, du Halde edited the "*Lettres édifiantes et curieuses écrites des missions étrangères par quelques missionaires de la Compagnie de Jésus*" which had a great impact on their times.

Especially in progressive France these reports were received with eager interest, and Confucius's "practical philosophy" was highly praised. The patres took hardly any notice of Taoism at that time and regarded Buddhism, in a way, as a heterodox variety of Catholic Christianity—a heterodoxy which, they believed, was due to the instigation of the devil.

Eminent thinkers like Pierre Bayle (1647-1706), Malebranche (1638-1715), Fénélon (1651-1715), Montesquieu (1689-1755), Voltaire (1694-1778) and others drew attention to Confucius's China, and Voltaire regarded Confucianism as an ideal philosophy of reason.

There seems to be little doubt that Francois Quesnay (1694-1774), who first set forth the political aspects of physiocracy, was strongly influenced by Chinese ideas. The physiocrats set great store on landed property, agriculture, and natural religion. Quesnay believed an "enlightened despotism" to be the ideal form of government, and he traced this idea back to the "despotic", but not "arbitrary and tyrannical" power of the Chinese Emperor.

The influence of Confucian thinking which was by no means mutilated by the reports to such an extent as was sometimes claimed, can also be felt in LEIBNITZ's work "*Novissima Sinica historiam nostri temporis illustratura*" (1697). And when, in 1721, his pupil CHRISTIAN WOLFF placed Confucian morals on the same level as Christian morals in his address to the University of Halle on the subject of "De Sinarum philosophica practica", he was relegated from the university.

Towards the end of the 18th century and during the 19th, general interest in Confucianism declined, although one more great work on Chinese history reflecting Confucian thoughts was presented, namely the "*Histoire Générale de la Chine*" (1777-1785) written by J.A.M. DE MORIAC DE MAILLA. It is a political-moralistic book which presents all events in terms of formulae and valuations derived from Neoconfucianism in its most orthodox form. In the light of this work where nothing of a lively, historical development is to be felt, G.F. HEGEL stated in his "*Philosophie der Weltgeschichte*": "We have before us the oldest state and yet it seems to have no past, a state which seems to exist today just as in ancient times". And LEOPOLD VON RANKE counts the Chinese among the nations in a state of "eternal standstill". Not unjustifiably they were all referring to the façade of the Confucian Empire behind which, however, a very lively development was taking place which makes these statements appear wrong.

In the second half of the 19th century it was mainly missionaries, consulate and embassy officials, and holders of other high-ranking positions who gave us reports on China and Confucianism. Two pioneering works must be mentioned here: "*The Middle Kingdom*" (2 vols., 1948) by WELLS WILLIAMS and "*The Chinese Classics*" (8 vols., 1861-1885), a translation of a great part of the Confucian canonical literature, by JAMES LEGGE.

In this context we must praise the outstanding achievement of MAX MÜLLER who, in 1879, edited the "*Sacred Books of the East*", which were less concerned with criticism or praise of Chinese wisdom than with religious science and history.

In those days Sinology mainly confined itself to the interpretation of texts, restricting itself principally to the Confucian classics. A new approach to Chinese religions, above all to Confucianism, was opened up by a non-Sinologist, MAX WEBER (1864-1920), whose works on economic ethics and world religions began to appear in 1915. He used the translations which had been done in accordance with the orthodox method, and with the sagacity of a genius, he was able to draw conclusions from them which have had strong, lasting effects on Chinese studies. In the course of this century scholars have succeeded more and more in detaching themselves from the rigid clichés of Chinese orthodoxy and in following and broadening the way MAX WEBER indicated.

Scholars like A.F.Wright (U.S.A.), John K. Fairbank (U.S.A.), and D. Twichett (England) see the history of Confucian thought as a superstructure resting on a sociological and economic basis whereas J.R. LEVENSON (U.S.A.) with his three-volume work on "*Confucian China and Its Modern Fate*" (1958-1965) again switches the emphasis to the history of Confucian thought which he treats from the beginning of the Manchu time until the extinction of Confucian remnants in Mao's empire.

TAOISM

I. Essence of Taoism

The words "*han san wei i*", "(China) comprising three (religions) has made (them) one", indicate how difficult, or sometimes impossible, it was even for the Chinese to draw a clear line of distinction between Confucianism, Taoism, and Buddhism, especially at the later stage of their development. Both Taoism and Buddhism with their doctrines of redemption penetrated into State Confucianism. Yet both of them have survived the revolutions and changes of the past few decades far better than Confucianism. Their lasting success is due to the fact that they complied to a greater degree with the religious needs of the people than did Confucianism, which merely regarded the individual as a member of the family and as a social animal in state and society.

In contrast to Buddhism which sees life as suffering and demands that, when he attains the ideal stage of ultimate reality, man ought to be "dead" to the things of this world, Taoism holds that life is valuable and ought to be enjoyed in the right way, and prolonged. The World and the individual's Ego are not illusions but are very agreeable realities. He who has understood the teaching of *Yang* and *Yin* and their interaction in the Five Elements and in the all-embracing (Taoist) *Tao*, is able to procure for himself a glorified body so that he may enjoy immortality or at least longevity. The gods themselves were at work in these forces of nature and were worshipped because of their effectiveness.

Since the Taoist religion never developed a supreme canonical authority, no uniform "pantheon" of gods was established. As in the Buddho-Taoist folk religion, with which folk Taoism merged more and more, deities of ancient mythology lived at all times beside historical and legendary Taoist masters or figures of fairy tales who had been raised to the status of gods; gods of stars were worshipped beside philosophers, gods of mountains and weather gods beside war heroes. The influence of Confucian bureaucracy upon this assembly of gods is unmistakably reflected in the strict hierarchical order which was introduced during the Han era. Time and again the emperor himself would intervene and "promote" or "degrade" one or other of the Taoist gods, depending on whether or not they had proved useful to the state.

The differences between the Taoist religion (*Tao Chiao*) and the Taoist philosophy (*Tao Chia*) of Lao-tzu, Chuang-tzu, and Lieh-tzu were bridged by the mythical ideas which the two had in common as well as by magical and practical exercises or techniques in the psychical and physical spheres. These practices included meditation, dietetics, gymnastics as well as certain sexual techniques all of which are intended to fortify and dam up man's vitality so that it cannot escape.

Although the Taoist moral doctrine took over from the time of the Fathers of Taoism (Lao-tzu, Chang-tzu, Lieh-tzu) a number of concepts, for example the *Wu Wei*, "non-action" in the sense of not incurring guilt, of preserving one's integrity, the individualistic adepts and immortality practitioners neglected the question of morals. Influenced by Buddhism and Confucianism, however, folk Taoism developed morals in order to make monastic life in the monasteries possible which had grown up in the country under the influence of Buddhism.

II. Historical Development

In the years between 350 B.C. and 250 B.C. the names of Lao-tzu, Chuang-tzu, and Lieh-tzu were connected with texts which even today are still the basis of so-called "philosophical Taoism". These early texts express ideas which had presumably been formulated in certain schools in eastern China. The texts contain what we would today call philosophical and psychological aphorisms and words of practical wisdom. In addition to this they also give information about the fact that a "hygiene school" existed at that time, which had formulated a set of instructions on how to attain longevity. Respiratory techniques and other Yoga-like practices are recommended in order to preserve or recover youthful vigour and, if not do away with death completely, to defer it as long as possible.

In those years, early Taoism also followed the theories of Tsou Yen (350-270 B.C.) who, together with his adherents, is said to have initiated the search for the elixir of life and allegedly developed a special form of alchemy based upon speculations on the elements. In the eastern provinces bird myths were prevalent which gave rise to the legend of the immortals (*Hsien*), who are often pictured with wings, and to the myth of the paradises in the sea. In pre-Christian China, expeditions were equipped to set out for these places to search for the mushroom that prevents death.

The mythical patron of the Taoist school was the Yellow Emperor, *Huang Ti*, the ideal type of emperor in the kingdom of Utopia at the beginnings of time, a master of medicine and alchemy, of the art of war, and of sexual practices. Toward the end of the Han era he was superseded by Lao-tzu who was also given the title of a master of medicine and alchemy. In the Han era the *Tao Teh Ching*, a book which has been translated so many times and often in such a fanciful way, was known as "The Sayings of Huang Ti and Lao-tzu", and these teachings were called the Huang-Lao doctrine.

As we have seen, it was not at all easy to present a biography of Confucius of but fair reliability; however, in the case of Lao-tzu it seems to be an absolutely hopeless task. According to the *Shih Chi*, "Memoirs of the Historian", he was court archivist to the Chou kings; he received Confucius in Lo-yang and went to the West when the dynasty fell. The *Shih Chi* also says that before leaving the country he handed the *Tao Teh Ching* to the mythical pass commander Kuan Ling Yin Hsi upon the latter's urgent request. All these reports were for the most part invented for the benefit of the Taoists. Likewise, his surname and given name Li Erh or his surname and public name Li Tan are not identical with the author of the *Tao Teh Ching*. In earlier texts we merely find allusions to a mythical Lao-tzu (Master Lao) or Lao Tan. It seems that the entry in the *Shih Chi* was brougth about by a certain family Li in Shantung around 100 B.C. who claimed to be descendants of Lao-tzu. However, even the historiographer expresses certain doubts about these statements. When this somewhat unreliable biography goes on to say that, according to Lao-tzu's teaching, man ought to lead an anonymous and obscure life, this is possibly a reference to the group of people to which Lao-tzu and his circle may well have belonged, for there had always been people in China who had renounced the world. Among them we may also include Lao Lai-tzu who in the text *Chuang-tzu* reprimands Confucius because of his false morals, and also that "madman from Ch'u" who attacks the moral philosophy of Confucius (*Lun Yü* XVIII, 5). Lao-tzu is certainly to be numbered among those people who preferred the "simple life" to political and public life and who were fishermen at lakes or rivers or who lived in distant mountain regions and were, according to the general belief of the people, invulnerable because of their saintliness. As true Taoists they lived in solitude and were in no way embittered or frustrated, but they led this life out of conviction. Lao-tzu and Chuang-tzu, whom we present not as historical personalities but as protagonists of a certain group of early Taoists, differed from hermits in that they founded schools where their teaching was at first transmitted orally and was written down later. Judging from its style and contents, the text *Lao Tzu*, which did not receive the title of *Tao Teh Ching* until the Later Han era (in order to upgrade it and incorporate it in the set of canonical books, "*Ching*"), cannot have been written by LAO TAN, who was a contemporary of Confucius, but it seems certain that it is identical with a text that appears toward the end of the Warring States period although some of the aphorisms, which belonged to the oral tradition of the *Tao Chia* of that time, may date back at least to the 6th century B.C.

By the 3rd century B.C., the Huang-Lao teaching had become established in a close religious group. Strangely enough, their philosophy of the *Wu Wei*, non-action, and of the all-embracing *Tao* merged with the ideas of the legalists, the doctrine of the centralized police state of the Ch'in. Strict laws were to guarantee that the state functioned automatically so that the sovereign could practice *Wu Wei*.

Probably, however, it was the bent for alchemy and the desire for immortality which induced the first Ch'in emperor to receive theTaoists benevolently who practised such arts. At that time the Taoist ideas were enriched by Shamanistic traditions which infiltrated from the southern, non-Chinese country of Ch'u. For example, there were reports of "Wanderings through Heaven", which possibly were undertaken under the influence of narcotic mushrooms and which were construed as an ecstatic union with *Tao* and with the primordeal chaos. This tradition was especially cultivated at the court of Huai Nan, who was the grandson of the founder of the Han dynasty (died 122 B.C.), and it was written down in the book *Huai Nan Tzu*.

During the 400 years of the Han era, when public life was controlled by the Confucian state doctrine which had some legalist features, Taoism retreated into the sphere of private life, not only among the people but also with the emperor, empress, princes, and officials of the court. Lao-tzu was already deified at that time, and an inscription of the year 165 A.D. describes him as "an emanation of primordeal chaos" and "co-eternal with the Three Luminaries (Sun, Moon, and Stars)". At the same time Emperor Huan had altars erected to Lao-tzu and to Buddha who was at that time seen to be Taoist. A little later, when rivalries broke out between Taoism and Buddhism, the book "Lao-tzu's Conversion of the Barbarians" (*Lao-tzu Hua Hu Ching*) was written. Alluding to Lao-tzu's legendary journey to the West, the

Chinese Lao-tzu was identified with the Indian Buddha in order to steal the show from the Buddhists.

Taoism also spread among the people, and its Messianic and utopian ideas incited the rebellions which brought about the fall of the Han dynasty. At the time of Emperor Huan (147-67 B.C.), Chang Tao Ling was active as a teacher and missionary in the province of Sse-ch'uan. Since his converts' tribute to him was five bushels of rice his sect was called the "Five Bushel Sect" or also "Heavenly Master Sect", the latter name being an allusion to the Pope-like position of Chang Tao Ling's successors. It became the nucleus and starting point of the Taoist folk church. In 215 A.D. it was forced to give up its political autonomy but continued to exist under the episcopal dynasty of the Chang family who had their seat near the Dragon and Tiger Mountains (Lung Hu Shan) (Kiangsi) until they were expelled from the mainland by the Communists.

In 184 A.D. the Taoist sect of the Yellow Turbans rose in rebellion in central and eastern China. They longed for the utopia described in the *T'ai P'ing Ching* (Classical Text of Great Peace and Justice). However, they could not stand their ground for long against the armies of the central government. The leaders of both the Yellow Turbans and the Heavenly Master Sects were healers. They distributed talismans, and in their opinion illness was the toll of sin; therefore, confession and penitence were necessary if one wanted to be cured. Priest-magicians were placed at the head of small communities which were at the same time military units. These communities with collective ceremonies also attached value to the Confucian virtues, above all to *Hsiao*, filial piety. These virtues were construed as being magical powers and contributed towards the unity of the community.

The lively interchange of ideas which the Taoist religion was carrying on, more or less voluntarily, with Buddhism as well as with Confucianism is reflected in scholars like Ho Yen (190-225 A.D.) or Wang Pi (226-249) who wrote commentaries on the Confucian as well as on the Taoist classics. Following Buddhist examples, Taoist monasteries were established, and the communal life of the monks was governed by the maxims of Confucianism.

In the period from the fourth century A.D. until the seventh, while Sinicized foreign dynasties governed in the North of the country and Chinese dynasties in the South, Taoism continued to exist on different levels. The *Hsüan Hsüeh* (Dark Learning) philosophy concerned itself with the study of the exegesis of so-called philosophical Taoism (Lao-tzu, Chuang-tzu, Lieh-tzu) whereas other intellectuals and poets devoted themselves to practices aimed at attaining longevity and studied the text *Pao P'u Tzu* by Ko Hung. They despised Chuang-tzu for being far too speculative.

In folk Taoism the *Mao Shan* Sect near present-day Nanking came into vogue. At that time the *Shan Ch'ing Ching* (Book of the Heaven of Superior Purity) largely replaced the *T'ai P'ing Ching*. Now the will and instructions of the immortals and of the gods are revealed through the automatic writing of a medium .The *Hung Wan Tzu Hui* (Red Swastika Society), a sect which is wide-spread in East Asia and which with respect to its religious activity is also called *Tao Yüan*, seems to preserve this tradition in Taiwan, Hongkong, and Japan. The texts thus revealed are liturgical poems. The *Mao Shan* Sect wants to concentrate, in the corpus of the adept, the good, helpful spirits who live in Heaven, on holy mountains and in the body of the adept at the same time. An interesting phenomenon is the rôle of the female immortals in this sect, who are able to bring about this desired union in themselves and in others. It is not surprising, therefore, that a woman, Lady Wei, was the first leader of this sect. At that time the remarkable text *Ling Pao Tu Jen Ching* (The Marvellous Talisman Book of the Salvation of Men) was en vogue, in which Taoist deities are depicted according to the model of Buddhas and Boddhisattvas.

When in the 7th century the T'ang dynasty which had created a new Imperium Sinicum traced back the ancestral line of the imperial family to Lao-tzu, just because they happened to bear the family name of Li, Taoism temporarily enjoyed special importance. In 667 A.D. Emperor Kao Tsung bestowed the high-sounding name of "*Tai Shang Hsüan Yüan Huang Ti*", "Very Noble Celestial and Primordeal Emperor" on Lao-tzu. The books of the Taoist Fathers (Lao-tzu, Chuang-tzu, Lieh-tzu) were temporarily included in the list of state examination texts, and it became the fashion for "surplus" princesses to retire to Taoist nunneries.

During the Sung era, the emperors Chen Tsung (988-1022) and Hui Tsung (1101-1126), the great painter, furthered Taoism in a special way. At that time the *Cheng I* Sect (Great Unity Sect) flourished, which was a continuation of the Folk Church of the Heavenly Master Chang (*Chang T'ien shih*). The Heavenly Masters were enfeoffed with the whole area around the Dragon and Tiger Mountains.

The other great Taoist sect which, like the *Cheng I* Sect, has continued to exist up to this very day is the *Ch'üan Chen* Sect (Perfect

Realization Sect) which is also called the Internal Alchemy Sect. It has many things in common with *Ch'an* (=Zen) Buddhism and, in contrast to the *Cheng I* Sect, demands of its monks the strict observance of celibacy. Meditation and charitable works have priority over great collective religious services. The famous White Clouds Monastery, which even today houses Taoist monks, was a centre of this sect.

The Taoist canon (*Tao Tsang*) was also compiled during this era, and it was first printed in 1019.

The greatest political importance ever attained by a Taoist was conferred on the monk Ch'ang Ch'un who, in 1227, was ordered by the Mongol ruler Chingiz Khan "to control all priests and persons of religion in his empire". At that time only the northern parts of China belonged to the Mongol empire which did not annex the whole of China until 1278. Since both Ch'ang and Chingiz died in 1227, i.e. in the very same year, Chang only held this exceptional, powerful position for a very short time.

During the reign of Khubilai Khan (1214-1294), the old rivalry between Buddhists and Taoists, who both endeavoured to win the sovereign's favour, flared up again, and the fore-mentioned book which claimed that Lao-tzu as a Buddha had converted the Indian barbarians, played a special rôle in that controversy. The Taoists were defeated in the disputes of 1255, 1256, and 1258. And when, in impotent rage, they put fire to their own temples in order to be able to accuse the Buddhists, it was decreed in 1281 that the Taoist canon should be burnt. Only the *Tao Teh Ching* was spared. As a result, only 1120 volumes of the *Tao Tsang* survived in the Ming edition whereas the Sung edition had comprised 4565 volumes. With this burning of the books the old feud between Taoism and Buddhism came to an end. Since the end of the 13th century approximately, the Taoist religion has not played an eminent, independent rôle. While Taoist philosophy underwent a certain renaissance in Neoconfucianism and *Ch'an* (=Zen) Buddhism and was also developed in specific directions, the Tao religion gradually degenerated. The Taoist gods merged into the syncretistic folk religion. There were but few centres, e.g. in the Dragon Tiger Mountains and in the monasteries of the Lao Shan, where a folk religion was observed in which not Buddhism, but Taoism was preponderant. Generally speaking, this has remained the case right up into the 20th century.

The *Tao Tsang*

All the texts of Taoism, but also many other texts which actually belong to the legalists, the Mohists, even the Manichees, and Nestorian Christians in China, are to be found in the present-day edition of the *Tao Tsang* which dates from 1445 and 1596. Manichees as well as Christians concealed their syncretistic texts in the *Tao Tsang* after the tolerant Mongol dynasty had been superseded by the Ming dynasty.

450 out of the total number of 1120 volumes are liturgical texts which, partly, have also been handed down outside the *Tao Tsang*. The name *Tao Tsang*, Taoist Canon, was inspired by the example of the *San Tsang*, Buddhist Tripitaka, and today it comprises 1464 titles. The whole corpus of texts is divided into three *Tung*. The Chinese character for *Tung* actually means "cave", as well as "to communicate" and "to see through the mysteries". Since people believed that many texts were hidden in mountain caves, the word *Tung* conjures up "mysterious caves with unknown treasures of books" and "sacred powers which are revealed in these books".

III. Conception of the Deities

Although the Taoist pantheon has displayed a strict hierarchical order since the time of the Han era, this order has continually changed and varies from sect to sect. What they all have in common is their bureaucratic structure, for the Taoist gods do not rule the world, but are rather its administrators. The course of the world ougth best to be left to itself, i.e. to the spontaneity with which the Great *Tao* (the Way) gives expression (*Teh*) to itself, the spontaneity which thrives best in the undisturbed interaction of *Yin* and *Yang*, the succession of the seasons and the circulation of the Five Elements.

It is impossible to offer within the scope of this treatise a detailed discussion of the Taoist concept of *Tao* which belongs more to the field of philosophy than to that of the history of religion. In order to give a rough outline of this comprehensive concept of *Tao* which, in itself, is but an auxiliary term for something that cannot be expressed, let me explain the two aspects of *Tao* by drawing on the concepts of "natura naturans" and "natura naturata" as they are understood by Master Ekkehart who speaks of "Gottes ungenatûrte natûre" and "genatûrte natûre", in the sense of "*Tao* absconditus" and "*Tao* revelatus".

During the Han era, it was Lao-tzu and *Huang Ti* (Yellow Emperor) who presided over the pantheon. While *Huang Ti* was a cosmic deity, Lao-tzu became, so to speak, an incarnation of *Tao*. His emergence out of the primordeal chaos was the prime cause of all creation, and he was given the title of *Tao Chün* (Lord Tao). Since he soon became merged with *Huang Ti*, he also got the title of *Huang Lao Chün*. According to the opinions of that time, "this *Huang Lao Chün* could also be perceived by means of meditation in the microcosm of the human body". Whereas such ideas continued to be cultivated in esoteric Taoism, in the 5th century the *San Ch'ing*, the Three Pure Ones, were made the highest trinity of gods. These gods are within the body of the individual, but at the same time as redeemer gods for all men, aloof in the distant solitude of Heaven. No doubt, Buddhist ideas of the Bodhisattva have already played a rôle in the conception of this triad.

The first and supreme deity is the *Yüan Shih T'ien Ts'un* (Heavenly Elder of the Primal Origin). He is a hypostasis of *Tao* and is able to read the very first revelation in "jade characters". When the ordered world emerged out of chaos, not only gods, men, and the rest of the visible world came into existence, but also the sacred books. And it is the task of the gods to hand down these books (*Ling Pao* = Sacred Jewels) through other, inferior gods to men. The second deity is *Ling Pao Chün*, Lord of the Sacred Jewels, also called *T'ai Shang Tao Chün*, Very Noble Lord Tao, who passes the highest wisdom to the lower gods. The third person of the *San Ch'ing*, finally, is Lao-tzu, who bears the high-sounding title of *T'ai Shang Lao Chün*, Very Noble Lord Lao. He reveals the teaching of *Tao* to those men who have already proved themselves and have been entered into the list of the immortals. The composition of the Great Three varies, but this composition is the most Taoist. The three deities mentioned are the patron saints of the three sections of the *Tao Tsang*, a fact which shows how closely literature and higher reality were also connected in Taoism, which is also expressed in the text and the symbols of the *I Ching*, a text which belongs neither exclusively to Confucianism nor to Taoism.

However concise our description of the Taoist pantheon may be, the goddess *Hsi Wang Mu* must not be missed who, as "Queen Mother of the West", rules over a paradise in the K'un Lun mountains, a paradise inhabited by myriads of immortals. It is there, too, that the Peaches of Immortality are cultivated under her supervision. Furthermore, she is a mediator between the deities mentioned above and men who are striving for immortality. Such people whose endeavours are acknowledged by her—as, it is claimed, was the case with Emperor Mu of the Chou dynasty and Emperor Wu of the Han dynasty—will receive from her sacred texts which will prove to be excellent talismans, and they will come to eat the Peaches of Immortality. Especially during the Liu Ch'ao era (3rd-6th century A.D.) she plays the rôle of a mediator of texts, as can be concluded from many half-legendary textual histories. Today, *Hsi Wang Mu* is no longer worshipped; she only survives in a few works of art for which she served as a model.

As early as the 6th century A.D., stone steles were erected in honour of *Yü Huang*, the Jade Emperor. However, it was not until the Sung era that he gained the emperors' favour when, in 1012 A.D. he was introduced into the official cult that was under imperial protection. In the course of time he came to be the supreme god of folk religion and has remained so up to our days. In the purer, pre-Sung Taoism he held the office of "Head of the Personnel Department" on the staff of the god *Yüan Shih T'ien Tsun*, and it was his duty to keep the registers of gods and immortals. In the meantime the Jade Emperor has superseded his former "boss", and although in the Buddho-Taoist folk religion he was assimilated into the Indian god Indra, his Taoist origin is prevalent, and the places where he is worshipped are regarded as being principally places of the Taoist cult.

In 1115 A.D., still during the Sung era, the aspiring god was given the title of Supreme Emperor by the romantic painter-emperor Hui Tsung – very much to the annoyance of the Confucians who were of the opinion that this title could only be claimed by Heaven. However, even today he has not yet given up his rôle as an official of the record office, since the Gods of Hearth as well as those of the towns and the surrounding districts come once a year to the Jade Emperor, who is their superior, in order to report on the good and evil deeds of men.

Taoism is acquainted with three types of deification: a) of natural forces, b) of metaphysical concepts, c) of men, who are on the lowest rung of the hierarchical ladder. The latter, however, are familiar to the people through stories and theatre, and the people prefer to seek refuge in them.

The two texts "On Actions and Retributions" (*T'ai Shang Kan Ying P'ien*) and "Text on Determining (to do good deeds) in Secret" (*Yin Chih Wen*), which both originated in the 11th century, contain a great deal of popular morals embracing Taoism, Buddhism, and Confucianism; Buddhism, however, being restricted to the punishments of hell and having the same catalogue of sins as Confucianism. Both texts, however, were written from a Taoist standpoint, and they have been read by the people more than the *Tao Teh Ching*, let alone the text *Chuang Tzu*.

IV. Worship

In the temples which are regarded as Taoist, not only the Jade Emperor (*Yü Huang*) and Lao-tzu are worshipped, but also very often deified men (*Shen* or *Shen Ming*) who were famous in history and were made popular by the theatre. In addition, there is the special God of Earth (*T'u Ti Kung*) who is regarded as the personification of the place where Heaven and Earth meet.

The most important object in the temple is not the image of the deity but the incense burner, which often bears a date and thus offers reliable information regarding the foundation date of the temple. For this reason, the head of the temple is called the "Superintendent of the Incense Burner" (*Lu Chu*). Privileged members of the community are allowed to take ashes from the incense burner in order to fill their private incense burner at home with them. In this way they remain in constant communication with the main altar and the deities as well as with the other members of the community. It should be mentioned that in Taoism the burning of incense is an act of purification and not one of sacrifice as in Buddhism.

Among the many religious temple festivals, the so-called *Chiao* festivals deserve special mention as they serve to safeguard the unity of the religious community throughout the ecclesiastical year. There are *Chiao* for peace and against catastrophes and pestilence, *Chiao* for the restauration and reconsecration of temples.

In Taiwan even today the central and most important liturgy on the occasion of such festivals is performed by *Tao Shih*, i.e. Tao priests who are invited from monasteries and centres of cult, where a comparatively pure religious Taoism is still observed. The supreme Taoist priest – formerly in Mainland China and now in Taiwan – is the Taoist "Pope", the Heavenly Master (*T'ien Shih*), who has already been mentioned in the historical survey. He is entitled to delegate his functions.

An ordained priest must know the liturgical texts by heart and in addition to this he must be a virtuous drummer. The proceedings of the service are regulated by drum beats to even a greater degree than in Confucian sacrificial ceremonies, and the drummer must be a Tao priest. The ritual dances are acrobatic in character; the holy texts are sung.

The most important passages are read by the supreme priest who, among other things, must have an intelligent appearance and, as a rule, comes from a rich family and is married. In most cases he has studied for twenty years during which he copied the liturgical texts by hand and learned them by heart. At his ordination the priest receives a high-sounding title, and he is allocated to one of the fictitious administrative districts of the theocratic Taoist realm, which have corresponding zones in the microcosm of the human body.

Most of the texts lie on the altar table during the ceremony and are read aloud; others which are secret and have only been passed down orally are recited by heart. Ordained priests abstain at all times from eating the meat of geese, dogs, and eel, and above all they avoid eating the meat of the water buffalo, because Lao-tzu allegedly went to the West on a water buffalo. The petitions to the deities are made in the form of official applications—a fact which proves that in this respect Taoist practices are orientated more towards the Confucian state than towards the Buddhist church.

The Tao priest alone is allowed to invoke and implore the *San Ch'ing*, the Three Aspects of *Tao*, directly, in a kind of litany, without first turning to the deities sitting enthroned in the temple. The religious ceremonies which take place in the temple after the Tao priests have left, as well as the ceremonies and theatrical performances which take place outside the temple during the Tao service, all belong primarily to the Buddho-Taoist folk religion, and their multifarious aspects cannot be dealt with here.

V. Conception of Man

The Taoist religion has innumerable variations concerning the creation of the world. The majority of the Taoist sacred books begin by describing how the world was created. After the dissolution of primordeal chaos the pure, light *Yang* particles soar up to Heaven where they form the community of gods and form the divine revelation in precious jade characters whereas the coarse and heavy emanations of *Yin* sink down to form the terrestrial world. Moreover, the female *Yin*, which in Lao-tzu's philosophical Taoism has preference over *Yang*, becomes the principle of death in religious Taoism. Everything physical originates from the emanations of *Yin* and *Yang* in primordeal chaos, which liquefy and vaporize and then coagulate and solidify again.

While this conception was widespread in the Liu-ch'ao era, another version of the creation of the world, which originated from the time of the Han era, was also current. This version sees Lao-tzu as a demiurge from the parts of whose body the features of nature derive. His eyes become the sun and the moon, his head the massive K'un Lun mountains; his hair makes the stars, and his bones become the vitally important dragons. The animals originate from his flesh, and the snakes in the sea from his intestines. The hair of his body forms the plants, his genitals men, etc. This cosmic conception of Lao-tzu is a Taoist version of the Indian Purusha (Primeval Man, Chinese: *P'an Ku*) of the Indian Yumir Myth.

The Taoist sees the highest happiness in attaining longevity or immortality in this world. Han mirrors or lacquer boxes show in their ornamentation the *Hsien Jen*, the immortals, who are depicted as winged human beings (like angels in Christianity). In order to attain immortality, the body must be transformed by means of complicated physical and mental practices. By eating gold and cinnabar one tries to give the body the durability of gold and the chemical adaptability of cinnabar in order to ward off old age and death. These practices have a long tradition in China; they sprang up among the circles of metallurgists and potters. The classical text of life-prolonging alchemy is the text *Pao P'u Tzu* by Ko Hung (283-343 A.D.) who considers the safest way to physical immortality to lie in eating cinnabar which has been transformed nine times into mercury and back again. Many Chinese emperors and princes involuntarily reached the Yellow Springs (eternity, death) prematurely by poisoning themselves with cinnabar and gold drugs.

During the T'ang era (7th century) this exoteric alchemy, also called methods of the "outer elixir" (*Wai Tan*), was superseded by esoteric alchemy, methods of the "inner elixir" (*Nei Tan*), which is opposed to the consumption of drugs and which attaches importance to the equilibrium between the dual forces *Yin* and *Yang* and the elements in the microcosm of the human body. Wei Po Yang's book *Chou I Ts'an T'ung Ch'i* ("Kinship of the Three Ways of Heaven, Earth, and Man" or "Kinship of the Three Ways of the *I Ching*, Taoism, and Alchemy"), which dates from the 2nd century B.C. and deals with speculative rather than with experimental alchemy, became the principal text of the *Nei Tan* school. For the adept of esoteric alchemy, it is of the utmost importance to prevent any substance of vigour from escaping out of the body. Instead of expending vital energies, for example on begetting children, the adept observes wise restraint. Specific bedroom techniques are recommended which are designed to spare the sperms and at the same time to enhance vitality.

Another technique which is aimed at the same goal but which employs different methods is so-called "embryonic respiration" which means that the breath is made to circulate in a closed circuit through the "cinnabar fields" of the head, breast, and abdomen, while external respiration is limited to a minimum. Such practices are said to reverse the normal process of life from birth to death, for by means of these endeavours the adept produces an embryo of immortality, a homunculus, which at the moment of death is released from the body like a sabre from the sheath. This "new man" which has been systematically produced in one's own body is also called the Golden Flower (*Chin Hua*). These miraculous processes going on in his own body, which are furthered or obstructed by good or bad spirits and demons, can be perceived by the Tao master by means of meditation into his viscera in an Internal Vision. If the adept sees the good regents, the Three Ones: One of Heaven, One of Earth, and the *T'ai I* (Supreme One), who are seen as a trinity, together with all the other healing spirits sitting in majestic tranquillity in the key points of his body, he will know that everything is in order and that he is on his way to immortality. In contrast to Confucianism, the *Nei Tan* Taoists believe that man's destiny is not dependent on Heaven (*T'ien Ming*) but on man himself.

Many Taoist devotees practise a great number of gymnastic exercises, e.g. so-called Chinese boxing (*T'ai Chi Ch'üan*) which is still practised today by many people in Chinese East Asia, usually in parks and public gardens. It is performed in accordance with Lao-tzu's motto "weak like water" and is part of the Taoist mode of behaviour of the *Jou Tao* (Japanese: *Jû Dô*), "soft way" or "yielding way" at the basis of which is the ancient Taoist law of *Wu Wei*, non-action. The flexible and yielding posure, e.g. in boxing, is intended to prevent man's growing old and stiff.

The common rule for drug-eaters, esoterics, meditators, and practitioners of religious mechano-therapy is that they should reduce their intake of food as much as possible. It is particularly important not to eat any cereals because they nourish the malevolent spirits in the human body which cause death and decay.

VI. The Present Situation of Taoism

The decline of the Buddho-Taoist folk religion and its persecution by the Communists in Mainland China also affected "pure" Taoism. The Taoist priests are regarded as agents for the perpetuation of gross superstition which, according to materialistic Maoism, has to be replaced by modern medicine and hygiene.

When in 1949 representatives from all classes of the people convened in order to discuss a new, Communist form of government, seven out of the 585 delegates representated the following religious communities: Buddhism, Islam, Protestantism, Catholicism. Taoism received neither public nor official attention.

During the fifties, various semi-religious and semi-political secret societies based on Taoist-Messianic ideas (Yellow Turbans, Christian ideas) caused the police force much trouble and worry. Societies like "The Way of Pervading Unity" (*I Kuan Tao*) or "Heavenly Gate" (*T'ien Men*), or the "Eight Trigrams Sect" (*Pa Kua*) were recklessly and cruelly fought by the Communist rulers. It is very difficult to say today how important the rôle of such secret societies still is in the People's Republic. The belief in the physical invulnerability of the members of these sects, which comes from *Wai Tan* and *Nei Tan* Taoism, gives them an unimaginable, death-defying courage, as was also the case with the Boxers in 1901.

In the non-Communist countries of East and South East Asia, Taoist ideas survive in the so-called Societies of World Religion, e.g. the *Tao Yüan* and the *T'ung Shan Hui* sects which claim that they have distilled the essence from all the religions of the world and that they have syncretized them the into the very best religion.

A really religious form of Taoism only exists in Taiwan. Centres of the religion are, e.g., in Mushan near Taipei, where the magnificent *Chih Nan Kung* (Compass Temple) towers above the surrounding countryside, and in Tainan, where the Heavenly Master (*T'ien Shih*) has his see. There a Taoist liturgy is cultivated which is almost 2000 years old, and the ceremonies performed by Taoist priests (*Tao Shih*) are essentially different from those of the folk religion which is only permitted outside the Taoist temples. Great merit for the flourishing of Taoism is due to the late Heavenly Master Chang En P'u, who died in 1970 and who advocated a more spiritualized form of Taoism. He was allegedly the 63rd Heavenly Master since Chang Tao Ling at the end of the Han era. The *T'ien Shih* is the spiritual head of the *Cheng I* Sect. This sect, together with the *Ch'üan Chen* Sect, are the most important Taoist sects to have survived from the Sung era. Broadly speaking, they represent the exoteric as well as the esoteric alchemy in Taoism, but it is significant that exoteric alchemy, i.e. the external application of elixirs, was able to assert itself better under the influence of European allopathic medicine.

Furthermore, there is a society of "Adepts of Taoism" which has about 200 members, and a Taiwan Taoist Association with almost 5000 members.

The younger generation in Taiwan and in the entire Far East thinks little of Taoist practices. It seems, that the religion is doomed.

The sole surviving aspect is the interest in philosophical Taoism, especially in that of Lao-tzu and Chuang-tzu. Whereas the issue in Communist China is whether *Tao* ought to be interpreted in a materialistic or an idealistic way, and which "class conscience" the Taoist texts represent, in the non-Communist countries of East Asia and in Europe the *Tao* is usually explained psychologically. Emphasis is given to the healing power which may emanate from an all-embracing *Tao* experience in our troubled world. In this emphasis on the wholesome and healing forces, the old magic Taoism is also *mutatis mutandis* preserved in "philosophical Taoism" as it is understood today.

VII. Short History of the Study of Taoism

Whereas the Jesuit Matteo Ricci (1552-1610), who was perhaps the first Western Sinologist, values Confucianism highly, he condemns Taoism as well as folk religion for their paganism and detestable idolatry in his book "*Storia dell' Introduzione del Cristianesimo in China*". Athanasius Kircher (1601-1680), too, is of the same opinion, and he makes the derogatory remark that Taoism only appealed to the common people ("... respondet plebeis"), and this opinion is shared by all early Jesuit missionaries. And although the mendicant orders did not idealize Confucianism in the way the Jesuits did, they agreed with them in their rejection of Taoism as devilry.

The—probably—earliest translation of the *Tao Teh Ching* which is ascribed to the "founder of Taoism" Lao-tzu, was done by P. François Noël (1651-1729), who was a Belgian Jesuit and an excellent Sinologist. The 18th century symbolists among the Jesuits also tried to find the "lumen naturale" in the *Tao Teh Ching*, as can be concluded from the title of an unsigned manuscript in the British Museum "*Textus quidam ex libro antiquissimo Tao te kim exerpti quibus probatur SSmae Trinitatis Mysterium Sinicae genti olim notum fuisse*". The clerical symbolist began to take Taoism seriously because they hoped it would be possible to harness it to their missionary task. One excellent representative of this school is P. DE PRÉMARE with his "*Documents relatifs aux missions chinoises et remarques en latin sur le livre Tao-te-King*" which was published in 1707. He was one of the first to write a Chinese grammar and, on account of his rudimentary knowledge of Chinese phonology and the transcription of foreign names, he read the name of Jehova from the phonemes *Yi Hsi Wei* which appear in the *Tao Teh Ching* (chapt. 14).

Towards the end of the 18th century, P. Jos. M. AMIOT (1718-1793) gave the first detailed description of Taoism in a letter written to the minister M. Bergin on October 16, 1787. Although on the whole he gives a disparaging report on the religion, he voices his approval of celibacy and the search for immortality in Taoism. His sagacious mind recognizes that "dans la Chine moderne" the three Chinese religions are merging together more and more, and it is in this fact that he sees the actual reason of this decadence.

The Jesuit LÉON WIEGER (1856-1933) offers thorough scientific investigations in his two-volume work on Taoism; Vol. I: "*Bibliographia, Le Canon, Les Index*" (1911) and Vol. II: "*Les Pères du système taoiste*" (1913). Neither this work nor JAMES LEGGE's "*The Texts of Taoism*" (1891) has been outdated yet.

The two great works by H. DORÉ "*Recherches sur les Superstitions en Chine*" (15 vols., Shanghai 1914-29) and by J.J.M. DE GROOT "*The Religious System of China*" (6 vols., 1892) offer much material without any missionary motives, but also without giving detailed interpretation.

It was H. MASPERO who made a new departure in the investigation of Taoism, and basing his opinion on the old texts, he depicted it as a religion which had been lively and active in the Chinese people since the Han era (see *Langues Posthumes*, Vol. II, *Le Taoisme*, Paris 1950), and for the first time he clearly elaborated the individualistic aspect of Taoism, the striving for self-redemption and personal immortality. His work "*Les procédés de 'nourrire le principe vital' dans la religion taoiste ancienne*" (1937) can claim the merit that it disclosed for the first time to Sinology the right way of understanding such concepts as *Wai Tan* and *Nei Tan*. It was also MASPERO who broke down the wall between philosophical and religious Taoism and who found interrelations which had not been noticed up till then.

P. Eugen Feifel (a) and James R. Ware (b) concerned themselves with the important tractate *Pao P'u Tzu*, a) in Monumenta Serica 1941, 1944, 1946; b) "*Alchemy, Medicine, Religion*" (1966). These works are a methodical approach to Taoism of the Liu-ch'ao era.

Max Kaltenmark with his book "*Le Lie-sien tchouan*", Pékin 1953, presented to us the Taoist hagiography, which supplies a wealth of interesting ideal conceptions. By these works Sinology concerned with history of religion has finally freed itself and is now working along the lines of a non-engaged systematic history of religion.

SELECTED BIBLIOGRAPHY

I. *General:*

Chan, Wing-tsit, *Religious Trends in Modern China*, New York 1953
De Groot, J.J.M., *The Religious System of China*, 6 vols., Leiden 1892, repr. Taipei, Taiwan 1964
Eberhard, W., *Religious Activities and Religious Books in Modern China*, *Zeitschrift für Missionswissenschaft* No. 4, (1965)
——, *Guilt and Sin in Traditional China*, Berkeley and Los Angeles 1967
Needham, J., *Science and Civilisation in China*, Vol. 2, Cambridge 1956
Thompson, L.G., *Chinese Religion: An Introduction*, Belmont, Calif. 1969
Waley, A., *Three Ways of Thought in Ancient China*, London 1939
Werner, E.T.C., *Dictionary of Chinese Mythology*, Shanghai 1932

II. *Confucianism:*

Biallas, F.X., *Konfuzius und sein Kult*, Peking/Leipzig 1928
Creel, H.G., *Confucius and the Chinese Way*, *Harper Torchbook Edition* 1960
De Groot, J.J.M., *Universismus*, Berlin 1918
Dobson, w.a.c.h., *Mencius*, Oxford 1963
Fairbank, J.K., (ed.) *Chinese Thought and Institutions*, Chicago 1957
Hsiao, Kung-chuan, *Rural China*, *Imperial Control in the Nineteenth Century*, Seattle 1960 (Chapter Local Sacrifices)
Kramers, R.P., *K'ung Tzu Chia Yü* (tr.), Leiden 1950
Legge, J., *The Chinese Classics*, 5 vols., Oxford 1861-72, repr. Hong-Kong 1960
Nivison, D.S. and Wright, A.F., (ed.) *Confucianism in Action*, Stanford 1959
Waley, A., *The Analects of Confucius*, London 1938
Williams, E.T., *The State Religion of China during the Manchu Dynasty*, *Journal of the North China Branch*, *Royal Asiatic Society*, Vol. XLIV, 1913
Wright, A.F., (ed.) *Studies in Chinese Thought*, Chicago 1953
——, (ed.) *Confucian Persuasion*, Stanford 1960
——, and Twichett, D., (ed.) *Confucian Personalities*, Stanford 1962

III. *Taoism:*

Creel, H.G., *What is Taoism? Journal of the American Oriental Society*, Vol. 76, No. 3, 1956

Duyvendak, J.J.L., *Tao Tö King: Le Livre de la Voie et de la Vertu*, Paris 1953

Kaltenmark, M., *Le Lie-sien tchouan*, Peking 1953

——, *Lao Tzu and Taoism*, Stanford 1969 (original ed.: *Lao tseu et le taoisme*, Paris 1965)

Kramers, R.P., *Die Lao-Tzu Diskussion in der chinesischen Volksrepublik*, *Etudes Asiatiques* XXII, 1968

Legge, J., *The Texts of Taoism*, London 1881

Maspero, H., *Les Procédés de 'nourrire le principe vital' dans la religion taoiste ancienne*, *Journal Asiatique* 1937

——, *Le taoisme*, Paris 1950

Stein, R.A., *Remarques sur les mouvements du Taoisme politico-religieux au IIe siècle ap. J.C.*, *T'oung-pao*, 50 (1963)

Ware, J.R., *Alchemy, Medicine, Religion in the China of A.D.* 320. *The Nei P'ien of Ko Hung (Pao P'u Tzu)*, Cambridge, Mass., 1966

Welch, H., *The Parting of the Way*, Boston 1957

Wilhelm, R., *The Secret of the Golden Flower*, transl. Londen 1931

Wu, L.C. and Davis, T.L., *Translation of the Ts'an-t'ung-ch'i*, in: *Isis*, Vol. 18, Sept. 1930

For much of the first-hand information I am indebted to the Deutsche Forschungsgemeinschaft; a DFG-grant enabled me to travel to South East and East Asia in 1968/69 and pursue field studies there.

THE RELIGIONS OF JAPAN

BY

CARMEN BLACKER

Cambridge, England

I. Essence of Japanese Religion[1]

The essence of Japanese religion has always been a successful and viable syncretism. The chief components have been Shinto, the native cult, mingled with various sects of Mahayana Buddhism. The term Shinto itself implies a fusion of many cults and practices of different ethnic origins, while Japanese Buddhism survives in a bewildering multiplicity of sects and schools. Until 1870 the two religions were almost indistinguishably blended in the minds of most Japanese, the resulting cult being not the precarious patchwork that might be imagined, but an integrated whole with an inner logic and impetus of its own. Since 1945 when for the first time for some 70 years complete religious freedom was granted to the Japanese, this same tendency towards successful syncretism has reasserted itself in the many new movements and groups which immediately made their appearance. The two traditional components, Shinto and Buddhism, still predominate, though groups professing Christian ethical principles are numerous. In the formation of these new movements a typical pattern emerges which seems to assert itself persistently throughout the history of Japanese religion.

II. Historical Development

The religious cult native to the Japanese and practised at the time of the introduction of Buddhism in the 6th century is usually termed 'early Shinto'. The term is misleading in so far as it implies a homo-

1 The complex nature of religion in Japan has made it necessary to depart in certain respects from the scheme laid down the contributions to this Handbook. The 'Concept of Man', for example, has not been treated as a separate section, but incorporated in the long section on historical development. Certain other sections too have been ommitted because it was not thought possible to give them meaningful treatment.

geneous cult, uniformly practised throughout Japan. Early Shinto was not a uniform system of belief. It was a complex amalgram of different traditions brought by the different ethnic groups which during the previous 500 years had gone to compose the Japanese race. The exact composition of this race, and hence of the 'native' religious system, is still a matter of controversy among scholars, but it seems comparatively clear that we have ethnic elements of Melanesian, of Tungusic and of South-east Asian origin, with a further invasion in the late prehistoric period of the 3rd or 4th centuries A.D. of Altaic peoples from Manchuria and Korea. The mixed origins of the native cult should therefore be borne in mind in any discussion of early Shinto.

Our materials for the study of the native cult fall into two distinct categories. In the first place we have a number of literary sources which give an account of what is taken to be the cult of the Imperial House and the dominant clans on the central Yamato plain. These sources comprise first the two earliest examples of writing in Japan, the chronicles known as the Kojiki and the Nihon Shoki. These books, though committed to writing as late as the early 8th century, undoubtedly contain material of great antiquity previously transmitted orally by professional reciters. They include several important cycles of myths, describing *inter alia* the creation of the Japanese islands and people, and the descent of the Japanese Emperors from the Sun Goddess. We also have the earliest anthology of poetry, the Manyōshu, again committed to writing during the 8th century, and containing many songs and poems of obvious antiquity which shed light on the early religion. We also have the two works known as the Jōganshiki and the Engishiki. The latter, the 'institutes of the Engi Period' (901-923) contains a detailed description of a number of Shinto rituals, and 27 Shinto prayers or *norito*. The Jōganshiki compiled in 871 contains prescriptions for the celebration of Shinto rituals, but no *norito*.

From these works it has been possible to reconstruct with fair accuracy the religious system centering round the Imperial family during the 5th and 6th centuries. Recent Japanese scholarship however has insisted that these literary sources reveal only a narrow segment of the early religious cult. In remoter districts variations of the cult were practised which were never committed to writing, but which can be studied through certain surviving rites and practices, orally transmitted, of what was previously dismissed as 'folk religion'. It was the great scholar and ethnologist Yanagida Kunio who first showed that field studies of living practices in various remote districts could shed a new and unsuspected light on the ancient cult. His own voluminous works and those of his distinguished followers such as Hori Ichirō have proved the importance of what Robert Redfield called the 'little tradition' in illuminating our knowledge of the important ancient cult of mountains, for example, and of Japanese shamanism, neglected until recent times because they survived only on the non-literary folk level.

Though the details of worship and practice certainly differed widely in different parts of the country, we can at least reconstruct certain basic beliefs which were widely established at the time when written records started. The following description will be based largely on the literary sources.

From the myths in the early chronicles we gather that the Japanese of the Yamato plain, following a pattern reminiscent of North Asian shamanism, envisaged a three-layered universe. In the middle lay the world of man, where there was a small sphere of things that human beings could successfully control. A far larger sphere lay outside their control, and this lay in the gift of the beings who inhabited the worlds above and below. The upper world, known as Takamagahara or the High Plain of Heaven, was inhabited by beings known as *kami*, which were the primary objects of worship within the cult. The lower world was the place where the dead went, a filthy and polluted region called Yomi. With regard to the destination of the dead however, it should be remembered that this was by no means the same in all variations of the cult. In many places the dead were conceived to go to certain mountains. In others there survived a tradition of Tokoyo, a land beyond the sea where the dead were believed to go and whence they would return at certain seasons of the year to bless the homes and fertilise the seed—a survival, as some scholars believe, of an early Melanesian ethnic strain. The conception of a lower world, however, gloomy and defiled, seems to have been the dominant one in the aristocratic cult.

The nature of the *kami* will be described in more detail in a later section. Here suffice to say that in their early form they appear to have been spiritual forces, devoid of specific shape, which shadowily personified those aspects of the natural world and human society which lay beyond the understanding of primitive man. These forces could be invoked at certain seasons to visit the human world and to grant such otherwise unattainable boons as a good rice harvest, seasonable rains, freedom from pestilence and male children.

The power of these superior beings however was not uniformly benign. They could grant blessings when duly and correctly worshipped, but they could also blast with curses (*tatari*) when offended. What caused them offence were 'pollutions' of various kinds, acts or states which rendered a man ceremonially impure and unfit to approach a shrine.

The sources of pollution are set out in one of the most important of the early rituals preserved in the Engishiki, the Oharai or Great Purification. They are divided broadly into *amatsutsumi* or Heavenly Offences and *kunitsutsumi* or Earthly Offences. The former are mostly crimes which would threaten the livelihood of a primitive rice growing community, such as breaking down the divisions between the rice fields, and opening the gates of the sluices. They are mentioned in the early myths as having been committed by the unruly god Susanoo, to the offence of the Sun Goddess. The Earthly Offences comprise a number of apparently miscellaneous acts, such as wounding or killing, desecration of a corpse, incest, bestiality, leprosy, tumours, snake bite, calamity from thunder or birds and witchcraft. The great 18th century scholar Motoori Norinaga classified these offences into the three categories of moral sin, physical pollution and disaster. In practice, however, most of these items seem to have been ignored, and the sources of pollution to have been reduced broadly to two: death and blood. Contact with a corpse, with a woman in childbirth, or with a wounded person or animal, contaminated a man so that he must undergo ritual isolation from his fellows for a stated period, and for an even longer time refrain from approaching a shrine. Any violation of these rules was liable to incur the danger of a sudden *tatari* from the offended deity, striking in the form of sickness, madness, accident or fire.

With early Shinto therefore we are still in a pre-moral stage of religious development. Ceremonial impurity, with penalties directed equally against the man who inflicts a wound on another and the man who suffers the wound, stood in place of what later developed into a religious sense of moral wrong. The development of an ethical code in Shinto came only later with the influence of Buddhism and Confucianism. Indeed, very few Japanese words for moral qualities are of native origin. Benevolence, justice, propriety, compassion—words for these qualities only appeared in the Japanese language with the arrival of the Confucian classics and Buddhist scriptures.

The cult could thus be correctly described as archaic. Preliterary and pre-moral, it was concerned primarily with the pacification and rejoicing of vague spiritual forces, conceived to dwell in a realm other than the human but closely impinging on it, and in whose gift lay the large sphere of life which lay outside human control.

When during the latter half of the 6th century Buddhism made its first appearance in Japan, it is hardly surprising that a religion so remote from such beliefs should have been at first misunderstood. The *kami*, after all, were regarded as spiritual powers, external to the human mind, capable of bestowing worldly benefits beyond the human grasp. The Buddha, on the other hand, had taught that worldly prosperity, the accumulation of what seem to be the blessings of this world, was in the long run of little account. The world as experienced in the ordinary human manner was invariably full of suffering. Only by a profound internal transformation of consciousness achieved by meditational disciplines on a basis of moral purification, could one arrive at the illumination which comes from knowledge of the reality lying behind the illusory veil of appearances, and in which alone wisdom and bliss can be discovered.

When Buddhism was first introduced into Japan in the form of an image and copies of sutras sent by the king of one of the Korean kingdoms—the date is given in the Nihon Shoki as 552 A.D.—it was for some years regarded as no more than a new version of the native cult. The figures of the Buddha and his attendant Bodhisattvas were seen not as images symbolising a different and more sublime state of consciousness, but as potential bestowers of abundant harvests, male heirs and due monsoon rains, and as saviours from famine and pestilence. The sublime Buddhist art of this period, and the work of Prince Shōtoku, whose Constitution of 604 counsels reverence for the Three Treasures as keys to a harmonious world, indicate that even at this early date there was some understanding of the gentler side of Buddhist teaching; of the compassion for suffering and the reverence for life which is so integral a part of Mahayana doctrine.

More prominent however seems to have been the state cult of Buddhism which established itself in the course of the 7th century in Japan. A glance at the official chronicles will show that Buddhism in this state cult was called upon to fulfil two main functions. Neither of these have anything to do with the original teaching of the Buddha, but curiously both have survived until today as the two main duties which the average Japanese expects Buddhism to perform in his daily life.

The first of these is the disposal of the dead and the pacification of ghosts and spirits. The ancient Shinto cult with its horror of the pollution of death had provided no means for the repose of the dead, nor anything in the way of a comforting eschatology. It is clear from the archeological finds of the pre-Buddhist period, however, that the dead were greatly feared. All dead spirits were apparently believed to be potentially harmful, but especially those who had died a violent or untimely death. It was Buddhism therefore which fulfilled the urgent need of providing special requiem masses (*kuyō*) by which the spirit could find its proper rest and join the benevolent ranks of the 'ancestors', to whom offerings were made every day in household shrines to ensure their constant benign protection.

As early as the 6th century we find references in the chronicles of Buddhist sutras being read or Buddhist rituals performed for the repose of dead members of the Imperial family or the aristocracy. That it should have continued to perform this function for 1400 years is perhaps strange when we remember that according to the early Buddhist doctrine in India such steps were irrelevant, since the dead person was believed to be soon reborn in the state prescribed by his past karma. But so insistent has always been the demand of Japanese religion for some means to help the dead, with all their terrors, to final peace, that until today Buddhist temples have found one of their most lucrative functions to lie here. Some indeed may be said to subsist almost entirely on fees for funerals and other obsequies.

The second function with which Buddhism was charged as early as the 7th century and which it still discharges today was to provide magical spells for the production of mundane benefits. The early Mahayana sutras to reach Japan—the Lotus Sutra, for example, the Daihannyakyō or Large Prajñāpāramitā Sutra, the Ninnōkyō or Sutra of Benevolent Kings—were used not as guides towards an internal transformation revealing the vanity of the world, but as spells for rain, for the Emperor's recovery from sickness, for the birth of a male heir, for the arrest of an epidemic. Throughout the history of Japanese religion the same stress on benevolent productive magic has always persisted. The only Buddhist sects today to repudiate spells for *genseriyaku*, present worldly blessings, are the Amidist sects and the Rinzai sect of Zen. For all the others it is one of their chief sources of wealth. Even in the Sōtō sect of Zen, for example, the richest and most celebrated temples are not those which shelter a wise and saintly teacher capable of guiding disciples towards spiritual illumination, but those which enshrine an image reputed to be *arataka*, efficacious in granting, for a stated sum of money, such boons as prosperity in business, harmony in the family and freedom from traffic accidents.

The functions which Buddhism was destined to fulfil for the average Japanese were thus defined within a century of its introduction. Side by side with these practices, however, there grew up in certain temples a literary tradition whereby teachings more nearly approaching the Buddha's original message were disseminated to a learned and religiously enthusiastic few.

In the course of the 7th century, and the greater part of the 8th when the capital was established at Nara, the Six Schools were introduced by monks from China and established in various temples in the vicinity.

Without exception they were too abstruse and metaphysical to be comprehensible by anyone outside the small groups of monks set to study them in the temples. The Sanron or Mādhyamika School, introduced as early as 625 by a Korean monk, taught the Middle Path of the Eightfold Negation, wherein there was no production, no extinction, no annihilation, no permanence, no unity, no diversity, no coming, no going. The disciple must perceive the truth to be the Void. The Jōjitsu School, introduced about the same time, taught not only the Voidness of Elements, but also the Voidness of Self. The Hossō or Yogācāra School, brought to Japan in 654 by Dōshō, a pupil of the celebrated Hsüan-tsang, taught the doctrine of *vijñapti-mātra*, that nothing exists beyond thought. The Kusha sect, introduced in 658, was based on the Abhidharmakośa of Vasubandhu, wherein it was stated that once reality is seen in its myriad component parts, self too will be seen to be illusory, a mere aggregate of atoms. The Ritsu or Vinaya sect, introduced by the saintly monk Ganjin in 753, prescribed the minute rules by which the lives of monks and nuns should be ordered. Finally the Kegon sect, reputedly introduced into Nara in 736 by an Indian monk called Bodhisena, was based on the Avataṃsaka Sutra which taught the sublime doctrine of a world in which there was no distinction between things, *jiji-muge-hokkai*, and other teachings such as the Sixfold Specific Nature of all Dharmas.

Such metaphysical deliverances, the product of minds which have reached advanced stages of enlightened consciousness, are not easily understood by those who have not. They have left no permanent imprint on Japanese Buddhism at all, beyond the temples at Nara, some ceremonies of extreme antiquity and interest, and the great image in the Tōdaiji temple fashioned after the vision of the Buddha seen in the Kegon Sutra. On the lives of ordinary Japanese the Six Schools have made no impression.

The oldest Buddhist schools still to survive as a meaningful religion in Japan are the two sects of esoteric Buddhism introduced from China during the 9th century, after the capital had been moved from Nara to Kyoto. The Tendai sect, based on the Chinese T'ien T'ai school founded in the 6th century by Chih-i, was brought to Japan in 805 by the eminent priest Saichō, known later as Dengyō Daishi. The Shingon sect, following the Chinese version of the right-handed Tantra, was introduced three years later by the even more remarkable priest Kūkai, who had studied the esoteric teachings for two years in China. Both these sects claim to transmit the real core of the Buddha's teaching—the experience of enlightenment and the path of leading towards it. Both sects declare that the essential nature of every man is identical with that of the cosmic Buddha, the Dharmakaya, visualised as Dainichi Nyorai or Vairocana Buddha. This perfect Buddha nature in man has been obscured and beclouded by the delusions of the phenomenal world, so that we do not realise its presence within us. We can recover it by the complex discipline known as the *sammitsu*, the Three Secrets; a process of ritual imitation, by which we can come to identify our three activities of action, speech and thought with those of the cosmic Buddha. Our actions we can identify by means of the ritual gestures known as mudra; our speech by mantras, or magical sounds, and our thoughts by certain modes of meditation such as gazing at the Sanscrit letter A. By these means we can achieve the state of *sokushin-jōbutsu*, becoming a Buddha in this very body.

Both sects are described as esoteric in so far as their more profund mysteries were, at any rate untill very recently, revealed only orally and in secret to those who had undergone the requisite initiations.

It is not surprising however that such a complex spiritual discipline should have been undertaken only by a few priests of more than usual sanctity and inspiration. For the layman, the two sects provided what he had always demanded: spells, often potent sounding corruptions of Sanscrit mantras, for the warding off of plague, fire, drought and the malevolent ghosts which were thought at the time to be the cause of nearly all sickness and calamity. In this form Buddhism virtually for the first time began to penetrate to the level of the ordinary Japanese, carried by peripatetic ascetics known as *hijiri* or *genja*.

Doctrinally, the Tendai sect was more catholic than the Shingon. The only path taught by the Shingon was the esoteric one based on the teaching of the *sammitsu*. The Tendai offered a broader choice, including a form of walking meditation based on the worship of

Amida known as *jōgyō-zammai*, and another known as *shikan*, 'stopping and insight'. Unlike the Shingon sect, the Tendai gave supreme reverence and priority to the Lotus Sutra, the Saddharma Pundarika, which it considered to expound the highest and deepest forms of truth, and compared with which the other doctrines and disciplines it embraced in its catholic fold were mere preliminary steps.

The truly Japanese forms of Buddhism which appeared in such profusion during the 12th and 13th centuries ultimately derived, therefore, from the Tendai sect—the seedpod from which arose the schools which now embrace the enormous majority of Japanese who call themselves Buddhist. For although Buddhism under the influence of these tantric sects was more widely disseminated than ever before, it was still predominantly an aristocratic cult, magically catering for the needs of the elegant ruling class in the Capital. The way to salvation which it offered was, moreover, by no means an easy one. The technique taught by Shingon for 'becoming a Buddha in this very body' were too complex and esoteric for any but dedicated priests.

It was only at the beginning of the 13th century that Buddhism evolved in such a way as to reach the ordinary man. The curious upsurge of new sects and movements which occurred at this time marked an important new stage in the development of Buddhism in Japan. For although these new sects differed from each other in ways which seem on first glance to be fundamental yet they have certain important traits in common which we now know to be characteristically Japanese.

In the first place, they all arose at a time of special misery and crisis. They may hence be regarded as a specific response to the anxieties of civil war, starvation, earthquake, pestilence and maladministration. Secondly, they all arose at the inspiration of a charismatic figure, the Founder, who was later accorded reverence on a par with a Bodhisattva. And thirdly, they preached *salvation*, in the sense of a complete change in man's state, rather than the merely local and temporary benefits which we have seen to be so characteristic of the earlier sects.

Further than this common structural basis, the Kamakura sects tend to fall into three distinct categories, each advocating a different path towards salvation.

First there were the Amidist sects, the Jōdo and Shin which worship the Buddha Amida. These are also known as the *tariki* schools, schools of 'other strength', because, like the prototype of the Amidist cult in China, they teach that there is nothing whatever that we ourselves can do to escape from the horrors of the ordinary human state, or from the horrors of a rebirth somewhere worse. We must rely entirely on the superior power of Amida Buddha to enable us to be reborn in his own paradise, the Pure Land in the west. There, under idyllically perfect conditions, we can be sure of eventually attaining nirvana. We can rely on Amida's saving grace by simply repeating, with complete faith and purity of heart, the mystic invocation *Namu Amida Butsu*. If we do this with complete faith, we need have no fears, whether of hell, the realm of hungry ghosts or any other limbo. Amida will come to meet us at our death and escort us to his paradise. Our own efforts are completely negligible in the present age, for the world has entered the depraved period of *mappō*, the Latter Days of the Law, when, as predicted in the sutras, the Buddha's law would lose its force. Our only hope of salvation therefore lies in the grace of Amida to save all those who call on his name.

It should be noted that this doctrine envisages salvation as only attainable after death. Also that the Pure Land, although strictly speaking only a stage on the way to final nirvana, was considered by most Japanese as quite good enough a place to pass the rest of eternity. There are several minor differences between the two Amidist sects, most conspicuous of which perhaps is the teaching as to the number of times it is necessary to recite the sacred formula before one can be sure of achieving *ōjō*, or rebirth in paradise. Hōnen, the founder of the Jōdo sect, always insisted that it should be recited as many times as possible. Shinran, the founder of the Shin sect, declared that only one invocation, provided it was made with true faith, was enough to ensure a joyous rebirth. This is not such a travesty of Buddhist teaching as it might appear, for the quality of faith which Shinran had in mind is by no means easy to achieve; it is a complete surrender of the self attainable only by few.

The complementary path to that of the Amidist sects is that of *jiriki*, self help, a phrase usually used to describe the two sects of Zen which arose at this time. Far from totally surrendering his will in self-abnegating devotion to Amida, the Zen disciple is taught that through strenuous *zazen*, sitting and struggling with various meditational exercises designed to lead the mind to hitherto unsuspected depths, he can by his own efforts, guided by a qualified master, bring about in himself successively deepening experiences of illumination. It is here that we find the most profound and distinctive indication of Japanese spirituality. The Zen sect with its unique and practical teaching towards 'sudden enlightenment' has deeply influenced much of the best Japanese art.

Of the two schools of Zen which took root in Japan, the Rinzai is the better known in the West owing to the writings of Dr Suzuki Daisetsu. Here we find the teachings of the Chinese school of Lin-chi transmitted to Japan with little admixture of native elements. The disciple must grapple with the meditational exercises known as *kōan*, problems without logical or rational content designed to awaken the Buddha nature by stilling the mind through concentration, and then rousing it to realise levels beyond the discriminating intellect. The *kōans* customarily used in Rinzai monasteries are all of Chinese origin, though the order in which they are given to the disciple is based on the classification of the great Japanese Zen master of the 18th century Hakuin. Most of the details of the meditational discipline too have come to Japan from China.

The Rinzai teaching was first introduced by the monk Eisai, who began preaching in Kyūshū at the end of the 12th century. He later founded temples in Kyoto and Kamakura by which the teaching was propagated. It found some of its most ardent disciples among the warrior class, which was rising to prominence at the time.

The Sōtō school of Zen was founded in Japan a few years later by the eminent priest Dōgen (1200-1253). Although Chinese in origin, its development in Japan has been very different from the Rinzai school. It is today far wealthier, with twice as many temples and believers. The reason is not far to seek. It is that it has allowed its teachings to become so mingled with folk beliefs and practices that sometimes there is scarcely any trace of anything that is recognisably Zen. Its biggest temples are geared to the lucrative business of reciting spells for worldly blessings, and in the large Toyokawa Inari temple the presiding deity is Inari, the Shinto rice spirit in fox form. In its meditational practices too the Sōtō school differs interestingly from the Rinzai. *Kōans* of every kind are scorned, and instead a discipline known as *shikan-taza* is practised. The disciple does not attempt to concentrate his mind on any focal point, but simply sits in the faith that he is here and now a Buddha, observing objectively such thoughts as may pass through his mind. Whereas the Rinzai school relies almost exclusively on Chinese sources for its sutras and books of *kōans*, in the rituals of the Sōtō sect little is heard beyond the words of the Founder Dōgen, whose status has been raised, in the typically Japanese manner, virtually to that of a Bodhisattva. Indeed the voluminous writings of

Dōgen are among the most profound and subtle in Japanese religious literature.

The third distinctive current of Buddhism during the Kamakura period is that comprising the Nichiren sect, best described as based on the Lotus Sutra. Nichiren was a turbulent priest who again flourished during the disturbed period of the 13th century, and who vehemently declared that all Japan's ills, particularly the Mongol invasions under Kublai Khan, were all due to neglect of the true faith. This was nothing more nor less than complete faith in the Lotus Sutra, to be expressed in the mystic formula *Namu Myōhō Rengekyō*. Nichiren's vehement intolerance of all other forms of Buddhism and all other religions is curiously unBuddhist and unJapanese. Yet it is obvious that it has a compelling appeal, for the Nichiren sect has flourished since the 13th century and is today the best subscribed of all the older sects. Furthermore it has had numerous offshoots which have split from the original Nichiren sect on some minor point of doctrine but which still preserve the basic faith in the power and efficacy of the Lotus Sutra. The latest and most celebrated of these is Sōka Gakkai, which has pushed its intolerance to even more fanatical lengths.

The salvation preached by these Lotus Sutra sects is in interesting contrast to the other modes we have noticed. The Amidist sects promised salvation in the next world after death. The Zen school proclaimed that the Buddha nature lay within us, obscured and unrecognised, but could be released through meditational discipline so that we can be fully enlightened in this life. The Nichiren sect vehemently denounced both these teachings and proclaimed instead a future terrestrial paradise, a millennium in which our descendants, once they have learnt to embrace the right faith, will enjoy perfect peace and bliss.

A word about what is known as the Christian Century in Japan is necessary at this point. This period stretched from 1549, when St Francis Xavier arrived in Japan, to 1639 when the final edict of expulsion and proscription of all Christians was issued. Christian missionary work was at first the monopoly of the Portuguese Jesuits, a natural outcome of the Portuguese conquests in India and their successful commercial ventures further east to Malacca and Macao. Many of the Jesuit missionaries were men remarkable for courage, faith and determination, yet to the last their efforts met with only very limited success. In the first years of their mission no obstacles were placed in the way of their preaching, and several of the feudal lords in Kyūshū seem to have become genuine converts. In other cases it was more difficult to distinguish enthusiasm for Christianity from enthusiasm for the material goods, silk and gold, brought by the Portuguese Great Ship once a year from Macao, the visits of which were for some time made conditional on a kindly reception to the Jesuits. Later in the century the missionary ranks were swelled by a number of Spanish friars. All were kindly received by Nobunaga, the military ruler of most of the country during the middle 16th century, but largely because he detested Buddhism and saw in the missionaries a welcome ally against the common enemy. His successor Hideyoshi at first received them with equal cordiality, until 1587 when with inexplicable suddenness he issued an edict expelling all missionaries. The real persecution however did not start until 1614, after the first Tokugawa Shogun Ieyasu had come to power. The reason for his ruthless banishment of all foreign missionaries and proscription of all native Christians was largely the suspicion that the missionaries were the forerunners of a political conquest by Spain such as had befallen Manila. The story of the persecution is one of horrifying cruelty, culminating in the Shimabara rebellion of 1637-8, when a number of native Japanese Christians were massacred to a man. The following year, 1639, the final edict of expulsion and proscription was issued.

The effects of the proscription of Christianity on Buddhism were twofold. In the 250 years of isolation from the outside world under the feudal rule of the Tokugawa Shoguns which succeeded the expulsion, the position of Buddhism was materially strengthened and formalised by the edict that all families must register at a Buddhist temple of the sect of their choice as *danka* or supporters. But at the same time the growth and organisation of the sects and temples were subjected to a minute political control, which resulted before long in a sorry spiritual stagnation. Such religious enthusiasm as survived seems to have been directed more towards the purely academic and theoretical study of doctrine, at the expense of the cultivation of spiritual wisdom and illumination which is the proper end of the Buddhist disciple's striving, but which the authorities considered might lead to a dangerous religious charisma.

Far more potent than Buddhism during the Tokugawa period were the doctrines of Neo-Confucianism, particularly those of the Sung philosopher Chu Hsi. It was Neo-Confucianism which provided the first really vigorous system of social ethics that the Japanese had known. We have seen that early Shinto provided no ethical rules at all. Nor had Buddhism in Japan ever provided a viable *social* ethic. Mahayana teaching emphasised compassion for suffering, respect for the sanctity of life, whether of man or beast, and prescriptions for a pure if solitary life. But it had failed to provide detailed precepts whereby the relations between ruler and vassal, father and son, husband and wife, elder and younger should be regulated. Moral behaviour in Buddhism was in any case regarded as a merely preparatory and purificatory step towards the more important business of training and opening the mind through meditation.

Hence the doctrines of Neo-Confucianism fulfilled a genuine need, and filled it at the same time in a way very acceptable to the Tokugawa authorities. The underlying philosophy of Chu Hsi's teaching that the universe was naturally and essentially hierarchical, and that in consequence human society was similarly vertical, with all men naturally unequal, was a suitable creed for maintaining the existing relations between rulers and ruled, with the Tokugawa rulers securely in power.

The religious and intellectual situation during the 18th and early 19th centuries was further complicated by a movement which became known as *fukko-Shintō*, the revival of Shinto. For centuries the cult we described as 'early Shinto' had been virtually neglected by educated people. The early chronicles, poems and rituals which transmitted the cult were no longer legible or comprehensible to scholars. The cult had become unrecognisably mingled with Buddhist elements, in forms such as Ryōbu-Shintō and Ichijitsu-Shintō which had grown up since medieval times. The Shinto Revival of the 18th century was an attempt by scholars to rediscover the Shinto cult in all its ancient purity, stripped of the foreign accretions which had debased and distorted it. At the same time they developed two powerful myths. The first was of a Japanese golden age in the past; a state of simple innocent perfection and bliss which, they averred, had been the Japanese 'state of nature' before the corruption and innate viciousness of Chinese ideas had caused a 'fall' from these idyllic conditions. The second myth was that the message of the ancient myths pointed towards the unique superiority of the Japanese race over all other peoples of the world. The special act of divine creation which had gone to produce Japan, the direct descent of the Emperor from Amaterasu the Sun Goddess, all proved that the Japanese were qualitatively different from other races and peoples, and hence ineluctably destined to rule the world.

These compelling doctrines were advanced mainly by three notable scholars, Kamo Mabuchi (1697-1769), Motoori Norinaga (1730-1801) and Hirata Atsutane (1776-1843). All produced monumental works of exegesis of the ancient texts. The Kojiki, which had long lain in a limbo of neglect and incomprehension, was resuscitated by Motoori, the poems of the Manyōshu by Mabuchi, while it fell to Hirata to emphasise and extend the two myths underlying the movement in a manner which was years later to yield momentous and terrifying consequences.

By the mid 19th century the creed which functioned most powerfully as a 'religion' in Japan was the combination of Confucian ethical teachings with Shinto myth known as Mitogaku. It was these doctrines, which were not the loose amalgam that might be supposed but an organic whole with explosive power, which became the creed underlying the movement to abolish the feudal system, overthrow the Shogun and restore the Emperor to the pristine and numinous power which they mistakenly imagined he had enjoyed in ancient times.

The policy of the Meiji government in the early 1870s was therefore to foster a spirit of national identity centring on the Emperor. To this end they set about a drastic scheme for 'separating' Shinto from Buddhism (*shimbutsu-bunri*), and persecuting Buddhism as a foreign and undesirably other-worldly creed. Until this time the two religions had been amicably and viably combined for the great majority of Japanese in what was known as *shimbutsu-konkō*, union of gods and Buddha. At no time since the first introduction of Buddhism had there been hostility with the native cult beyond minor political skirmishes of a local and temporary kind. Various formal theologies were propounded during the early middle ages whereby this union was defined. But by and large the Shinto *kami* settled down in the comfortable position of local guardians of the Buddhist cult, or as temporary manifestations (*gongen*) of Buddhist deities. Thus until 1870 every Buddhist temple always contained one or more Shinto shrines, and in the minds of many the two supernatural orders were only vaguely distinguished.

The policy of the Meiji government ended this amicable harmony. Buddhist temples were forcibly converted into Shinto shrines, and monks and nuns compelled to return to lay life. In many places the persecution of Buddhism (*haibutsu-kishaku*) was severe, and the destruction of temples and humiliation of priests wanton and deplorable. Even though the first fury of the persecution soon died down, Buddhism remained under certain restrictions which grew increasingly severe as the nationalist fever mounted. It is interesting to note, however, that it was always valued for the part it played in promoting the repose of the dead.

Severe restrictions on religious liberty, particularly the liberty to form new religious groups and movements, lasted until 1945. In that year General MacArthur promulgated the *Shūkyō Hōjinrei* or Religious Bodies Law, which granted complete freedom to the Japanese to form or join what religious groups they pleased. The result was an extraordinary upsurge of new groups and cults, which increased year by year in so spectacular a manner that by 1951 the number of officially registered groups had risen to 720. A good many of these were quickly discovered to be entirely fraudulent, being merely commercial enterprises exploiting the loose wording of the law of 1945 to pose as religious 'bodies' in order to avoid paying taxes. Further legislation in 1951 weeded out these bogus concerns, and the latest available figures, from the Year Book of 1964, is the comparatively modest one of 378-145 Shinto groups, 165 Buddhist, 39 Christian and 29 'others'. This fourfold classification imposed by the Ministry of Education is not always helpful, sometimes positively misleading. Few of the Buddhist groups, for example, could be easily recognisable as such. The new movements can more usefully be considered to be a reaction of Japanese society to the state of acute crisis into which it was thrown by the defeat, occupation by a foreign power and the collapse of the reputedly invincible cult of State Shinto.

The wealthier and more successful groups are markedly messianic, promising to the faithful not only a rain of divine favours here and now, but a fairly imminent shift to a terrestrial paradise in the future. The message is proclaimed by the powerful figures of the Founders and Foundresses who claim unique divine revelation. These charismatic personages, of which Mrs Kitamura Sayo, the Foundress of the Dancing Religion, is a good example, are by no means new to the Japanese religious scene. Their counterparts can be traced back to the 8th and 9th centuries, and have continued to appear during the intervening years, particularly in periods of crisis. Indeed, many of the prominent characteristics of these groups—the divinely inspired Founder, the stress on miraculous worldly favours—can be found persistently appearing in emergent movements throughout Japanese history. New, of course, are the modern methods of propaganda and organisation employed by the movements, which combine in a curious way patterns of belief of great antiquity with vast concrete cathedrals of startling modern design, missionary tours to California, networks of closed circuit television and huge rallies reminiscent of an American football match. Most of the cults are tolerant and innocuous, providing comfort, fellowship and hope in otherwise wretched and humdrum lives. Only the now notorious Sōka Gakkai, with its intolerance, its militancy, its ruthlessly threatening propaganda and its obscure political ambitions, strikes an increasingly fanatical and sinister note.

The new cults are therefore a remarkable feature of the postwar religious scene in Japan, their constantly increasing wealth and swelling ranks of believers appearing in marked contrast to the depleted registers and dilapidated structures of many temples of the older Buddhist sects.

III. Conception of Deity

A. *Shinto*

We have already briefly described the 'deities' of early Shinto as the shadowy spiritual forces known as *kami*. The word is a particularly difficult one to define adequately in English, and even among Japanese scholars there is still much variety of interpretation. There seems to be general agreement, however, that in the early cult they were conceived to be spiritual forces, superior to man in both knowledge and power, dwelling in a realm of their own which was higher than the human world. In what we have described as the 'literary' cult of Shinto this high place was believed to be a region called Takamagahara, the High Plain of Heaven, presumably identified with the sky. In other versions of the ancient cult the high place was the local mountain, conceived to be in itself the Other World and probably at this early period a realm forbidden and inviolate to human beings.

The *kami* could however at stated seasons be cajoled to leave their own world and visit that of man. Having no specific shape of their own they could only manifest themselves if 'called down' into some object of an appropriately inviting shape. These vehicles for the *kami* were called *yorishiro*. There seem to have been an interesting variety of objects used for this purpose, most of which were of a tall, thin shape a little reminiscent of a lightning conductor.

We may mention a few examples of these vehicles in view of their importance in the later development of the cult. First, natural objects such as trees and stones were frequently used. That trees, particularly pine trees, were a favorite vehicle of the *kami* is attested even today by their invariable presence round a Shinto shrine, and the survival of a number of place names associating trees closely with a numinous presence. Stones used as *yorishiro* seem to have been usually of a long and thin shape, though very huge rocks or rocks with a suggestively sexual shape were also used. Certain mountains and volcanic islands were also believed to be *yorishiro*, their conical or thickly tree covered shape being considered suitable for inviting the descent of the *kami*.

Other *yorishiro* of later date are found in various artefacts. Flags, pillars and emblems of the usual long, thin shape were common, while the earliest dolls and puppets were used not for decoration or amusement, but for this sacred purpose of a temporary lodging for the *kami*. Other artefacts were the mirrors, swords and the mysterious curved jewel called *magatama*, found in such profusion in the great tombs of the 3rd and 4th centuries and clearly invested with magic power.

The most interesting category of *yorishiro* is that of human beings. Here we find the earliest evidence of what can be called shamanism in Japan. It differs however from its Siberian counterpart in so far as the role of the 'visitor to the other world' is reversed. Among the Siberian tribes it is the shaman whose soul leaves his body and travels to the other world of spirits. In Japan it is the deity or spirit who is persuaded to leave his realm and visit the human world. In both cases, however, the objective is the same—to obtain from the superior spiritual beings knowledge of a kind inaccessible to man, which will prove of direct benefit to the community. Knowledge of the coming harvest, for example, of the rains, and of the pests and epidemics which in the hidden future threaten the livelihood of the village.

The earliest shamans in Japan were called *miko*. They seem to have been predominantly women, and to have played a part both in the literary aristocratic Shinto cult, as well as in the more remote versions practised in villages. In some cases the reigning queen herself seems to have acted as a *miko* in order to seek an oracular answer to a question. In a later section we shall see how the *takusen-matsuri*, or ritual wherein a *kami* is invited to possess a medium in order to answer questions, was a widespread cult in ancient times.

There seems to have been little conception of individuality in the *kami*. Incalculable numbers of them were believed to dwell in the high realm, but apart from their qualities of superior power and knowledge they were endowed with few distinctively personal characteristics. The *kami* in the myths are given names, it is true, but they are blurred and shadowy beings nevertheless. The *kami* worshipped in remoter districts are thought not even to have had names; they were simply the local tutelary deity.

At this early period they were not thought to prolong their visit to the human world for longer than the duration of the ritual of 'calling down'. Indeed, an essential part of the early rituals was that of sending the deity away after he had received the offerings and transmitted the oracular answers to questions.

An important stage in the development of the cult was therefore that by which the *kami* came to be thought to reside for the greater part of the year in fixed shrines constructed in suitable places for their convenience. Instead of the temporary *yorishiro*, a more permanent dwelling place known as a *shintai* or 'god body' came into prominence. It is with this development that we are first confronted with the bewildering problem of proliferating categories of *kami*. *Kami* are found in natural objects, in the potent shapes of phallicism, in certain human beings, in ancestors. Hence attempts by earlier scholars to give a neat overall description of Shinto such as nature worship or ancestor worship were all doomed to at least acrimonious controversy.

Let us look briefly at a few of the apparently disparate categories of beings subsumed under the name of *kami*, and see how they have developed from the earlier stage we examined above.

In the first place we have *kami* which are obviously manifestations of the incomprehensible forces of nature. A tree which is particularly huge or old, or twisted into an odd or mysterious shape, is thought to enshrine a *kami*. Stones of an odd, huge or phallic shape are thought to be the dwelling places of *kami*. In the early myths the majority of *kami* come under this heading. The Sun Goddess Amaterasu Omikami was described as the supreme Ruler of Heaven, paramount in dignity. The unruly deity Susanoo is thought to represent the storm, though as we shall see in a later section he belongs to a different mythical cycle from that centring on the Yamato plain, and hence in all likelihood to a different people. Tsukiyomi no Mikoto was the moon god, while deities are mentioned of the harvest, rice, fire, water, wind and grass. Occasionally, as in the case of Amaterasu and Susanoo, the deity is given faint beginnings of a personality. But in most cases, as we have indicated, the nature *kami* remain a depersonalised hierophany. These mysterious forces and shapes of nature were thought to manifest something 'other', a reality belonging to a world different from the human. Hence the *kami*, originally thought to descend only momentarily into certain ritual objects, were now thought to 'show through' the object in which they constantly inhered. Because they thus showed through, the object itself was recognised to be mysterious and awesome.

Another prominent category of *kami* is that concerned with fertility and growth. The *sae-no-kami* or phallic deities represent not only procreative power, but also vigorous animal life, the vitality that can triumph over death and disease. Hence they are used, as their name implies, as 'preventions' of the forces which threaten life, as magical prophylactics. The *sae-no-kami* are hence often found in traditionally dangerous spots such as crossroads and bridgeheads.

Certain superior men are also conceived to be *kami*. This can happen either while they are still alive or after they are dead. The Emperor, for example, with all the numinous charisma of his office, is a *kami* during his lifetime. So are certain others who prove their superiority to ordinary men by heroic abstentions, charity or creative power. Others whose fame lives after them may become *kami* after their death. Indeed, a large category of *kami* is that of deified ancestors or founders of new communities.

This brings us to the vexed question of the relation of the *kami* to dead spirits. Here there is every evidence of wide variation due to mixed origin. In the myths of the Kojiki there would seem to be a strict separation between the two. The *kami* dwelt in the upper realm, dead spirits went to the lower, and the attempt of the god Izanagi to visit his dead wife in the lower realm was in every way disastrous. Elsewhere, however, particularly in the districts where the dead are believed to go to certain mountains, there seems to be a curious intermingling of the two categories of supernatural being. The introduction of Buddhism obscured the issue still further. For now some people were believed to become *hotoke* or Buddhas after their death, and the line drawn between those who became *hotoke* and those who became *kami* was a very indistinct one. Always, however, it is necessary for the surviving descendants to perform the correct obsequies and requiem prayers. Without this help from the living, the dead spirits can be expected to join the terrifying and malignant ranks of unquiet ghosts, ever ready to molest the living out of envy for their continuing vitality. With the correct requiems however, potentially evil ghosts can be converted into a benign source of protection. Even today in many rural districts one hears stories of evil entities, notably foxes, neglected ancestors and the vaguely malevolent beings known as *sawari*, which can, through correct exorcism and requiem prayers be transmuted into a *kami* of a benevolently protective kind.

Of the dislike which all *kami* have for the 'pollutions' of death and blood, and of the curses with which they will blast men when offended by these impurities, we have already spoken in a previous section.

Throughout the various categories of *kami*, disparate though they may at first appear, we can find a basic common character. The *kami* is a superior spiritual force which firstly can control those movements of nature—the succession of seasons, the growth of crops, the timely onset of the rains, the vanquishing of pestilence—which are beyond the control and understanding of man. Secondly, they have knowledge of the things of the future hidden from man. Hence they can be invoked for protection from disaster, for specific favours, for specific information. And they dwell for most of the year in certain objects and places which *show* by their numinous shape or their mysterious and awesome associations that they are the vehicle for a power from another world.

B. *Buddhist*

Each sect among the many which comprise Japanese Buddhism worships its own particular form of the Buddha and his attendant pantheon. But before we briefly describe the most important a few general remarks are necessary. It should always be borne in mind that in all levels of Japanese society save the most spiritual and the most sophisticated, the distinction between *kami* and *hotoke*, Buddhas, is a blurred one. The Buddha and his surrounding Bodhisattvas are invested with the same qualities that were originally ascribed to the *kami*. Contrary to the original teaching of the Buddha, they are transmuted into external magical bestowers of worldly goods or useful worldly knowledge. The Mahayana figure of the Bodhisattva has for this reason become particularly popular in Japan, images of those most celebrated for their 'efficacy' and compassion, Kannon and Jizō for example, being found scattered all over the country regardless of divisions of sect.

The distance between the conception of the Buddha as the illuminated wisdom within oneself which when awakened will reveal the vanity of worldly goods and the emptiness of form, and that of the magical dispenser of an ever increasing store of this world's goods, seems at first sight a wide one. No understanding of Japanese Buddhism is complete which does not comprehend both.

Shingon

The two sects of esoteric Buddhism which made their appearance in Japan during the 9th century inherit the large pantheon of deities so characteristic of the Tantric Buddhist schools in China. In Shingon, however, iconography is more prominent than in Tendai. At the centre is the Buddha Vairocana, rendered in Japanese as Dainichi Nyorai. Dainichi is conceived as the *dharmakaya*; the whole universe is in its essential nature a manifestation of this Buddha, who is present in every part of the cosmos. Hence we are also, in our essential nature, Buddha, and our supreme task in life is to realise this Buddha in ourselves, to become a Buddha in this very body' (*sokushin-jōbutsu*). This we can do, as recounted in a previous section, by a process of ritual imitation of the actions, words and thoughts of the Buddha.

Prominent also in the esoteric pantheon are the Four Dhyāni Buddhas found in all schools of Tantric Buddhism. Round Vairocana in the centre are Akṣobhya (Ashuku) in the east, Ratnasambhava (Hōshō) in the south, Amitābha (Amida) in the west and Amoghasiddhi (Fukūjōju) in the north. The rest of the large pantheon are ultimately 'emanations' of Vairocana. The popular class of deities known as the Five Myōō, for example, are fundamentally 'wheel bodies' of the Buddha, their fearful appearance being designed to destroy passion and delusion. Of these five the most celebrated is Fudō Myōō, whose cult is widespread throughout Japan. In black, blue or red form he is revered as an efficacious bestower of worldly boons. The gentler class of Bodhisattvas too are prominently worshipped in the Shingon sect, notably the various forms of Kannon or Avalokiteśvara—Eleven-faced Kannon, Thousand-handed Kannon and Horse-headed Kannon. In Shingon temples can also be found a number of Hindu deities imported into Tantric Buddhism, while a further proliferation is to be found in the two mandalas, the Kongōkai or Diamond-world and the Taizōkai or Womb- world mandalas, used in the sect for purposes of initiation.

a) Jōdo and Shin

Both these sects naturally reserve their foremost homage for the Buddha Amida. Amida, in his Indian form Amitābha or Amitāyus, the Lord of Measureless Light or Life, we have already seen figuring in the Tantric pantheon as the Dhyāni Buddha of the west. The Jōdo and Shin sects have singled him out for special worship as the saviour who will rescue us from the horrors of repeated incarnation into various realms of the suffering world, and by leading us after our death straight to his Pure Land in the west will enable us in idyllic conditions to attain ultimate nirvana. Both sects rely for their doctrine on the three Amidist sutras. The Muryōjukyō or Greater Sukhāvatīvyūha Sutra describes how Amida in a former incarnation countless ages ago as a monk called Dharmakara, made a series of vows that he would become a Buddha on condition that he should be able to help all other sentient beings to enlightenment. The Amidakyō or Lesser Sukhāvatīvyūha Sutra stresses the principle of salvation by faith in Amida's mercy alone, not by any effort of one's own. The Kammuryōjukyō or Amitāyurdhyāna Sutra is largely concerned with descriptions of the delights of Amida's paradise. Also with meditations on Amida which are ignored by Jōdo and Shin practice in favour of repetition of the *nembutsu* with 'a sincere heart, a deep believing heart and a longing heart'. Only thus, the Founders averred, could one be sure of rebirth in the Pure Land.

b) Zen

The central activity of the Zen disciple being zazen, sitting in meditation in order to awaken the Buddha nature within oneself, worship of the Buddha as a deity or saviour is less stressed than in other sects. In temples of the Rinzai sect Buddha images are few, though the *zendō* or meditation hall always enshrines a figure of Monju or Manjuśri, the Bodhisattva representing enlightened wisdom. It is the Buddha within ourselves that we must discover and awaken, and this is to be done less by contemplating the image and outward representation of the Buddha than by looking into our own minds.

c) Nichiren

The 'deity' for the sects deriving from the teachings of Nichiren is in fact a sutra. The Lotus Sutra or Hokekyō, is held to be the expression of supreme truth, the worship of which will bring not only a rain of worldly blessings, but for those who care for it, ultimate enlightenment. Veneration for the Lotus Sutra began in the Tendai sect, where as we have seen it stood for the crown and quintessence of the Buddha's teaching. The eleven years that Nichiren spent on Mt Hiei convinced him that this scripture was indeed all that it declared itself to be—and Watanabe Shōkō has pointed out that the Lotus excells in exaggerated praise of itself. Worship of the sutra would ensure not only personal salvation, but deliverance from almost all mundane evils as well. This sutra was indeed the *only* proper object of worship, so that failure to give it due reverance would result in both loss of salvation and in innumerable worldly calamities, among which invasion by a foreign foe like the Mongols was prominent. Hence Nichiren's vehement intolerance of all other sects of Buddhism, succinctly expressed in his quatrain: Nembutsu leads to the lowest hell; Zen disciples are devils; Shingon brings the ruin of the country; Ritsu are traitors and assassins.

In a secondary manner the Nichiren sects also reverence the various deities mentioned in the Lotus Sutra. The Bodhisattva Kannon, for example, is described in the famous chapter *Kanzeon Bosatsu Fumonbon* as promising to deliver all mankind from every conceivable disaster —fire, water, demons, passions, dragons, pestilence and thunder. This passage is widely used as an efficacious protective spell, and worship is duly accorded to Kannon.

It is an odd paradox that the Lotus, whose message is fundamentally the catholic one of universal salvation, should in Japan have given rise to the most narrowly and militantly intolerant of all the sects of Buddhism.

IV. Worship

A. *Cult—Shinto*

From the description of the nature of the *kami* in the previous section it is clear that two types of ceremonial observance must be necessary for their worship. First, they are beings superior in power in knowledge to men, who dwell in another world or plane, but who can be summoned at due seasons to the human world and cajoled by correct treatment into giving the community the benefit of their powers. Second, they are easily offended by various pollutions, which no man in the ordinary course of living can avoid.

From these premises we should expect to find prominent in their cult (i) rituals for summoning the *kami* from their own world and sending them back at the close of the ceremony, together with rituals for placating them during their visit and requesting them for favours. And (ii) rituals for purifying people of the pollutions they wittingly or unwittingly acquire. These two basic rites can be said to cover the essentials of the cult of early Shinto.

The rites in the first category are broadly called *matsuri*, a term which means basically 'to worship'. The *matsuri* is the most widespread and colourful of the Shinto rituals, being found in infinite variety throughout the length and breadth of Japan. Basically however its structure consists of the following stages. First the officiating priest, purified in a manner we will later describe, recites the appropriate invocations summoning the *kami* down into the *yorishiro*, nowadays often a ceremonial wand bedecked with streamers of cut white paper, which has been prepared within the sacred enclosure. This enclosure is cordoned off by the particular rope (*shimenawa*) which in Shinto marks the boundary between sacred and profane space. Once the *kami* has descended he is presented with suitable placatory offerings. These always include food and drink of various kinds—rice, seaweed and certain fish together with *sake* or rice-wine. In early times certain rites required more elaborate offerings among which various kinds of cloth, swords, spears and horses were prominent. Food and drink were always essential, since in ancient times the *matsuri* usually included a communion meal, in which worshippers partook of food with their god. The offerings may also include music and dancing, many *matsuri* being uniquely distinguished by their traditional dances and tunes.

In the early cult the next stage of the rite usually took the form of inducing the *kami* to grant oracular answers (*takusen*) to questions concerning the future welfare of the community. The oracle was frequently obtained through a *miko* or female medium, who in a state of divine possession delivered the god's answers about the future harvest, monsoon rains, summer epidemics and seasonal pests. Today these *takusen-matsuri* have become regrettably rare, surviving in only some half dozen remote villages. But there is every possibility that in the early form of the cult this use of the shamanic medium was a widespread method of divining the future and the will of the *kami*. Other forms of divination were also practised, however, some of which survive today in the form of contests (*kyōgi*). In many *matsuri* the highlight is a wrestling match, a tug-of-war, a horse race or a contest with swords or bows and arrows. The origin of these contests is believed to be not merely the diversion and entertainment of the *kami*, but also the divination of his will by the outcome of the contest.

Another important stage of many *matsuri* is the *miyuki*, wherein the *kami* is transported in an ornamental palanquin round the village by shouting young men dressed in *matsuri* clothes. The journey of the palanquin, which often includes a short sea voyage, is marked by wild and erratic plunges, a survival of the time when the whole community was virtually in a state of ecstatic possession.

Petitionary prayers are always a feature of the *matsuri*—the god is implored to arrange the unknowable future in a manner satisfactory to the village—after which the officiating priest recites the final valedictory spell which 'sends the *kami* back' to his usual abode.

The rites surrounding this ceremonial visit of the *kami* to the human world have developed into some of the most distinctive and beautiful of the Japanese arts and skills. Many forms of dance and drama which today seem completely secular originated in the dances of the *miko* to induce a divine possession, or in the magical 'imitations' to obtain good fishing catches and crops, or to frighten away demons of plague and calamity.

The second ritual essential to the Shinto cult is that of purification. We have seen how the *kami* are offended by various pollutions, many of which—death, sexual intercourse and birth, for example, arise unavoidably in the course of ordinary daily life. The need for purification therefore arises in two different ways.

First, a priest who is to officiate at a *matsuri*, summoning and welcoming a *kami*, must take special precautions to ensure that he is thoroughly cleansed of all pollution. For a stated number of days before the *matsuri* he must undergo what is known as *imi*, 'avoidance of pollution'. This used to involve isolation in a particular part of the house, where he cooked his own meagre food on a separate fire. Nowadays however the restrictions are confined to mere abstinence from meat and strong smelling vegetables. Further purification may be obtained by means of the lustration known as *mizugori*, standing under a waterfall or tipping buckets of cold water over oneself for a stated period.

Imi is also required by those who have actually been in contact with one of the sources of pollution, death or blood, and who are therefore more impure than the rest of the community—unlike the priest who seeks merely to become more pure for the purposes of the rite. The taboos customary after contact with death and blood naturally differ widely throughout the country, but without exception they have become far less exacting in modern times. In most sections of the urban communities such customs have almost disappeared. Only in some remote islands and villages are they strictly observed, the community believing that ritually unclean persons will be blasted by severe curses should they approach a shrine.

These taboos include, as in the cases of the priest, isolation and lustration. The performance of certain rituals for removing impurity is also necessary, however, and of these the oldest known is the Ōharai or Great Purification, which as we have seen numbers among the 23 ancient Shinto rituals preserved in the Engishiki. It is designed to cleanse the whole population, high and low alike, of the pollutions which they may knowingly or unknowingly have acquired. The text of the ritual is of particular interest in the detailed list it gives of the Heavenly and Earthly Offences, mentioned in a previous section, which it prays may be purged "as wind blows away clouds and mist, as dense bushes are cleared by a sickle."

Other important rituals preserved in the Engishiki include several prominently concerned with fertility and food. The Niiname or tasting of the First Fruits, and the Daijōe or ceremony of First Fruits on the accession of the Emperor are examples.

By and large therefore, we can say that the cult of Shinto is chiefly concerned with summoning and petitioning the *kami* for favours, among which fertility and the foreknowledge of it figure largely, and with placating the *kami* by avoiding the physical impurities which offend them.

B. *Myth*

The myths recorded in the Kojiki and Nihon Shoki are believed to be the result of a long tradition of oral transmission by the guild of *kataribe* or reciters, who memorised the words originally uttered by priestesses in a state of divine possession, wherein the gods explain their own origin and that of the country and the people. Clearly however the myths are not of homogeneous origin. They comprise in the first place two cycles of obviously different derivation together with other minor themes to which scholars have assigned parallels among south east Asian Melanesian, Altaic or Austroasian peoples.

In the space available it is not possible to give a detailed analysis of the structure of the myths, as has been done by Japanese scholars such as Matsumoto Nobuhiro, Higo Kazuo or Ōbayashi Taryō. We can attempt only a brief outline of the different groups into which the myths tend to fall, and a broad indication of the dominant themes and categories.

1) Cosmogonic myths of a confused kind start both chronicles. The Kojiki tells us simply that three *kami* appeared in the High Plain of Heaven when Heaven and Earth began. They and the succeeding six generations of *kami*, all with immensely long names, quickly fade into oblivion. The Nihon Shoki, after a description of obviously Chinese inspiration of inchoate chaos becoming separated into heaven and

earth, declares that the first deity came into being from a thing like a reed. The Kojiki version is thought to be of south east Asian origin, the Nihon Shoki one to derive the part of central Asia whence came the Imperial clan.

2) The creation of the Japanese islands, with their mountains, rivers and trees, and of myriads more *kami* is attributed in both Chronicles to the two deities of the 7th generation after the beginning, Izanagi and Izanami. These deities were both brother and sister and husband and wife. By means of a jewelled spear stirring the ocean they created the islands—a theme which has southern parallels. Next they created Amaterasu the Sun Goddess, later to become the paramount deity in the pantheon, and the moon god. These were both sent up to the High Plain of Heaven. They then produced the turbulent deity Susanoo, who behaved with such violence that he was banished to the underworld. Izanami then gave birth to the Fire god, who burnt her so that she died and descended herself to the gloomy underworld known as Yomi. Izanagi followed her to try to bring her back, but recoiled on finding her putrefying amid maggots with eight kinds of thunder gods seated upon her. He escaped safely from his underworld pursuers, and purified himself in a stream, creating more deities in the process.

3) There follows an account of the struggle between the Sun Goddess Amaterasu and her brother Susanoo. The latter behaved so outrageously, committing all the crimes which in the Ōharai ritual are stated to be sources of pollution, that the Sun Goddess hid herself in a cave and the world was plunged into darkness. She was finally persuaded to emerge by the inspired dance and utterance of the goddess Amenouzumenomikoto. Susanoo was fined heavily for his crimes and once more banished to the underworld.

4) The so-called Izumo myths follow, with a number of incidents connected with the deity Susanoo and his progeny. The Kojiki relates that he begged food from the Food Goddess, who offered him various delicacies produced from different parts of her body. This offended Susanoo, who promptly killed the Food Goddess. He then proceeded to the Izumo area, where he rescued a maiden about to be devoured by an eight headed serpent. A miraculous sword was discovered in the tail of the serpent, which has since become one of the Imperial regalia and which some authorities consider indicates the advent of an iron culture.

5) The protagonist in the next group is one of the sons of Susanoo,

Ōkuninushi also known as Ōnamochi. He succoured a suffering hare, and was consequently given a princess in marriage. The jealous schemes of his eighty brothers to destroy him were all foiled. In an eerie sequence he then joins his father Susanoo in the underworld, where he is subjected to a number of ordeals, in a snake chamber and in a centipede chamber. All of these he successfully surmounts an escapes safely out of the underworld.

Aided by a dwarf called Sukunabikona, clothed in feathers and coming in a boat from the Otherworld of Tokoyo, he then assumes authority over the land of Izumo.

6) Two deities were then despatched from Heaven to request Ōkuninishi to deliver up his domain of Izumo to the Grandson of the Sun Goddess, Ninigi-no-mikoto. Ōkuninushi at first refused, but eventually consented to allow Ninigi to rule public matters provided he continued to direct divine affairs.

7) The Hyūga myth, as it is called, describes how Ninigi descended, "cleaving his way through the eight-piled clouds with an awful way-cleaving," on to a mountain in Hyūga in Kyūshū. He was attended by five *kami* who later became the ancestors of the chief hereditary corporations in ancient Japan, and carried with him the Three Sacred Treasures, the mirror, sword and jewel given him by the Sun Goddess. These have since become the Imperial regalia of Japan. He married a lady called Konohanasakuyahime, rejecting her ugly but longer-lived sister, who in resentment cursed their progeny to short life.

8) Stories follow concerning the conflict between two sons of Ninigi, one a hunter and the other a fisher, and the visit of the latter to the sea god's daughter.

9) The last stage of the mythical narrative brings us to a dim outer boundary of historical fact. It describes the progress of the Emperor Jimmu, the great-grandson of Ninigi, from Kyūshū to the Yamato plain, beset by various enemies on the way and preceded by a three legged crow. Here we undoubtedly have "a legendary echo of a real movement of population from Kyūshū eastwards." At Kashiwabara in Yamato Jimmu became the first legendary Emperor of Japan, in the year 660 B.C. From this year, however fanciful, Japanese history is said to start.

No detailed analysis of the structure of these myths is possible here. Nor can we trace the many analogous themes by which Japanese scholars have sought to distinguish the various ethnic strands. We will simply draw attention to the most obvious division in the narrative—that which distinguishes the cult of the Sun Goddess, celebrated by the Imperial family on the Yamato plain, from that of Izumo, where the principal deities, Susanoo and Ōkuninushi, seem to have been connected with water and storm. Matsumoto Nobuhiro in particular has drawn attention to the peculiar structure of the Izumo myths, with their predominating components of thunder, water and serpents so distinct from the elements pertaining to the worship of the Sun Goddess. The mythical narrative points clearly towards the final subjugation of the Izumo cult by that of the Imperial clan, with the banishment of Susanoo to the underworld and the ceding by Ōkuninushi of all public authority to the grandson of the Sun Goddess.

We may repeat here that it was due entirely to the extraordinary work of the scholars of the Shinto revival in the 18th and early 19th centuries that these myths were rescued from the limbo of forgotten incomprehension in which they had lain for centuries. The ultimate result of these labours was, however, to invest the narratives with a numinous power which it is very unlikely that they ever possessed in the early times when they were chanted at banquets and ceremonies by members of the *kataribe*. They then became myths in a different sense. They were seen to embody truths of a timeless and archetypal kind: the golden age in the past, before the 'fall' from pristine perfection was brought about by vicious foreign creeds. And the corollary that the Japanese race was qualitatively different and superior to all others, and hence destined to rule the world. Today, we may add, the myths have entirely lost their charisma, and are subjected by a number of scholars to structural and comparative analysis which a generation ago would have been unthinkable. It is one of the paradoxes of the history of thought that the primitive and heterogeneous narratives which we have here outlined should have been partially instrumental in inspiring the totalitarian nationalism of the 1930s, with its disastrous and tragic consequences.

V. Short History of the Study of Religion

The objective study of religion in Japan dates only from the Meiji period. It was only in the 1880s that the first works appeared which could properly be said to treat the science or history of religion. Even then, despite the stimulus of contact with the discipline newly founded in the west under the auspices of Max Müller, Japanese scholars still laboured under peculiar difficulties. The disinterested investigation of the origins of Shinto, for example, was hampered during the Meiji period by the policy of the government of reinterpreting Shinto as a cult of national morality rather than as a religion, and of surrounding the resulting artefact of 'State Shinto' with a mystique which rendered objective study parlous. The case of Professor KUME KUNITAKE, dismissed from his chair at Tokyo Imperial University in 1893 for publishing an article arguing that Shinto was a survival of a primitive form of sun worship, illustrates the hazards to which Japanese historians of religion were subject.

On the science of religion as a whole, however, a number of pioneering studies appeared during the 1880s, notable among which were the works of ANEZAKI MASAHARU, KATŌ GENCHI and INOUE TETSUJIRŌ. In 1896 the Society for the Study of Comparative Religion (*Hikaku Shūkyō Kenkyūkai*) was founded through the initiative of ANEZAKI, and nine years later the discipline was given formal recognition by the establishment of a chair in the Science of Religion (*Shūkyōgaku*) at Tokyo Imperial University with ANEZAKI as its first occupant.

Buddhist studies too made a new beginning during the Meiji period, largely owing to contact with western scholarship in the Pali canon. As early as 1876 NANJŌ BUNYU, a priest of the Shin sect, travelled to Oxford to study Sanscrit under MAX MÜLLER, producing seven years later his celebrated *Catalogue of the Chinese Translations of the Buddhist Tripitaka*. Western scholarship in Theravada Buddhism, with its strict canons of linguistic discipline and its stress on the historicity of the Buddha, opened up an entirely new approach to Japanese Buddhologists. The work of ANEZAKI and of TAKAKUSU JUNJIRŌ, under whose auspices the monumental task of compiling the Taishō Tripitaka was later undertaken, were notable contributions to the study of primitive Buddhism on the new historical principles.

To the field of Mahayana scholarship too a number of distinguished names contributed among whom that of SUZUKI DAISETSU became during this century of world wide repute. His *Essays in Ẓen Buddhism*, published during the 1920s, were the first exposition in a western language of the principles and meditational disciplines of the Zen sect. It was only after the war, however, after 30 years of relative obscurity, that Dr SUZUKI's writings became truly instrumental in 'bringing Zen to the West', and indeed in touching off a new social movement there. His books on Mahayana doctrine in general and on the Lankavatara sutra have also become definitive.

Western work on Japanese religion started with two remarkable achievements, B. H. CHAMBERLAIN's translation of the *Kojiki* and W. G. ASTON's translation of the *Nihongi*, both basic texts of primitive Shinto. Both scholars were considerably helped by the exegetical work of the theologians of the Shinto Revival, whose tendentious interpretations of the ancient texts did not affect the value of their work of linguistic reconstruction and elucidation. The first systematic exposition of Shinto in a western language was ASTON's *Shinto, the Way of the Gods*, published in 1905 when arguments as to the 'origin of religion' were rife among western scholars. ASTON, while considering Shinto to be "perhaps the least developed of religions which have an adequate literary record," was careful to record his disagreement with HERBERT SPENCER as to its origin. The latter's sweeping reduction of all deities to the single origin of ancestor worship ASTON considered to be particularly invalid in the case of Shinto, whose *kami* could more meaningfully be traced back to 'nature worship.'

In western work on Japanese Buddhism, DE VISSER's *Ancient Buddhism in Japan* and SIR CHARLES ELIOT's *Japanese Buddhism* are outstanding studies of doctrine, philosophy and formal observance.

Studies of Japanese religion by western scholars have tended to follow certain fixed trends. First, they have invariably treated Shinto and Buddhism as two separate entities, making little attempt to discover a phenomenology which would treat Japanese religion, particularly its most characteristically syncretic manifestations, as an organic and coherent whole. Second, they have concentrated attention almost entirely on the literary aspects of Shinto and Buddhism. Studies of Buddhism have been concerned with doctrine and philosophy. Studies of Shinto have treated the myths and their interpretations and the formal organisation of recorded worship. The non-literary traditions of the folk religion have been almost entirely ignored.

The same tendencies were followed by Japanese scholars during the Meiji period. From about 1910 however, they were to some extent offset by the work of YANAGIDA KUNIO. This remarkable man was fired by a passionate conviction that it was in surviving practices both religious and secular handed down from ancient times by means other than the written word that knowledge of the ancient ways of the Japanese people could be discovered. The material which he collected and collated in the course of journeys all over Japan he published in an immense volume of writing stretching over a period of some forty years. This great work inaugurated a new approach to the study of religion in Japan, embodying as it did the assumptions that written records were not the only valid sources of investigation, and that the rigid separation of the 'great' from the 'little' tradition was no longer viable.

Since the war religious studies in Japan have advanced on all fronts. Among the scholars who have made outstanding contributions we can mention in this short space only a few. In the field of Buddhist studies the work of SUZUKI DAISETSU remained prominent until his death in 1966; also that of NAKAMURA HAJIME and TSUKAMOTO ZENRYŪ. In the philosophy and science of religion ISHIZU TERUJI has written important books, and on the subject of Japanese shamanism, mountain worship and Japanese religion as a whole the work of HORI ICHIRŌ is of the first importance; also that of the late KISHIMOTO HIDEO. HARADA TOSHIAKI and ISHIDA EICHIRO have also made valuable contributions to the study of Japanese folk religion, myth and symbol.

SELECT BIBLIOGRAPHY[1]

ANEZAKI MASAHARU, *A History of Japanese Religion.* London 1930, rep. Tokyo 1963.
——, *Japanese Mythology.* (Vol. 8 of *The Mythology of all Races.* ed. C. J. MacCullough). Boston 1928.
ASTON, W. G., *Shinto, the Way of the Gods.* London 1905.
BOXER, C. R., *The Christian Century in Japan.* London 1951.
CAREY, OTIS, *A History of Christianity in Japan.* New York 1909.
CHAMBERLAIN, B. H., *Kojiki, or Records of Ancient Matters.* (Supplement to Vol. 10 of *Transactions of the Asiatic Society of Japan,* 1882.)
COATES, H. H. and ISHIZUKA RYUGAKU, *Honen the Buddhist Saint,* Kyoto 1925.
DE BARY, W. T. et al., *Sources of the Japanese Tradition.* New York 1958.
DORSON, RICHARD, M., *Studies in Japanese Folklore.* Indiana 1963.
DUMOULIN, HEINRICH, *A History of Zen.* London 1964.
ELIOT, Sir CHARLES, *Japanese Buddhism.* London, 1935, rep. 1959.
FLORENZ, KARL, "Ancient Japanese Rituals", *Transactions of the Asiatic Society of Japan,* Vol. 27, 1899.
HOLTOM, D. C., "The Meaning of Kami," in three parts, *Monumenta Nipponica* Vols. 3 and 4, 1940 and 1941.
——, *Modern Japan and Shinto Nationalism.* London 1947.
——, *The National Faith of Japan. A Study in Modern Shinto.* London 1938.
HORI ICHIRÓ, "On the concept of the Hijiri." *Numen,* Vol. 5, 1958.
——, "Japanese Folk Beliefs." *American Anthropologist,* Vol. 61, No. 3, 1959.
KISHIMOTO HIDEO, ed., *Japanese Religion in the Meiji Era.* Tokyo 1956.

[1] Only references in European languages have been included in the bibliography.

KITAGAWA, J. M., "The Prehistoric Background of Japanese Religion," *History of Religions*, Vol. 2, No. 2, 1963.
— —, *Religion in Japanese History*. New York 1966.
MATSUMOTO NOBUHIRO, *Essai sur la Mythologie Japonaise*. Paris 1928.
MURAOKA TSUNETSUGU, *Studies in Shinto Thought*. Tokyo 1964.
NAKAMURA HAJIME, *The Ways of Thinking of Eastern Peoples*. Tokyo 1963.
OFFNER, C. B. and VAN STRAELEN, H., *Modern Japanese Religions*. Tokyo 1963.
REISCHAUER, E. O., *Ennin's Travels in T'ang China*. New York 1955.
Religious Studies in Japan. ed. by Japanese Association for Religious Studies. Tokyo 1959.
SANSOM, Sir GEORGE, *Japan, a Short Cultural History*. London 1946.
SATOW, E. M., "Ancient Japanese Rituals," *Transactions of the Asiatic Society of Japan*. Vol. 7, 1879. Part 4, 1881.
——, "The Revival of Pure Shintau." *Transactions of the Asiatic Society of Japan*, Vol. 3. 1875.
SAUNDERS, E. DALE, "Japanese Mythology," in *Mythologies of the Ancient World*, ed. Samuel Kramer, New York 1961.
SASAKI, RUTH FULLER, *The Zen Kōan*. Kyoto 1965.
SUZUKI, D. T., *Essays in Zen Buddhism*. Series 1-3. Rep. London 1950-3.
SCHURHAMMER, GEORG, *Shinto, the way of the Gods in Japan. According to the Printed and Unprinted Reports of Jesuit Missionaries in the Sixteenth and Seventeenth Centuries*. Bonn. 1923.
TAJIMA RYUJUN, *Les Deux grands mandalas et le doctrine de l'esoterisme Shingon*. Tokyo 1959.
THOMSON, HARRY, *The New Religions of Japan*. Tokyo 1963.
VISSER, M. W. DE, *Ancient Buddhism in Japan*. Leiden 1935.

RELIGIONS OF ILLITERATE PEOPLE

BY

E. G. PARRINDER

I. Short Description

Illiterate people are to be found in every country and all ages. Many members of some of the most important "higher" religions are illiterate, and cannot read the sacred texts of their faith. However, distinctions can be made between those religious traditions which have written texts and some recorded history, and those which have neither. The "higher" religions would then be those that have "scriptures" which embody the wisdom of past sages. The religions of illiterate peoples include the personal faith of individuals, but they have a continuity of tradition which is almost wholly oral.

Since such religions which depend on oral tradition are found in every continent outside Europe, there are great differences between the manifestations of religion in various places. The difficulties that are encountered in describing supposed entities such as Hinduism or Confucianism, are much greater in encompassing or analysing the faith of those who have no literature. Only the broadest generalizations can be made, and some of these may apply to literate religions as well.

The absence of literature has sometimes been taken to indicate that these religions are "primitive." But the art of writing is a rare and comparatively recent human acquisition; it has been invented only in a few places, though borrowed and adapted in many others. Lack of writing may be due not to primitiveness but to cultural isolation. The Aztecs, Incas and Mayas of America were illiterate through isolation, and so were Africans isolated by the Sahara desert and tropical forests, and aboriginal Australians cut off by the sea. Hill and forest tribes of Asia may have been secluded both by geography and by manmade barriers.

The religions of these illiterate peoples are not necessarily "primitive," in the sense that they have no complex culture. Nor are they primordial in the sense that they can give information about the nature of religion in its first appearances among mankind. It used to be assumed that illiterates were superstitious and uncritical in their thinking, and primitive in that they acted as men did in the childhood of the race. Modern research has changed this picture. All races of men have had a long history, even if it is unrecorded, and many developments have occurred down the ages. Even "higher" religions contain survivals or revivals of ancient customs, though these are modified in changing contexts. The description "primitive" is misleading and should be abandoned. The Nuer of the Sudan are a naked cattle-herding people, but their religious thought is remarkably subtle and complex. The Australian aboriginals are nomadic food-gatherers, but A. P. ELKIN holds that their philosophy and ceremonial life are in some ways no lower or less complicated than our own.

Other names have been coined or borrowed to describe the religions: Fetishism, Animism, Totemism, Mana, Taboo. Some of these will be referred to again under the history of the study. Animism is still a popular term, and is taken to mean that people consider each phenomenon of nature to be activated by a soul (anima); the sun, hills, trees, rivers, and so on, all having manikins or spirits living in them. Since this is clearly wrong, some writers conclude that religion is based on a delusion. If these animistic notions were primitive, and were the origins of religion, then all religion would be in error. But while some such beliefs may be held, there is more to the religions of illiterate peoples than animistic fantasies. If there is belief in one or more creating deities this faith cannot be dismissed as mere Animism, for God need not be located anywhere or regarded merely in an anthropomorphic manner. Then there are worldwide rituals connected with the dead, and these also cannot be described as Animism. It is better to use some neutral phrase, such as the "traditional religons" of illiterate peoples, and to seek more precision in detailed studies of particular tribes.

Only the broadest generalizations can be made about the religious beliefs of all illiterate peoples. That there are religious beliefs and practices is undoubted. Suggestions of a few early explorers that some remote peoples, in the state of nature, and presumably innocence, had no thoughts about the purpose of man and the universe, have been discarded. Sir SAMUEL BAKER, the African explorer, said in 1866 of the northern Nilotes: "Without any exception they are without belief in a Supreme Being, neither have they any form of worship or idolatry; nor is the darkness of their minds enlightened by even a ray of superstition." Modern scientific studies show this to be nonsense.

Religious beliefs are concerned with the universe and man, among both literates and illiterates. There are ideas of supernatural beings, and myths of creation and mankind. It seems natural to look up to the sky, and so some deities are celestial and transcendent. Sun, moon and stars are often, though not always, revered. The earth and its fertility are important, and often related to human fertility. Manifestations of the divine are believed to take place in many places and times. There are sacrifices, prayers, sacred shrines and holy persons. The spirits of the dead are related still to the living family. Religion is both personal and social, and is concerned with both belief and conduct.

In addition to such basic concepts and customs, there are many local variations. Even where there are comparable practices they may differ so much as to be virtually distinct phenomena. Totemism in Australia is very different from that of America. Detailed description of these religious phenomena must be sought under the separate headings where they are discussed.

II. Historical Development

Absence of religious literature means that not only are there no written texts which transmit the thoughts of one generation to another, but there is no history of the religion and its development. It need not be doubted that there have been outstanding thinkers, priests, prophets, and poets, in Africa, America and Australia. But they have disappeared with scarcely a trace, wasting their sweetness on the desert air. If they effected any changes in the direction of religious development, little or nothing is known of them. It seems that their thoughts have not usually been embodied in set texts or fixed rituals. This accounts, partly, for the apparent casualness of much religious observance where there are no prescribed liturgies or unchanging written prayers to recite.

Since there was no writing there are no religious autobiographies. There is nothing from the inside, to tell what it is like to belong to an illiterate religion, and what are the most vital beliefs and important customs. Reliance must be placed almost entirely on outside observation. There is, however, religious expression in tangible and lasting form in art, and to some degree in architecture. The wealth of sculpture in wood, clay, bronze and stone gives some clues to important elements of religious life. Plastic art, like music, is not easy to understand from the viewpoint of an alien tradition; but the grotesque masks, for example, used in many parts of the world in the impersonation of spirits, arouse feelings of awe and fear that are no doubt part of their intention.

Absence of written history means that changes in religious practice have not been recorded, and so it is vain to suppose that modern illiterate religion is certainly the same as religion was in its origins. Even modern changes are hard to assess. Whether there is more devotion, or less, in the amount of attention paid to ancestral rituals under modern conditions is largely a matter of conjecture. For there are few records of practice even as recently as the last century. Even today the incidence of practice and the variations in different localities remain largely unrecorded.

In the article "Present Religious Situation," Paragraph I, some attempt will nevertheless be made to compare the present religious situation with what is known of the recent past. All religions, like all human activities, are in a state of transition. Some new developments can be observed, alongside old continuing customs. This is particularly true of illiterate religions, for they have been subjected in the past two centuries to new or increasing pressures from the literate religions: Christianity or Islam, Hinduism or Buddhism.

One aspect of history that can be partly traced is the present knowledge of these illiterate religions. This is chiefly the product of European exploration of the world in modern times. It dates from the sixteenth century, but it is not very extensive or useful till the nineteenth century, or scientific till the twentieth century. The Portuguese navigators who sought a route to the Indies, and the Spaniards who sailed to America, and led the way for the rest of the world, were looking for gold or spices. They also hoped to make contacts with Prester John or Christian kings of India. They tried to make political and religious alliances, extend the realms of their monarchs, and spread the domains of the Pope. Their impact was military, occasionally missionary, but they were not interested in studying the religions of the lands they invaded or touched on.

The early missions were unsuccessful, or eventually died out, in most of the contacts with Asia and Africa. In America the Spanish priests finally recorded something of the ancient civilizations, but knowledge of the forest tribes or plainsmen had to wait till later, and still much of the religion of the tropical peoples of America is unknown. Traders occasionally picked up information or made superficial deductions. The Dutch trader BOSMAN in 1705 remarked that "almost all the [West African] Coast Negroes believe in one true God, to whom they attribute the creation of the world, and all things in it, though in a crude indigested manner, they not being able to form a just idea of a deity." Yet in 1887 Sir ARTHUR ELLIS thought that the Supreme Being of these same peoples was a "loan-god," introduced by the missionaries. Later he revised this opinion, but the idea remained current, and it had to await the investigations of R. S. RATTRAY on Ashanti in 1923 to put it finally out of court.

Serious study of the religions hardly began before the nineteenth century, and even then it was often so loaded with preconceived theory and inadequate observation as to be practically useless. The history of the study is largely a history of theory. It will be considered further in the article, Paragraph II.

Few of the theorists who wrote eloquently about "primitive religion" had been anywhere near a primitive people. They wove hypotheses without observing facts or conducting experiments. Their information came from stories sent by explorers, traders, missionaries, administrators, and finally anthropologists. The evidence taken from these sources was suspect in many ways. European travellers were on the look out for strange if not prodigious customs, and they made much of unusual dress or dance, often misunderstood. Globetrotters, journalists and photographers still do the same, looking for the colourful and exotic. Interpretation of religion was biased in favour of superstition. It was out of perspective, stressing the exceptional, casually observed, and overlooking the humdrum rites and affairs of everyday life. Even intelligent and highly trained observers, like Darwin or Livingstone, Caillié or Frobenius, were often careless in their remarks about religion.

Very few European travellers had any knowledge of the language of the people about whom they wrote with such confidence, as "knowing the native mind." They worked through interpreters, or interrupters. In the later nineteenth century missionaries and administrators began to settle down and learn the languages. They did a great work in putting many languages into writting and creating the rudiments of a literature. Today the spread of English, French, and other languages has tended to hinder this process. But even when the missionary spoke the language of his people, that did not necessarily give him much knowledge of their religion. He might not be interested in it, regarding it as an evil or outdated thing, to be destroyed or replaced by his own faith. Even if he was able and willing to talk about indigenous religion, the very words used might mean one thing to himself and another to his hearers. A missionary in Blantyre, MALAWI, said in 1882: "In all our translations of Scripture where we found the word God we used *Mulungu*, but this word is chiefly used by the natives as a general name for spirit. The spirit of a deceased man is called his Mulungu." This usage has affected interpretation of the religion ever since, but it illustrates cultural influence as much as indigenous idea.

After a great deal of superficial observation and writing, including snippets on religious customs along with descriptions of elephants and spiders, marriage and miasma, serious study began towards the end of the last century. Canon CALLAWAY wrote on the Zulu in 1870, Bishop CODRINGTON on the Melanesians in 1891, BOAS on the Kwakiutl Indians in 1894, and SPENCER and GILLEN on the Australian Arunta in 1899. These works have been made obsolete, or seriously modified, by later study. But in their day they provided correctives to some former theories and they gave material for further speculation. These theories are examined further in Paragraph VII. According to the present standard of the study of this subject the religions of the illiterate people of Africa, Asia, North America and Australia are treated separately in the chapters A, B, C and D.

A

AFRICA

BY

E. G. PARRINDER

I. Concepts of the Deity

The continent of Africa divides naturally at the Sahara desert, and the peoples of tropical and southern Africa are the subject of this section. Early travellers sometimes suggested that Africans had no religion, or if they found a clear belief in God this was said to come from Islam or Christianity. But a supreme God is named in a Bantu dictionary of 1650, and Bosman's observations in 1705 in West Africa have been mentioned. It is now generally agreed that most, if not all, African peoples have had a belief in a Supreme Being, though how active this belief is in cultus and daily life differs from place to place.

Exceptions may be found among the Bushmen and Pygmies, but very little is known about their religion. The Hottentots among the Bushmen have nearly all become Christians and information about their earlier beliefs depends upon scrappy notes left by the first travellers and missionaries. They believed in a personal spirit, Tsui'goab, whom some writers have called God and others an ancient hero. He was invoked as lord and rain-giver, and sacrifices were made to him.

The Pygmies of the Congo forests believe in a great spirit and have myths of creation and of heaven and earth. Some of these myths may derive from their negro neighbours. Schebesta says that the Mbuti Pygmies believe in God, called Tore, who created men and from whom fire came to mankind.

African negroes, Bantu and Sudanese, use many names for God. A common name in East Africa is Mulungu, which has been adopted in over thirty translations of the Bible. The etymology of Mulungu is not known, but the concept includes both a High God and an impersonal spirit. Mulungu is creator and ruler, but he is also omnipotent and omnipresent. His voice is heard in thunder and his power appears in lightning. He is just, rewarding the good and punishing the wicked.

Another African name for God is Leza, used from the northern Kalahari through the Congo to Tanzania. The name may derive from a verb "to cherish," and it designates the divine providence. Leza created everything, lives in heaven, and is called upon for rain, being manifested in thunder and lightning. He is called incomprehensible, but also "mother of all beasts."

A different divine name is Nyambe, found in western equatorial Africa, from Botswana to Cameroun, and used in many Bible translations. It may be related to a name Nyame, used for God in Ghana and the Ivory Coast. Its basic meaning seems to be power or creation, and God is both the almighty dweller in heaven and a mysterious power in all things.

West African peoples have many names for God, according to the language: Amma, Ngewo, Mawu, Olorun, Chukwu, all used of the Supreme Being. Sometimes the meaning is clear; Ol-orun of the Yoruba of Nigeria is "owner of heaven." But others are obscure, and both Mawu of Dahomey and Chukwu of the Nigerian Ibo are used of God and also of the soul in man, regarded as an emanation of the deity. In the complex mythology of the Dogon of the Upper Volta the God Amma created the universe and earth, and then united himself with the earth to produce a series of mortal twins.

Although there are widespread myths of the withdrawal of God from the world, after an original dwelling near to man, yet God is not a remote deity to many Africans. While sacrifices and cults directed to God alone are rare, yet in proverbs, riddles, and salutations the name of God is used daily by many people. God is the first cause but also the continuing providence. He is giver of morality and judge of human actions. God is spoken of personally, and often with a wife and family. Names and titles of God, which have been collected from many parts of the continent, show him first of all as moulder of men's bodies and giver of breath. Then his power is seen in nature, not only in creating the world in the past, but in the storms and seasons of today. Generally he is a God of comfort, both father and mother, the "one on whom men lean and do not fall." But he is also mysterious, the one beyond all thanks, the inexplicable, "the great pool contemporary with everything."

Placide Tempels has emphasized the importance of power, vital force, dynamism, in African philosophy. The world is the realm of powers, of different kinds, and the best life is the one that has the most power and harmony. Life and power are requested in prayers, maintained by good medicine, and threatened by evil magic and witchcraft. But there is a hierarchy of powers, and God is the greatest of all, the strong one, for he has life in himself, and every other power in the universe is derived from him. After God come other powers, spirits of nature and ancestors, and then come impersonal forces. Man tries to live at peace with all these forces and become strong with their help. But they all depend on the great God.

Although Africans believe in a supreme God, they also believe in other spiritual beings. The organization of worship of gods is most marked in West Africa, and in other places spirits may be feared but receive only occasional worship. Ancestors also are propitiated, but whether ancestral cults are "worship" is as debatable in Africa as it was in China. Both Christians and Muslims demand renunciation of the worship of other gods from their converts, but varieties of respect for the ancestors continue in the new religions.

It is remarkable that not much attention is given to the sun and moon in African belief and worship. The sun is always present in the tropics and there is no need to call it back from its decline in winter, as was done in ancient Europe and Japan. The Bushmen have myths about the moon, in which a message is sent to men concerning death, which is told in other negro myths about the supreme God. Some of the Pygmies say that the moon created the first man and taught the mysteries of procreation. The sun rules the heaven, and sometimes appears in a role like that of God, and negro myths tell of men going up to heaven to see either God or the sun. But these are unusual, and the sun plays little role in cultus.

God is sometimes spoken of as mother, and a writer in Ghana spoke of Father-Mother God. The Fon of Dahomey speak of God, Mawu, as the moon, mother, kindly and wise. Paired with her is Lisa, the sun, strong and harsh. From this pair came seven other twins; the gods of storm, earth, iron and water being the most important. But although there are temples of Lisa in central Dahomey, many Dahomeans know little of this deity and hold that Mawu is the sole supreme God.

The spirits of the storm are often the most important nature gods, because of the tropical tornadoes which bring the expected rains, but also cause damage with lightning and thunderbolts. The Yoruba of Nigeria believe in Shango, who is both a storm deity and the fourth ruler of their ancient kingdom. Having ruled tyrannically he retired to the forest and hanged himself, or ascended to heaven by a chain. Thunderbolts are his axes, and symbolical axes are carried by his followers. Rainbows are divine manifestations; sometimes they are symbols of celestial snakes, and there are fantasies of treasure to be found where the rainbow ends.

The spirit of the earth is important, and it may be that myths of God retiring from the world echo ancient beliefs of the separation of heaven and earth after the creation of mankind. The Ashanti of Ghana speak of Earth Thursday, because that day is sacred to mother earth. Although they have no temples for this deity, yet libations are poured out on the ground at planting, harvesting, and digging graves. For the Ibo of Nigeria the most important of all the spirits is Ala, the ruler of men, source of morals, and giver of harvests. She is a mother who sends fertility to crops and to men, and who takes the dead into her pocket or womb. Ala is often depicted in painting and sculpture as a mother with a child in her arms.

Earth spirits include those of hills and rocks, trees and forest. Great mountains, such as Mount Cameroun, Mount Kenya, Kilimanjaro, and many lesser hills, are thought to be the abodes of powerful spirits. There is often a simple stone altar or a sacred tree where offerings are placed, by occasional travellers or by regular priests. Hunters propitiate the forest spirits and are often weather prophets and rain-makers. The god of iron is important to hunters, soldiers and blacksmiths, and in these more peaceful days he is invoked by lorry drivers and cyclists.

Spirits of the water are revered by fishermen, and often by those who live far from the sea. There are myths of the sea invading the land, and in the sea mermen and mermaids are believed to dwell. Rivers have their presiding spirits; most of the Buganda rivers were said to have originated from divine or royal beings. All the great lakes have stories told about them of supernatural beings who live beneath their surface. Snakes are often connected with the waters, and the python cults of West Africa are found along the rivers and in the delta regions.

Other important gods are the intermediaries between heaven and earth, the oracles and guardian spirits. Methods of divination, to discover the past or prepare horoscopes for the future are very popular. One of the most complex systems, which has spread to other countries, is practised by the Yoruba and connected with a semi-divine being called Ifa, who founded the sacred town of Ilé-Ifé. But divination is found right across Africa, from Senegal to Malagasy, and one of the commonest methods is to cast strings of nuts to the ground and interpret the meaning of the concave and convex faces which appear uppermost. Divining bowls are used in many places, and some of those employed by the Venda of the Transvaal resemble stone bowls unearthed in the ruins of the stone cities of Zimbabwe in Rhodesia.

The many deities are sources of power, they may be beneficent or otherwise, but their help is sought by prayer and sacrifice and it is thought that even the most fierce, like lightning or smallpox, may turn away harmful actions from their worshippers. Many houses and villages have images or symbols of guardian spirits, which are usually dangerous forces whose attentions are turned against intruders and in favour of the householders.

II. Worship

1. *Cult*

Regular worship of the supreme God is not usual in Africa, but there are exceptions, such as the Ashanti of Ghana, the Gikuyu of Kenya, and the Shona of Rhodesia. All of these have places and people designated for the worship of God. The places of worship are small buildings, wayside altars, groves of trees, or mountain peaks. Simple gifts are made, on ordinary occasions, and prayers are offered for life and health. Priests or elders lead the devotions and represent the people.

Since belief in pantheons of gods is most prominent in West Africa, it is this region that has the most numerous temples. The storm god Shango has many shrines, small mud and wood buildings, since tropical Africa has hardly any ancient building in stone. The temples contain wood and clay images, brightly painted, of the storm and other gods. A central altar bears stones which are called thunderbolts, "God's axes," and it is smeared with oil, flour and blood.

The earth mother Ala has shrines in all parts of Ibo Nigeria and there are special houses, called Mbari, which are not temples but are built to the glory of Ala on the advice of priests or oracles. Mbari houses are constructed by designated men and women, who live together in chastity for weeks or months while the work is being done. They are filled with clay figures, of which the central one is always Ala, usually with a child in her lap. Many other figures depict divine, human and animal figures, all modes of life, sexual and political, natural and fantastic. Once the Mbari house is completed it is left and in a few years collapses, and new ones are made.

Many Africans pray regularly every day, standing or kneeling in front of the house shrine of the guardian spirit or other deities. A few beans, a little oil, water or alcohol, are put on the shrine or on a metal stand in front of it. Diviners cast their strings of nuts and place gifts at the symbols of the oracle, morning and evening, and when consulted by clients. In many families the senior or oldest person, man or woman, performs devotions on behalf of the family. Other people may watch, join in, or utter a few informal petitions.

Many of the West African temples are small, sometimes a tiny hut into which only a priest can enter by stooping, or place a gift on a small altar. Other people stand outside, and in such hot countries communal rituals are performed in the open air. In many places there are days sacred to the worship of one divinity or other but, as in Hinduism and Buddhism, there is no obligation on all the faithful to attend any regular worship. Only on great festivals are there large audiences who watch, or join in dances and chants.

Prayers are simple and not fixed. The supreme God may be first invoked, since it is not uncommonly held that all sacrifice is ultimately destined to him. Other spirits may be associated with him, the spirits of earth and sky, and particular tutelary gods. Petitions are made for the health of the nation, of the elders and family, for women to bear children, for the young to be preserved from sickness, for preservation from accidents in agriculture and at home, for safety in travel, for success in business or examinations, for general grace. In the absence of any written liturgy the words of the prayers may vary, but the sense is often the same. It is rare to find a magical conception that insists on literal repetition of a fixed prayer.

Sacrifice is made of various ingredients. The simplest are libations of water, milk or alcohol, which are poured out at a shrine, a grave, or on the ground as part of a larger sacrifice. Cereals are offered, as thanksgiving or to avert danger. In particular the offering of first-fruits is made to gods and ancestors, before any of the people taste of the newly gathered harvest. Blood sacrifices are made for important occasions, a fowl, goat, sheep or ox. Human sacrifices have never been widespread, and in the olden days they were nearly all made at the funerals of important people, to provide them with companions to the afterlife, and so they were not religious, or not intended to propitiate any deity.

Sacrifices are made in sickness, at childbirth, when a woman is barren to remove sin or ritual offence, at family ceremonies, and to honour or propitiate ancestors. A great sacrifice may be offered at regular intervals, an annual festival, or on special occasions of need, in drought or disease. Most sacrifices are preventive, to stop danger coming or to get rid of misfortune, by imploring the help of a spirit. Sacrifices are either individual or collective, to deal with dangers threatening a person or family, or on behalf of the whole community as in time of epidemic disease.

The sacraments are the festivals of family life, the *rites de passage*: birth, adolescence, marriage and funeral. They are mostly performed at home, and led by an elder of the family and not by a priest in a public building. When a child is conceived and born offerings are made to the ancestors by the parents, and a diviner may be consulted to discover which deity the child is to worship. In adolescence initiation ceremonies for boys and girls, often within "secret societies," are performed with the aim of introducing the youth into adult membership of the community and informing him of social duties and ancestral customs. There are not many specifically religious ceremonies for marriage, but at different stages offerings may be made to tutelary or ancestral spirits. At funerals offerings are made to the spirit of the dead person, and a final sacrifice may be performed to get rid of any contamination from death and bring mourning to an end.

The sacraments affirm communion with the ancestors. The officiants are the leaders of the family group or elderly persons. Priests are attached to temples of gods, and they are intermediaries who sacrifice on behalf of those who come to consult the deity. Diviners may also be priests, and they are often engaged in the fulltime service of the oracle whose will they interpret on behalf of individuals or communities. There are persons of prophetic character, such as rain-makers and other oracular figures who live close to nature and bring messages at times. The witch-doctors, who figure prominently in popular presentations of African customs, are respected and public figures, also connected with oracles and ordeals. They are not themselves witches, though they may be credited with supernatural powers, but their task is to cure those who have been bewitched and prevent the activities of people thought to be witches. Priests and witch-doctors may use the services of mediums, who in trance states declare the will of the spirits. Priests themselves may do this, but in some of the highly organized cults of West Africa the priests do not go into trances, but interpret and control the mediums who give messages at their orders.

Both religious cult and priestly persons are different from magic and its practitioners. The magician is also a recognized figure, who prepares protective or offensive charms, "medicines," for individuals and communities. He is distinct from the evil magician, or sorcerer, who works in secret at anti-social purposes and is feared.

2. *Ethics*

Ethical teachings are not codified, since there is no writing. Moral virtues and offences vary considerably from place to place, but they are always present. Those connected with marriage, in particular, are complex; with rules of affinity within which marriage is forbidden, prohibitions of incest and adultery, but general permission of polygamy outside the forbidden relationships.

The importance of God and the spirit world in general for human behaviour must be noted. Morality is not only convention, independent of God or the ancestors. Breach of customs and commands is regarded as sin, because there is a divine sanction against wrongdoers. A man who suffers is believed to have offended against God and propitiation must be made for his cure. This shows again that God is not merely a *Deus remotus*, having retired from the world after creation. He is indeed transcendent and fearful, but he is also near to men, knows all that they do, and punishes them for offences. So moral law has divine backing, and this is illustrated further by the belief that God is the judge of men after death and rewards or punishes them according to their deeds. Sin means both deliberate wrongdoing and also breach of a taboo, either knowingly or unknowingly. In either case it is an offence against God. A sinner is polluted, and the purpose of sacrifice is to remove contamination and restore man to full communion with God.

3. *Myth*

There are countless African myths which, in the absence of written doctrine, help to give an idea of religious beliefs and attitudes which are not always clear from an external observation of rituals. Collections of myths have been made in many parts of Africa, though there are still peoples whose mythology is hardly known. Influences have come from the outside, from the Arabian and Asian world to East African and Sudanese Hamites, and from Europe through Portuguese, Spanish, English and French colonization and education. Nowadays myths may include modern details, such as sending a letter to heaven where in olden times it would simply have been a message. But despite the growth of literacy myths are very popular and are told at all levels of society. They include animal fables and traditions of national heroes, but attention is given here to the religious myths.

The primordial myth is that of the creation of the world and man, and most peoples have their own version of this. The Yoruba say that the supreme God sent a demiurge to the watery marsh that was the earth, with a bag that lay between the thighs of the Almighty. When this divinity arrived here below he shook soil out of the bag, and then took out a cock and a pigeon who scratched the soil abroad till the earth was covered. The Dogon story is that God created the sun and moon like pots, the sun white hot with bright red copper rings and the moon with white copper rings. To make the stars he flung pellets of clay into space, and the earth also was made from a lump of clay. The Fon speak of a great snake which gathered the earth together, after God had made it, and which still supports the earth by thousands of coils above and below. The snake made courses for rivers and carried God in its mouth, creating mountains where they stopped.

The Gikuyu of Kenya speak of God as the divider of the universe, who created a great mountain as sign of his wonders and resting-place for himself. This is the "mountain of brightness," Mount Kenya, where God dwells and towards which men turn and raise their hands in prayer. From this mountain God showed the fathers of the different tribes the places of the earth, and gave them the choice of tools for their future occupations and habitations. The Luyia of Kenya say that God created his own dwelling in heaven by himself, and then made two assistants to help in other work. Pillars were put round heaven to support it, like the posts which support the roofs of large Luyia houses. God made the sun, but wondered for whom it would shine, so he made the first man and later a woman as companion for him. He made a red cock to live in the clouds, which makes the thunder when it crows and lightning by shaking its wings. God made two rainbows, the male is narrower than the female rainbow, and if it appears first the rain is stopped.

A myth of the sun and moon is found among the Luyia, saying that God made the moon first and it was brighter and bigger than the sun, its younger brother. The sun was jealous and wrestled with the moon till the sun was thrown down and begged for mercy. When they wrestled again the moon was thrown into the dirt and splashed all over. Then God told the brothers to stop fighting, and said that henceforth the sun would be brighter and would shine during the day for kings and chiefs, while the moon with its muddy face would shine at night for thieves and witches. The theme of a younger brother gaining the advantage over the elder is common in African mythology.

Other myths say that God gave food to men, but either they wasted it and became hungry, or else they had to find by painful experience which food and work was appropriate to each class of men: farmers, hunters and fishermen. The discovery of fire marks an important stage, and many stories say that there was no fire at first. The Dogon cycle of myths says that the first ancestor stole a piece of the sun from the Nummo spirits, who were children of God and earth and were the heavenly smiths. The Nummos threw thunder and lightning at the ancestor but he slid with the fire down a rainbow to earth, landing with such force that he broke his arms and legs, thus forming the joints in his previously sinuous limbs. A pygmy story says that one of their ancestors seized a brand of fire from the village of God, but God pursued him and took it back. Then the Pygmy made wings from bird feathers and learnt to fly. He stole fire again and God chased him in a cosmic pursuit, but the Pygmy finally escaped. Meanwhile the mother of God, who had been warming herself at the celestial fire, died of the cold when it was stolen. When God returned and found her he decreed that men too should die as a punishment.

A divine family often occurs in the myths, and this shows again that in African belief God is not just a cosmic force, but he has personality, life and consciousness like man. God is thought of in anthropomorphic fashion, but it is significant that in African art, with all its great wealth of sculpture, the supreme God is not represented, though other gods are frequently.

Myths of God's withdrawal from the earth are widespread. In ancient times God lived on earth among men, but he left the world through some human, usually female, misdeed. The Mende of Sierra Leone say that men were always bothering God, so he moved away while they slept, and when they awoke they saw him spread out above in all directions. But God gave man and woman a fowl each, so that they might sacrifice to him in time of need. In Ghana and Nigeria it is said that men were too familiar with God, for the sky was just above their heads. Children wiped their greasy hands on the sky after eating, and women tore pieces off the sky for their soup. Women also hit the sky when pounding grain with their pestles, and the limit was reached when a woman had a very long pole and hit the sky in the eye, so that it moved far away. It is remarkable that the Nuba and kindred people of the upper Nile, thousands of miles away, tell a similar story of women hitting the sky with their porridge spoons, till at last the heaven was pierced and retreated to the distance. A myth from Burundi in central Africa says that men plotted to kill God because a crippled baby had been born, but God knew of the plot and went far away.

In these myths God is practically identified with the sky; but they are explanatory stories, giving reasons for the distance of God in the heavens, and in many other tales the sky is the dwelling place for God who has houses or villages there. A common theme is that of a rope or spider's web hanging from heaven to earth. Many peoples of central and southern Africa who call God Mulungu, say that when he was leaving the earth he asked the spider to spin a thread, and then God climbed up to heaven that way. The great spider's webs that are seen hanging from trees on misty mornings give an easy explanation of how to get to the world above. But in other stories a rope hangs from the sky, and men and women climb up it in some great emergency to seek the help of God. Although God is transcendent, yet communications have been kept open with the earth, and God often appears in other myths, as those of man and death will show.

III. Concept of Man

1. *Creation*

Some myths tell of man having been created by God or his assistants. The Yoruba say that an assistant divinity made men from clay and moulded their features, but God alone breathed life into these dummies. Despite efforts by the divinity to find out how this was done, whenever he hid to watch God at work he fell asleep, and so God still sends the vital breath into man. Dogon myths say that men and women were born of the union of God and earth, and that the original pair bore a series of twins, four males and four females, who were the ancestors of the tribe. The Dinka of the Sudan say that the first man and woman were made of clay and placed in a pot, and when it was opened they became big. God gave them one grain of corn a day, but when the woman was greedy and pounded more corn, her pestle hit the sky, which went away. Their neighbours, the Shilluk, have a story which says that in the beginning men lived in heaven with God, but they offended him by eating fruit which made them ill and God sent them away. Despite the resemblance to the myth in Genesis, this story is found among people that seem to have had no Muslim or Christian influence.

Different myths of the origins of men suggest that they came not from heaven but out of the ground. The Zulu and Thonga, of South Africa and Mozambique, used to say that the first man and woman came out of a reed or reed-bed, which exploded and there they were. The Herero of South-west Africa say that their ancestors and cattle came out of a tree which still exists in the veld, though sheep and goats came from a hole in the ground. There is a Pygmy story which associates the first men with the chameleon, a reptile which often figures in African myth. The chameleon heard a whispering noise in a tree, like birds chirping or water running, and this was strange since there was no water on earth at that time. With an axe the chameleon cut the tree open and a great flood of water came out which spread all over the world. The first man and woman also came out of the tree, light-skinned, and the parents of the rest of men.

In Ghana there are Ashanti myths which say that the first men came from holes in the ground; seven men, some women, a dog and a leopard emerged from the earth on a Monday night. The men and women were frightened at the strange sight of the earth, but their leader laid his hands on them on Tuesday and allayed their fears. However on Wednesday when they began to build houses a tree fell on their leader and he was killed. Next the dog went out to search for fire and brought it back. It seems that the God of creation met these people and took one of them as his assistant. Annual ceremonies are held in the forest in memory of these ancestors, and their names are repeated on Mondays and Tuesdays only. The leopard is sacred to some of their clans.

2. *Nature*

African religion is world-affirming. Despite the calamities of human and natural life, there is no renunciation of the world for an ascetic life. Marriage and the family are the proper lot of man; to have many children and material wealth are the greatest blessings. It is hoped that after death rebirth will bring men back to their previous family and property, from the cold world of shades to the warm sunlit earth. The heavenly world with God is but a larger and happier version of the present life on earth.

Numerous myths say that men and women originally had no knowledge of the process of procreation. In Ashanti myth it was the python, the non-poisonous snake, which brought the knowledge, in a phallic symbolism. The python sprayed the man and woman with water and sent them to lie together. Children were born and since then some clans hold the python as sacred, and if they find a dead python they sprinkle it with white clay and bury it almost in human fashion. A Pygmy story says that God taught the first Pygmy the mystery of birth and he taught it to his negro brother.

Man should be perfect by nature, and any physical abnormality is enough to disqualify a person from office. Children born with extra bodily members may be exposed or neglected, for fear of the bad luck they might bring. "Born-to-die" children are those who come after several other babies have died. It is thought to be the same child that reappears, and marks are made on the body to show this. Such children are laden with protective charms, and may be called by offensive names so as to suggest to the spirit of disease that they are not worth taking away. Twins, and other multiple births, are regarded as abnormal, if not of animal nature. In some places twins have been exposed or neglected, but in others, by reversal of the taboo, they have been honoured and taken into official service. Wooden images of twins are among the commonest of curios bought by collectors and museums, for they are in daily use during the lifetime of the twins. Twin cults are practised by placing food or liquid in joined earthenware pots, outside the door of a house. If a child dies his twin wears a wooden image of the other in his belt, or the mother of both twins who have died wears two images, one in front and one behind, tucked in her skirt.

Although the material world and the physical nature of man are important, African thought does not believe man to be only a body. There is a soul, or souls, the animating principle of man. Beliefs in the soul vary greatly from place to place. The Fon of Dahomey speak of the human spirit (*sɛ*) which is a part of God (Mawu), the great spirit of the world. This spirit is brought to the newborn child by the heavenly snake, and it has an individual character during the life of the man but at death it is absorbed again into God. Individual qualities, personality, facial character, tone of voice, are made possible by a spiritual faculty (*sɛlidō*) which is the vehicle of the fate of an individual and cannot enter another man. Then there is the shadow (*yɛ*) which becomes invisible at death and leaves the body, to be reborn in the next life and pass on the resemblance of an ancestor to a child. A further refinement is the soul (*joto*) of the ancestor which comes to the living man who is his representative. The soul is always reborn in the same clan, for this social system was divinely founded, and those who are to die and those to be reborn are arranged in heaven. The ancestral cult must be maintained, since it ensures the continuity of the family, which is reinforced by spiritual power coming from the ancestors.

3. *Destiny; Salvation*

God and the divinities are all credited with superhuman powers. They can help men or afflict them, and both happiness and misery are attributed to their activity. If a man is struck with lightning it is obvious that he is a sinner, and if he has no apparent misdeed then he must be a secret offender. If he survives the misfortune sacrifices are made to clear away all contamination. The deity is inexplicable, but he may also be gracious and can forgive and restore man to happiness.

The very popular oracle divinity of the Yoruba is called Orun-mila, "heaven knows salvation." He is a beneficent and saving God, who assisted in creation, restored the world after a flood, and calls death to account. He is saluted every day as the being whom all men honour, and his coming brings joy and thankfulness. Being the divinity of the oracle he is still very popular for divination on social occasions, such as choosing a new chief, and for individuals interested in fortune-telling.

The tragic destiny of some people is reflected in myths which show them trying to get an explanation from God for the troubles of life. The stories show, incidentally, a good deal more freedom and variety of individual action than is sometimes thought to be possible in tribal society. The Ila of Zambia tell of an old woman who had lost all her family because God (Leza), "the One who besets," had taken them all away. After her relatives, children, and even grandchildren, had died the woman thought that she would follow them. But then she began to grow younger, a rejuvenation that some people might have attributed to witchcraft, taking the soul-substance of one's relatives. The woman resolved to use her new energies in searching for God and demanding an explanation for her tragedies. She cut down tall trees and piled them on top of one another to reach the sky, but they all fell down. So she wandered about looking for the road to heaven, where it touches the earth at the horizon. She never reached it, and as she told her story to different tribes they assured her that it was not strange to suffer, for the bereavements that had come to her were the lot of all mankind, and all came from God. A similar story by the Chaga of Kenya tells of a man whose sons died, and he determined to shoot God. But when he found God at the daybreak he saw his sons behind him, more glorious than they had ever been on earth. God told the man to go home and more sons were born to him.

4. *Personal and General Eschatology*

Belief in the survival of death is found everywhere in Africa, and so is the notion that death is unnatural. It is generally believed that death was not known in the earliest times, and often that even now death does not happen naturally but by the maleficence of some evil person or power. Two themes are found in widely separated regions. One resembles the story of Pandora's Box, of a hidden mystery. The Lamba people of Zambia say that the first man sent to God for some seeds, and these were given to his messengers in small bundles, with instructions that one of them in particular was not to be opened. But the messengers were curious and opened the forbidden bundle, and death came out. The Kono of Sierra Leone say that God sent new skins for men and entrusted them to a dog. But on the way to earth the dog put down his bundle and joined in a feast. He told his companions that he was taking new skins to men, and when the snake heard this he slipped out, stole the skins, and distributed them to his family. Ever since then snakes have changed their skins and are immortal, while man dies but destroys snakes if he can.

The failure of animal messengers is stated in many myths. The Mende of Sierra Leone say that God sent a dog to tell men that they would not die, and a toad to say that they would die. The dog stopped on the way to eat food, but the toad kept on and gave men the message of their mortality first, and this could not be changed. A Zulu myth says that God sent a chameleon with the message that men would not die. But the chameleon walks slowly and it ate food on the way. Then God sent a lizard with the message that men would die, and it got there first.

Many similar myths are told, from Senegal to Malagasy, with great variety of narrative and detail, but all with the theme that death came into the world after an original period when it did not exist. However there is always belief in life after death, sometimes in a heavenly world, sometimes underground. There is little general eschatology of the end of the world, but belief in a personal judgement after death is found. Reincarnation, of the whole or part of the soul, is believed in in some places, but where there is speculation about its length it may be said to last only ten or twelve reappearances in the same family.

African myths about creation and death have many resemblances, and these are as important as their differences. In reaction against earlier attempts to reduce all variety to uniformity, as suggested by Frazer and his followers, it is now sometimes assumed that all African myths, beliefs, and art forms, are completely different and narrowly tribal. But African tribes did not all live in isolation from one another in the past. There were many migrations, considerable negro empires, contact with Europeans during the last five hundred years and with Asians much longer on the east coast.

It is not possible to say much of the religions of Africa in the past. The material now available has all been collected within the last hundred years. The history of the religion, as has been said elsewhere, is the history of the modern study of the religion, because there are no ancient records. But the myths preserve many old themes, and they reveal attitudes to life, to human being, eternity and God which are of great significance.

In modern times new religions, universal and historical, Islam and Christianity, have made many inroads into Africa. It is estimated that the numbers of Christians in the whole of Africa in 1900 was not more than ten millions, but today it is more than sixty millions. The number of Muslims south of the Sahara is at least as great, and these two religions are expanding rapidly because of the decline of the old traditional religion under modern pressures. But old beliefs and attitudes remain and they prevail not only among the remaining millions who still follow the old religions, but they also influence the converts to the new faiths, in their attitudes to life and death.

SELECTED BIBLIOGRAPHY

BAUMANN, H., *Schöpfung und Urzeit des Menschen im Mythus der Afrikanischen Völker*, 1936.
DIETERLEN, G., *Notes sur la Religion Bambara*, 1951.
EVANS-PRITCHARD, E. E., *Nuer Religion*, 1956.
FORDE, D., ed., *African Worlds*, 1954.
GRIAULE, M., *Dieu d'Eau*, 1948.
IDOWU, E. B., *Olódumarè, God in Yoruba Belief*, 1962.
LIENHARDT, G., *Divinity and Experience*, 1961.
NADEL, S. F., *Nupe Religion*, 1954.
PARRINDER, E. G., *African Traditional Religion*, 1954.
——, *African Mythology*, 1968.

Rattray, R. S., *Ashanti*, 1923.
Rouch, J., *La Religion et la Magie Songhay*, 1960.
Schapera, I., *The Khoisan Peoples of South Africa*, 1930.
Schebesta, P., *Les Pygmées du Congo Belge*, 1952.
Smith, E. W. and Parrinder, E. G., eds., *African Ideas of God*, 3rd edition, 1967.
Zahan, D., ed., *Réincarnation et vie mystique en Afrique noire*, 1965.

B

ASIA (NORTH AND CENTRAL)

BY

A. CLOSS

Graz, Austria

Historical facts about the religion of illiterate tribes can only be found in the pre-historical ethnology and the historical ethnology relating to culture. In the first field have J. MARINGER [7b] discovered the older conditions for North-Eurasia and K. JETTMAR besides for Siberia (*RNA* 307-336), JETTMAR [5c] for the Steppes and the Altai [5a], and J. MARINGER those for Mongolia [7a]. In the second field J. HAEKEL (*AV* 1, 1946, 131-142) dealt with the Obugrians (see *RNA* 331 etc.) and, on the 2nd Austrian Symposium for Anthropologists in Wartenstein (Horn 1961, 211 etc.), with the Kets who had come from North China to the central part of the Yenisei River. The spread of breeders of large animals, initially of reindeer breeders, i.e. the pre-finnish Samoyeds from the Sayan area, is discussed by W. SCHMIDT (III, 340 etc.), also the later movement of the Tunguses (*Schm* XI, 679-682) from their original settlements on both sides of the Baykal Sea (JETTMAR, *WBKL* 9, 1952, 484-511) and finally of the Turkish horse and cattle breeders, the Yakuts (W. SCHMIDT XI, 3-5). The development phases of the Finns who settled in the areas stretching from the higher River Kama to the Urals, their change-over to agriculture within the permian group and their advancement along the River Volga is reviewed by I. PAULSON (*RNA* 148-157). Additional information by JETTMAR (*RNA* 311, 313-320).

Relatively older conceptions and customs have most likely been kept on the one side in connexion with Uralians by the pre-Samoyedic Yukagirs, on the other side among the Paläoasiatic peoples by the Koryaks. The type of early hunter civilisation with an appropriate communal religion, which A. FRIEDRICH (1941, *RNA* 140) put in the beginning, did, according to JETTMAR (*RNA* 347), not develop until later through a secondary assimilation of preyers of the food "Wildbeuter" and hunters who, originally, had different myths and rites and who, from West of the River Ob, had followed the retreating ice and, to the East of the ice, striven towards the Arctic Ocean, where, along the Bering Strait, the Eskimoes are said to have developed (*RNA* 345) of whom three groups have survived in the extreme East of Asia.

Based on these ethnohistorical findings it is not only possible to assess the approximate time relationship of tribal religions, but also the appearance of communal "primitive" forms of piety and the development of these.

I. Regional Popularities in Ethnological Categories of Religion

First to be mentioned is the ecstatic type of these categories, the Shamanism. The most thorough description of the phenomenon in this area is given by H. Findeisen (1957, *RNA* 140) who has made use of the comprehensive older Russian literature; traces in archeology are noted by K. Jettmar (*RNA* 318 and 340. farther 320, 325, 328, 333, 339, 342 & 350). As early as 1797 the first German university lecturer in science of religion C. W. Flügge from Göttingen, described the Shamanism as the most outstanding piece of paganism of the Lapps and Finns, after J. G. Georgi had previously reported its general existence in these areas in his "Beschreibung aller Nationen des russischen Reiches" (Description of all nations of the Russian Kingdom 1771). However, less traces of it can be found with the Finns, even though one would, according to traditional conception, have thought them to be most prominent there because of the agricultural character of the Finnish civilisation. No mention of it is made in the general description of Shamanism by M. Eliade [2] pointing out its peculiarities within the separate national groups. The Obugrians (l.c. 213-218), however, and especially the Hungarians (J. Fakezas in Studies of Shamanism [16] were deeply involved in it. The assumption that the epic Vainemoinen of the Finns (M. Haavio [4a]), who travelled into the underworld, was a typical Shaman is only supported by the closer linguistic relationship of the Finns with the Samoyeds whose Shamanism described (Eliade, l.c. 213-220), but is in several points—e.g. alluring of the spirits by songs and the pronounced preference for fortune-telling—closer linked with that of the Lapps (*RNA* 297-299). Ecstatic "prophetism" based on shamanism at Finnougriens claims A. F. Puukko [13].

On the other hand, there is the considerably different Shamanism of the Eskimoes (*RNA* 397-405) in which, for instance, esctacy is evoked by rubbing a stone on a rock in the direction of the sun's orbit (l.c. 400). Greater similarity to the Samoyedic Shamanism shows the Yukagiric Shamanism (ELIADE l.c. 236-240) which primarily serves hunting, calls the assistant spirits, which are in the shape of animals, by imitating the voices of these animals, finds its climax in a flight to the "master of the animals" and also employs fortune-telling (l.c. 239). Hardly anything of interest can be found in the Koryakic Shamanism.

In South Siberia and in the Steppes, with the Altaians and Mongols, but also with the Tunguses and Kets more exciting forms can be found, including the fanaticism (*RNA* 440, 461), which PAULSON (*RNA* 129 etc.) attributes to the Pre-Tungusic and Pre-Yakutic tribes, as well as the Shamanistic costume (FINDEISEN 30-86), farther the Shamanistic drum, the pictures on which are, for reasons unknown remarkably similar in Lapland and in Minusinsk, (FINDEISEN 156-160).

The Shamanism of this entire continent shows more than that of any other area that the speciality of the Shamanistic ecstacy is based on its aim at communication with the spirits, for which usually animal shaped assistant spirits are used. Further important qualities of this comparatively widely spread phenomenon in our area are: dominance of the so-called "send-out" Shamanism over the "possession" Shamanism (J. MARINGER, 7a, 420) and by some sterns the relative unimportance of an underworld orientation (described as black Shamanism by D. BANZAROW in 1846) in comparison to the celestial orientation (white Shamanism) which in the Altai finds its climax in the presentation of the soul of an animal to a high-god of the "upper world" (*Schm* Ix, 278-306). For this, steps leading to heaven are ascended which have their counterpart in the underworld. Both are linked by the mythical Shamanistic tree which is sometimes imagined upside down (KAZAROW) and which the Dolgans call turu (FINDEISEN 112 & 119); an earthly variety—a birch tree—which is held in great awe (l.c. 105) stands in front of a Shaman's house. Furthermore, traces of a macro-microcosmic parallelism can be found in the Shaman's costume. Characteristic are also the spirit alluring songs, the use of a stick (even before the drum, FINDEISEN 149), the fights of the Shamans and the close connection between the profession of a blacksmith with that of a Shaman (FINDEISEN 94-97). One of these blacksmith-Shamans was Ghengis-Khan whose ancestor Bodontshar procreated with a female falcon. Another speciality is the coexistense of the bird- and the skeleton-Shamanism. The latter is connected with the main ritual of early hunting, when the bones were laid together in order to achieve a resuscitation of the animal (H. NACHTIGALL, *ZE* 77, 1952, 188 etc.) by which the death and resurrection of the Shaman (LEHTISALO *T* 1937) are symbolised. The bird Shamanism, on the other hand, is based on animal shaped assistant spirits and the magical flight.

According to L. VAJDA (*UAJB* 31, 1959) all these elements were combined by an integrating process during the Bronze Age. The basic phenomenon, however, extacy during contact with the spirits, is older in all cases; it was initially not so much directed towards spirits of the dead as towards the species spirits of animals in order to gain their favour for hunting and fishing. This, however, does not justify the assumption that the Shamanism rooted in the lives of hunters was *the* religion of early hunting as such. GEORGI was also wrong when he called the Shamanism a religion of its own; present day advocates of this opinion exaggerate the true facts (E. STIGLMAYR, *Ethn.* 1962). Every time more information comes to hand about a tribe Shamanism is, even in Siberia, connected with trends and conceptions which are not rooted in it. The assumption that it might have taken the character of a salvationary religion with the tribe of the Buriats (FINDEISEN 15) also exceeds reality; the factor of salvation did not occur here in the foreground until it was brought about by Buddhism.

With regard to the animal relations in the Shamanism, they seem to have their roots in these areas but also include the bear (FINDEISEN 22-25) which, according to K. NARR (*S* 10, 1959) originated as far back as the palaeolithic era. However, only in rare instances is an ideological relationship or a primitive affinity between human groups and animal species (totemism in its true sense) assumed; the Shamanistic trends have, both here and in the theriomorphic ideology of the animal style (ALFÖLDI [1]), their roots in the general category of animalism. Without denying completely the presence of totemism within the outlined areas of Siberia, or even for the Turko-Mongols, JETTMAR rejects, as being wrong, RADONIKAS ideas and ANISIMOWS even stronger opinion that the totemism goes back to the beginning of a religious development in this continent and especially to the onset of Shamanism (*RNA* 112).

On the other hand, the closer relationship of Shamanism with religion (*K* 1, 1960, 29-38), as opposed to the true god-opposing magic which W. SCHMIDT had in mind, is not abolished by the fact that the spirits were forced to obey which is described in the various Shamanistic stories collected by KSENOFONTOW and correlated by BUDRUSS. This force is administered for the benefit of the souls of the dead against those spirits who have taken possession of them and against sickness demons; and this is done in the institutional way in the service of religion. The assistant spirits, on the other hand, of which the Eskimoes worship the Tornasuk who stands behind all Shamans (E. HOLTVED in: *Studies* 16, 28 etc.) were, just as other higher beings, more likely to be called upon than forced.

II. DEITIES

The species spirits of animals and their guardian spirits which existed in large numbers and many variations in these areas, mainly with tribes who had not yet gone over to animal breeding, but also with the Yakuts, cannot be rated as animal shaped gods, not even in their position as lord (A. HULTKRANTZ, 1961, *RNA* 412) and master of the animals, because their range of power does not include people but animals, and only certain kinds of them. Although their favour and disfavour has an influence on the luck in hunting, they are not real hunting gods.

Only "masters of all animals," with regard to shape anthropomorphically higher beings, such as the Pičvučin of the Koryaks and the Chukchi and the god Kalgama of the Tungusic Goldens, have a claim to this title. Pičvučin is even thought of as tending his flock from the Pole star (l.c. 70). This connects him with the Uranic gods. However, in this position as a hunting master and food donor from heaven he is surpassed in divine qualities by the Mayin of the Tunguses. The Ilibem-Berti of the Samoyeds does not quite reach this status, in as far as he tends his reindeers on the peninsula of Yamal but otherwise lives in the forest (l.c. 89). He cannot, simply because some natives compare him with the heavenly god Num, be described as a hypostasis of a god of heaven as has been tried by W. SCHMIDT, for others contradict this and there is not enough proof of a central godliness of heaven for this figure to justify this concept. There is not even evidence that he has been a habitant of a heavenly plane.

He is, however, closer to the deities of hunting than to other different god-like beings, such as the lords of terrestrial areas of earth, fresh water and seas, who have already been known to the Yukagirs who, with regard to language, preceded the Samoyeds. These are, in many cases, male, such as the *künc*, the earth spirit of the Kets. Female varieties are mainly found with agricultural tribes, but the Tunguses also have their lady mistress of the earth called *dunne mulun*. Masters of the water are: the *ütkyllos* of the Eastyak-Samoyeds; the *Jenkvort* (water lord) of the Ugric Eastyaks; the ruler of the seas, *anquaken-etin* (*etin* = owner), of the coastal Koryaks and Keretkun of the Chukchi, who has his match in kacak of the Eskimos (l.c. 72). There are also numerous water gods ruling over fish. With the Finnish tribes (HOLMBERG (= *HARVA*, *RNA* 140), but also with the Karagasses, the Buriats and the Yakuts these gods do not only have the function of donors of fish; the Yakuts even know of a water bull, *ogusa* (*RNA* 404). The lords of the forest who are subordinate to the earth lords, on the other hand, are more similar to the hunting gods, such as the Pargä of the Samoyeds, the East Finnish-Karelic forest master Tapio and the West Finnish Hissii. The Gilyaks have Rai-ya as lord of the mountains and the Tayga in the role of an animal owner and hunting god, similar to the Hinkon of the Yenisei Tunguses.

The above mentioned Num of the Samoyeds, who is worshipped as the god of heaven by the natives, is also asked for luck in hunting. The Tunguses also pray to their god of heaven Mayin for hunting luck, but only as one of other things, and they do not at all ask Buga, the "world god" (*RNA* 40), for it. To see in Buga nothing but an impersonation of the universe would be wrong, since creative acts, such as the creation of the Pole star and the erection of the world column (*Schm* X, 529), are attributed to him. Nor can he be imagined as the representative of the supporting pillar of the world and its base. This conception could perhaps be attributed to the name of Tuntu of the Ainu (*RNA* 52 etc.) who is a high god there. The function of a god includes everywhere the preservation and guidance of the universe which, in the Tungusic belief, is carried out by turu (*RNA* 38), although he is not the embodiment of it. However, with him the world relation is not only one aspect among others as it is with the Koryakic Naininen (*RNA* 48). The world relation is more important for the Radien of the Lapps (*RNA* 295) and the highest beings of the Obugrians, and PAULSON has recognised this relationship (*RNA* 142) and called these gods world gods. This name is probably most suited to the Num-turem of the Woguls in as far as the two words *num* and *tur*—perhaps originating from the Samoyedic substratum—are connected.

With regard to the Finnish god Ilmarinen the world relation is accompanied by his ties to atmospheric phenomena, as is also the case with the god Pon of the Yukagirs. Impersonations of the appearance of events in the air, e.g. of wind, thunder and lightning, are especially frequent in the Finnish area. The Lapps know a wind man Bieggolmai and a thunderstorm god Tiermes as well as a thunder god Ukko who is also known by the Esthonians, for whom lightning is a deity called Pikne. In the Altai lightning is something impersonal—the arrow of the god of heaven (*RNA* 236).

The highest position, however, is held by the impersonations of the day sky which are similar to the great Indo-Germanic gods of light. These are even present when the luminaries, sun, moon and stars, themselves are worshipped, as it was done, for instance, by the Koryaks. They had, besides the already mentioned cult-less Pon and their own sun god Pugu, who was also worshipped as a master reigning over morality (l.c. 47), a heavenly god Kuju, whom they worshipped through prayer. The light itself also appears in the shape of Memdeye-Ecie, the father of fire in the popular belief of the Yukagirs, an impersonation of the heavenly fire believed to be alive, from which the Northern Lights are shining (l.c. 47). The Northern Lights themselves are not impersonated—the Eskimos see in them the torches of soul escorts and the Esthonians the blood of fallen warriors.

Of the gods believed to live or be impersonated in heaven mainly those of the Finns, but also those of the Ugrians are light accentuated, while the Eastyaks call their highest god saenki-turen, which means the bright and luminous turen. In the same way the expression **jumala*, on which the name of the East Finnish god of heaven is based, means something like "shining reflection" (l.c. 230). It is, however, difficult to explain the derivation of the name Jumo, the god of the Cheremisses, from the Indo-European names of the gods of heaven by H. Paasonen (*RNA* 216). It is also just as disputable whether the Ugrian expression for heaven, i.e. turen, which seems to be matched by the Lappish word tiermes, goes back to a Turkish-Tartaric influence (l.c. 212). The word *tengere* which is supposed to have influenced it is also used by the Turko-Mongols (J. S. Roux [14]). These highly dynamic tribes use it to describe the god represented by the vault of heaven. Vambery claimed a connection of this name with Tan, which means light (*Schm* X, 129-131), but this is not proved.

The father figure status so closely linked with Indo-European gods of heaven is not very pronounced here, although the West-Yakuts call their highest god their best father while the East-Yakuts call theirs the wise father (*Schm* XI, 38 etc.).

Other gods without any proven special links to light also belong in this area, such as the Samoyedic Num, the receiver of reindeer sacrifices (l.c. 57), and the cult-less Es (l.c. 41 etc.) of the Kets as well as the Koryakic Gicholan, which means "master up there" (*RNA* 48) the Pase-kamui of the Ainu (l.c. 51), whose connection with Tuntu, i.e. pillar of the world, is rather not transparent, and finally the Eskimo high god Sila.

Only a vague similarity can be found between the numerous "God's sons" in the range of the "Burkans" (the first part of this expression goes back to Buddha) and the Indo-European Dioscuri, and this is found in the figure of the horse riding hero of the Buriats, Solbon (*Schm* X, 266 etc.), who is connected with the morning and evening star (*RA* 198 etc.). But he has no twin brother with him, only a servant, Dogedei. There are further the god-like brothers shown in the contrast of light and dark moon (*Schm* IX, 266 etc.) who have no similarity to the Ašvins.

The agricultural Finns imagine their heavenly god to live in holy matrimony with the "mother of earth" (*RNA* 238). No proof is given for a similar marriage between the earth goddess of the Mongols, Ötygen, and the highest Tengri. The choice of a human bridegroom for the mother of earth found among the Turkicised Chuwashes (with Finnish origin) can hardly be called a repetition of the holy wedding with a god of heaven.

An earth deity is found with the Turko-Mongols in the group of the Jersub, which means land and water spirits, and only occasionally as gods of the underworld. The goddess of earth and death, Hosadam, of the Kets lives on a death island near the mouth of the Yenisei river (*RNA* 44 etc.), whilst the goddess Sedna of the Eskimoes lives at the bottom of the sea. The view expressed by W. Schmidt that the Turkish tribes had their own earth god religion as well as their religion of heavenly gods (*Schm* IX, 172 etc.) is seriously opposed by A. v. Gabain. The figure of Ngaa of the Samoyeds (*Schm* X, 667) and the malicious, demonised "black" Khan Erlik of the Altaians, who is master of the evil spirits called *körmös*, are interpreted by W. Schmidt as dark moon figures opposite the light moon figure of the high god Ülgän who exists next to the Tengri (*Schm* IX, 446 etc.). The genetic relationship of this god Ülgän living in the East (*Schm* IX, 337) to the universally Uranic Tengri remains obscure. The Tengri of the Buriats is split up into 99 hypostases.

The tribe goddess Ummai of the Altaians (*Schm* IX, 875) and the spring goddess Tomam of the Kets (*Schm* IX, 686 etc.) are not found in "Weltbild einer frühen (Pflanzer)-Kultur" (Theory of life of an early (planter-) civilisation) by JENSEN. JENSEN says that the goddess Sedna of the Eskimos and the girl out of whose cut-off fingers the sea animals are also supposed to have originated can "only with reservations" and "from outside" be understood as "demagods." The Chuwashes, he continues, had the independent figure of a slain ancestor out of whoses ashes a tree is growing (A 62, 1967 ...), but again the cult is missing just as with the epic Lemminkainen of the Finns (HAAVIO 9a). Nothing living or nourishing grows out of his dead body, and in this he conforms with the type of Balder and, seen in this light, with the myth of Osiris (*K* 7, 1965, 226), not, however, with the demagods. Nor can any roots in the original Finnish myth be recognised.

III. MYTH

The presentations of the mythology of the Finns and Siberians by HOLMBERG, of the Hungarians by KATONA, KANDRA, IPOLYI, SOLYMOSSY, ROHEIM, BERSE-NAGY, of the Yurak-Samoyeds by LEHTISALO, the Lapps by QUIGSTAD and REUTERSKJÖLD, the Eskimos by RASMUSSEN, the Kazakhstan-Tatars by KOBLOV, and the cosmology of the Altaians by LANDYSEV are not restricted to the criterion "cult traditions." A paper by CHUDJAKOW (*G.* 44, 1883) deals with the motives of the Altaians who are poor in myth but have a wealth of epic poetry. Even FINDEISEN classes the motif of the swan ladies, which is found in the "Mongolian Area," to fairy stories (260), although he usually refers to an animal myth of Shamanism. Of higher religious importance are, even without any history of cult, the traditions concerning gods and higher beings and, in this connection, the structure of the world, since it is being lived in or even created by them.

Subject of mythical phantasy was also the god of heaven, originally in the family connection. In the toadstool song of the Irtyshostyaks seven daughters of a god of heaven are mentioned and, in the fairy story, a son as well (KARJALAINEN 1922, *FFC* 44, 266). The heavenly god of the Manchuria-Tunguses, Apaki-Enduri, has seven daughters, the highest being of the Buriats, Esege Malan, a wife with sons and daughters. A large family is also attributed to the lunar-mythological being Jedai of the Kets (*Schm* IX, 539) and to the lunar Ülgän of the Altaians, as well as to his opponent in the underworld, Erlik. The heavenly gods are connected with heroes in the hero cult of the Ugrian (*RNA* 333) and in customs of the Abakan-Tatars (*Schm* IX, 731 etc.). In the sun myths of the Yukagirs a closer connection between the solar sphere and the hunters and warriors can be recognised. Sun and moon are the eyes of the highest god of the Buriats, Esege-Malan (*Schm* X, 456).

The West Eskimoes regard the moon as the highest god and worship it by cult (*RNA* 379). In all Eskimo-areas many stories are told about sun and moon as sister and brother, but few of them religious ones, although they seem to have influenced the ritual, since the festival of extinguishing the fire (lamp festival, *RNA* 370) is based on them.

The Buriats have a story about a hedgehog who has given effective advice to the highest being as to how to bring back sun and moon to their proper place after both celestial bodies had been carelessly given away (*Schm* X, 345). The Mongols have been handed down the story that, at one time, there were several suns of which some had been shot down or captured because their heat had caused damage (*RA* 180). The Shamans wear two metal mirrors, representing sun and moon, on their chest in the belief that these are mirrors in themselves. The concept of the breast of a hare (e.g. with the Kachintsen, *Schm* IX, 632 etc.) refers to a lunar tribal father.

The origin of the motif that the world was created from the body of a giant, which the Kalmucks believed, is rather abstruse (*RA* 110). Generally, the origin and world creating myths both in Northern and in Central Asia refer not so much to the astral universe as to the earth with its stream of life symbolised by the tree of life (HOLMBERG). The Esege of the Buriats is said to have created sun and moon from a handful of earth. Mythical connections can also be applied to the main elements of the world image of these tribes, i.e. apart from the concept of the world pillar and the world tree to the partition of the upper and the lower world into initially seven and later nine steps (*Schm* IX, 96 etc.). This differentiation has been preceded by the simple tripartite division into heaven, earth and the underworld, which was still believed by the Kets. The Altaians imagine a milky lake in the centre of the graduated structure of heaven.

According to the tradition of the Woguls and Itelmes, the earth was lowered from above (*RNA* 35), which, as the Kets believe, was done by Es (*Schm* XI, 485). According to other traditions it was nearly always drawn up from the sea by means of divers animals (in Emasia L. WALK, *Magw* 63, 1933, 60-76; in universal comparison W. SCHMIDT, *Studia Instit. Anthropos.* 20, 1964). The creation and consolidation of the world is usually done in the presence of an enemy. In rare instances a trickster himself acts as the creator, like the cultural demigod Rabe (*RNA* 369) in North Alaska and North East Asia who is worshipped by sacrifices; and the original Shaman Doh of the Kets who usally wrests the souls from the earth goddess Hosadam (*Schm* XI, 510 etc.). He is said to have flown over the primeval sea together with birds called divers and directed the pulling up of the earth. Among the transformers the cultural-hero raven of the Eskimoes from Alaska mostly shows of a saviour, for there he is bringing the light and arranging the other world (*RNA* 277).

Of the separate mythical points emerging from the legend of creation it is worth mentioning the heavenly mammoth in the belief of the Woguls (KARJALAINEN *FFC* 8, 41, 16), and the belief of the Tunguses and Samoyeds that, in prehistoric times, the world was formed by "horns" of mammoths (*RNA* 35). The concept, held by the Tunguses, of two snakes embracing the earth in the ocean goes back to Southern influence (*RNA* 38 and 315). The same explanation applies to the isolated occurrence, e.g. with the Tunguses, of the idea of a final world fire (*Sch* X, 530, 557) and the concept of the end of the world which the Altai-Tatars had (*Schm* IX, 281).

In ethical connection the claim that the Eskimoes' best qualities—working skill, courage and perseverance, tact and generosity—are determined by the religion, is opposed by the view that only their ritual behaviour is a result of their ideas about their higher beings (*RNA* 372). According to W. RADCLOFF there is no justice in the world of Shamanism. For not only the gods of darkness but also those of the light do by no means always act in accordance with ethical principles. A. v. GABAIN even talks of the bad disposition of the gods. This can perhaps be applied to the lunar Ülgän but not so much to the Tengri. He, in the belief of the Yukagirs even surpasses the sun in his demands for moral behaviour and his control over the orderliness of life.

IV. The Cult

By no means unimportant in the moral respect is the fact that the prayer is so much in the foreground in these areas and often takes on really impressive forms. Examples are quoted by W. Schmidt (IX, 142 etc., 344 etc., 354 etc. 581 etc.; X, 87 etc., 284 etc., 331 etc., 483 etc., 537 etc., 706 etc.; XI, 84 etc., 912 etc.). The inao of the Ainu have their counterparts in the pole cult of the North Asians (*AV* 1, 1946, 150), they are considered as mediators between god and man (Obayashi 1965, *RNA* 142). The most impressive of the cult acts are the very ancient hunting rites (C. Lot-Falck 1953, *RNA* 142), as for instance the placing together of the bones in order to achieve the reincarnation of the hunting animals (A. Friedrich 1943, *RNA* 140; Paulson 1950, *RNA* 142). Most experts regard this as nothing more than a magical performance, Schmidt and his school see in it an expression of the sacrifice idea—perhaps the bones were offered back to the donator of hunting luck asking him to reincarnate them.

Above all perhaps the disposition of the skulls can be explained as an offering (F. Gahs 1928, *RNA* 140). But also the submersion offering goes far back (Al. Closs, *WBKL* 9, 1952, 66 etc.). The Yukagirs offer blood to the river mother (Findeisen 20). In connection with fishing the Eskimoes celebrate their bladder festival on which occasion the bladders of the seals are given back to the sea. The youngest type of Eskimo-tribes also observes a whale cult (M. Lantis 1958, *RNA* 413). In some areas a cult is also devoted to the elk (Woguls, Haekel *AV* 1, 1946, 115) and the eagle (Sternberg *L* 1925, *RNA* 381), by the Lebed-Tatars as a clan animal and otherwise often as sun animal represented in the world column.

The most important act among the hunting sacrifices, before the change-over to animal breeding, was the offering of the reindeer. Even afterwards it still shows the style of the hunting sacrifice (RNA 58) more so than the offering of a horse by the Altaians, which was already influenced by the cow sacrifice (W. Koppers 1936, *WBKL* 6). According to W. Schmidt (15, 1942, 127-148) offerings to heaven had already this form in Central Asia before the time of Shamanism. Thus the oldest Turk tribes had their animal consecration when they freed a captured or reared animal for the Tengri. The killing of the animal by strangulation, known from the reindeer rite, was also taken over for horse sacrifices, when Ülgän was the receiver and was presented with the soul of the sacrificed horse by the Shamans. Exceptions are the offering of a dog to the sun, done by the coastal Koryaks and the Yukagirs, the cattle sacrifice within the cult for the dead of the Yakuts (*Schm.* XI, 190, 196) and the offering of a pig which was done by the Tunguses (*Schm* X, 665 etc.). The most likely custom to have played a part as a prime sacrifice in the religion of the Turks was perhaps the milk offering at the Yakutic Isyach festival (*Schm* XI, 115-118). Koumiss (JOCHELSON 1906, *R* 618) is also used as a sacrificial drink (*RA* 572 etc.). Not clarified in the history relating to civilisation is the isolated human sacrifice by the Buriats (P. MELNIKOV, G. 1875; anything traces in Soil Discoveries: *RNA* 341).

In the sociological respect the cult of the hunters is centred on the family, while the agricultural people have extended it to a village cult. Personalities with such a wide sphere of influence as can be found with some Shamans, e.g. a highly respected person of the Golds (FINDEISEN 121) or the "Ten Drum Old Woman" of other Tunguses (l.c. 90 etc.), are rare with agricultural people, and, as a rule, even the Turko-Mongols have no formal tribal priesthood.—In addition to the above mentioned festivals, which also include a fairly widely spread bear festival and the wolf festival of the Koryaks (*Schm* II, 335), there are also a New Year festival celebrated in Spring by the Kets (*RN* 43) and an Autumn festival of the Samoyeds and the Turko-Mongols. A Shaman festival was celebrated by the Buriats (FINDEISEN 75).

With regard to the widely scattered Finns the most outstanding factor is the housecult observed by the planters, which is described by G. RÄNK (*RNA* 143). The holy corner in the house, which the Esthonians devote to the original farmer (*RNA* 251), the containers erected by the Votyaks for the hut spirit (*RNA* 242) and the cult of the stable and washroom masters and the corn man (*RNA* 247) as well as the holy groves are characteristics of the ancestor and kinship cult and its events, which are associated with the yearly cycle and the field fertility. However, the stone labyrinths of the Samoyeds living on the Barents Sea (*RNA* 313) can probably not be explained as an ancestral cult and are therefore not megalithic in the ethnological sense. Everywhere in these areas the fire is worshipped as a hearth fire. This cult is also prominent with the Mongols who have probably developed from former plant growers to horse riding herdsmen (*Schm* X, 71 etc. according to N. POPPE 1925). The Turk tribes have taken over, from their hunting past, not only the impersonation of the hearth fire (*Sch* IX, 228 etc. according to DYRENKOVA 1927) but also a universal fire spirit, omniscient and venerable, who stands in high esteem and is offered white sheep sacrifices. Both nations offer a gift of butter to the hearth fire and believe it to have cleaning powers. By rubbing wooden sticks (according to the older method) the herdsmen nomads produce fire in order to drive away animal pests.

Most cult idols, even the theriomorphic ones, have their roots in the family, kinship and clan association and their relations to the spirits. HAEKEL (*AV* 1, 1946) reviews these customs as observed by the Ugrian. According to him the seida of the Lapps and the sjadei of the Samoyeds, both of them representing nature spirits, can be counted in this category. Related to nature spirits, especially earth spirits, are probably the obo of the Mongols, which are heaps of stones at the road side (KAZAROW 1927, *RA* 68). The cult idols of the Ugrians also represent assistant spirits of the Shamans. In this case theriomorphy predominates. The corresponding ongone of the Buriats represent, among others, higher assistants of the historic Shamans (*Schm* X, 365). The Lamaism strengthens this trend.

One part of the animal shaped cult idols, including the Pasker cut out of felt, the glutton from the graves of sovereigns in the Noin Ula at the snow line of the Altai mountains (JETTMAR 5c, 76), is related to a tribal history. In the Ugrian tribe the glutton has the same role as the wolf of the Old Turks, i.e. that of a tribal father. These cult images are not so much subject of the belief in spirits as of the religious anthropology.

V. THE RELIGIOUS IMAGE OF MAN

Everywhere in North and Central Asia the whole of the prehistoric myths, of which the Eskimos according to the ethnologist BOAS had very few, were centred more around the earth than the human race. The human race was either brought up with the earth from the depth or let down with it from heaven. The Chukchi (*Schm* III, 392) and the Ainu (*Schm* III, 453) believe in the creation of man by a heavenly being. The Koryaks have two opposing interpretations: according to one man was created by god, according to the other by a raven which itself had emerged from dust. Some Eskimo tribes, and several Polar tribes (W. KOPPERS, *WBKL* 1, 1930, 359-399), regard the dog as the creator of man. The decline in the perfection intended by god is blamed on the carelessness of the otter instructed to stand guard (*Schm* III, 453). Usually the source of the evil and the deterioration of mankind is blamed on an opponent.

Body and soul are judged differently in this connection. While the

Tawgy-Samoyeds believe the souls of all men to be ready made in heaven before incarnation is effected by a goddess of birth, the Turks and the Lebed-Tatars and, of the Mongol race, the Buriats believe that the soul is infused into the body, which was created by the god of heaven through the amalgamation of several earthly substances, by the opponent " in one case through the nostrils, in another through a tube from the rectum.

The belief in the soul, which is extensively covered by PAULSON, is highly developed and differentiated in these tribes. Here culminates the pluralism of the souls. The soul is not seen as a single substance, but it is believed that there are several souls next to one another within the individual. In early hunting days the concept of a soul made of bones was very prominent, while later different organs of the human body are attributed soul qualities. PAULSON has claimed a close connection between the "free soul," which was of great importance with the Shamans, the shadow soul and the soul of the dead (spirit) clinging more to the body (*RNA* 114). All three together form the figurative soul. The "double" soul and the dream soul can also be regarded as a figurative soul (*RNA* 257). The breath soul, on the other hand, is of a pneumatic kind, the principle of living, which the Yukagirs think lies in the heart, while they believe the free soul to be located in the head. The guardian spirit of the Finns, the haltja, discussed by VILKUNA, is no human spiritual being, although a man's luck depends on the spirit's connection with him. He is also regarded as a fate soul (PAULSON, *Scripta Inst. Donneriani Aboensis* II, 1963, 133-149; more about fate on pages 89-96, M. KUUSI).

When the breath soul escapes, death occurs which, in the belief of the Eskimoes, higher beings had after consultation considered to be the best thing for the man (*RNA* 406). The Altaians see in Erlik (*RNA* 265) an impersonation of death, i.e. a god of death, while the Finns regard their god of death, Kalma, the embodiment of sickness spirits (*RNA* 265). Some other tribes regard illness as such as the real cause of death.

One Eskimo woman had explained to Rasmussen that death was either the end of life or the transition into another form of life and one therefore need not be afraid (*RNA* 410). There are many different ideas about the place of residence of the dead. Most concepts are connected with the central world, i.e. the earth, either immediately beneath the surface in the zone of fertility where, strangely, especially the restless souls and those of people having died a "gruesome death" are suspected to be, in the mountains " believed by the Finns and Lapps (*RNA* 294)—or on an island to be reached by going down-stream. The kingdom of death of the Eskimoes, where the goddess Sedna reigns, however, is in the depth of the sea. The underworld of Erlik stands just as much outside the central world as the heaven or the moon, both of which also play a part in tribal religions as collecting centres of souls. The kingdom of Erlik is the most likely one to be regarded as a place of punishment for wrong-doers, where, however, good souls as well can be forcefully taken to, while on the other hand, the heaven also beckons to the dead fallen in fight. Thus it does not seem to be a place for the good alone, and even less does the moon. Some tribes believe in rebirth (*K* 7 1965, 221-225, prehistorically indicated *RNA* 338). The reincarnation belief of the Eskimoes has been monographically dealt with by A. Wachtmeister (1956 *RNA* 415).

The Finns (*RNA* 250) and the Altaians (Kazanow, *RA* 628) buried their dead bodies under the earth, the Tunguses had a platform and tree burial (*Schm* X, 558) which is also found in other tribes of this continent (H. Nachtigall, 1953, *RNA* 142). Embalmment is carried out by the Eskimoes (*RNA* 363). Some Mongolic tribes (Soyots: *Schm* X, 422; Kalmucks: *Schm* X, 104) left their dead bodies to wild animals. A. Friedrich recognised in this a remainder of the bone preservation of the hunting cult (1938, *WBKL* 5, 226 etc.), although no belief in resuscitation is connected with it. The Altaian belief in resuscitation (*Schm* IX, 128 etc.) goes back to a contact with the Iran. The same is suspected of the stories concerning a deluge believed by the Samoyeds, Woguls and Ketes (W. Anderson, Flutsagen 1923, *RA* 615), although this has not always been sufficiently proved. However, the myth of a prehistorical fire flood believed to have been caused by the devil (*RNA* 37) seems to be fairly substantial.

VI. Influences

Apart from influences between neighbouring tribes, e.g. Koryaks and Yukagirs, there seems to be an influence from the religions of previous populations, some of which can only be recognised prehistorically, e.g. among the Samoyeds, the Kets, the Obugrians and the Abakan-Tatars. In the same way the Perchten figures of Central Asia, which are discussed by R. Bleichsteiner (1953, *AV* 8, 58-75), could be explained as a legacy of Indo-European tribes of the East. The concept of the division into layers of the universe stands in remarkably close connection with Mesopotamia (M. ELIADE, 2.257), and the Ugrians were inspired by the Hittites with regard to their idol cult (J. HAEKEL, *AV* 1, 134-137 (J. MARINGER, 7a, 407). The Lapp sand the Finnish tribes of the Baltic provinces, on the other hand, have adapted many customs from the Teutons, although, however, the basic mutuality must not be overlooked.

The strongest influence probably came from the Irani. Through their Shamanism, especially the send-off Shamanism (W. NÖLLE, [9], they themselves have obvious connections with the old North. Furthermore, the word *bangha*, with which they describe the main medium for achieving pre- en ex-Zarathustrian ecstacy, i.e. the hemp, became a loan-word which spread far to the North. The Ugrians, the Mordvinians and the Cheremisses also use it to describe the delirium which they however do not produce by the hemp. The names for the deity in the Pahlavi form, kudai (*Schm* IX, 839 etc.) and Hormuzda (*Schm* XI, 43 etc.), also penetrated into Central Asia, the first one to the people of the North Altai and the second to the Buriats. According to K. DONNER (*Studia Orientala*, Helsinki 1925) the name of the Samoyedic god of heaven Num is supposed to have been taken over by the Sogdians in a similar way. This would mean that the Samoyeds had given to their god who, in their belief, is the ruler of the world, a name which in both the Greek and the Sogdian language means law. The Turko-Mongols received probably even more important inspiration from the Persian eschatology and demonology. The suscitation resuscitation belief of the Altaians (K. HAEKEL, 7, 1965, 236 etc.) has already been mentioned.

The world religions (see map on page 10 of FINDEISEN) of Islam and Christianity strengthened and spiritualised these beliefs considerably. The Arabian expression *kijamat* for resurrection is still used by the Finns (*RNA* 272), and the word *Shaitan* for the devil by the Kirghiz, Chuwashes and Volga-Finns. The Turk tribes, however, also use the name Šimnu (i.e. Shaman, H. JUNKER, *UAJb* 5, 1925, 49 etc.) for the Iranian figure of Ahriman. Influenced by Orthodox Christianity the Esthanian Setekuses changed their festival for the dead from Autumn to Eoner Eve (*K* 7, 1965, 232).

The Turk tribes were apparently influenced by the Islam to include into their Ülgän belief (*Schm* IX, 118, 172) the idea of a holy book of wisdom, "Nom," after they had developed epigraphically some kind of runic characters along the river Orchon as early as the 7th century A.D. Of the Mongolians, most of whom have changed over to Buddhism, the only tribe to have experienced any kind of reform is that of the polytheistic Buriats, where the Lamaist Mindiu (*Schm* XI, 215) successfully fought for the white against the black Shamanism still in existence today, e.g. in the monastery of the black Chan in Mongolia, South of the River Yenisei.

Research history is comprehensively covered in *RNA*, for Siberia and the remaining North (7-24) as well as for the Finns (148-173) by PAULSON, for the Lapps (287 etc.) and the Eskimoes (363 etc.) by HULTKRANTZ. No reference is made to the tribal religions of Central Asia in *Handbuch der Orientalistik* (Guide to Orientalism) and one therefore has to refer to the information given in the volumes by W. SCHMIDT The earliest information about Mongols and Tatars has been collected by W. SCHOTT (Berlin 1845), the most important, however, by P. S. PALLAS (1776-1801). Hero legends of the Minusinsk-Tatars were collected by A. SCHIEFNER (Petersburg 1859). Systematic research was first started by VAMBERY. Most thorough use of the epigraphic material for historical purposes was made by BARTHOLD.

LITERARY INDEX

I. *Complete representations*

RA HARVA, UNO
1938 Die religiösen Vorstellungen der altaiischen Völker. FFC125.— 1953 French translation, Paris.

RNA PAULSON, IVAR; HULTKRANTZ, AKE; JETTMAR, KARL
1961 Die Religionen Nordeurasiens und der amerikanischen Arktis. Stuttgart (Religionen der Menschheit, published by Ch. M. Schröder, 3).

Schm SCHMIDT, W., *Ursprung der Gottesidee*. Münster, Westphalia.
1931 III Asien etc.
1949 IX Primäre Hirtenvölker (Turks and Tatars)
1925 X Sekundäre Hirtenvölker (Mongols, Tunguses and in addition Yukagirs)
1954 XI Jakuten, Sojoten, Karagassen, Jenisseier (= Vets) ("Primärsekundäre Hirtenvölker")

Critical review by A. v. GABAIN (A 1956, 106 etc., 10/11) and O. PRITSAK (UAH 27, 1955 etc.).

This literature covers all monographs on religions of the various tribes introduced in this paper which have appeared to date, as well as publications on the concepts, myths and rites contained therein and related special questions in exact bibliographical order. The paper refers to them by the name of the author and in the first quotation the year of publication in front of the symbol for the complete representation under which it appears in the index.

II. *Later publications of importance for the historical momentum*

[1] ALFÖLDI, A., 1931, "Die theriomorphe Weltbetrachtung in den hochasiatischen Kulturen." *Jb. des deutschen archäol. Institutes.* Berlin.
[2] ELIADE, M., 1957, *Schamanismus und archaische Ekstasetechnik*, Zurich and Stuttgart. - 2. Ed. (englisch) New York 1964, 181-258.
[3] GJESSING, G., 1944, "Circumpolare Stone Age." *Acta Arctica* II, Kfibenhavn.
[4a] HAAVIO, M., 1952, "Vainemoinen Eternal Sage." *FFC* 144.
[4b] ——,1965, *Lemminkainen.* Helsinki.
[5a] JETTMAR, K., 1951, "The Altai before the Turks." *Bull. Mus. of Far Eastern Antiqu.* 135-223, Stockholm.
[5b] ——,1964, *Die frühen Steppenvölker. Kunst der Welt.* Baden-Baden.
[5c] ——,1966, "Mittelasien und Sibirien in vortürkischer Zeit." *Handbuch der Orientalistik*, 1. Abt. V. Bd. 5. Section, Geschichte Mittelasiens.Leiden-Köln, 1-105.
[6] LOORITS, O., 1958, "Hauptzüge und Entwicklungswege der uralischen Religion." *Folklore Studies* 17. Tokyo.
[7a] MARINGER, J., 1963, "Mongolian before the Mongols." *Arctic Anthropology* (Madison) 1, 75-85.
[7b] ——,1963, "Zur Religion der bronzezeitlichen Bewohner der Waldzone Osteuropas," *Studia Instituti Anthropos* 18, 401-420, Wien-Mödling.
[8a] MICHAEL, H. N., ed., 1962, *Studies in the Siberian Ethnogenesis.* Including: TOKAREV, "Ursprung der burjatischen Nation."
[8b] ——,ed., 1963, *Studies in Siberian Shamanism.* Toronto. Including VASILJEV on the concept of the universe by the Ewenki.
[9] NÖLLE, W., 1953, "Iranisch-nordasiatische Beziehungen im Schamanismus." *Jahrbuch des Musaeum für Völkerkunde zu Leipzig*, 12, 86-90.
[10] PALLISEN, N., 1953, "Die alte Religion der altaischen Völker etc." *Microbibliotheca Anthropos.* Feiburg i.S., volume 7.
[11] PAULSON, I., 1963, "Der Mensch im Volksglauben der finnischen Völker." *ZE* 88, 49-65.
[12] PAPROTH, H. J. R., 1964, "En Gammal Jägarit." *Skrifter Human. Fak.* Uppsala.
[13] PUUKKO, A. F., 1935, "Ekstatische Propheten mit besonderer Berücksichtigung der finnisch-ugrischen Parallelen." *Zt. für die alttestamentl. Wissenschaft*, Berlin 53, 23-35.
[14] ROUX, J. S., 1956, "Tengri. Essai sur le Ciel-Dieu des peuples altaiques." *Revue de l'histoire des religions*, 173-212. Paris.
[15] SCHMIDT, W., 1942, "Das Himmelsopfer bei den asiatischen Pferdezüchtern." *Eth.* 7, 127-148. Stockholm.
[16] *Studies in Shamanism* 1967, Ed. C. M. Edsman. Scripta Instituti Donneriani Aboensis 1., Stockholm.

The above works are referred to in the text, if necessary, by the name of the Author and the list number.

III. *Abbreviations of journals*

A	*Anthropos*
ARW	*Archiv für Religionswissenschaft*
AV	*Archiv für Völkerkunde, Wien*
Eth	*Ethnos*, Stockholm
FFC	*FF Communications*, Helsinki

G	*Globus*
K	*Kairos*, Salzburg
MAGW	*Mitteilungen der Anthropologischen Gesellschaft Wien*
S	*Saeculum*
UAJb	*Ural-Altaische Jahrbücher*
WBKL	*Wiener Beiträge für Kulturgeschichte und Linguistik*
WVM	*Wiener Völkerkundliche Mitteilungen*
ZE	*Zeitschrift für Ethnologie*

C

NORTH AMERICA

BY

J. R. FOX

New Brunswick, New Jersey, USA

I. Essence of the Religion

It is important to understand from the outset that we are not dealing with one religion but with many religious systems. These vary in complexity from simple shamanistic practices to intricate calendrical ceremonies; from simple animistic concepts to elaborate pantheons. A rough division can be made between the religions of the hunters and gatherers on the one hand, and those of the settled agriculturalists on the other. Extreme elaboration of belief and rite naturally belongs to the latter, although there is an underlying substratum of concepts and practices common to all the varieties. Of these the notion of an impersonal, a-moral power (Keresan *'ianyi*, Siouan *wakan*, Algonquian *orenda*, etc.) is perhaps the most pervasive. The concept is akin to that of *mana* in Polynesia. This power is usually thought of as independent of both men and supernatural beings, but it is inherent in some things and can be acquired in various ways. It can be used to good and evil ends. The perverted use of it is witchcraft, a universally recognized phenomenon. The use of fetishes (images, bundles etc.) is also common.

The essence of the religions of the aboriginal Americans lies in the idea of harmony in the universe. Harmony between nature, Man and the supernatural, means fertility of men and crops, and success in hunting, war, and personal achievement. Disharmony—often caused by witchcraft—leads to tribal, personal and even cosmic disaster. Ritual therefore is a means of either maintaining or restoring this basic harmony.

I will confine myself here to the religion of the Indians of North America, but many features are common to both halves of the continent (shamanism, for example.) It will not be possible to do more than give a brief introduction to the basic elements of religious life in North America.

II. Historical Development

The majority of the ancestors of the American Indians entered the continent over the Bering Straits land-bridge between 25,000 and 9,000 years ago. They were upper-paleolithic hunters largely of mongoloid extraction. Certain of the beliefs, myths and rituals of the simplest groups today have recognizable counterparts in the religions of the Siberian tribes (the creation myth of Earth Diver for example.) [15] The original religion then must have been that of simple hunters. The elements of this must have been rituals concerned with hunting and warfare, and individual shamanistic practices largely concerned with divination and curing. Even as the religions became more elaborated these elements were not lost: Navaho religion is still primarily concerned with healing, [12] while the Zuni *Shalako* ceremony, one of the most elaborate of the ceremonials of the settled agriculturalists, is thought to be in essence a hunting ritual. [3] Amongst the agriculturalists, however, calendrical rites and fertility rituals began to dominate the religions, and more positive pantheons appeared. The individualistic religion of the hunters became overlaid with collectivist ideologies and communal rites. With the coming of the Europeans, Catholicism in particular exerted a profound influence. In most parts of Spanish America aspects of Catholicism were incorporated into the native religions, and in some cases (e.g. Yacqui) synthetic religions were produced.

The acquisition of the horse and the development of an extensive buffalo-hunting culture by the Plains Indians, led to an elaboration of ceremony centered on various war cults and the Sun Dance. In the late nineteenth-century, after a series of military reverses, these groups developed the Ghost Dance Religion—an eschatological movement aimed at restoring the "old ways." More recently a synthetic religion based on the taking of Peyote has flourished amongst the survivors. (See section 6).

III. Conception of the Deity

Belief in supernatural beings is universal in the Americas, but it varies in complexity and definiteness. Except in the higher religions there is not much evidence for a belief in a supreme being, and even in these the supreme God is essentially *primus inter pares*. Ideas concerning supreme beings are reported for several tribes, but it is difficult to know how to assess these. Missionaries, for example, who were interested in aboriginal religious ideas were ever ready to translate Indian notions of "spirit" and "power" into more familiar concepts such as "God.' Also they may have been reporting the ideas of outstanding individuals rather than commonly held tribal beliefs. The idea of a supreme "power" of some kind, associated with the sky or the sun, is certainly present in some of the agricultural tribes.

There are often creator spirits which manifest at least this aspect of deity. Amongst the northern hunter-gatherers the commonest of these is Earth Diver, or a spirit associated with Earth Diver. [17] This story—known also in Eastern Asia—tells how the world was once only water but how a diving animal or bird brought up earth out of which the world was made. [15] Some versions have a spirit who guides Earth Diver and his subsequent operations. Other creator spirits are equally vague. The Zuni creator willed himself into existence, and once his task was done he vanished. In most myths the creator either vanishes or is disposed of, and lesser but more tangible deities take his place.

Of these more tangible deities we might single out three types: the Hero Twins or Culture Hero; the animal spirit and especially the "owner" or "leader"; the trickster. It is difficult to know whether to treat the latter as part of religion or simply of mythology. He rarely has ceremonies or prayers devoted to him, so I will deal with him under myth (section 4 para. 3). The Hero Twins on the other hand do figure in ritual in many tribes, and in some religions (e.g. Navaho) they are central deities who were instrumental in the creation and early socialization of Man. [12] The hunters obviously specialized in animal spirits (wolf; thunderbird; salmon; bear etc.) These were rich in "power" and had to be placated in various ways by positive ritual and the observance of taboos. Prominent among them was the "owner" of the animals (e.g. the Deer Maiden amongst the Keres, or Sedna of the eastern Eskimo). This spirit—half human, half beast—was appropriately the link between men and animals (birds, fish). Properly treated and respected this spirit would ensure success in hunting. These spirits were often totemistic and hence in the care of a particular clan.

With the Plains Indians the idea of Guardian spirits flourished (probably derived from Algonkian sources.) These were individual animal spirits obtained in a vision quest.

As we move up the scale of religious complexity the array of animal and nature spirits is supplemented by the concept of "power" inherent in heavenly bodies, directions, winds, rain, and the earth itself. Sometimes this is not personalized, or not to any high degree, and sometimes it develops into a definite pantheon. Thus in the Pueblos there is a sky/sun father and an earth/corn mother; with the Pawnee the morning and evening stars were personalized. Finally there are supernaturals which are "pure" spirits—like the *katsinas* of the Pueblos. [10] These are not personifications of natural phenomena, but spiritual beings deriving from early episodes in the creation story. They are, however, conceived in anthropomorphic form and are imitated in ritual. In a similar category, but malevolent rather than benevolent, is the notorious *windigo* spirit of the Ojibwa (which has counterparts amongst the northwest coast Indians.) This is a cannibal spirit which devours men who are then regurgitated. As a result they themselves become cannibals. [16]

Sacred rulers do not occur in North America, with the possible exception of the Natchez whose ruler was identified with the Sun and carried in a litter, thus echoing features found in Middle and South American religions. The most definite conception of a "High God" perhaps occurred among the Pawnee, whose supreme being, *Tirawa-atius*, had many of the attributes of deity. Again, this tribe shows affinities with the high religions of the South. [4]

IV. Worship

1. *Cult*

By "worship" I understand the various means employed by men for entering into some relationship with the supernatural. This can include relationships of avoidance, and some tribes employed various rituals of purification to rid contaminated persons of dangerous "power." Warriors and homicides were usually purified in this way, and the notorious "scalp ceremonies" were directed to this end. Very often avoidance magic was practiced against ghosts of the dead. But it was more usual to seek a relationship of intimacy with the supernatural. To this end *visions* were sought, and the *vision quest* is perhaps the most typical and fundamental aspect of Amerindian worship. [1]

Visions as a source of ritual power were common throughout the continent, but there was considerable difference in emphasis. It is difficult to generalize, but we can say very roughly that north of Mexico visions were deliberately sought after (hence the concept of the "quest"), while south of Mexico they were not sought after but were accepted if they came through dreams or hallucinatory experience. There were exceptions to this general rule; for example, on the Northwest coast *spirit possession* was a common mode of obtaining power, with a corresponding belief in *soul loss* as a cause of disease. [15] Behind all the variations however lay the idea that an individual could gain spiritual power by means of a vision of a supernatural entity. In some cultural areas (e.g. the Plains) this was the pre-eminent religious idea. Amongst the Plains Indians it was not only the religious practitioners (shamans or medicine men) who sought visions, but every man of the tribe. Indeed, initiation into full adult status depended on the obtaining of a suitable vision in which the potential warrior saw a supernatural animal which became his *guardian spirit*. Some commentators have assumed that visions were only sought after in order to obtain guardian spirits, but this is a misconception. It led however to the idea that the seeking of visions was essentially a *rite de passage*, but again this was only one of its functions. It is essential to grasp that the vision itself was the basic feature and that it could be put to many uses. It was used in California by shamans wishing to effect a cure; among the Montagnais to achieve success in hunting; among the Plains Indians for a variety of purposes including mourning, success in war or vengeance, curing, hunting and artistic effort.

The idea that visions were peculiarly associated with both initiation and with guardian spirits derives from the extreme elaboration of the vision quest amongst the Algonkians and the Plains Indians. [2] The "classical" quest was in fact undertaken by a boy at puberty or by a young warrior. Among the Crow for example a boy would fast for four days and supplicate the spirits to "take pity on him." He would often hack off a finger joint in order to arouse supernatural pity. [7] Among certain of the Sioux the supplicant would stand for two days and nights praying for a vision. Whatever the means employed—and they inevitably involved mortification of the flesh—the vision usually appeared on the fourth night. The spirit usually appeared in the form of an animal: buffalo, elk, deer, bear, eagle or sparrow hawk were popular, but even insects such as the mosquito might be the vehicle of supernatural power. From the spirit the supplicant learned a song and certain taboos, and was told to obtain a token—buffalo hair, eagle's wing etc—which would serve as a talisman throughout life.

This vision experience was the true initiation rite for the tribes around the Great Lakes and was seen primarily as a preparation for life. On the Plains however a man might continue to seek supernatural aid in this way throughout his life. In doing so he collected a number of "tokens" and wrapped these into a bundle. This "sacred" or "medicine" bundle became his most important possession, and the bundles of chiefs were often thought to have very special powers. These sacred packages could only be opened with special ceremony. Various versions of the sacred bundle are found all over North America—often described as "fetishes" by observers. They are all clearly derived from the hunter's basic "bundle" of ceremonial objects—a kind of travelling altar appropriate to a nomadic people. [18]

The sincerity of the vision experience cannot be doubted, as there were often individuals who failed to receive supernatural communications. Among some tribes this was handled by allowing a very successful visionary to sell part of his power to a less successful tribesman. He would make a replica of his bundle and teach his songs and taboos, and generally take on the role of guardian spirit to his client.

I have concentrated on the role of the vision as this is the most distinguishing feature of Amerindian religion and has rarely reached this degree of elaboration in any other tribal peoples. Visionary experience was largely confined to men. In some tribes women sought visions, but this was not common. Among the hunters women were regarded as "powerful" in their own right by virtue of their ability to give birth. But this power was antithetical to "male" power. The most positive evidence of it was menstruation, and many hunting tribes surrounded the menstruating woman with taboos and avoidances. Menstrual blood was particularly feared as harmful to war and hunting enterprises, but it was so powerful that a fearless hunter might even turn it to advantage by "taming" it and carrying some with him on the hunt (Northwestcoast). Among some hunting peoples, particularly the Athabascans, the girl's puberty ceremony was of considerable importance and ranked as a major ceremonial.

Shamanistic practices are found in most of the hunting and gathering tribes—and in others—over the whole of the continent. [9] The Shaman sometimes functions primarily as a healer who sucks objects from the bodies of victims of witchcraft or ghostly attack. In other cases he is primarily a prophet, diviner and visionary rather than a healer. The "sucking shaman" is perhaps best designated "medicine man" (French médecin), and the title of shaman proper reserved—as it is amongst the Tungus of Siberia from whom the term originates—for the seer, confessor, medium and miracle worker. In either case the "power" to heal or prophesy was usually obtained in a vision, although this had to be followed by intensive training at the hands of an experienced shaman or healer. The shaman amongst the Tungus and the Eskimo received his vision without a quest and usually as the result of a mysterious illness. After a period of fasting and training he was able to see visions regularly and to control spirits. From older shamans he learned conjuring tricks, swallowing feats, fire walking and the like. Among other miracles the Eskimo shaman could perform the spirit flight, and visit, in spirit, other places. He could even go down into the sea and speak to the "owners" of the fish and seals, or travel over-land to find caribou. (This "spirit flight" is also well known in central Asia.) The recovering of lost souls—a common cause of illness—and the hearing of confessions were also part of the shaman's task.

This miracle-working seer was more common in the extreme north and the sub-arctic than elsewhere. But elements of the shaman complex proper are found elsewhere amongst the "medicine men" of other culture areas. As we move south however, the idea of the medicine man as a specialist healer (albeit with spirit aid) is most common. Conjuring was common in the tribes around the Great Lakes where the medicine men formed a trans-tribal cult (especially among the Winnebago, Ojibwa and Menomini) known as the *Midéwiwin.* [5] The Navaho and other Apachean tribes of the Southwest also incorporated wonder working into the repertoire of the "singers" or medicine men, thus reflecting their connections with their linguistic cousins the Athabaskans in Northwest Canada [12].

The above patterns were commonest amongst the hunters. The planters, as we have already seen, relegated the individualistic visionary shaman to a minor place or dispensed with him altogether. They were much more concerned with calendrical fertility rituals, and these tended to be in the hands of priests or priestly organizations. In some cases however these priestly cults were obviously derived from a shamanistic source—a development perhaps foreshadowed by the Midéwiwin society. The most striking case of this is with the Keresan-speaking Pueblo Indians of the Rio Grande in New Mexico. The priestly societies here (which still function) are organizations of medicine men who perform the sucking cures, recover lost or stolen souls, and put on annual wonder-working performances. But their organization is essentially that of priestly cult. Initiates do not require a vision, but they must undergo a long training in word-perfect ritual accompanied by the familiar disciplines of fasting and abstinence. One of their number is the spiritual head of the tribe, and they excercise governmental as well as ritual functions. They are also concerned with the fertility rituals. This is a clear case in which the shamanistic functionaries have evolved into an organized ritual-governmental organ of the tribe. [10]

There is also continuity between the rituals of the hunters and the agriculturalists in the areas of hunting and war; for many of the agricultural tribes continued to hunt, and some of the Prairie tribes—such as the Omaha—had a completely mixed economy. Both hunting and war rituals were similar in both types of culture, but again there was a definite tendency for these ceremonies to be taken over by cult groups with priestly officers as the societies became more complex. It is this growth of ritual specialization that marks out the more elaborate of the agriculturalists from their hunter cousins. At one end of the scale we have the completely individualistic religions in which each man could commune directly for his own benefit with the spirits, and at the other the collectivist religions in which the welfare of the community at large was the aim, and this aim was achieved by the ritual activity of the priests. Many of the elements and symbols may have been the same in each case, but the overall organization was different.

The hunters and nomads however did not lack collective rituals for the benefit of the whole group. The most spectacular of these was undoubtedly the Sun Dance of the Plains Indians. [14] Although composed of ancient elements, this ceremony must have been of fairly recent elaboration as many of the most famous Plains tribes only took to the horse at the end of the eighteenth century, moving into the Plains from the Desert or the Woodlands. Many elements such as the reverence for the Sun, the use of a sacred pole, and the obtaining of visionary power through ordeal and mortification were woven into the ceremony. It took place just after the great buffalo hunt during eight days in midsummer. The various scattered groups of the tribe came together to relax after their exertions. There were many variations but a few elements were common: a lodge was erected or a sacred enclosure made, usually circular. The main feature of this was a centre pole which became the focus of attention in the rituals. Usually the ceremony was "sponsored" by an individual as a result of a vow in time of sickness or war, but the whole tribe joined the sponsor. Past sponsors acted as officiants at the ceremonies. After several days of preliminary ceremonial (including much smoking—a ritual act common to most tribes) the climax was reached in the actual dance itself. The dancers danced while looking fixedly at the sun or the pole, and they blew on bone whistles. In some tribes thongs would be attached to the top of the pole and some dancers would fasten these thongs through their chest muscles and pull outwards while dancing until the muscles tore. One is inevitably reminded here of the amputations and other mortifications practiced on the vision quest, and indeed much of the prayer involved was the same in each case: a plea for "pity" from the sun and other supernaturals.

The sacrificial elements here are obvious, but sacrifice as such did not figure as largely in North America as it did in the middle American religions. The nearest equivalents to the human sacrifices of the Aztecs occurred in the Pawnee ceremony of the sacrifice to the Morning Star. A girl captive representing the Evening Star was shot through the heart with an arrow and then clubbed to death. Her spirit joined that of her "husband" the Morning Star. The Iroquois "sacrificed" brave captive warriors, but it is uncertain whether or not this was really a religious ceremony. There are hints of human sacrifice in some Pueblo ceremonies where symbolic victims are slain, but no direct evidence that this is a substitution for previous practice. There is no animal sacrifice, but among many of the planting tribes there was a first-fruits offering not unlike those observed in the old world.

The settled agriculturalists—of whom we may take the Pueblos as an example—represent the high point of the development of priestly religions in north America. It should be realized however that it was rare for these priests to be full time professionals; they were mostly members of cult groups or medicine societies, each group having charge of a particular ceremony. Very often the priesthoods were hereditary offices, and clans, for example, were often said to "own" ceremonies. Sometimes the connection was very direct as among the Hopi where the snake clan was in charge of the snake ceremonies. Among the Pueblos the practice of giving ceremonies at the instigation of individual sponsors still existed, but the major ceremonies were connected with calendrical observances, and in particular with the summer and winter equinoxes and the spring and autumn solstices.

Each ceremony followed a similar pattern. The priestly society went into retreat for a fixed period, fasted, smoked, made sand paintings, "prayer sticks" and "prayer feathers." This making of pure "prayer offerings" was a feature of Southwestern religious practice.) On the final day or days of the ceremony there would be public dancing. In the winter many of these dances would take place in the *Kiva*, the ceremonial chamber of a society or moiety. Prominent among the Pueblo cults was that of the *Katsinas* (*kachinas*): the "masked gods" or "dancing gods" that we have mentioned earlier. These beings are associated with the clouds and with rain, and are imitated by initiates in the public dances. The Pueblos show probably the greatest complexity in north America of priesthoods, cults, medicine societies, and other ritual organizations all interlocking into a vast ceremonial complex. The worship of the sun and the corn (who is also Mother Earth), the hero twins, sacred tobacco, shamanism and sacred fires, are all woven into this complex of rites which revolve around the themes of harmony and fertility. [10]

The neighbours of the Pueblo Indians, the Navaho, are noted as ceremonialists and are a good example of a hunting tribe which has settled and adopted more elaborate religious practices to supplement and extend its basic shamanism. The focus of Navaho ceremonial is the curing rite, and it is sponsored by the sick person and his clansmen. But it is directed by a paid specialist—a "singer"—who knows the chants and the appropriate sand paintings. The making of the latter is an art borrowed from the Pueblos but elaborated to a high degree. Masked impersonations of the Navaho deities (which include the Hero Twins) accompany the curing ceremony in its closing stages. These ceremonies can be for a variety of illnesses and the appropriate cure is diagnosed in shaman fashion. The ritual details however, are more reminiscent of the Pueblos, but lack their concern with fertility and the sun and corn. [12]

We have seen throughout this discussion how forms of prayer vary. Amongst the Iroquoian tribes recorded prayers are largely of thanksgiving; the Alongkians and Plains Indians prayed for "pity" (largely as individuals) and for success—they were supplicants; Pueblo and Navaho prayer was much more a statement of ritual fact—nearer indeed to an incantation, the proper performance of which ensured the ends desired. Most highly developed Indian ceremonials were symbolic re-enactments of myths, and especially of the myths of creation.

2. *Ethics*

It is almost impossible to generalize about the ethical standards and ideas of the American Indians. It was rare for these to be specifically connected with ideas of religious merit or demerit. There was no hell or punishment in after life for wrongdoers, nor were the inducements of paradise very specific despite the notion of a "happy hunting ground" held by sentimental whites. All one can say by way of generalization is that each group had socially approved ends and modes of behaviour, and that usually supernatural "power" could be used to promote those ends. This could either be power sought for individual success as on the Plains, or power sought by communal action for the communal good as in the Pueblos. Where power was utilized for socially disapproved ends, this was almost universally treated as witchcraft and severely punished. There was no group in which it was not believed that there were evil persons who would misuse supernatural power to harm their fellows. The ideas about sorcery and the techniques of witchcraft were not peculiar to America but were similar to those found elsewhere. Outside this sphere of the evil use of power, however, the beliefs and rituals about the supernatural were not concerned with any ethical code. (In some of the revivalist religions, strongly influenced by Christianity, ethical considerations did become important). Kindliness, honesty, forgiveness, chastity, duty to parents etc. were all enjoined in some measure, and a code of ethics was usually supposed to have been laid down "in the beginning" by the Creator or the culture heroes. But the rituals were not concerned with these matters except incidentally; that is, "harmony" of human relationships was often considered essential to a successful ritual performance. There was no idea of a code of conduct which if kept would incur the favour of the deities or spirits, or if broken would incur their wrath.

3. *Myth*

Some myths have already been mentioned, including those of creation, but these are only a part of the vast body of Amerindian mythology. [17] They are however the most important part, and most of the myths connected with rituals deal in fact with the "dawn" period of creation and the activities of the culture heroes and first people. As might be expected from what we have said about ethics, these are not "moral" tales; indeed the activities of many of the actors run counter to the conventional morality of the tribes. Typically they describe the origins of natural phenomena or pieces of ritual, or the exploits of holy people. As in many other parts of the world the theme of a deluge destroying the world crops up almost universally. Other myths tend to appear in clusters with characteristic "distributions." Thus the Algonkian and Siouan tribes share a series of myths including the story of the woman who married a sky being (or "star husband") and also of an attempt to snare the sun. Some themes are more widely distributed than others (we have mentioned the flood) and among these are the stories of the testing of the hero twins, and the exploits of the trickster. Both these themes have a distribution outside north America and the latter in particular has attracted attention because the principal character shows affinities with Hermes and Loki and related figures of European mythology. He appears in many guises—on the northwest coast as a Raven, in the eastern forests as a Rabbit and in many areas as a Coyote. This great archetypical figure is at once the creator of all order and at the same time the epitome of disorder; he is both immensely clever and a simple dupe; he defies every known convention and yet is the founder of convention. Typically he has enlarged intestines wound around him and an enormous and insatiable appetite; with this goes an uncontrollable and again extended penis which often becomes detached and has its own adventures. He cannot control his bowels or bladder; he stoops to low pranks and humbles proud maidens. He is in short the impulsive, instinctively cunning and yet simple aspect of Man's nature. Jung suggests that the Winnebago trickster cycle illustrates the gradual growth of social and sexual maturity in the human being from a completely a-social to an at least partly socialized creature. But Trickster is never completely socialized: he remains the simple, primitive energy of human personality. The variations on this theme are legion and some very attenuated, but it is in many ways the most typical and widespread myth. [11]

V. Conception of Man

1. *Creation*

Myths of the creation of man vary considerably. Only in the Pueblos do we get the classic tale of mankind being begotten by the Sky Father on the Earth Mother, the first beings ascending from the womb of earth through a reed. In most of the tribes around the Great Lakes it was naturally some kind of emergence from water that was involved, and often this was achieved by Earth Diver under the direction of the Creator Spirit or a culture hero. In other tales the first creatures were animals, some of whom took human form later. On the Plains and the Prairies it was common for the first men to have descended from the sky, passing through various "heavens" or "worlds" until they landed in this one—just as the Pueblo Indians rose up through several worlds. In most of these myths the idea of man entering into a watery world with no place to land is found. An animal or hero helps to find a dry place for man to settle. Where a clan organization exists it is common to find each clan with its own origin myth and some idea of an orderly chronology of creation which establishes an order of precedence amongst the clans. Perhaps the only generalization one can make about the creation of man is that there is rarely any idea of a specific act of creation by a higher being for a specific purpose. Man "emerges" from various sources in various ways.

2. *Nature*

Philosophical ideas about human nature are not common except among a few gifted "thinkers." By and large the order of nature and society is assumed to be laid down and fixed. There is therefore no idea of man striving for a better condition of life. His aim is to live harmoniously and successfully within the tribal framework. He is capable of both good and evil but is not particularly prone to either. Human nature is seen if anything as a mixture of good and evil tendencies. There is no notion of human beings as creatures born in sin against which curse they must struggle nor are they born essentially innocent and only later corrupted by the world. Thus there is no fall of man. In fact man is seen as having evolved from a child-like state on the model of individual ontogeny.

In the beginning the first men were relatively helpless. The culture hero often had to complete their physical development and then to teach them even the rudiments of culture. The most important things he taught were the rituals and other observances, and to the Indian, if these rituals are performed and observances kept, then the order laid down in the beginning will be maintained. And this order is essentially good, and life is essentially good. The great danger lies in the misuse of this power by evil individuals and hence the greatest crime is witchcraft.

3. *Destiny and Eschatology*

Most tribes had some conception of an afterlife but in many of the hunting tribes this was not well defined. Nor was the "soul" thought of as eternal. It might survive for some time, but it might also "fade away" after a time. (Most tribes in fact believed that man possessed more than one soul). With few exceptions (e.g. the Sioux) the dead were feared in various degrees, and their "power" was dangerous. This could be nullified by various processes such as the adoption of a substitute relative for the dead one, the substitute taking over the "soul" of the dead person. The idea of reincarnation was also present in some areas—but it was not an elaborate conception of a "wheel" of reincarnation from which escape was possible, but rather a Pythagorean notion that one of the "souls" might return as an animal or be inherited by a kinsman. Dead infants among the Hopi were buried in the house in the hope that their souls would be reincarnated in the next child born. It is only among the Pueblos that a definite and at all elaborate conception of a happy afterlife appears.The dead here joined the *katsinas* or became clouds and hence bringers of rain. Amongst the Hopi a woman was buried in her bridal dress, and this was essential to ensure her passage to the next world.

With such an attenuated or shadowy conception of an afterlife there could be no notion of a life on earth devoted to reward in heaven, or of a Nirvana-like escape from the toils of incarnation. Human destiny, therefore, personal or general, did not point to some end state to be achieved. Certainly there was no idea of supernatural reward or salvation which ensured eternal life. It is a fair generalization to say that the Indian valued this life and that reward if any was desired in order to make it more successful, as, for example, in the vision quest. As we have seen in the previous paragraph, there was no notion of mankind moving from or toward any particular state of grace. The "ways" or "roads" of life had been laid down and were followed not for reward in eternity but because they made life on earth happy and harmonious.At best death was a peaceful state of rest: at worst it was a nihilistic state which offered nothing and was not welcomed.

The "destiny" of man, therefore, was to live a successful life in harmony with the natural and moral order as conceived by his culture; an order essentially unchanging and usually unchallenged. Within this framework he found his fulfilment. The idea of "salvation" is clearly irrelevant in such a system.

VI. Present Religious Situation

Some of the aboriginal traits mentioned above still survive in certain tribes. The Pueblo Indians have maintained a quite remarkable continuity of religious belief and practice which runs in harness with adopted Catholicism. The Navaho—most successful of the surviving tribes—retain their rituals intact. Other groups in the Southwest (e.g. the Yaqui) have amalgamated Catholic and indigenous elements. The Iroquois still maintain an impressive ceremonial cycle, and among some surviving Plains groups the Sun Dance is still performed. But by and large the aboriginal religion of the hunters, and the planters of the Southeast, collapsed as an integrated system when these societies were destroyed.

Two modern movements however should be noted: one was a religion of despair while the other may well become the unified religion of the surviving Americans. I allude to the Ghost Dance Religion and the Peyote Religion. Various "prophets" had arisen throughout the eighteenth century preaching the eventual success of the Indian in his struggle with the white man. In the nineteenth century however it became obvious that this could not be achieved unaided and a different brand of prophesy arose. This was based on the old shamanistic experience of trance and spirit message. The message usually laid down a strict code of ethics for the Indian and an injunction to observe the old "Indian ways." Along with this code went a dance ritual the performance of which would ensure the survival of the Red Man when the whites were destroyed by flood, and/or the return of the Indian dead to help defeat the whites. With this victory would come the return of the buffalo. The most successful of these prophets was Wovoka, a Paiute, who started his own version in Nevada in 1886. The Ghost Dance spread through the Plains and finally reached the Sioux. In 1890 the last Sioux uprising occurred and after its failure the Ghost Dance with its promise of the return of the Old Ways disappeared. [8]

Another tradition of prophesy had been pacific. It produced the Shaker Religion, but its most significant modern development has been the growth of the Peyote Religion. The fruit and roots of the Peyote cactus (*Lophophora williamsii*) contain hallucinogens and had been used in Mexico for obtaining religious visions. It was introduced into the U.S.A. in the late nineteenth century by Apache tribes who raided and traded over the Mexican border. There grew up around the taking of peyote a definite series of rituals deriving from Plains sources, which involved confession, singing, drumming, smoking, praying and the ceremonial taking of the "button" of the peyote cactus. The movement spread through the tribes settled in the Oklahoman Indian Territory, and then through the other Plains tribes, filling the vacuum left by the failure of the Ghost Dance. Missionaries went out to the Utes and the Navaho and now both have versions of the cult. It is now a nationally organized religion and has been incorporated as the Native American Church of the United States. Its ethics and creed are a mixture of Indian and Christian elements, but its form and inspiration clearly derive from native sources. [13]

SELECTED BIBLIOGRAPHY

[1] Benedict, Ruth, "The Vision in Plains Culture," *American Anthropologist*, 24, 1-23, 1922.

[2] Benedict, Ruth, *The Concept of the Guardian Spirit in North America*, Memoirs of the American Anthropological Association No. 29, 1923.

[3] Bunzel, Ruth L., "Introduction to Zuni Ceremonialism," *47th Annual Report of the Bureau of American Ethnology*, 1932.

[4] Dorsey, George A., *Traditions of the Skidi Pawnee*, Memoirs of the American Folklore Society, Vol. 8, 1904.

[5] Hoffman, W. J., "The Mide'wiwin or Grand Medicine Society of the Ojibwa," *7th Annual Report of the Bureau of American Ethnology*, 1891.

[6] Hultkrantz, Ake, *Conceptions of the Soul among North American Indians*, Stockholm, 1953.

[7] Lowie, Robert H., *The Religion of the Crow Indians*, Anthropological Papers of the American Museum of Natural History, 25, Part 2, 1922.

[8] Mooney, James, "The Ghost-Dance Religion and the Sioux Outbreak of 1890," *14th Annual Report of the Bureau of American Ethnology*, Part 2, 1896.

[9] Park, Willard Z., *Shamanism in Western North America*, Evanston, 1938.

[10] Parsons, E. C., *Pueblo Indian Religion* (2 vols.) Chicago, 1939.

[11] Radin, Paul, *The Trickster: A Study in American Indian Mythology*, New York, 1956.

[12] Reichard, Gladys A., *Navaho Religion* (2 vols.) New York, 1950.

[13] Slotkin, J. S., *The Peyote Religion*, Glencoe, 1956.

[14] Spier, Leslie, *The Sun Dance of the Plains Indians: Its Development and Diffusion*, Anthropological Papers of the American Museum of Natural History, Vol. 16, Part 7, 1921.

[15] Tax, Sol, (Ed.) *Indian Tribes of Aboriginal America*, Chicago, 1952.

[16] Teicher, Morton I., *Windigo Psychosis*, Seattle, 1960.

[17] Thompson, Stith, *Tales of the North American Indians*, Cambridge, (Mass.), 1929.

[18] Wissler, Clark, *Ceremonial Bundles of the Blackfoot Indians*, Anthropological Papers of the American Museum of Natural History, Vol 7, Part 2, 1912.

D

AUSTRALIA

BY

T. G. H. STREHLOW

Adelaide, Australia

I. General Introduction

A study of Australian aboriginal beliefs presents many problems. One of these arises from the attitudes of the European observer which are always apt to colour his observations. As Professor Stanner has expressed it, the older anthropological writers who described the beliefs of the aboriginal population were baffled to find among the Australian tribes a religion without God, without any creeds or church or priests, without any concern for "sin" or sexual morals (in the European sense), and without any "material show." Yet modern anthropologists are undoubtedly correct in stating that in each Australian aboriginal group religion "is a living faith, something quite inseparable from the pattern of everyday life and thought" (Berndt). Consequently, "it penetrates all facets of aboriginal life and has little to fear from distinctions which are both abstract and disunitive and which we, with our philosophical education, often make" (Worms).

Two other difficulties arise from the special nature of the observed aboriginal material and the character of the worshippers: the European observer is, firstly, bewildered by the manifold variety of the totemic clans among the numerous Australian tribal units, and, secondly, hindered by the veil of deep secrecy behind which many of the most important parts of the sacred beliefs and ritual are hidden by the totemic clan leaders. Secrecy in all things regarded as sacred was indeed one of the most striking—and for the European observers one of the most frustrating—characteristics of aboriginal religion.

In consequence, all episodes related in the sacred myths, all verses found in the sacred songs, and all acts found in the sacred ceremonial cycles, were carefully graded in point of sacredness and secrecy. Young men were taught only those sections of belief and ritual that were open to the novices. Middle-aged men knew most of the sacred lore appropriate to their totemic clan area. But there were probably never more than two or three elderly leaders to be found at any one time in one of the major local totemic groups who possessed that fulness of knowledge which enabled them to function as the final repositories of the complete body of sacred lore which was the property of their group. Only a handful of European observers have ever been honoured by being admitted to the final mysteries of aboriginal religion in any Australian area.

Nevertheless, though the aboriginal religious beliefs have been studied in depth only in a few parts of the Australian continent—notably in Central Australia (Spencer and Gillen, C. Strehlow, Róheim, T. G. H. Strehlow), Arnhem Land (Elkin, Berndt, Stanner), and north-western Australia (Worms)—certain facets of these beliefs may be regarded as being both reasonably authenticated and as having a wide currency over the whole of the continent. (Stanner indicates seven characteristics of aboriginal religion in *Aboriginal Man in Australia*, pp. 213-21).

II. Conception of the Supernatural: the Immortal Beings, the Eternal Totemic Landscape, and Time as an Element of Eternity

The religious concepts of the aboriginal Australians in most parts of the continent were based on beliefs about the eternal existence in the landschape of supernatural beings (generally known as "totemic ancestors") who were normally linked indivisibly with specific totemic animals, totemic plants, or natural phenomena.

These supernatural beings had originally slept under the crust of an eternal and uncreated earth at sites marked today by soaks, waterholes, springs, rock plates, and other natural features. Time began when they awakened from their sleep and burst to the surface, "born out of their own eternity." These supernatural beings varied greatly in appearance. Some rose in animal shapes, resembling kangaroos, emus, and the like. Others emerged in human guise, looking like perfectly formed men and women. Both sexes were represented among them: for the female ancestresses already formed "a second sex" in their own right, and were not merely inferior, imperfect, or less powerful editions of the males. In most of the supernatural beings there existed an indivisible linking between elements found in animals (or plants) on the one hand and in humans on the other. Those beings that looked like animals, for instance, generally thought and acted like humans: conversely, those in human form could change at will into the particular animals with which they were indivisibly linked. Only plant shapes were unknown in this assembly: since plants cannot move or speak, the ancestors and ancestresses linked with them were invariably visualized as being human or animal in form. Their food, however, consisted exclusively of the plants that formed their totem. Finally, there existed some sacred sites which had given birth to human-shaped supernatural beings that were not linked with either plants or animals, though they were in all other respects the equals of the earth-born totemic ancestors.

The earth had been in the beginning a featureless, desolate, barren plain, covered in eternal darkness; for the sun, the moon, and certain other heavenly bodies, too, had originally slumbered under the earth's crust. Neither had any animals, birds, or plants existed at this stage. This barren, lifeless earth was now transformed by the creative labours of the newly emerged totemic ancestors, who began to wander about on its surface. They filled the earth with the animals and plants of their totems. Mountains, sandhills, plains, salt lakes, swamps, river courses, springs, and soakages, all came into being to mark the deeds of the roving totemic ancestors and ancestresses. In reasonably well-watered portions of Australia every landscape feature was associated with some mythical episode or some sacred verse. Hence Australian mythology was everywhere validated and fixed by the geography of the countryside.

The sacred songs were accepted as compositions first intoned by these supernatural personages. Their verses were hence believed to include both historical accounts of supernatural events and the original creative words of supernatural beings. Similarly, all sacred ritual in which the totemic ancestors were represented in later times by their human reincarnations was believed to have been instituted by the supernatural personages honoured in them. In consequence, great care was taken to ensure that the oral tradition prevented changes being made in the episodes related in the sacred myths, in the verses of which the sacred songs were composed, and in all ritual acts in which those supernatural personages made their appearance. All alterations of myths, songs, and ceremonies, and all revelations of sacred matters to persons not entitled to receive them, were regarded as constituting sacrilege; and sacrilege was punishable by death—a penalty exacted by no means infrequently even in historical times.

Despite their great powers, the supernatural ancestors were not completely masters of the world to which they had given its final shape. In the first place, though the totemic ancestors and ancestresses were not accountable for any of their actions to any superior Power, and though the paths of their wanderings lay "beyond the borders of good and evil," as it were, it is clear from the concluding episodes of many of the sacred myths that aboriginal religion everywhere envisaged and assumed the existence of some indefinable, nameless Force that was capable of bringing about the final downfall of even the most powerful earth-born supernatural beings who had deliberately committed breaches of those moral laws which governed the conduct of their later human reincarnations. This Force was neither explained in specific terms nor even given a name in aboriginal mythology: it was merely implicit in the retribution that overtook some of those ancestral transgressors who had committed criminal actions, such as cannibalism or murder of close kinsfolk.

Secondly, the earth-born totemic ancestors were subject to age, sickness, and decay. They could be hurt and wounded, and they knew the meaning of pain. Again, their wanderings on the surface of the earth were only of limited duration. All the earth-born supernatural beings, after they had accomplished their labours and completed their wanderings, were overpowered by weariness. It is true that they were by their very nature immortal, and that even those of them who were "killed" by other totemic ancestors continued their existence in the form of rocks or sacred objects (often called by their Aranda name of *tjurunga*). All of them, however, sank back into their first state of sleep, and their bodies either vanished into the ground (often at the sites where they had first emerged) or turned into rocks, trees, or tjurunga objects. Like the birthplaces of the totemic ancestors, these final resting places were regarded as sacred centres and had to be avoided on pain of death by humans, except on special ceremonial occasions. Before the final disappearance of the totemic ancestors from the surface of the earth, death (for the human beings of later days) had been brought into the world by the acts of some of them. The sun, the moon, and the rest of the earth-born celestial bodies now rose to the sky; and the world of birth, labour, pain, and death that men and women have known ever since came into being.

Local variations of these general beliefs about the nature of the supernatural beings were considerable. In the northern Kimberley region, for instance, the cult of the Wondjina was of the highest importance. The Wondjina were supernatural beings closely associated with the sky, the rainbow, spirit children, and the increase of natural species. These Wondjina were believed to continue their existence as visible rock and cave paintings: their pictures, in short, represented "the very essence or spirit of the beings and creatures depicted" (BERNDT).

Some of the most widely publicized totemic ancestors in recent anthropological literature are those associated with localities in the northern section of the Northern Territory, where the sacred ritual was largely connected with various fertility cults. These cults honoured personages such as the Fertility Mother and the Rainbow Serpent, the Lightning Brothers, the Wawalag Sisters, the Kunapipi Mother, and the Djanggawul Sisters and Brother. It was in this area that bark paintings, *mimi* or stick figure paintings, and the so-called "X-ray" pictures were the dominant forms of art. These paintings, incidentally, represent the very peak of Australian visual art.

While these totemic ancestors were not represented by carved human figures, except in eastern Arnhem Land, they were believed to have imparted some of their supernatural powers to various symbolical objects, both permanent and temporary. Among the former were the rocks, trees, and tjurunga (slabs of stone or wood, both engraved and plain) into which they had turned, also the Wondjina paintings already mentioned. Among the latter were the objects made for use in the sacred ceremonies—tnatantja poles, waningga thread crosses, and ground paintings. These temporary objects were all regarded as replicas, made by totemites, of originals created by their totemic ancestors.

If the term "tjurunga" is applied to the sacred wooden boards generally, then it may be stated that they were in use in almost all parts of Australia. The only areas where they were not found were Bathurst and Melville Islands, also Tasmania; and they were rarely used in western Arnhem Land. The smaller boards that were swung at sacred ceremonies are known as bullroarers.

Three general observations may now be made on the sacred myths themselves.

(a) The time when these supernatural beings wandered about on earth has often been labelled in anthropological literature as "the dream time"—a term first coined by Spencer and Gillen. This is a wrong translation of the Aranda *altjiranga ngambakala* ("having originated out of eternity," "having originated out of one's own self," "born out of one's own eternity"), which was often shortened to *altjiranga* ("ever from eternity," "ever from the very beginning"). The root meaning of *altjira* is "eternal," "uncreated." The Aranda verb *altjira rama* (to dream) is a transitive verb requiring an object. It means literally either "I see eternal things" (without a stated object) or "I see with eternal vision" (with an added object); for during a dream the mortal soul (see below) was believed to leave the body of the sleeper and to have the experiences seen in the dream. The term "dream time" is hence an unfortunate misnomer. The English translations suggested above would give the exact renderings. Even the translation "in the beginning" for *altjiranga* would point to the fact that human time began only after the totemic ancestors had sunk back into eternal sleep.

(b) The sacred myths were known only in general outline by the aboriginal women, since only the adult initiated men were eligible for full instruction in sacred matters. Some of the most significant portions of the sacred myths were known only to a handful of elderly men in each totemic clan. The women probably preserved additional mythical episodes as part of their own secret lore.

(c) In order to protect the most secret portions of their sacred myths even more, certain Australian local groups circulated traditional false versions among the younger men. This was true particularly in the Aranda-speaking area. Thus in one of the most important Western Aranda myths the native cat ancestor Pmalbungka of Ltalaltuma was described as sending his sons out to hunt wallabies and as eating the cooked game with them. This traditional "false version" served as a cover for the correct tradition, which informed the elderly Ltalaltuma totemites that neither Pmalbungka nor his sons ever ate any wallabies: Pmalbungka opened his arm veins each day and fed his sons with his own blood. Here we come upon one form of the concept of blood as a symbol of life. Another form is to be found in those Australian myths where totemic ancestors are described as shedding their blood on the ground in order to produce their progeny.

Though there existed divine sky dwellers also, these in most parts of Australia took no interest in human affairs nor wielded any power over men. Only in the eastern Australian religious systems—among whose believers circumcision was unknown—did the sky beings assume central importance.

The main authority for the beliefs and rites in eastern Australia is

HOWITT, who described the exploits of such sky-heroes as Baiame, Daramulun, and others. These were honoured in special cults, in which bullroarers, carved trees, and clay figures of animals and Daramulun featured prominently. Though the records about them are rather sketchy, it is certain that these sky-heroes were intimately associated with *bora* ground initiation ceremonies, which differed considerably from the initiation rites of inland Australia; for in eastern Australia circumcision was not carried out. Tooth evulsion largely took its place. Failure to practise circumcision meant that the eastern Australians were separated by strong social and religious barriers from their inland neighbours.

Outside the eastern Australian region, no traces can be found of any single Supreme Being that exercised an overriding control over the powers and functions of the great multitude of the earth-born totemic ancestors. This fact can be expressed in another way by the statement that the powers and the functions of the Supreme Being (God) venerated in the Higher Religions were, in Australian religion, shown as "splintered" and parcelled out among a host of lesser supernatural personages, each with his or her own well-defined orbit. (Hence in Australia men believed in οἱ Θεοί rather than in ὁ Θεός). These personages were all tied to local sacred centres, and they respected one another's spheres of power.

III. MAN

The aboriginal forms of religious worship were determined by the Australian conception of man and his personal relationship to the supernatural beings.

Mankind, like the totemic ancestors, was believed to have eternal origins. For instance, in Central Australia the first human beings were believed to have come into existence in the shape of semi-embryonic masses of half-developed infants, all joined together in their hundreds, lying helplessly at places which later took on their present shapes of salt lakes or great waterholes. These masses were sliced up into individual infants by certain totemic ancestors so that they would develop into full human beings. Thus mankind in its present form came into existence.

While the myths concerning the origin of mankind differed in various parts of Australia, there existed everywhere the belief that, since the time when the totemic ancestors returned to their eternal sleep, all individual men and women had stood in some intimate and unbreakable personal relationship with one or the other of the supernatural earth-born personages which figured in their worship.

For a full understanding of this relationship in any given area detailed knowledge of the conception and reincarnation beliefs held in that locality is necessary. Over most (perhaps the whole) of Australia it was believed that the supernatural beings had left an invisible trail of life behind them in the eternal landscape shaped by their wanderings. Pregnant women received some of this supernatural life, and passed it on to their unborn infants.

Since the Australian tribes have so often been accused by anthropological writers of complete ignorance of physiological paternity, it is necessary to emphasize the fact that, at least in those regions where more careful research has recently been undertaken, it has been shown that the facts of conception were adequately understood. In the Aranda-speaking area of Central Australia, for instance, it has always been accepted that intercourse between a man and a woman resulted in a foetus which had a mortal human "life" (or "soul") of its own: in other words, man came into being initially like the animals, whose existence also resulted from mating between male and female parents. But man differed from the animals in acquiring the greater part of his personality from his all-important second "life" (or "soul"), which was immortal. This second soul was part of the "life" of one of the immortal supernatural ancestors, who had entered the body of an already pregnant woman at some definite point of the eternal landscape. In other words, a totemic ancestor seeking rebirth chose not just a married woman, but rather a pregnant woman, as his mother.

There were several ways in which this spark of supernatural life was believed to make its entry. It might enter into the future mother either at her first bout of morning sickness in a given pregnancy (brought on, it was believed, by food containing some of the "life" of a supernatural being), or while she was experiencing the first stabs of pain of more advanced pregnancy (caused by a bullroarer hurled at her by a supernatural being), or while she (or, in some areas, her husband) was experiencing a dream-vision of the future child (brought on by the supernatural being who was seeking rebirth). Every person's second "soul" was therefore a part of the total living and immortal essence of a totemic ancestor or ancestress who had sought reincarnation in a new human being. Hence in Central Australia, and probably in most other parts of the continent also, every person was believed to have received most of his personality, and also much of his physical shape, from the supernatural personage from whom he had become re-incarnated in one of the above ways. He was hence believed to have two "lives" (or "souls"): the first was human and mortal, the second was immortal and eternal.

As a result, *all* human beings in Australian religion achieved a personal dignity probably unequalled in other systems. The very multiplicity of the supernatural beings ensured that every man (and woman) was considered to have a personal link with the divine and the eternal.

Since in Australia the supernatural beings were associated with boulders, trees, and tjurunga objects, their human incarnations were linked with them also. They acted as symbols of the link existing between each person and the supernatural being from whom he had derived his second "soul," and hence also his totemic animal or plant. The place where this second "soul" had entered into his body (as, for instance, in the Aranda-speaking area), or where the person himself had been born (as, for instance, among the Western Desert tribes), was regarded as his special home ground. Its sacred traditions became his property after initiation, if he was a male: women, though they also owned sacred traditions, were normally kept in imperfect awareness of the nature of these, and had their appropriate sacred totemic acts carried out on their behalf by close male relatives.

Over most of interior Australia sacred tjurunga slabs (and stones) constituted the visible links between men and women and their supernatural beings. Here every individual possessed one of these symbolic objects, which were kept in sacred caves or on tree platforms. In some areas sea shells were used for a similar purpose.

IV. Worship

The Australian conception of the nature of the supernatural beings and of the nature of man inevitably determined the whole shape of Australian worship.

Even in their secular activities the aboriginals believed that they were imitating at every point activities instituted by certain of their supernatural beings. All forms of hunting and food gathering, all processes of making tools and weapons, and even the various methods of cooking the game animals, were thought to have been instituted by these beings, and some of them—who thus assumed the role of culture heroes—had taught these skills to the first men and women. Since in Australia mankind was, by reincarnation, indivisibly linked with the supernatural beings, religious worship naturally assumed outward forms rather different from those found elsewhere on the globe, where special intermediaries (for instance, priests) were regarded as necessary to provide efficient links between divinities and mortals. Again, there was in Australia no real dichotomy between the world of everyday activities and the sacred sphere: man's role in both was to make his behaviour as closely similar as he could to that of the supernatural beings.

Propitiation of remote supernatural beings, and prayers to unwilling, angry, or jealous deities, could form no part of Australian religious worship: men do not propitiate themselves or pray to themselves.

The religious acts hence fell, in the main, into four categories:

a. *Initiation rites*

Here novices underwent physical ordeals which were believed to have been prescribed by the supernatural beings, before instruction could be given to them to explain their relationship to these beings and to the physical world created by them. The ordeals themselves varied considerably. Over most of Australia circumcision was the main initiatory rite, and most of the tribes in this area also practised subincision. The eastern Australian tribes, however, did not practise either circumcision or subincision. Here tooth-evulsion and blood-letting rites (which, together with head gashing, were also practised in the circumcision area) often formed part of the initiatory rites. Whatever the nature of the physical ordeals might be, they were always inflicted on special initiation grounds, after days or weeks of preparatory singing and ritual carried out by the fully initiated men. The *bora* initiatory grounds of eastern Australia have already been mentioned.

These initiatory rites affected all males, who generally went through them soon after reaching puberty. They had the object of preparing youths for admission to full social status as men and of introducing them into full communion with that spiritual world which was open to them by reason of their reincarnation from the supernatural beings.

The religious importance of these initiatory rites varied very considerably from region to region. In eastern Australia, where the sky-beings were revered, and where the sounds of the bullroarers swung on the *bora* grounds were believed to be the voices of these beings, the initiatory rites were regarded as being of the highest religious importance: they represented the full introduction of the novices into the spiritual world that controlled their whole lives. This was largely true also of the circumcision rites of the Western Desert tribes of inland Australia, where the special acts shown to the novices before circumcision were regarded as the most sacred rites which they would ever witness. Among the Pitjantjara and allied tribes, for instance, they were called *ngalungka*, and the objects and even some of the verses associated with these rites could not be revealed on pain of death, except on these special occasions. In certain parts of northern Australia, too, the initiation rites were regarded as constituting perhaps the most important part of the sacred ritual.

But other tribes, such as the numerous Aranda-speaking communities of the Centre, valued the initiation rites mainly as ceremonies ensuring the correct physical preparation of the males (through circumcision and subincision) for participation in the sacred commemorative and increase rites in which the religious worship of the initiated men found its full expression. Even here, however, evidence can be found that these initiatory rites may once have been credited with a much more important religious function. Thus, among the Western Aranda, the non-sacred Tuanjiraka legend was compulsorily taught to all women and children. According to this legend, supernatural beings assembled on the circumcision ground, roaring loudly (their roars being imitated by the swinging of large bullroarers). Their one-legged leader Tuanjiraka finally cut off the heads of the initiates with a stone knife. He stuck the heads back several days later, after they had begun to decay; and the initiates, miraculously restored to life, were now in a fit state to establish communication with the secret world of the supernatural beings. The continued transmission of this false account to the Western Aranda women and children was claimed to be essential for the full achievement of the purpose of circumcision.

b. *Commemorative ceremonies*

These were dramatic performances organized into cycles, each of which was associated with one of the more important sacred myths. These cycles were tied to the sacred centres mentioned in the myths, and presented the supernatural personages celebrated in the myths before the eyes of the men who were believed to be reincarnated from them, also before those of their relatives and friends.

All acts in a cycle were carefully graded. The early acts, portraying the minor figures of a myth, or the less important episodes in the stories of the major characters, were freely shown to all members of the appropriate audience, including young initiates. The later acts, in which the major personages in the most important episodes (also the most sacred ceremonial objects) were revealed, were shown only to carefully selected audiences of older totemic clansmen; and some of the concluding acts were never revealed to more than three or four of the most trusted senior members and leaders of the appropriate totemic clans.

In most areas of Australia the actors in these ceremonies had their bodies decorated with birds' down or pulverized plant-matter stuck on with blood. Decorations of this nature served to obliterate the human lineaments of the actors, who were, in addition, precluded from speaking with their own voices from the time when their decorating had begun till after the conclusion of their acts. Only the appropriate sacred verses, believed to have been composed for such occasions by the supernatural beings honoured by these acts, could be intoned by the men taking part in the decoration and in the ritual.

Probably because of the use of human blood, drawn off to the accompaniment of sacred verses, the belief was widespread that the tufts of down or plant-matter that were scattered from the persons of the actors or from their ceremonial objects during the performances of these sacred commemorative acts had acquired the power of turning themselves into the appropriate animals or plants. Thus the down shed by actors during bandicoot, emu, snake, and other ceremonies, was believed to be capable of turning into bandicoots, emus, snakes, and other animals, after the ceremonial ground had been, in addition, quickened by heavy rains. Similarly, commemorative acts in which the sun (in Australia always an earth-born being, translated to the sky only at the end of his or her earthly exploits) was represented were staged only very sparingly by sun totemites, since it was feared that these acts had the power of bringing about a great increase of summer heat.

c. *Increase ceremonies*

In these ceremonies the members of a totemic clan carried out special rites relating to the increase of the animals or plants of their own totem at sites where it was believed that these creative rites had been instituted by the local totemic ancestors. Thus Aranda men who believed that they had become reincarnated from kangaroo totemic ancestors that had emerged from the Krantji soak would assemble from time to time near this soak. They would sing the kangaroo increase charms and perform the kangaroo increase ritual appropriate to Krantji. Both charms and increase ritual were believed to have been first used by the Krantji kangaroo totemic ancestors for the increase of kangaroos. The blood used for the sacred ground paintings and the sacred objects used in the Krantji ceremonies had to be given by men regarded as reincarnations of the Krantji kangaroo totemic ancestors or by close male relatives of such men: for it was believed that "kangaroo life"—symbolized by the blood of human kangaroo clansmen—had to be poured on the ground, and that all original actions and words of the local kangaroo supernatural beings had to be repeated exactly, before new kangaroos would emerge from the ground at Krantji as they had done at the beginning of time.

At many local increase centres in Central Australia both ground paintings and totem poles figured in the increase ritual. The former had the function of the feminine symbol, the latter of the male symbol.

The use of human blood donated by the totemites was a striking feature of religious ritual throughout Australia. Whereas in many non-Australian religious systems animals were sacrificed to propitiate deities, the Australian totemite had to use his own blood in his ritual. It was drawn by himself either from his arm veins or from his subincised urethra, normally to the intonation of sacred verses. It was hence regarded not merely as human blood, but as a sacred liquid which contained the power to create new life, just as the blood of the original supernatural beings had done. And just as animals had emerged at the beginning of time from ground saturated with the blood of the totemic ancestors, and from objects used by them, so it was believed that animals of the appropriate species could be created by the use of painted shields, ground paintings, or totem poles, whose sacred designs had been applied on surfaces anointed with the blood of human totemites to the accompaniment of the creative words left behind by the totemic ancestors. Because of these features, it would seem reasonable to classify increase ceremonies of this kind as being of a sacramental rather than of a magical nature.

Other ways of promoting the increase of plants and animals consisted in rubbing with stones or striking with branches rocks and boulders representing the changed bodies of the ancestral beings, or in sprinkling these rocks and boulders with blood given by the totemites. In both cases, the appropriate creative verses of the ancestral beings had to be intoned. In the Kimberleys and in western Arnhem Land, the sacred paintings in caves and on rocks used to be retouched with their proper colours from time to time to ensure similar increases of animals and plants, and also of rain.

In all cases it was believed that man could bring about the increases of plants and animals, and also of rain, only through the supernatural beings, by repeating their original creative actions and by intoning their original creative words. He derived his right to carry out the ritual from the fact that, through reincarnation, some of the "life" of these totemic ancestors was residing in his own person.

d. *Magic and sorcery*

There were some forms of sacred ritual, however, where more conventionally "magic" ideas permeated the acts. Thus, the charms sung by medicine men to heal diseases were, like all other sacred verses, believed to have been composed by totemic ancestors. But they became fully effective only when chanted by specially initiated medicine men: these medicine men derived their powers either directly from visionary contacts with the supernatural beings who had first composed these healing charms or by direct transference from older medicine men.

In certain areas it was believed that there existed special totemic ancestors or ancestral spirits who were responsible for transferring these magic powers to the medicine men. Thus among the Wuradjeri of eastern Australia Baiame himself was believed to have given out the magic quartz crystals used for magic purposes. Here we come upon the idea of a *magica successio*; for it was not necessary for a medicine man to be regarded as the reincarnation of one of those particular totemic ancestors who had left these healing charms behind.

The symbols of the magic powers that had been transferred to the medicine men varied in different parts of Australia: quartz crystals, pearlshells, australites, bones, and stones were all used for this purpose. Just as varied were the claims made in different areas for the magic powers themselves. They ranged from the power of divination (for instance, indicating a murderer after someone had died) to the more normal powers of curing patients and of making rain.

Since these magic powers had been derived, not by reincarnation from the supernatural beings but only by later transference from older medicine men or from special ancestral spirits, it is not surprising to find that, in Central Australia at any rate, the magic powers were not necessarily regarded as being of a permanent nature. The Western Aranda, for instance, believed that a medicine man could lose his magic powers completely if he broke some of the food restrictions placed on him (such as eating fat or marrow). In this area a medicine man who had lost his special powers could never hope to regain them.

The Australian attitude towards the totemic ancestors or ancestral spirits that had transferred their magic powers to medicine men always remained one of awe and reverence. Like all supernatural beings, they could not be coerced against their will by man's use of their magic charms. If the charms failed to work in a given instance, it was the medicine man who was blamed. Such a failure was attributed either to the more powerful magic of a rival medicine man, to some mistake made by the medicine man while he was carrying out his magic ritual, or to the loss by the medicine man of his magic powers.

Other forms of Australian magic ritual included love magic and the death rite of bone-pointing. These two forms of magic ritual, too, were believed to depend for their efficacy upon the singing of the correct verses and the exact repetition of the appropriate symbolic actions handed down by certain supernatural beings. But the persons carrying out such ritual did not have to belong personally to the totems of these supernatural beings.

e. *Other rites*

Under this heading come the fertility rites of northern Australia, particularly of Arnhem Land. These included the Kunapipi cult, and the rites based on the myths of the Rainbow Serpent, the Wawalag Sisters, and the Djanggawul Sisters and Brother. The Djanggawul ritual made extensive use of rangga poles, decorated with ochre patterns and hung with feathered strings (the rangga poles and posts were the most prominent sacred objects of eastern Arnhem Land). Here sex was invested with a religious significance. The ritual laid stress on the symbolic representation of intercourse, which was intended to fertilize both human beings and the earth. Birth and spiritual rebirth were also emphasized in the Kunapipi cult: "the sacred ground is the 'Mother place' through which men pass to be reborn" (BERNDT).

The women's secret rites also belonged to this group. These included women's love magic (designed to attract a sweetheart or to renew a husband's affection, such as the *djarada* and *jawalju*), charms to destroy rivals in love, fertility ritual intended to promote having babies, and, at least in some areas, commemorative acts celebrating certain ancestresses.

In certain types of love-magic performances, both men and women took part. In addition, the presence of dancing women was essential in the Aranda area at some stage of such specifically male ceremonies as circumcision and the ritual preparations of men who were about to be despatched on avenging expeditions.

Far too little is still known of the women's secret rites: only skilled female investigators, who have gained the confidence of the older aboriginal female guardians, can hope to be admitted to the fulness of their secrets.

Finally there were the mortuary rites—the rites which were performed to bring about the severing of the last social ties with the dead by their surviving family members and friends. These reached their highest complexity in Arnhem Land, and on Bathurst and Melville Islands. The *bugamani* or grave posts of Bathurst and Melville Islands sometimes attained a length of eighteen feet, and their decorative patterns were highly ornamental. In north-central Arnhem Land the skulls of dead persons were painted with special designs and carried about by close relatives for about a year before they were deposited in the waterhole from which the dead person's soul had come, or in a cave. An additional aim of the mortuary rites everywhere was to speed the spirits of the departed to whatever future environment awaited them: the character of this land of the dead varied from tribe to tribe.

f. *Summary*

If we except the medicine men, there was no special class of holy persons to be found in Australia: *all* human beings had the high personal status derived from close personal association with the supernatural beings.

All sacred acts carried out by humans were believed to be exact repetitions of acts first instituted by the supernatural beings. At no level of religious ritual was there any suggestion that the supernatural beings were being compelled by human activities to yield to the wishes and demands of their human worshippers.

No sacrifices of animals, plants, or human beings were made to the supernatural beings by their human worshippers: because of their personal links with the supernatural beings the human worshippers used their own "sacred" blood whenever it was required for the ceremonies.

Since the human totemites believed themselves to be, at least to a significant degree, of the same substance as the personages who figured in their sacred songs and ritual, aboriginal religion established a deeply personal relationship between, every human individual and the world of eternity. Totemic ancestors, totemic animals and plants, and the sacred landscape were all linked with mankind by personal bonds; and it was these personal bonds which distinguished the aboriginal Australian beliefs sharply from the nature religions found in other parts of the world.

Probably over most of Australia, every individual, in spite of the multiplicity of supernatural beings in his tribal community, was linked indivisibly with only one of these personages. His ritual rights and duties and his whole social status were determined by this personal link (STREHLOW, T. G. H., *Personal Monototemism in a Polytotemic Community*).

As might be expected, the ideal conduct of a worshipper was one that could be described (as has been done in the religious context of non-Australian communities) as "ritual holiness." The death penalty was commonly imposed on the more serious ritual offences classifiable as sacrilege. Moral offences in our sense brought down merely the wrath of organized human society upon the offender, not the anger of the supernatural beings. Hence there was among the Australian aboriginals no real feeling of "sin" in the Christian sense. However, the basic elements of the social structure of the Australian tribes were also believed to have been instituted by some of the supernatural beings; and moral offences that were held to endanger the very foundations of society could be punished severely, even the death penalty being imposed for certain grave offences, such as incest.

A tribute should be paid to the aboriginal attitude of religious toleration: every person's religious beliefs and ritual duties were, to a significant degree, of a private nature, and hence largely secure against outside interference. At the same time, every man had to act as a ceremonial assistant to men of other totems, whenever called upon to do so. The very nature of the religious beliefs thus acted as a barrier to religious fanaticism and authoritarianism.

V. DESTINY AND ESCHATOLOGY

It was man's destiny to live in harmony and in identification with the supernatural powers that had shaped his physical environment, and that were still sustaining it. Only in this way could he achieve happiness and security.

Man's emulation of the way of life first instituted by the supernatural beings also helped to sustain nature. Animals and plants needed to be multiplied from time to time through the intonation of the creative words and the performances of the creative acts that had first brought them into being. Similarly rain depended on the words and acts of those human clansmen who had been reincarnated from the rain ancestors. Any failure or neglect by the human clansmen to repeat the creative ritual of the supernatural beings would lead, it was believed, to the eventual drying up of the landscape and to the death of the local animals and plants. Creation time and human time were, in a vital sense, continuous.

The close ties between man and the supernatural beings were broken at death. After death mortuary rites ensured both that the survivors could, after a traditionally fixed interval of mourning, return to their normal way of life, and that the spirits of the departed, after being appeased by the sorrowing of their relatives and friends, could be induced to seek out their new future environment. A convenient illustration of the meaning of death as explained in the Australian religious context may be taken from the normal Aranda beliefs as to what happened to man's two souls after death. The "immortal" soul went back to the site at which it had first passed into the unborn infant, and the "mortal" soul turned into a "ghost". Both among the Aranda and in other Australian tribes it was this ghost whose possible malicious anger towards its former friends and relatives had to be averted by various mourning ceremonies; and these culminated in some final act that marked the end of the period during which the ghost could exert its influence on the survivors. After that no more account was taken of a deceased person; and in many communities it was assumed that the ghost ceased to exist in its former haunts, or even to exist at all.

How greatly religious beliefs differed even between tribal groups closely akin to each other may be seen in the fact that, while the Western Aranda groups believed that the mortal soul was finally destroyed by lightning and that the immortal soul went back to the place whence it had first sprung, the north-eastern Aranda groups believed that the immortal souls of all their departed (now called *erintarinja* and *arambaranga*) kept on roaming about in the country where they had once dwelt in human bodies, and that they continued watching over the ceremonial acts of the survivors. These north-eastern Aranda groups had no firm traditions about the fate of the mortal souls: it was, however, accepted that, after the mortuary rites, these mortal souls ("ghosts") could be disregarded completely.

In the final analysis man, in Australian totemistic religion, was linked with the animals and the plants of his environment, and with the eternal landscape in which he lived, because he carried in him a vital spark of one of the supernatural beings that had created all life. Life as such could not be conquered by death: only its temporal manifestations (men, animals, and plants) suffered destruction.

Australian religion inspired in its aboriginal worshippers a vital sense, and a deep conviction, of personal contact with verities and values passionately believed to be eternal: the eternity *motif* was one of the most striking basic elements of Australian religion.

The concept of a future existence after death did not influence men's actions in this world: Australian religion was a religion for men and women living in a land which had never ceased being inhabited by supernatural beings. Human time was only a part of eternity, and all values motivating society were believed to be timeless and unalterable.

In spite of Tillich's dictum that "there are no societies which possess the eternal," every Australian totemite firmly believed that he "possessed the eternal" in his own life span.

BIBLIOGRAPHY

BASEDOW, H., *The Australian Aboriginal*, Preece, Adelaide. 1925.

BERNDT, R. M. and C., *The World of the First Australians*, Ure Smith, Sydney, 1964.

——,"Wuradjeri Magic and 'Clever Men'", *Oceania*, Vol. XVII, No. 4; Vol. XVIII No. 1, 1941.

——,*Kunapipi*, Cheshire, Melbourne, 1951.

——,*Djanggawul*, Routledge and Kegan Paul, London, 1952.

EBERLE, O., *Cenalora*, Otto Walter, Olten und Freiburg, 1954.

ELKIN, A. P., *Aboriginal Men of High Degree*, Australasian Publishing Company, Sydney, 1945.

——,*The Australian Aborigines: How to understand them*, Angus and Robertson, Sydney, 1964.

HOWITT, A. W., *The Native Tribes of South-East Australia*, Macmillan, London, 1904.

MEGGITT, M. J., *Desert People*, Angus and Robertson, Sydney, 1962.

MOUNTFORD, C. P., *Arnhem Land: Art, Myth and Symbolism*, Melbourne University Press, Melbourne, 1956.

RÓHEIM, G., *Australian Totemism*, George Allen and Unwin, London, 1925.

——,*The Eternal Ones of the Dream*, International Universities Press, New York, 1945.

SCHMIDT, W., *Ursprung der Gottesidee*, Münster, 1926-35.

SPENCER, B. and GILLEN, F. J., *The Native Tribes of Central Australia*, Macmillan, London, 1899.

— —,— —,*The Northern Tribes of Central Australia*, Macmillan, London, 1904.

STANNER, W. E. H., *On Aboriginal Religion*, Oceania Monograph No. 11, Sydney, 1963.

— —,"Religion, Totemism and Symbolism" in *Aboriginal Man in Australia* (chap. 8), Angus and Robertson, Sydney, 1965.

STREHLOW, C., *Die Aranda- und Loritja-Stämme in Zentral-Australien*, Veröffentlichungen des Frankfurter Museums für Völkerkunde, Frankfurt, 1907-21.

STREHLOW, T. G. H., "Ankotarinja, an Aranda Myth," *Oceania*, Vol. IV, No. 2. 1933.

— —,*Aranda Traditions*, Melbourne University Press, Melbourne, 1947.

— —,"Personal Monototemism in a Polytotemic Community," in *Festschrift für Ad. E. Jensen*, Klaus Renner Verlag, Munich, 1964.

WARNER, W. L., *A Black Civilization*, Harper, New York, 1937/58.

WORMS, E. A., "Religion", in *Australian Aboriginal Studies*, Oxford University Press, Melbourne, 1963.

THE PRESENT RELIGIOUS SITUATION

BY

E. G. PARRINDER

I

Since there is no written history of the religions of illiterate peoples, little can be known about their past. In some places they have been isolated from the literary religions. But in the hills and jungles of India, Burma and China, or the steppes of Siberia, they have been in closer contact with literate peoples and may have absorbed some of their religious ideas. Yet until modern times it seems that the illiterate peoples remained relatively isolated, for contact would have brought some missionary attempts at conversion or the introduction of writing.

The modern picture is one of mingling cultures and rapid change. The old isolation has gone and there are few "untouched" peoples. Modern exploration, imperialism, nationalism, communications, all have contributed to make wide contacts inevitable. The most remote markets have on sale Swedish matches, Jamaican sugar, Manchester cloths, or Marseille cooking pots.

The political and commercial influences bring about social changes and enlarge mental horizons. Not only are illiterate peoples visited from the outside, they themselves travel as their fathers never could. Many go to the towns, and work in mines and ports. There is more money, and goods to buy. There are international languages to be learnt: English or Swahili, Spanish or Hindi. Even in country villages new laws may change old customs; the land may be alienated, as it never was under traditional custom, to allow the creation of large plantations. This affects ancestral beliefs, for the ancestors were the owners of the land.

More important is the arrival of missionaries of the "higher" religions, seeking to educate people and change them from their old faith. Christian missions began again effectively in the last century, and they have continued till the present with the result, as a church historian says, that the Church, in extent and numbers, has spread more in the present than in any previous century. The greatest successes of the Church have been among illiterate peoples; there has been much less conversion from the literate faiths. The prestige of written tradition, of scriptures, and of universality, have given both Christianity and Islam great advantages. Christianity has also used the authority of imperialism, or the superiority of Western material culture, as powerful weapons in conversion in every continent. Hardly less important has been its use of education. The churches have built countless schools, and have taught their faith to the crowds of young people who sought self-improvement through the schools. The old religion was often looked down upon as the province of the old and the ignorant. Such wisdom as they had tends to be swamped or forgotten.

Other world religions have revived their missionary zeal also. Islam has gathered in millions of converts in tropical Africa, and Buddhists have advanced in south-east Asia. Even Hindus have sought to bring within their religion the non-caste hill and forest tribes, imposing their own dress and customs on them.

The considerable numbers of conversions from the old religions to the new, have inevitably weakened the former. Within living memory religions have declined, if not disappeared. It is not now possible to describe the pre-Christian religion of, say, the Hottentots. This process seems bound to continue. There have been some revivals of ancient cults, but the forces of modernism are strong and growing.

However, a significant feature of the mingling of old and new is the formation of hybrid cults. The Cargo Cults of the Pacific Islands reflect old beliefs with new religious aspirations, hoping for supernatural goods and superhuman powers coming from over the sea. Ethiopian sects in South Africa reflect black nationalism, and Zionist sects express revivalism and faith-healing. Organizations, such as the Cao Dai of Vietnam and the Tenri Kyo of Japan, have mingled old and new social and religious hopes. They are often originated or led by powerful charismatic leaders.

The great numbers of such religious movements, and their indigenous rather than foreign leadership, suggest to some writers that they are "religions of the oppressed," if not the "opium of the people." But it is not as simple as that. The countless small religious groups all over the world cannot all be attributed to social oppression. If there are many sects in South Africa, so there are in America, and there have been many in Europe. Sectarianism is not merely a feature of Protestantism, or of Christianity, but of religion in general.

Some writers who have written about sectarianism should have looked more closely at the indigenous background of the religion. It would have shown that there was remarkably little organization, many priests and prophets, and different rituals and healing shrines; these might later have been called sectarianism. In the old religion there was concern for physical as well as spiritual health, and so in the new sects there is great pre-occupation with healing by faith. Some modern sects are millenarian and messianic; others have no trace of such hopes. All give an indigenous expression to religion, yet they freely borrow such elements of a new faith as suit their purposes.

Syncretism is inevitable in modern circumstances, and it is a feature of much religious history. Christian sects may help to root Christianity deeper into an indigenous environment, and remove the marks of foreign origins from its local expression. Islamic sects may give Islam a wider outlook, by adopting Western methods, such as education, to the needs of Muslim communities. New prophets and cults may meet spiritual needs of their followers. But there are also dangers of obscurantism, by rejecting Western medicine and returning to magic.

It is hard to estimate the numbers of those who follow the old religions, the converts to the new, and those who make a deliberate synthesis. At the beginning of this century the numbers of Christians in Africa south of the Sahara would hardly have been reckoned at a million, and Muslims not many more. In 1968 a survey concluded that there were more than sixty million Christians in sub-Saharan Africa, and Muslims must have been at least as many. Many "tribalists" remained, but their numbers were constantly decreasing and most of them could be reckoned potential Christians or Muslims. Christianity has claimed many aboriginal Australians and most Pacific Islanders, and increasing missionary efforts are being made in South America. The largest numbers of those who follow the old faiths are probably to be found in Africa, but they are more vulnerable to the new religions than are the inhabitants of the forests of South America.

The religions of illiterate peoples are declining. Their outward forms seem bound to disappear, though perhaps not all before the end of this century. But many of the old religious attitudes will remain, and they will condition the mentality of many who have embraced new religions, and even of those who have abandoned most formal religious practice altogether.

II. History of the Study of the Religion

"Laymen may not be aware that most of what has been written in the past, and with some assurance, and is still trotted out in colleges and universities, about animism, totemism, magic, etc., has been shown to be erroneous or at least dubious." So declares E. E. EVANS-PRITCHARD in his important book *Theories of Primitive Religion*. The history of the study of the religions of illiterate peoples shows a strong preponderance of theory over established fact. Perhaps this was almost inevitable, since the scope was worldwide, and comprehensive theories were useful. But there was the danger of undue generalization, or forcing all facts into the same mould. Today, however, there is such concern for fact and particularity that it is hard to arrive at any theory at all.

Interest in the ways of unlettered people dates at least from STRABO writing on the Troglodytes or CAESAR on the Druids. Later writers often had felicitous styles but less experience of travel than these classical models. ROUSSEAU spun theories about natural religion, and De BROSSES in 1760 concluded that the "dieux fétiches" of the negroes and of Egypt showed that religion originated in fetishism. This theory held the field for a long time, at least down to Comte in 1908, who tried to show that there was an evolutionary development from fetishism to polytheism to monotheism. As the basis of fetishism was supposed to be ignorance, due to the inability of primitive man to think straight, so the goal of evolution would be positivism or atheism, by abolishing all cosmology.

The word Fetish was introduced by the Portuguese trading round Africa, and describing as *feitiço* (from Latin *facticius*) the African cult objects that they saw. These were artificial objects, and their name could hardly be adequate as a description of the religion as a whole. Later E. B. TYLOR tried to confine the use of the word fetish to "the doctrine of spirits, embodied in, or attached to, or conveying influence through, certain material objects. Fetishism will be taken as including the worship of 'stocks and stones' and thence it passes by an imperceptible gradation into idolatry." But clearly this description could be applied to many of the "higher" religions that use "stocks and stones" or believe that spirits convey influence through "certain material objects." It is unfair to apply this description simply to "primitive" peoples, and inadequate to use it for a whole religious complex. This word Fetish has generally been abandoned today as misleading.

TYLOR's *Primitive Culture* was one of the most influential studies of the subject. He himself was dissatisfied with the word Fetish and coined Animism, "the theory of souls," as "a minimum definition of religion" and a "fundamental concept of primitive belief." It was suggested in Paragraph I that this word also is unsatisfactory as a description of any system of religion. It will be noted that TYLOR was trying to do two things, at least. He sought the nature of "primitive" belief, and hoped from that to arrive at a basic definition of all religion and so to get back to the origins of religion.

TYLOR took Animism to refer to the souls of man and natural objects. Other writers gave variations on similar themes. Some held that all gods, in antiquity and modern times, were derived from personifications of the phenomena of nature. MAX MÜLLER was regarded as a leader of this position, though he seems to have thought that since natural objects gave a feeling of the infinite they served as best symbols of it. HERBERT SPENCER took up the idea of ghosts, maintaining that religious myths had historical origins, and that gods had developed out of deified ancestors. This Euhemerism, which could not be proved as the origin of all religion, was put in the shade by TYLOR's Animism, which seemed more scientific or likely. But TYLOR's theory, though supported with illustrations from the Stone Age hunters to modern tropical peoples, was also an attempted explanation of how "natives" think, without proof that the idea of soul or God had arisen in the way suggested. It might be objected that the supposition that animals have souls like human beings belongs to an advanced stage of human culture, and that some peoples at a low cultural level believe in an impersonal Supreme Being.

A modification of Animism was suggested by MARETT in 1899 who invented the term Animatism, to indicate the belief that nature is animated not by personal souls but by vaguer impersonal forces. MARETT disliked the assumption that appeared to be behind TYLOR's theory, that primitive man was a philosopher, spinning hypotheses about souls. He said that "savage religion is something not so much thought out as danced out," though he had never seen any of it in action. MARETT adopted from CODRINGTON a Melanesian word *mana*, to indicate an impersonal force behind all things. It seems clear from later research that *mana* did not mean this, and MARETT's theory was as conjectural as that of TYLOR.

Also from the Pacific came the word Taboo (*tapu*), for a religious prohibition. While from the North American Indians came Totem, used of an animal or plant symbol. Great play was made with these as primitive or original to religion.

Even better known than TYLOR for his writings on all kinds of religion was Sir JAMES FRAZER. His immense works contain masses of story culled from all over the world and fitted into Frazerian patterns. FRAZER had never been out of Europe, and expressed repugnance at the thought of meeting one of the "natives" about whom he wrote so finely. His *Totemism* appeared in 1887 and *The Golden Bough* first in 1890. Yet FRAZER added little of value to TYLOR's theory, and he added confusion by new suppositions. He accepted, perhaps from COMTE, a theory of the progress of mankind, from magic to religion, and from religion to science. According to FRAZER magic came first in man's dealings with nature. It was a kind of primitive science, trying to manipulate material things for human ends, but based on false premises. When magic failed man turned to religion, believing that there were supernatural powers greater than himself, whose almighty will needed propitiation. But this religious supposition must itself in turn give way to the purer knowledge of science, which at last has both the knowledge and the effective method. But there was no solid basis for FRAZER's theory, no proof that magic preceded religion, or was abandoned in favour of religious devotion. In fact magic and religion can be found at most, perhaps all, stages of human culture. FRAZER's theory of development has been abandoned, although some of his terms, like "sympathetic magic", have been useful.

The fascination of simpler forms or early developments of religion is well displayed in the writings of LÉVY-BRUHL. His *Mentalité Primitive* did not appear till 1922, after his philosophical writing, but he challenged the British School for trying to explain other cultures in their own way. They imagined how they would have thought and acted had they been primitive people; what is called the "if I were a horse" fallacy. LÉVY-BRUHL thought that human societies could be classified into two main types, the primitive and the civilized. TYLOR and others had considered that primitives would react as they did themselves, or vice versa, but in fact both would be conditioned by vastly different environments. LÉVY-BRUHL spoke of "pre-logical" modes of thought, to describe mental processes that appear natural in primitives but absurd to Europeans. His critics took this to mean that illiterates cannot think logically; LÉVY-BRUHL meant that they are logical, but with a different kind of logic from our own. Religious facts are social rather than psychological, as DURKHEIM said also, and illiterates reason incorrectly because their society is backward. However, LÉVY-BRUHL was also theorizing without ever visiting the peoples about whom he wrote. He made illiterates more superstitious than they are, and Europeans less than they are, and enlarged the gulf between us which is wide enough already.

EMILE DURKHEIM in *Les Formes élémentaires de la Vie religieuse* in 1911 stressed the social fact of religion. He rejected theories which tried to show it to be an illusion, for if it were it could never have survived so long, or have produced law, science and morals. DURKHEIM noted that illiterates often took little notice of some of the most striking phenomena of nature, and so they were not animists. On the other hand they divinized animals, often humble ones who could hardly have inspired religious feeling. DURKHEIM based much of his theory on SPENCER and GILLEN's *Native Tribes of Central Australia*, and he held that the Totemism there studied was the most elementary form of religion. Other writers of the period thought the same. Religion does not worship an illusion, said DURKHEIM, but its object is society itself. The power of society arouses feelings of respect and concepts of deity. The totem creatures are not worshipped, but their designs engraved on bull-roarers are symbols of the impersonal power of society, of clans and god, which are the same thing.

DURKHEIM's theory was criticized by VAN GENNEP, but this was ignored. His nephew MARCEL MAUSS tried to show that it was valid for a different society, the Eskimos. And MAUSS with HENRI HUBERT applied similar analyses to Vedic and Hebrew religion. The gods represent societies, sacrifices strengthen social forces, which in turn confer strength on individuals.

It was unfortunate that DURKHEIM relied almost entirely on Australian totemism, and that of a particular people, the Arunta. The ceremonies they perform seem to have different meanings elsewhere, and these peoples have still not been adequately studied. But DURKHEIM made a number of unwarrantable assumptions. He assumed that religion was a reflection of society; but if this were so the beliefs of religion would change with every society, whereas universal religions are found in very different social organizations. Further, DURKHEIM thought that totemism was the earliest form of religion, but there is no proof of this. In fact it is not known what were the earliest forms of religion, say, in the Old Stone Age. But there seems no reason to suppose that religion then did not have diverse forms, as it has done usually in its later history. Then, DURKHEIM's belief that because the Australian aboriginals had a fairly simple food-gathering culture therefore their religious ideas were the simplest of all, and reveal the original form of totemism, is also unwarranted. Also the identification of totemism with a clan, and therefore with a society, ignores the fact that some societies have clans but not totems, and others have totems but no clans.

Then came SIGMUND FREUD's theory of the origins of religion, in his *Totem and Taboo* in 1913. This was even more hypothetical than his *Moses and Monotheism*, which experts had dismissed with scorn. Yet FREUD's totem theory has had more effect, though it is psychological rather than social as in the writings of DURKHEIM. From his experience with neurotic patients FREUD considered that magical rituals had been invented to relieve tensions. He thought that religion in like manner arose from feelings of guilt. ROBERTSON SMITH in his *Religion of the Semites* (1889) had assumed a primordial totemism, which culminated in a cannibalistic feast. FREUD's story, for which there was no historical foundation provable, followed this but postulated that primitive men were dominated by the father of the clan who kept all the females to himself. The sons rose against him, killed and ate him, but then in a fit of remorse (the original Oedipus Complex), they deified the father. Religion was thus based on guilt and its rituals commemorated the guilt in communion feasts. FREUD gave no historical evidence for this amazing theory, though he drew some analogies from the behaviour of horses. But in the nature of the case it could only be a theory, relying on faith in Freudian psycho-analysis, for there are no remains of what the earliest, prehistoric, really primitive men, did. Few serious anthropologists accepted the Freudian dogma; it was rejected by KROEBER and MALINOWSKI, by BOAS and SCHMIDT yet FREUD did not modify it. There is no evidence for universal primitive totemism, no history of totemism, no cannibalistic totem feasts.

A reaction against animist and other theories of primitive religion was made by ANDREW LANG in *The Making of Religion*, in 1898. He accepted the belief in the importance of souls, which might have arisen from dreams or psychical phenomena. But LANG rejected the notion that the idea of God arose at a late stage in human history, by a general process of evolution from souls and ghosts. From his missionary and other correspondents, he showed that the idea of a fatherly, omnipotent, High God is found among peoples of low material culture. It may have originated from reflection on creation and design. Indeed LANG thought that the idea of God came first, and was corrupted later by animistic ideas. This too was theory.

LANG's theme was taken up and developed by WILHELM SCHMIDT in *Der Ursprung der Gottesidee*, from 1912 onwards. SCHMIDT tried to establish a chronology for primitive cultures, holding that food-gathering peoples, like the Pygmies, Australian aboriginals, and Eskimos, are the "ethnologically oldest" people. These people then being shown as monotheists prove that monotheism was the original pattern of religion, from which mankind degenerated in a Fall. There were several fallacies among much material. It is an intellectualist reconstruction, without sufficient grounding in prehistory. Food-gathering peoples today are not necessarily the most primitive. SCHMIDT tried to force every kind of religion into a monotheistic mould, even where it was the clearest polytheism. And monotheism and polytheism are found in many different times and places. As PETTAZZONI said: "What we find among uncivilized peoples is not monotheism in its historically legitimate sense, but the idea of a Supreme Being, and the erroneous identification, the misleading assimilation, of this idea to true monotheism can only give rise to misunderstandings."

Most of the nineteenth century writers who founded the science of anthropology were armchair theorists. If they had been able to spend even a few weeks among the people of whom they wrote, their methods and conclusions might have been very different. They were both intellectualist and romantic, as the titles of some of their books show: *The Golden Bough*, *The Mystic Rose*, *How Natives Think*, *At the Back of the Black Man's Mind*. Curiously enough few were experts in the study of religion, its history or theology. EVANS-PRITCHARD declares that "with one or two exceptions, whatever the background may have been, the persons whose writings have been most influential have been at the time they wrote agnostics or atheists. Primitive religion was with regard to its validity no different from any other religious faith, an illusion...Religious belief was to these anthropologists absurd, and it is so to most anthropologists of yesterday and today." There was the hope, sometimes scarcely veiled, that by discrediting the origins of religion, or showing the religion of illiterates to be an intellectual aberration, the "higher" religions would also be undermined. The difference of this approach from that of serious students of Buddhism or Islam, in the same period, is significant.

Father SCHMIDT, however, was a Roman Catholic priest and he tried to show that religious belief was not simply a reflection of social organization. Whatever the faults of his theories, he succeeded in collecting a great deal of evidence to show that many peoples of simple organization, hunters and food-gatherers who had no political model for a monarchic deity, believed in a Supreme Being, though also in other spirits.

A powerful theological influence came from RUDOLF OTTO in *Das Heilige* in 1917. OTTO followed SCHLEIERMACHER in opposing a purely rationalistic interpretation of religion, though he criticized SCHLEIERMACHER's beginning with human experience rather than with divine action. OTTO drew most of his examples from Indian and Semitic thought, but he claimed that the experience of the *mysterium tremendum et fascinans* was characteristic of the "religion of primitive man."

Some of the field anthropologists of the twentieth century express similar ideas. R. H. LOWIE studied the American Crow Indians at first hand, and wrote in his *Primitive Religion* (1925) that their religion was marked by "a sense of the Extraordinary, Mysterious, or Supernatural." But he held that only religious feelings were important, and that there was no specifically religious behaviour. PAUL RADIN in a study of the Winnebago Indians also rejected explanations of religious behaviour in favour of "a thrill". And A. GOLDENWEISER characterized both religion and magic by the "religious thrill".

At the present time the amount of anthropological study on the religions of illiterate peoples is incalculable. Anthropologists have been to every continent and penetrated some of the most remote places. But they have tended to concentrate on illiterates, and very few have ventured to apply anthropological techniques to the "higher" religions. Perhaps they were repelled by the need of acquiring classical languages and studying masses of scripture. With illiterate peoples there were no scriptures or history to study. But it is curious that the study of the historical religions of Asia has been undertaken by philologists, historians, and to some extent theologians and philosophers. They have studied scriptures and doctrines, and paid rather less attention to rituals. While the religions of Africa, Australia and tribesmen generally were the provinces of anthropologists, who studied the organization of society, marriage customs and inheritance, and the observable rituals and dances of religion.

However, some anthropologists, with training in the study of social customs, and linguistic competence through long residence among their people, have devoted whole volumes to the examination of religious practice. A great deal of valuable material has been gathered, and its importance will remain, for in the absence of written history these are the first documents of the religion studied. There has often been some over-riding point of view which was foreign to the material collected. MALINOWSKI followed the psychological interpretations of his predecessors, and RADCLIFFE-BROWN the sociological theories of DURKHEIM.

Whether for the proper study of a religion the student needs himself to sympathize with a religious viewpoint will continue to be debated. But EVANS-PRITCHARD points out that while believer and unbeliever can observe and record happenings, when they go further into explanations some bias may appear. Here it is the unbeliever who seeks a theory, biological, psychological, or sociological, to explain the religious illusion. "The believer seeks rather to understand the manner in which a people conceives of reality and their relations to it." He makes a proper comparative study, and puts the ritual into a universal religious context.

Missionaries were usually better equipped in theology and philosophy than anthropologists. But, as was suggested earlier, they have often been selective in the study of the religion of their people, or even firmly opposed to it. There are still some who regard it all as the work of the Devil, and many others who think it unimportant because it is declining before the advance of western civilization. However, religion has a habit of persisting, under changed forms, and in any case its customs and beliefs are of historical interest. Some missionaries have produced impartial works of great scientific value. A notable example is SMITH and DALE's *Ila-speaking Peoples of Northern Rhodesia* (1920).

There have been few attempts, by field workers, to draw out the general principles of the religious thought of the peoples they studied. A remarkable attempt is made in PLACIDE TEMPELS' *La Philosophie Bantoue* of 1945. TEMPELS found that a constant theme in the language of people in tropical Africa was "force, potent life, vital energy." This was the possession of God, the object of prayers, the nature of the ancestors, and the source of magic. Tempels called it "force vitale", and E. W. SMITH had already noted a similar theme which he called "dynamism". TEMPELS was criticized as imposing a European interpretation upon an innocent people, but he retorted that he had done just the contrary. Europeans had given a static interpretation to indigenous religion, whereas their whole attitude to life was dynamic. Moreover, Bantu thought did not simply suppose that there were multitudes of independent monads or blind powers, but it postulated a hierarchy of beings, informed by intelligence. God is the supreme cause, and man the most powerful of dependent beings, but vitally related to the animal and inanimate worlds.

The study of the religions of illiterate peoples having been liberated from nineteenth century theorists, in part, then passed mainly to field anthropologists. But the limitations of their outlook tended to isolate the study of these religions from the work being done among the "higher" religions. Very few historians of religion have entered these fields, for their extent is frightening. Few have been able to span the worlds both of the "primitive" and the historical religions as MIRCEA ELIADE has done. His works seem to be endless, and they have the great merit of drawing upon the studies of Eastern European and Asian writers, as well as those of the West. Already his early specializations in Hindu religion revealed the wider horizons that were to be surveyed. In *Le Chamanisme* in 1951 ELIADE excused himself for not considering the African field, as too vast, but he ranged easily across Siberia, India, Australia and North America. In *Traité d'Histoire des Religions* (translated as *Patterns in Comparative Religion* in 1958) ELIADE examined "the complexity of 'primitive' religion." He insisted that it shares many concepts with all religions: the difference of sacred and profane, the dialogue between them, the complex and superior "hierophanies" or manifestations of the divine, systems into which hierophanies are fitted, theories, myths, rites, and moral notions.

The importance of the study of the religions of illiterate peoples is becoming clearer. Some earlier scholars were repelled by "savages", and though, their rituals tedious, while others were pleased if there was "a welcome bit of obscenity in their rites." EVANS-PRITCHARD ridicules these pretensions at superiority, and also the theological assumptions that some religions are revealed while others are natural. "There is a good sense in which it may be said that all religions are religions of revelation." The task of the historian of religion is to study the religious beliefs and practices of any society, and to discover how they affect the lives of members of that society. From the anthropologist it can at least be learnt that comparative religion should not be just a study of history and texts, but of ordinary people and the role that religion plays in their lives. "Religion is what religion does."

MIRCEA ELIADE also has called on historians of religion to rise to the opportunities that are open to them, with the great amount of material made available by modern study. The hopes aroused by the beginnings of comparative religion have not been fulfilled. There is no modern MAX MÜLLER or JAMES FRAZER, he says, modestly. Specialists have been afraid of enlarging their horizons. They become "timid", lost in detail, afraid of drawing conclusions, and failing to contribute to the general advance of culture. If historians of religion fail to take up the creative interpretation of the material now at hand, their work will be left to ill-equipped anthropologists and probably neglected altogether. There will continue to be collections of facts about religions, but their understanding as spiritual universes will disappear.

EPILEGOMENA

BY

C. J. BLEEKER
Amsterdam, Holland

In his able and commendable book "Ancient Mesopotamia, Portrait of a Dead Civilization," A. Leo Oppenheim has included a paragraph entitled "Why a 'Mesopotamian Religion' should not be written." There he argues that there are two reasons for not attempting a description of the Mesopotamian religion, these being "the nature of the available evidence, and the problem of comprehension across the barriers of conceptual conditioning." In other words he believes that the data impart too little information about the religious notions of the ancient Mesopotamians and that the Western man of this century lacks the conceptual dimension needed to fathom a polytheistic religion such as that of ancient Mesopotamia. In principle this judgment passed by a highly competent Assyrologist deprives the existing descriptions of the ancient Mesopotamian religion of their value and condemns all new attempts to characterise this religion.

All things considered, Oppenheim's judgment can be applied to this manual on the history of religions. Primarily this is of course the case with Volume I dealing with "The Religions of the Past," though the said view is equally applicable to Volume II, which is devoted to "The Religions of the Present." Firstly it is usually difficult to interpret the various forms in which religions are expressed, including those of the living religions, and, moreover, these forms are susceptible to diverse interpretations. Secondly it is doubtful whether, in practice, one can fully absorb the essence of a type of religion one does not profess. Consequently a growing scepticism can be discerned regarding the value of syntheses of the history of religions. A scientific love of truth deters many scholars from writing major studies on the history of religions. More than ever before they recognise the limitations of their knowledge and insight. At most they hazard the composition of a modest monograph or a few annotations on an isolated religious phenomenon that has caught their attention.

Viewed in this light, the publication of "Historia Religionum" is a risky enterprise. The editors are fully aware of this. Nevertheless they believe that this publication is, in every respect, a meaningful one. Although, obviously, its content and standard of scholarship will have to prove its worth and significance, it is nevertheless useful, in this "Epilegomena" to look back on the two parts of this work and to give a reasoned explanation of the principles underlying it. Only such an argumentation can demonstrate that there are solid grounds for publishing this new manual of the history of religions and that mature consideration has been paid to its basic structure.

The first thing to note is that certain sectors of the vast field of the history of religions are not included within the scope of this handbook. For example no special treatment is given of such newer forms of religion as theosophy, anthroposophy, Caodaism in south-east Asia (Viet-Nam), or the numerous sects which have sprung up like mushrooms in Japan since the second world war. Their omission does not imply a judgment on these religious phenomena. From the viewpoint of the history of religions they are certainly of interest. Considerations of practice and principle, however, have convinced the editors that the material dealt with in the present work should be limited to those salient religions of the past and the present usually selected to form the subject matter of such handbooks. On the one hand it is obvious that the scope of this work—sufficiently voluminous in itself—is limited to a certain size and that, on the other hand, research in the field of the history of religions should first of all be focussed on religions whose importance is evidenced by the numbers of their followers, their historic function and their characteristic form. Limiting the subject also meant setting aside all sorts of interesting questions of a general nature pertaining to the history of religions. Such a question is the influence exercised by one religion on another, or that of the phenomena covered by the term "Dynamik der Religionen" used by G. van der Leeuw, being "Synkretismus, Mission, Erweckungen, Reformationen." [9] These problems are so important and at the same time so complex and difficult to elucidate that they require a separate treatment and would not receive their dues in a sort appendage to this manual. It was quite impossible to include phenomenological surveys in this work regardless of how fascinating these are and how strongly they can be inspired by the structural parallelism of the subjects dealt with. [9, 20]

In the second place a few remarks should be added to what is said in the Preface about the basic pattern of all the articles in this manual. Needless to say a certain phenomenological principle and a particular view of the structure of religion are inherent in this pattern. The question arising therefrom will be dealt with presently. Meanwhile it can be stated that there were three reasons for selecting this pattern. First, it accords with the structural image of religion presented by such authoritative scholars of the history of religion as W. B. Kristensen [7] and, in particular, G. van der Leeuw in his "Phänomenologie der Religion"; second, it is one which immediately springs to mind, being readily discernible in diverse types of religion and, third, its merit is that it clearly brings out the points of similarity and dissimilarity between the religions dealt with. This, then, is the unique feature of this manual, that it renders possible a real comparison between the religions, because it sharply delineates the parallel lines of structure.

While on the subject of the formal structure of this work, it might be useful to consider further its division in two parts: "Religions of the Past" and "Religions of the Present." It is common knowledge that there are innumerable different classifications of the world religions. Leaving aside the earlier works, one need only glance through a few of the more recent manuals on the history of religion by, for example, G. Mensching [11], W. B. Kristensen, [8] and H. Ringgren and Å. V. Ström [14] to discover that religions can be classified according to different viewpoints. In doing so the critical reader cannot fail to see that a certain principle, a particular view of the factors determining the structure of religion, forms the basis of each classification. No matter how unbiased the historian who makes the classification is, such a view always tends to be a covert appraisement which really should be avoided. Of the classifications now current, the one selected appeared to be the most impartial and unbiased. It implies nothing and its only merit is that it records that there are two groups of religions, the obsolete and the extant. As we have seen, this fact makes it possible to construct a balanced classification.

Thirdly it is desirable that the position of the present work in the development of this branch of study be determined. Anyone using the word "development," must clearly realise the fact that he is handling a heavily-charged concept. Perhaps with scarcely any appreciation of the confusion he thereby stirs up. For this problem has many aspects and has been the subject of an unmanageable volume of publications. One viewpoint clearly emerges: no matter how great the importance of the concept "development" may be in the natural sciences, it is a dubious concept in the historical sciences, and hence also the history of religions. It is very difficult to discern a clear line of progress in history. And in the present context we are concerned with a special type of history, namely the history of the study of the history of religions. The course of this study has often been described in works of both reference and criticism. Surveys have been compiled by E. Lehmann, [10] Fr. Heiler, [5], J. de Vries, [19] and K. Rudolph. [15] These teach us that the study of the history of religions has been deeply and alternatingly influenced by certain theories, like animism, dynamism, totemism, fetishism, or by certain ideas like the conception of the Supreme Being, the sacred kingship, or the mythic-ritual pattern. Furthermore it is quite apparent that no rational line can be traced in the succession of studies on the history of religions in the sense that later researchers consciously elaborate on what has been published by earlier scholars. Unless, of course, we take it in the sense of gradually learning from the mistakes of our forerunners, so that present-day scholars of the history of religions are more critical and circumspect in their works. In other words, they are aware of certain fashionable theories, and their approach to the material is purely historical, albeit guided by the general phenomenological principle that the nature and structure of a religion can only be fathomed if the relative data are studied with an open mind in order to understand, as W. B. Kristensen has phrased it, "the belief of the believer." It is at this juncture in the "development" of this branch of study that the present manual should be located. It proffers a series of articles which are not obscured by inaccurate pre-conceptions and which provide a scientifically well-founded and religiously penetrating picture of the religions of the past and present.

Following on these more formal comments something might be said of the principia underlying "Historia Religionum." Besides this is the best means of repudiating such sceptical views as those of Oppenheim.

The first point to be noted is that the history of religions is a distinct branch of study with a special task to perform. The independent character of the history of religions is a direct consequence of the autonomous nature of religion. Religion has to be understood as religion. The task of fathoming the purport and structure of the religious phenomena can be entrusted only to a science competent to fulfil it. R. Pettazzoni rightly said: "The peculiar, the very character, of religious facts as such give them the right to form the subject of a special science. That science is the science of religion in the proper sense of the word; the essential character of religious facts is the necessary and sufficient reason for its existence. This science cannot be philological nor archeological nor anything else. Nor can it be the sum total of the particular religious facts studied by philology, archeology, ethnology and so on. Its definition in contrast to these various sciences is not a matter of quantity but of quality, being connected with the special nature of the data which constitute its subject-matter." [13] This quotation really refers to a science with a broader horizon than the history of religions, namely: the science of religion. Still it is equally applicable to the history of religions, it being a component part of the "science of religion," which, for that matter is a complex of sciences, all concerned with the unbiassed study of the phenomenon of religion. These are the history, psychology, sociology, phenomenology and the philosophy of religion. There is a continual interaction between these sciences. Hence the history of religions cannot do without the assistance of its related sciences. Moreover the history of religions must repeatedly call in the ancillary assistance of other, independent sciences such as philology, archeology and ethnology. In the last resort, however, only the history of religions is competent to assess the religious purport of the phenomena.

Secondly, then, the essential thing is to understand the "belief of the believers," as noted above. This implies that every explanation that attributes the significance of the religious data to non-religious factors —psychological or sociological for example—is unsound. Admittedly psychological and sociological motives can play an important role in the religious process, for religion is a phenomenon of human culture. But the meaning of these phenomena is determined by the fact that they are the testimonials of religious people about their encounter with the Holy, with a deity, with God. This thesis proceeds from the presupposition that the research worker is capable of understanding believers of different types. Doubts are sometimes voiced about whether anyone can adequately sense the essence of a religion he does not profess. Something will be said presently about the limitations of the concept of the history of religions .In principle Th. P. van Baaren is right in arguing that one must proceed from the axioma that mutual understanding is possible. [1] This holds good not only for profane intercourse between people, but also for the scientific "discourse" which the historian of religions conducts with adherents of diverse religions in the past and the present.

Thirdly it should be borne in mind that there are certain limitations to the insight of the history of religions. Not only has each type of faith its arcana known to none but its adherents, but also the material is often extremely refractory. This is particularly true of the religious heritage of dead beliefs. The data pertaining to them are often fragmentary. In most cases the adherents of these religions have not passed on to us any explanation of their myths and rituals, and understandably for they were thoroughly conversant with their meaning. So they have taken the secret of their faith with them to their grave. Even though it usually does not require much effort to understand certain religious feelings and convictions—of ancient peoples for example—which are universally human, great acumen and mental agility are needed to learn how to detect the characteristic pattern of thinking of certain religions. In principle we disagree wholly with the quotation from Oppenheim cited above that the western man of this century lacks the conceptual conditioning needed to comprehend, for example, ancient Mesopotamian polytheism. The results of historical research in the field of religion prove irrefutably that this capacity is indeed present. Admittedly the researcher must bear in mind that he is dealing with concepts borrowed from typically modern western terminology. To cite an example, the ancient Egyptian language had no words to express belief, religion, piety. Still this does not prevent us from finding clues to the Egyptian religion, for this quantity is of course present. When engaged in practical study, however, every scholar undergoes the painful experience of being frustrated by enigmatical data. This should be a continual stimulus for him to burrow into the incomprehensible material with a mind ever more unbiassed and sympathetically inclined until its meaning emerges. There are times, also, when he must acknowledge he has reached the absolute limit of his insight and must admit a "non-liquet."

Although the majority of the historians of religions are scarcely aware of the fact, it is manifest that, fourthly, their research rests on a certain conception of religion. If this were not so they would have no criterion for distinguishing between religious phenomena and non-religious data. One can agree with those who maintain that religion is an abstract conception proper to philosophy and theology. For the historian of religions knows only of religions in the plural. [18] This does not alter the fact that every historian of religions operates with an intuitive notion of what religion is, a latent comprehension of which he gradually must become conscious and which will become purer and profounder as his studies progress. Still this brings up an interesting question which seldom receives close attention. That question is whether it is possible to devise and formulate a conception of religion that covers all the heterogeneous religious phenomena, or whether a distinction should be drawn between true and pseudo-religious phenomena. The latter need not necessarily imply the thesis postulated by certain Christian theologians that Christianity is the only true and veritable religion and that all non-Christian religions are pious, human aspirations lacking any metaphysical background. This question becomes particularly relevant when it is held that no proper religion is to be found beyond the Indus, since all Oriental religiousness is really wisdom and human self-realisation. Now the problem of a universally-valid conception of religion is not an isolated one. Here, in fact, we come up against one of the cruces with which every science has to wrestle, namely the arduous task of formulating the precise conceptions of classification. Much can be said on this subject. Briefly the issue is that, although all things are interrelated in practice, and hence the contours of the material and spiritual quantities are always blurred, there is no conceivable science which does not draw distinctions specifically by using certain conceptions of classification. Consequently the science of the history of religions would be paralysed if it possessed no criterion for recognising religious phenomena. Since its approach is characterised by neutrality and freedom from prejudice, this criterion must be as inclusive as possible, for example in the form of a simple "Key Word of Religion." [3]

This question rises once more in a different guise in the observations of W. Cantwell Smith. [17] After his critical treatment of the concept religio and the terms used for the great world religions, this author arrives at the conclusion what words like Christendom, Buddhism and even the concept religion should be dropped, since they constitute a barrier to true insight. Hence they should be replaced by two factors: "an historical-cumulative tradition" and "the personal faith of men and women." Another passage reveals just what induced Smith to make this pronouncement. [18] In it he attacks the impersonal character of much research on the history of religions and goes on to propose that "the study of a religion is the study of persons;" in other words he sees the issue as the living faith of people. In his opinion this can be learnt only by discussion with professors of the religion in question. In this way can be found the only practicable definition of religion. His conclusion is therefore: "No statement about religion is valid unless it can be acknowledged by that religion's believers... It is the business of comparative religion to construct statements about religion that are intelligible within at least two traditions simultaneously." This is certainly not an objectionable a-proach, but it is not one that can be applied in all circumstances. It cannot be utilised in the study of dead religions, for the simple reason that their adherents cannot be interviewed. And these religions still constitute a powerful bloc in the world of religious phenomena. As for the living religions, it is not certain that even intelligent believers are fully acquainted with, and can take an overall view of, their own religion. The specialist often knows of essential peculiarities that have escaped the notice of the believers. The judgment passed by a believer about his belief is anything but infallible. Definitely it must be supplemented with and verified by the expert insight of the historian of religions. Therefore, the criterion recommended by Smith for a sound definition of religion has no absolute validity. And his proposal to eliminate the concept religion and the terms for the world religions is inapplicable in historical research in the field of religion. Of course one cannot ignore the problems inherent in the term "Islam," for example. Nevertheless the history of religions would be deprived of a valuable apparatus, no matter how faulty, if the terms to which Smith takes objection were discarded. After all one must work with the tools at hand. Should the history of religions be denied the use of such a universal concept as religion, then it is doomed to inactivity and sterility.

Fifthly, even intelligent votaries of the history of religions entertain misconceptions about the business and function of this study which should be removed. Some believe that the purpose of the science of religion and also of the history of religions is to create a form of religion that satisfies the needs of the modern, spiritually-uprooted man. Others expect that the history of religions should be used to promote mutual understanding among the faithful and thus strengthen world peace. Our branch of study cannot satisfy these demands. Every suggestion of this nature should be emphatically rejected. It is not the task of the history of religions to construct a prognosis of the future form of religion, nor to consolidate mutual understanding between the adherents of the world religions. A sharp, clearly-defined line separates the purely scientific work of the historian of religions from the activities of those who labour on behalf of the Ecumenical Movement or the World Congress of Faith. [12] As a science, the history of religions is guided by the principle of the "epochè": the suspension of judgment, i.e. impartiality, the attitude of listening. Nonetheless the historian of religions is not unaffected by the subject of his study. On the contrary, he is engaged in it, for he realises that he is dealing with the highest values of mankind, and he is also aware of the social significance of religion. [6] That is why he can feel himself under an obligation to provide his contemporaries with some knowledge of the essence and structure of religion. "But his task is not conversion to faith whatsoever, but simply enlightening." [12] The present work is meant to be a contribution to that end.

The final question is what is the advantage offered by this manual. Obviously there is no concrete answer to this question, for the importance of the present work will only become manifest after repeated reading and comparison between articles in it. A general formulation can be given, however, of the value of "Historia Religionum." It offers a more lucid insight into the structure of the world religions than that found in foregoing handbooks, mainly because the differences and similarities are made more manifest. If, in addition, the reader bears in mind the four factors which the present writer believes to be determinative of the structure of religions, namely the constant forms of expression, the irreducible factors, the types of religious orientation, i.e. the various ways in which one acquires a knowledge of god, and the characteristic features, [4] then he perceives a certain relief in the chaotic world of religious phenomena and discovers the "logic" in the structure of religion.

SELECTED BIBLIOGRAPHY

[1] BAAREN, TH. P. VAN, *Doolhof der goden*, 1960, p. 9.
[2] BLEEKER, C. J., "The Phenomenological Method" (*The Sacred Bridge*, 1963)
[3] ——, "The Key Word of Religion" (*The Sacred Bridge*, 1963).
[4] ——, "La structure de la religion" (*The Sacred Bridge*, 1963).
[5] HEILER, FR., *Erscheinungsformen und Wesen der Religion*, 1961, Einleitung II.
[6] JAMES, E. O., *Comparative Religion*, 1938, p. 350.
[7] KRISTENSEN, W. B., *The Meaning of Religion. Lectures on the Phenomenology of Religion*, 1960.
[8] ——, *Inleiding tot de godsdienstgeschiedenis*, 1953.
[9] LEEUW, G. VAN DER, *Phänomenologie der Religion*, 1933, § 93, 94.
[10] LEHMANN, E., "Zur Geschichte der Religionsgeschichte" (Chantepie de la Saussaye, *Lehrbuch der Religionsgeschichte* I).
[11] MENSCHING, G., *Allgemeine Religionsgeschichte*, 1948/2.
[12] *Numen*, Vol. VII, Fasc. 2-3, Dec. 1960, pp. 220 sq.

[13] Pettazzoni, R., "History and Phenomenology in the Science of Religion" (*Essays on the History of Religions*, 1954).
[14] Ringgren, H. och Ström, Å. V., *Religionerna i historia och nutid*, 1957.
[15] Rudolph, K., *Die Religionsgeschichte an der Leipziger Universität und die Entwicklung der Religionswissenschaft, Ein Beitrag zur Wissenschaftsgeschichte und zum Problem der Religionswissenschaft*, 1962.
[16] ——, "Die Probleme der Religionswissenschaft als akademisches Lehrfach" (*Kairos*, IX Jahrgang, 1967, Heft 1).
[17] Cantwell Smith, W., *The Meaning and End of Religion, A New Approach to the Religious Tradition of Mankind*, 1964.
[18] ——, "Comparative Religion, Whither- and Why?" (*The History of Religion, Essays in Methodology*, 1959.
[19] Vries, J. de, *Godsdienstgeschiedenis in vogelvlucht*, 1961.
[20] Widengren, Geo, *Religionsphänomenologie*, 1969.

INDEX OF AUTHORS

INDEX OF SUBJECTS

Abbreviations

Preh.r. = Prehistoric Religion, Eg = Egypt, Mes = Mesopotamia, Syr = Syria, Isr = Israel, Hit = Hittites, Ir = Iran, Gr = Greek, R = Roman, H = Hellenistic, Gn = Gnosticism, Ma = Manichaeism, G = German, Ce = Celts, Sl = Slaw, Me = Mexican, Pe = Peru, Ju = Judaism, Chr = Christianity, Isl = Islam, Zo = Zorastrianism, Hi = Hinduism, Ja = Jainism, Bu = Buddhism, Chin = China, Jap = Japan, Ill = Illiterate

594 (Ma), 613, 615, 617f, 620f (Germ), 630, 633, 636f, 640ff, 646 (Ce), 685, 689 (Pe), II 24f, 39 (Ju), 155f (Isl), 228 (Zo), 250ff, 258ff, 262, 276, 286, 289, 310, 328ff, 333 (Hi), 360, 363f (Ja), 391, 414, 436 (Bu), 477, 487ff, 501 (Chin), 521, 523, 526, 535f (Jap), 558, 562, 576f, 584, 596, 622f, 631f, 634, 636, 638f (Ill)
bowls I 183
magister sacrorum I 512
Maqlû collection I 153, 188
Magna Mater I 462, 485, 502
magu I 357
magupat I 329
māh I 341, 347
Mahābhārata II 269, 271, 277
Maha Bodhi Society II 453, 456
Mahā-Kāśyapa II 375f, 397
mahāpuruṣa I 3
Mahāsabhā II 281
Mahāsāṃghika II 377, 382, 440
Mahāvibhāṣa II 378
Mahāvīra II 348ff, 358, 360ff, 366, 368
Mahāvīra Brotherhood II 369
mahāyajñas II 326
Mahāyāna II 273f (Hi), 380, 384, 386, 388f, 392, 396ff, 402, 407, 409, 415, 417, 420, 424, 428, 432, 439f, 443, 445, 450f, 453, 457ff, 461 (Bu), 520f, 529, 536, 546 (Jap)
scriptures II 378f, 383 (Bu)
Mahdī II 186, 196
Maheśamūrti, *triśīrṣa* II 245
Maḥmūd of Ghazna II 134
Mahound II 200
Maia, myth of I 545
Maimonides II 13, 21ff, 29f, 42
Maitreya I 588, *see also* Buddha Maitreya
Malachi I 307f
Malakbel I 504, 527
Malalas, Chronicle of I 654, 658
Malāmatīya II 140
Malebranche II 494
Mālik ibn Anās II 134
malikites II 134
malkaṭ šamīn I 284
Mama Quilla I 684
mambūhā I 586
Mami I 139f, 162
Mami-Nintu I 166
Mamluks II 135ff, 163
Ma'mūn II 132
Man, conception of I 34-37 (Preh.r.), 93-107 (Eg), 165-181 (Mes), 218 (Syr), 321f (Hit), 426-438 (Gr), 480-485 (R), 555-564 (Gn), 603-606 (Ma), 623ff (Germ), 644ff (Ce), 661f (Sl), 673-677 (Me), 688f (Pe), II 36-42 (Ju), 103-118 (Chr), 178-190 (Isl), 231ff (Zo), 311-338 (Hi), 364-368 (Ja), 428-452 (Bu), 489f, 508ff (Chin), 579-584, 586ff ,604-608, 615ff (Ill)
origin of I 93ff (Eg), 165f (Mes), 218 (Syr), 250 (Isr), 426-430 (Gr), 555-558 (Gn), 603f (Ma), 623 (Germ), 673 (Me), 688 (Pe), II 36ff (Ju), 103-107 (Chr), 178f (Isl), 231 (Zo), 311-316 (Hi), 428ff (Bu), 508f (Chin), 579f, 586, 604f, 615 (Ill), *see also* creation
being of I 95-102 (Eg), 166-171 (Mes), 218 (Syr), 250, 309f (Isr), 321f (Hit), 358 (Ir), 430ff (Gr), 480-484 (R), 604f (Ma), 623f (Germ), 674 (Me), II 103-107 (Chr), 179ff (Isl), 231f (Zo), 311-316 (Hi), 364-368 (Ja), 430ff (Bu), 489f (Chin), 580ff, 586f, 605, 616 (Ill)
destiny of I 102-104 (Eg), 171-178 (Mes), 273-277, 288, 292 (Isr), 321 (Hit), 358 (Ir), 432-437 (Gr), 624 (Germ), 646 (Ce), 674ff (Me), II 38f (Ju), 107-112 (Chr), 181-184 (Isl), 232 (Zo), 316-337 (Hi), 364-368 (Ja), 432-446 (Bu), 509f (Chin), 582f, 606, 617 (Ill), *see also* salvation
future of I 104-107 (Eg), 178-181 (Mes), 218 (Syr), 311f (Isr), 322 (Hit), 366ff (Ir), 437f (Gr), 485 (R), 514 (H), 558-564 (Gn), 605f (Ma), 624f (Germ), 646 (Ce), 676f (Me), 688f (Pe), II 40ff (Ju), 112-118 (Chr), 184-190 (Isl), 233 (Zo), 337f (Hi), 446-452 (Bu), 583f, 587f (Ill), *see also* eschatology
mana I 490 (R), II 551, 593, 633 (Ill)
Mānā, the Great I 586, cf. 558
Mana-rabba I 558, cf. 586
manas I 337
Manasā II 300
Manasseh II 293, 304
mandā I 586